RELEVANT DATES

28 November 1995	Budget Statement
4 January 1996	Publication of Finance Bill
29 April 1996	Royal Assent

A Guide to
The Finance Act 1996

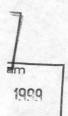

1999

A GUIDE TO
THE FINANCE ACT 1996

(excluding provisions relating to excise duties and certain miscellaneous provisions not relating to taxation)

Contributors
CHARLES BARCROFT, ATII
DEREK BOND, ATII, Solicitor
GILES CLARKE, MA, PhD, Barrister
COLIN DAVIS, MA, FCA
NIGEL DORAN, MA, LLM, AIB, ACCA, ATII, Solicitor
CAREY GROSSE, LLB, ATII
ANDREW HUBBARD, BMus, PhD, ATII
ZIGURDS KRONBERGS, MA, BSc, ARCS, ACA, FCCA
JOHN LABRUM, FCAA, ATII
ROBERT MURGATROYD, formerly one of HM Inspectors of Taxes
MICHAEL NEWSTEAD, BA, formerly one of HM Inspectors of Taxes
GEOFF PENNELLS, FCCA, ATII
IAN PURVES, FCA, ATII, APMI
GARY RICHARDS, MA, LLB, ATII, Solicitor
CHARLES VITEZ, FCA
RICHARD WALLINGTON, MA, Barrister
DAVID F WILLIAMS, MA (CANTAB), FCA, FCCA, FTII, FRSA

BUTTERWORTHS
LONDON, DUBLIN AND EDINBURGH
1996

United Kingdom	Butterworths, a Division of Reed Elsevier (UK) Ltd, Halsbury House, 35 Chancery Lane, LONDON WC2A 1EL and 4 Hill Street, EDINBURGH EH2 3JZ
Australia	Butterworths Pty Ltd, SYDNEY, MELBOURNE, BRISBANE, ADELAIDE, PERTH, CANBERRA and HOBART
Canada	Butterworths Canada Ltd, TORONTO and VANCOUVER
Ireland	Butterworth (Ireland) Ltd, DUBLIN
Malaysia	Malayan Law Journal Sdn Bhd, KUALA LUMPUR
New Zealand	Butterworths of New Zealand Ltd, WELLINGTON and AUCKLAND
Singapore	Reed Elsevier (Singapore) Pte Ltd, SINGAPORE
South Africa	Butterworth Publishers (Pty) Ltd, DURBAN
USA	Michie Butterworth, CHARLOTTESVILLE, Virginia

A CIP Catalogue record for this book is available from the British Library.

ISBN 0 406 99313 0

Typeset by Kerrypress Ltd, Luton and William Clowes Ltd, Beccles and London
Printed and bound in Great Britain by Mackays of Chatham plc, Chatham, Kent.

CONTENTS

Contents

INTRODUCTION

EXCISE DUTIES

Alcoholic liquor duties.   The excise duty on spirits is reduced to £19.78 per litre of alcohol in the spirits as from 28 November 1995 (s 1). The duty on wine exceeding 15% strength but not 22% strength is reduced to £187.24 per hectolitre. The duty on wine exceeding 22% strength is £19.78 per litre of alcohol in the wine (s 2). The rate of duty on cider is £35.67 per hectolitre in the case of cider exceeding 7.5% strength and £23.78 per hectolitre on other cases.

Hydrocarbon oil duties.   The rates of duty on light oil and heavy oil are increased, with effect from 28 November 1995, to 39.12p per litre for light oil and 34.30p per litre on heavy oil (s 4(1)). The rate of duty on road fuel is reduced to 28.17p per kilogram from the same date (s 4(2)). The rate of rebate on light oil delivered for home use is 1.81p per litre less than the rate at which duty is charged. The corresponding figure for gas oil is 2.33p per litre (s 4(3)). The rate of rebate on unleaded petrol is 1.5p per litre for high octane unleaded and 4.82p per litre for ordinary unleaded from 15 May 1996.

The rebate of duty for heavy oil supplied for home use is now subject to restrictions. If the fuel is to be used for propelling an "excepted vehicle" or if it is to be used for an engine not used for propelling a vehicle or for heating , then the rebate is at the rate for rebated gas oil. Where a rebate for heavy oil has been obtained, the fuel may not be used as described above unless duty at the rebated gas oil rate is paid (s 5). Penalties are imposed for the misuse of kerosene under the above provisions.

A charge to excise duty is imposed where leaded and unleaded petrol are mixed otherwise than by an approved mixing. The rates are set out in a new Sch 2A Part III of the Hydrocarbon Oil Duties Act 1979. The person producing the mixture is responsible for paying the duty and must notify Customs who are given powers to raise an assessment where they consider that a mixing has taken place and duty is payable (s 6 introducing new ss 20AA, 20AB of the 1979 Act).

Penalties are imposed for the misuse of oil which contains a marker prescribed for duty-free and rebated oil. Such oil must not be used as fuel for a road vehicle (s 7).

The special provisions relating to fuel for ships in home waters and fuel for use in fishing boats etc (ss 18 and 19 of the 1979 Act) are repealed with effect from an appointed day (s 8).

Tobacco products duty.   The rates of duty are increased with effect from 28 November 1995 (s 9 and new table to Sch 1 Tobacco Products Duty Act 1979).

Betting duties: rates.   The rate of general betting duty is reduced to 6.75% as from 1 March 1996 (s 10). The rate of pool betting duty is reduced to 27.5% as from 3 December 1995 and to 26.5% from the first Sunday after the Act is passed (s 11).

Amusement machine licence duty.   A special amusement machine licence is required for small prizes machines and for amusement machines which are not gaming machines. This licence applies to the machine rather than the premises in which it is situated (s 12).

Air passenger duty (APD).   Flights which depart from and return to the same airport, and which last not more than 60 minutes, are exempt from APD (s 13).

Vehicle excise duty.   For licences taken out after 28 November 1995, the rate of duty on private cars and other vehicles in the same category is increased from £135 to £140 (s 14). The rate of duty for electrically-propelled motor cycles is the same as the rate for motor cycles of up to 150ccs. An electrically-assisted pedal cycle is exempt from duty (s 15). Steam powered vehicles are included in the "special concessionary" class from 28 November 1995 (s 16).

The definition of "special vehicle" in the Vehicle Excise and Registration Act 1994 Sch 1 para 4(2) is widened to include any goods vehicles which are not used for hire or reward and any vehicle designed or adapted for use with a semi-trailer where the semi-trailer is not used for the conveyance of goods or burden. Such vehicles qualify for the basic goods vehicle rate. This rate also applies to any rigid goods vehicle used only in connection with a person learning to drive or taking a driving test. Similarly it applies only to any tractive unit to which a semi-trailer is attached if used loaded only in connection with a person learning to drive or taking a driving test. The declarations required when applying for a licence to drive a goods vehicle are to apply also in relation to "special vehicles" (s 17).

The classes of exempt vehicles are to include a new class of vehicles over 25 years old from 28 November 1995 (s 18). However, with effect from 1 June 1996, however, certain vehicles over 25 years old are not exempt under the new class: these are Hackney carriages, recovery vehicles, vehicles used for exceptional loads, haulage vehicles or goods vehicles and certain special vehicles (s 19).

A vehicle is exempt from vehicle excise duty under the Vehicle Excise and Registration Act 1994 Sch 2 para 22 when it is being used solely for the purposes of taking it for a relevant examination and bringing it away from such an examination. It is exempt when used by an authorised person for warming up its engine in preparation for carrying out a compulsory test or relevant examination (s 20). There are corresponding amendments to Sch 2 para 22 and s 42 in relation to vehicle testing in Northern Ireland (ss 21, 22).

The legislation relating to vehicle licensing and regulation is amended to include a provision requiring a person keeping a vehicle off the road to notify the Department giving details of the vehicle. This will be covered by new regulations. The Secretary of State is given power to obtain information from any person by or through whom a vehicle is sold or a licence holder who is not renewing his licence (new s 46A to the 1994 Act). Where a person fails to comply with new s 46A, and later signs a written statement of admission, that statement is evidence that he was keeping the vehicle at the relevant time (new s 51A). The Secretary of State may compound any proceedings for an offence against the regulations and accept a financial penalty (s 23 and Sch 2).

Repeal of certain drawbacks and allowances.   A number of minor provisions, some of which are spent, are repealed (s 24).

VALUE ADDED TAX

EC Second VAT Simplification Directive.   Provisions are introduced into VATA 1994 to facilitate "fiscal warehousing" (new ss 18A–18F and

Sch 5A). A person wishing to operate a fiscal warehouse must first obtain approval from Customs. Acquisitions and supplies of eligible goods which are within the fiscal warehousing regime are treated as taking place outside the UK. Eligible goods are those listed in new Sch 5A—mainly commodities. A charge to VAT arises when the goods are removed from the fiscal warehousing regime unless they are transferred to a fiscal warehouse in another member state. The services of a fiscal warehouse keeper or customs warehouse keeper are zero rated if performed whilst the goods are subject to either warehousing regime. The legislation, which contains numerous definitions and anti-avoidance provisions, will be backed up by Regulations. It will come into effect on an appointed day (s 26 and Sch 3).

With effect from 1 January 1996, the value of goods imported from outside the EC includes all incidental expenses including commission, packaging, transport and insurance costs incurred up to the first destination in the UK and to any further known destination within the EC (s 27).

The special provisions of VATA 1994 s 22 relating to the valuation of aircraft or hovercraft adapted for recreational use, are repealed as from 1 January 1996 (s 28).

The zero-rating provisions of VATA 1994 s 30 are extended to include the application of a treatment or process to another person's goods where the result is to produce goods falling within Sch 8 (the zero-rating schedule). The rule which deems such an application to be a supply of goods to which the treatment or process is applied is repealed. These changes take effect from 1 January 1996 (s 29).

Other provisions relating to charges to VAT. A person carrying out a conversion of a building for residential use otherwise than in the course of a business may claim a refund of any VAT paid on the costs of the conversion, including contractors' invoices. This will enable persons carrying out DIY conversions to claim refunds (s 30).

Customs are given power to counteract the avoidance of non-recoverable input tax by partially exempt groups (VATA 1994 new Sch 9A). Counteraction is by way of a "direction" issued by Customs which may be to the effect that a particular company shall, or shall not, be treated as a member of the group for any specified period. A direction may specify that a particular supply shall fall outside the protection of VATA 1994 s 43(1)(*a*), with the result that it is not ignored for VAT purposes. Customs may then raise an assessment to recover any tax due as a result of the direction. There is a right of appeal against the direction and the assessment (VATA 1994 s 83(*wa*)). Customs may not make a direction if they are satisfied that any relevant transaction or change in group membership was effected for genuine commercial purposes and not the avoidance of VAT (s 31 and Sch 4).

The definition of "supply of gold", for the purposes of the accounting provisions of VATA 1994 s 55, is widened to include the supply of goods consisting of gold grain of any purity or in gold coins of any purity, with effect for supplies made after 28 November 1995 (s 32).

The exclusion from the charge to VAT of small gifts of goods is extended to cover goods costing up to £15. This limit may be increased by Treasury order (s 33).

Payment and enforcement. Customs are given power to require persons within the payment on account provisions of VATA 1994 s 28 to make those payments in a particular manner—eg by electronic transfer of funds (s 34).

New default surcharge provisions are to apply to persons within the payment on account rules, in place of the existing provisions which continue to apply to persons who account quarterly (VATA 1994 new s 59A). The new provisions render a taxable person liable to a default surcharge if he is late making a payment on account and a surcharge liability notice has been served on him. The rules work in the same way as the existing default surcharge rules and the percentage surcharges are the same. A new s 59B deals with the interaction of the new payment on account surcharge provisions with the existing surcharge provisions. The new provisions apply in relation to prescribed accounting periods ending on or after 1 June 1996 (s 35).

The repeated misdeclaration penalty provisions are strengthened by a new provision which allows a prescribed period for which a serious misdeclaration penalty has been imposed to be taken into account when determining whether any subsequent period is subject to the persistent misdeclaration penalty (s 36).

The penalty for failure to notify liability (VATA 1994 s 67) is to apply in particular to a failure to notify liability on a transfer of a business as a going concern under Sch 1 para 7 (s 37).

Customs may allow businesses to omit some of the information which is presently required to be included on VAT invoices. This matter will be dealt with in new Regulations (s 38).

LANDFILL TAX

The basic provisions. Landfill tax is under the care and management of Customs (s 39). It is charged on disposals of waste in landfill sites on or after 1 October 1996 (s 40). It is payable by the site operator (s 41). The standard rate is £7 per tonne of waste disposed. Certain waste will be charged at £2 per tonne. Waste qualifying for the reduced rate will be specified by Treasury order (s 42).

Exemptions. Materials dredged from rivers, canals, watercourses, docks and harbours is exempt, as is material removed from the sea in the interests of navigation. Material removed from the sea bed in order to extract minerals therefrom is also exempt (s 43). Material extracted in the course of commercial mining or quarrying is exempt (s 44). The remains of dead domestic pets are exempt (s 45). These exemptions may be varied by Treasury order (s 46).

Administration. Any person carrying out taxable activities must register with Customs. A person who intends to commence or cease such activities must notify Customs. Regulations will set out the procedure for registration and notification (ss 47,48).

The accounting for, and payment of, landfill tax will be also governed by Regulations (s 49). Customs are given power to assess any site operator who fails to comply with the Regulations or where the amount of tax paid is considered to be incorrect (s 50).

Regulations will provide for the granting of credits against landfill tax liabilities and the refund of tax in certain circumstances. Credits must be claimed, and the Regulations will set out the claims procedure (s 51). In particular, a landfill site operator is entitled to a credit where an invoice including an element of landfill tax becomes a bad debt (s 52). An operator is also entitled to a credit in relation to payments which he makes to approved bodies which are concerned with the protection of the environment (s 53).

Review and appeal. Most decisions of Customs in relation to landfill tax are subject to a review procedure. The operator may require Customs to review a decision by notice in writing within 45 days of the date of the decision (s 54). There is then a right of appeal to the VAT Tribunal against Custom's decision by notice in writing within 45 days of the date of the decision. As with VAT appeals, the disputed tax must normally be paid before the appeal may proceed (s 55).

On an appeal against an assessment, the Tribunal may increase or decrease the amount of the tax liability. Any unpaid tax carries interest at such rate as the Tribunal may determine. Appeals may be settled by agreement. Either party may appeal to the Court against the decision of the Tribunal (s 56).

The above rules come into force on 1 October 1996 unless an earlier date is appointed by order (s 57).

Miscellaneous. The treatment of partnerships will be dealt with in Regulations, as will bankruptcies, receiverships and liquidations. A company carrying on business in several divisions may register each division separately. The Regulations will also deal with the transfer of a business as a going concern (s 58).

Companies under common control may apply to be treated as a group. Where they are so treated, one company files consolidated returns for the group and pays the tax on behalf of the group. However, each group member becomes jointly and severally liable for the whole of the group's tax (s 59).

Site operators will be required to keep proper records in connection with landfill tax. Anyone concerned with landfill disposal may be required to produce relevant documents for inspection. In cases of suspected fraud, Customs are given power to enter and search premises, to arrest persons suspected of fraud and to apply for an order giving access to recorded information etc. Documents may be removed from premises which are searched and samples of waste material may be taken. The normal recovery procedures are available to Customs and penalties, both civil and criminal, are imposed for evasion of the tax. Interest on overdue tax is imposed. Various other administrative rules are set out (s 60 and Sch 5).

The date of disposal of waste is taken to be the date on which the invoice relating to the disposal is issued, provided that it is issued within fourteen days of the actual date of disposal. However, the site operator may elect to ignore this rule and pay tax by reference to the actual date (s 61).

Regulations may provide that certain temporary disposals of waste should be non-taxable (s 62).

Customs may direct that certain materials which consist largely of materials qualifying for the reduced rate of tax, but which contain small amounts of standard-rated materials, should be treated as wholly taxable at the reduced rate (s 63).

Interpretation. The legislation defines "disposal of material as waste", "disposal by way of landfill", "landfill site" and "operator of a landfill site" (ss 64-67). Regulations will be issued prescribing rules for ascertaining the weight of waste disposed (s 68). There are various other definitions of terms (ss 69,70). Finally, s 71 determines which Orders and Regulations are to be made by Customs and which are to be made by the Treasury.

INCOME TAX, CORPORATION TAX AND CAPITAL GAINS TAX

CHAPTER I PRINCIPAL PROVISIONS

Income tax charge, rates and reliefs. For 1996–97, the lower, basic and higher rates of income tax are 20%, 24% and 40% respectively. The lower rate band is extended to £3,900 and the threshold for the higher rate is increased to £25,500. Tax deductions from payments to sub-contractors are to be made at the rate of 24% with effect from 1 July 1996 (s 72).

For 1996–97 and subsequent years, income chargeable to income tax under Schedule D Case III, Schedule F, or equivalent foreign income is to be taxed at the lower rate instead of at the basic rate. However, such income is treated as the top slice of the taxpayer's income in determining the liability at the higher rate. The income tax deductible at source from such income is deductible at the lower rate. There are numerous consequential amendments to TA 1988. In particular, new ss 689A and 689B deal with trustees' expenses. Further, a new s 88A deals with the rate of corporation tax on the policyholders' share of certain profits of life assurance companies (s 73 and Sch 6).

For 1996–97, the single personal allowance is increased to £3,765. The age allowance is £4,910 for persons aged 65 or over and £5,090 for persons aged 75 or over (s 74). The blind person's allowance is increased to £1,250 (s 75). The limit of tax relief for home loans is based on a loan of £30,000.

Corporation tax charge and rate. The rate of corporation tax for the year ending on 31 March 1997 is 33% (s 77). The small companies rate is 24% and the marginal relief fraction is 9/400 (s 78).

Abolition of Schedule C charge etc. Schedule C is abolished with effect from 1996–97 for income tax purposes and for accounting periods ending on or after 1 April 1996 for corporation tax purposes. There are numerous consequential amendments to the tax legislation. In particular, TA 1988 s 18 (the main Schedule D charging section) is amended to eliminate the exclusions from Cases III–VI of income chargeable under Schedule C. Further, the scope of Cases IV and V are widened to include the proceeds from the sale, by a bank of coupons for foreign dividends and the sale to a dealer in coupons by a person who is not a dealer in coupons (s 79 and Sch 6).

CHAPTER II LOAN RELATIONSHIPS

Introductory provisions. With the exception of s 102 and Sch 13 (discounted securities), the provisions of this chapter apply for corporation tax purposes only. Profits from loan relationships entered into for the purposes of a trade are included in trading profits. Profits from other loan relationships are brought into charge under Schedule D Case III (s 80). The definition of "loan relationship" is widely drawn (s 81).

Taxation of gains and relief for deficits. In the case of a trade, the credits and debits relating to loan relationships are treated as trading receipts and trading expenses. Under Case III, the credits and debits are aggregated. A net credit is a Case III profit and a net debit is a "deficit" which may be set off against the total profits of the same accounting period, surrendered under the group relief provisions or carried back or forward against Case III profits from loan relationships (ss 82, 83 and Sch 8).

Computational provisions etc. The credits and debits to be brought into the tax computations are those which are brought into the accounts in accordance with an "authorised accounting method". Capital items are included. Allowable expenses include expenses of setting up the loan relationship and abortive costs. There are special rules dealing with matters such as late interest, options, FOREX gains and losses, bad debts, sovereign debts, non-arm's length transactions, groups, repos etc (s 84 and Sch 9).

There are two authorised accounting methods: the accruals basis and the mark-to-market basis.

Companies should adopt the basis which is appropriate under normal accountancy practice (s 85). The method used in the company's accounts will be followed for tax purposes if it is one of the above methods. Otherwise, the method used will be the one which "equates with" the method used in the accounts, as defined (s 86). However, if the parties to a loan relationship are connected with each other (as defined), the accruals basis must be used in relation to that loan relationship (s 87). The connection is disregarded in the case of a dealer in assets representing loan relationships and in the case of a life assurance company where the loan relationship is linked to its basic life assurance business or general annuity business (s 88).

Where an accounting method is not applied consistently in successive accounting periods, a balancing credit or debit must be brought into account to reflect the change (s 89). A similar rule applies on the occasion of a change of accounting method (s 90).

Where interest is received under deduction of tax at source, and the interest is received more than two years after the end of the accounting period in which it, or any part of it, has been credited in the accounts, the credit for the tax deducted is set off in the accounting period in which the interest is received. There are special rules for identifying interest receipts with amounts credited in the accounts (s 91).

Special cases. The accruals basis must be used in relation to convertible securities, and the charge to tax is restricted to interest only. For CGT purposes, the acquisition or disposal consideration is adjusted to exclude accrued interest. This rule does not apply in relation to certain discounted securities or to securities which are held as trading stock (s 92).

In the case of a loan relationship which is linked to the value of chargeable assets, only interest debits and credits are brought into account under the new legislation. Gains and losses on disposal of such a relationship are dealt with under the CGT legislation. The consideration for the acquisition or disposal are adjusted to exclude accrued interest (s 93).

In computing the Case III income or deficit relating to an index linked gilt, any debits or credits relating to the value of the gilt are to be adjusted by reference to the movement in the RPI during the period by reference to which the change in value is reflected in the accounts. The Treasury is given power, by order, to exclude certain indexed gilts from the benefit of this adjustment (s 94).

Where the accruals basis applies to a gilt or to strips of a gilt, any exchange of the gilt for strips, or any consolidation of strips into a single security is deemed to involve a disposal and reacquisition at market value of the assets concerned. The Treasury has the power to make regulations for determining the market value of a gilt or strips of a gilt (s 95).

As regards $3\frac{1}{2}$% Funding Stock 1999-2004 and $5\frac{1}{2}$% Treasury Stock 2008-2012, held otherwise than as trading stock, the accruals basis must be adopted and only interest credits are brought into the Case III computation (s 96).

Payments of manufactured interest are treated as interest payments for the purposes of this legislation (s 97).

The Treasury is given power to approve different accounting methods for investment trusts. Authorised unit trusts will continue to be dealt with under the income tax rules applicable to unauthorised unit trusts. There are provisions dealing with holdings in offshore funds (s 98 and Sch 10).

The taxation of loan relationships in the hands of life assurance companies is dealt with specifically in Sch 11 (s 99).

Miscellaneous other provisions. The new legislation applies to interest on money debts which did not arise from loan relationships, and in particular it applies to interest treated as arising by reason of a transfer pricing adjustment under TA 1988 s 770 (s 100).

The FA 1994 provisions relating to financial instruments are extended to cover certain debt contracts and options, with effect from 1 April 1996 (see FA 1994 new s 147A and s 150A). However, where a contract falls under the new provisions, it is excluded from the 1994 provisions (s 101 and Sch 12).

Where a person other than a company within the charge to corporation tax realises a profit from the discount on a security, that profit is chargeable to income tax under Schedule D Case III or Case IV. Losses arising on a transfer of such securities are available for set off against his general income for the year of loss. Certain securities are excluded from these provisions. There are various definitions and provisions dealing with trustees, transfers between connected persons, non-arm's length transactions, gilt strips etc (s 102 and Sch 13).

Various terms are defined for the purposes of the loan relationships provisions (s 103). There are a great number of minor and consequential amendments (s 104 and Sch 14) and transitional provisions s 105 and Sch 15). The new legislation applies to accounting periods ending on or after 1 April 1996. There are special rules dealing with accounting periods straddling that date, with loan relationships in existence at that date and with discounted securities held on that date (Sch 15).

CHAPTER III PROVISIONS RELATING TO THE SCHEDULE E CHARGE

From 1996–97, where an employee is provided with living accommodation by reason of his employment, the amount of his fringe benefit is to be computed in accordance with ss 145,146 even if he is chargeable under the general principles of Schedule E. Only if the amount chargeable under general principles exceeds the charge under ss 145,146 will that amount become chargeable. This counteracts certain "cash alternative" schemes (s 106).

From 1996–97, where an employee is provided with two or more beneficial loans by the same lender, he may elect to aggregate the loans and have the fringe benefit calculated on the aggregate amount rather than separately for each loan. The time limit for electing for aggregation is 92 days from the end of the tax year. The time limit for electing for the averaging basis of calculation is shortened to coincide with the time limit for filing an amended return for the year (s 107).

From 1996–97, any person holding an office in HM Government in the UK, and certain other office holders, are exempt from tax under Schedule E in respect of transport and subsistence provided by the Crown (s 108).

The limit for charitable payroll deductions is increased to £1,200 from 1996–97 (s 109).

The PAYE Regulations are to be amended to include provisions relating to the payment by employers of employees' liabilities in respect of fringe benefits and expenses following an Inland Revenue investigation. Such PAYE settlements are common and the new Regulations will simply provide a formal basis for them. Presumably, they will enable the Revenue to take formal proceedings for recovery as if the tax liability was a liability of the employer (s 110).

CHAPTER IV   SHARE OPTIONS, PROFIT SHARING AND EMPLOYEE SHARE OWNERSHIP

Share options.   For CGT purposes, the acquisition cost of an option is the price actually paid for it, rather than its market value. This applies to options granted on or after 28 November 1995 (s 111). Where an option is released in consideration for the grant of a new option, no gain or loss arises, but the cost of the new option is the cost of the old one plus any further consideration given on the grant of the new one (s 112).

Savings related share option schemes.   The scheme rules may provide that an option may be exercised where, at a bonus date, the holder is employed by an associate company of the grantor or a company under the grantor's control. The rules of existing schemes may be altered to include such a provision (s 113).

Other share option schemes.   For approved schemes, the limit on the value of share options is now reduced to £30,000: the four times remuneration limit is repealed. The exercise price of the options must not be manifestly less than the market value of the shares on the date the option was granted: the existing 85% rule is repealed (s 114). There are transitional rules for existing schemes (Sch 16) and for options acquired between 17 July 1995 and the passing of the Finance Act (s 115).

Profit sharing schemes.   The "release date" under TA 1988 s 187(2) is to be the third anniversary of the date of appropriation of the shares to the participant, rather than the fifth anniversary, where that third anniversary falls after the passing of the Act. Where the third anniversary falls before that time, but the fifth anniversary falls after it, the release date is the date of Royal Assent (s 116). The charge to tax on shares withdrawn before the new release date is on 100% of the value of the shares except where the individual resigns or retires in which case it is based on 50% of that value (s 117). The appropriate allowance under TA 1988 s 186(12), in calculating the tax on any capital receipt, is reduced to £60 maximum and the number of years in the formula is reduced to a maximum of three—both changes applying as from 1997–98 (s 118).

Employee share ownership trusts.   There is no longer a requirement for a minimum period of one year's service in relation to trusts established after the passing of the Finance Act (s 119). Trust deeds may provide that an employee may be a beneficiary if he is eligible to participate in a savings related share option scheme. A transfer of securities is made on "qualifying terms", and is therefore exempt from the charge to tax under FA 1989 s 69, if such an employee exercises his options as against the trustees and pays the acquisition price to them (s 120).

Chapter V Self assessment, general management etc

General.   There are minor amendments to TMA 1970 ss 8, 9, 11AA and 12AA to ensure that returns include all details required to compute the tax liabilities for the year concerned (s 121). There are detailed amendments to TA 1988 reflecting the change to self assessment (s 122). There are minor detailed amendments to TMA 1970 ss 12AA–12AC dealing with partnership returns, partnership statements and the inspector's powers of enquiry (s 123). Amendments to TMA 1970 s 12B require taxpayers to keep and retain records and documents necessary to complete self assessment returns and claims for relief (s 124). There are minor amendments to TMA 1970 s 28C, which enables an inspector or collector to issue a "determination" of the tax payable where a self assessment return has not been filed by the due date (s 125). The provisions requiring payments on account of income tax (TMA 1970 s 59A) are amended to ensure that any tax deducted under the PAYE regulations can be adjusted for the purpose of calculating the payments on account required under s 59A (s 126). Where a self assessment return shows that a refund is due, but the inspector institutes an enquiry, no refund need be made until the enquiry is complete (s 127 amending TMA 1970 s 59B).

Where a claim for relief affects two or more tax years, it is given in tax terms for the later year. The rules are set out in TMA 1970 new Sch 1B which deals with claims for loss relief, farmers' averaging claims, carry back of post cessation receipts and backward spreading of payments for copyrights etc. There are consequential amendments to the time limits for making such claims (s 128 and Sch 17).

The general rules relating to claims (TMA 1970 s 42 and Sch 1A) are not to apply to claims for relief for medical insurance premiums under FA 1989 s 54(6)(*b*) or for relief for allowable costs of vocational training under FA 1991 s 32. Such claims will be dealt with in regulations which will take effect from an appointed day (s 129).

The provisions for making claims under the self assessment rules are not to apply to the giving of "notices". Existing practice will continue (s 130).

As regards interest on overdue tax, the new version of TMA 1970 s 86 (substituted by FA 1995 s 110) applies as from 1997–98 so far as it relates to partnerships whose trades, professions or businesses commenced before 6 April 1994 (s 131).

There are minor amendments to TMA 1970 dealing with the recovery of tax not postponed, and the calculation of payments on account. TMA 1970 s 88 (interest on overdue tax in cases of fraudulent or negligent conduct) becomes redundant with the introduction of self assessment and is repealed. There are various other detailed amendments (s 132 and Sch 18).

The provisions enabling an inspector to enquire into returns are extended to cover claims and elections included in returns and amended returns. There are consequential amendments to the provisions dealing with the production of documents, amendment of self assessment etc (s 133 and Sch 19).

There are numerous amendments of detail to various provisions relating to the giving of reliefs (s 134 and Sch 20).

The time limits for certain claims, which used to be two years or six years after the end of the year of assessment, are shortened to 31 January one year and ten months after the end of the year. It is important to note, however, that the following six year time limits relating to chargeable gains have been reduced to two years or one year and ten months—

- rollover of gain or loss on appropriation to trading stock (s 161)
- small part disposals (ss 242–244).

New rules are provided for assigning proceedings to the General or Special Commissioners, and to the various divisions in the case of the General Commissioners. These are to be found in TMA 1970 new ss 46B–46D and new Sch 3 (s 136 and Sch 22).

There are detailed changes in the provisions relating to CT 61 returns, including provisions requiring a company to file an amended return if it discovers an error in a return (s 137 and Sch 23).

Detailed provisions deal with the situation where the Revenue are not aware of a company's accounting periods and where a s 11 notice specifies a period which is not an accounting period, or where the inspector initiates an enquiry into a specified period which is not an accounting period (TMA 1970 new ss 28AA, 28AB). There are also provisions enabling the Revenue to make "determinations" of corporation tax payable where no return is filed or where a return notice is only partially complied with (TMA 1970 new ss 28D–28F). Other minor amendments are made (s 138 and Sch 24).

Surrenders of ACT are to be dealt with in accordance with the procedures set out in TA 1988 new Sch 13A. A claim to surrender ACT may be withdrawn within the time limit for making the claim (TA 1988 s 240 new sub-ss (5A)–(5C)) (s 139 and Sch 25).

Chargeable gains. On a transfer of a business or part of a business to a company which becomes an investment trust, the gains and losses arising on the deemed sale and reacquisition of assets is taken to arise in the accounting period which ends immediately before the company becomes an investment trust. This applies from the "appointed day" for self assessment of companies (s 140).

Relief for replacement of business assets may be claimed in a self assessment on a provisional basis. If the new assets are not acquired within the rollover period then the self assessment is adjusted to reduce or eliminate the relief (TCGA 1992 new s 247A) (s 141).

Where a capital sum is paid by a tenant to a landlord for the variation, waiver or surrender of a lease, it is taxable in the year in which it is paid rather than the year in which the lease is granted. This rule applies from 6 April 1996 (s 142).

CHAPTER VI MISCELLANEOUS PROVISIONS

Reliefs. Annual payments under insurance policies insuring "qualifying risks" are to be exempt from tax from 1996–97. A qualifying risk is a risk of physical or mental illness or disability or a risk of becoming unemployed. The conditions to be satisfied by the policy are drawn tightly so as to prevent abuse for tax avoidance purposes. In particular, the policy must be "self contained". This means that it may not insure risks other than qualifying risks and the terms of the policy must be commercial (s 143 and TA 1988 new ss 580A, 580B).

From 6 May 1996, relief for vocational training costs is available to anyone over 30 who pays for full time vocational training in a course which consists of or includes four consecutive weeks (s 144).

The provisions allowing Commonwealth citizens resident abroad etc to claim personal allowances (TA 1988 s 278) are extended to cover nationals of states within the European Economic Area (s 145).

The exemption for the investment income of charities is extended to cover short interest which enacts Concession B9 (s 146).

Relief from income tax for Class IV National Insurance Contributions is withdrawn from 1996–97 (s 147).

Compensation payments for mis-sold personal pensions are exempt from tax where the recipient acted on bad advice given during the period from 28 April 1988 to 30 January 1994 (s 148).

Payments made after 5 April 1996 under a court order made prior to 15 March 1988 to or for the benefit of a person who reached the age of 21 before 6 April 1994 are no longer to be treated as charges on the income of the taxpayer, nor as the income of the recipient (s 149).

Payments of damages for personal injury, under an agreement or court order, are exempt from tax in the hands of the recipient. This applies to payments received after the passing of the Finance Act (TA 1988 new s 329AA). The same exemption applies to annuity payments under an award of compensation under the Criminal Injuries Compensation Scheme (new s 329AB) (s 150 and Sch 26).

Taxation of benefits. Certain benefits payable under Government "pilot" schemes are to be made wholly or partly exempt. These will be specified by Treasury order (s 151).

The jobfinder's grant is exempt from tax from its starting date in April 1995 (s 152).

Investments. The rules of the foreign income dividend scheme relating to the calculation of distributable foreign profit and notional foreign source ACT are amended. There is a minor relaxation of the requirements for a company to be an international headquarters company, and a provision enabling foreign income dividends to be included in the computation of the Case I profits of a company's life assurance business (s 153 and Sch 27).

The exemption for Government securities issued free of tax to residents abroad ("FOTRA" securities) is not to be overridden by the tax legislation. In the case of any particular issue, the Treasury may provide that a non-resident holder is exempt from tax irrespective of his country of domicile. There are consequential amendments to other legislation (s 154 and Sch 28).

A direction by the Treasury under TA 1988 s 50 or s 51, that interest on certain Government securities may be paid gross, may specify a date from which payments may be made gross (s 155 and TA 1988 new s 51AA).

Following the repeal of Schedule C, new legislation is included to deal with the deduction of tax by banks and other UK paying and collecting agents from public revenue dividends and foreign dividends (s 156, Sch 29 and TA 1988 new ss 118A–118K). These will be supplemented by regulations following consultation between the Revenue and the banks etc.

Stock lending fees received by pension funds under an approved stock lending agreement are to qualify for the same exemption as any interest arising on the same stock (s 157 and TA 1988 new s 129B).

The accrued income scheme rules do not apply to the vesting of securities in a person's personal representatives where the deceased died on or after 6 April 1996. If the personal representatives transfer the securities to legatees within the interest period in which the death occurs, the accrued income scheme rules do not apply to that transfer (s 158).

The bond washing provisions of TA 1988 s 729 are repealed, as are the corresponding provisions of s 786(4), but sales and purchases which would have been caught by those provisions are brought within s 737A (deemed manufactured payments). The provisions of s 737 are extended to cover the case where the recipient of the manufactured dividend is a non-resident but carries on a trade through a branch or agency in the UK. There are other detailed amendments and the dividend manufacturing regulations will also be amended in relation to overseas dividends (s 159).

The definition of investment trust in TA 1988 s 842 is widened to include companies whose income derives wholly or mainly from shares or securities or eligible rental income. Further, the rate of corporation tax chargeable on the eligible rental income of an investment trust is the small companies rate. Broadly speaking, eligible rental income is from the letting of property which would have qualified under the old BES rules—residential properties let under the assured tenancy rules (s 160 and Sch 30).

There are minor changes to the Venture capital trust provisions dealing with the requirements as to subsidiaries of the relevant company and the definition of "control" (s 161).

Insurance policies. The ending of certification of insurance policies, scheduled for 5 May 1996, is postponed until an "appointed date" which will be specified by an order of the Board (s 162).

Insurance companies. The provisions introduced in 1989 relating to the taxation of life assurance business are amended and there are new provisions dealing with the application of surpluses in reduction of certain losses (s 163 and Sch 31).

There are detailed changes in the rules for ascertaining the limit of relief for management expenses of a life assurance business (s 164).

Annual payments under insurance policies may now be deducted in computing profits under the provisions of Schedule D Case I (s 165).

There is a new scheme of relief for equalisation reserves maintained in connection with general insurance business. The new legislation (TA 1988 new ss 444BA–444BD) will be supplemented by regulations to be issued by the Treasury (s 166 and Sch 32).

Industrial assurance business is no longer treated as a separate business for the purposes of the provisions of TA 1988 dealing with insurance companies. There are detailed consequential amendments (s 167).

There is a new definition of "capital redemption business" and consequential amendments to the I minus E basis of the tax computation. The Treasury is given power to issue regulations providing for capital redemption business to be taxed as life assurance business (s 168).

There are detailed changes to the rules governing the making of quarterly refunds of tax to an insurance company in respect of its pensions business (s 169 and Sch 34).

The time limit for an inspector to initiate an enquiry into the return of an insurance company or friendly society is extended where a non-annual method of accounting is adopted or where actuarial valuations are carried out on a biennial or triennial basis (s 170 and TMA 1970 ss 11AC–11AE).

Friendly societies. There is a new definition of "life or endowment business" in TA 1988 s 466. With effect from 1 September 1996, certain policies providing for sickness or infirmity are excluded. There is a corresponding amendment to TA 1988 s 266 which grants relief for premiums paid on certain policies issued by friendly societies (s 171).

Personal pension schemes. The rules relating to the return of contributions after the death of a member (TA 1988 s 637A) are redrafted to take account of possible annuity purchases under s 636. Also, where a spouse or dependant is entitled to benefits after the member's death, but has elected to defer any annuity and dies during the period of deferral, a lump sum may now be paid to his heirs (s 172).

Participators in close companies.   Tax due under TA 1988 s 419 on a loan to a participator is payable nine months and one day after the end of the accounting period in which the loan was made. If the loan is repaid before the due date, the tax is not payable. If the loan is repaid after the due date, the tax is repayable nine months after the end of the accounting period in which it was repaid. This applies in relation to accounting periods ending on or after 31 March 1996 (s 173).

TCGA 1992 s 13 enables the Revenue to apportion amongst shareholders the gains arising to a non-resident company which would be a close company if resident in the UK. The basis of apportionment is changed in relation to gains arising on or after 28 November 1995. Such gains are apportioned in accordance with participators' "interests" in the company as participators. A participator's interest is determined in accordance with "all of the factors by reference to which he falls to be treated as a participator" (s 174).

Cancellation of tax advantages.   There are technical amendments to the "dividend stripping" provisions of TA 1988 s 704 to exclude from the ambit of paragraph D only those companies whose shares are listed in the Official List of the Stock Exchange and which are under the control of five or fewer persons (s 175).

Chargeable gains: reliefs.   The qualifying age for retirement relief under TCGA 1992 ss 163, 164 is reduced to 50 for disposals on or after 28 November 1995 (s 176).

Reinvestment relief is available where a chargeable gain arises on a disposal of qualifying corporate bonds which were acquired in exchange for shares. This change is back-dated to the introduction of reinvestment relief (s 177).

Special cases.   Sub-contractors are to be required to carry registration cards if they do not qualify for an exemption certificate. A sub-contractor will have to present his registration card to his contractor when seeking payment even where payment is made under deduction of tax. These new rules are to be introduced by regulations (s 178).

There are detailed amendments to the capital allowances legislation relating to rollover relief for ships (s 179 and Sch 35).

A balancing charge will be imposed where an asset representing allowable scientific research expenditure ceases to belong to the trader who incurred the expenditure. The disposal of an interest in an oil licence is deemed to be a disposal of such an asset (s 180 and CAA 1990 new ss 138A,138B).

For the purposes of TCGA 1992 s 194, a foreign oil licence relates to an undeveloped area if no development has taken place in any part of the area and no condition for carrying out development in the area has been satisfied by the grant of any consent or the approval of any programme of development (s 181).

There are detailed amendments to the controlled foreign companies legislation. In particular, the distributions required to satisfy an acceptable distribution policy are 90% of net chargeable profits for accounting periods beginning on or after 28 November 1995. As regards the exempt activities test, there is a tightening of the requirements relating to wholesale, distributive and financial businesses. There is a tightening of the wording of s 748(3)(*a*) regarding the effects of two or more transactions (s 182 and Sch 36).

PART V INHERITANCE TAX

The nil rate band is increased to £200,000 for chargeable transfers made after 5 April 1996 (s 183).

From 6 April 1996 all unquoted shares qualify for the 100% business property relief, as do unquoted securities forming part of a controlling holding (s 184).

The 100% agricultural property relief for tenanted land is extended to cases where, after 31 August 1995, a tenant dies and another person succeeds to the same tenancy. It also covers cases where, on the death of a tenant after 31 August 1995, another person obtains a tenancy under an enactment (otherwise than in relation to land in Scotland) (s 185).

PART VI STAMP DUTY AND STAMP DUTY RESERVE TAX

Stamp duty.   Transfers of securities to an electronic transfer system on or after 1 July 1996 are exempt from stamp duty (s 186).

Stamp Duty Reserve Tax (SDRT).   From 1 July 1996, SDRT is chargeable whether the agreement, transfer etc is executed within or outside the UK, and whether or not any party to the transfer is resident in the UK (s 187).

The two-month expiry period in FA 1986 s 87(2) is removed from 1 July 1996 so that the charge to SDRT arises on the "relevant day". There is a corresponding amendment to the repayment provisions of s 92 (s 188).

The exemption from stamp duty on the transfer of securities to an electronic system does not prevent the transfer being charged to SDRT if it is made for money or money's worth (s 189).

Where shares or securities are acquired by a marketmaker or broker free of stamp duty or SDRT, a subsequent intra-group transfer by that company will be chargeable to SDRT. This applies as from 4 January 1996 (s 190).

In a stock lending agreement, the return of stock to the lender and the transfer of collateral to the lender are both exempt from SDRT from 1 July 1996 (s 191 and FA 1986 new s 89B).

The provisions relating to the repayment or cancellation of SDRT are amended in consequence of the elimination of the two-month expiry period (s 192).

From 1 July 1996, the charge to SDRT on depositary receipts arises when the relevant shares are held by the issuer of the depositary receipts as arises when they are held by a nominee (s 193).

The rates of SDRT are converted from fixed amounts per £100 or part of £100 to flat percentages as from 1 July 1996 (s 194).

SDRT regulations may include provisions imposing on the Board functions involving the exercise of discretion (s 195).

Clearance services.   A person providing clearance services may, with the Board's approval, elect to pay stamp duty and SDRT on transfers within the service under the normal rules rather than paying the 1.5% duty on entry into the service (s 196 and FA 1986 new s 97A).

PART VII MISCELLANEOUS AND SUPPLEMENTAL

Miscellaneous: indirect taxation.   The Treasury is given power to make regulations determining the rate of interest on air passenger duty, insurance premium tax, VAT recoverable by assessment and landfill tax (s 197).

Miscellaneous: direct taxation. The term "bank" is defined for various tax purposes. It includes certain European banks and certain international organisations of which the UK is a member (s 198 and Sch 37).

The references in the tax legislation to quoted securities are replaced by references to securities listed in the Official List of the Stock Exchange (s 199 and Sch 38).

A person's domicile status is not to be affected by the fact that the person is or becomes eligible to vote in the UK (s 200).

The following Concessions are enacted:

B19 capital allowances for buildings

B28 Leased cars costing over £12,000

B39 Contributions to overseas pension schemes

D1, D19 Replacement of buildings destroyed

D28 Assets of negligible value

D48 Retirement relief

D36 Relief for irrecoverable loans to traders

G1,G2 Stamp allowance for lost or spoiled documents

(s 201 and Sch 39).

Miscellaneous: other matters. The Treasury is given power to make regulations to facilitate the exchange of gilts for stripped versions of the same gilts and the consolidation of strips into a single security. There are corresponding amendments to the accrued income scheme (s 202 and Sch 40).

There are amendments to the tax provisions relating to the reorganisation of the Milk Marketing Board (s 203).

FINANCE ACT 1996
(1996 Chapter 8)

ARRANGEMENT OF SECTIONS

PART I
EXCISE DUTIES

Air passenger duty

PART II
VALUE ADDED TAX

EC Second VAT Simplification Directive

Other provisions relating to charges to VAT

Payment and enforcement

PART III
LANDFILL TAX

The basic provisions

Exemptions

17

Finance Act 1996

PART IV

INCOME TAX, CORPORATION TAX AND CAPITAL GAINS TAX

CHAPTER I

PRINCIPAL PROVISIONS

18

CHAPTER II
LOAN RELATIONSHIPS

CHAPTER III
PROVISIONS RELATING TO THE SCHEDULE E CHARGE

CHAPTER IV
SHARE OPTIONS, PROFIT SHARING AND EMPLOYEE SHARE OWNERSHIP

Finance Act 1996

CHAPTER V
SELF-ASSESSMENT, GENERAL MANAGEMENT ETC

CHAPTER VI
MISCELLANEOUS PROVISIONS

Arrangement of Sections

Taxation of benefits

Investments

Insurance policies

Insurance companies

Friendly societies

Personal pension schemes

Participators in close companies

Cancellation of tax advantages

Chargeable gains: reliefs

Special cases

PART V

INHERITANCE TAX

PART VI

STAMP DUTY AND STAMP DUTY RESERVE TAX

Stamp duty

Stamp duty reserve tax

Clearance services

PART VII

MISCELLANEOUS AND SUPPLEMENTAL

Miscellaneous: indirect taxation

Miscellaneous: direct taxation

Miscellaneous: other matters

Supplemental

SCHEDULES

Arrangement of Sections

An Act to grant certain duties, to alter other duties, and to amend the law relating to the National Debt and the Public Revenue, and to make further provision in connection with Finance. 29th April 1996

PART I

EXCISE DUTIES

Air passenger duty

13 Pleasure flights

(1) In section 31 of the Finance Act 1994 (air passenger duty: exceptions for certain passengers) after subsection (4) there shall be inserted—

"(4A) A passenger is not a chargeable passenger in relation to a flight if under his agreement for carriage (whether or not it is evidenced by a ticket)—

(*a*) the flight is to depart from and return to the same airport, and
(*b*) the duration of the flight (excluding any period during which the aircraft's doors are open for boarding or disembarkation) is not to exceed 60 minutes."

(2) In section 32 of that Act (change of circumstances after ticket issued etc)—

(*a*) in subsection (1) (which provides that that section applies where a person's agreement for carriage is evidenced by a ticket) for the words "This section applies" there shall be substituted the words "Subsections (2) and (3) below apply";
(*b*) after subsection (3) there shall be added—

"(4) Where—

(*a*) at the time a passenger's flight begins, by virtue of section 31(4A) above he would not (assuming there is no change of circumstances) be a chargeable passenger in relation to the flight, and
(*b*) by reason only of a change of circumstances not attributable to any act or default of his, the flight does not return to the airport from which it departed or exceeds 60 minutes in duration (excluding any period during which the aircraft's doors are open for boarding or disembarkation),

He shall not by reason of the change of circumstances be treated as a chargeable passenger in relation to that flight."

GENERAL NOTE
This section gives statutory effect to a concession which has operated since the introduction of air passenger duty on 1 November 1994 (Customs and Excise News Release 42/94, see *Simon's Tax Intelligence* 1994, p 1287). Through an amendment to FA 1994 s 31, it exempts short pleasure flights from the duty, provided that the flight is to depart from and return to the same airport, and that the planned duration of the flight does not exceed 60 minutes. There is also provision for an unexpected change of circumstances, such that the flight does not return to the departure airport, or the permitted duration is exceeded. In this case, an amendment to FA 1994 s 32 maintains the exemption, provided that the change of circumstances has not been caused by an act or default of the passenger concerned.
Apart from this provision, many pleasure flights are outside the duty, under the exemption for aircraft which have an authorised take-off weight of less than ten tonnes or an approved passenger seating capacity of less than 20.

PART II

VALUE ADDED TAX

EC Second VAT Simplification Directive

25 EC Second VAT Simplification Directive

Sections 26 to 29 of and Schedule 3 to this Act are for the purpose of giving effect to requirements of the directive of the Council of the European Communities dated 17th May 1977 No 77/388/EEC and the amendments of that directive by the directive of that Council dated 10th April 1995 No 95/7/EC (amendments with a view to introducing new simplification measures with regard to value added tax).

GENERAL NOTE
   Sections 26–29 and Sch 3 give effect to Directive 77/388/EEC (the Sixth Directive) as amended by Directive 95/7/EC (the Second Simplification Directive).

26 Fiscal and other warehousing

(1) The provisions of Schedule 3 to this Act shall have effect.

(2) Subject to subsection (3) below, this section and Schedule 3 to this Act shall come into force on such day as the Commissioners of Customs and Excise may by order made by statutory instrument appoint, and shall apply to any acquisition of goods from another member State and any supply taking place on or after that day.

(3) In so far as the provisions inserted by Schedule 3 to this Act confer power to make regulations they shall come into force on the day this Act is passed.

GENERAL NOTE
   This section introduces Sch 3, which has effect from a day to be appointed by statutory instrument. It applies to supplies and acquisitions taking place on or after the appointed day. However, the power to make regulations under provisions inserted by Sch 3 has effect from the date of Royal Assent.

27 Value of imported goods

(1) Section 21 of the Value Added Tax Act 1994 (value of imported goods) shall be amended as follows.

(2) In subsection (2) of that section at the end of paragraph (*a*) the word "and" shall be omitted.

(3) For paragraph (*b*) of that subsection there shall be substituted—

"(*b*) all incidental expenses, such as commission, packing, transport and insurance costs, up to the goods' first destination in the United Kingdom; and
(*c*) if at the time of the importation of the goods from a place outside the member States a further destination for the goods is known, and that destination is within the United Kingdom or another member State, all such incidental expenses in so far as they result from the transport of the goods to that other destination;

and in this subsection 'the goods' first destination' means the place mentioned on the consignment note or any other document by means of which the goods are imported into the United Kingdom, or in the absence of such documentation it means the place of the first transfer of cargo in the United Kingdom."

(4) This section shall have effect in relation to goods imported on or after 1st January 1996.

GENERAL NOTE
This section amends VATA 1994 s 21(2). It makes two changes to the rules for valuing goods imported after 31 December 1995.

First, the substituted s 21(2)(*b*) provides that the taxable amount now includes all incidental expenses incurred up to the first place of destination in the UK. This is the place identified on the consignment note or other documentation under which the goods were imported. In the absence of such documentation, the first place of destination is the place in the UK where cargo is first transferred. This is normally the place where the goods are first landed or unloaded (Budget Notice 103/94 para 4).

Second, the new s 21(2)(*c*) provides that, where a further place of destination within the European Communities is known, the taxable amount must also include the incidental expenses associated with transporting the goods to that place.

For the foregoing purposes, "incidental expenses" include commission, packing, transport and insurance. The Commissioners consider that transport costs include ancillary services such as handling, loading and storage (Budget Notice 103/95, para 3).

28 Adaptation of aircraft and hovercraft

(1) Section 22 of the Value Added Tax Act 1994 shall be omitted.

(2) This section shall apply to supplies made on or after 1st January 1996.

GENERAL NOTE
This section repeals VATA 1994 s 22 in relation to supplies made after 31 December 1995.

29 Work on materials

(1) The Value Added Tax Act 1994 shall be amended as follows.

(2) After subsection (2) of section 30 there shall be inserted the following subsection—

"(2A) A supply by a person of services which consist of applying a treatment or process to another person's goods is zero-rated by virtue of this subsection if by doing so he produces goods, and either—

(*a*) those goods are of a description for the time being specified in Schedule 8; or
(*b*) a supply by him of those goods to the person to whom he supplies the services would be of a description so specified."

(3) In subsection (5) of section 55 (supplies of gold), after paragraph (*b*) there shall be inserted the following—

"; or
(*c*) any supply of services consisting in the application to another person's goods of a treatment or process which produces goods a supply of which would fall within paragraph (*a*) above.";

and the word "or" at the end of paragraph (*a*) shall be omitted.

(4) Paragraph 2 of Schedule 4 (which provides that the treatment or processing of another person's goods shall in certain circumstances be a supply of goods) shall be omitted.

(5) This section shall apply to supplies made on or after 1st January 1996.

GENERAL NOTE
This section repeals VATA 1994 Sch 4 para 2 and inserts new ss 30(2A) and 55(5)(*c*) in relation to supplies made after 31 December 1995. A trader now makes a supply of services rather than a supply of goods when he applies a treatment or process to another person's goods. Such supplies continue to be zero-rated and to be included in the special accounting scheme for gold to the same extent as previously.

The repeal of the word "or" by the proviso to sub-s (3) applies to VATA 1994 s 55(5)(*a*) as substituted with effect from 29 November 1995 by s 32(1).

Other provisions relating to charges to VAT

30   Refunds in connection with construction and conversion

(1) For subsection (1) of section 35 of the Value Added Tax Act 1994 (refund of VAT to persons constructing certain buildings) there shall be substituted the following subsections—

"(1) Where—

(*a*) a person carries out works to which this section applies,
(*b*) his carrying out of the works is lawful and otherwise than in the course or furtherance of any business, and
(*c*) VAT is chargeable on the supply, acquisition or importation of any goods used by him for the purposes of the works,

the Commissioners shall, on a claim made in that behalf, refund to that person the amount of VAT so chargeable.

(1A) The works to which this section applies are—

(*a*) the construction of a building designed as a dwelling or number of dwellings;
(*b*) the construction of a building for use solely for a relevant residential purpose or relevant charitable purpose; and
(*c*) a residential conversion.

(1B) For the purposes of this section goods shall be treated as used for the purposes of works to which this section applies by the person carrying out the works in so far only as they are building materials which, in the course of the works, are incorporated in the building in question or its site.

(1C) Where—

(*a*) a person ('the relevant person') carries out a residential conversion by arranging for any of the work of the conversion to be done by another ('a contractor'),
(*b*) the relevant person's carrying out of the conversion is lawful and otherwise than in the course or furtherance of any business,
(*c*) the contractor is not acting as an architect, surveyor or consultant or in a supervisory capacity, and
(*d*) VAT is chargeable on services consisting in the work done by the contractor,

the Commissioners shall, on a claim made in that behalf, refund to the relevant person the amount of VAT so chargeable.

(1D) For the purposes of this section works constitute a residential conversion to the extent that they consist in the conversion of a non-residential building, or a non-residential part of a building, into—

(*a*) a building designed as a dwelling or a number of dwellings;
(*b*) a building intended for use solely for a relevant residential purpose; or
(*c*) anything which would fall within paragraph (*a*) or (*b*) above if different parts of a building were treated as separate buildings."

(2) In subsection (2) of that section (method of making claim), after "may by regulations prescribe" there shall be inserted "or, in the case of documents, as the Commissioners may determine in accordance with the regulations".

(3) After subsection (3) of that section there shall be inserted the following subsections—

"(4) The notes to Group 5 of Schedule 8 shall apply for construing this section as they apply for construing that Group.

(5) The power of the Treasury by order under section 30 to vary Schedule 8 shall include—

(*a*) power to apply any variation made by the order for the purposes of this section; and

(*b*) power to make such consequential modifications of this section as they may think fit."

(4) This section applies in relation to any case in which a claim for repayment under section 35 of the Value Added Tax Act 1994 is made at any time on or after the day on which this Act is passed.

GENERAL NOTE
    This section replaces VATA 1994 s 35(1) with a new s 35(1)–(1D), amends s 35(2) and inserts new s 39(4), (5). It gives statutory effect to a concession effective from 1 March 1995 (see VAT Information Sheet 10/95, 11 April 1995, para 2) which replaced an earlier concession effective from 21 July 1994 (see VAT Information Sheet 4/94, 1 December 1994, para 7). The provisions relating to refund of VAT to do-it-yourself builders have been redrafted and extended to include residential do-it-yourself conversions. The new provisions apply to refunds claimed on or after the date of Royal Assent.

REFUND IN RESPECT OF GOODS
    The new VATA 1994 s 35(1)–(1B) provide that a person may claim a refund of VAT in respect of goods if—

(*a*) he lawfully carries out any of the following works otherwise than in the course or furtherance of business:

(i)   constructing a building designed as one or more dwellings,
(ii) constructing a building for use solely for a relevant residential purpose,
(iii) constructing a building for use solely for a relevant charitable purpose,
(iv) a residential conversion;

(*b*) the goods are building materials which are incorporated in the building or its site in the course of carrying out the works; and

(*c*) VAT is chargeable on the purchase, acquisition or importation concerned.

REFUND IN RESPECT OF SERVICES
    A person (referred to as a "relevant person") may carry out a residential conversion lawfully and otherwise than in the course or furtherance of business. He may arrange for another person (referred to as a "contractor") to carry out all or part of the conversion works. If so, the new VATA 1994 s 35(1C) provides that the relevant person may claim a refund of VAT in respect of the contractor's services if VAT is chargeable on them and the contractor does not act as an architect, surveyor, consultant or supervisor.

CLAIMS
    VATA 1994 s 35(2) is amended to provide that a claim for refund must be accompanied by such documents as the Commissioners may determine in accordance with regulations. For the regulations currently in force, see the VAT Regulations, SI 1995/2218, regs 200, 201.

DEFINITIONS
    The new VATA 1994 s 35(1D) provides that a person carries out a "residential conversion" for the foregoing purposes if he converts a non-residential building, or the non-residential part of any other building, into one or more dwellings or into accommodation intended for use solely for a relevant residential purpose.
    The new VATA 1994 s 35(4) provides that the foregoing provisions are construed in accordance with the Notes to VATA 1994 Sch 8 Group 5. For buildings designed as one or more dwellings, see Notes 2, 3. For a relevant residential purpose, see Notes 4, 5. For a relevant charitable purpose, see Note 6. For non-residential buildings and parts of buildings, see Notes 7, 8. For construction, see Notes 16–18. For building materials, see Notes 22, 23.

29

31   Groups: anti-avoidance

(1) In section 43 of the Value Added Tax Act 1994 (groups of companies), after subsection (8) there shall be inserted the following subsection—

"(9) Schedule 9A (which makes provision for ensuring that this section is not used for tax avoidance) shall have effect."

(2) After Schedule 9 to that Act there shall be inserted the Schedule set out in Schedule 4 to this Act.

(3) In section 83 of that Act (appeals), after paragraph (*w*) there shall be inserted the following paragraph—

"(wa) any direction or assessment under Schedule 9A;".

(4) In section 84 of that Act (further provisions relating to appeals), after subsection (7) there shall be inserted the following subsection—

"(7A) Where there is an appeal against a decision to make such a direction as is mentioned in section 83(wa), the cases in which the tribunal shall allow the appeal shall include (in addition to the case where the conditions for the making of the direction were not fulfilled) the case where the tribunal are satisfied, in relation to the relevant event by reference to which the direction was given, that—

(i) the change in the treatment of the body corporate, or
(ii) the transaction in question,

had as its main purpose or, as the case may be, as each of its main purposes a genuine commercial purpose unconnected with the fulfilment of the condition specified in paragraph 1(3) of Schedule 9A."

(5) Subsection (1A) of section 43 of that Act shall not have effect in relation to supplies on or after the day on which this Act is passed.

GENERAL NOTE
    VATA 1994 s 43 allows companies under common control to register as a group and disregards supplies made between group members. It has given rise to a number of tax avoidance schemes. VATA 1994 s 43(1A) was introduced by FA 1995 s 25(2) to counteract one such scheme. This section repeals VATA 1994 s 43(1A) in relation to supplies made on or after Royal Assent (sub-s (5)) and replaces it with new provisions designed to "provide a more flexible and comprehensive response to the mischief without affecting valid commercial transactions involving movement from a group" (Budget Notice 129/95 para 6). The new provisions are set out in a new VATA 1994 s 43(8) and Sch 9A (sub-ss (1), (2)). The text of Sch 9A is set out in Sch 4 of this Act. A right of appeal is given by new VATA 1994 ss 83(wa) and 84(7A) (sub-ss (3), (4)).

APPEALS
    The new VATA 1994 s 83(wa) provides that an appeal lies to a VAT and Duties Tribunal with respect to—

(a) any direction made by the Commissioners under VATA 1994 Sch 9A para 1 (as inserted by sub-s (2) and Sch 4); and
(b) any assessment made by the Commissioners under VATA 1994 Sch 9A para 6 (as inserted by sub-s (2) and Sch 4) as a consequence of such a direction.

    The new VATA 1994 s 84(7A) provides that the tribunal must allow an appeal if the conditions for making a direction were not fulfilled. A tribunal must also allow an appeal if it is satisfied that the main purpose (or each of the main purposes) for a body corporate joining or leaving a VAT group, or entering into a transaction, was a genuine commercial purpose unconnected with the making of a supply which meets the conditions set out in VATA 1994 Sch 9A para 1(3) (as inserted by sub-s (2) and Sch 4). The word "includes" seems to indicate that a tribunal may allow an appeal on other grounds.

32   Supplies of gold etc

(1) In section 55 of the Value Added Tax Act 1994 (supplies of gold), for paragraph (*a*) of subsection (5) there shall be substituted the following paragraph—

"(*a*) any supply of goods consisting in fine gold, in gold grain of any purity or in gold coins of any purity; or".

(2) This section applies in relation to any supply after 28th November 1995.

33 Small gifts

(1) In Schedule 4 to the Value Added Tax Act 1994 (matters to be treated as supply of goods or services), in paragraph 5(2)(*a*) (gift of goods in the course or furtherance of a business not a supply if cost to donor is not more than £10), for "£10" there shall be substituted "£15".

(2) At the end of paragraph 5 of Schedule 4 to that Act there shall be inserted the following sub-paragraph—

"(7) The Treasury may by order substitute for the sum for the time being specified in sub-paragraph (2)(*a*) above such sum, not being less than £10, as they think fit."

(3) In section 97(4) of that Act (orders which are subject to affirmative procedure), after paragraph (*a*) there shall be inserted the following paragraph—

"(ab) an order under paragraph 5(7) of Schedule 4 substituting a lesser sum for the sum for the time being specified in paragraph 5(2)(*a*) of that Schedule;".

(4) Subsection (1) above shall apply where a gift is made after 28th November 1995.

Payment and enforcement

34 Method of making payments on account

In section 28 of the Value Added Tax Act 1994 (payments on account of VAT), after subsection (2) there shall be inserted the following subsection—

"(2A) The Commissioners may give directions, to persons who are or may become liable by virtue of any order under this section to make payments on account of VAT, about the manner in which they are to make such payments; and where such a direction has been given to any person and has not subsequently been withdrawn, any duty of that person by virtue of such an order to make such a payment shall have effect as if it included a requirement for the payment to be made in the manner directed."

duty to make payments in the specified manner if a direction has been given to him and it has not been withdrawn.

Directions will require traders to make payments on account by electronic means such as clearing house automated payment system (CHAPS), bankers automated clearing system (BACS), standing order or bank giro credit, but not by direct debit (Budget Notice 10/95 para 3; HC Official Report, Standing Committee E (Fifth Sitting), cols 145, 146).

35 Default surcharges

(1) The Value Added Tax Act 1994 shall be amended as follows.

(2) After section 59 (default surcharge) there shall be inserted the following section—

"59A Default surcharge: payments on account

(1) For the purposes of this section a taxable person shall be regarded as in default in respect of any prescribed accounting period if the period is one in respect of which he is required, by virtue of an order under section 28, to make any payment on account of VAT and either—

(a) a payment which he is so required to make in respect of that period has not been received in full by the Commissioners by the day on which it became due; or

(b) he would, but for section 59(1A), be in default in respect of that period for the purposes of section 59.

(2) Subject to subsections (10) and (11) below, subsection (4) below applies in any case where—

(a) a taxable person is in default in respect of a prescribed accounting period; and

(b) the Commissioners serve notice on the taxable person (a 'surcharge liability notice') specifying as a surcharge period for the purposes of this section a period which—

(i) begins, subject to subsection (3) below, on the date of the notice; and

(ii) ends on the first anniversary of the last day of the period referred to in paragraph (a) above.

(3) If—

(a) a surcharge liability notice is served by reason of a default in respect of a prescribed accounting period, and

(b) that period ends at or before the expiry of an existing surcharge period already notified to the taxable person concerned,

the surcharge period specified in that notice shall be expressed as a continuation of the existing surcharge period; and, accordingly, the existing period and its extension shall be regarded as a single surcharge period.

(4) Subject to subsections (7) to (11) below, if—

(a) a taxable person on whom a surcharge liability notice has been served is in default in respect of a prescribed accounting period,

(b) that prescribed accounting period is one ending within the surcharge period specified in (or extended by) that notice, and

(c) the aggregate value of his defaults in respect of that prescribed accounting period is more than nil,

that person shall be liable to a surcharge equal to whichever is the greater of £30 and the specified percentage of the aggregate value of his defaults in respect of that prescribed accounting period.

(5) Subject to subsections (7) to (11) below, the specified percentage referred to in subsection (4) above shall be determined in relation to a prescribed accounting period by reference to the number of such periods during the surcharge period which are periods in respect of which the taxable person is in default and in respect of which the value of his defaults is more than nil, so that—

(*a*) in relation to the first such prescribed accounting period, the specified percentage is 2 per cent;

(*b*) in relation to the second such period, the specified percentage is 5 per cent;

(*c*) in relation to the third such period, the specified percentage is 10 per cent; and

(*d*) in relation to each such period after the third, the specified percentage is 15 per cent.

(6) For the purposes of this section the aggregate value of a person's defaults in respect of a prescribed accounting period shall be calculated as follows—

(*a*) where the whole or any part of a payment in respect of that period on account of VAT was not received by the Commissioners by the day on which it became due, an amount equal to that payment or, as the case may be, to that part of it shall be taken to be the value of the default relating to that payment;

(*b*) if there is more than one default with a value given by paragraph (*a*) above, those values shall be aggregated;

(*c*) the total given by paragraph (*b*) above, or (where there is only one default) the value of the default under paragraph (*a*) above, shall be taken to be the value for that period of that person's defaults on payments on account;

(*d*) the value of any default by that person which is a default falling within subsection (1)(*b*) above shall be taken to be equal to the amount of any outstanding VAT less the amount of unpaid payments on account; and

(*e*) the aggregate value of a person's defaults in respect of that period shall be taken to be the aggregate of—

(i) the value for that period of that person's defaults (if any) on payments on account; and

(ii) the value of any default of his in respect of that period that falls within subsection (1)(*b*) above.

(7) In the application of subsection (6) above for the calculation of the aggregate value of a person's defaults in respect of a prescribed accounting period—

(*a*) the amount of outstanding VAT referred to in paragraph (*d*) of that subsection is the amount (if any) which would be the amount of that person's outstanding VAT for that period for the purposes of section 59(4); and

(*b*) the amount of unpaid payments on account referred to in that paragraph is the amount (if any) equal to so much of any payments on account of VAT (being payments in respect of that period) as has not been received by the Commissioners by the last day on which that person is required (as mentioned in section 59(1)) to make a return for that period.

(8) If a person who, apart from this subsection, would be liable to a

surcharge under subsection (4) above satisfies the Commissioners or, on appeal, a tribunal—

(*a*) in the case of a default that is material for the purposes of the surcharge and falls within subsection (1)(*a*) above—

(i) that the payment on account of VAT was despatched at such a time and in such a manner that it was reasonable to expect that it would be received by the Commissioners by the day on which it became due, or

(ii) that there is a reasonable excuse for the payment not having been so despatched,

or

(*b*) in the case of a default that is material for the purposes of the surcharge and falls within subsection (1)(*b*) above, that the condition specified in section 59(7)(*a*) or (*b*) is satisfied as respects the default,

he shall not be liable to the surcharge and for the purposes of the preceding provisions of this section he shall be treated as not having been in default in respect of the prescribed accounting period in question (and, accordingly, any surcharge liability notice the service of which depended upon that default shall be deemed not to have been served).

(9) For the purposes of subsection (8) above, a default is material to a surcharge if—

(*a*) it is the default which, by virtue of subsection (4) above, gives rise to the surcharge; or

(*b*) it is a default which was taken into account in the service of the surcharge liability notice upon which the surcharge depends and the person concerned has not previously been liable to a surcharge in respect of a prescribed accounting period ending within the surcharge period specified in or extended by that notice.

(10) In any case where—

(*a*) the conduct by virtue of which a person is in default in respect of a prescribed accounting period is also conduct falling within section 69(1), and

(*b*) by reason of that conduct, the person concerned is assessed to a penalty under section 69,

the default shall be left out of account for the purposes of subsections (2) to (5) above.

(11) If the Commissioners, after consultation with the Treasury, so direct, a default in respect of a prescribed accounting period specified in the direction shall be left out of account for the purposes of subsections (2) to (5) above.

(12) For the purposes of this section the Commissioners shall be taken not to receive a payment by the day on which it becomes due unless it is made in such a manner as secures (in a case where the payment is made otherwise than in cash) that, by the last day for the payment of that amount, all the transactions can be completed that need to be completed before the whole amount of the payment becomes available to the Commissioners.

(13) In determining for the purposes of this section whether any person would, but for section 59(1A), be in default in respect of any period for the purposes of section 59, subsection (12) above shall be deemed to apply for the purposes of section 59 as it applies for the purposes of this section.

(14) For the purposes of this section references to a thing's being done by any day include references to its being done on that day.''

(3) In section 59, at the beginning of subsection (1) (circumstances amounting to a default in respect of any prescribed accounting period), there shall be inserted "Subject to subsection (1A) below''; and after that subsection there shall be inserted the following subsection—

"(1A) A person shall not be regarded for the purposes of this section as being in default in respect of any prescribed accounting period if that period is one in respect of which he is required by virtue of any order under section 28 to make any payment on account of VAT.''

(4) After subsection (10) of that section there shall be inserted the following subsection—

"(11) For the purposes of this section references to a thing's being done by any day include references to its being done on that day.''

(5) After the section 59A inserted by subsection (2) above there shall be inserted the following section—

"59B Relationship between sections 59 and 59A

(1) This section applies in each of the following cases, namely—

(*a*) where a section 28 accounting period ends within a surcharge period begun or extended by the service on a taxable person (whether before or after the coming into force of section 59A) of a surcharge liability notice under section 59; and

(*b*) where a prescribed accounting period which is not a section 28 accounting period ends within a surcharge period begun or extended by the service on a taxable person of a surcharge liability notice under section 59A.

(2) In a case falling within subsection (1)(*a*) above section 59A shall have effect as if—

(*a*) subject to paragraph (*b*) below, the section 28 accounting period were deemed to be a period ending within a surcharge period begun or, as the case may be, extended by a notice served under section 59A; but

(*b*) any question—

(i) whether a surcharge period was begun or extended by the notice, or
(ii) whether the taxable person was in default in respect of any prescribed accounting period which was not a section 28 accounting period but ended within the surcharge period begun or extended by that notice,

were to be determined as it would be determined for the purposes of section 59.

(3) In a case falling within subsection (1)(*b*) above section 59 shall have effect as if—

(*a*) subject to paragraph (*b*) below, the prescribed accounting period that is not a section 28 accounting period were deemed to be a period ending within a surcharge period begun or, as the case may be, extended by a notice served under section 59;

(*b*) any question—

(i) whether a surcharge period was begun or extended by the notice, or
(ii) whether the taxable person was in default in respect of any

35

prescribed accounting period which was a section 28 accounting period but ended within the surcharge period begun or extended by that notice,

were to be determined as it would be determined for the purposes of section 59A; and

(c) that person were to be treated as having had outstanding VAT for a section 28 accounting period in any case where the aggregate value of his defaults in respect of that period was, for the purposes of section 59A, more than nil.

(4) In this section 'a section 28 accounting period', in relation to a taxable person, means any prescribed accounting period ending on or after the day on which the Finance Act 1996 was passed in respect of which that person is liable by virtue of an order under section 28 to make any payment on account of VAT.''

(6) In section 69(4)(a) and (9)(b) (disregard in connection with penalties for breach of regulations of conduct giving rise to a surcharge), after the words "section 59", in each case, there shall be inserted "or 59A".

(7) In section 76(1) and (3)(a) (assessments for surcharges), after the words "section 59", in each case, there shall be inserted "or 59A".

(8) This section applies in relation to any prescribed accounting period ending on or after 1st June 1996, but a liability to make a payment on account of VAT shall be disregarded for the purposes of the amendments made by this section if the payment is one becoming due before that date.

GENERAL NOTE
This section inserts new VATA 1994 ss 59A, 59B and makes consequential amendments to ss 59, 69, 76. It introduces a new default surcharge system for traders who are required to make payments on account of their VAT liabilities in relation to prescribed accounting periods ending after 31 May 1996.

VATA 1994 s 59
A new VATA 1994 s 59(1A) provides that a person is not regarded as being in default for a prescribed accounting period, so as to trigger a surcharge liability notice or liability for surcharge under s 59, if he is required to make payments on account for that period (sub-s (3)).
A new VATA 1994 s 59(11) provides that anything required to be done by a specified day is deemed to be so done if it is done on or before that day (sub-s (4)).

VATA 1994 s 59A (INSERTED BY SUB-S (2))
A person required to make payments on account in respect of a prescribed accounting period is in default if, on or before the due date, the Commissioners have not received—

(a) the full amount of a payment on account due for the period;
(b) a return for the period; or
(c) (if a return has been received by the due date) the full amount of VAT shown thereon as payable (s 59A(1)).

A payment received on or before the due date is not deemed to be so received if something remains to be done after the due date so as to enable the whole amount of the payment to become available to the Commissioners (s 59A(12), (13)), eg where an unsigned cheque must be returned for signature.
A default under heads (a), (b) or (c) above may lead to service of a surcharge liability notice (s 59A(2)). A default under heads (a) or (c) above gives rise to a liability to default surcharge if the prescribed accounting period concerned ends within the surcharge period specified in, or extended by, a surcharge liability notice and the aggregate value of defaults for the prescribed accounting period is more than nil (s 59A(4)).
A default does not give rise to these consequences if—

(a) the time and mode of despatch were such that it was reasonable to expect that the payment or return would be received by the Commissioners on or before the due date (s 59A(8)(a)(i), (b) and (9));

(*b*) there is a reasonable excuse for the payment or return not having been so despatched (s 59A(8)(*a*)(ii), (*b*) and (9));
(*c*) the default gives rise to a penalty under VATA 1994 s 69 (s 59A(10)); or
(*d*) the prescribed accounting period is specified in a direction made by the Commissioners (s 59A(11)).

Any surcharge liability notice or surcharge assessment which depends upon such a default is accordingly set aside (s 59A(8), (10), (11)).

The Commissioners may serve a surcharge liability notice if a person is in default for a prescribed accounting period (referred to here as a "default period"). The surcharge liability notice must specify a surcharge period. This begins on the date of the surcharge liability notice and ends on the first anniversary of the last day of the default period (s 59A(2)). If a default occurs in respect of a prescribed accounting period ending at or before the end of the surcharge period, the existing surcharge period may be extended by service of another surcharge liability notice. The existing surcharge period and its extension are regarded as a single surcharge period (s 59A(3)).

Default surcharge is an amount equal to 2 per cent, 5 per cent, 10 per cent or 15 per cent of the aggregate value of defaults for the default period (according to whether this is respectively the first, second, third or later default in the surcharge period) subject to a minimum of £30 (s 59A(4), (5)). It should be noted that a late return, being a default, affects the rate of surcharge on a subsequent default.

The aggregate value of defaults for a prescribed accounting period is the aggregate of (s 59A(6)(*e*))—

(*a*) (as regards such payment on account giving rise to a default) the amount of the payment, or that part of it, which is received late (s 59A(6)(*a*)–(*c*) and (7)(*b*)); and
(*b*) (as regards the balance of VAT due for the prescribed accounting period) the amount of the payment due, or that part of it, which is received late (s 59A(6)(*d*) and (7)(*a*)).

The balance of VAT due for the purpose of head (*b*) above is the VAT shown as due on the return for the prescribed accounting period concerned less the payments on account due for payment (whether or not paid) in respect of the period (s 59A(6)(*d*)).

EXAMPLE

X's return for a prescribed accounting period shows VAT due of £3.9 m. He is required to make two payments on account of £1.2 m. He makes part payments of £0.9 m in respect of each payment on account and £1.4 m in respect of the balance, all by the due dates, and a final payment of £0.7 m in respect of the arrears after the due date for furnishing the return. The aggregate value of his defaults for the period is—

	Amount due £m	Paid by due date £m	Paid late £m
First payment on account	1.2	0.9	0.3
Second payment on account	1.2	0.9	0.3
Due when furnishing return	1.5	1.4	0.1
	£3.9	£3.2	£0.7

The aggregate value of his defaults for the period is £0.7 m. It should be noted that the calculation in s 59A(6), (7) arrives as the same aggregate value by a more convoluted route.

VATA 1994 s 59B (INSERTED BY SUB-S (5))

For the purpose of the following provisions, a "section 28 accounting period" is a prescribed accounting period ending on or after the date of Royal Assent in respect of which a person is liable to make payments on account (s 59B(4)).

Where a section 28 accounting period ends within a surcharge period begun or extended by a surcharge liability notice served under VATA 1994 s 59, s 59A has effect as if the period ended within a surcharge period begun or extended by a notice served under s 59A. However, any question whether a surcharge period was begun or extended by the notice is determined in accordance with s 59. Similarly, any question whether the person was in default in respect of a prescribed accounting period which is not a section 28 accounting period is determined in accordance with s 59 (s 59B(1)(*a*) and (2)).

Where a prescribed accounting period which is not a section 28 accounting period ends within a surcharge period begun or extended by a surcharge liability notice served under VATA 1994 s 59A, s 59 has effect as if the period ended within a surcharge period begun or extended by a surcharge liability notice served under s 59. However, any question whether the surcharge period was begun or extended by the notice is determined in accordance with s 59A. Similarly, any question whether the person was in default in respect of a section 28 accounting period is determined in accordance with s 59A. Furthermore, for the purposes of s 59, the person is treated as having outstanding VAT for a section 28 accounting period if the aggregate value of his defaults for the period was more than nil (s 59B(1)(*b*) and (3)).

VATA 1994 s 69

VATA 1994 s 69(9)(*b*) is amended to provide that a person liable to default surcharge under s 59A is not liable to a penalty under s 69(1) in respect of the same default. Similarly, s 69(4)(*a*) is amended to provide that the default is disregarded in determining the amount of any daily penalty to which the person becomes liable under s 69(1) in respect of a subsequent default (sub-s (6)).

VATA 1994 s 76

VATA 1994 s 76(1)(*a*) is amended to provide that a liability to default surcharge under s 59A is assessed under s 76(1). Similarly, s 76(3)(*a*) is amended to provide that the assessment is made for the prescribed accounting period in respect of which the return or payment was received late (sub-s (7)).

36 Repeated misdeclaration penalty

(1) In section 64 of the Value Added Tax Act 1994 (repeated misdeclaration penalty), the following subsections shall be substituted for subsections (6) and (7) (inaccuracies treated as not material)—

"(6) Subject to subsection (6A) below, where by reason of conduct falling within subsection (1) above—

(*a*) a person is convicted of an offence (whether under this Act or otherwise), or

(*b*) a person is assessed to a penalty under section 60 or 63,

the inaccuracy concerned shall not be regarded as material for the purposes of this section.

(6A) Subsection (6) above shall not prevent an inaccuracy by reason of which a person has been assessed to a penalty under section 63—

(*a*) from being regarded as a material inaccuracy in respect of which the Commissioners may serve a penalty liability notice under subsection (2) above; or

(*b*) from being regarded for the purposes of subsection (3) above as a material inaccuracy by reference to which any prescribed accounting period falling within the penalty period is to be treated as the first prescribed accounting period so falling in respect of which there is a material inaccuracy.

(7) Where subsection (5) or (6) above requires any inaccuracy to be regarded as not material for the purposes of the serving of a penalty liability notice, any such notice served in respect of that inaccuracy shall be deemed not to have been served."

(2) This section has effect in relation to inaccuracies contained in returns made on or after the day on which this Act is passed.

GENERAL NOTE

This section replaces VATA 1994 s 64(6), (7) with a new s 64(6), (6A), (7). It has effect in relation to inaccuracies contained in returns made on or after the date of Royal Assent. The existing provisions have been redrafted and one change made.

VATA 1994 s 64(6), (6A), (7)

A person assessed to a serious misdeclaration penalty under VATA 1994 s 63 is not liable to a repeated misdeclaration penalty under s 64 in respect of the same inaccuracy (new s 64(6)). However, the Commissioners may serve a penalty liability notice by reason of it (new s 64(6A)(*a*)). If a penalty liability notice has already been served, the inaccuracy is now taken into account in determining whether a subsequent inaccuracy is the first material inaccuracy (so as to be exempt from liability to a penalty by virtue of s 64(3)) for the penalty period specified in the notice (new s 64(6A)(*b*)).

37 Penalties for failure to notify

(1) In section 67 of the Value Added Tax Act 1994 (penalty for failure to notify liability to be registered under Schedule 1, etc)—

(*a*) in subsection (1)(*a*), after "6" there shall be inserted ", 7"; and
(*b*) in subsection (3)(*a*), for "or 6" there shall be substituted ", 6 or 7".

(2) Subject to subsection (3) below, subsection (1) above shall apply in relation to—

(*a*) any person becoming liable to be registered by virtue of sub-paragraph (2) of paragraph 1 of Schedule 1 to the Value Added Tax Act 1994 on or after 1st January 1996; and
(*b*) any person who became liable to be registered by virtue of that sub-paragraph before that date but who had not notified the Commissioners of the liability before that date.

(3) In relation to a person falling within subsection (2)(*b*) above, section 67 of the Value Added Tax Act 1994 shall have effect as if in subsection (3)(*a*) for the words "the date with effect from which he is, in accordance with that paragraph, required to be registered" there were substituted "1st January 1996".

GENERAL NOTE

FA 1985 s 15(1)(*a*) originally provided that a person was liable to a penalty if he failed to notify liability to registration when a business was transferred to him as a going concern. This ceased to be so as a result of a drafting error made when enacting FA 1990 s 10 (repealed). FA 1985 s 15(1)(*a*) (repealed) should have been amended to include a reference to VATA 1983 Sch 1 para 4A (repealed) when paras 3, 4 of that Schedule were replaced by paras 3–4B. This situation is corrected by including a reference to VATA 1994 Sch 1 para 7 (formerly VATA 1993 Sch 1 para 4A) in VATA 1994 s 67(1)(*a*) (formerly FA 1985 s 15(1)(*a*)) and making a corresponding amendment to VATA 1994 s 67(3)(*a*) (sub-s (1)).

A person who fails to notify the Commissioners of his liability to registration by the due date following the transfer of a business to him as a going concern is liable to a penalty under VATA 1994 s 67 if (sub-s (2))—

(*a*) he became liable to registration after 31 December 1995; or
(*b*) he became liable to registration, before 1 January 1996 but had not notified the Commissioners of his liability to registration before that date.

In relation to a person within head (*b*) above, "relevant VAT" for the purpose of determining the amount of the penalty under s 67(1) is the VAT (if any) for which he is liable for the period beginning on 1 January 1996 and ending on the date when the Commissioners received his notification or otherwise became fully aware of his liability to registration (sub-s (3)).

38 VAT invoices and accounting

(1) Paragraph 2 of Schedule 11 to the Value Added Tax Act 1994 (regulations about accounting for VAT, VAT invoices etc) shall be amended as follows.

(2) After sub-paragraph (2) there shall be inserted the following sub-paragraph—

"(2A) Regulations under this paragraph may confer power on the Commissioners to allow the requirements of any regulations as to the statements and other matters to be contained in a VAT invoice to be relaxed or dispensed with."

(3) In sub-paragraph (10) (adjustments of VAT accounts), at the end of paragraph (*c*) there shall be inserted

"and
(*d*) for a person, for purposes connected with the making of any such entry or financial adjustment, to be required to provide to any prescribed person, or to retain, a document in the prescribed form containing

prescribed particulars of the matters to which the entry or adjustment relates; and

(*e*) for enabling the Commissioners, in such cases as they may think fit, to dispense with or relax a requirement imposed by regulations made by virtue of paragraph (*d*) above."

GENERAL NOTE

This section inserts new VATA 1994 Sch 11 para 2(2A) and (10)(*d*), (*e*). It extends the Commissioners' powers to make regulations in connection with VAT invoices, the making of entries in accounts and the making of financial adjustments.

PART III

LANDFILL TAX

The basic provisions

39 Landfill tax

(1) A tax, to be known as landfill tax, shall be charged in accordance with this Part.

(2) The tax shall be under the care and management of the Commissioners of Customs and Excise.

GENERAL NOTE

Introduction of landfill tax

Landfill tax is a new tax on the disposal of waste in landfill sites such as tips and disused quarries. Its introduction was first announced in November 1994 (*Simon's Tax Intelligence* 1994, Budget Issue p 1554). Site operators will be accountable for the tax which applies to disposals on or after 1 October 1996 (see s 40). All waste disposed of by landfill at licensed sites is liable to tax whether or not a charge is made for its disposal (CCE Budget Notice 114/95 dated 28 November 1995, *Simon's Weekly Tax Intelligence* 1995, Budget Issue p 1925).

The stated objective of the tax is, at least in part, to act as an incentive to reduce waste and to encourage other means of waste disposal less damaging to the environment than landfill disposal.

The revenue expected from the new tax will be offset by a general reduction in the main rate of employers' NICs from April 1997.

Administration

The new tax will be administered by Customs & Excise (sub-s (2)). In the context of landfill tax references to "the Commissioners" are to the Commissioners of Customs and Excise (s 70(1)).

40 Charge to tax

(1) Tax shall be charged on a taxable disposal.

(2) A disposal is a taxable disposal if—

(*a*) it is a disposal of material as waste,
(*b*) it is made by way of landfill,
(*c*) it is made at a landfill site, and
(*d*) it is made on or after 1st October 1996.

(3) For this purpose a disposal is made at a landfill site if the land on or under which it is made constitutes or falls within land which is a landfill site at the time of the disposal.

GENERAL NOTE

Landfill tax is charged on disposals of waste material made at landfill sites on or after 1 October 1996. The waste may consist of all kinds of material including objects, substances and products (see s 70(1)).

A taxable disposal is a disposal of material as waste (see s 64) made by way of landfill (see s 65) at a landfill site (see s 66). The tax only applies where the land on or under which the waste material is disposed of is a landfill site at the time of the disposal (sub-s (3)).

The time when the waste is landfilled will be the basic tax point for the tax. The precise physical location of the tax point will be agreed with the site operator (CCE Budget Notice 114/95 dated 28 November 1995, *Simon's Weekly Tax Intelligence* 1995, Budget Issue p 1925 and see ss 61, 62).

41 Liabililty to pay tax

(1) The person liable to pay tax charged on a taxable disposal is the landfill site operator.

(2) The reference here to the landfill site operator is to the person who is at

the time of the disposal the operator of the landfill site which constitutes or contains the land on or under which the disposal is made.

GENERAL NOTE
Landfill tax is payable by the person who is the site operator (see s 67) at the time of the disposal.

42   Amount of tax

(1) The amount of tax charged on a taxable disposal shall be found by taking—

(*a*) £7 for each whole tonne disposed of and a proportionately reduced sum for any additional part of a tonne, or
(*b*) a proportionately reduced sum if less than a tonne is disposed of.

(2) Where the material disposed of consists entirely of qualifying material this section applies as if the reference to £7 were to £2.

(3) Qualifying material is material for the time being listed for the purposes of this section in an order.

(4) The Treasury must have regard to the object of securing that material is listed if it is of a kind commonly described as inactive or inert.

GENERAL NOTE
There are two rates of landfill tax. The standard rate of tax is £7 per tonne of material disposed of. A lower rate of £2 per tonne will apply to disposals of certain specified waste materials.
The list of waste materials qualifying for the lower rate ("qualifying material") will be set out in a Treasury order (sub-s (3)).
In principle the lower rate is intended to apply to inactive or inert waste (sub-s (4)) which does not decay producing methane gas, and does not have the potential to pollute groundwater or contaminate the land (CCE Budget Notice 114/95 dated 28 November 1995, *Simon's Weekly Tax Intelligence* 1995, Budget Issue p 1925). However, the categories of waste qualifying for the lower rate have been extended to include some waste materials outside the "inactive waste" category of the Department of the Environment's waste classification scheme.
Wastes which will qualify for the lower rate include (see *Simon's Weekly Tax Intelligence* 1996, p 591)—

(*a*) naturally occurring rocks and soils;
(*b*) ceramic or cemented materials;
(*c*) processed or prepared mineral materials;
(*d*) furnace slags;
(*e*) bottom ash and fly ash from wood or coal combustion;
(*f*) certain low activity organic compounds;
(*g*) gypsum and plaster disposed of in sites licensed only to take inactive or inert waste.

Further categories may be added to this list. To qualify for the lower rate, the listed waste must not be mixed with or contaminated by, any non-listed waste materials—apart from small quantities with no potential for pollution.

Exemptions

43   Material removed from water

(1) A disposal is not a taxable disposal for the purposes of this Part if it is shown to the satisfaction of the Commissioners that the disposal is of material all of which—

(*a*) has been removed (by dredging or otherwise) from water falling within subsection (2) below, and
(*b*) formed part of or projected from the bed of the water concerned before its removal.

(2) Water falls within this subsection if it is—

(*a*) a river, canal or watercourse (whether natural or artificial), or
(*b*) a dock or harbour (whether natural or artificial).

(3) A disposal is not a taxable disposal for the purposes of this Part if it is shown to the satisfaction of the Commissioners that the disposal is of material all of which—

(*a*) has been removed (by dredging or otherwise) from water falling within the approaches to a harbour (whether natural or artificial),
(*b*) has been removed in the interests of navigation, and
(*c*) formed party of or projected from the bed of the water concerned before its removal.

(4) A disposal is not a taxable disposal for the purposes of this Part if it is shown to the satisfaction of the Commissioners that the disposal is of material all of which—

(*a*) consists of naturally occurring mineral material, and
(*b*) has been removed (by dredging or otherwise) from the sea in the course of commercial operations carried out to obtain substances such as sand or gravel from the seabed.

GENERAL NOTE
This section provides exemptions from landfill tax for disposals of certain materials dredged, or otherwise removed from, water. The exemptions are intended to cover landfill disposals of natural accumulations of material removed from harbours and waterways in order to keep the waterway clear for navigation or to prevent flooding. They are not intended to apply to, for example, the disposal of waste material removed from stagnant ponds and lakes (HC Official Report, 27 March 1996, col 1062). The three specific sets of circumstances in which the disposal is exempted from landfill tax are as follows.
The first (sub-ss (1), (2)) relates to material from rivers, canals or watercourses, or from docks or harbours. This material must have projected from, or formed part of, the bed of the water from which it was removed.
The second head of exemption (sub-s (3)) relates to material from harbour approaches which is removed in the interests of navigation. Again the material must have projected from, or formed part of, the bed of the water from which it was removed.
The third head of exemption (sub-s (4)) applies to naturally occurring mineral material removed from the sea in the course of commercial operations to extract substances, such as sand or gravel, from the seabed.
To be exempt, the disposal must consist only of the qualifying material under each head.

44 Mining and quarrying

(1) A disposal is not a taxable disposal for the purposes of this Part if it is shown to the satisfaction of the Commissioners that the disposal is of material all of which fulfils each of the conditions set out in subsections (2) to (4) below.

(2) The material must result from commercial mining operations (whether the mining is deep or open-cast) or from commercial quarrying operations.

(3) The material must be naturally occurring material extracted from the earth in the course of the operations.

(4) The material must not have been subjected to, or result from, a non-qualifying process carried out at any stage between the extraction and the disposal.

(5) A non-qualifying process is—

(*a*) a process separate from the mining or quarrying operations, or
(*b*) a process forming part of those operations and permanently altering the material's chemical composition.

GENERAL NOTE
This section exempts landfill disposals of waste materials from mines and quarries subject to certain conditions (sub-s (1)).
The exemption applies only to waste extracted from the earth in the course of a commercial mining or quarrying operation (sub-ss (2), (3)). The waste must be naturally occurring material

(sub-s 3)) and must not have been processed either separately from the mining or quarrying operation or in such a way as to alter its chemical composition between extraction and disposal (sub-s (5)). Processing which forms part of the mining or quarrying operation need not necessarily be carried out at the mine or quarry (HC Official Report, 27 March 1996, col 1064).

45 Pet cemeteries

(1) A disposal is not a taxable disposal for the purposes of this Part if—

(*a*) the disposal is of material consisting entirely of the remains of dead domestic pets, and

(*b*) the landfill site at which the disposal is made fulfils the test set out in subsection (2) below.

(2) The test is that during the relevant period—

(*a*) no landfill disposal was made at the site, or

(*b*) the only landfill disposals made at the site were of material consisting entirely of the remains of dead domestic pets.

(3) For the purposes of subsection (2) above the relevant period—

(*a*) begins with 1st October 1996 or (if later) with the coming into force in relation to the site of the licence or resolution mentioned in section 66 below, and

(*b*) ends immediately before the disposal mentioned in subsection (1) above.

GENERAL NOTE
This section exempts disposals of waste consisting only of the remains of dead domestic pets (s 45(1)(*a*)). This exemption is intended for pet cemeteries licensed as landfill sites (CCE Budget Notice 114/95 dated 28 November 1995, *Simon's Weekly Tax Intelligence* 1995, Budget Issue, p 1925). If the site has also been used for landfill disposal of other kinds of waste materials since 1 October 1996 or, if later, the date on which the site's waste deposit or disposal licence was granted, the exemption does not apply (s 45(1)(*b*), (2)–(3)).

46 Power to vary

(1) Provision may be made by order to produce the result that—

(*a*) a disposal which would otherwise be a taxable disposal (by virtue of this Part as it applies for the time being) is not a taxable disposal;

(*b*) a disposal which would otherwise not be a taxable disposal (by virtue of this Part as it applies for the time being) is a taxable disposal.

(2) Without prejudice to the generality of subsection (1) above, an order under this section may—

(*a*) confer exemption by reference to certificates issued by the Commissioners and to conditions set out in certificates;

(*b*) allow the Commissioners to direct requirements to be met before certificates can be issued;

(*c*) provide for the review of decisions about certificates and for appeals relating to decisions on review.

(3) Provision may be made under this section in such way as the Treasury think fit (whether by amending this Part or otherwise).

GENERAL NOTE
Landfill tax exemptions may be extended or restricted by Treasury order (sub-s (1)).

In particular it is proposed to introduce a certification procedure (sub-s (2)) for exempting disposals of waste from the clearance of previously contaminated land. The procedure would enable exemption to be given where clearance is necessary for reclamation of the land while ensuring that it did not benefit those responsible for the pollution of the land (*Simon's Weekly Tax Intelligence* 1996, p 529, HC Official Report, 27 March 1996, col 1053).

Administration

47 Registration

(1) The register kept under this section may contain such information as the Commissioners think is required for the purposes of the care and management of the tax.

(2) A person who—

(*a*) carries out taxable activities, and
(*b*) is not registered,

is liable to be registered.

(3) Where—

(*a*) a person at any time forms the intention of carrying out taxable activities, and
(*b*) he is not registered,

he shall notify the Commissioners of his intention.

(4) A person who at any time ceases to have the intention of carrying out taxable activities shall notify the Commissioners of that fact.

(5) Where a person is liable to be registered by virtue of subsection (2) above the Commissioners shall register him with effect from the time when he begins to carry out taxable activities; and this subsection applies whether or not he notifies the Commissioners under subsection (3) above.

(6) Where the Commissioners are satisfied that a person has ceased to carry out taxable activities they may cancel his registration with effect from the earliest practicable time after he so ceased; and this subsection applies whether or not he notifies the Commissioners under subsection (4) above.

(7) Where—

(*a*) a person notifies the Commissioners under subsection (4) above,
(*b*) they are satisfied that he will not carry out taxable activities,
(*c*) they are satisfied that no tax which he is liable to pay is unpaid,
(*d*) they are satisfied that no credit to which he is entitled under regulations made under section 51 below is outstanding, and
(*e*) subsection (8) below does not apply,

the Commissioners shall cancel his registration with effect from the earliest practicable time after he ceases to carry out taxable activities.

(8) Where—

(*a*) a person notifies the Commissioners under subsection (4) above, and
(*b*) they are satisfied that he has not carried out, and will not carry out, taxable activities,

the Commissioners shall cancel his registration with effect from the time when he ceased to have the intention to carry out taxable activities.

(9) For the purposes of this section regulations may make provision—

(*a*) as to the time within which a notification is to be made;
(*b*) as to the form and manner in which any notification is to be made and as to the information to be contained in or provided with it;
(*c*) requiring a person who has made a notification to notify the Commissioners if any information contained in or provided in connection with it is or becomes inaccurate;
(*d*) as to the correction of entries in the register.

(10) References in this Part to a registrable person are to a person who—

(*a*) is registered under this section, or

(*b*) is liable to be registered under this section.

Any person who carries out taxable activities (see s 69) is liable to be registered (sub-s (2)). There is, of course, no turnover threshold for landfill tax registration (CCE Budget Notice 114/95 dated 28 November 1995, *Simon's Weekly Tax Intelligence* 1995, Budget Issue p 1925). Landfill site operators will be required to notify liability to register by the end of August 1996 (CCE Budget Notice 114/95 dated 28 November 1995, *Simon's Weekly Tax Intelligence* 1995, Budget Issue, p 1925).

An unregistered person who intends to start carrying out taxable activities must give notice of that intention to the Commissioners (sub-s (3)). The Commissioners must also be notified when the intention to carry out taxable activities ceases (sub-s (4)).

The Commissioners may cancel the registration of a person who has ceased to carry out taxable activities (sub-s (6)). Where a person has given notice that he no longer intends to make taxable supplies, cancellation of registration is mandatory (sub-ss (7)–(8)) provided the Commissioners are satisfied that the person concerned will not carry out taxable activities and there is no unpaid tax or credit outstanding.

The time limits for giving the required notices to the Commissioners, the form of notice, and the information to be supplied, will be set out in regulations made by the Commissioners. The regulations may also provide for notification of inaccuracies and for correction of the register (sub-s (9)).

A "registrable person" is defined as one who is registered or liable to be registered for the purposes of the tax (sub-s (10)).

48 Information required to keep register up to date

(1) Regulations may make provision requiring a registrable person to notify the Commissioners of particulars which—

(*a*) are of changes in circumstances relating to the registrable person or any business carried on by him,

(*b*) appear to the Commissioners to be required for the purpose of keeping the register kept under section 47 above up to date, and

(*c*) are of a prescribed description.

(2) Regulations may make provision—

(*a*) as to the time within which a notification is to be made;

(*b*) as to the form and manner in which a notification is to be made;

(*c*) requiring a person who has made a notification to notify the Commissioners if any information contained in it is inaccurate.

The Commissioners may make regulations requiring registrable persons to supply prescribed information to keep the landfill tax register up to date. The information covered relates to changes in the circumstances of the registrable person or any business carried on by him.

The regulations may impose time limits for supplying the information, set out the method of notifying it, and require notification of any inaccuracies in the information provided.

49 Accounting for tax and time for payment

Regulations may provide that a registrable person shall—

(*a*) account for tax by reference to such periods (accounting periods) as may be determined by or under the regulations;

(*b*) make, in relation to accounting periods, returns in such form as may be prescribed and at such times as may be so determined;

(*c*) pay tax at such times and in such manner as may be so determined.

The Commissioners may make regulations about accounting periods, the form and making of returns, and the time and manner of payment of the tax.

ACCOUNTING PERIODS

It is expected that accounting periods will be quarterly and the tax will be payable one month after the end of the period. The Commissioners will allow accounting periods to be aligned with existing periods for VAT returns or returns required by waste regulatory authorities. Monthly returns may be required where the Commissioners consider the tax to be at risk (CCE Budget Notice 114/95 dated 28 November 1995, *Simon's Weekly Tax Intelligence* 1995, Budget Issue, p 1925).

50 Power to assess

(1) Where—

(*a*) a person has failed to make any returns required to be made under this Part,

(*b*) a person has failed to keep any documents necessary to verify returns required to be made under this Part,

(*c*) a person has failed to afford the facilities necessary to verify returns required to be made under this Part, or

(*d*) it appears to the Commissioners that returns required to be made by a person under this Part are incomplete or incorrect,

the Commissioners may assess the amount of tax due from the person concerned to the best of their judgment and notify it to him.

(2) Where a person has for an accounting period been paid an amount to which he purports to be entitled under regulations made under section 51 below, then, to the extent that the amount ought not to have been paid or would not have been paid had the facts been known or been as they later turn out to be, the Commissioners may assess the amount as being tax due from him for that period and notify it to him accordingly.

(3) Where a person is assessed under subsections (1) and (2) above in respect of the same accounting period the assessments may be combined and notified to him as one assessment.

(4) Where the person failing to make a return, or making a return which appears to the Commissioners to be incomplete or incorrect, was required to make the return as a personal representative, trustee in bankruptcy, receiver, liquidator or person otherwise acting in a representative capacity in relation to another person, subsection (1) above shall apply as if the reference to tax due from him included a reference to tax due from that other person.

(5) An assessment under subsection (1) or (2) above of an amount of tax due for an accounting period shall not be made after the later of the following—

(*a*) two years after the end of the accounting period;

(*b*) one year after evidence of facts, sufficient in the Commissioners' opinion to justify the making of the assessment, comes to their knowledge;

but where further such evidence comes to their knowledge after the making of an assessment under subsection (1) or (2) above another assessment may be made under the subsection concerned in addition to any earlier assessment.

(6) Where—

(*a*) as a result of a person's failure to make a return in relation to an accounting period the Commissioners have made an assessment under subsection (1) above for that period,

(*b*) the tax assessed has been paid but no proper return has been made in relation to the period to which the assessment related, and

(*c*) as a result of a failure to make a return in relation to a later accounting period, being a failure by the person referred to in paragraph (*a*) above or a person acting in a representative capacity in relation to him, as mentioned in subsection (4) above, the Commissioners find it necessary to make another assessment under subsection (1) above,

then, if the Commissioners think fit, having regard to the failure referred to in paragraph (a) above, they may specify in the assessment referred to in paragraph (c) above an amount of tax greater than that which they would otherwise have considered to be appropriate.

(7) Where an amount has been assessed and notified to any person under subsection (1) or (2) above it shall be deemed to be an amount of tax due from him and may be recovered accordingly unless, or except to the extent that, the assessment has subsequently been withdrawn or reduced.

(8) For the purposes of this section notification to—

(a) a personal representative, trustee in bankruptcy, receiver or liquidator, or

(b) a person otherwise acting in a representative capacity in relation to another person,

shall be treated as notification to the person in relation to whom the person mentioned in paragraph (a) above, or the first person mentioned in paragraph (b) above, acts.

(9) Subsection (5) above has effect subject to paragraph 33 of Schedule 5 to this Act.

(10) In this section "trustee in bankruptcy" means, as respects Scotland, an interim or permanent trustee (within the meaning of the Bankruptcy (Scotland) Act 1985) or a trustee acting under a trust deed (within the meaning of that Act).

GENERAL NOTE

The Commissioners can make estimated assessments of landfill tax to the best of their judgment (sub-s (1)) where—

(a) returns have not been made; or

(b) the Commissioners have been prevented from verifying returns because the necessary records have not been kept or they have not been allowed access to such records; or

(c) the returns made are incomplete or incorrect.

The Commissioners may also make assessments to recover overpaid credit as tax due (sub-s (2)).

An estimated assessment of tax and an assessment to recover overpaid credit may be combined and notified together.

The power to make an estimated assessment applies equally where a person acting in a representative capacity (eg on behalf of a deceased or insolvent person) fails to make a return or makes a return which is incomplete or incorrect. References to tax due from the representative include tax due from the taxpayer (sub-s (4)) and notification to the representative is notice to the taxpayer (sub-s (8)). If a person acting in a representative capacity fails to make a return for an accounting period after the taxpayer has paid an estimated assessment without making the return due for an earlier accounting period, the Commissioners may increase the amount which they would otherwise have assessed for the later period (sub-s (6)). The increase in the estimate for that period is presumably to allow for the possibility that the earlier assessment was an underestimate of the tax due.

Subject to any subsequent reduction or withdrawal of the assessment, the tax assessed is recoverable as tax due (sub-s (7)).

TIME LIMITS FOR ASSESSMENTS

Subject to an overriding limit of six years (sub-s (9), Sch 5 para 33), the time limit for assessments is two years after the end of the accounting period for which the tax was due or, if later, one year after evidence of facts justifying the making of the assessment came to the Commissioners' knowledge (sub-s (5)).

Credit

51 Credit: general

(1) Regulations may provide that where—

(*a*) a person has paid or is liable to pay tax, and

(*b*) prescribed conditions are fulfilled,

the person shall be entitled to credit of such an amount as is found in accordance with prescribed rules.

(2) Regulations may make provision as to the manner in which a person is to benefit from credit, and in particular may make provision—

(*a*) that a person shall be entitled to credit by reference to accounting periods;

(*b*) that a person shall be entitled to deduct an amount equal to his total credit for an accounting period from the total amount of tax due from him for the period;

(*c*) that if no tax is due from a person for an accounting period but he is entitled to credit for the period, the amount of the credit shall be paid to him by the Commissioners;

(*d*) that if the amount of credit to which a person is entitled for an accounting period exceeds the amount of tax due from him for the period, an amount equal to the excess shall be paid to him by the Commissioners;

(*e*) for the whole or part of any credit to be held over to be credited for a subsequent accounting period;

(*f*) as to the manner in which a person who has ceased to be registrable is to benefit from credit.

(3) Regulations under subsection (2)(*c*) or (*d*) above may provide that where at the end of an accounting period an amount is due to a person who has failed to submit returns for an earlier period as required by this Part, the Commissioners may withhold payment of the amount until he has complied with that requirement.

(4) Regulations under subsection (2)(*e*) above may provide for credit to be held over either on the person's application or in accordance with directions given by the Commissioners from time to time; and the regulations may allow directions to be given generally or with regard to particular cases.

(5) Regulations may provide that—

(*a*) no benefit shall be conferred in respect of credit except on a claim made in such manner and at such time as may be determined by or under regulations;

(*b*) payment in respect of credit shall be made subject to such conditions (if any) as the Commissioners think fit to impose, including conditions as to repayment in specified circumstances;

(*c*) deduction in respect of credit shall be made subject to such conditions (if any) as the Commissioners think fit to impose, including conditions as to the payment to the Commissioners, in specified circumstances, of an amount representing the whole or part of the amount deducted.

(6) Regulations may require a claim by a person to be made in a return required by provision made under section 49 above.

(7) Nothing in section 52 or 53 below shall be taken to derogate from the power to make regulations under this section (whether with regard to bad debts, the environment or any other matter).

GENERAL NOTE

The Commissioners can provide by regulations for a system of landfill tax credits under which a person who has paid or is liable to pay tax would be entitled to credit in circumstances to be specified (sub-s (1)). The credit system would be used, eg to ensure that an operator would be taxed only once where the waste disposed of was transferred to another landfill site (CCE Budget

Notice 114/95 dated 28 November 1995, *Simon's Weekly Tax Intelligence* 1995, Budget Issue, p 1926). The total credit for an accounting period would be deducted from the tax due for the period. If there is no tax due, or it is less than the credit, the balance of the credit would be paid to the taxpayer or held over to a later period. The regulations may also provide for the treatment of credits due to a person who ceases to be registrable for landfill tax (sub-s (2)). Credits may be withheld if returns are outstanding for earlier accounting periods (sub-s (3)), or at the election of the taxpayer, or by direction of the Commissioners (sub-s (4)).

The regulations may require landfill tax credit to be claimed, prescribe the method and timing of claims, and impose conditions as to the payment and repayment of credit and as to deduction of credit (sub-s (5)). A claim to credit may be required to be made in the return (sub-s (6)).

Specific regulation-making powers given as regards credits for bad debts (s 52) and for payments to approved environmental bodies (s 53) are additional to the general powers described above (sub-s (7)).

52   Bad debts

(1) Regulations may be made under section 51 above with a view to securing that a person is entitled to credit if—

(*a*) he carries out a taxable activity as a result of which he becomes entitled to a debt which turns out to be bad (in whole or in part), and

(*b*) such other conditions as may be prescribed are fulfilled.

(2) The regulations may include provision under section 51(5)(*b*) or (*c*) above requiring repayment or payment if it turns out that it was not justified to regard a debt as bad (or to regard it as bad to the extent that it was so regarded).

(3) The regulations may include provision for determining whether, and to what extent, a debt is to be taken to be bad.

GENERAL NOTE
Credit may be allowed for the landfill tax element of a bad debt which results from a taxable activity. This is subject to conditions to be prescribed by regulations including conditions requiring repayment of credit if all or part of the debt later appears to be recoverable.

53   Bodies concerned with the environment

(1) Regulations may be made under section 51 above with a view to securing that a person is entitled to credit if—

(*a*) he pays a sum to a body whose objects are or include the protection of the environment, and

(*b*) such other conditions as may be prescribed are fulfilled.

(2) The regulations may in particular prescribe conditions—

(*a*) requiring bodies to which sums are paid (environmental bodies) to be approved by another body (the regulatory body);

(*b*) requiring the regulatory body to be approved by the Commissioners;

(*c*) requiring sums to be paid with the intention that they be expended on such matters connected with the protection of the environment as may be prescribed.

(3) The regulations may include provision under section 51(5)(*b*) or (*c*) above requiring repayment or payment if—

(*a*) a sum is not in fact expended on matters prescribed under subsection (2)(*c*) above, or

(*b*) a prescribed condition turns out not to have been fulfilled.

(4) The regulations may include—

(*a*) provision for determining the amount of credit (including provision for limiting it);

(*b*) provision that matters connected with the protection of the environment include such matters as overheads (including administration) of environmental bodies and the regulatory body;

(*c*) provision as to the matters by reference to which an environmental body or the regulatory body can be, and remain, approved (including matters relating to the functions and activities of any such body);

(*d*) provision allowing approval of an environmental body or the regulatory body to be withdrawn (whether prospectively or retrospectively);

(*e*) provision that, if approval of the regulatory body is withdrawn, another body may be approved in its place or its functions may be performed by the Commissioners;

(*f*) provision allowing the Commissioners to disclose to the regulatory body information which relates to the tax affairs of persons carrying out taxable activities and which is relevant to the credit scheme established by the regulations.

GENERAL NOTE
Credit will be allowed in respect of payments to approved bodies. These bodies will have objects which include the protection of the environment (sub-s (2)). These may include research and development of, and provision of information about, more sustainable waste management practices—such as recycling, composting, energy recovery and minimisation of waste production (HC Official Report, Standing Committee E, 8 February 1996, col 180).

The regulations to be made by the Commissioners may impose conditions on the right to credit in these circumstances, lay down requirements for approval of environmental bodies by regulatory bodies approved by the Commissioners, and prescribe the environmental matters on which such payments may be spent (sub-s (2)). The prescribed environmental matters may include overheads of the approved environmental or regulatory body (sub-s (4)(*b*)). Repayment of the credit may be required where the payment is not spent on the prescribed matters or the conditions for credit are not met (sub-s (3)).

The regulations as to credits for payments to environmental bodies may also cover matters affecting the approval of environmental and regulatory bodies, withdrawal of approval, disclosure of information by the Commissioners to regulatory bodies, and the amount of the credit (sub-s (4)). It is proposed that a site operator who makes a payment to an environmental trust will be able to claim a rebate of up to 90 per cent of the payment, subject to a maximum of 20 per cent of the landfill tax (CCE Budget Notice 114/95 dated 28 November 1995, *Simon's Weekly Tax Intelligence* 1995, Budget Issue, p 1927).

Review and appeal

54 Review of Commissioners' decisions

(1) This section applies to the following decisions of the Commissioners—

(*a*) a decision as to the registration or cancellation of registration of any person under this Part;

(*b*) a decision as to whether tax is chargeable in respect of a disposal or as to how much tax is chargeable;

(*c*) a decision as to whether a person is entitled to credit by virtue of regulations under section 51 above or as to how much credit a person is entitled to or as to the manner in which he is to benefit from credit;

(*d*) a decision as to an assessment falling within subsection (2) below or as to the amount of such an assessment;

(*e*) a decision to refuse a request under section 58(3) below;

(*f*) a decision to refuse an application under section 59 below;

(*g*) a decision as to whether conditions set out in a specification under the authority of provision made under section 68(4)(*b*) below are met in relation to a disposal;

(*h*) a decision to give a direction under any provision contained in regulations by virtue of section 68(5) below;

(*i*) a decision as to a claim for the repayment of an amount under paragraph 14 of Schedule 5 to this Act;

(*j*) a decision as to liability to a penalty under Part V of that Schedule or as to the amount of such a penalty;

(*k*) a decision under paragraph 19 of that Schedule (as mentioned in paragraph 19(5));

(*l*) a decision as to any liability to pay interest under paragraph 26 or 27 of that Schedule or as to the amount of the interest payable;

(*m*) a decision as to any liability to pay interest under paragraph 29 of that Schedule or as to the amount of the interest payable;

(*n*) a decision to require any security under paragraph 31 of that Schedule or as to its amount;

(*o*) a decision as to the amount of any penalty or interest specified in an assessment under paragraph 32 of that Schedule.

(2) An assessment falls within this subsection if it is an assessment under section 50 above in respect of an accounting period in relation to which a return required to be made by virtue of regulations under section 49 above has been made.

(3) Any person who is or will be affected by any decision to which this section applies may by notice in writing to the Commissioners require them to review the decision.

(4) The Commissioners shall not be required under this section to review any decision unless the notice requiring the review is given before the end of the period of 45 days beginning with the day on which written notification of the decision, or of the assessment containing the decision, was first given to the person requiring the review.

(5) For the purposes of subsection (4) above it shall be the duty of the Commissioners to give written notification of any decision to which this section applies to any person who—

(*a*) requests such a notification,

(*b*) has not previously been given written notification of that decision, and

(*c*) if given such a notification, will be entitled to require a review of the decision under this section.

(6) A person shall be entitled to give a notice under this section requiring a decision to be reviewed for a second or subsequent time only if—

(*a*) the grounds on which he requires the further review are that the Commissioners did not, on any previous review, have the opportunity to consider certain facts or other matters, and

(*b*) he does not, on the further review, require the Commissioners to consider any facts or matters which were considered on a previous review except in so far as they are relevant to any issue not previously considered.

(7) Where the Commissioners are required in accordance with this section to review any decision it shall be their duty to do so; and on the review they may withdraw, vary or confirm the decision.

(8) Where—

(*a*) it is the duty under this section of the Commissioners to review any decision, and

(*b*) they do not, within the period of 45 days beginning with the day on which the review was required, give notice to the person requiring it of their determination on the review,

they shall be deemed for the purposes of this Part to have confirmed the decision.

GENERAL NOTE

The right to a review and appeal applies to decisions of the Commissioners on the following (sub-s (1))—

(*a*) registration and cancellation of registration;
(*b*) whether tax is chargeable, and the amount of tax;
(*c*) entitlement to credit, the amount of credit, and how it is to be given;
(*d*) assessment of tax or credit, and the amount assessed;
(*e*) refusal of a company's request for separate registration of its business divisions;
(*f*) refusal of group registration;
(*g*) whether conditions for the application of specified rules for determining the weight of materials disposed of are met;
(*h*) a direction that agreed rules for determining weight of materials shall cease to apply;
(*i*) claims for repayment of tax overpaid;
(*j*) liability to penalties;
(*k*) apportionment of a penalty for tax evasion between a company and its officers;
(*l*) liability to interest on underdeclared or unpaid tax, and the amount of such interest;
(*m*) interest payable by the Commissioners;
(*n*) requirement of security as a condition of carrying out taxable activities; and
(*o*) the amount of penalties or interest assessed.

Any person affected by such a decision may require the Commissioners to review the decision. The person requiring the review must do so by notice in writing to the Commissioners within 45 days starting with the day on which written notification of the decision (or an assessment containing the decision) was given to him (sub-ss (3)–(4)); but the Commissioners may nevertheless agree to review the decision notwithstanding that the time for giving notice has expired (see s 55(1)(*b*)). If a person affected by a decision has not already been given written notification of it, he may request the Commissioners to do this (sub-s (5)).

On reviewing the decision the Commissioners may withdraw, vary or confirm it (sub-s (7)). If they do not give notice of their determination on the review within 45 days starting with the day on which the review was required, they are treated as having confirmed the decision (sub-s (8)). A further review may only be required if there are facts or matters which the Commissioners did not have the opportunity to consider on their previous review. The Commissioners cannot be required to reconsider facts or matters considered on a previous review unless they are relevant to issues not previously considered (sub-s (6)).

55 Appeals: general

(1) Subject to the following provisions of this section, an appeal shall lie to an appeal tribunal with respect to any of the following decisions—

(*a*) any decision by the Commissioners on a review under section 54 above (including a deemed confirmation under subsection (8) of that section);
(*b*) any decision by the Commissioners on such review of a decision referred to in section 54(1) above as the Commissioners have agreed to undertake in consequence of a request made after the end of the period mentioned in section 54(4) above.

(2) Where an appeal is made under this section by a person who is required to make returns by virtue of regulations under section 49 above, the appeal shall not be entertained unless the appellant—

(*a*) has made all the returns which he is required to make by virtue of those regulations, and
(*b*) has paid the amounts shown in those returns as payable by him.

(3) Where an appeal is made under this section with respect to a decision falling within section 54(1)(*b*) or (*d*) above the appeal shall not be entertained unless—

(*a*) the amount which the Commissioners have determined to be payable as tax has been paid or deposited with them, or
(*b*) on being satisfied that the appellant would otherwise suffer hardship the Commissioners agree or the tribunal decides that it should be entertained notwithstanding that that amount has not been so paid or deposited.

(4) On an appeal under this section against an assessment to a penalty under paragraph 18 of Schedule 5 to this Act, the burden of proof as to the matters specified in paragraphs (*a*) and (*b*) of sub-paragraph (1) of paragraph 18 shall lie upon the Commissioners.

GENERAL NOTE
There is a right to appeal to a VAT and duties tribunal (see s 70(1)) against the outcome of the Commissioners' review (sub-s (1)). The tribunal may not generally hear an appeal where the appellant has failed to submit returns or to pay the tax shown as due on his returns (sub-s (2)). If the appeal relates to tax chargeable or assessed as due, the tax must be paid or deposited with the Commissioners; this requirement can, however, be waived by the Commissioners or the tribunal if satisfied that the appellant would otherwise suffer hardship (sub-s (3)).

On an appeal against the assessment of a penalty for tax evasion, the burden of proof (as to the act or omission giving rise to the penalty and that the conduct involved dishonesty) is on the Commissioners (sub-s (4)).

56 Appeals: other provisions

(1) Subsection (2) below applies where the Commissioners make a decision falling within section 54(1)(*d*) above and on a review of it there is a further decision with respect to which an appeal is made under section 55 above; and the reference here to a further decision includes a reference to a deemed confirmation under section 54(8) above.

(2) Where on the appeal—

(*a*) it is found that the amount specified in the assessment is less than it ought to have been, and

(*b*) the tribunal gives a direction specifying the correct amount,

the assessment shall have effect as an assessment of the amount specified the direction and that amount shall be deemed to have been notified to the appellant.

(3) Where on an appeal under section 55 above it is found that the whole or part of any amount paid or deposited in pursuance of section 55(3) above is not due, so much of that amount as is found not to be due shall be repaid with interest at such rate as the tribunal may determine.

(4) Where on an appeal under section 55 above it is found that the whole or part of any amount due to the appellant by virtue of regulations under section 51(2)(*c*) or (*d*) or (*f*) above has not been paid, so much of that amount as is found not to have been paid shall be paid with interest at such rate as the tribunal may determine.

(5) Where an appeal under section 55 above has been entertained notwithstanding that an amount determined by the Commissioners to be payable as tax has not been paid or deposited and it is found on the appeal that that amount is due the tribunal may, if it thinks fit, direct that that amount shall be paid with interest at such rate as may be specified in the direction.

(6) Without prejudice to paragraph 25 of Schedule 5 to this Act, nothing in section 55 above shall be taken to confer on a tribunal any power to vary an amount assessed by way of penalty except in so far as it is necessary to reduce it to the amount which is appropriate under paragraphs 18 to 24 of that Schedule.

(7) Without prejudice to paragraph 28 of Schedule 5 to this Act, nothing in section 55 above shall be taken to confer on a tribunal any power to vary an amount assessed by way of interest except in so far as it is necessary to reduce it to the amount which is appropriate under paragraph 26 or 27 of that Schedule.

(8) Sections 85 and 87 of the Value Added Tax Act 1994 (settling of appeals by agreement and enforcement of certain decisions of tribunal) shall have effect as if—

   (*a*) the references to section 83 of that Act included references to section 55 above, and

   (*b*) the references to value added tax included references to landfill tax.

GENERAL NOTE
   Where the appeal tribunal increases an assessment of tax due, the assessment is treated as having been notified to the appellant in the increased amount (sub-ss (1)–(2)).
   If the outcome of an appeal is that the tax paid or deposited is not due, it is repayable with interest; and similarly credit found to be due to the appellant is to be paid with interest. The rate of interest in these cases is decided by the tribunal (sub-ss (3)–(4)). The tribunal may direct payment of interest by the appellant where tax not already paid or deposited is found on appeal to be due to the Commissioners (sub-s (5)).
   The powers of the tribunal to vary amounts assessed as penalties (see Sch 5 paras 18–25) and interest (see Sch 5 paras 26–28), otherwise than by way of mitigation, are limited (sub-ss (6)–(7)).
   As for VAT, the settling of an appeal by agreement has effect as a determination by the tribunal, and the provisions for enforcement of a VAT tribunal's decisions also apply to decisions on landfill tax appeals (sub-s (8)).

57   Review and appeal: commencement

Sections 54 to 56 above shall come into force on—

   (*a*) 1st October 1996, or

   (*b*) such earlier day as may be appointed by order.

GENERAL NOTE
   The review and appeals procedures come into force on 1 October 1996 unless the Commissioners make an order (see s 71(1)) providing for an earlier commencement date.

Miscellaneous

58   Partnership, bankruptcy, transfer of business, etc

(1) As regards any case where a business is carried on in partnership or by another unincorporated body, regulations may make provision for determining by what persons anything required by this Part to be done by a person is to be done.

(2) The registration under this Part of an unincorporated body other than a partnership may be in the name of the body concerned; and in determining whether taxable activities are carried out by such a body no account shall be taken of any change in its members.

(3) The registration under this Part of a body corporate carrying on a business in several divisions may, if the body corporate so requests and the Commissioners see fit, be in the names of those divisions.

(4) As regards any case where a person carries on a business of a person who has died or become bankrupt or incapacitated or whose estate has been sequestrated, or of a person which is in liquidation or receivership or in relation to which an administration order is in force, regulations may—

   (*a*) require the first-mentioned person to inform the Commissioners of the fact that he is carrying on the business and of the event that has led to his carrying it on;

   (*b*) make provision allowing the person to be treated for a limited time as if he were the other person;

   (*c*) make provision for securing continuity in the application of this Part where a person is so treated.

(5) Regulations may make provision for securing continuity in the application of this Part in cases where a business carried on by a person is transferred to another person as a going concern.

(6) Regulations under subsection (5) above may in particular—

(*a*) require the transferor to inform the Commissioners of the transfer;
(*b*) provide for liabilities and duties under this Part of the transferor to become, to such extent as may be provided by the regulations, liabilities and duties of the transferee;
(*c*) provide for any right of either of them to repayment or credit in respect of tax to be satisfied by making a repayment or allowing a credit to the other;

but the regulations may provide that no such provision as is mentioned in paragraph (*b*) or (*c*) of this subsection shall have effect in relation to any transferor and transferee unless an application in that behalf has been made by them under the regulations.

GENERAL NOTE
For businesses carried on by partnerships or other unincorporated bodies, the Commissioners can make regulations to determine who is responsible for landfill tax compliance (sub-s (1)). An unincorporated body which is not a partnership may be registered in the name of the body and changes in its membership will not affect its registration as a person carrying out taxable activities (sub-s (2)).

A company which carries on its business in several divisions may apply to register for landfill tax in the names of the divisions; but the Commissioners are apparently not obliged to agree to this (sub-s (3)).

Regulations can also be made to deal with the position where a business is carried on by someone else after the death, bankruptcy or incapacity of the original owner or under a liquidation, receivership or administration order. The regulations may require the person carrying on the business to notify the Commissioners and may provide for continuity in the treatment of the business for landfill tax purposes (sub-s (4)).

Similarly, where a business is transferred to another person as a going concern, regulations may be made generally to ensure continuity in the treatment of the business for landfill tax purposes. In particular the regulations may require the transferor to notify the Commissioners of the transfer; and they may provide that, subject to an application by the parties, liabilities and duties of the transferor with regard to landfill tax shall pass to the transferee and one party's repayments or credits shall be paid or allowed to the other (sub-ss (5)–(6)).

59 Groups of companies

(1) Where under the following provisions of this section any bodies corporate are treated as members of a group, for the purposes of this Part—

(*a*) any liability of a member of the group to pay tax shall be taken to be a liability of the representative member;
(*b*) the representative member shall be taken to carry out any taxable activities which a member of the group would carry out (apart from this section) by virtue of section 69 below;
(*c*) all members of the group shall be jointly and severally liable for any tax due from the representative member.

(2) Two or more bodies corporate are eligible to be treated as members of a group if the condition mentioned in subsection (3) below is fulfilled and—

(*a*) one of them controls each of the others,
(*b*) one person (whether a body corporate or an individual) controls all of them, or
(*c*) two or more individuals carrying on a business in partnership control all of them.

(3) The condition is that the prospective representative member has an established place of business in the United Kingdom.

(4) Where an application to that effect is made to the Commissioners with respect to two or more bodies corporate eligible to be treated as members of a group, then—

(*a*) from the beginning of an accounting period they shall be so treated, and
(*b*) one of them shall be the representative member,

unless the Commissioners refuse the application; and the Commissioners shall not refuse the application unless it appears to them necessary to do so for the protection of the revenue.

(5) Where any bodies corporate are treated as members of a group and an application to that effect is made to the Commissioners, then, from the beginning of an accounting period—

(*a*) a further body eligible to be so treated shall be included among the bodies so treated,
(*b*) a body corporate shall be excluded from the bodies so treated,
(*c*) another member of the group shall be substituted as the representative member, or
(*d*) the bodies corporate shall no longer be treated as members of a group,

unless the application is to the effect mentioned in paragraph (*a*) or (*c*) above and the Commissioners refuse the application.

(6) The Commissioners may refuse an application under subsection (5)(*a*) or (*c*) above only if it appears to them necessary to do so for the protection of the revenue.

(7) Where a body corporate is treated as a member of a group as being controlled by any person and it appears to the Commissioners that it has ceased to be so controlled, they shall, by notice given to that person, terminate that treatment from such date as may be specified in the notice.

(8) An application under this section with respect to any bodies corporate must be made by one of those bodies or by the person controlling them and must be made not less than 90 days before the date from which it is to take effect, or at such later time as the Commissioners may allow.

(9) For the purposes of this section a body corporate shall be taken to control another body corporate if it is empowered by statute to control that body's activities or if it is that body's holding company within the meaning of section 736 of the Companies Act 1985; and an individual or individuals shall be taken to control a body corporate if he or they, were he or they a company, would be that body's holding company within the meaning of that section.

GENERAL NOTE

Companies may apply for group registration for landfill tax purposes. As for VAT, the effect of group registration is to treat the taxable activities of member companies as carried out by the representative member. The latter assumes liability for the tax incurred by all the group members; but each member of the group is jointly and severally liable for the tax due from the representative member (sub-s (1)).

Two or more companies form a group where one controls the others, or all of them are owned by one individual or company or by a partnership of individuals (sub-s (2)). If a company is a member of a group because it is controlled by a particular person, the Commissioners may give notice to that person terminating the company's inclusion in the group registration when it is no longer so controlled (sub-s (7)). One company controls another if it is the latter's holding company (under the Companies Act 1985 s 736) or has power to control its activities. Control by an individual or individuals is determined by analogy with the position of a holding company (sub-s (9)).

The representative member responsible for tax compliance on behalf of the group must have an established place of business in the UK (sub-s (3)).

Group registration takes effect from the start of an accounting period. The Commissioners can only refuse group registration where necessary for the protection of the revenue (sub-s (4)).

Once a group registration is in place, application may be made to the Commissioners to add new members, to remove or replace existing members, or to discontinue the group treatment. The Commissioners can only refuse to add or substitute a new group member where such refusal appears to them necessary for the protection of the revenue (sub-ss (5)–(6)).

Applications relating to group registration must be made by one of the companies or by the person controlling the companies. The application must be made at least 90 days before the start of the accounting period from which it is to take effect; but the Commissioners have a discretion to allow a late application (sub-s (8)).

60   Information, powers, penalties, etc

Schedule 5 to this Act (which contains provisions relating to information, powers, penalties and other matters) shall have effect.

GENERAL NOTE

This section introduces Sch 5 which deals with the enforcement of landfill tax, including—

(a) record keeping and production of documents;
(b) powers of entry, inspection, search, arrest, access to information, removal of documents, and taking samples;
(c) recovery of tax;
(d) criminal and civil penalties;
(e) interest;
(f) security for tax;
(g) disclosure and publication of information.

These provisions and other administrative matters are described in more detail in the notes on the Schedule below.

61   Taxable disposals: special provisions

(1) Where—

(a) a taxable disposal is in fact made on a particular day,
(b) within the period of 14 days beginning with that day the person liable to pay tax in respect of the disposal issues a landfill invoice in respect of the disposal, and
(c) he has not notified the Commissioners in writing that he elects not to avail himself of this subsection,

for the purposes of this Part the disposal shall be treated as made at the time the invoice is issued.

(2) The reference in subsection (1) above to a landfill invoice is to a document containing such particulars as regulations may prescribe for the purposes of that subsection.

(3) The Commissioners may at the request of a person direct that subsection (1) above shall apply—

(a) in relation to disposals in respect of which he is liable to pay tax, or
(b) in relation to such of them as may be specified in the direction,

as if for the period of 14 days there were substituted such longer period as may be specified in the direction.

TAX POINT

The basic tax point for landfill tax is the time of the landfill disposal of the waste. But if a landfill invoice is issued later, within the period of 14 days starting on the date of the disposal, the disposal is treated as made when the invoice was issued (sub-s (1)). At the request of the taxpayer the Commissioners may extend the 14-day period in relation to specific disposals or to all disposals on which the taxpayer is liable to tax (sub-s (3)).

The taxpayer may elect by notice in writing to the Commissioners for the tax point to remain unaffected by the issue of landfill invoices (sub-s (1)(c)).

LANDFILL TAX INVOICE
A landfill invoice will have to contain certain particulars to be specified by regulations made by the Commissioners (sub-s (2)). These will include the registered site operator's name, address and landfill tax registration number, and the date of issue. The invoice will not need to show the amount of landfill tax charged on the disposal; but if this does appear on the invoice, it must be accompanied by a statement that it is not deductible as input VAT (CCE Budget Notice 114/95 dated 28 November 1995, *Simon's Weekly Tax Intelligence* 1995, Budget Issue, p 1926).

62   Taxable disposals: regulations

(1) For the purposes of this Part, regulations may make provision under this section in relation to a disposal which is a taxable disposal (or would be apart from the regulations).

(2) The regulations may provide that if particular conditions are fulfilled—

(*a*) the disposal shall be treated as not being a taxable disposal, or
(*b*) the disposal shall, to the extent found in accordance with prescribed rules, be treated as not being a taxable disposal.

(3) The regulations may provide that if particular conditions are fulfilled—

(*a*) the disposal shall be treated as made at a time which is found in accordance with prescribed rules and which falls after the time when it would be regarded as made apart from the regulations, or
(*b*) the disposal shall, to the extent found in accordance with prescribed rules, be treated as made at a time which is found in accordance with prescribed rules and which falls after the time when it would be regarded as made apart from the regulations.

(4) In finding the time when the disposal would be regarded as made apart from the regulations, section 61(1) above and any direction under section 61(3) above shall be taken into account.

(5) The regulations may be framed by reference to—

(*a*) conditions specified in the regulations or by the Commissioners or by an authorised person, or
(*b*) any combination of such conditions;

and the regulations may specify conditions, or allow conditions to be specified, generally or with regard to particular cases.

(6) The regulations may make provision under subsections (2)(*b*) and (3)(*b*) above in relation to the same disposal.

(7) The regulations may only provide that a disposal is to be treated as not being a taxable disposal if or to the extent that—

(*a*) the disposal is a temporary one pending the incineration or recycling of the material concerned, or pending the removal of the material for use elsewhere, or pending the sorting of the material with a view to its removal elsewhere or its eventual disposal, and
(*b*) the temporary disposal is made in an area designated for the purpose by an authorised person.

GENERAL NOTE
The Commissioners may make regulations exempting an otherwise taxable disposal wholly or to a limited extent (sub-s (2)) where the disposal is temporary. This applies to disposals made on a temporary basis pending incineration or recycling of the waste material, pending its removal for use elsewhere, or pending sorting of the material with a view to its removal or later disposal. The temporary disposal must be made in an area of the site designated for that purpose (as a tax-free zone) by a person authorised by the Commissioners (sub-s (7), s 70(1)). Generally, storage for up to 12 months would be regarded as temporary (HC Official Report, Standing Committee E, 8 February 1996, col 211).
Regulations may also be made to defer the tax point in respect of the whole or part of a disposal;

but the regulations cannot provide for a tax point earlier than that given by the actual time of the disposal or issue of a landfill invoice (sub-ss (3)–(4)).

The application of the regulations in both cases may be subject to conditions specified in the regulations, or by the Commissioners, or by a person authorised by them. Such conditions may be of general application or relate to particular cases (sub-s (5)). Under the regulations a disposal may also be exempted in part and deferred in part (sub-s (6)).

63 Qualifying material: special provisions

(1) This section applies for the purposes of section 42 above.

(2) The Commissioners may direct that where material is disposed of it must be treated as qualifying material if it would in fact be such material but for a small quantity of non-qualifying material; and whether a quantity of non-qualifying material is small must be determined in accordance with the terms of the direction.

(3) The Commissioners may at the request of a person direct that where there is a disposal in respect of which he is liable to pay tax the material disposed of must be treated as qualifying material if it would in fact be such material but for a small quantity of non-qualifying material, and—

(*a*) a direction may apply to all disposals in respect of which a person is liable to pay tax or to such of them as are identified in the direction;

(*b*) whether a quantity of non-qualifying material is small must be determined in accordance with the terms of the direction.

(4) If a direction under subsection (3) above applies to a disposal any direction under subsection (2) above shall not apply to it.

(5) An order may provide that material must not be treated as qualifying material unless prescribed conditions are met.

(6) A condition may relate to any matter the Treasury think fit (such as the production of a document which includes a statement of the nature of the material).

GENERAL NOTE
This section is concerned with the treatment of waste material as qualifying for the lower rate of landfill tax (see s 42).

Where the waste disposed of is mostly qualifying material but includes a small quantity of non-qualifying material, it may be treated as qualifying for the lower rate by direction of the Commissioners. The Commissioners may make general directions for this purpose (sub-s (2)). In response to a request by a particular taxpayer, they may also make directions specific to some or all of the disposals of that taxpayer (sub-s (3)). A specific direction overrides a general one (sub-s (4)).

Conditions to be met for material to be treated as qualifying material may be imposed by Treasury order (sub-ss (5)–(6)).

Interpretation

64 Disposal of material as waste

(1) A disposal of material is a disposal of it as waste if the person making the disposal does so with the intention of discarding the material.

(2) The fact that the person making the disposal or any other person could benefit from or make use of the material is irrelevant.

(3) Where a person makes a disposal on behalf of another person, for the purposes of subsections (1) and (2) above the person on whose behalf the disposal is made shall be treated as making the disposal.

(4) The reference in subsection (3) above to a disposal on behalf of another person includes references to a disposal—

(*a*) at the request of another person;

(*b*) in pursuance of a contract with another person.

GENERAL NOTE

The disposal of material as waste is a disposal made with the intention of discarding the material, whether or not the material has any residual value or use (sub-ss (1)–(2)).

Where the disposal is made by one person on behalf of another, the latter must intend the material to be discarded. This includes disposals made at the request of, or by agreement with, the other party (sub-ss (3)–(4)).

65   Disposal by way of landfill

(1) There is a disposal of material by way of landfill if—

(*a*) it is deposited on the surface of land or on a structure set into the surface, or

(*b*) it is deposited under the surface of land.

(2) Subsection (1) above applies whether or not the material is placed in a container before it is deposited.

(3) Subsection (1)(*b*) above applies whether the material—

(*a*) is covered with earth after it is deposited, or

(*b*) is deposited in a cavity (such as a cavern or mine).

(4) If material is deposited on the surface of land (or on a structure set into the surface) with a view to it being covered with earth the disposal must be treated as made when the material is deposited and not when it is covered.

(5) An order may provide that the meaning of the disposal of material by way of landfill (as it applies for the time being) shall be varied.

(6) An order under subsection (5) above may make provision in such way as the Treasury think fit, whether by amending any of subsections (1) to (4) above or otherwise.

(7) In this section "land" includes land covered by water where the land is above the low water mark of ordinary spring tides.

(8) In this section "earth" includes similar matter (such as sand or rocks).

GENERAL NOTE

Material is disposed of by way of landfill if it is deposited on or under the land, or on a structure set into the surface of the land. It makes no difference if the waste material is in a container when disposed of (sub-ss (1)–(2)).

For this purpose "land" includes land under water but above the low water mark of ordinary spring tides (sub-s (7)).

Material which is deposited in a cavity (eg a cavern or mine), or which is covered with earth after being deposited, is nevertheless treated as deposited under the land. In the case of waste material covered with earth, the disposal is treated as made when the waste is deposited, not when it is covered over (sub-ss (3)–(4)). For this purpose "earth" includes sand, rocks and other similar matter (sub-s (8)).

The Treasury may by order vary the meaning of the expression "disposal by way of landfill" (sub-ss (5)–(6)).

66   Landfill sites

Land is a landfill site at a given time if at that time—

(*a*) a licence which is a site licence for the purposes of Part II of the Environmental Protection Act 1990 (waste on land) is in force in relation to the land and authorises disposals in or on the land,

(*b*) a resolution under section 54 of that Act (land occupied by waste disposal authorities in Scotland) is in force in relation to the land and authorises deposits or disposals in or on the land, (*c*) a disposal licence issued under Part II of the Pollution Control and Local Government (Northern Ireland) Order 1978 (waste on land) is in force in relation to the land and authorises deposits on the land,

(*d*) a resolution passed under Article 13 of that Order (land occupied by district councils in Northern Ireland) is in force in relation to the land and relates to deposits on the land, or

(*e*) a licence under any provision for the time being having effect in Northern Ireland and corresponding to section 35 of the Environmental Protection Act 1990 (waste management licences) is in force in relation to the land and authorises disposals in or on the land.

GENERAL NOTE
    A landfill site is land in respect of which the disposal of waste is authorised by a site licence for the purposes of the Environmental Protection Act 1990 Part II. Land occupied by a waste disposal authority in Scotland covered by a resolution (under the Environmental Protection Act 1990 s 54) is also a landfill site; and in Northern Ireland land on which deposits are authorised by a disposal licence or by resolution (under Pollution Control and Local Government (Northern Ireland) Order 1978) or by the equivalent of a waste management licence is a landfill site.
    The land is a landfill site only so long as the licence or resolution remains in force.

67　Operators of landfill sites

The operator of a landfill site at a given time is—

(*a*) the person who is at the time concerned the holder of the licence, where section 66(*a*) above applies;

(*b*) the waste disposal authority which at the time concerned occupies the landfill site, where section 66(*b*) above applies;

(*c*) the person who is at the time concerned the holder of the licence, where section 66(*c*) above applies;

(*d*) the district council which passed the resolution, where section 66(*d*) above applies;

(*e*) the person who is at the time concerned the holder of the licence, where section 66(*e*) above applies.

GENERAL NOTE
    The operator of the landfill site is the holder of the waste management licence in respect of it. For landfill sites occupied by waste disposal authorities in Scotland, the operator is the authority concerned. In Northern Ireland the site operator is the holder of the licence, or the district council which passed the resolution, authorising the deposit of waste on the land.

68　Weight of material disposed of

(1) The weight of the material disposed of on a taxable disposal shall be determined in accordance with regulations.

(2) The regulations may—

(*a*) prescribe rules for determining the weight;

(*b*) authorise rules for determining the weight to be specified by the Commissioners in a prescribed manner;

(*c*) authorise rules for determining the weight to be agreed by the person liable to pay the tax and an authorised person.

(3) The regulations may in particular prescribe, or authorise the specification or agreement of, rules about—

(*a*) the method by which the weight is to be determined;

(*b*) the time by reference to which the weight is to be determined;

(*c*) the discounting of constituents (such as water).

(4) The regulations may include provision that a specification authorised under subsection (2)(*b*) above may provide—

(*a*) that it is to have effect only in relation to disposals of such descriptions as may be set out in the specification;
(*b*) that it is not to have effect in relation to particular disposals unless the Commissioners are satisfied that such conditions as may be set out in the specification are met in relation to the disposals;

and the conditions may be framed by reference to such factors as the Commissioners think fit (such as the consent of an authorised person to the specification having effect in relation to disposals).

(5) The regulations may include provision that—

(*a*) where rules are agreed as mentioned in subsection (2)(*c*) above, and
(*b*) the Commissioners believe that they should no longer be applied because they do not give an accurate indication of the weight or they are not being fully observed or for some other reason,

the Commissioners may direct that the agreed rules shall no longer have effect.

(6) The regulations shall be so framed that where in relation to a given disposal—

(*a*) no specification of the Commissioners has effect, and
(*b*) no agreed rules have effect,

the weight shall be determined in accordance with rules prescribed in the regulations.

GENERAL NOTE
The amount of landfill tax charged is calculated by reference to the weight of the waste material disposed of (see s 42). Rules for determining the weight of material are to be set out in regulations made by the Commissioners. The installation of weighbridges will not be required (CCE Budget Notice 114/95 dated 28 November 1995, *Simon's Weekly Tax Intelligence* 1995, Budget Issue, p 1926).
The rules may cover the method of determining the weight, the time at which this is to be done and the discounting of water and other constituents of the material (sub-s (3)).
The regulations may include provisions authorising the Commissioners to provide special rules by specification or by agreement with the taxpayer (sub-ss (1)–(2)). Rules contained in a specification by the Commissioners may apply to particular disposals, or particular disposals may be excluded unless certain conditions are met (sub-s (4)). The Commissioners may direct that rules agreed with the taxpayer shall cease to apply, eg where they do not provide an accurate indication of the weight or are not being fully observed (sub-s (5)).
Where no specification or agreement applies, the weight of material is to be determined in accordance with the general rules in the regulations (sub-s (6)).

69   Taxable activities

(1) A person carries out a taxable activity if—

(*a*) he makes a taxable disposal in respect of which he is liable to pay tax, or
(*b*) he permits another person to make a taxable disposal in respect of which he (the first-mentioned person) is liable to pay tax.

(2) Where—

(*a*) a taxable disposal is made, and
(*b*) it is made without the knowledge of the person who is liable to pay tax in respect of it,

that person shall for the purposes of this section be taken to permit the disposal.

Registration for landfill tax is required when a person carries out taxable activities (see s 47). This section defines the circumstances in which a person carries out a taxable activity.

A taxable activity is carried out by a person who makes a taxable disposal (see s 40) for which he is liable to pay landfill tax. Where the person making the taxable disposal is not the person liable to pay the tax in respect of it, the latter carries out the taxable activity if he permitted the disposal or it was made *without* his knowledge.

70 Interpretation: other provisions

(1) Unless the context otherwise requires—

"accounting period" shall be construed in accordance with section 49 above;
"appeal tribunal" means a VAT and duties tribunal;
"authorised person" means any person acting under the authority of the Commissioners;
"the Commissioners" means the Commissioners of Customs and Excise;
"conduct" includes any act, omission or statement;
"material" means material of all kinds, including objects, substances and products of all kinds;
"prescribed" means prescribed by an order or regulations under this Part;
"registrable person" has the meaning given by section 47(10) above;
"tax" means landfill tax;
"taxable disposal" has the meaning given by section 40 above.

(2) A landfill disposal is a disposal—

(*a*) of material as waste, and
(*b*) made by way of landfill.

(3) A reference to this Part includes a reference to any order or regulations made under it and a reference to a provision of this Part includes a reference to any order or regulations made under the provision, unless otherwise required by the context or any order or regulations.

(4) This section and sections 64 to 69 above apply for the purposes of this Part.

GENERAL NOTE
This section contains several definitions (sub-s (1)) which are used or explained elsewhere in the commentary. A "landfill disposal" (sub-s (2)) is a disposal of material as waste (see s 64) made by way of landfill (see s 65).

Supplementary

71 Orders and regulations

(1) The power to make an order under section 57 above shall be exercisable by the Commissioners, and the power to make an order under any other provision of this Part shall be exercisable by the Treasury.

(2) Any power to make regulations under this Part shall be exercisable by the Commissioners.

(3) Any power to make an order or regulations under this Part shall be exercisable by statutory instrument.

(4) An order to which this subsection applies shall be laid before the House of Commons; and unless it is approved by that House before the expiration of a period of 28 days beginning with the date on which it was made it shall cease to have effect on the expiration of that period, but without prejudice to anything previously done under the order or to the making of a new order.

(5) In reckoning any such period as is mentioned in subsection (4) above no

account shall be taken of any time during which Parliament is dissolved or prorogued or during which the House of Commons is adjourned for more than four days.

(6) A statutory instrument containing an order or regulations under this Part (other than an order under section 57 above or an order to which subsection (4) above applies) shall be subject to annulment in pursuance of a resolution of the House of Commons.

(7) Subsection (4) above applies to—

(a) an order under section 42(3) above providing for material which would otherwise be qualifying material not to be qualifying material;
(b) an order under section 46 above which produces the result that a disposal which would otherwise not be a taxable disposal is a taxable disposal;
(c) an order under section 63(5) above other than one which provides only that an earlier order under section 63(5) is not to apply to material;
(d) an order under section 65(5) above providing for anything which would otherwise not be a disposal of material by way of landfill to be such a disposal.

(8) Any power to make an order or regulations under this Part—

(a) may be exercised as regards prescribed cases or descriptions of case;
(b) may be exercised differently in relation to different cases or descriptions of case.

(9) An order or regulations under this Part may include such supplementary, incidental, consequential or transitional provisions as appear to the Treasury or the Commissioners (as the case may be) to be necessary or expedient.

(10) No specific provision of this Part about an order or regulations shall prejudice the generality of subsections (8) and (9) above.

GENERAL NOTE

This section sets out the procedures for making subordinate legislation on landfill tax.

The Treasury is responsible for making orders relating to landfill tax, except for an order bringing forward the commencement date for the review and appeals provisions (see s 57) which would be made by the Commissioners. The Commissioners are also responsible for making regulations (sub-ss (1)–(2)).

Orders and regulations relating to landfill tax are made by statutory instrument (sub-s (3)). With certain exceptions, the statutory instrument containing the order or regulations may be annulled by resolution of the House of Commons (sub-s (6)). This does not apply to a commencement order made by the Commissioners as above. A different procedure is laid down for Treasury orders excluding waste material from qualifying for the lower rate by list (under s 42(3)) or by imposing conditions (under s 63(5)), for orders restricting the application of exemptions from landfill tax (under s 46(1)(b)), and for Treasury orders extending the meaning of the expression "disposal of material by way of landfill" (under s 65(5)). These Treasury orders have to be approved by the House of Commons within 28 days of being made (sub-ss (4)–(5), (7)).

The powers of the Treasury and the Commissioners to make orders and regulations for landfill tax purposes are widely drawn (sub-ss (8)–(10)).

PART IV

INCOME TAX, CORPORATION TAX AND CAPITAL GAINS TAX

CHAPTER I

PRINCIPAL PROVISIONS

Income tax charge, rates and reliefs

72   Charge and rates of income tax for 1996–97

(1) Income tax shall be charged for the year 1996–97, and for that year—

(*a*) the lower rate shall be 20 per cent;
(*b*) the basic rate shall be 24 per cent; and
(*c*) the higher rate shall be 40 per cent.

(2) For the year 1996–97 section 1(2) of the Taxes Act 1988 shall apply—

(*a*) as if the amount specified in paragraph (*aa*) (the lower rate limit) were £3,900; and
(*b*) as if the amount specified in paragraph (*b*) (the basic rate limit) were £25,500;

and, accordingly, section 1(4) of that Act (indexation) shall not apply for the year 1996–97.

(3) Section 559(4) of the Taxes Act 1988 (deductions from payments to subcontractors in the construction industry) shall have effect—

(*a*) in relation to payments made on or after 1st July 1996 and before the appointed day (within the meaning of section 139 of the Finance Act 1995), with "24 per cent" substituted for "25 per cent"; and
(*b*) in relation to payments made on or after that appointed day, as if the substitution for which section 139(1) of the Finance Act 1995 provided were a substitution of "the relevant percentage" for "24 per cent".

GENERAL NOTE
This section reimposes income tax for the year of assessment 1996–97 and sets the rates at which income tax is to be charged for that year. The lower and higher rates remain at 20 per cent and 40 per cent respectively. The basic rate is reduced from 25 per cent to 24 per cent, the first reduction since the year 1988–89 (sub-s (1)).

The section extends the lower rate band for the year 1996–97 to the first £3,900 of taxable income (increased from £3,200 for 1995–96); the basic rate band is extended to cover the next £21,600 of taxable income so that the higher rate threshold is raised to £25,500 (£24,300 for 1995–96). Since these increases exceed the amounts by which the bands would have been increased under the statutory indexation provisions (by £500 and £200 respectively), those indexation provisions (TA 1988 s 1(4)) are accordingly disapplied for the year 1996–97 (sub-s (2)).

DEDUCTIONS FROM PAYMENTS TO SUBCONTRACTORS
In consequence of the reduction in the basic rate of tax, the rate of deductions from payments to subcontractors in the construction industry who do not hold valid certificates of exemption is also reduced to 24 per cent. This change is effective for payments after 30 June 1996 (sub-s (3)). With effect from a date to be appointed (not before 1 August 1998: see FA 1995 s 139(3)), new provisions are to be introduced which will empower the Treasury to determine by order the rate of deductions from subcontractors' payments (although the rate determined cannot exceed the basic rate of income tax in force at the time) (TA 1988 s 559(4A) inserted by FA 1995 s 139(1)).

73   Application of lower rate to income from savings

(1) After section 1 of the Taxes Act 1988 there shall be inserted the following section—

"1A Application of lower rate to income from savings and distributions

(1) Subject to sections 469(2) and 686, so much of any person's total income for any year of assessment as—

(*a*) comprises income to which this section applies, and
(*b*) in the case of an individual, is not income falling within section 1(2)(*b*),

shall, by virtue of this section, be charged for that year at the lower rate, instead of at the rate otherwise applicable to it in accordance with section 1(2)(*aa*) and (*a*).

(2) Subject to subsection (4) below, this section applies to the following income—

(*a*) any income chargeable under Case III of Schedule D other than—

(i) relevant annuities and other annual payments that are not interest; and
(ii) amounts so chargeable by virtue of section 119 or 120;

(*b*) any income chargeable under Schedule F; and
(*c*) subject to subsection (4) below, any equivalent foreign income.

(3) The income which is equivalent foreign income for the purposes of this section is any income chargeable under Case IV or V of Schedule D which—

(*a*) is equivalent to a description of income falling within subsection (2)(*a*) above but arises from securities or other possessions out of the United Kingdom; or
(*b*) consists in any such dividend or other distribution of a company not resident in the United Kingdom as would be chargeable under Schedule F if the company were resident in the United Kingdom.

(4) This section does not apply to—

(*a*) any income chargeable to tax under Case IV or V of Schedule D which is such that section 65(5)(*a*) or (*b*) provides for the tax to be computed on the full amount of sums received in the United Kingdom; or
(*b*) any amounts deemed by virtue of section 695(4)(*b*) or 696(6) to be income chargeable under Case IV of Schedule D.

(5) So much of any person's income as comprises income to which this section applies shall be treated for the purposes of subsection (1)(*b*) above and any other provisions of the Income Tax Acts as the highest part of his income.

(6) Subsection (5) above shall have effect subject to section 833(3) but shall otherwise have effect notwithstanding any provision requiring income of any description to be treated for the purposes of the Income Tax Acts (other than section 550) as the highest part of a person's income.

(7) In this section 'relevant annuity' means any annuity other than a purchased life annuity to which section 656 applies or to which that section would apply but for section 657(2)(*a*)."

(2) In section 4 of that Act (construction of references to deduction of tax), after subsection (1) there shall be inserted the following subsection—

"(1A) As respects deductions from, and tax treated as paid on, any such amounts as constitute or (but for the person whose income they are) would constitute income to which section 1A applies, subsection (1) above shall have effect with a reference to the lower rate in force for the relevant year of assessment substituted for the reference to the basic rate in force for that year.''

(3) Subsection (1) above has effect in relation to the year 1996–97 and subsequent years of assessment and subsection (2) above has effect in relation to payments on or after 6th April 1996.

(4) Schedule 6 to this Act (which makes further amendments in connection with the charge at the lower rate on income from savings etc) shall have effect.

(5) Where any subordinate legislation (within the meaning of the Interpretation Act 1978) falls to be construed in accordance with section 4 of the Taxes Act 1988, that legislation (whenever it was made) shall be construed, in relation to payments on or after 6th April 1996, subject to subsection (1A) of that section.

GENERAL NOTE

This section inserts a new section, TA 1988 s 1A. The effect of the new section (together with supplementary amendments made by Sch 6) is that certain savings income of individuals, personal representatives and trustees of interest in possession trusts will be subject to income tax at the lower rate only with effect from the year 1996–97. It effectively extends the tax treatment which has applied to dividend income received by such persons with effect from 1993–94 (TA 1988 s 207A, which is superseded by the new s 1A).

INCOME SUBJECT TO LOWER RATE CHARGE

In relation to individuals, this tax treatment applies only to the extent that the income does not fall within the higher rate band (TA 1988 s 1A(1)(b) inserted by sub-s (1)). For this purpose, any income within the scope of the new section is treated as the highest part of the individual's income (leaving out of account any termination payment relating to an office or employment (within TA 1988 s 148) and gains on certain non-qualifying life insurance policies (within TA 1988 s 547(1)(a)) (TA 1988 s 1A(5), (6) inserted by sub-s (1))).

The new section applies to the following sources of income—

(a) income chargeable under Schedule D Case III, subject to the exceptions mentioned below;
(b) income chargeable under Schedule F (that is, distributions made by UK resident companies);
(c) "equivalent foreign income". This comprises income chargeable under Schedule D Case IV or V which would have been chargeable under Schedule D Case III had the source been in the UK (subject to the exceptions below) and distributions of any non-resident company which would have been chargeable under Schedule F if the company had been UK resident. However, it does not include income chargeable on the remittance basis (by virtue of TA 1988 s 65(4)) or income paid to a beneficiary in respect of his interest in the residue of a foreign estate and deemed to be chargeable under Schedule D Case IV (by virtue of TA 1988 s 695(4)(b) or s 696(6)) (TA 1988 s 1A(2)(c), (3), (4) inserted by sub-s (1)).

The new section applies to purchased life annuities within TA 1988 s 656 (or annuities which would be within that section but for the fact that they would (apart from s 656) be treated as consisting to any extent of the payment or repayment of a capital sum). However, it does *not* apply to other annuities or annual payments which are not interest. It also does *not* apply to rents receivable in respect of land or easements in connection with mines, quarries etc or electric line wayleaves (ie income chargeable under Schedule D Case III by virtue of TA 1988 s 119 or 120) (sub-ss (2)(a), (7)).

The Revenue have confirmed that investment income of Scottish liferent trusts is subject to the lower rate charge under TA 1988 s 1A on the same basis as the income of English interest in possession trusts (HC Official Report, Standing Committee E (Ninth sitting), cols 267, 270, 271, *Simon's Weekly Tax Intelligence* 1996, p 330).

It is expressly provided that income arising to the trustees of unauthorised unit trusts which would otherwise be within the scope of TA 1988 s 1A is to be charged at the basic rate of income tax rather than the lower rate (TA 1988 s 1A(1) and s 469(2) as amended by FA 1996 Sch 6 para 12, see commentary to that provision below).

Income arising to the trustees of discretionary trusts which is liable to income tax at the special rate applicable to such trusts (34 per cent from 1996–97) is also expressly excluded from the lower rate charge under TA 1988 s 1A (TA 1988 s 1A(1) and s 686(1) as amended by FA 1996 Sch 6 para 13, see commentary to that provision below).

PAYMENTS SUBJECT TO DEDUCTION OF TAX AT SOURCE

Where payments of income within TA 1988 s 1A are made subject to deduction of tax at source (eg bank and building society interest), the rate of deduction for payments made after 5 April 1996 is the lower rate of income tax in force for the relevant year of assessment (ie 20 per cent for the year 1996–97) (TA 1988 s 4(1A) inserted by sub-ss (2), (3)). Individuals who are liable to higher rate tax will therefore be assessable to tax at a further 20 per cent on such income, to the extent that it exceeds the basic rate limit.

References in subordinate legislation to the deduction of income tax from payments of income within the scope of TA 1988 s 1A are similarly to be construed as requiring deduction at the lower rate of tax in respect of payments made after 5 April 1996 (sub-s (5)).

74   Personal allowances for 1996–97

(1) For the year 1996–97 the amounts specified in the provisions mentioned in subsection (2) below shall be taken to be as set out in that subsection; and, accordingly, section 257C(1) of the Taxes Act 1988 (indexation), so far as it relates to the amounts so specified, shall not apply for the year 1996–97.

(2) In section 257 of that Act (personal allowance)—

(*a*) the amount in subsection (1) (basic allowance) shall be £3,765;

(*b*) the amount in subsection (2) (allowance for persons aged 65 or more but not aged 75 or more) shall be £4,910; and

(*c*) the amount in subsection (3) (allowance for persons aged 75 or more) shall be £5,090.

GENERAL NOTE

This section specifies the 1996–97 rates of the basic personal allowance (£3,765) and the personal age allowances for individuals aged 65–74 (£4,910) and 75 or over (£5,090) respectively. The increases in each of these allowances exceed the amounts by which they would have been increased under the statutory indexation provisions by £100. Accordingly the indexation provisions (TA 1988 s 257C(1)), in so far as they relate to those allowances, are disapplied for the year 1996–97.

In the absence of express statutory provision to the contrary, the amounts of the basic married couple's allowance and the enhanced married couple's allowances where either spouse is aged 65–74 or over 74 respectively are increased in line with the Retail Prices Index under the statutory indexation provisions (TA 1988 s 257C(1)), as are those allowances which are fixed at the amount of the basic married couple's allowance (the additional personal allowance, widow's bereavement allowance and relief in respect of maintenance payments under post-14 March 1988 obligations).

The income limit for age-related allowances (above which the personal and married couple's age allowances are progressively abated to the level of the basic allowances for persons under 65) is also increased in line with the Retail Prices Index under the statutory indexation provisions.

In summary, the personal allowances for 1996–97 are as follows—

Personal allowance (age under 65)	£3,765
Personal allowance (age 65–74)	£4,910
Personal allowance (age 75 and over)	£5,090
Married couple's allowance (age under 65)	£1,790
Married couple's allowance (age 65–74)	£3,115
Married couple's allowance (age 75 and over)	£3,155
Income limit for age-related allowances	£15,200
Additional personal allowance	£1,790
Widow's bereavement allowance	£1,790

75   Blind person's allowance

(1) In section 265(1) of the Taxes Act 1988 (blind person's allowance), for "£1,200" there shall be substituted "£1,250".

(2) This section shall apply for the year 1996–97 and subsequent years of assessment.

GENERAL NOTE

This section increases the amount of the blind person's allowance from £1,200 to £1,250 with effect for the year 1996–97 and subsequent years of assessment.

The allowance is available to individuals who are registered blind for all or part of the year of assessment concerned (TA 1988 s 265(1)). A husband and wife who are both blind may each claim the allowance.

76 Limit on relief for interest

For the year 1996–97 the qualifying maximum defined in section 367(5) of the Taxes Act 1988 (limit on relief for interest on certain loans) shall be £30,000.

GENERAL NOTE

Interest paid on certain loans is eligible for relief only to the extent that the amount of the loan does not exceed the "qualifying maximum". The loans to which this limit applies are—

(*a*) a loan used to purchase the borrower's only or main residence (or a loan made before 6 April 1988 and used to improve such a residence);
(*b*) a loan used to purchase a private residence when the borrower is living in job-related accommodation;
(*c*) a loan to a person aged 65 or over, secured on the borrower's main residence, to purchase a life annuity (TA 1988 s 365).

In relation to most interest paid after 31 July 1988 the limit applies to a residence irrespective of the number of borrowers who have loans in respect of that residence. In relation to certain loans made before 1 August 1988 to joint borrowers (other than a married couple living together) the limit applies separately to each borrower (TA 1988 s 357).

The qualifying maximum must be set for each year of assessment (TA 1988 s 367(5)). This section sets it at £30,000 for the year 1996–97, the level at which it has remained since 1983–84.

Corporation tax charge and rate

77 Charge and rate of corporation tax for 1996

Corporation tax shall be charged for the financial year 1996 at the rate of 33 per cent.

GENERAL NOTE

This section reimposes corporation tax for the financial year 1996. It sets the main rate of corporation tax at 33 per cent, the rate which has applied since the financial year 1991.

78 Small companies

For the financial year 1996—

(*a*) the small companies' rate shall be 24 per cent; and
(*b*) the fraction mentioned in section 13(2) of the Taxes Act 1988 (marginal relief for small companies) shall be nine four-hundredths.

GENERAL NOTE

This section reduces the small companies' rate of corporation tax to 24 per cent for the financial year 1996, in line with the reduction in the basic rate of income tax (see s 72).

The profits limit for the small companies' rate is unchanged at £300,000 and the upper limit on profits for the purposes of marginal relief remains at £1,500,000 (TA 1988 s 13(3)).

However, in consequence of the reduction in the small companies' rate, the marginal relief fraction is changed to nine four-hundredths and the marginal rate of tax on profits between the lower and upper limits for marginal relief has increased from 35 per cent to 35·25 per cent.

Abolition of Schedule C charge etc

79 Abolition of Schedule C charge etc

(1) The charge to tax under Schedule C is abolished—

(*a*) for the purposes of income tax, for the year 1996–97 and subsequent years of assessment;
(*b*) for the purposes of corporation tax, for accounting periods ending after 31st March 1996.

(2) Schedule 7 to this Act (which, together with Chapter II of this Part of this Act, makes provision for imposing a charge under Schedule D on descriptions of income previously charged under Schedule C, and makes connected amendments) shall have effect.

GENERAL NOTE

This section abolishes the charge under Schedule C with effect from the year 1996–97 for income tax purposes and for accounting periods ending after 31 March 1996 for corporation tax purposes.

It introduces Sch 7, which provides for income previously charged under Schedule C to be charged to income tax under Schedule D Cases III, IV and V. (Different provision is made in relation to corporation tax: see Sch 14 para 5.)

The Schedule also makes a number of consequential amendments, some of which are applicable for both income and corporation tax purposes.

CHAPTER II

LOAN RELATIONSHIPS

INTRODUCTION

Part IV Chapter II, which comprises ss 80–105 and Schs 8–15, contains fundamental changes to the taxation of interest and gains from gilts and bonds. They are effectively the third stage of radical changes to the taxation of the financial markets. The process began with the introduction of the foreign exchange legislation contained in FA 1993 and the financial instrument legislation contained in FA 1994 and the Finance Act 1996 effects the operation of these earlier provisions.

The changes have their genesis in the November 1993 Budget. The Chancellor proposed a review of the taxation of interest paid and received by companies which would also consider the rules for the taxation of the return to investors in securities, with the objectives—

"(*a*) to simplify the tax system by removing unnecessary distinctions between different ways of meeting the cost of borrowing and between loans from different types of lender;
(*b*) to allow the interest shown in the commercial accounts as a deduction for tax purposes;
(*c*) to remove the need to apportion the return on securities between capital and revenue;
(*d*) to rationalise the treatment of cross-border flows of interest to reflect international developments;
(*e*) to make it easier, in consequence, for businesses to comply with their taxation responsibilities."

Consultation took place with representative bodies but no wide-ranging reform resulted.

On 25 May 1995, the Revenue published a consultative document which set out their proposal for the reform of the taxation of gilts and bonds. In the accompanying Press Release, the Financial Secretary commented—

"The current tax rules for gilts and bonds originate in the 19th century. As the financial markets and the tax system have evolved, more and more special rules have been added. As a result, on a foundation designed for the circumstances of over a century ago, we have a top-heavy superstructure which makes for complexity and anomaly, has traps for the unwary, and inhibits financial innovation."

The changes were linked to the announcement by the Bank of England that it planned to introduce a strips market for gilts (allowing the principal and coupons of gilt-edged securities to be detached and owned separately) and FA 1996 contains provisions to allow this to take place. It should be noted that the scope of the changes exceeds those simply necessary for the introduction of a strip market.

The consultative process attracted much comment, particularly from individual investors, and led to the Press Release of 10 July 1995 in which it was announced that the changes would proceed but with some changes. In particular, "the changes would not apply to the overwhelming majority of private investors", by excluding those with holdings of £200,000 or less, although in the event this last aspect was subject to further change.

The Budget Press Release on 28 November 1995 announced that the new rules would in general apply to companies only and would be effective from 1 April 1996. Apart from some simplifications individuals and trusts will continue to be subject to the present rules. It also indicated that the process may not yet be complete, in that "the Government will continue to consider the scope for other simplifications of the tax rules for loan interest".

The process of consultation in respect of these changes, was, particularly significant as changes were introduced subject to much debate in Standing Committee. The measures have a broad range of support but one extreme view was quoted—

"The Chartered Institute of Accountants in Scotland was even more eloquent in its expression of despair. Its submission on clauses 72 to 97 and schedules 7 to 14 simply reads: 'delete all Clauses and Schedules relating to Loan Relationships.' That was its view of the way in which the matter was progressing."

The Minister proceeded to provide an overview of the changes and the intention behind them—

"The basic rules are, first, that the tax system should recognise all debit and credit that arise from borrowing and lending, although in more complex deals, it does not necessarily do that. Secondly, they should be calculated according to authorised accounting methods. We have spoken particularly of accruals because far and away the vast majority of businesses account in that way. Thirdly, the figures should follow those that are produced for non-tax purposes wherever they are acceptable. That may be bad news for my hon. Friend the Member for Beaconsfield, because it means one set of accounts and one set of principles. We cannot have the accounts saying one thing and the tax man saying another, which happens now to a certain extent.

We are moving to a more simplified method of ensuring that debits, credits and taxation follow accounts. My hon. Friend mentioned some of the far more complicated was of raising money by a variety of routes. They have provided accountants with a great deal of business, but they are no longer relevant. That is important for British industry because it means that it is cheaper and easier to raise money. This country will become more attractive to businesses. The clause simplifies our tax code, repeals some exising legislation and allows the strips gilts market to proceed. Those matters are of great importance to us all.

The important question of how the clause will affect the larger company with more complex borrowing comes down to the first basic rule that tax should recognise all debits and credits arising from borrowing and lending. In the complex methods of funding, companies that borrow find that the costs of their borrowing are not totally accounted for when it comes to tax relief. I shall not give an example of that because there is not time: it is complicated and it would be better if it were written down. A company will benefit if it can be more certain that the costs of raising the finance it needs will be fully catered for in the tax system.

As for winners and losers, with any reform there will be changes. This reform is not about raising additional tax revenue. We estimate its overall effect to be broadly neutral. It will undoubtedly benefit everyone in the long run in that it is more coherent. But one group of people who will certainly lose will be the people who have set up tax-driven arrangements designed to profit at the Exchequer's expense from the weaknesses of the currency. We have not heard a word from any of them.

The CBI, which is likely to have a considerable number of members who fall into the complex money-raising category, is very much in favour of these reforms. The gainers are clear: they are companies that currently sell bonds at a loss and will now get tax relief. The gainers are a minority of companies which will get tax relief on the borrowings of their costs earlier. We can be certain that the gainers will be small businesses and medium-sized companies that are getting into the more complicated side of financing or are already involved in fairly complicated deals, and the losers will be those who have been trying to fiddle the system.''

Some of the key changes are the abolition, at least for companies, of the Accrued Income Scheme, deep gain securities, deep discount securities, Schedule C, Schedule D Case IV and the distinction between short and yearly interest for the purposes of establishing deductibility, but it is retained with regard to withholding tax. In addition, there is provision for the introduction of ''loan relationships''.

Introductory provisions

80   Taxation of loan relationships

(1) For the purposes of corporation tax all profits and gains arising to a company from its loan relationships shall be chargeable to tax as income in accordance with this Chapter.

(2) To the extent that a company is a party to a loan relationship for the purposes of a trade carried on by the company, profits and gains arising from the relationship shall be brought into account in computing the profits and gains of the trade.

(3) Profits and gains arising from a loan relationship of a company that are not brought into account under subsection (2) above shall be brought into account as profits and gains chargeable to tax under Case III of Schedule D.

(4) This Chapter shall also have effect for the purposes of corporation tax for determining how any deficit on a company's loan relationships is to be brought into account in any case, including a case where none of the company's loan relationships falls by virtue of this Chapter to be regarded as a source of income.

(5) Subject to any express provision to the contrary, the amounts which in the case of any company are brought into account in accordance with this Chapter as respects any matter shall be the only amounts brought into account for the purposes of corporation tax as respects that matter.

GENERAL NOTE

This section provides the framework for the assessment of gains and losses for the purposes of corporation tax of ''loan relationships''.

All profits and gains arising from a ''loan relationship'' are to be assessable for corporation tax as income under Chapter II.

Where the company is party to the loan relationship for the purposes of its trade, profits and gains are to be included in the computation of trading profits and gains. Where such loan relationship gives rise to a "deficit", the Chapter provides that relief will be given, even where none of the company's loan relationships are regarded as a source of income (see s 82).

Where the company is party to the loan relationship outside the course of its trade then assessment of profits and gains will be under Schedule D Case III. Again, relief is to be given for deficits on loan relationships (see ss 82 and 83).

The provisions of Chapter II shall be the only basis of subjecting profits and losses from loan relationships to corporation tax unless expressly provided.

81   Meaning of "loan relationship" etc

(1) Subject to the following provisions of this section, a company has a loan relationship for the purposes of the Corporation Tax Acts wherever—

   (*a*) the company stands (whether by reference to a security or otherwise) in the position of a creditor or debtor as respects any money debt; and

   (*b*) that debt is one arising from a transaction for the lending of money;

and references to a loan relationship and to a company's being a party to a loan relationship shall be construed accordingly.

(2) For the purposes of this Chapter a money debt is a debt which falls to be settled—

   (*a*) by the payment of money; or

   (*b*) by the transfer of a right to settlement under a debt which is itself a money debt.

(3) Subject to subsection (4) below, where an instrument is issued by any person for the purpose of representing security for, or the rights of a creditor in respect of, any money debt, then (whatever the circumstances of the issue of the instrument) that debt shall be taken for the purposes of this Chapter to be a debt arising from a transaction for the lending of money.

(4) For the purposes of this Chapter a debt shall not be taken to arise from a transaction for the lending of money to the extent that it is a debt arising from rights conferred by shares in a company.

(5) For the purposes of this Chapter—

   (*a*) references to payments or interest under a loan relationship are references to payments or interest made or payable in pursuance of any of the rights or liabilities under that relationship; and

   (*b*) references to rights or liabilities under a loan relationship are references to any of the rights or liabilities under the agreement or arrangements by virtue of which that relationship subsists;

and those rights or liabilities shall be taken to include the rights or liabilities attached to any security which, being a security issued in relation to the money debt in question, is a security representing that relationship.

(6) In this Chapter "money" includes money expressed in a currency other than sterling.

GENERAL NOTE

This section provides the definition of loan relationship and associated terms.

A company will have a loan relationship where it stands in the position of creditor or debtor as respects any "money debt", which debt arises from the lending of money. It will apply regardless of whether the company is secured or otherwise.

A "money debt" is a debt which falls to be settled by payment of money or the transfer of another money debt. "Money" is not restricted to sterling. The term money debt includes certain debt securities which would not represent a loan under general law (ie where issued for non-cash consideration). However, this extended definition does not cover a debt arising from rights conferred by shares in a company.

The terms payment or interest under a loan relationship are payment and interest made or payable in pursuance to any rights or liabilities under that loan relationship under sub-s (5). The subsection also provides a definition of rights or liabilities under loan relationships. The terms refer to any of the rights or liabilities under the agreement or agreements representing the loan relationship, including the rights and liabilities attaching to any security to the loan relationship.

This particular aspect of the section generated some comment in Standing Committee as to its complexity. With regard to the definition of loan relationship, the Minister stated—

"I shall try to address some of the hon. Gentleman's points. Section 81 is not modified by Section 100 because Section 81 deals with loans for money whereas Section 100 deals with interest on things which are not loans for money. That same definition is used when considering the general list of every conceivable type of certificate . . . It does not extend to invoices or payments under guarantees, but it does extend to tradeable loan notes, for example when taken in exchange for a takeover bid. Whether promissory notes are covered by the new rules depends on whether there is a loan of money. If there is, the promissory note is covered; if there is not, then it is not. The answer to the question about certification is the same. Again, on contingency debt, one uses the same criteria."

Taxation of profits and gains and relief for deficits

82   Method of bringing amounts into account

(1) For the purposes of corporation tax—

    (*a*) the profits and gains arising from the loan relationships of a company, and

    (*b*) any deficit on a company's loan relationships,

shall be computed in accordance with this section using the credits and debits given for the accounting period in question by the following provisions of this Chapter.

(2) To the extent that, in any accounting period, a loan relationship of a company is one to which it is a party for the purposes of a trade carried on by it, the credits and debits given in respect of that relationship for that period shall be treated (according to whether they are credits or debits) either—

    (*a*) as receipts of that trade falling to be brought into account in computing the profits and gains of that trade for that period; or

    (*b*) as expenses of that trade which are deductible in computing those profits and gains.

(3) Where for any accounting period there are, in respect of the loan relationships of a company, both—

    (*a*) credits that are not brought into account under subsection (2) above ("non-trading credits"), and

    (*b*) debits that are not so brought into account ("non-trading debits"),

the aggregate of the non-trading debits shall be subtracted from the aggregate of the non-trading credits to give the amount to be brought into account under subsection (4) below.

(4) That amount is the amount which for any accounting period is to be taken (according to whether the aggregate of the non-trading credits or the aggregate of the non-trading debits is the greater) to be either—

    (*a*) the amount of the company's profits and gains for that period that are chargeable under Case III of Schedule D as profits and gains arising from the company's loan relationships; or

    (*b*) the amount of the company's non-trading deficit for that period on its loan relationships.

(5) Where for any accounting period a company has non-trading credits but no non-trading debits in respect of its loan relationships, the aggregate amount of the credits shall be the amount of the company's profits and gains for that period that are chargeable under Case III of Schedule D as profits and gains arising from those relationships.

(6) Where for any accounting period a company has non-trading debits but no non-trading credits in respect of its loan relationships, that company shall have a non-trading deficit on its loan relationships for that period equal to the aggregate of the debits.

(7) Subsection (2) above, so far as it provides for any amount to be deductible as mentioned in paragraph (*b*) of that subsection, shall have effect notwithstanding anything in section 74 of the Taxes Act 1988 (allowable deductions).

GENERAL NOTE

This section sets out the method by which profits, gains and deficits from loan relationships are to be brought into account for the purposes of corporation tax in any accounting period.

The section refers to "debits" and "credits" (see s 84) and the basis of assessment depends upon whether the company is party to the relevant loan relationship for the purposes of a trade. If the company is a party to loan relationship for the purposes of a trade carried on by it, any debits will be relieved as an expense of the trade and any credits will be taxed as a receipt of the trade. These rules will override the provisions of TA 1988 s 74, which deny relief for certain expenses in computing trading profits.

If the company has loan relationships to which it is party not for the purposes of its trade, the aggregate of any debits from these non-trading loan relationships is subtracted from the aggregate of any non-trading credits. An excess of credits is assessable under Schedule D Case III. An excess of debits is the company's non-trading deficit and relief is given as described in s 83 below. If the company only has debits or credits the aggregate is treated as the non-trading deficit or the Schedule D Case III income respectively.

During the debate, the Minister noted—

"I laid out the three basic rules underpinning the clause, one is that the figures should follow those produced for non-tax purposes whenever that is acceptable. No prescriptive rules exist to say what tax treatment should apply, as tax treatment will follow the accounts. That is the beauty of the clause— it provides the flexibility that companies have sought."

Further—

". . . whether one treats a specific type of loan in a specific way depends on the accounting treatment that is used for a specific company. That is the issue in question and the tax law follows the accounting treatment that has been used."

83   Non-trading deficit on loan relationships

(1) This section applies for the purposes of corporation tax where for any accounting period ("the deficit period") there is a non-trading deficit on a company's loan relationships.

(2) The company may make a claim for the whole or any part of the deficit to be treated in any of the following ways, that is to say—

(*a*) to be set off against any profits of the company (of whatever description) for the deficit period;

(*b*) to be treated as eligible for group relief;

(*c*) to be carried back to be set off against profits for earlier accounting periods; or

(*d*) to be carried forward and set against non-trading profits for the next accounting period.

(3) So much of the deficit for the deficit period as is not the subject of a claim under subsection (2) above shall be carried forward so as to be brought into account for the purposes of this Chapter as a non-trading debit ("a carried-forward debit") for the accounting period immediately following the deficit period.

(4) No claim shall be made under subsection (2)(*a*) to (*c*) above in respect of so much (if any) of the non-trading deficit of a company for any accounting period as is equal to the amount by which that deficit is greater than it would have been if any carried-forward debit for that period had been disregarded.

(5) No part of any non-trading deficit of a company established for charitable

purposes only shall be set off against the profits of that or any other company in pursuance of a claim under subsection (2) above.

(6) A claim under subsection (2) above must be made within the period of two years immediately following the end of the relevant period, or within such further period as the Board may allow.

(7) In subsection (6) above "the relevant period"—

(*a*) in relation to a claim under subsection (2)(*a*), (*b*) or (*c*) above, means the deficit period; and
(*b*) in relation to a claim under subsection (2)(*d*) above, means the accounting period immediately following the deficit period.

(8) Different claims may be made under subsection (2) above as respects different parts of a non-trading deficit for any period, but no claim may be made as respects any part of a deficit to which another claim made under that subsection relates.

(9) Schedule 8 to this Act (which makes provision about what happens where a claim is made under subsection (2) above) shall have effect.

GENERAL NOTE
This section which introduces Sch 8, provides for the relief available for an accounting period ("the deficit period") in which a company has a non-trading deficit on its loan relationships.
The company with a non-trading deficit may make a claim under sub-s (2) for the whole or part of the deficit—

(*a*) to be set off against any of its profits of the deficit period; or
(*b*) to be eligible for group relief; or
(*c*) to be carried back against Schedule D Case III profits from loan relationships of earlier accounting periods; or
(*d*) to be carried forward against non-trading profits of the next accounting period.

Different claims may be made for different parts of the deficit for any period. Claims must be made within two years of the end of the relevant period (or such longer period as the Board may allow). For the purposes of sub-s 2(*a*)–(*c*) the relevant period is the deficit period and for sub-s 2(*d*) is the accounting period immediately following the deficit period. These reliefs are explained further in Sch 8.
Where a claim is not made the deficit is carried forward and is treated as a non-trading deficit of the immediately following accounting period. Where a non-trading deficit is carried forward, it is not available for the more extensive relief under sub-s (2)(*a*)–(*c*) but a claim under sub-s 2(*d*) to carry it forward again may be made.
During the passage of the Bill through Parliament amendments were made to this section from its original draft. The changes effectively allow a loss not used under sub-s (2)(*a*)–(*c*) to be used in the next accounting or carried forward again by election.
A non-trading deficit accruing to a company established for charitable purposes is excluded from relief under this sub-s (2).

Computational provisions etc

84 Debits and credits brought into account

(1) The credits and debits to be brought into account in the case of any company in respect of its loan relationships shall be the sums which, in accordance with an authorised accounting method and when taken together, fairly represent, for the accounting period in question—

(*a*) all profits, gains and losses of the company, including those of a capital nature, which (disregarding interest and any charges or expenses) arise to the company from its loan relationships and related transactions; and
(*b*) all interest under the company's loan relationship and all charges and expenses incurred by the company under or for the purposes of its loan relationships and related transactions.

(2) The reference in subsection (1) above to the profits, gains and losses arising to a company—

(*a*) does not include a reference to any amounts required to be transferred to the company's share premium account; but

(*b*) does include a reference to any profits, gains or losses which, in accordance with normal accountancy practice, are carried to or sustained by any other reserve maintained by the company.

(3) The reference in subsection (1)(*b*) above to charges and expenses incurred for the purposes of a company's loan relationships and related transactions does not include a reference to any charges or expenses other than those incurred directly—

(*a*) in bringing any of those relationships into existence;

(*b*) in entering into or giving effect to any of those transactions;

(*c*) in making payments under any of those relationships or in pursuance of any of those transactions; or

(*d*) in taking steps for ensuring the receipt of payments under any of those relationships or in accordance with any of those transactions.

(4) Where—

(*a*) any charges or expenses are incurred by a company for purposes connected—

(i) with entering into a loan relationship or related transaction, or

(ii) with giving effect to any obligation that might arise under a loan relationship or related transaction,

(*b*) at the time when the charges or expenses are incurred, the relationship or transaction is one into which the company may enter but has not entered, and

(*c*) if that relationship or transaction had been entered into by that company, the charges or expenses would be charges or expenses incurred as mentioned in subsection (3) above,

those charges or expenses shall be treated for the purposes of this Chapter as charges or expenses in relation to which debits may be brought into account in accordance with subsection (1)(*b*) above to the same extent as if the relationship or transaction had been entered into.

(5) In this section "related transaction", in relation to a loan relationship, means any disposal or acquisition (in whole or in part) of rights or liabilities under that relationship.

(6) The cases where there shall be taken for the purposes of this section to be a disposal and acquisition of rights or liabilities under a loan relationship shall include those where such rights or liabilities are transferred or extinguished by any sale, gift, exchange, surrender, redemption or release.

(7) This section has effect subject to Schedule 9 to this Act (which contains provision disallowing certain debits and credits for the purposes of this Chapter and making assumptions about how an authorised accounting method is to be applied in certain cases).

GENERAL NOTE
    This section introduces Sch 9 and provides definitions of "debits" and "credits".
    The "debits" and "credits" for an accounting period shall be the sums which "fairly represent" all profits, gains and losses (capital or otherwise) arising from, and all charges and expenses incurred by the company under its loan relationships and "related transactions" and interests under its loan relationships. This is to be determined by reference to an "authorised accounting method".

A "related transaction" in relation to a loan relationship is any disposal or acquisition of rights or liabilities under that loan relationship (including transfers or extinguishment by sale, gift, exchange, surrender, redemption or release).

The profits, gains and losses arising include those which in accordance with normal accountancy practice are carried to or sustained by any other reserve maintained by the company but excludes amounts required to be transferred to the company's share premium account.

The charges and expenses under sub-s (3) are only those which are incurred "directly"—

(*a*) in bringing the loan relationships into existence;
(*b*) in entering into or giving effect to those transactions;
(*c*) in making payments under the relationships or in pursuance of those transactions; or
(*d*) in taking steps to ensure receipts under the relationships or in accordance with the transactions.

The relief for charges and expenses is extended for those incurred by a company in connection with entering into or giving effect to any obligations which might arise under a loan relationship or related transaction which does not yet exist. It applies to such charges or expenses incurred at a time when the relationship or transaction may be entered into and where they would be eligible under sub-s (3) if the relationship had been entered into. There is no requirement for the loan to be entered into subsequently.

The section is subject to Sch 9 which provides guidance on how an authorised accounting method is to be applied and disallowing certain items.

85   Authorised accounting methods

(1) Subject to the following provisions of this Chapter, the alternative accounting methods that are authorised for the purposes of this Chapter are—

(*a*) an accruals basis of accounting; and
(*b*) a mark to market basis of accounting under which any loan relationship to which that basis is applied is brought into account in each accounting period at a fair value.

(2) An accounting method applied in any case shall be treated as authorised for the purposes of this Chapter only if—

(*a*) it conforms (subject to paragraphs (*b*) and (*c*) below) to normal accountancy practice, as followed in cases where such practice allows the use of that method;
(*b*) it contains proper provision for allocating payments under a loan relationship to accounting periods; and
(*c*) where it is an accruals basis of accounting, it does not contain any provision (other than provision comprised in authorised arrangements for bad debt) that gives debits by reference to the valuation at different times of any asset representing a loan relationship.

(3) In the case of an accruals basis of accounting, proper provision for allocating payments under a loan relationship to accounting periods is provision which—

(*a*) allocates payments to the period to which they relate, without regard to the periods in which they are made or received or in which they become due and payable;
(*b*) includes provision which, where payments relate to two or more periods, apportions them on a just and reasonable basis between the different periods;
(*c*) assumes, subject to authorised arrangements for bad debt, that, so far as any company in the position of a creditor is concerned, every amount payable under the relationship will be paid in full as it becomes due;
(*d*)   secures the making of the adjustments required in the case of the relationship by authorised arrangements for bad debt; and
(*e*) provides, subject to authorised arrangements for bad debt and for writing off government investments, that, where there is a release of any liability under the relationship, the appropriate amount in respect of the

release is credited to the debtor in the accounting period in which the release takes place.

(4) In the case of a mark to market basis of accounting, proper provision for allocating payments under a loan relationship to accounting periods is provision which allocates payments to the accounting period in which they become due and payable.

(5) In this section—

(*a*) the references to authorised arrangements for bad debt are references to accounting arrangements under which debits and credits are brought into account in conformity with the provisions of paragraph 5 of Schedule 9 to this Act; and

(*b*) the reference to authorised arrangements for writing off government investments is a reference to accounting arrangements that give effect to paragraph 7 of that Schedule.

(6) In this section "fair value", in relation to any loan relationship of a company, means the amount which, at the time as at which the value falls to be determined, is the amount that the company would obtain from or, as the case may be, would have to pay to an independent person for—

(*a*) the transfer of all the company's rights under the relationship in respect of amounts which at that time are not yet due and payable; and

(*b*) the release of all the company's liabilities under the relationship in respect of amounts which at that time are not yet due and payable.

GENERAL NOTE

This section specifies the accounting methods which are authorised for the purposes of the Chapter, being accruals or mark-to-market, subject to certain conditions. (Section 86 provides guidance as to which method is to be used.)

To be authorised the accounting method must conform with normal accountancy practice and make "proper provision" for the allocation of payments under a loan relationship to accounting periods. In addition, where an accruals basis is used it must not allow debits, other than for bad debts, by reference to the value of any asset representing the loan relationship.

"Proper provision" for the allocation of payments where an accruals basis is used requires that—

(*a*) payments are allocated to the period to which they relate, regardless of when they are paid or received or are due and payable;

(*b*) there is a just and reasonable apportionment between accounting periods of payments relating to two or more periods;

(*c*) for the creditor, every payment is assumed to be paid in full as it becomes due, subject to authorised arrangements for bad debt relief (see Sch 9 para 5);

(*d*) adjustments are made for bad debts by authorised arrangements (see Sch 9 para 5); and

(*e*) any release of a liability is credited in the appropriate amount to the debtor in the period of the release, subject to authorised arrangements for bad debt (see Sch 9 para 5) and for writing off government investments (see Sch 9 para 7).

"Proper provision" for the allocation of payments where a mark-to-market basis is used requires that payments are allocated to periods in which they become due and payable.

To be authorised the mark-to-market method must value the loan relationship in each accounting period at its "fair value". For this purpose, "fair value" is the amount which, at the time of valuation, would be obtained from an independent person for the transfer of all of the company's rights under the loan relationship or would have to be paid to such a person for the release of amounts not yet due and payable.

During the debate in Standing Committee, the Minister was asked—

"about the use of mark-to-market and whether that accounting method had to be used previously in order for a business to decide to use it. Companies can choose their method, provided that they follow their accounts. There is no requirement that mark-to-market should have been used before."

In the debate on s 90 (cl 81) it was "a fair value is what a company could expect to sell its holdings for on the open market".

86 Application of accounting methods

(1) This section has effect, subject to the following provisions of this Chapter, for the determination of which of the alternative authorised accounting methods that are available by virtue of section 85 above is to be used as respects the loan relationships of a company.

(2) Different methods may be used as respects different relationships or, as respects the same relationship, for different accounting periods or for different parts of the same accounting period.

(3) If a basis of accounting which is or equates with an authorised accounting method is used as respects any loan relationship of a company in a company's statutory accounts, then the method which is to be used for the purposes of this Chapter as respects that relationship for the accounting period, or part of a period, for which that basis is used in those accounts shall be—

(*a*) where the basis used in those accounts is an authorised accounting method, that method; and

(*b*) where it is not, the authorised accounting method with which it equates.

(4) For any period or part of a period for which the authorised accounting method to be used as respects a loan relationship of a company is not determined under subsection (3) above, an authorised accruals basis of accounting shall be used for the purposes of this Chapter as respects that loan relationship.

(5) For the purposes of this section (but subject to subsection (6) below)—

(*a*) a basis of accounting equates with an authorised accruals basis of accounting if it purports to allocate payments under a loan relationship to accounting periods according to when they are taken to accrue; and

(*b*) a basis of accounting equates with an authorised mark to market basis of accounting if (without equating with an authorised accruals basis of accounting) it purports in respect of a loan relationship—

(i) to produce credits or debits computed by reference to the determination, as at different times in an accounting period, of a fair value; and

(ii) to produce credits or debits relating to payments under that relationship according to when they become due and payable.

(6) An accounting method which purports to make any such allocation of payments under a loan relationship as is mentioned in subsection (5)(*a*) above shall be taken for the purposes of this section to equate with an authorised mark to market basis of accounting (rather than with an authorised accruals basis of accounting) if—

(*a*) it purports to bring that relationship into account in each accounting period at a value which would be fair value if the valuation were made on the basis that interest under the relationship were to be disregarded to the extent that it has already accrued; and

(*b*) the credits and debits produced in the case of that relationship by that method (when it is properly applied) correspond, for all practical purposes, to the credits and debits produced in the case of that relationship, and for the same accounting period, by an authorised mark to market basis of accounting.

(7) In this section "fair value" has the same meaning as in section 85 above.

(8) In this section "statutory accounts", in relation to a company, means—

(*a*) any accounts relating to that company that are drawn up in accordance with any requirements of the Companies Act 1985 or the Companies (Northern Ireland) Order 1986 that apply in relation to that company;

(*b*) any accounts relating to that company that are drawn up in accordance with any requirements of regulations under section 70 of the Friendly Societies Act 1992 that apply in relation to that company;

(*c*) any accounts relating to that company which are accounts to which Part I of Schedule 21C to the Companies Act 1985 or Part I of Schedule 21D to that Act (companies with UK branches) applies;

(*d*) in the case of a company which—

(i) is not subject to any such requirements as are mentioned in paragraphs (*a*) or (*b*) above, and

(ii) is a company in whose case there are no accounts for the period in question that fall within paragraph (*c*) above,

any accounts relating to the company drawn up in accordance with requirements imposed in relation to that company under the law of its home State; and

(*e*) in the case of a company which—

(i) is not subject to any such requirements as are mentioned in paragraphs (*a*), (*b*) or (*d*) above, and

(ii) is a company in whose case there are no accounts for the period in question that fall within paragraph (*c*) above,

the accounts relating to the company that most closely correspond to the accounts which, in the case of a company formed and registered under the Companies Act 1985, are required under that Act.

(9) For the purposes of subsection (8) above the home State of a company is the country or territory under whose law the company is incorporated.

GENERAL NOTE

This section specifies when either an authorised accruals or mark-to-market basis of accounting is to be used by a company in respect of its loan relationships. It is, however, subject to the following provisions of the Chapter which may override it.

Different methods may be used for different loan relationships or for the same loan relationship in different accounting periods or part thereof.

Where an authorised accounting method has been used by a company in its "statutory accounts", then it is to be followed for the purposes of this Chapter. If the basis of accounting used in the statutory accounts "equates" to an authorised accounting method, that authorised accounting method will be used. Otherwise an authorised accruals basis must be used.

An accounting basis equates to an authorised accruals basis if it purports to allocate payments under the loan relationship to accounting periods when they are taken to accrue.

An accounting basis equates to an authorised mark-to-market basis if it purports to produce credits and debits—

(*a*) by reference to the fair value (as defined by s 85) of the loan relationship; and

(*b*) for payments as they become due and payable under the loan relationship.

During the passage of the Bill through Parliament, sub-s (6) was introduced. It provides that where an accounting method is used which allocated payments under a loan relationship to accounting periods as they accrue (under sub-s (5)(*a*)) but which marks the relationship, to fair value, disregarding interest, it will be treated as an authorised mark-to-market basis of accounting.

"Statutory accounts" are defined as those drawn up in accordance with the Companies Act 1985, Companies (Northern Ireland) Order 1986 and the Friendly Societies Act 1992 s 70. Where none of these are applicable and the company draws up accounts in accordance with the law of its home State (ie that State under whose laws it is incorporated), those accounts are "statutory accounts". Where none of these are applicable, the "statutory accounts" are the accounts which most closely correspond to the accounts required of a company formed and registered under the Companies Act 1985.

87 Accounting method where parties have a connection

(1) This section applies in the case of a loan relationship of a company where for any accounting period there is a connection between the company and—

(*a*) in the case of a debtor relationship of the company, a person standing in the position of a creditor as respects the debt in question; or

(*b*) in the case of a creditor relationship of the company, a person standing in the position of a debtor as respects that debt.

(2) The only accounting method authorised for the purposes of this Chapter for use by the company as respects the loan relationship shall be an authorised accruals basis of accounting.

(3) For the purposes of this section there is a connection between a company and another person for an accounting period if (subject to subsection (4) and section 88 below)—

(*a*) the other person is a company and there is a time in that period, or in the two years before the beginning of that period, when one of the companies has had control of the other;

(*b*) the other person is a company and there is a time in that period, or in those two years, when both the companies have been under the control of the same person; or

(*c*) there is a time in that accounting period, or in those two years, when the company was a close company and the other person was a participator in that company or the associate of a person who was such a participator at that time.

(4) Two companies which have at any time been under the control of the same person shall not, by virtue of that fact, be taken for the purposes of this section to be companies between whom there is a connection if the person was the Crown, a Minister of the Crown, a government department, a Northern Ireland department, a foreign sovereign power or an international organisation.

(5) The references in subsection (1) above to a person who stands in the position of a creditor or debtor as respects a loan relationship include references to a person who indirectly stands in that position by reference to a series of loan relationships.

(6) Subsections (2) to (6) of section 416 of the Taxes Act 1988 (meaning of control) shall apply for the purposes of this section as they apply for the purposes of Part XI of that Act.

(7) Subject to subsection (8) below, in this section "participator" and "associate" have the meanings given for the purposes of Part XI of the Taxes Act 1988 by section 417 of that Act.

(8) A person shall not for the purposes of this section be regarded as a participator in relation to a company by reason only that he is a loan creditor of the company.

GENERAL NOTE

This section provides that an authorised accruals basis of accounting must be used for tax purposes when there is a "connection" between the parties to the loan relationship in specified circumstances.

The section applies where the debtor company is connected with the creditor under the loan relationship or vice versa. These include a creditor or debtor standing in such a position indirectly by reference to a series of loan relationships.

The term "connection" is defined very widely, being referenced to the other person party to a company's loan relationship. It applies where the other person—

(*a*) is a company and either has "control" of the other;

(*b*) is a company and they are under the "control" of the same person; or

(*c*) is a "participator" in the company, which is a close company, or is an "associate" of such a participator.

These tests are applied at any time in the accounting period in question or within two years before the beginning of the period. As originally drafted this period had been six years.

"Participator" and "associate" are as defined by TA 1988 s 417, except that a participator which is such only by reason of being a creditor of the company is excluded from the definition. "Control" is as defined by TA 1988 s 416(2)–(6).

During the passage of the Bill through Parliament, exemptions were introduced. First, sub-s (4) was introduced so that two companies are not connected if they are considered to be under common control solely because they have been under the control of the Crown, a Minister of the Crown, a government department, a Northern Ireland department, a foreign sovereign power or an international organisation. Second, s 88 was introduced.

88   Exemption from section 87 in certain cases

(1) Subject to subsection (5) below, where a creditor relationship of a company is one to which that company is a party in any accounting period in exempt circumstances, any connection for that accounting period between the company and a person who stands in the position of a debtor as respects the debt shall be disregarded for the purposes of section 87 above.

(2) A company having a credit relationship in any accounting period shall, for that period, be taken for the purposes of this section to be a party to that relationship in exempt circumstances if—

(a) the company, in the course of carrying on any activities forming an integral part of a trade carried on by that company in that period, disposes of or acquires assets representing creditor relationships;
(b) that period is one for which the company uses an authorised mark to market basis of accounting as respects all the creditor relationships represented by assets acquired in the course of those activities;
(c) the asset representing the creditor relationship in question was acquired in the course of those activities;
(d) that asset is either—

(i) listed on a recognised stock exchange at the end of that period; or
(ii) a security the redemption of which must occur within twelve months of its issue;

(e) there is a time in that period when assets of the same kind as the asset representing the loan relationship in question are in the beneficial ownership of persons other than the company; and
(f) there is not more than three months, in aggregate, in that accounting period during which the equivalent of 30 per cent or more of the assets of that kind is in the beneficial ownership of connected persons.

(3) An insurance company carrying on basic life assurance and general annuity business and having a creditor relationship in any accounting period shall, for that period, be taken for the purposes of this section to be a party to that relationship in exempt circumstances if—

(a) assets of the company representing any of its creditor relationships are linked for that period to its basic life assurance and general annuity business;
(b) that period is one for which the company uses an authorised mark to market basis of accounting as respects all the creditor relationships of the company represented by assets that are so linked;
(c) the asset representing the creditor relationship in question is so linked;
(d) that asset is either—

(i) listed on a recognised stock exchange at the end of that period; or
(ii) a security the redemption of which must occur within twelve months of its issue;

(e) there is a time in that period when assets of the same kind as the asset representing the creditor relationship in question are in the beneficial ownership of persons other than the company; and

(*f*) there is not more than three months, in aggregate, in that period during which the equivalent of 30 per cent or more of the assets of that kind is in the beneficial ownership of connected persons.

(4) For the purposes of subsections (2) and (3) above—

(*a*) assets shall be taken to be of the same kind where they are treated as being of the same kind by the practice of any recognised stock exchange, or would be so treated if dealt with on such a stock exchange; and

(*b*) a connected person has the beneficial ownership of an asset wherever there is, or (apart from this section) would be, a connection (within the meaning of section 87 above) between—

(i) the person who has the beneficial ownership of the assets, and

(ii) a person who stands in the position of a debtor as respects the money debt by reference to which any loan relationship represented by that asset subsists.

(5) Where for any accounting period—

(*a*) subsection (1) above has effect in the case of a creditor relationship of a company, and

(*b*) the person who stands in the position of a debtor as respects the debt in question is also a company,

that subsection shall not apply for determining, for the purposes of so much of section 87 above as relates to the corresponding debtor relationship, whether there is a connection between the two companies.

(6) Subsection (5) of section 87 above shall apply for the purposes of this section as it applies for the purposes of that section.

(7) In this section "basic life assurance and general annuity business" and "insurance company" has the same meanings as in Chapter I of Part XII of the Taxes Act 1988, and section 432ZA of that Act (linked assets) shall apply for the purposes of this section as it applies for the purposes of that Chapter.

GENERAL NOTE

This section provides exemption from the application of s 87, which section provides for an accruals basis of accounting must be used for tax purposes when there is a "connection" between the parties to the loan relationship in the circumstances specified.

It was introduced during the passage of the Bill through Parliament. Section 88 provides that where a creditor company is party to loan relationship in any accounting period in exempt circumstances, any connection for that accounting period is disregarded for the purposes of s 87.

Exempt circumstances arise where the company—

(*a*) in that period acquires or disposes of creditor relationships as an integral part of its trade;

(*b*) in that period it has used authorised mark-to-market accounting for all of its loan relationships;

(*c*) the loan relationship was acquired in the course of the trade;

(*d*) the asset is listed on a recognised stock exchange at the end of the period or is due for redemption within 12 months of issue;

(*e*) at some time during the period, another person beneficially owned assets of the same kind (ie it is treated as the same kind by practice of any recognised stock exchange or would be so treated if it was so dealt on such an exchange); and

(*f*) there is not more than three months in the accounting period in which 30 per cent or more of the loan relationships are in the beneficial ownership of connected persons (as defined ins 87 and referring to the relationship between the owner and the debtor).

Similar conditions apply to an insurance company carrying on a basic life assurance business and general annuity business where assets representing any of its creditor relationships are linked to its basic life assurance or general annuity business.

Where the debtor is a company, s 88(1) does not apply in respect of the debtor for determining whether there is a connection between the two companies for the purposes of s 87. Section 87(5) continues to apply.

89 Inconsistent application of accounting methods

(1) Where there is any inconsistency or other material difference between the way in which any authorised accounting method is applied as respects the same loan relationship in successive accounting periods, a balancing credit or balancing debit shall be brought into account in the second of those periods ("the second period").

(2) The amount of the balancing credit or debit shall be computed as respects the relationship in question by—

(*a*) taking the amount given by subsection (3) below and the amount given by subsection (4) below; and

(*b*) then aggregating those amounts (treating any debit as a negative amount) to produce a net credit or net debit.

(3) The amount given by this subsection is whichever of the following is applicable—

(*a*) a debit equal to the amount (if any) by which the first of the following amounts exceeds the second, that is to say—

(i) the aggregate of the credits actually brought into account for all previous periods in which the accounting method was used; and

(ii) the aggregate of the credits that would have been brought into account if that method had been applied in those periods in the same way as it was applied in the second period;

(*b*) a credit equal to the amount (if any) by which the second aggregate mentioned in paragraph (*a*) above exceeds the first; or

(*c*) if both those aggregates are the same, nil.

(4) The amount given by this subsection is whichever of the following is applicable—

(*a*) a credit equal to the amount (if any) by which the first of the following amounts exceeds the second, that is to say—

(i) the aggregate of the debits actually brought into account for all previous periods in which the accounting method was used; and

(ii) the aggregate of the debits that would have been brought into account if that method had been applied in those periods in the same way as it was applied in the second period;

(*b*) a debit equal to the amount (if any) by which the second aggregate mentioned in paragraph (*a*) above exceeds the first; or

(*c*) if both those aggregates are the same, nil.

(5) In this section "previous period" means any accounting period before the second period.

GENERAL NOTE

This section ensures that when a company alters the application of its authorised accounting method no debits or credits fall out of account as a result.

It applies where there is any inconsistency or material difference in the way that the method is applied in succeeding accounting periods. It causes a "balancing debit" or "balancing credit" to be brought into account in the second of those periods.

The balancing debit or credit is the difference between the aggregate of the debits and credits given in respect of the loan relationship in previous accounting periods under the existing method and the aggregate of the debits and credits which would have been given under the new method.

90 Changes of accounting method

(1) This section applies where different authorised accounting methods are used for the purposes of this Chapter as respects the same loan relationship for different parts of the same accounting period or for successive accounting periods.

(2) Where, in the case of any loan relationship, the use of any authorised accounting method is superseded in the course of any accounting period by the use of another—

(*a*) the assumptions specified in subsection (4) below shall be made;

(*b*) each method shall be applied on those assumptions as respects the part of the period for which it is used; and

(*c*) the credits and debits given by the application of those methods on those assumptions shall be brought into account in the accounting period in which the change of method takes effect.

(3) Where, in the case of any loan relationship, the use of any authorised accounting method is superseded as from the beginning of an accounting period by the use of another—

(*a*) a net credit or debit shall be computed (treating any debit used in the computation as a negative amount) by—

(i) aggregating the credits and debits which, on the assumptions specified in subsection (4) below, would have been given in respect of that relationship for the successive accounting periods by the use for each period of the accounting method actually used for that period;

(ii) aggregating the credits and debits so given without the making of those assumptions; and

(iii) substracting the second aggregate from the first;

and

(*b*) the net credit or debit shall be brought into account for the purposes of this Chapter in the accounting period as from the beginning of which the change of method takes effect.

(4) The assumptions mentioned in subsections (2) and (3) above are—

(*a*) that the company ceased to be a party to the relationship immediately before the end of the period, or part of a period, for which the superseded method is used;

(*b*) that the company again became a party to that relationship as from the beginning of the period or, as the case may be, part of a period for which the other authorised accounting method is used;

(*c*) that the relationship to which the company is deemed to have become a party is separate and distinct from the one to which it is deemed to have ceased to be a party;

(*d*) that the amount payable under the transaction comprised in each of the assumptions specified in paragraphs (*a*) and (*b*) above was equal to the fair value of the relationship; and

(*e*) so far as relevant, that that amount became due at the time when the company is deemed to have ceased to be a party to the relationship or, as the case may be, to have again become a party to it.

(5) Where—

(*a*) a mark-to-market basis of accounting is superseded by an accruals basis of accounting in the case of any loan relationship, and

(*b*) the amount which would have accrued in respect of that relationship in the period or part of a period for which the accruals basis of accounting is used falls to be determined for the purposes of this section in accordance with the assumptions mentioned in subsection (4) above,

that amount shall be taken for those purposes to be equal to the amount resulting from the subtraction of the amount given by subsection (6)(*a*) below from the amount given by subsection (6)(*b*) below.

(6) Those amounts are—

(*a*) the amount which by virtue of the assumptions mentioned in subsection (4) above is given as an opening value for the period or part of a period; and
(*b*) the amount equal to whatever, in the computation in accordance with an authorised accruals basis of accounting of the amount accruing in that period or part of a period, would have been taken to be the closing value applicable as at the end of that period or part of a period if such a basis of accounting had always been used as respects the relationship.

(7) In this section "fair value" has the same meaning as in section 85 above.

GENERAL NOTE
This section ensures that when a company changes from one authorised accounting method to another no debits or credits fall out of account as a result.

It applies where there is a change in the accounting method used in the course of or at the beginning of an accounting period. In doing so it assumes under sub-s (4)—

(*a*) the company ceased to be a party to the loan relationship immediately before the end of the period (or part period) for which the superseded method was used;
(*b*) the company became party to the loan relationship from the beginning of the period (or part period) for which the new method is used;
(*c*) the loan relationship after the change is treated as separate and distinct from the loan relationship before the change; and
(*d*) the deemed transactions at (*a*) and (*b*) take place at "fair value" (as defined under s 85), which becomes due on the deemed cessation or when the company is deemed to become party to the loan relationship again.

Where the change takes place during the accounting period each method is applied using these assumptions for the part of the period for which it is used and the resulting debits and credits are recognised in the accounting period of the change.

Where the change takes place with effect from the beginning of an accounting period the credits and debits that would be due for each of the successive periods are calculated and aggregated for both accounting methods and the difference is brought into account in the accounting period at the beginning of which the change takes place.

During the debate, sub-ss (5) and (6) were introduced which provide special rules for switches from a mark-to-market to an accruals basis of accounting. The amount which would have accrued for the period (or part) for which an accruals basis is used is the closing value assuming the accruals basis had always been used less the opening value under the assumptions in sub-s (4).

It should also be noted that discussions are taking place between the Revenue and the Institute of Chartered Accountants over interpretation of the provision and the Revenue will be writing to the Institute explaining how the provision works.

91 Payments subject to deduction of tax

(1) This section applies where—

(*a*) any company receives a payment of interest on which it bears income tax by deduction; and
(*b*) in the case of that company, a credit relating to that interest has been brought into account for the purposes of this Chapter for an accounting period ending more than two years before the receipt of the payment.

(2) On a claim made by the company to an officer of the Board, section 7(2) or, as the case may be, 11(3) of the Taxes Act 1988 (deducted income tax to be set against liability to corporation tax) shall have effect in relation to the income tax on the payment as if the interest had fallen to be taken into

account for the purposes of corporation tax in the accounting period in which the payment of that interest is received.

(3) In determining for the purposes of this section which accounting period is the accounting period for which a credit relating to interest paid subsequently was brought into account, every payment of interest to a company under a loan relationship of that company shall be assumed to be a payment in discharge of the earliest outstanding liability to that company in respect of interest payable under the relationship.

(4) For the purposes of this section, the earliest outstanding liability to interest payable under a loan relationship of a company shall be identified, in relation to any payment of such interest, according to the authorised accounting method most recently used as respects that relationship, so that—

(*a*) if that method is an authorised accruals basis of accounting, it shall be determined by reference to the time when the interest accrued; and

(*b*) if that method is an authorised mark to market basis of accounting, it shall be determined by reference to the time when the interest became due and payable.

(5) In subsection (4) above the reference, in relation to a payment of interest made to a company in any accounting period, to the authorised accounting method most recently used as respects that relationship is a reference to the authorised accounting method which, in the case of that company, has been used as respects that relationship for the accounting period which, when the payment is made, is the most recent for which amounts in respect of that relationship have been brought into account for the purposes of this Chapter.

(6) A claim under this section shall not be made in respect of any payment of interest at any time after the later of the following, that is to say—

(*a*) the time two years after the end of the accounting period in which the payment is received; and

(*b*) the time six years after the end of the accounting period for which the credit in respect of the interest was brought into account for the purposes of this Chapter.

(7) Where—

(*a*) there is a payment of interest to a company under a loan relationship of that company, and

(*b*) the company is prevented by virtue of subsection (6) above from making any claim under this section in respect of that payment,

the company shall not be entitled to make any claim under paragraph 5 of Schedule 16 to the Taxes Act 1988 (set off of income tax borne against income tax payable) in respect of that payment.

GENERAL NOTE

This section provides for the basis on which income tax will be available for set-off against corporation tax where the income is recognised for corporation tax purposes more than two years before it is received.

The company can claim for the provisions which allow for the set-off of income tax against the company's corporation tax liability (TA 1988 s 7(2), for UK resident companies, or s 11(3), for non-UK companies) to apply by regarding the interest as recognised for tax purposes in the period in which it is received. The claim must be made by the later of two years after the end of the accounting period in which it is received and six years after the end of the accounting period in which the credit is recognised.

Payments of interest will be deemed to be in discharge of the earliest outstanding tax liability. This will be done by reference to the most recently used authorised accounting method, which is that used for the accounting period, when the payment was made, in which amounts have been brought into account under this Chapter.

Where a claim is out of time, relief for the income tax will not be given by set-off against income tax payable by the company in the CT 61 return, under TA 1988 Sch 16 para 5.

Special cases

92 Convertible securities etc

(1) This section applies to an asset if—

(*a*) the asset represents a creditor relationship of a company;

(*b*) the rights attached to the asset include provision by virtue of which the company is or may become entitled to acquire (whether by conversion or exchange or otherwise) any shares in a company;

(*c*) the extent to which shares may be acquired under that provision is not determined using a cash value which is specified in that provision or which is or will be ascertainable by reference to the terms of that provision;

(*d*) the asset is not a relevant discounted security within the meaning of Schedule 13 to this Act;

(*e*) at the time when the asset came into existence there was a more than negligible likelihood that the right to acquire shares in a company would in due course be exercised to a significant extent; and

(*f*) the asset is not one the disposal of which by the company would fall to be treated as a disposal in the course of activities forming an integral part of a trade carried on by the company.

(2) The amounts falling for any accounting period to be brought into account for the purposes of this Chapter in respect of a creditor relationship represented by an asset to which this section applies shall be confined to amounts relating to interest.

(3) Only an authorised accruals basis of accounting shall be used for ascertaining those amounts.

(4) Amounts shall be brought into account in computing the profits of the company for the purposes of corporation tax as if the Taxation of Chargeable Gains Act 1992 had effect in relation to any asset to which this section applies as it has effect in relation to an asset that does not represent a loan relationship.

(5) For the purposes of that Act the amount or value of the consideration for any disposal or acquisition of the asset shall be treated as adjusted so as to exclude so much of it as, on a just and reasonable apportionment, relates to any interest which—

(*a*) falls to be brought into account under subsections (2) and (3) above as accruing to any company at any time; and

(*b*) in consequence of, or of the terms of, the disposal or acquisition, is not paid or payable to the company to which it is treated for the purposes of this Chapter as accruing.

(6) In subsection (5) above the references to a disposal, in relation to an asset, are references to anything which—

(*a*) is a disposal of that asset (within the meaning of the Taxation of Chargeable Gains Act 1992); or

(*b*) would be such a disposal but for section 127 or 116(10) of that Act (reorganisations etc);

and the references to the acquisition of an asset shall be construed accordingly.

GENERAL NOTE

This section deals with securities with rights which entitle, or may entitle the holder to acquire shares in a company and provides that only interest should be accounted for under this Chapter, using an authorised accruals basis.

The section applies where the asset represents a creditor relationship of the company, includes the rights noted above (by conversion, exchange or otherwise) and it is not a "relevant discounted security" within Sch 13. Further, for the section to apply, at the time when the asset came into existence, there must have been "a more than negligible likelihood" that the right would in due course be exercised to a "significant extent". As can be seen, the criteria are rather subjective and at present no formal guidance is available.

The section does not apply where the asset is held for trading purposes, but it should be noted that the wording of the exclusion requires that the disposal of the asset would be treated as a disposal in the course of activities forming an "integral part" of the company's trade.

The asset representing the loan relationship will be subject to corporation tax on capital gains as if it were not a loan relationship. For this purpose the acquisition price or sales proceeds will be adjusted on a "just and reasonable apportionment" to exclude interest recognised under this section but which is not paid or payable to the company as a result of an acquisition or disposal. For this purpose, disposals are defined by TCGA 1992 or would be other than for the application of the reorganisation provisions of TCGA 1992 ss 127 or 116(10) and acquisitions are construed accordingly.

93   Relationships linked to the value of chargeable assets

(1) This section applies in the case of any loan relationship of a company that is linked to the value of chargeable assets unless it is one the disposal of which by the company would fall to be treated as a disposal in the course of activities forming an integral part of a trade carried on by the company.

(2) The amounts falling for any accounting period to be brought into account for the purposes of this Chapter in respect of the relationship shall be confined to amounts relating to interest.

(3) Only an authorised accruals basis of accounting shall be used for ascertaining those amounts.

(4) Amounts shall be brought into account in computing the profits of the company for the purposes of corporation tax as if the Taxation of Chargeable Gains Act 1992 had effect in relation to the asset representing the relationship as it has effect in relation to an asset that does not represent a loan relationship.

(5) For the purposes of that Act the amount or value of the consideration for any disposal or acquisition of the asset shall be treated as adjusted so as to exclude so much of it as, on a just and reasonable apportionment, relates to any interest which—

(*a*) falls to be brought into account under subsections (2) and (3) above as accruing to any company at any time; and
(*b*) in consequence of, or of the terms of, the disposal or acquisition, is not paid or payable to the company to which it is treated for the purposes of this Chapter as accruing.

(6) For the purposes of this section a loan relationship is linked to the value of chargeable assets if, in pursuance of any provision having effect for the purposes of that relationship, the amount that must be paid to discharge the money debt (whether on redemption of a security issued in relation to that debt or otherwise) is equal to the amount determined by applying a relevant percentage change in the value of chargeable assets to the amount falling for the purposes of this Chapter to be regarded as the amount of the original loan from which the money debt arises.

(7) In subsection (6) above the reference to a relevant percentage change in the value of chargeable assets is a reference to the amount of the percentage change (if any) over the relevant period in the value of chargeable assets of any particular description or in any index of the value of any such assets.

(8) In subsection (7) above "the relevant period" means—

(*a*) the period between the time of the original loan and the discharge of the money debt; or

(*b*) any other period in which almost all of that period is comprised and which differs from that period exclusively for purposes connected with giving effect to a valuation in relation to rights or liabilities under the loan relationship.

(9) If—

(*a*) there is a provision which, in the case of any loan relationship, falls within subsection (6) above,

(*b*) that provision is made subject to any other provision applying to the determination of the amount payable to discharge the money debt,

(*c*) that other provision is to the effect only that the amount so payable must not be less than a specified percentage of the amount falling for the purposes of this Chapter to be regarded as the amount of the original loan, and

(*d*) the specified percentage is not more than 10 per cent,

that other provision shall be disregarded in determining for the purposes of this section whether the relationship is linked to the value of chargeable assets.

(10) For the purposes of this section an asset is a chargeable asset, in relation to a loan relationship of a company, if any gain accruing on the disposal of the asset by the company on or after 1st April 1996 would, on the assumptions specified in subsection (11) below, be a chargeable gain for the purposes of the Taxation of Chargeable Gains Act 1992.

(11) Those assumptions are—

(*a*) where it is not otherwise the case, that the asset is an asset of the company;

(*b*) that the asset is not one the disposal of which by the company would fall to be treated for the purposes of corporation tax as a disposal in the course of a trade carried on by the company; and

(*c*) that chargeable gains that might accrue under section 116(10) of that Act (postponed charges) are to be disregarded.

(12) In subsection (5) above references to a disposal, in relation to an asset, are references to anything which—

(*a*) is a disposal of that asset (within the meaning of the Taxation of Chargeable Gains Act 1992); or

(*b*) would be such a disposal but for section 127 or 116(10) of that Act (reorganisations etc);

and the references to the acquisition of an asset shall be construed accordingly.

(13) For the purposes of this section neither—

(*a*) the retail prices index, nor

(*b*) any similar general index of prices published by the government of any territory or by the agent of any such government,

shall be taken to be an index of the value of chargeable assets.

GENERAL NOTE

This section applies to loan relationships which are "linked to the value" of "chargeable assets", providing that only interest should be accounted for under this Chapter, using an authorised accruals basis.

As originally drafted, the section would have applied to financial traders but this was amended (sub-ss (1) and (10)) to ensure that it does not apply where a disposal of such an asset would be treated as forming an integral part of a trade.

A "chargeable asset" for this purpose is an asset in relation to a loan relationship of the company if any gain on its disposal on or after 1 April 1996 would be a chargeable gain under TCGA 1992 assuming that the asset is an asset of the company (if it is not), its disposal would not be treated as in the course of a trade for tax purposes and the deferral provisions of TCGA 1992 s 116(10) did not apply.

A loan relationship is "linked to the value" of a chargeable asset, if in pursuance of any provision having effect for the purposes of the relationship the amount payable to discharge the money debt (see s 81(2)) is determined by applying a "relevant percentage change in the value of chargeable assets" to the amount of the original loan from which the money debt arises(sub-s (6)). This applies whether the discharge of the money debit is on redemption of a security issued in relation to the money debt or otherwise, further, special provisions apply where there is a provision falling within sub-s (6), which is subject to any "other provision" determining the amount payable to discharge the money debt. Where the "other provision" requires that the amount payable cannot be less than the original loan by up to and including 10 per cent, the "other provision" is to be disregarded in determining whether the relationship is linked to the value of chargeable assets.

For this purpose, the "relevant percentage change in the value of chargeable assets" is the percentage change in the "relevant period" in the value of any chargeable assets. This also includes changes in value of an index of the value of such assets, but such index excludes the RPI or similar general index of prices published by the government of any territory or by the agent of any such government.

The "relevant period" is the time between the original loan and the discharge of the money debt or such other period in which "almost all" of that period is comprised, where it differs exclusively to effecting the valuation of the rights or liabilities under the loan relationship.

The asset representing the loan relationship will be subject to corporation tax on capital gains as if it were not a loan relationship. For this purpose the acquisition price or sales proceeds will be adjusted on a "just and reasonable apportionment" to exclude interest recognised under this section but which is not paid or payable to the company as a result of an acquisition or disposal. For this purpose, disposals are as defined by TCGA 1992 or would be other than for the application of the reorganisation provisions of TCGA 1992 ss 127 or 116(10) and acquisitions are construed accordingly.

94   Indexed gilt-edged securities

(1) In the case of any loan relationship represented by an index-linked gilt-edged security, the adjustment for which this section provides shall be made in computing the credits and debits which fall, for any accounting period, to be brought into account for the purposes of this Chapter in respect of that relationship as non-trading credits or non-trading debits.

(2) The adjustment shall be made wherever—

(*a*) the authorised accounting method applied as respects the index-linked gilt-edged security gives credits or debits by reference to the value of the security at two different times, and

(*b*) there is any change in the retail prices index between those times.

(3) Subject to subsection (4) below the adjustment is such an adjustment of the amount which would otherwise be taken for the purposes of that accounting method to be the value of the security at the earlier time ("the opening value") as results in the amount in fact so taken being equal to the opening value increased or, as the case may be, reduced by the same percentage as the percentage increase or reduction in the retail prices index between the earlier and the later time.

(4) The Treasury may, in relation to any description of index-linked gilt-edged securities, by order provide that—

(*a*) there are to be no adjustments under this section; or

(*b*) that an adjustment specified in the order (instead of the adjustment specified in subsection (3) above) is to be the adjustment for which this section provides.

(5) An order under subsection (4) above—

(*a*) shall not have effect in relation to any gilt-edged security issued before the making of the order; but (*b*) may make different provision for different descriptions of securities.

(6) For the purposes of this section the percentage increase or reduction in the retail prices index between any two times shall be determined by reference to the difference between—

(*a*) that index for the month in which the earlier time falls; and
(*b*) that index for the month in which the later time falls.

(7) In this section "index-linked gilt-edged securities" means any gilt-edged securities the amounts of the payments under which are determined wholly or partly by reference to the retail prices index.

GENERAL NOTE

This section deals with index-linked gilt-edged securities and provides that non-trading debits and credits arising are to be adjusted by reference to the movement in the RPI as prescribed.

Index-linked gilt-edged securities are gilts giving rise to payments which are determined by reference, in whole or part, to the RPI.

The adjustment is made where there is a change in the RPI between two different times at which the gilt is valued for the purposes of the authorised accounting method. The adjustment causes the value of the gilt at the earlier of the two times to be increased or decreased by the percentage movement in the RPI between the two times.

The percentage movement in the RPI between the two times is determined by reference to the RPI for the month in which those times fall.

During the passage of the Bill through Parliament, amendments were made to allow Treasury regulations to be made which can provide that no such adjustment, or a modified adjustment as specified in the order, is to be made in respect of any description of index-linked gilts. The regulations will not apply to any gilts in issue at the time of making the order, but may apply to different descriptions of securities.

95 Gilt strips

(1) This section has effect for the purposes of the application of an authorised accruals basis of accounting as respects a loan relationship represented by a gilt-edged security or a strip of a gilt-edged security.

(2) Where a gilt-edged security is exchanged by any person for strips of that security—

(*a*) the security shall be deemed to have been redeemed at the time of the exchange by the payment to that person of its market value; and
(*b*) that person shall be deemed to have acquired each strip for the amount which bears the same proportion to that market value as is borne by the market value of the strip to the aggregate of the market values of all the strips received in exchange for the security.

(3) Where strips of a gilt-edged security are consolidated into a single gilt-edged security by being exchanged by any person for that security—

(*a*) each of the strips shall be deemed to have been redeemed at the time of the exchange by the payment to that person of the amount equal to its market value; and
(*b*) that person shall be deemed to have acquired the security received in the exchange for the amount equal to the aggregate of the market values of the strips given in exchange for the security.

(4) References in this section to the market value of a security given or received in exchange for another are references to its market value at the time of the exchange.

(5) Without prejudice to the generality of any power conferred by section 202 below, the Treasury may by regulations make provision for the purposes of this section as to the manner of determining the market value at any time of any gilt-edged security (including any strip).

(6) Regulations under subsection (5) above may—

(*a*) make different provision for different cases; and
(*b*) contain such incidental, supplemental, consequential and transitional provision as the Treasury may think fit.

(7) In this section "strip" means anything which, within the meaning of section 47 of the Finance Act 1942, is a strip of a gilt-edged security.

GENERAL NOTE
  This section provides for the taxation of a company which strips or reconstitutes a gilt while an authorised accruals basis is used.
  The term "strip" is defined by FA 1942 s 47. The Bank of England issued a parallel paper to the May 1995 Inland Revenue consultative document on the development of a gilts strip market. The stripping of a gilt causes the entitlements to payment of future interest and repayment of principal to be separated and allows them to be held separately. This is beneficial in that it allows holders of gilts to structure their holdings so that they more closely match their future cash flow requirements. The stripped gilt can be reconstituted into its original form.
  The section provides where the holder of the gilt exchanges it for strips of that security, the security is deemed to have been redeemed at its market value at the time of the exchange and the strips are deemed to be acquired for the same value. The value is attributed to the strips by apportionment based upon the value of any particular strip and the aggregate value of the strips.
  Where the gilt is reconstituted the process is similar. Each of the strips are deemed to have been redeemed for their market values at the time of the exchange and the gilt received will be deemed to be acquired for the aggregate of the market values of the strips.
  The Treasury may make regulations for the determination of market value of the gilts or the strips and these may make different provisions for different cases and contain associated provisions as the Treasury thinks fit.

96   Special rules for certain other gilts

(1) This section applies as respects any loan relationship of a company if—

(*a*) it is represented by a security of any of the following descriptions—

(i) 3¼% Funding Stock 1999–2004; or
(ii) 5½% Treasury Stock 2008–2012;

and

(*b*) it is one to which the company is a party otherwise than in the course of activities that form an integral part of a trade carried on by the company.

(2) The amounts falling for any accounting period to be brought into account for the purposes of this Chapter in respect of a loan relationship to which this section applies shall be confined to amounts relating to interest.

(3) Only an authorised accruals basis of accounting shall be used for ascertaining those amounts.

GENERAL NOTE
  This section applies in respect of two specific gilt-edged securities, providing that only interest should be accounted for under this Chapter, using an authorised accruals basis.
  The gilts are the 3.5 per cent Funding Stock 1999–2004 and the 5.5 per cent Treasury Stock 2008–2012. The section applies only where the gilts are not held in the course of activities forming an integral part of a trade.
  These gilts were grandfathered at a stage when the provisions were going to apply to individuals and these low coupon gilts had been widely purchased by individuals in anticipation of a tax free capital gain on redemption.

97   Manufactured interest

(1) This section applies where—

(*a*) any amount ("manufactured interest") is payable by or on behalf of, or to, any company under any contract or arrangements relating to the transfer of an asset representing a loan relationship; and (*b*) that amount is, or (when paid) will fall to be treated as, representative of interest under that relationship ("the real interest").

(2) In relation to that company the manufactured interest shall be treated for the purposes of this Chapter—

(*a*) as if it were interest under a loan relationship to which the company is a party; and
(*b*) where that company is the company to which the manufactured interest is payable, as if that relationship were the one under which the real interest is payable.

(3) Any question whether debits or credits falling to be brought into account in the case of any company by virtue of this section—

(*a*) are to be brought into account under section 82(2) above, or
(*b*) are to be treated as non-trading debits or non-trading credits,

shall be determined according to the extent (if any) to which the manufactured interest is paid for the purposes of a trade carried on by the company or is received in the course of activities forming an integral part of such a trade.

(4) Where section 737A(5) of the Taxes Act 1988 (deemed manufactured payments) has effect in relation to a transaction relating to an asset representing a loan relationship so as, for the purposes of section 737 of, or Schedule 23A to, that Act, to deem there to have been a payment representative of interest under that relationship, this section shall apply as it would have applied if such a representative payment had in fact been made.

(5) This section does not apply where the manufactured interest is treated by virtue of paragraph 5(2)(*c*) or (4)(*c*) of Schedule 23A to the Taxes Act 1988 (manufactured interest passing through the market) as not being income of the person who receives it.

GENERAL NOTE
This section provides for the treatment of manufactured payments by, to, or on behalf of a company arising in respect of loan relationships.
The section applies to such manufactured interest, which is payable under a contract or arrangement relating to the transfer of an asset representing a loan relationship and which is to be treated as representative of the real interest.
The effect of the section is to treat the manufactured interest as the real interest. Trading assessment of the ensuing debits or credits will be made by—

(*a*) the paying company if it is paid for the purposes of a trade carried on by it; and
(*b*) by the receiving company if it is received in the course of activities forming an "integral part of such a trade".

The section further provides that where the asset representing a loan relationship is sold and repurchased such that it would be within TA 1988 s 737A, s 737A(5) will apply by deeming there to have been a payment representative of interest. This is for the purpose of applying the withholding provisions of TA 1988 s 737 and Sch 23A.
Section 737A causes the sales and repurchases of securities (as defined) which extend over a coupon date to be subject to the withholding tax provisions of TA 1988 s 737 and Sch 23A. Such arrangements may provide any payment representative of the interest not be paid separately, but be rolled up into the repurchase price. In this case, without s 737A the withholding tax provisions would not apply, s 737A(5) deeming the manufactured payment of interest to have been made.
However, the section does not apply where the "passing on" provisions of TA 1988 Sch 23A para 5 apply. This paragraph causes the manufactured payments to be treated as not being income of the recipient, because the real dividend is effectively treated as being passed on.

98 Collective investment schemes

The provisions of this Chapter have effect subject to the provisions of Schedule 10 to this Act (which makes special provision in relation to certain collective investment schemes).

GENERAL NOTE
This section introduces Sch 10, which provides special rules with regard to the taxation of loan relationships for—

(*a*) authorised investment trust companies and venture capital trusts;
(*b*) authorised unit trusts;
(*c*) distributing offshore funds; and
(*d*) holders of authorised unit trusts and offshore funds.

99   Insurance companies

The preceding provisions of this Chapter have effect subject to Schedule 11 to this Act (which makes special provision in relation to certain insurance companies and in relation to corporate members of Lloyd's).

GENERAL NOTE
This section introduces Sch 11 which modifies the new legislation on loan relationships in the case of certain insurance companies and corporate members of Lloyd's.

Miscellaneous other provisions

100   Interest on judgments, imputed interest, etc

(1) This Chapter shall have effect in accordance with subsection (2) below where—

(*a*) interest on a money debt is payable to or by any company;
(*b*) that debt is one as respects which it stands, or has stood, in the position of a creditor or debtor; and
(*c*) that debt did not arise from a loan relationship.

(2) It shall be assumed for the purposes of this Chapter—

(*a*) that the interest is interest payable under a loan relationship to which the company is a party; but
(*b*) that the only credits or debits to be brought into account for those purposes in respect of that relationship are those relating to the interest.

(3) References in this section to interest payable on a money debt include references to any amount which, in pursuance of sections 770 to 772 of the Taxes Act 1988 (transactions at an undervalue or overvalue), as those sections have effect by virtue of section 773(4) of that Act, falls to be treated in pursuance of those sections as—

(*a*) interest on a money debt; or
(*b*) interest on an amount which is treated as a money debt.

(4) Any question whether debits or credits falling to be brought into account in accordance with this section in relation to any company—

(*a*) are to be brought into account under section 82(2) above, or
(*b*) are to be treated as non-trading debits or non-trading credits,

shall be determined according to the extent (if any) to which the interest in question is paid for the purposes of a trade carried on by the company or is received in the course of activities forming an integral part of such a trade, or (in the case of deemed interest) would be deemed to be so paid or received.

(5) This section has effect subject to the provisions of Schedules 9 and 11 to this Act.

GENERAL NOTE
This section provides that certain amounts taxed as interest will be so taxed even though no loan relationship exists.
The section applies to interest payable by or to a company in respect of a money debt, which

does not arise from a loan relationship. The company must be or must have been a debtor or creditor under the debt.

The section specifically covers notional imputed interest under the transfer pricing provisions of TA 1988 ss 770–772 where s 773(4) causes amounts to be treated as interest on a money debt (real or deemed). Schedule 9 para 16 deals with interest on pre-existing loan relationships.

Trading assessment of the ensuing debits or credits will be made by—

(*a*) the paying company if it is paid (or deemed to have been paid) for the purposes of a trade carried on by it; and

(*b*) the receiving company if it is received (or deemed to have been received) in the course of activities forming an "integral part" of such a trade.

The section is subject to Schs 9 and 11.

101   Financial instruments

(1) Chapter II of Part IV of the Finance Act 1994 (provisions relating to certain financial instruments) shall not apply to any profit or loss which, in accordance with that Chapter, accrues to a company for any accounting period on a qualifying contract by virtue of which the company is a party to any loan relationship if—

(*a*) an amount representing that profit or loss, or

(*b*) an amount representing the profit or loss accruing to the company on that contract,

is brought into account for that period for the purposes of this Chapter.

(2) After section 147 of that Act (qualifying contracts) there shall be inserted the following section—

"147A   Debt contracts and options to be qualifying contracts

(1) For the purposes of this Chapter a debt contract or option is a qualifying contract as regards a qualifying company if the company becomes entitled to rights, or subject to duties, under the contract or option at any time on or after 1st April 1996.

(2) For the purposes of this Chapter a qualifying company which is entitled to rights, or subject to duties, under a debt contract or option both immediately before and on 1st April 1996 shall be deemed to have become entitled or subject to those rights or duties on that date.

(3) This section has effect subject to paragraph 25 of Schedule 15 to the Finance Act 1996 (transitional provisions)."

(3) After section 150 of that Act (qualifying contracts) there shall be inserted the section set out in Schedule 12 to this Act (which defines debt contracts and options by reference to contracts and options conferring rights and duties to participate in loan relationships).

(4) In section 151 of that Act (provisions that may be included in contracts and options), for the words "or a currency contract or option,", in each place where they occur, there shall be substituted "a currency contract or option or a debt contract or option".

(5) In section 152(1) of that Act (disregard of provisions for relatively small payments in contracts and options), after "150" there shall be inserted "or 150A".

(6) In section 153(1) of that Act (qualifying payments), for the word "and" at the end of paragraph (*c*) there shall be substituted—

"(*ca*) in relation to a qualifying contract which is a debt contract, a payment falling within section 150A(5) or (6) above; and".

GENERAL NOTE
This section makes amendments to the financial instruments provisions introduced by FA 1994 and introduces Sch 12, thereby extending those rules to "debt contracts and options".

First, the section excludes the financial instrument provisions from applying to a "qualifying contract" where the profit or loss from it is assessable under this Chapter.

The section introduces Sch 12 which makes amendments to FA 1994, specifically to define "debt contracts" and "debt options".

The section inserts a new s 147A into FA 1994, which provides that a debt contract or option will be a "qualifying contract" for the purposes of FA 1994, where the company becomes entitled to rights or subject to duties at any time after 1 April 1996. Where the company was party to the contract immediately before and after that date, it is deemed to have become subject to it on 1 April 1996 and transitional provisions are provided by Sch 15 para 25.

Finally, the section makes amendments to the definitions in FA 1994 to accommodate this extension, specifically by—

(*a*) ensuring that the "provisions which may be included" (FA 1994 s 150) in a financial instrument contract and it still be considered a "qualifying contract" extend to debt contracts and options;

(*b*) ensuring that the "provisions that may be disregarded" (which relate to relatively small payments which would otherwise cause a financial instrument contract to not be treated as qualifying) in FA 1994 s 152(1) extend to debt contracts and options; and

(*c*) providing that the definition of "qualifying payments" which may be made under a financial instrument extends to the payments defined by FA 1994 s 150A(5) and (6) (see Sch 12) in respect of debt contracts and options.

102 Discounted securities: income tax provisions

Schedule 13 to this Act (which, in connection with the provisions of this Chapter relating to corporation tax, makes provision for income tax purposes about discounted securities) shall have effect.

GENERAL NOTE
This section introduces Sch 13 which provides for the income tax treatment of discounted securities on their transfer or redemption.

Supplemental

103 Interpretation of Chapter

(1) In this Chapter—

"authorised accounting method", "authorised accruals basis of accounting" and "authorised mark to market basis of accounting" shall be construed in accordance with section 85 above;

"creditor relationship", in relation to a company, means any loan relationship of that company in the case of which it stands in the position of a creditor as respects the debt in question;

"debt" includes a debt the amount of which falls to be ascertained by reference to matters which vary from time to time;

"debtor relationship", in relation to a company, means any loan relationship of that company in the case of which it stands in the position of a debtor as respects the debt in question;

"gilt-edged securities" means any securities which—

(*a*) are gilt-edged securities for the purposes of the Taxation of Chargeable Gains Act 1992; or

(*b*) will be such securities on the making of any order under paragraph 1 of Schedule 9 to that Act the making of which is anticipated in the prospectus under which they are issued;

"an independent person" means a knowledgeable and willing party dealing at arm's length;

"international organisation" means an organisation of which two or more sovereign powers, or the governments of two or more sovereign powers, are members;

"loan" includes any advance of money, and cognate expressions shall be construed accordingly;

"money" shall be construed in accordance with section 81(6) above and subsection (5) below;

"money debt" shall be construed in accordance with section 81(2) above;

"non-trading credit" and "non-trading debit" shall be construed in accordance with section 82(3) above;

"retail prices index" has the same meaning as it has, by virtue of section 833(2) of the Taxes Act 1988, in the Income Tax Acts;

"share", in relation to a company, means any share in the company under which an entitlement to receive distributions may arise.

(2) For the purposes of this Chapter a company shall be taken to be a party to a creditor relationship for the purposes of a trade carried on by that company only if it is a party to that relationship in the course of activities forming an integral part of that trade.

(3) For the purposes of this Chapter, and of so much of any other enactment as contains provision by reference to which amounts fall to be brought into account for the purposes of this Chapter, activities carried on by a company in the course of—

(*a*) any mutual trading, or

(*b*) any mutual insurance or other mutual business which is not life assurance business (within the meaning of Chapter I of Part XII of the Taxes Act 1988),

shall be deemed not to constitute the whole or any part of a trade.

(4) If, in any proceedings, any question arises whether a person is an international organisation for the purposes of any provision of this Chapter, a certificate issued by or under the authority of the Secretary of State stating any fact relevant to that question shall be conclusive evidence of that fact.

(5) For the purposes of this Chapter the European currency unit (as for the time being defined in Council Regulation No 3180/78/EEC or in any Community instrument replacing it) shall be taken to be a currency other than sterling.

GENERAL NOTE
This section provides definitions and other interpretative guidance for the Chapter.
For the purposes of the Chapter—

(*a*) a company is considered to be party to a creditor relationship for the purposes of a trade only if it is so in the course of activities forming an integral part of that trade;

(*b*) mutual trading and mutual insurance or other mutual business other than life assurance business does not constitute the whole or part of a trade;

(*c*) in determining whether a person is an international organisation, a certificate issued by or under the authority of the Secretary of State shall be conclusive evidence of any fact it contains; and

(*d*) the ECU or any replacement is a currency other than sterling.

104   Minor and consequential amendments

Schedule 14 to this Act (which, for the purposes of both corporation tax and income tax, makes certain minor and consequential amendments in connection with the provisions of this Chapter) shall have effect.

GENERAL NOTE
This section introduces Sch 14 which makes consequential amendments to existing corporation tax and income tax legislation.

It should be noted that the Revenue's commentary on the draft legislation when it was released stated—

"The Section and Schedule make minor and consequential amendments to existing legislation. Their effect, generally, is to adapt existing provisions to the new structure and terminology of Chapter II without materially changing their substantive effect or to repeal provisions made obsolete by the extended changes and reliefs provided by the Chapter."

In introducing the changes to the schedule at the Committee Stage, the Minister noted "This is a rag bag Schedule into which all minor and inconsequential matters have been placed—it consists of 74 paragraphs."

105 Commencement and transitional provisions

(1) Subject to Schedule 15 to this Act, this Chapter has effect—

(*a*) for the purposes of corporation tax, in relation to accounting periods ending after 31st March 1996; and

(*b*) so far as it makes provision for the purposes of income tax, in relation to the year 1996–97 and subsequent years of assessment.

(2) Schedule 15 to this Act (which contains transitional provisions and savings in connection with the coming into force of this Chapter) shall have effect.

GENERAL NOTE

This section provides that the Chapter is operative for corporation tax for accounting periods ending after 31 March 1996 and for income tax from the year 1996–97 onwards discounted security, subject to the transitional provisions of Sch 15, which it introduces.

CHAPTER III

PROVISIONS RELATING TO THE SCHEDULE E CHARGE

106   Living accommodation provided for employees

(1) In subsection (1) of section 145 of the Taxes Act 1988 (living accommodation provided for employees), the words "and is not otherwise made the subject of any charge to him by way of income tax" shall be omitted.

(2) After section 146 of that Act there shall be inserted the following section—

"146A   Priority of rules applying to living accommodation

(1) This section applies where, within the meaning of section 145, living accommodation is provided in any period for any person by reason of his employment.

(2) The question whether the employee is to be treated under section 145 or 146 as in receipt of emoluments in respect of the provision of the accommodation shall be determined before any other question whether there is an amount falling to be treated in respect of the provision of that accommodation as emoluments.

(3) Tax under Schedule E in respect of the provision of the accommodation shall be chargeable on the employee otherwise than in pursuance of sections 145 and 146 to the extent only that the amount on which it is chargeable by virtue of those sections is exceeded by the amount on which it would be chargeable apart from those sections."

(3) This section applies for the year 1996–97 and subsequent years of assessment.

GENERAL NOTE
    TA 1988 ss 145 and 146 charge to tax the benefit arising to employees by the provision of living accommodation. This section is designed to counteract avoidance schemes whereby a lower charge under the general Schedule E charging section (TA 1988 s 19) is deliberately attracted by the offer of a cash alternative to the accommodation.
    The announcement of this anti-avoidance measure was accompanied by the publication of an extra-statutory concession relaxing the operation of TA 1988 ss 145 and 146 in two particular circumstances.

THE CASH ALTERNATIVE
    The avoidance scheme(s), said to be costing the Treasury some £10 million a year, which this section is intended to counteract, work(s) on the same principle as the similar scheme to avoid the car-benefit charge counteracted by FA 1995 s 43.
    An employee for whom it is intended to provide living accommodation that would otherwise attract a charge under ss 145 and 146 is given the option of either taking the accommodation or an amount of extra salary. The extra salary is usually set at a lower level than the amount of the charge under ss 145 and 146. By taking the accommodation, the employee forgoes the salary. The intention behind the scheme is that, in these circumstances, the rule in *Heaton v Bell* (1969) 46 TC 211 would come into play, to tax the employee on the amount of salary forgone. This would be because under the *ratio* in that case, the perk (the accommodation) is readily convertible into cash, giving rise to a charge under s 19. Where there is a charge under s 19 (or indeed any other provision), there is no charge under s 145 (which applies only in the case where there is no charge to income tax otherwise) or s 146 (which applies only if s 145 applies).

THE PROVISIONS
    This section removes (by sub-s (1)) the words from s 145(1) that restrict its application to instances where the provision of living accommodation for an employee by reason of his employment "is not otherwise made the subject of any charge to him by way of income tax". It then inserts (by sub-s (2)) a new TA 1988 s 146A.
    Section 146A applies where there would be a charge under s 145. It provides that—
    (*a*) the charge to tax under s 145 (and where appropriate s 146) has priority over any other question whether the provision of the accommodation gives rise to emoluments, and that

(*b*) where there would also be a charge to Schedule E otherwise than under ss 145 or 146, that other charge is limited to the amount (if any) by which the other charge exceeds the charge under ss 145 and 146.

TAKING EFFECT

These provisions take effect from the year of assessment 1996–97 (sub-s (3)).

NEW EXTRA-STATUTORY CONCESSION

The new concession, first published in Budget Press Release REV 38, 28 November 1995, "Living accommodation provided by reason of employment", deals with two separate situations.

Where the same living accommodation is provided in circumstances in which a charge to TA 1988 s 145 and, where appropriate, s 146 arises to two or more employees within the same period, there is nothing to prevent a full charge on both or all of those employees. The concession limits the charge to that which would apply if it had been provided to one employee only. The amount of the charge will then be apportioned between the relevant employees with regard to all the relevant facts.

The charge to tax under s 145 is based on the annual value of the property or (where greater) the rent paid by the person at whose cost the accommodation is provided. For property in the UK, the "annual value" is (under TA 1988 s 837(2)) the gross rateable value under General Rate Act 1967 s 23 (or an estimate of what this would have been, for newer properties); Extra-statutory concession A56 deals with property in Scotland, where there was a rating revaluation in 1985.

For property abroad, however, the definition in s 837(1) would lead to use of the open-market rental value; as it would for property in the UK also if the employer (or other person at whose cost the accommodation was provided) paid a market rent for it. Where this applies, and there is a charge under s 146 also (because the cost of providing the accommodation exceeds £75,000), it is felt that the combined charge to tax is disproportionately high. In such circumstances, the new concession waives the charge under s 146.

The concession applies for the year of assessment 1995–96 (and presumably subsequent years, although the press release does not say so) and to earlier years in cases where the tax liability is still to be agreed.

107   Beneficial loans

(1) For section 160(1B) of the Taxes Act 1988 (aggregation of loans) there shall be substituted the following subsections—

"(1B) Where, in relation to any year—

(*a*) there are loans between the same lender and borrower which are aggregable with each other,
(*b*) the lender elects, by notice given to the inspector, for aggregation to apply in the case of that borrower, and
(*c*) that notice is given before the end of the period of 92 days after the end of that year,

all the loans between that lender and that borrower which are aggregable with each other shall be treated for the purposes of subsections (1) and (1A) above and Part II of Schedule 7 as a single loan.

(1BA) For the purposes of subsection (1B) above loans are aggregable with each other for any year where—

(*a*) in the case of each of the loans, there is a time in that year, while the loan is outstanding as to any amount, when the lender is a close company and the borrower a director of that company;
(*b*) the benefit of each of the loans is obtained by reason of the borrower's employment;
(*c*) in the case of each of the loans, there is no time in that year when a rate of interest is applied to the loan which is equal to or more than whatever is the official rate at that time;
(*d*) the loans are loans made in the same currency; and
(*e*) none of the loans is a qualifying loan."

(2) In paragraph 5 of Schedule 7 to that Act (alternative method of calculation)—

(*a*) in sub-paragraph (1)(*a*), for the words from "for the purpose" to "appeal)" there shall be substituted "at a time allowed by sub-paragraph (2) below"; and

(*b*) in sub-paragraph (1)(*b*), for "within the time allowed by sub-paragraph (2) below" there shall be substituted "at such a time".

(3) For sub-paragraph (2) of that paragraph there shall be substituted the following sub-paragraph—

"(2) A notice containing a requirement or election for the purposes of sub-paragraph (1) above is allowed to be given at any time before the end of the period of 12 months beginning with the 31st January next following the relevant year."

(4) This section has effect for the year 1996–97 and subsequent years of assessment and applies to loans whenever made.

GENERAL NOTE

This section makes amendments to TA 1988 s 160 and Sch 7 (the provisions charging employer-provided beneficial loans for employees earning £8,500 or more and directors to tax under Schedule E).

With the introduction of self-assessment, employers will be required to compute the amount of all benefits on the form P11D or P9D, so that the employee, to whom a copy will have to be furnished, will be provided with the necessary information for his self-assessment return.

This section is designed to simplify calculation of the amount chargeable ("the cash equivalent") where more than one loan to the same employee is in existence. It does so by making the aggregation of such loans optional rather than mandatory.

AGGREGATION OF LOANS

Under the previous provisions of TA 1988 s 160(1B), where there has been more than one loan between the same lender and the same borrower outstanding as to any amount at any time in any year and a charge to tax has arisen from them, they have been treated as a single loan for this purpose, provided only that they were made in the same currency and were not "qualifying loans" (that is, broadly, loans in respect of which the interest would qualify for tax relief).

Subsection (2) replaces the existing s 160(1B) by two subsections ((1B) and (1BA)). Taken together, they provide that loans are only to be aggregated where the lender (and not the borrower) elects for aggregation. Also, the type of loan in respect of which the election is available is narrowly defined (particularly restricting aggregation to loans from close companies to their directors).

The election may be exercised only in respect of loans that are "aggregable with each other" (new sub-s (1B)(*a*)). Subsection (1BA) defines aggregable loans in any year as loans where in respect of each loan—

(*a*) the lender is a close company and the borrower a director of that company for any time in that year during which any part of the loan is outstanding;

(*b*) the benefit of the loan is obtained by reason of the borrower's employment;

(*c*) there is no time in that year when interest charged on the loan equals or exceeds the official rate at that time;

(*d*) the loan is made in the same currency; and

(*e*) the loan is not a qualifying loan.

If the lender wishes to elect for aggregation in respect of any one borrower, and the conditions above are satisfied, he must give written notice to the inspector within 92 days of the end of the relevant year of assessment (new sub-s (1B)(*c*)). Where the election is not made, not made on time, is not valid, or cannot be made, each loan will be treated separately.

THE ALTERNATIVE METHOD OF CALCULATION

Subsection (2) makes amendments to the time limits for the election to have the cash equivalent of the benefit calculated under the "alternative method" described in TA 1988 Sch 7 para 5 (which is more exact than the averaging method of Sch 7 para 4).

Until now, the alternative method has been applied if the Revenue so required in respect of any assessment or at the employee's election (former para 5(1)). The employee's election has had to be made either within the time allowed for appealing against an assessment in which the averaging method had been used, or, in the absence of such an assessment, within six years of the end of the relevant year of assessment. Where an assessment had been made, the inspector could allow an extension (former para 5(2)).

In order to align these provisions with self-assessment time limits, a time limit is now imposed on the inspector and the same time limit applies to the employee. This time limit (new para 5(2)) is the second 31 January after the end of the year of assessment (eg 31 January 1999 for the year of assessment 1996–97). This is the normal time limit for both inquiring into the self-assessment return (on the part of the Revenue) and amending the self-assessment return (on the part of the taxpayer).

TAKING EFFECT
These changes take effect from 1996–97 and apply to loans whenever made (sub-s (4)).
See also Budget Press Release REV 24 (para 7), 28 November 1995, "Self-assessment".

108   Incidental benefits for holders of certain offices etc

(1) After section 200 of the Taxes Act 1988 (expenses of Members of Parliament) there shall be inserted the following section—

"200AA   Incidental benefits for holders of certain offices etc

(1) A person holding any of the offices mentioned in subsection (2) below shall not be charged to tax under Schedule E in respect of—

(*a*) any transport or subsistence provided or made available by or on behalf of the Crown to the office-holder or any member of his family or household; or
(*b*) the payment or re-imbursement by or on behalf of the Crown of any expenses incurred in connection with the provision of transport or subsistence to the office-holder or any member of his family or household.

(2) Those offices are—

(*a*) any office in Her Majesty's Government in the United Kingdom, and
(*b*) any other office which is one of the offices and positions in respect of which salaries are payable under section 1 of the Ministerial and other Salaries Act 1975 (whether or not the person holding it is a person to whom a salary is paid or payable under the Act).

(3) Nothing in this section shall prevent a person from being chargeable to tax under Schedule E in respect of the benefit of a mobile telephone (within the meaning of section 159A).

(4) References in this section to a member of the family or household of an office-holder shall be construed in accordance with section 168(4).

(5) References in this section to the provision of transport to any person include references to the following—

(*a*) the provision or making available to that person of any car (whether with or without a driver);
(*b*) the provision of any fuel for a car provided or made available to that person;
(*c*) the provision of any other benefit in connection with a car provided or made available to that person.

(6) In this section—

'car' means any mechanically propelled road vehicle; and
'subsistence' includes food and drink and temporary living accommodation."

(2) This section has effect for the year 1996–97 and subsequent years of assessment.

GENERAL NOTE
This section was inserted with some haste into the Finance Bill at Report Stage in order to safeguard ministers of the Crown and certain other parliamentary officeholders from a possible charge to tax on benefits received while they are travelling on official business.

Since the introduction in 1976 of the benefits legislation relating to directors and "higher-paid" employees (now found in TA 1988 Part V Chapter II), it has been accepted that the legislation did not impose a charge under Schedule E on transport, meals and temporary accommodation (such as hotel rooms) provided at public expense to the Speaker, government ministers and officeholders of the official Opposition, or members of their families, while they were performing official duties.

However, a review by the Revenue must clearly have suggested that the legal grounds for this practice were questionable, hence the need to introduce this section, which inserts a new section 200AA into the Taxes Act.

See also IR Press Release, 25 March 1996, "Confirmation of Tax Treatment of Official Travel".

EXEMPTION FROM SCHEDULE E CHARGE
Section 200AA applies to persons holding—

(a) an office in Her Majesty's Government in the United Kingdom; and
(b) any other office in respect of which an official salary is payable under the Ministerial and Other Salaries Act 1975 s 1.
(S 200AA(2).)

The chief offices under (b) are those of the Speaker of the House of Commons and the Leader of Her Majesty's Opposition. The section applies whether or not a salary is actually paid under the Act to the person holding the office.

Exemption from a charge under Schedule E is provided to the relevant officeholders in respect of—

(a) transport or subsistence provided or made available from the public purse ("by or on behalf of the Crown") to them or to members of their family or household; and
(b) payment or reimbursement from the public purse of expenses incurred in connection with such transport or subsistence to them or members of their family or household.
(S 200AA(1).)

MEANING OF TRANSPORT AND SUBSISTENCE
For the purposes of s 200AA, transport includes (but is not limited to)—

(a) the provision of a car, with or without a driver, and fuel for such a car; and
(b) the provision of any other benefits in connection with such a car.
(S 200AA(5).)

"Subsistence" includes food, drink and temporary living accommodation (s 200AA(6)).

MOBILE TELEPHONES
No exemption is provided by this section in respect of mobile telephones (s 200AA(3)).

EFFECT
Section 200AA has effect from 1996–97 (sub-s (2)). Travel and subsistence for previous years will be dealt with under the previous (and now suspect) practice.

109 Charitable donations: payroll deduction schemes

(1) In section 202(7) of the Taxes Act 1988 (which limits to £900 the deductions attracting relief), for "£900" there shall be substituted "£1,200".

(2) This section has effect for the year 1996–97 and subsequent years of assessment.

GENERAL NOTE
This section increases the annual limit for donations under the payroll-giving scheme (sometimes also known as "GAYE" (give as you earn)) from £900 to £1,200, with effect from 1996–97.

The limit was last changed (from £600 to £900) with effect from 1993–94.

See also Budget Press Release REV 10, 28 November 1995, "Charities: higher limit for payroll giving".

110 PAYE settlement agreements

After section 206 of the Taxes Act 1988 there shall be inserted the following section—

"206A PAYE settlement agreements

(1) PAYE regulations may make provision falling within subsection (2) below about the sums which, as sums in respect of income tax under

Schedule E on emoluments of a person's employees, are to be the sums for which the employer is to be accountable to the Board from time to time.

(2) That provision is provision under which the accountability of the employer, and the sums for which he is to be accountable, are to be determined, to such extent as may be prescribed, in accordance with an agreement between the Board and the employer ('a PAYE settlement agreement'), instead of under PAYE regulations made otherwise than by virtue of this section.

(3) PAYE regulations may provide for a PAYE settlement agreement to allow sums for which an employer is to be accountable to the Board in accordance with the agreement—

(*a*) to be computed, in cases where there are two or more persons holding employments to which the agreement relates, by reference to a number of those persons all taken together;

(*b*) to include sums representing income tax on an estimated amount taken, in accordance with the agreement, to be the aggregate of the cash equivalents and other amounts chargeable to tax in respect of—

(i) taxable benefits provided or made available by reason of the employments to which the agreement relates; and

(ii) expenses paid to the persons holding those employments;

and

(*c*) to be computed in a manner under which the sums for which the employer is accountable do not necessarily represent an amount of income tax payable in respect of income which (apart from the regulations) is assessable under Schedule E on persons holding employments to which the agreement relates.

(4) PAYE regulations may provide—

(*a*) for an employer who is accountable to the Board under a PAYE settlement agreement for any sum to be so accountable without that sum, or any other sum, being treated for any prescribed purpose as tax deducted from emoluments;

(*b*) for an employee to have no right to be treated as having paid tax in respect of sums for which his employer is accountable under such an agreement;

(*c*) for an employee to be treated, except—

(i) for the purposes of the obligations imposed on his employer by such an agreement, and

(ii) to such further extent as may be prescribed,

as relieved from any prescribed obligations of his under the Income Tax Acts in respect of emoluments from an employment to which the agreement relates; and

(*d*) for such emoluments to be treated as excluded from the employee's income for such further purposes of the Income Tax Acts, and to such extent, as may be prescribed.

(5) For the purposes of any PAYE regulations made by virtue of this section it shall be immaterial that any agreement to which they relate was entered into before the coming into force of the regulations.

(6) PAYE regulations made by virtue of this section may—

(*a*) make different provision for different cases; and

(*b*) contain such incidental, supplemental, consequential and transitional provision as the Board may think fit.

(7) Without prejudice to the generality of subsection (6) above, the transitional provision that may be made by virtue of that subsection includes transitional provision for any year of assessment which—

(*a*) for the purposes of the regulations, treats sums accounted for in that year before the coming into force of the regulations as accounted for in accordance with an agreement as respects which the regulations have effect after they come into force; and

(*b*) provides, by reference to any provision made by virtue of paragraph (*a*) above, for income arising in that year before the coming into force of the regulations to be treated as income in relation to which modifications of the Income Tax Acts contained in the regulations apply.

(8) Without prejudice to the generality of subsection (6) above, any power of the Board to make PAYE regulations with respect to sums falling to be accounted for under such regulations shall include power to make the corresponding provision with respect to sums falling, by virtue of this section, to be accounted for in accordance with a PAYE settlement agreement.

(9) In this section—

'employment' means any office or employment the emoluments from which are (or, apart from any regulations made by virtue of this section, would be) assessable to tax under Schedule E, and cognate expressions shall be construed accordingly;

'PAYE regulations' means regulations under section 203;

'prescribed' means prescribed by PAYE regulations;

'taxable benefit', in relation to an employee, means any benefit provided or made available, otherwise than in the form of a payment of money, to the employee or to a person who is, for the purposes of Chapter II of this Part, a member of his family or household;

and references in this section to a time before the coming into force of any regulations include references to a time before the commencement of section 110 of the Finance Act 1996 (by virtue of which this section was inserted in this Act)."

GENERAL NOTE

Where employers have found it difficult to make returns of relatively minor expenses paid and benefits provided to employees, including cases where a particular benefit has been shared by a number of individuals and apportionment has proved impracticable, the Revenue's practice has been to encourage the employer to make lump-sum voluntary settlements (hitherto known as "annual voluntary settlements"). The negotiated lump sum, which includes a "grossed-up" element, since tax is being paid on behalf of an employee, is taken in complete settlement of the tax due on the items covered. The individual employee is relieved of the duty to declare those items in his tax return and the employer likewise does not have to include them in his return of expenses and benefits.

These settlements have been negotiated under the Revenue's general care and management powers (TMA 1970 s 1(1)), but are now to be put on a statutory footing by regulation. Apparently, the need to do this follows legal advice to the Revenue that the existing arrangements may be *ultra vires*.

CHANGE OF NAME

The settlements are now to be known as PAYE Settlement Agreements (PSAs).

POWER TO MAKE REGULATIONS

A new section (s 206A) is inserted into TA 1988 under which these regulations may be laid. Somewhat unusually, the section prescribes in some detail what the regulations may or may not contain.

For example, under a PSA, the employer's accountability in respect of income tax under Schedule E on employees' remuneration and the sums for which the employer is accountable is to be determined not under the normal PAYE regulations but under the regulations to be made under s 206A (s 206A(2)).

The regulations will apply to taxable benefits and expenses payments from and of the employments to which the PSA relates (s 206A(3)).

Sums paid under a PSA are not to be treated for any prescribed purpose as tax deducted from emoluments. Employees are to have no rights to be treated as having paid tax in respect of such sums, but are to be treated as being relieved of any prescribed obligations under the Income Tax Acts in respect of emoluments to which the PSA relates, except to the extent of the obligations imposed on the employer by the PSA and anything further in the regulations themselves. The regulations will also prescribe to what extent the emoluments covered by the PSA are to be excluded from the employee's income for income-tax purposes (s 206A(4)).

The regulations will also apply to settlements made before they come into force (s 206A(5)).

CONSULTATIONS AND STATEMENT OF PRACTICE

The Revenue is consulting on the content of the regulations, which have been published in draft form (see the Consultative Document published on 12 March). The aim is to introduce the regulations in the summer of this year.

The Consultative Document also contains a draft Statement of Practice, setting out how the statutory scheme is to operate.

It is confirmed that PSAs will cover only benefits and expenses payments, and that these will generally be "minor". "Non-minor" benefits and payments will occasionally be included if payable on an irregular basis in such a way that applying PAYE to them or apportioning the value of benefits between individual employees is impractical. "Major" benefits, such as company cars, car fuel and beneficial loans are definitely excluded from coverage, as are round-sum allowances.

A cap of 5 per cent of total remuneration payable to the employee for that year is proposed for the aggregate value of items that can be covered by a PSA.

NATIONAL INSURANCE CONTRIBUTIONS

Payment by an employer of an employee's tax liability on benefits or expenses payments constitutes earnings liable to NICs, because it is the discharge of a personal debt. Upon the introduction of PSAs, the liability becomes the employer's, so no NICs will be due.

It remains a moot point whether there is an NIC liability in respect of current settlements. There is some dispute as to this.

Some items to be covered by a PSA may themselves constitute earnings for NIC purposes. The government has undertaken to introduce primary NIC legislation to allow PSAs to settle NIC liabilities also, but until this takes effect, NICs on any items covered by a PSA remain remain to be calculated and paid separately.

PARLIAMENTARY PROCEEDINGS

It may be worth quoting from ministerial assurances given by the Financial Secretary to the Treasury, Mr Michael Jack, in the course of the Standing Committee debates. He said, inter alia—

"... it is not our aim to try to do away with the benefits of the discussions that currently take place between companies and the Revenue... the flexibility and informality [of the current informal arrangements] are of benefit to the 2,500 employers who have that type of agreement and we do not intend our proposals to remove that...

The essence of the arrangements will remain unchanged; it is the legal framework within which they will operate that will change. Existing agreements will normally be continued until the following year...

It will still be possible to negotiate the arrangements with the Revenue. The [section] will give *vires* to the current schemes."

(HC Official Report, 15 February 1996, Standing Committee E (tenth sitting), cols 318, 319.)

CHAPTER IV

SHARE OPTIONS, PROFIT SHARING AND EMPLOYEE SHARE OWNERSHIP

Share options

111   Amount or value of consideration for option

(1) Section 149A of the Taxation of Chargeable Gains Act 1992 (consideration for grant of option under approved share option schemes not to be deemed to be equal to market value of option) shall be amended as follows.

(2) In subsection (1)(*b*) (restriction to approved share option schemes) for "as mentioned in section 185(1) of the Taxes Act (approved share option schemes)" there shall be substituted "by an individual by reason of his office or employment as a director or employee of that or any other body corporate".

(3) In subsection (2) (grantor to be treated as if the amount or value of the consideration was its actual amount or value) for "The grantor of the option" there shall be substituted "Both the grantor of the option and the person to whom the option is granted".

(4) Subsection (4) (section not to affect treatment under that Act of person to whom option granted) shall cease to have effect.

(5) For the side-note to that section there shall be substituted "Share option schemes."

(6) This section has effect in relation to any right to acquire shares in a body corporate obtained on or after 28th November 1995 by an individual by reason of his office or employment as a director or employee of a body corporate.

GENERAL NOTE
   Under previous rules a capital gain could arise on the grantor of an unapproved share option by reference to its market value (TCGA 1992 s 17(1)). In the case of Revenue approved schemes the actual amount or value of the consideration received was substituted for market value (with the result that capital gains rarely arose in practice (TCGA 1992 s 149A(1) and (2)). This use of actual consideration is now extended, for options granted on or after 28 November 1995, to any option obtained by an individual by reason of his office or employment as a director or employee of a company (whether or not that is the company to whose shares the option relates) (sub-ss (2) and (6)).
   This use of actual consideration extends, for approved or unapproved options granted on or after that date, to the calculation of any gain or loss on a subsequent disposal of shares acquired by the exercise of the option (or, indeed, a disposal of the option itself) by the person to whom the option is granted (sub-ss (3), (4), (6)). In the case of approved options the same result was previously achieved, in general, by TA 1988 s 185(3)(*b*)).

112   Release and replacement

(1) After section 237 of the Taxation of Chargeable Gains Act 1992 there shall be inserted—

"237A   Share option schemes: release and replacement of options

(1) This section applies in any case where a right to acquire shares in a body corporate ('the old right') which was obtained by an individual by reason of his office or employment as a director or employee of that or any other body corporate is released in whole or in part for a consideration which consists of or includes the grant to that individual of another right ('the new right') to acquire shares in that or any other body corporate.

(2) As respects the person to whom the new right is granted—

   (*a*) without prejudice to subsection (1) above, the new right shall not be regarded for the purposes of capital gains tax as consideration for the release of the old right;

(*b*) the amount or value of the consideration given by him or on his behalf for the acquisition of the new right shall be taken for the purposes of section 38(1) to be the amount or value of the consideration given by him or on his behalf for the old right; and

(*c*) any consideration paid for the acquisition of the new right shall be taken to be expenditure falling within section 38(1)(*b*).

(3) As respects the grantor of the new right, in determining for the purposes of this Act the amount or value of the consideration received for the new right, the release of the old right shall be disregarded.''

(2) Section 238(4) of that Act (which provides that the release of an option under an approved share option scheme in exchange for another option, in connection with a company take-over, is not to involve a disposal, and which is superseded by subsection (1) above) shall cease to have effect.

(3) This section has effect in relation to transactions effected on or after 28th November 1995.

GENERAL NOTE

New provisions give a capital gains rollover on the exchange, on or after 28 November 1995, of an option which was obtained by an individual by reason of his office or employment as a director or employee of a company (whether or not that is the company to whose shares the option relates). The rules apply when such an "old option" is released in whole or in part for a consideration which consists of or includes the grant to that individual of a "new option" over shares in the same or any other company, for example on a takeover (sub-s (1), inserting new TCGA 1992 s 237A(1), and sub-s (3)).

In these circumstances the new option is not treated for capital gains purposes as consideration for the release of the old option. Instead, the new option takes over the base cost of the old option. If any additional consideration is given for the new option this is added to the base cost (sub-s (1), inserting new TCGA 1992 s 237A(2)). It is not absolutely clear how these rules apply in a case where the old option is released only in part, or where cash is given for the old option in addition to the new option.

In calculating any capital gains charge on the grantor of the new option (as to which, see s 111 above) the value of the old right is ignored. A charge will therefore arise only if there is additional consideration (sub-s (1), inserting new TCGA 1992 s 237A(3)).

Previous provisions allowing for a capital gains rollover in certain circumstances where approved options were exchanged under the terms of a scheme (for example, on a takeover) are superseded by the new rules, and are therefore repealed with effect for transactions taking place on or after the same date (sub-ss (2) and (3)).

The new rules parallel existing provisions in TA 1988 s 136(1) which prevent an income tax charge arising under TA 1988 s 135 on the exchange of unapproved options.

Savings-related share option schemes

113   Exercise of rights by employees of non-participating companies

(1) In paragraph 21 of Schedule 9 to the Taxes Act 1988 (provisions which an approved savings-related share option scheme may make with respect to the exercise of rights under the scheme) in sub-paragraph (1), the word "and" immediately preceding paragraph (*e*) shall be omitted and after that paragraph there shall be inserted—

"and

(*f*) if, at the bonus date, a person who has obtained rights under the scheme holds an office or employment in a company which is not a participating company but which is—

(i) an associated company of the grantor, or

(ii) a company of which the grantor has control,

those rights may be exercised within six months of that date.''

(2) After sub-paragraph (3) of that paragraph there shall be inserted—

"(4) Where a scheme approved before the date of the passing of the Finance Act 1996 is altered before 5th May 1998 so as to include such a provision as is specified in sub-paragraph (1)(*f*) above, the scheme may apply the provision to rights obtained under the scheme before the alteration takes effect, whether the bonus date in relation to the rights occurred before or after the passing of that Act; and where the provision is applied to such rights by virtue of this sub-paragraph, its application to such rights shall not itself be regarded as the acquisition of a right for the purposes of this Schedule.

This sub-paragraph has effect subject to paragraph 4 above."

(3) In paragraph 26(3) of that Schedule (only directors or employees of grantor or participating company to be eligible to participate, except as provided by paragraph 19 or pursuant to such a provision as is referred to in paragraph 21(1)(*e*)) after "21(1)(*e*)" there shall be inserted "or (*f*)".

GENERAL NOTE

Under a Revenue approved savings-related share option scheme options may not be exercised by an individual who has ceased to hold the office or employment by virtue of which he was eligible to participate in the scheme (TA 1988 Sch 9 para 26(3)). This rule is subject to various exceptions allowing early exercise (within six months of the cessation) where the office or employment ceases to be held in certain defined circumstances (TA 1988 Sch 9 paras 19, 21(1)(*e*)).

Schemes approved (or altered) after Royal Assent may now also provide that if, at the bonus date, an option holder holds an office or employment in a company ("his current employer") which is not a participating company in the scheme, his options may be exercised within six months of the bonus date if his current employer is (sub-s (1), inserting new TA 1988 Sch 9 para 21(1)(*f*), and sub-s (3))—

(*a*) an associated company of the grantor (ie the company which has established the scheme); or

(*b*) a company of which the grantor has control.

"Control" and "associated company" are defined by the current legislation (TA 1988 ss 187(2), 416, 840). The "bonus date", broadly, is the date on which repayments under the related certified contractual savings scheme are due (TA 1988 Sch 9 para 17).

Where a scheme which was approved before Royal Assent is altered before 5 May 1998 to include such a provision, the scheme may apply that provision to options granted before the alteration takes effect, whether the relevant bonus date occurred before or after Royal Assent. Where a scheme takes advantage of this facility, this will not be regarded for the purpose of the legislation dealing with approved option schemes as giving rise to any additional rights on the part of the existing option holder. Any such alteration of a scheme is subject to the normal requirement for Revenue approval (sub-s (2), inserting new TA 1988 Sch 9, para 21(4)).

Other share option schemes

114 Requirements to be satisfied by approved schemes

(1) Part IV of Schedule 9 to the Taxes Act 1988 (requirements applicable to approved share option schemes which are not savings-related) shall be amended in accordance with subsections (2) and (3) below.

(2) In paragraph 28 (scheme must impose limit on aggregate market value of shares which may be acquired in pursuance of rights obtained under the scheme or certain related schemes)—

(*a*) in sub-paragraph (1) (aggregate market value of shares not to exceed the appropriate limit) for "the appropriate limit" there shall be substituted "£30,000"; and

(*b*) sub-paragraphs (2) and (4) (meaning of the appropriate limit and, for the purposes of that definition, the relevant emoluments) shall cease to have effect.

(3) In paragraph 29 (price at which shares may be acquired to be stated and to be not manifestly less than the market value, or, in certain circumstances, 85 per cent of the market value, of shares of the same class) for sub-paragraphs (1) to (6) there shall be substituted—

"(1) The price at which scheme shares may be acquired by the exercise of a right obtained under the scheme—

(*a*) must be stated at the time the right is obtained, and
(*b*) must not be manifestly less than the market value of shares of the same class at that time or, if the Board and the grantor agree in writing, at such earlier time or times as may be provided in the agreement."

(4) Section 185 of the Taxes Act 1988 (approved share option schemes) shall be amended in accordance with subsections (5) to (7) below.

(5) In subsection (2), for "Subject to subsections (6) to (6B) below" there shall be substituted "Subject to subsection (6) below".

(6) For subsections (6) to (6B) there shall be substituted—

"(6) Where, in the case of a right obtained by a person under a scheme which is not a savings-related share option scheme, the aggregate of—

(*a*) the amount or value of any consideration given by him for obtaining the right, and
(*b*) the price at which he may acquire the shares by exercising the right,

is less than the market value, at the time he obtains the right, of the same quantity of issued shares of the same class, he shall be chargeable to tax under Schedule E for the year of assessment in which he obtains the right on the amount of the difference; and the amount so chargeable shall be treated as earned income, whether or not it would otherwise fall to be so treated."

(7) In subsections (7) and (8) for "(6A)" there shall be substituted "(6)".

(8) In section 120 of the Taxation of Chargeable Gains Act 1992 (increase in expenditure by reference to tax charged in relation to shares etc) in subsection (6) (which defines the applicable provision) for paragraph (*b*) (which refers to subsection (6A) of section 185 of the Taxes Act 1988) there shall be substituted—

"(*b*) subsection (6A) of that section (as that subsection has effect in relation to rights obtained before the day on which the Finance Act 1996 was passed), or
(*c*) subsection (6) of that section (as that subsection has effect in relation to rights obtained on or after that day);".

(9) Schedule 16 to this Act, which makes provision with respect to share option schemes approved before the day on which this Act is passed, shall have effect.

(10) Subsections (3) to (7) above have effect in relation to rights obtained on or after the day on which this Act is passed.

GENERAL NOTE
Various changes are made to the conditions to be satisfied by approved share option schemes which are not savings-related. (These were previously referred to by the Revenue as "executive" schemes, and are now referred to as "company share option plans" to reflect the reduction in the maximum benefit available. Neither term is used in the relevant legislation, however.)

THE £30,000 LIMIT
Under the previous legislation there was a limit on the value of shares over which an individual could hold options of, broadly, £100,000 or four times emoluments (TA 1988 Sch 9 para 28). (This

related to the value of the shares at, broadly, the time the option was granted.) With effect from Royal Assent (and, in practice, for schemes seeking approval since the Budget Statement of 28 November 1995) there is substituted a single limit of £30,000 (sub-s (2)). See also the transitional provisions in s 115 below.

ABOLITION OF DISCOUNTED OPTIONS
Under previous legislation the price at which shares could be acquired on the exercise of an option was required to be not manifestly less than the market value of shares of the same class at (broadly) the time of grant. In certain circumstances where the grantor company also operated an approved "all-employee" share scheme this figure was reduced to 85 per cent of the market value (TA 1988 Sch 9 para 29). For options granted on or after the date of Royal Assent the 85 per cent alternative is removed (sub-ss (3) and (10)). See also the transitional provisions in s 115 below.

THE INCOME TAX CHARGE ON DISCOUNTED OPTIONS
Existing legislation in TA 1988 s 185(6)–(6B) imposes an income tax charge on the participant where the aggregate of—

(*a*) the consideration given for an option under an approved executive scheme, and
(*b*) the price which would be paid for the shares on exercise of the option

is less than the market value of the shares at the time of the grant. The charge is made under Schedule E, for the year of assessment in which the option is granted, on an amount equal to that by which the aggregate figure in paras (*a*) and (*b*) above falls short of the market value. Where the scheme permitted the grant of options with an exercise price not less than 85 per cent of market value, this charge was calculated by comparison of the aggregate consideration with 85 per cent of the market value, rather than with the full amount of that value. With the removal of the 85 per cent alternative for the exercise price, the legislation dealing with the charge on the grant is similarly amended (again, for options granted on or after the date of Royal Assent) to compare the aggregate consideration only to the full market value (sub-ss (5), (6) and (10)). In any case such charges are rare, as a result of the prohibition on the grant of options with an exercise price at a *manifest* discount to market value, as discussed above.
Existing legislation gives an allowance for such a charge when calculating a capital gain on a subsequent disposal of the shares, or an income tax charge under TA 1988 s 135 or s 162 (ie, broadly, when the option is exercised in circumstances such that the benefits of the approved scheme regime do not apply). This legislation is amended, again in relation to grants of options on or after the date of Royal Assent, to take account of the change discussed above to the charge on the grant (sub-ss (7) and (10)). For historic reasons the provisions giving a capital gains allowance appear not only in TA 1988 s 185(7) but also in TCGA 1992 s 120. The latter is also amended to take account of this change (sub-s (8)).
Subsection (9) introduces Sch 16, which deals with the position of schemes approved before Royal Assent.

115   Transitional provisions

(1) If, during the period—

(*a*) beginning with 17th July 1995, and
(*b*) ending with the day preceding the passing of this Act,

any rights have been obtained by a person under an approved share option scheme in circumstances falling within subsection (2) below, the rights shall be treated for the purposes of sections 185 to 187 of, and Schedule 9 to, the Taxes Act 1988 as being rights obtained otherwise than in accordance with the provisions of an approved share option scheme.

(2) The circumstances mentioned in subsection (1) above are circumstances such that, on the assumptions in subsection (3) below, there would, by virtue of paragraph 28 or 29 of Schedule 9 to the Taxes Act 1988 (limit on what may be obtained and requirements with respect to price), have been, with respect to the operation of the scheme, a contravention of any of the relevant requirements or of the scheme itself.

(3) The assumptions mentioned in subsection (2) above are—

(*a*) that the amendments made by subsection (2) of section 114 above had effect at all times on and after 17th July 1995;

(*b*) that the amendments made by subsections (3) to (7) of that section had effect in relation to rights obtained at any time on or after that date; and
(*c*) that the provisions of paragraphs 1(1) and 2 to 5 of Schedule 16 to this Act had effect at all times on and after 17th July 1995, but with the substitution for references to the day on which this Act is passed of references to that date.

(4) For the purposes of this section, rights obtained by a person on or after 17th July 1995 shall be treated as having been obtained by him before that date if—

(*a*) the scheme in question is one approved before that date;
(*b*) an offer of the rights or an invitation to apply for them was made in writing to that person before that date; and
(*c*) he obtained the rights within the period of thirty days beginning with the day on which the offer or invitation was made.

(5) In this section—

"approved share option scheme" means an approved share option scheme, within the meaning of section 185 of the Taxes Act 1988, other than a savings-related share option scheme;
"relevant requirements" has the meaning given in paragraph 1(1) of Schedule 9 to the Taxes Act 1988;
"savings-related share option scheme" has the meaning given by Schedule 9 to the Taxes Act 1988.

GENERAL NOTE
Transitional provisions deal with the position of options granted under an approved executive scheme in the period beginning on 17 July 1995 (when the Chancellor of the Exchequer announced the withdrawal of relief from such schemes) and ending on the day before Royal Assent. In certain circumstances such options are treated as not having been granted under an approved scheme (and thus as not eligible for the relevant tax reliefs) (sub-s (1)).

The circumstances in question are where, on the assumptions set out below, there would, by virtue of TA 1988 Sch 9 para 28 or 29 have been, with respect to the operation of the scheme, a contravention of any of the statutory requirements by reference to which the scheme was approved, or a contravention of the rules of the scheme itself. Paragraph 28 relates to the limit on the value of shares over which options may be granted, and para 29 relates to the exercise price (ie prohibiting a manifest discount or, formerly, a discount of more than 15 per cent to the market value of the shares at the time of the grant of the option) (sub-s (2)).

The assumptions referred to in the previous paragraph are (sub-s (3))—

(*a*) that the imposition of the £30,000 limit by s 114(2) above had effect at all times on and after 17 July 1995 (this limit will, of course, relate to all outstanding options, and not merely to those granted on or after 17 July 1995);
(*b*) that the abolition of the 15 per cent discount facility, and the making of consequential amendments, by s 114(3)–(7) above had effect in relation to options granted at any time on or after 17 July 1995; and
(*c*) that the provisions of Sch 16 below deeming the £30,000 limit and the "no discount" rule to be included in pre-existing schemes applied (without the facility in para 1(2) and (3) for the grantor to "opt out") with effect from 17 July 1995 rather than from the date of Royal Assent.

The effect is that although for technical reasons the two major restrictions made by s 114 do not take effect until Royal Assent, in practice they apply also in the period from 17 July 1995 to Royal Assent (with the difference that if they are breached the scheme remains approved but options granted during that time are treated as if it had not been).

For these purposes options granted on or after 17 July 1995 are treated as granted before that date if (sub-s (4))—

(*a*) the scheme was approved before that date;
(*b*) the option was offered to the option holder, or he was invited to apply for it, before that date (in writing); and
(*c*) the option was in fact granted within the period of 30 days beginning with the day on which that offer or invitation was made.

Profit sharing schemes

116   The release date

(1) In section 187(2) of the Taxes Act 1988 (interpretation of sections 185 and 186 of, and Schedules 9 and 10 to, that Act) in the definition of "release date" (the fifth anniversary of the date on which shares were appropriated to a participant in a profit sharing scheme) for "fifth" there shall be substituted "third".

(2) The amendment made by subsection (1) above shall have effect in relation to shares of a participant in a profit sharing scheme if the third anniversary of the appropriation of the shares to the participant occurs on or after the day on which this Act is passed.

(3) If the third anniversary of the appropriation of any shares to a participant in a profit sharing scheme has occurred, but the fifth anniversary of their appropriation to him has not occurred, before the passing of this Act, then, in the application of sections 186 and 187 of, and Schedules 9 and 10 to, the Taxes Act 1988 in relation to those shares, the release date shall be the day on which this Act is passed.

GENERAL NOTE
   The "release date" after which the participant in a Revenue approved profit sharing scheme may dispose of his shares without an income tax charge becomes the third anniversary of the date on which the shares were appropriated to him, rather than the fifth as previously (sub-s (1)).
   The change has effect where the third anniversary falls on or after the date of Royal Assent (sub-s (2)). If the third anniversary falls before the date of Royal Assent and the fifth anniversary on or after that date, then the release date is the date of Royal Assent itself (sub-s (3)).

117   The appropriate percentage

(1) In Schedule 10 to the Taxes Act 1988 (further provisions relating to profit sharing schemes) for paragraph 3 (the appropriate percentage) there shall be substituted—

   "3.—(1) For the purposes of any of the relevant provisions charging an individual to income tax under Schedule E by reason of the occurrence of an event relating to any of his shares, the 'appropriate percentage' in relation to those shares is 100 per cent, unless sub-paragraph (2) below applies.

   (2) Where the individual—

   (*a*) ceases to be a director or employee of the grantor or, in the case of a group scheme, a participating company as mentioned in paragraph 2(*a*) above, or
   (*b*) reaches the relevant age,

   before the event occurs, the 'appropriate percentage' is 50 per cent, unless paragraph 6(4) below applies."

(2) In section 187(8) of that Act (determination of certain values and percentages where shares are appropriated to a participant at different times) paragraph (*b*) (which relates to the appropriate percentage), and the word "and" immediately preceding it, shall cease to have effect.

(3) Subsections (1) and (2) above have effect in relation to the occurrence, on or after the day on which this Act is passed, of events by reason of whose occurrence any provision of section 186 or 187 of, or Schedule 9 or 10 to, the Taxes Act 1988 charges an individual to income tax under Schedule E.

GENERAL NOTE
   When a participant disposes of scheme shares (or obtains a capital receipt from his shares) before the release date, a tax charge arises on the "appropriate percentage" of the value of his

shares (or of the capital receipt). Hitherto, that percentage has been 100 per cent if the relevant event occurred before the fourth anniversary of the appropriation of the shares, and 75 per cent if it occurred between the fourth and fifth anniversaries. For disposals or receipts on or after the date of Royal Assent (and as a consequence of the change to the definition of the release date made by s 116 above) the appropriate percentage becomes 100 per cent for any event before the release date. Existing rules reduce this figure to 50 per cent in the case of an individual who, before the event in question, has either reached the "relevant age" (broadly, a retirement age laid down in the scheme) or ceased employment on the ground of injury, disability or redundancy. This provision is retained in a recast form, removing a slight ambiguity of wording (sub-s (1), inserting new TA 1988, Sch 10, para 3, and sub-s (3)).

Previously the definition of the "appropriate percentage" was subject to an overriding 100 per cent figure which applied under TA 1988 Sch 10 para 6(4)(*a*) in the case of excess or unauthorised shares. Clearly, this is now only of relevance in the case of the 50 per cent limit, and the legislation is rephrased to reflect this (sub-s (1), inserting new TA 1988 Sch 10 para 3).

Existing provisions in TA 1988 s 187(8) provide an identification rule where a disposal before the release date is made from a holding of shares which were appropriated to the participant at different times. For events on or after the date of Royal Assent, this rule no longer applies in determining the appropriate percentage, as that percentage will now be the same (either 100 per cent or 50 per cent) for all the shares concerned (sub-ss (2) and (3)).

118　The appropriate allowance

(1)　In section 186(12) of the Taxes Act 1988 (determination of the appropriate allowance for the purposes of the charge to tax on capital receipts by a participant in an approved profit sharing scheme)—

(*a*)　for "£100" there shall be substituted "£60"; and
(*b*)　for "five years" there shall be substituted "three years".

(2)　Subsection (1) above has effect for the year 1997–98 and subsequent years of assessment.

GENERAL NOTE
Under existing legislation a participant is charged to income tax not on the appropriate percentage of the whole of any capital receipt, but on the appropriate percentage of what remains of the receipt after deducting the "appropriate allowance" for the year of assessment in question (so far as not utilised against a previous receipt in that year) (TA 1988 s 186(3) and (12)). The principal effect is to prevent charges arising on very small receipts.

The appropriate allowance for any year of assessment is currently £20 for each year in which shares were appropriated to the participant under the scheme within the five-year period immediately preceding the year of assessment in question, plus £20. This gives a theoretical maximum of £120, but the legislation provides an overriding maximum of £100 (TA 1988 s 186(12)).

For 1997–98 onwards (and following the change in the release date made by s 116 above) the allowance will be £20 for each year in which shares were appropriated to the participant under the scheme within the three-year period immediately preceding the year of assessment in question, plus £20; the overriding maximum will be £60. Implementation is deferred until 1997–98 as that will be the first full year throughout which the new three-year release date will apply.

Employee share ownership trusts

119　Removal of requirement for at least one year's service

(1)　In Schedule 5 to the Finance Act 1989 (employee share ownership trusts) in paragraph 4(5)(*a*) (for a trust to be a qualifying ESOT, its beneficiaries must have been employees or directors of the company for at least one year) the words "not less than one year and" shall cease to have effect.

(2)　This section applies to trusts established on or after the day on which this Act is passed.

GENERAL NOTE
Under previous legislation the trust deed of a qualifying employee share ownership trust was required to provide that a person was a beneficiary at a particular time (the "relevant time") if he met various conditions, one of which was that at each given time in a qualifying period he was an employee or director of a company falling within the founding company's group (FA 1989 Sch 5

para 4(2)(*b*)). A "qualifying period" was a period which ended at the relevant time and was of a length (specified in the trust deed) of not less than one year and not more than five years (FA 1989 Sch 5 para 4(5)). For trusts established on or after the date of Royal Assent the requirement for the qualifying period to be not less than one year is removed. For the purposes of the existing legislation a trust is considered to be established when the deed under which it is established is executed (FA 1989 Sch 5 para 17). While, strictly, this rule is not relevant for the present purpose, it is assumed that it will apply in practice (and it is difficult to see what other criteria could be in point).

120   Grant and exercise of share options

(1) In Schedule 5 to the Finance Act 1989 (employee share ownership trusts), in paragraph 4 (the trust deed must contain provision as to the beneficiaries) after sub-paragraph (2) there shall be inserted—

"(2A) The trust deed may provide that a person is a beneficiary at a given time if at that time he is eligible to participate in a savings-related share option scheme within the meaning of Schedule 9 to the Taxes Act 1988—

(*a*) which was established by a company within the founding company's group, and
(*b*) which is approved under that Schedule.

(2B) Where a trust deed contains a rule conforming with sub-paragraph (2A) above it must provide that the only powers and duties which the trustees may exercise in relation to persons who are beneficiaries by virtue only of that rule are those which may be exercised in accordance with the provisions of a scheme such as is mentioned in that sub-paragraph."

(2) In consequence of the amendment made by subsection (1) above, section 69 of, and Schedule 5 to, the Finance Act 1989 (which respectively make provision about chargeable events in relation to the trustees of qualifying employee share ownership trusts and the requirements to be satisfied by such trusts) shall be amended in accordance with the following provisions of this section.

(3) In subsection (4) of that section (meaning of "qualifying terms" for the purposes of the provision that the transfer of securities to beneficiaries is a chargeable event if it is not on qualifying terms)—

(*a*) in paragraph (*a*) (securities which are transferred at the same time must be transferred on similar terms) after "time" there shall be inserted "other than those transferred on a transfer such as is mentioned in subsection (4ZA) below";
(*b*) in paragraph (*b*) (securities must have been offered to all the persons who are beneficiaries), after "trust deed" there shall be inserted "by virtue of a rule which conforms with paragraph 4(2), (3) or (4) of Schedule 5 to this Act"; and
(*c*) in paragraph (*c*) (securities must be transferred to all such beneficiaries who have accepted the offer) for "beneficiaries" there shall be substituted "persons".

(4) After subsection (4) of that section there shall be inserted—

"(4ZA) For the purposes of subsection (1)(*b*) above a transfer of securities is also made on qualifying terms if—

(*a*) it is made to a person exercising a right to acquire shares, and
(*b*) that right was obtained in accordance with the provisions of a savings-related share option scheme within the meaning of Schedule 9 to the Taxes Act 1988—

(i) which was established by, or by a company controlled by, the company which established the trust, and

(ii) which is approved under that Schedule, and

(c) that right is being exercised in accordance with the provisions of that scheme, and

(d) the consideration for the transfer is payable to the trustees.''

(5) In sub-paragraph (4) of paragraph 4 of that Schedule (trust deed may provide for charity to be beneficiary if there are no beneficiaries falling within a rule conforming with sub-paragraph (2) or (3)) after "sub- paragraph (2)" there shall be inserted ", (2A)".

(6) In sub-paragraph (7) of that paragraph (trust deed must not provide for a person to be a beneficiary unless he falls within a rule conforming with sub-paragraph (2), (3) or (4)) after "sub-paragraph (2)" there shall be inserted ", (2A)".

(7) In sub-paragraph (8) of that paragraph (trust deed must provide that person with material interest in founding company cannot be a beneficiary) after "at a particular time (the relevant time)" there shall be inserted "by virtue of a rule which conforms with sub-paragraph (2), (3) or (4) above".

(8) In paragraph 5(2) of that Schedule (trust deed must be so expressed that it is apparent that the general functions of the trustees are as mentioned in paragraphs (a) to (e)) after paragraph (c) there shall be inserted—

"(cc)   to grant rights to acquire shares to persons who are beneficiaries under the terms of the trust deed;".

(9) In paragraph 9 of that Schedule (trust deed must provide that transfers of securities to beneficiaries must be on qualifying terms and within the qualifying period) in sub-paragraph (2) (meaning of qualifying terms)—

(a) in paragraph (a) (securities which are transferred at the same time must be transferred on similar terms) after "time" there shall be inserted "other than those transferred on a transfer such as is mentioned in sub-paragraph (2ZA) below";

(b) in paragraph (b) (securities must have been offered to all the persons who are beneficiaries) after "trust deed" there shall be inserted "by virtue of a rule which conforms with paragraph 4(2), (3) or (4) above"; and

(c) in paragraph (c) (securities must be transferred to all such beneficiaries who have accepted the offer) for "beneficiaries" there shall be substituted "persons".

(10) After sub-paragraph (2) of that paragraph there shall be inserted—

"(2ZA) For the purposes of sub-paragraph (1) above a transfer of securities is also made on qualifying terms if—

(a) it is made to a person exercising a right to acquire shares, and

(b) that right was obtained in accordance with the provisions of a savings-related share option scheme within the meaning of Schedule 9 to the Taxes Act 1988—

(i) which was established by, or by a company controlled by, the founding company, and

(ii) which is approved under that Schedule, and

(c) that right is being exercised in accordance with the provisions of that scheme, and

(d) the consideration for the transfer is payable to the trustees.''

(11) In paragraph 10 of that Schedule (trust deed must not contain features not essential or reasonably incidental to purposes mentioned in that paragraph)—

(*a*) after "acquiring sums and securities," there shall be inserted "granting rights to acquire shares to persons who are eligible to participate in savings-related share option schemes approved under Schedule 9 to the Taxes Act 1988, transferring shares to such persons,"; and

(*b*) for "Schedule 9 to the Taxes Act 1988" there shall be substituted "that Schedule".

(12) This section has effect in relation to trusts established on or after the day on which this Act is passed.

GENERAL NOTE

Various amendments are made to the legislation dealing with qualifying employee share ownership trusts, to enable them to be operated in conjunction with Revenue approved savings-related share option schemes. These amendments apply in relation to trusts established on or after the date of Royal Assent (sub-s (12)). As to the date on which a trust is established, see the note on s 119 above.

BENEFICIARIES

Existing legislation provides for certain classes of person who must, or may, be beneficiaries of a qualifying trust. A new rule now indicates that the trust deed may provide that a person is a beneficiary at a time when he is eligible to participate in an approved savings-related share option scheme established by a company within the founding company's group. Where such a rule is included within the deed it must provide that, in relation to persons who are beneficiaries only by virtue of that rule, the only powers and duties which the trustees may exercise are those which may be exercised in accordance with the provisions of such an approved scheme (sub-s (1), inserting new FA 1989 Sch 5 para 4(2A)). The effect is to create two distinct categories of beneficiary, normally with a considerable overlap in terms of the identity of the individuals concerned; ie beneficiaries under the old rules and share-option scheme beneficiaries.

Under existing legislation the trust deed may provide for a charity to be a beneficiary if there is no person who is a beneficiary within any rule included in the deed under the other statutory provisions governing who must, or may, be a beneficiary, and if the trust is in consequence being wound up (FA 1989 Sch 5 para 4(4)). Similarly, existing legislation indicates that the trust deed must not provide for a person to be a beneficiary unless he falls within any rule which is included in the deed and conforms with those statutory provisions (or with the rule as regards charities) (FA 1989 Sch 5 para 4(7)). Both these provisions are now amended so that the statutory rules as to who may be a beneficiary which are taken into consideration for these purposes include the new rule that the deed may provide for participants in an approved savings-related scheme to be beneficiaries (sub-ss (5) and (6)).

Under existing legislation in FA 1989 Sch 5 para 4(8) the trust deed must provide, broadly, that a person cannot be a beneficiary if he has a "material interest" in the founding company, or has had such an interest within the previous year. This rule is now amended so that a person who has, or has had, such an interest need only be precluded by the trust deed from being a beneficiary under the old rules. He is not prevented from being a beneficiary under the new rule relating to persons eligible to participate in an approved savings-related share option scheme (sub-s (7)). A "material interest" for this purpose is, broadly, a five per cent interest (with or without associates) (FA 1989 Sch 5 para 16(1)). The legislation governing savings-related schemes itself excludes participation by an individual with a material interest in a relevant *close* company, but "material interest" in this context means, broadly, a 25 per cent interest (TA 1988 s 187(3) and (4) and Sch 9 paras 8 and 37–39).

TRANSFERS OF SECURITIES ON QUALIFYING TERMS

Existing legislation provides for a tax charge on the trustees when a "chargeable event" occurs. Various acts or omissions by the trustees give rise to a chargeable event, including a transfer of securities to beneficiaries otherwise than on "qualifying terms" (FA 1989 s 69(1)(*b*)). A transfer is made on qualifying terms if it meets three requirements (FA 1989 s 69(4)).

(*a*) The first requirement is that all the securities transferred at the same time be transferred on similar terms. An exception is now introduced to allow transfers on other terms where they fall within the new category set out below (ie, broadly, transfers on exercise of a savings-related share option) (sub-s (3)(*a*)).

(*b*) The second requirement is that securities have been offered to all the persons who are beneficiaries under the terms of the trust deed when the transfer is made. This is now limited to beneficiaries under the old rules, ie to persons who are beneficiaries otherwise than by virtue of their eligibility to participate in a savings-related share option scheme (sub-s (3)(*b*)).

(*c*) The third requirement is that securities are transferred to all beneficiaries who have accepted the offer. This is amended (by the substitution of "person" for "beneficiary") to make it clear that the reference is only to the restricted category of beneficiaries (ie beneficiaries under the old rules) to whom the offer is now required to be made (sub-s (3)(*c*)).

As indicated above, a new category of transfer is brought within the definition of a transfer on qualifying terms. This is a transfer made to a person exercising an option obtained under an approved savings-related share option scheme established by, or by a company controlled by, the company which established the trust, and where the option is being exercised in accordance with the provisions of that scheme and the consideration for the transfer is payable to the trustees (sub-s (4), inserting new FA 1989 s 69(4ZA)).

Not only does a transfer of securities give rise to a tax charge if it is not made on qualifying terms; in addition, under the existing legislation the trust deed must provide that where the trustees transfer securities to a beneficiary they must do so on qualifying terms. (A transfer on other terms thus lays the trustees open not only to a tax charge but also to the possibility of an action for breach of trust.) The legislation dealing with the requirements of the trust deed in this respect (FA 1989 Sch 5 para 9(2)) is in precisely the same terms as that dealing with the charge to tax as discussed above (FA 1989 s 69(4)), and is correspondingly amended by the present section, including the addition of the new category of transfer on qualifying terms; ie a transfer on exercise of a savings-related option (sub-ss (9) and (10), the latter inserting new FA 1989 Sch 5 para 9(2ZA)).

THE FUNCTION OF THE TRUSTEES

Under the existing legislation the trust deed must contain provision as to the function of the trustees, which must be so expressed that it is apparent that their general functions are within certain categories of transaction laid down in the statute (FA 1989 Sch 5 para 5(2)). To these categories there is now added the function of granting share options to persons who are beneficiaries under the terms of the trust deed (sub-s (8)). Although this provision is apparently widely drawn, it will not enable trusts to grant options otherwise than under approved savings-related schemes, as this would still involve the trustees in making subsequent transfers of shares otherwise than on qualifying terms (see above).

Existing legislation in FA 1989 Sch 5 para 10 provides that the trust deed must not contain features which are neither essential nor reasonably incidental to certain major purposes laid down in the statute. To these is now added the purpose of granting options to persons who are eligible to participate in approved savings-related share option schemes, and transferring shares to such persons (sub-s (11)).

CHAPTER V

SELF-ASSESSMENT, GENERAL MANAGEMENT ETC

General

121   Returns and self-assessment

(1) In subsection (1) of section 8 of the Taxes Management Act 1970 (personal return), and in subsection (1) of section 8A of that Act (trustee's return), after the words "year of assessment," there shall be inserted the words "and the amount payable by him by way of income tax for that year,".

(2) In subsection (1A) of each of those sections, the words from "and the amounts referred to" to the end shall cease to have effect.

(3) After that subsection of each of those sections there shall be inserted the following subsection—

"(1AA) For the purposes of subsection (1) above—

(*a*) the amounts in which a person is chargeable to income tax and capital gains tax are net amounts, that is to say, amounts which take into account any relief or allowance a claim for which is included in the return; and

(*b*) the amount payable by a person by way of income tax is the difference between the amount in which he is chargeable to income tax and the aggregate amount of any income tax deducted at source and any tax credits to which section 231 of the principal Act applies."

(4) For subsection (1) of section 9 of that Act (returns to include self-assessment) there shall be substituted the following subsection—

"(1) Subject to subsection (2) below, every return under section 8 or 8A of this Act shall include a self-assessment, that is to say—

(*a*) an assessment of the amounts in which, on the basis of the information contained in the return and taking into account any relief or allowance a claim for which is included in the return, the person making the return is chargeable to income tax and capital gains tax for the year of assessment; and

(*b*) an assessment of the amount payable by him by way of income tax, that is to say, the difference between the amount in which he is assessed to income tax under paragraph (*a*) above and the aggregate amount of any income tax deducted at source and any tax credits to which section 231 of the principal Act applies."

(5) In subsection (1)(*b*) of section 11AA of that Act (return of profits to include self-assessment), for the words ", allowance or repayment of tax" there shall be substituted the words "or allowance".

(6) In subsection (1)(*a*) of section 12AA of that Act (partnership return), after the words "so chargeable" there shall be inserted the words "and the amount payable by way of income tax by each such partner".

(7) For subsection (1A) of that section there shall be substituted the following subsection—

"(1A) For the purposes of subsection (1) above—

(*a*) the amount in which a partner is chargeable to income tax or corporation tax is a net amount, that is to say, an amount which takes into account any relief or allowance for which a claim is made; and (*b*) the amount payable by a partner by way of income tax is the difference between the amount in which he is chargeable to income tax and the aggregate amount of any income tax deducted at source and any tax credits to which section 231 of the principal Act applies."

(8) This section and sections 122, 123, 125 to 127 and 141 below—

(*a*) so far as they relate to income tax and capital gains tax, have effect as respects the year 1996–97 and subsequent years of assessment, and
(*b*) so far as they relate to corporation tax, have effect as respects accounting periods ending on or after the appointed day for the purposes of Chapter III of Part IV of the Finance Act 1994.

SUBSECTION (1)
TMA 1970 s 8(1) (individuals) and TMA 1970 s 8A(1) (trustees) are amended to provide that the purpose for which a return is required under the self-assessment procedure is extended to include not only the amounts in which a person is chargeable to income tax and CGT but to the amount of the tax he has to pay.

SUBSECTIONS (2) AND (3)
The definition in TMA 1970 ss 8(1A), 8A(1A) of the amounts in which a person is chargeable is deleted. New TMA 1970 ss 8(1AA) and 8A(1AA), are inserted and contain—

(*a*) a new definition of the amounts in which a person is chargeable to income tax and CGT as net amounts after deducting any relief or allowance claimed in the return; and
(*b*) a definition of the amount of income tax payable, which is the difference between the amount in which a person is chargeable and the total of any income tax deducted at source and of tax credits on company distributions under TA 1988 s 231.

SUBSECTION (4)
An amendment is made to TMA 1970 s 9(1) requiring the taxpayer's self-assessment to include both the amounts in which he is chargeable and the amount of income tax payable, using the same definitions.

SUBSECTION (5)
The amount of the self-assessment to corporation tax is to be calculated without reference to any claim for repayment of tax which may be included in the return. Reliefs and allowances continue to be deductible. The purpose of this amendment is presumably to prevent a company from reducing its payment of corporation tax by a claim for repayment which has not been agreed.

SUBSECTIONS (6) AND (7)
Similar amendments are made to TMA 1970 s 12AA (returns in respect of partnerships) to those described above for individuals, ie the need to return both amounts chargeable and net tax payable by an individual partner.

COMMENCEMENT
The provisions apply from the commencement of self-assessment (sub-s (8)).

122 Notional tax deductions and payments

(1) At the end of subsection (1) of section 9 of the Taxes Management Act 1970 (as substituted by section 121(4) above) there shall be inserted the words "but nothing in this subsection shall enable a self-assessment to show as repayable any income tax treated as deducted or paid by virtue of section 233(1), 246D(1), 249(4), 421(1), 547(5) or 599A(5) of the principal Act."

(2) At the end of subsection (1) of section 59B of that Act (payment of income tax and capital gains tax) there shall be inserted the words "but nothing in this subsection shall require the repayment of any income tax treated as deducted or paid by virtue of section 233(1), 246D(1), 249(4), 421(1), 547(5) or 599A(5) of the principal Act."

(3) In subsection (1) of section 233 of the Taxes Act 1988 (taxation of certain recipients of distributions), for paragraphs (*a*) and (*b*) there shall be substituted the following paragraphs—

"(*a*) that person shall be treated as having paid income tax at the lower rate on the amount or value of the distribution;

(*b*) no repayment shall be made of any income tax treated by virtue of paragraph (*a*) above as having been paid;".

(4) In paragraph (*a*) of subsection (1A) of that section—

(*a*) for sub-paragraph (i) there shall be substituted the following sub-paragraph—

"(i) income on which that person falls to be treated as having paid income tax at the lower rate by virtue of paragraph (*a*) of subsection (1) above, or";

and

(*b*) for the words "that assessment" there shall be substituted the words "that subsection".

(5) In the following enactments, namely—

(*a*) subsection (2)(*a*) of section 246D of that Act (individuals etc); and

(*b*) subsection (4)(*a*) of section 249 of that Act (stock dividends treated as income),

for the words from "no assessment" to "on it" there shall be substituted the words "the individual shall be treated as having paid income tax at the lower rate on that income".

(6) In subsection (1)(*b*) of section 421 of that Act (taxation of borrower when loan released), for the words "no assessment shall be made on him in respect of" there shall be substituted the words "he shall not be liable to pay".

(7) The following shall cease to have effect, namely—

(*a*) in subsection (5)(*a*) of section 547 of that Act (method of charging to tax), the words from "no assessment" to "but";

(*b*) in subsection (6) of section 599A of that Act (charge to tax: payments out of surplus funds), the words from "subject" to "and"; and

(*c*) subsection (7) of that section.

GENERAL NOTE

There are several receipts which are not liable to income tax at the lower rate, but the deemed lower rate tax is not repayable. Special provisions are required to deal with these receipts under self-assessment. They are—

(*a*) non-qualifying distributions (TA 1988 s 233(1));
(*b*) qualifying distributions received by a non-resident of the UK (TA 1988 s 233(1), (2));
(*c*) foreign income dividends (TA 1988 s 246D);
(*d*) stock dividends (TA 1988 s 249);
(*e*) release of close company loan (TA 1988 s 421);
(*f*) certain gains on insurance policies (TA 1988 s 547);
(*g*) payments out of surplus funds of a pension scheme (TA 1988 s 599A).

A self-assessment under TMA 1970 s 9 may not show as repayable the notional lower rate income tax applicable to receipts in (*a*)–(*g*) above (sub-s (1)), TMA 1970 s 59B is amended to deny repayment of such notional tax (sub-s (2)).

All the provisions listed above specify that no assessment shall be made on the recipient in respect of income tax at the basic rate; sub-ss (3)–(7) delete that specification and substitute a provision that the recipient shall be treated as having paid income tax at the lower rate (making it clear where it is not already provided that the notional tax is not repayable).

COMMENCEMENT

The provisions apply from the commencement of self-assessment (s 121(8)).

123   Liability of partners

(1) In subsection (2) of section 12AA of the Taxes Management Act 1970 (partnership return) after the words "with the notice" there shall be inserted the words "or a successor of his".

(2) In subsection (3) of that section after the words "the partner" there shall be inserted the words "or a successor of his".

(3) In subsection (7)(*a*) of that section, the words "any part of" shall cease to have effect.

(4) At the end of that section there shall be inserted the following subsections—

"(11) In this Act 'successor', in relation to a person who is required to make and deliver, or has made and delivered, a return in pursuance of a notice under subsection (2) or (3) above, but is no longer available, means—

(*a*) where a partner is for the time being nominated for the purposes of this subsection by a majority of the relevant partners, that partner; and
(*b*) where no partner is for the time being so nominated, such partner as—

(i) in the case of a notice under subsection (2) above, is identified in accordance with rules given with that notice; or
(ii) in the case of a notice under subsection (3) above, is nominated for the purposes of this subsection by an officer of the Board;

and 'predecessor' and 'successor', in relation to a person so nominated or identified, shall be construed accordingly.

(12) For the purposes of subsection (11) above a nomination under paragraph (*a*) of that subsection, and a revocation of such a nomination, shall not have effect in relation to any time before notice of the nomination or revocation is given to an officer of the Board.

(13) In this section 'relevant partner' means a person who was a partner at any time during the period for which the return was made or is required, or the personal representatives of such a person."

(5) In subsection (1) of section 12AB of that Act (partnership return to include partnership statement)—

(*a*) in paragraph (*a*), for the words "each period of account ending within the period in respect of which the return is made" there shall be substituted the words "the period in respect of which the return is made and each period of account ending within that period";
(*b*) in sub-paragraph (i) of that paragraph, for the words "that period" there shall be substituted the words "the period in question";
(*c*) after that sub-paragraph there shall be inserted the following sub-paragraph—

"(ia) the amount of the consideration which, on that basis, has accrued to the partnership in respect of each disposal of partnership property during that period,";

and

(*d*) in paragraph (*b*), after the words "such period" there shall be inserted the words "as is mentioned in paragraph (*a*) above" and after the word "loss," there shall be inserted the word "consideration,".

(6) In subsection (2) of that section—

(*a*) in paragraph (*a*) after the words "to that person" there shall be inserted the words "or a successor"; and

(*b*) in paragraph (*b*) for the words from "partnership statement" to "he" there shall be substituted the words "or a predecessor's partnership statement as to give effect to any amendments to the return in which it is included which he or a predecessor".

(7) In section 12AC of that Act (power to enquire into partnership return)—

(*a*) in subsection (1)(*b*), after the word "person" there shall be inserted the words "or a successor of that person"; and

(*b*) subsection (6) (which is superseded by subsection (4) above) shall cease to have effect.

(8) In subsection (1)(*b*) of section 93A of that Act (failure to make partnership return), after the word "he" there shall be inserted the words "or a successor of his".

(9) In subsections (3) and (4) of that section, after the words "the representative partner" there shall be inserted the words "or a successor of his".

(10) In subsection (6) of that section—

(*a*) after the words "the representative partner" there shall be inserted the words "or a successor of his"; and

(*b*) after the words "that partner", in both places where they occur, there shall be inserted the words "or successor".

(11) In subsection (7) of that section, for the words "the representative partner had a reasonable excuse for not delivering the return" there shall be substituted the words "the person for the time being required to deliver the return (whether the representative partner or a successor of his) had a reasonable excuse for not delivering it".

(12) In subsection (1)(*a*)(ii) of section 95A of that Act (incorrect partnership return or accounts), for the words "such a return" there shall be substituted the words "a return of such a kind".

(13) In subsection (3) of that section—

(*a*) after the words "the representative partner" there shall be inserted the words "or a successor of his"; and

(*b*) after the words "that partner", in both places where they occur, there shall be inserted the words "or successor".

(14) In subsection (1) of section 118 of that Act (interpretation), for the definition of "successor" there shall be substituted the following definition—

"'successor', in relation to a person who is required to make and deliver, or has made and delivered, a return under section 12AA of this Act, and 'predecessor' and 'successor', in relation to the successor of such a person, shall be construed in accordance with section 12AA(11) of this Act;".

PARTNER NOT AVAILABLE

TMA 1970 ss 12AA(2), (3), 12AB(2), 12AC(1) refer to notices etc being given by the Revenue to a partner in connection with a partnership return. Where the partner concerned is no longer available (presumably because he has left the partnership or ceased to be resident in the UK), those provisions are amended to enable such notices to be given to a "successor" (sub-ss (1), (2), (6) and (7)). A successor for this purpose is a partner nominated for the time being for that purpose by a majority of the relevant partners; such a nomination (or its revocation) cannot have effect until it is notified to the Revenue. If the partners do not nominate a successor, the Revenue may do so (sub-s (4)).

TMA 1970 ss 93A and 95A provide for the imposition of penalties where a representative partner has been called on to make partnership return and has either failed to do so or has rendered an incorrect return. Those provisions arc amended to enable penalties to be imposed where the return has been served on a successor to a representative partner (sub--ss (8)–(12)).

PERIOD OF PARTNERSHIP RETURN
TMA 1970 s 12AB requires a partnership return for a specified period to be accompanied by a partnership statement for each accounts period ending within the specified period. This requirement is now extended to require a statement to be produced for the specified period itself as well as for any accounts period ending within it (sub-s (5)(*a*), (*b*)). The partnership statement is also to include the amount of consideration accruing to the partnership from the disposal of property during the period in question (sub-s (5)(*c*), (*d*)).

124 Retention of original records

(1) The Taxes Management Act 1970, as it has effect—

(*a*) for the purposes of income tax and capital gains tax, as respects the year 1996–97 and subsequent years of assessment, and
(*b*) for the purposes of corporation tax, as respects accounting periods ending on or after the day appointed under section 199 of the Finance Act 1994 for the purposes of Chapter III of Part IV of that Act (self-assessment management provisions),

shall be amended in accordance with the following provisions of this section.

(2) In section 12B (records to be kept for purposes of returns) in subsection (4) (which permits the duty to preserve records to be discharged by the preservation of the information contained in them, and provides for the admissibility in evidence of copy documents) at the beginning there shall be inserted the words "Except in the case of records falling within subsection (4A) below,".

(3) After that subsection there shall be inserted—

"(4A) The records which fall within this subsection are—

(*a*) any statement in writing such as is mentioned in—

(i) subsection (1) of section 234 of the principal Act (amount of qualifying distribution and tax credit), or
(ii) subsection (1) of section 352 of that Act (gross amount, tax deducted, and actual amount paid, in certain cases where payments are made under deduction of tax),

which is furnished by the company or person there mentioned, whether after the making of a request or otherwise;

(*b*) any certificate or other record (however described) which is required by regulations under section 566(1) of the principal Act to be given to a sub-contractor (within the meaning of Chapter IV of Part XIII of that Act) on the making of a payment to which section 559 of that Act (deductions on account of tax) applies;

(*c*) any such record as may be requisite for making a correct and complete claim in respect of, or otherwise requisite for making a correct and complete return so far as relating to, an amount of tax—

(i) which has been paid under the laws of a territory outside the United Kingdom, or
(ii) which would have been payable under the law of such a territory but for a relief to which section 788(5) of the principal Act (relief for promoting development and relief contemplated by double taxation arrangements) applies."

(4) In subsection (5) of that section (penalty for failure to comply with section

12B(1) or (2A)) for "Subject to subsection (5A)" there shall be substituted "Subject to subsections (5A) and (5B)".

(5) After subsection (5A) of that section there shall be inserted—

"(5B) Subsection (5) above also does not apply where—

(*a*) the records which the person fails to keep or preserve are records falling within paragraph (*a*) of subsection (4A) above; and
(*b*) an officer of the Board is satisfied that any facts which he reasonably requires to be proved, and which would have been proved by the records, are proved by other documentary evidence furnished to him."

(6) In Schedule 1A (claims etc not included in returns) in paragraph 2A (keeping and preserving of records) in sub-paragraph (3) (which makes corresponding provision to section 12B(4)) at the beginning there shall be inserted "Except in the case of records falling within section 12B(4A) of this Act,".

(7) In sub-paragraph (4) of that paragraph (penalty for failure to comply with paragraph 2A(1)) at the beginning there shall be inserted "Subject to sub-paragraph (5) below,".

(8) After that sub-paragraph there shall be inserted—

"(5) Sub-paragraph (4) above does not apply where—

(*a*) the records which the person fails to keep or preserve are records falling within paragraph (*a*) of section 12B(4A) of this Act; and
(*b*) an officer of the Board is satisfied that any facts which he reasonably requires to be proved, and which would have been proved by the records, are proved by other documentary evidence furnished to him.".

(9) The amendments made by this section shall not have effect in relation to—

(*a*) any time before this Act is passed, or
(*b*) any records which a person fails to preserve before this Act is passed.

GENERAL NOTE
TMA 1970 s 12B(4) and Sch 1A para 2A(1) provide that a requirement to preserve records in support of a return or claim is satisfied if the information contained in them is preserved and that a copy of a document is admissible in evidence. Section 124 provides that in the case of certain records the original documents must be retained (sub-ss (2), (6)).
The documents to be retained are—

(*a*) (i) certificates of qualifying distributions and tax credit supplied by the company making the distribution;
(ii) certificates of deduction of tax under TA 1988 s 352;
(*b*) certificates given to a sub-contractor in the construction industry;
(*c*) records of tax paid under the laws of a foreign country (or that would have been paid but for relief for promoting development) necessary to substantiate a claim for double tax relief (sub-s (3)).

PENALTIES
TMA 1970 s 12B(5) and Sch 1A para 2A(4) provide for penalties for failure to keep and retain records. These penalties will not be imposed for failure to retain original documents listed above if a Revenue officer is satisfied that other evidence produced to him proves the facts which the original documents would have proved (sub-ss (4), (5), (7), (8)).

COMMENCEMENT
These provisions apply generally from the commencement of self-assessment (sub-s (1)), but not in relation to documents destroyed before the date of Royal Assent (sub-s (9)) (although it would still be necessary to preserve the information).

125 Determination of tax where no return delivered

(1) For subsection (1) of section 28C of the Taxes Management Act 1970 (determination of tax where no return delivered) there shall be substituted the following subsections—

"(1) This section applies where—

(*a*) a notice has been given to any person under section 8 or 8A of this Act (the relevant section), and

(*b*) the required return is not delivered on or before the filing date.

(1A) An officer of the Board may make a determination of the following amounts, to the best of his information and belief, namely—

(*a*) the amounts in which the person who should have made the return is chargeable to income tax and capital gains tax for the year of assessment; and

(*b*) the amount which is payable by him by way of income tax for that year;

and subsection (1AA) of section 8 or, as the case may be, section 8A of this Act applies for the purposes of this subsection as it applies for the purposes of subsection (1) of that section."

(2) In subsection (3) of that section the words "or 11AA" shall cease to have effect.

(3) In subsection (6) of that section for the words ", section 8A(1A) or, as the case may be, section 11(4)" there shall be substituted the words "or, as the case may be, section 8A(1A)".

(4) After subsection (5) of section 59B of that Act (payment of income tax and capital gains tax) there shall be inserted the following subsection—

"(5A) Where a determination under section 28C of this Act which has effect as a person's self-assessment is superseded by his self-assessment under section 9 of this Act, any amount of tax which is payable or repayable by virtue of the supersession shall be payable or (as the case may be) repayable on or before the day given by subsection (3) or (4) above."

GENERAL NOTE

TMA 1970 s 28C provides that a Revenue officer may make a determination of the amounts for which a person is chargeable to income tax, CGT and corporation tax where the person concerned has not delivered by the filing date a return served on him.

This section removes references to corporation tax from this provision so that it now only applies to income tax and CGT (sub-ss (1)–(3)).

Subsection (1) also inserts new TMA 1970 s 28C(1A) which provides that a determination by a Revenue officer may include both the amounts of income tax and CGT with which the person concerned is chargeable and the amount of income tax which is payable by that person for the year in question. This charge follows the introduction of a separate definition of income tax payable in TMA 1970 s 8(1AA) introduced by s 121 (see above).

Subsection (4) inserts new TMA 1970 s 59B(5A) which provides that where a determination by a Revenue officer is superseded by a self-assessment by the taxpayer, the tax payable (or repayable) in consequence is payable (or repayable) on or before 31 January following the end of the year of assessment. Where the taxpayer was not issued with a return form until after 31 October following the end of the year of assessment, the tax (or repayment) is not due until three months after the issue of the return form.

COMMENCEMENT

The provisions apply from the commencement of self-assessment (s 121(8)).

126 PAYE regulations

(1) After subsection (9) of section 59A of the Taxes Management Act 1970 (payments on account of income tax) there shall be inserted the following subsection—

"(10) Regulations under section 203 of the principal Act (PAYE) may provide that, for the purpose of determining the amount of any such excess as is mentioned in subsection (1) above, any necessary adjustments in respect of matters prescribed by the regulations shall be made to the amount of tax deducted at source under that section."

(2) After subsection (7) of section 59B of that Act (payment of income tax and capital gains tax) there shall be inserted the following subsection—

"(8) Regulations under section 203 of the principal Act (PAYE) may provide that, for the purpose of determining the amount of the difference mentioned in subsection (1) above, any necessary adjustments in respect of matters prescribed by the regulations shall be made to the amount of tax deducted at source under that section."

GENERAL NOTE
TMA 1970 s 59A provides for payments on account of tax for a year of assessment to be made where the amount of tax in the self-assessment for the preceding year exceeds tax deducted at source (which includes tax deducted under PAYE) for that year. Subsection (1) inserts new TMA 1970 s 59A(10) which enables the PAYE regulations to provide for any necessary adjustments to be made to the amount of tax deducted in the preceding year in calculating the excess; this could arise if the code number for the year in question (or a later year) has been adjusted to take account of an underpayment.

Subsection (2) inserts new TMA 1970 s 59B(7) which enables similar adjustments to the PAYE regulations to be made in calculating the further payment or repayment due when the actual liability for a year of assessment is compared with the payments on account.

COMMENCEMENT
The provisions apply from the commencement of self-assessment (s 121(8)).

127 Repayment postponed pending completion of enquiries

After subsection (4) of section 59B of the Taxes Management Act 1970 (payment of income tax and capital gains tax) there shall be inserted the following subsection—

"(4A) Where in the case of a repayment the return on the basis of which the person's self-assessment was made under section 9 of this Act is enquired into by an officer of the Board—

(*a*) nothing in subsection (3) or (4) above shall require the repayment to be made before the day on which, by virtue of section 28A(5) of this Act, the officer's enquiries are treated as completed; but

(*b*) the officer may at any time before that day make the repayment, on a provisional basis, to such extent as he thinks fit."

GENERAL NOTE
TMA 1970 s 59B(4) provides for repayment to be made where the payments on account for a year of assessment exceed the actual liability in the self-assessment for that year. This section inserts new TMA 1970 s 59(4A); this provides that where a Revenue officer makes enquiries into the return on which the self-assessment is based, the repayment need not be made until his enquiries are treated as completed, although the officer, if he thinks fit, may make a provisional repayment.

COMMENCEMENT
The provisions apply from the commencement of self-assessment (s 121(8)).

128 Claims for reliefs involving two or more years

(1) In section 42 of the Taxes Management Act 1970 (procedure for making claims etc)—

(*a*) subsections (3A) and (3B) (which are superseded by subsection (2) below) shall cease to have effect;

(*b*) in subsection (7)(*a*), the words "534, 535, 537A, 538" shall cease to have effect; and

(*c*) after subsection (11) there shall be inserted the following subsection—

"(11A) Schedule 1B to this Act shall have effect as respects certain claims for relief involving two or more years of assessment."

(2) After Schedule 1A to that Act there shall be inserted, as Schedule 1B, the provisions set out in Schedule 17 to this Act (claims for reliefs involving two or more years).

(3) For subsection (9) of section 96 of the Taxes Act 1988 (relief for fluctuating profits of farming etc) there shall be substituted the following subsection—

"(9) Where a person makes a claim under this section, any claim by him for relief under any other provision of the Income Tax Acts for either of the two years of assessment—

(*a*) shall not be out of time if made before the end of the period during which the claim under this section is capable of being revoked; and

(*b*) if already made, may be amended or revoked before the end of that period;

and, in relation to a claim made by being included in a return, any reference in this subsection to amending or revoking the claim is a reference to amending the return by amending or, as the case may be, omitting the claim."

(4) In section 108 of that Act (election for carry-back)—

(*a*) for the words "the inspector within two years after" there shall be substituted the words "an officer of the Board within one year from the 31st January next following"; and

(*b*) the words from "and, in any such case" to the end shall cease to have effect.

(5) For subsection (5) of section 534 of that Act (relief for copyright payments) there shall be substituted the following subsections—

"(5) A claim under this section with respect to any payment to which it applies by virtue only of subsection (4)(*b*) above—

(*a*) shall have effect as a claim with respect to all qualifying payments, that is to say, all such payments in respect of the copyright in the same work which are receivable by the claimant, whether before or after the claim; and

(*b*) where qualifying payments are so receivable in two or more years of assessment, shall be treated for the purposes of the Management Act as if it were two or more separate claims, each in respect of the qualifying payments receivable in one of those years.

(5A) A claim under this section may be made at any time within one year from the 31st January next following—

(*a*) in the case of such a claim as is mentioned in subsection (5) above, the latest year of assessment in which a qualifying payment is receivable; and

(*b*) in the case of any other claim, the year of assessment in which the payment in question is receivable.

(5B) For the purposes of subsections (5) and (5A) above, a payment shall be regarded as receivable in the year of assessment in computing the amount of the profits or gains of which it would, but for this section, be included."

(6) After subsection (6) of that section there shall be inserted the following subsection—

"(6A) In the case of persons carrying on a trade, profession or business in partnership, no claim may be made under any of the following provisions, namely—

(*a*) this section and section 535;
(*b*) section 537 as it has effect in relation to this section and section 535; and
(*c*) section 537A and section 538,

in respect of any payment or sum receivable on or after 6th April 1996; and nothing in any of those provisions shall be construed as applying to profits chargeable to corporation tax."

(7) In section 535 of that Act (relief where copyright sold after ten years or more), the following shall cease to have effect, namely—

(*a*) in subsection (4), the words "Subject to subsection (5) below";
(*b*) subsections (5) and (7); and
(*c*) in subsection (6), the words from "unless the author" to the end.

(8) After subsection (8) of that section there shall be inserted the following subsection—

"(8A) No claim for relief made under subsection (1) above shall be allowed unless it is made within one year from the 31st January next following the year of assessment in which the payment is receivable; and for the purposes of this subsection a payment shall be regarded as receivable in the year of assessment in computing the amount of the profits or gains of which it would, but for this section, be included."

(9) For subsection (5) of section 537A of that Act (relief for payments in respect of designs) there shall be substituted the following subsections—

"(5) A claim under this section with respect to any payment to which it applies by virtue only of subsection (4)(*b*) above—

(*a*) shall have effect as a claim with respect to all qualifying payments, that is to say, all such payments in respect of rights in the design in question which are receivable by the claimant, whether before or after the claim; and
(*b*) where qualifying payments are so receivable in two or more years of assessment, shall be treated for the purposes of the Management Act as if it were two or more separate claims, each in respect of the qualifying payments receivable in one of those years.

(5A) A claim under this section may be made at any time within one year from the 31st January next following—

(*a*) in the case of such a claim as is mentioned in subsection (5) above, the latest year of assessment in which a qualifying payment is receivable; and
(*b*) in the case of any other claim, the year of assessment in which the payment in question is receivable.

(5B) For the purposes of subsections (5) and (5A) above, a payment shall be regarded as receivable in the year of assessment in computing the amount of the profits or gains of which it would, but for this section, be included."

(10) After subsection (3) of section 538 of that Act (relief for painters, sculptors and other artists) there shall be inserted the following subsection—

"(4) No claim for relief made under subsection (1) above shall be allowed unless it is made within one year from the 31st January next following the year of assessment in which the payment is receivable; and for the purposes of this subsection a payment shall be regarded as receivable in the year of assessment in computing the amount of the profits or gains of which it would, but for this section, be included."

(11) This section (except subsections (1)(b) and (6) above) and Schedule 17 to this Act have effect as respects claims made (or deemed to be made) in relation to the year 1996–97 or later years of assessment.

(12) Subsection (1)(b) above has effect as respects claims made in relation to the year 1997–98 or later years of assessment.

GENERAL NOTE
Subsections (1) and (2) amend TMA 1970 s 42 (which sets out the provisions for making claims under the self-assessment scheme) in two ways—

(a) the provisions for dealing with claims involving more than one year are deleted and superseded by new TMA Sch 1B (inserted by FA 1996 Sch 17—see below);
(b) by deleting (for 1997–98 onwards) references in TMA 1970 a 42(7)(a) to claims by a trading partnership in respect of copyright and design royalties (see the comments on sub-s (6) below).

FARMING AND MARKET GARDENING
TA 1988 s 96 provides that a claim may be made to average over two consecutive years the profits of farming or market gardening assessable to income tax where the profits of the two years show a substantial fluctuation. Such a claim must be made within 12 months from the 31 January following the end of the second year of assessment concerned and may be revoked within the same time limit. Where such a claim is made, any claim for relief under any other provision of the Taxes Acts for either of the two years concerned may be made within the same time limit (and, if already made, may be revoked or amended within that time limit). Subsection (3) inserts new TA 1988 s 96(9) which provides that where the claim for other relief is made in a return, the amendment or revocation of that claim must be made by amending the return.

POST-CESSATION RECEIPT
Subsection (4) amends TA 1988 s 108 by providing that a claim to carry back a post-cessation receipt to the date of discontinuance is to be made to a Revenue officer within one year of the 31 January following the end of the year of assessment in which the payment was received (instead of two years from the end of that year).

COPYRIGHT AND DESIGN PAYMENTS
TA 1988 s 534 provides that a claim may be made to spread back copyright payments (in respect of literary, dramatic, musical or artistic work) where the author spent more than 12 months on the making of the work. Subsection (5) inserts new TA 1988 s 534(5), (5A) which provides—

(a) that a claim to spread back periodic payments on account of royalties must include all qualifying payments in respect of the same work received before or after the claim, and that where such payments are received in more than one year of assessment, a separate claim is needed for each of those years;
(b) that the time limit for a claim under (a) above is the 31 January following the end of the latest year in which a qualifying payment is receivable; and
(c) that the time limit for any other claim to spread back payments for copyright is the 31 January following the end of the year in which the payment is receivable.

Subsection (6) inserts new TA 1988 s 534(6) which provides that, where a trade, profession or business is carried on in partnership, no claim may be made to spread back or forward payments for copyright, lending rights or assignment of rights in a design. This denial of relief does not apply to corporation tax or to a payment or sum receivable before 6 April 1996.

TA 1988 s 535 provides for a claim to be made to spread forward a receipt from the sale or assignment of a copyright which takes place at least ten years after first publication of the work and the assignment is for at least two years. Where the author dies, any instalments deemed to arise on a date after the date of death are treated as receivable on the date of the last deemed instalment before death. Alternatively, the personal representatives could claim to spread the payment evenly over the period to the date of death; that alternative is withdrawn by sub-s (7) for 1996–97 onwards. Similarly, the right of the author on a cessation of his profession to claim to spread the payment evenly over the period to the date of cessation is also withdrawn.

Subsection (8) inserts new TA 1988 s 535(8A) which provides a time limit for making a claim to spread forward a receipt on sale or assignment of a copyright. The claim must be made within one

year from the 31 January following the end of the year of assessment in which the payment would
have been assessed but for the claim.

Subsection (9) inserts new TA 1988 s 537A(5), (5A), (5B) which repeat the provisions introduced
by sub-ss (5) and (8) (copyright payments—see above) for the purpose of claims to spread back
payments for the assignment of design rights.

TA 1988 s 538 provides for claims to spread back a receipt for the sale of a painting, sculpture
or other work of art. Subsection (10) inserts new TA 1988 s 538(4) which provides a time limit for
making a claim to spread backward such a receipt. The claim must be made within one year from
31 January following the end of the year of assessment in which the payment would have been
assessed but for the claim.

COMMENCEMENT
    The provisions apply to claims made (or deemed to be made) for 1996–97 and subsequent years,
except that for sub-s (1)(*b*) applies only for 1997–98 and subsequent years (sub-ss (11), (12)).

129   Claims for medical insurance and vocational training relief

(1) Nothing in section 42 of the Taxes Management Act 1970 (procedure for
making claims etc), or Schedule 1A to that Act (claims etc not included in
returns), shall apply in relation to—

   (*a*) any claim under subsection (6)(*b*) of section 54 (medical insurance relief)
   of the Finance Act 1989 ("the 1989 Act"); or

   (*b*) any claim under subsection (5)(*b*) of section 32 (vocational training
   relief) of the Finance Act 1991 ("the 1991 Act").

(2) In section 54(6)(*b*) of the 1989 Act and section 32(5)(*b*) of the 1991 Act,
after the words "on making a claim" there shall be inserted the words "in
accordance with regulations".

(3) In section 57(1) of the 1989 Act (medical insurance relief: supplementary),
after paragraph (*a*) there shall be inserted the following paragraph—

   "(*aa*) make provision for and with respect to appeals against a decision of
   an officer of the Board or the Board with respect to a claim under section
   54(6)(*b*) above;".

(4) In section 33(1) of the 1991 Act (vocational training relief: supplementary),
after paragraph (*a*) there shall be inserted the following paragraph—

   "(*aa*) make provision for and with respect to appeals against a decision of
   an officer of the Board or the Board with respect to a claim under section
   32(5)(*b*) above;".

(5) Subsection (1)(*a*) above shall not apply in relation to claims made before
the coming into force of regulations made by virtue of section 57(1)(*aa*) of the
1989 Act.

(6) Subsection (1)(*b*) above shall not apply in relation to claims made before
the coming into force of regulations made by virtue of section 33(1)(*aa*) of the
1991 Act.

GENERAL NOTE
    FA 1989 s 54 and FA 1991 s 32 provide respectively for relief in respect of medical insurance
and vocational training. In both cases the relief is governed by regulations made by the Revenue.
This section provides that and the regulations may make provision for appeals against a decision
by the Revenue or one of its officers on such a claim. Once such regulations are in force, the
making of a claim will not be governed by TMA 1970 s 42 but by the regulations themselves.

130   Procedure for giving notices

(1) Section 42 of, and Schedule 1A to, the Taxes Management Act 1970, as
they have effect—

   (*a*) for the purposes of income tax and capital gains tax, as respects the year
   1996–97 and subsequent years of assessment, and

(*b*) for the purposes of corporation tax, as respects accounting periods ending on or after the day appointed under section 199 of the Finance Act 1994 for the purposes of Chapter III of Part IV of that Act (self-assessment management provisions),

shall be amended in accordance with the following provisions of this section.

(2) In subsection (7) of section 42 (which contains a list of provisions, claims under which must be made in accordance with subsection (6)) the following words shall cease to have effect, that is to say—

(*a*) in paragraph (*a*), "62A," and "401,"; and
(*b*) in paragraph (*c*), "30,", "33,", "48, 49," and "124A,".

(3) In subsection (10) of that section (section 42 to apply in relation to elections and notices as it applies in relation to claims) the words "and notices" shall cease to have effect.

(4) In subsection (11) of that section (Schedule 1A to apply as respects any claim, election or notice made otherwise than in a return under section 8 etc) for the words ", election or notice" there shall be substituted "or election".

(5) In paragraph 1 of Schedule 1A (claims etc not included in returns), in the definition of "claim", for the words "means a claim, election or notice" there shall be substituted "means a claim or election".

GENERAL NOTE
TMA 1970 s 42 and Sch 1A provide the machinery for making claims under the Taxes Acts, and also for making elections and giving notices. Subsections (3), (4) and (5) provide that from the introduction of self-assessment those provisions no longer apply to the giving of notices.
TMA 1970 s 42(6) and (7) provide how claims, in respect of reliefs listed, are to be made where a trade, profession or business is carried on in partnership. Subsection (2) provides that claims by a partnership in respect of the following are not to be included in a partnership return—
TA 1988 s 62A (change of accounting date);
TA 1988 s 401 (relief for pre-trading expenditure);
CAA 1990 s 30 (first-year allowance for ships);
CAA 1990 s 33 (election to forego writing-down allowances in a single ship trade);
CAA 1990 ss 48, 49 (first-year allowances for certain expenditure on leased plant); and
CAA 1990 s 124A (initial allowance on certain expenditure on agricultural buildings).

131   Interest on overdue tax

(1) Section 110 of the Finance Act 1995 (interest on overdue tax) shall be deemed to have been enacted with the insertion after subsection (3) of the following subsection—

"(4) So far as it relates to partnerships whose trades, professions or businesses were set up and commenced before 6th April 1994, subsection (1) above has effect as respects the year 1997–98 and subsequent years of assessment."

(2) In subsection (3) of section 86 of the Taxes Management Act 1970 (which was substituted by the said section 110), for the words "section 93" there shall be substituted the words "section 92".

(3) In Schedule 19 to the Finance Act 1994, paragraph 23 (which is superseded by the said section 110) shall cease to have effect.

GENERAL NOTE
FA 1995 s 110 substituted new TMA 1970 s 86 revising the provisions for interest on overdue income tax and CGT under the self-assessment scheme. Subsection (1) provides that the new provisions apply to partnerships whose trades, professions or businesses commenced before 6 April 1994 only for 1997–98 onwards.
Subsection (2) corrects a misprint in TMA 1970 s 86(3).
Subsection (3) repeals FA 1994 Sch 19 para 23 which is superseded by FA 1995 s 110.

132 Overdue tax and excessive payments by the Board

Schedule 18 to this Act (which amends enactments relating to overdue tax or excessive payments by the Board) shall have effect.

GENERAL NOTE
This section introduces Sch 18.

133 Claims and enquiries

Schedule 19 to this Act (which, for purposes connected with self-assessment, further amends provisions relating to claims and enquiries) shall have effect.

GENERAL NOTE
This section introduces Sch 19.

134 Discretions exercisable by the Board etc

(1) Schedule 20 to this Act (which in connection with self-assessment modifies enactments by virtue of which a decision or other action affecting an assessment may be or is required to be taken by the Board, or one of their officers, before the making of the assessment) shall have effect.

(2) Subject to subsection (3) below, the amendments made by that Schedule shall have effect—

(a) for the purposes of income tax and capital gains tax, as respects the year 1996–97 and subsequent years of assessment; and
(b) for the purposes of corporation tax, as respects accounting periods ending on or after the day appointed under section 199 of the Finance Act 1994 for the purposes of Chapter III of Part IV of that Act (self-assessment management provisions).

(3) Paragraphs 22 and 23 of that Schedule shall have effect in relation to shares issued on or after 6th April 1996.

GENERAL NOTE
This section introduces Sch 20 and specifies from which time the provisions of that Schedule take effect.

135 Time limits for claims etc

(1) Schedule 21 to this Act (which in connection with self-assessment modifies enactments which impose time limits on the making of claims, elections, adjustments and assessments and the giving of notices, and enactments which provide for the giving of notice to the inspector) shall have effect.

(2) Subject to subsections (3) to (5) below, the amendments made by that Schedule shall have effect—

(a) for the purposes of income tax and capital gains tax, as respects the year 1996–97 and subsequent years of assessment; and
(b) for the purposes of corporation tax, as respects accounting periods ending on or after the day appointed under section 199 of the Finance Act 1994 for the purposes of Chapter III of Part IV of that Act (self-assessment management provisions).

(3) The amendments made to the Capital Allowances Act 1990 and the Finance Act 1994 by that Schedule, in their application to trades, professions or vocations set up and commenced before 6th April 1994, shall (so far as relating to income tax) have effect as respects the year 1997–98 and subsequent years of assessment.

(4) The Capital Allowances Act 1990, as it has effect for the year 1996–97 in

relation to trades, professions or vocations set up and commenced before 6th April 1994, shall (so far as relating to income tax) have effect as respects that year with the following modifications, that is to say, as if—

(*a*) in sections 25(3)(*c*), 30(1), 31(3) and 33(1) and (4), for "two years after the end of" there were substituted "the first anniversary of the 31st January next following";

(*b*) in section 37(2)(*c*), for "more than two years after the end of the chargeable period or its basis period" there were substituted "later than the first anniversary of the 31st January next following the year of assessment in which ends the basis period";

(*c*) in section 53(2), for "before the expiry of the period of two years beginning at the end of" there were substituted "on or before the first anniversary of the 31st January next following";

(*d*) in section 68(5), for "two years after the end of that period" there were substituted "the first anniversary of the 31st January next following the year of assessment in which the relevant period ends";

(*e*) in section 68(9A)(*b*), for "two years after the end of" there were substituted "the first anniversary of the 31st January next following the year of assessment in which ends";

(*f*) in section 129(2), for "not more than two years after the end of" there were substituted "on or before the first anniversary of the 31st January next following";

(*g*) in section 141(3), for "the inspector not later than two years after the end of" there were substituted "an officer of the Board on or before the first anniversary of the 31st January next following".

(5) Section 118 of the Finance Act 1994, as it has effect for the year 1996–97 in relation to trades, professions or vocations set up and commenced before 6th April 1994, shall (so far as relating to income tax) have effect as respects that year as if, in subsection (3), for "two years after the end of" there were substituted "the first anniversary of the 31st January next following".

GENERAL NOTE
  This section introduces Sch 21 and specifies from which times the provisions of that Schedule take effect.
  Subsection (2) provides that (with the exceptions in sub-ss (3) and (4)) the new time limits set in Sch 21 apply—

(*a*) as regards income tax and CGT, for 1996–97 onwards; and
(*b*) as regards corporation tax, for accounting periods ending on or after the date appointed for the introduction of self-assessment.

  Subsection (3) provides that amendments in Sch 21 to CAA 1990 and FA 1994, so far as they relate to trades etc which commenced before 6 April 1994, have effect for 1997–98 onwards.
  Subsection (4) provides that in specified sections of CAA 1990 references to time limits of two years after the end of a year of assessment are replaced (for 1996–97 onwards) by references to the first anniversary of the 31 January following the end of the year of assessment.
  Subsection (5) makes a similar amendment to FA 1994 s 118 so far as it relates to trades etc which commenced before 6 April 1994.

136 Appeals
Schedule 22 to this Act (which makes provision, in connection with self-assessment, about appeals) shall have effect.

GENERAL NOTE
  This section introduces Sch 22.

Companies

137 Schedules 13 and 16 to the Taxes Act 1988

(1) Schedule 23 to this Act shall have effect.

(2) The amendments made by that Schedule shall have effect as respects return periods ending on or after the appointed day for the purposes of Chapter III of Part IV of the Finance Act 1994.

(3) In subsection (2) above "return period" means—

(*a*) so far as relating to Schedule 13 to the Taxes Act 1988, a period for which a return is required to be made under paragraph 1 of that Schedule; and

(*b*) so far as relating to Schedule 16 to that Act, a period for which a return is required to be made under paragraph 2 of that Schedule.

GENERAL NOTE
   This section introduces Sch 23 which amends TA 1988 Sch 13 (collection of advance corporation tax) and TA 1988 Sch 16 (collection of income tax on company payments other than distributions). Schedule 23 has effect for return periods ending on or after the introduction of self-assessment for companies. A return period is an accounting period for which a company is required to make a return under TA 1988 Sch 13 or Sch 16 as the case may be.

138 Accounting periods

Schedule 24 to this Act (which makes provision, in connection with self-assessment, in relation to accounting periods) shall have effect.

GENERAL NOTE
   This section introduces Sch 24.

139 Surrenders of advance corporation tax

Schedule 25 to this Act (which makes provision, in connection with self-assessment, about surrenders of advance corporation tax) shall have effect.

GENERAL NOTE
   This section introduces Sch 25.

Chargeable gains

140 Transfer of company's assets to investment trust

(1) In section 101 of the Taxation of Chargeable Gains Act 1992 (transfer of company's assets to investment trust) after subsection (1) there shall be inserted—

"(1A) Any chargeable gain or allowable loss which, apart from this subsection, would accrue to the company on the sale referred to in subsection (1) above shall be treated as accruing to the company immediately before the end of the last accounting period to end before the beginning of the accounting period mentioned in that subsection."

(2) This section shall have effect as respects accounting periods ending on or after the day appointed under section 199 of the Finance Act 1994 for the purposes of Chapter III of Part IV of that Act (self-assessment management provisions).

GENERAL NOTE
   This section amends the rule which applies where the transferee company in a scheme of reconstruction or amalgamation subsequently becomes an investment trust. The rule is contained in TCGA 1992 s 101 and it is necessary because the scheme is treated as a no gain/no loss disposal (TCGA 1992 s 139) and gains accruing to investment trusts are not taxable (TCGA 1992 s 100). The effect of the rule is to impose a deemed disposal on all assets which were comprised in the scheme and are retained by the company at the time it becomes an investment trust.

At present the deemed disposal is deemed to occur immediately after the scheme was effected, and assessments are reopened as necessary. This clause brings the deemed disposal forward to the end of the accounting period immediately preceding the period in which the company becomes an investment trust. It will apply as respects accounting periods ending on or after the self-assessment appointed day (sub-s (2)). Its purpose is to avoid the reopening of assessments and to enable the rule in s 101 to fit better into self-assessment.

141   Roll-over relief

(1) In subsection (4) of section 152 of the Taxation of Chargeable Gains Act 1992 (roll-over relief)—

(*a*) after the word "making" there shall be inserted the words "or amending"; and

(*b*) after the word "assessments", in the second place where it occurs, there shall be inserted the words "or amendments".

(2) After section 153 of that Act there shall be inserted the following section—

"153A   Provisional application of sections 152 and 153

(1) This section applies where a person carrying on a trade who for a consideration disposes of, or of his interest in, any assets ('the old assets') declares, in his return for the chargeable period in which the disposal takes place—

(*a*) that the whole or any specified part of the consideration will be applied in the acquisition of, or of an interest in, other assets ('the new assets') which on the acquisition will be taken into use, and used only, for the purposes of the trade;

(*b*) that the acquisition will take place as mentioned in subsection (3) of section 152; and

(*c*) that the new assets will be within the classes listed in section 155.

(2) Until the declaration ceases to have effect, section 152 or, as the case may be, section 153 shall apply as if the acquisition had taken place and the person had made a claim under that section.

(3) The declaration shall cease to have effect as follows—

(*a*) if and to the extent that it is withdrawn before the relevant day, or is superseded before that day by a valid claim made under section 152 or 153, on the day on which it is so withdrawn or superseded; and

(*b*) if and to the extent that it is not so withdrawn or superseded, on the relevant day.

(4) On the declaration ceasing to have effect in whole or in part, all necessary adjustments—

(*a*) shall be made by making or amending assessments or by repayment or discharge of tax; and

(*b*) shall be so made notwithstanding any limitation on the time within which assessments or amendments may be made.

(5) In this section 'the relevant day' means—

(*a*) in relation to capital gains tax, the third anniversary of the 31st January next following the year of assessment in which the disposal of, or of the interest in, the old assets took place;

(*b*) in relation to corporation tax, the fourth anniversary of the last day of the accounting period in which that disposal took place.

(6) Subsections (6), (8), (10) and (11) of section 152 shall apply for the purposes of this section as they apply for the purposes of that section."

(3) In section 175 of that Act (replacement of business assets by members of a group)—

(*a*) in subsections (2A) and (2B), after the words "Section 152" there shall be inserted the words "or 153"; and
(*b*) in subsection (2C), for the words "Section 152 shall not" there shall be substituted the words "Neither section 152 nor section 153 shall".

(4) In section 246 of that Act (time of disposal or acquisition), the words from "or, if earlier" to the end shall cease to have effect.

(5) In subsection (5)(*b*) of section 247 of that Act (roll-over relief on compulsory acquisition), for the words "subsection (3)" there shall be substituted the words "subsections (3) and (4)".

(6) After that section there shall be inserted the following section—

"247A   Provisional application of section 247

(1) This section applies where a person who disposes of land ('the old land') to an authority exercising or having compulsory powers declares, in his return for the chargeable period in which the disposal takes place—

(*a*) that the whole or any specified part of the consideration for the disposal will be applied in the acquisition of other land ('the new land');
(*b*) that the acquisition will take place as mentioned in subsection (3) of section 152; and
(*c*) that the new land will not be land excluded from section 247(1)(*c*) by section 248.

(2) Until the declaration ceases to have effect, section 247 shall apply as if the acquisition had taken place and the person had made a claim under that section.

(3) For the purposes of this section, subsections (3) to (5) of section 153A shall apply as if the reference to section 152 or 153 were a reference to section 247 and the reference to the old assets were a reference to the old land.

(4) In this section 'land' and 'authority exercising or having compulsory powers' have the same meaning as in section 247."

GENERAL NOTE
This section amends the roll-over reliefs which are available on the replacement of business assets (TCGA 1992 ss 152–158 and 175) and on the compulsory acquisition of land (TCGA 1992 s 247). It has effect in relation to individuals and trustees from 1996–97 onwards, and in relation to companies as respects accounting periods ending on or after the appointed day for self-assessment purposes (s 121(8)). The main purpose of this clause is to allow roll-over claims on a provisional basis under self-assessment.

REPLACEMENT OF BUSINESS ASSETS
Section 141(2) introduces a new s 153A into the code for business assets. The new section allows a person carrying on a trade to declare in his return that the consideration for the disposal of old assets will be applied in acquiring new assets eligible for roll-over relief. The effect of such a declaration is that roll-over relief is treated as applying until the declaration ceases to have effect.
Under s 153A(3) the declaration ceases to have effect in one of three ways—

(*a*) if it is withdrawn;
(*b*) if it is superseded by a claim to roll-over relief arising out of an actual acquisition;
(*c*) on what is called the relevant day. This is defined in s 153A(5) as the third anniversary of 31 January next following the year of assessment in which the disposal took place or (in the case of companies) the fourth anniversary of the end of the accounting period in which the disposal took place.

When the declaration ceases to have effect, appropriate amendments to tax assessments are made and relevant time limits are lifted (s 153A(4)). Where, of course, the declaration has ceased to have effect by reason of an actual acquisition, an amendment to the assessment will only be required insofar as the amount expended on the actual acquisition is less than the amount claimed in the declaration.

It is intriguing that while s 153A(1) refers to the new assets in terms which echo the requirements for relief as laid down in s 152(1), it does not do so in relation to the old assets. It would seem therefore that a claim under s 153A could be made on the disposal of any asset used in the business, rather than merely one which is within the classes listed in TCGA 1992 s 155. Whether, however, there would be any advantage in this may be doubted, given that tax and interest would be payable when the declaration ceased to have effect.

Section 153A is expressed in terms of persons carrying on a trade. However, the existing TCGA 1992 s 158 extends it to professions and vocations and the various other activities there listed. Section 153A(2) specifically allows a declaration to extend to part only of the consideration from the old assets, in which case the rules as to partially replaced assets in s 153 will apply.

COMPULSORY ACQUISITION

Section 142(6) inserts a new s 247A into the code dealing with compulsory acquisitions. This makes similar provision to s 153A in relation to disposals to authorities having or possessing compulsory powers. As with s 153A, the old land is not defined in the same terms as in s 247 and so, for example, a claim under s 247A would seem to be competent even where the landowner has advertised.

OTHER AMENDMENTS

The remaining subsections of s 141 effect various minor amendments, and only sub-s (1) is concerned with self-assessment. It amends s 152(4), the subsection which allows roll-over relief to be applied on a provisional basis before completion where a contract for the acquisition of the new assets is entered into. It allows self-assessments to be amended when it is known whether or not the new assets have in fact been acquired in pursuance of the contract.

Subsection (3) amends last year's changes to TCGA 1992 s 175, the section dealing with roll-over relief and groups. It extends three rules to partial replacements under TCGA 1992 s 153. The rules concerned are the rule that all group trades are treated as one, the rule that a property-holding group member is treated as trading, and the prevention of relief for inter group acquisitions.

Subsection (5) makes a minor change to TCGA 1992 s 247. It extends to the roll-over relief on compulsory acquisitions the rule in s 152(4) (referred to above) allowing relief on a provisional basis once the contract for the acquisition of the new assets is entered into.

142   Premiums for leases

(1) Paragraph 3 of Schedule 8 to the Taxation of Chargeable Gains Act 1992 (premiums for leases) shall be amended as follows.

(2) In sub-paragraph (2), for the words "for the period" to the end there shall be substituted the words ", being a premium which—

(*a*) is due when the sum is payable by the tenant; and
(*b*) where the sum is payable in lieu of rent, is in respect of the period in relation to which the sum is payable."

(3) In sub-paragraph (3), for the words "for the period" to the end there shall be substituted the words ", being a premium which—

(*a*) is due when the sum is payable by the tenant; and
(*b*) is in respect of the period from the time when the variation or waiver takes effect to the time when it ceases to have effect."

(4) For sub-paragraphs (4) to (6) there shall be substituted the following sub-paragraphs—

"(4) Where under sub-paragraph (2) or (3) above a premium is deemed to have been received by the landlord, that shall not be the occasion of any recomputation of the gain accruing on the receipt of any other premium, and the premium shall be regarded—

(*a*) in the case of a premium deemed to have been received for the surrender of a lease, as consideration for a separate transaction which is effected when the premium is deemed to be due and consists of the disposal by the landlord of his interest in the lease; and

(b) in any other case, as consideration for a separate transaction which is effected when the premium is deemed to be due and consists of a further part disposal of the freehold or other asset out of which the lease is granted.

(5) If under sub-paragraph (2) or (3) above a premium is deemed to have been received by the landlord, otherwise than as consideration for the surrender of the lease, and the landlord is a tenant under a lease the duration of which does not exceed 50 years, this Schedule shall apply—

(a) as if an amount equal to the amount of that premium deemed to have been received had been given by way of consideration for the grant of the part of the sublease covered by the period in respect of which the premium is deemed to have been paid; and

(b) as if that consideration were expenditure incurred by the sublessee and attributable to that part of the sublease under section 38(1)(b).''

(5) This section has effect as respects sums payable on or after 6th April 1996.

GENERAL NOTE

This section amends the CGT lease premium rules in TCGA 1992 Sch 8. It focuses on two kinds of capital sum paid by the tenant to the landlord. The first is sums paid by the tenant to secure the variation or waiver of any of the terms of the lease. The second is sums payable under the terms of the lease to secure a surrender or the commutation of the rent. It applies as respect sums payable on or after 6 April 1996 (sub-s (5)). Its purpose is to avoid the need for adjustment to self-assessments.

Hitherto a sum paid by the tenant under the terms of the lease to secure the surrender of the lease has been treated as a disposal by the landlord at the time of the surrender of his rights under the lease (TCGA 1992 Sch 8 para 3(6)). Other sums to which this section applies have, with one exception, been treated as a premium paid on the grant of the lease and any gain accruing on the grant has had to be recomputed (Sch 8 para 3(4)). The one exception arose where the landlord was himself lessee under a lease whose duration was 50 years or less. Here the sum in question was treated as paid for a separate disposal, consisting of the "grant" of the part of the sub-lease to which the sum related (Sch 8 para 3(5)).

This section has changed the above rules as follows—

(a) Sums paid by the tenant under terms of the lease to secure a surrender will, as now, be treated as a disposal taking place when the surrender occurs. The property disposed of will continue to be the landlord's interest in the lease (Sch 8 para 3(4)(a), inserted by sub-s (4)).

(b) Other sums to which this section applies are now treated as due when payable, and paid in respect of the period of the lease which they cover (sub-ss (2) and (3)). The landlord is at that time treated as making a new part disposal of the freehold or other asset out of which the lease is created (Sch 8 para 3(4)(b) as inserted by sub-s (4)).

(c) As hitherto an exception is made where the landlord is himself tenant under a lease whose duration does not exceed 50 years. Here the sum continues to be treated as paid for a separate disposal consisting of the grant of the part of the sub-lease to which the sum relates. This is provided for by a new Sch 8 para 3(5), inserted with the same wording as the previous sub-para by sub-s (4).

CHAPTER VI

MISCELLANEOUS PROVISIONS

Reliefs

143 Annual payments under certain insurance policies

(1) After section 580 of the Taxes Act 1988 there shall be inserted the following sections—

"580A Relief from tax on annual payments under certain insurance policies

(1) This section applies (subject to subsection (7)(*b*) below) in the case of any such annual payment under an insurance policy as—

(*a*) apart from this section, would be brought into charge under Case III of Schedule D; or
(*b*) is equivalent to a description of payment brought into charge under Case III of that Schedule but (apart from this section) would be brought into charge under Case V of that Schedule.

(2) Subject to the following provisions of this section, the annual payment shall be exempt from income tax if—

(*a*) it constitutes a benefit provided under so much of an insurance policy as provides insurance against a qualifying risk;
(*b*) the provisions of the policy by which insurance is provided against that risk are self-contained (within the meaning of section 580B);
(*c*) the only annual payments relating to that risk for which provision is made by that policy are payments in respect of a period throughout which the relevant conditions of payment are satisfied; and
(*d*) at all times while the policy has contained provisions relating to that risk, those provisions have been of a qualifying type.

(3) For the purposes of this section and section 580B a qualifying risk is any risk falling within either of the following descriptions, that is to say—

(*a*) a risk that the insured will (or will in any specified way) become subject to, or to any deterioration in a condition resulting from, any physical or mental illness, disability, infirmity or defect;
(*b*) a risk that circumstances will arise as a result of which the insured will cease to be employed or will cease to carry on any trade, profession or vocation carried on by him.

(4) For the purposes of this section the relevant conditions of payment are satisfied in relation to payments under an insurance policy for so long as any of the following continues, that is to say—

(*a*) an illness, disability, infirmity or defect which is insured against by the relevant part of the policy, and any related period of convalescence or rehabilitation;
(*b*) any period during which the insured is, in circumstances insured against by the relevant part of the policy, either unemployed or not carrying on a trade, profession or vocation;
(*c*) any period during which the income of the insured (apart from any benefits under the policy) is less, in circumstances so insured against, than it would have been if those circumstances had not arisen; or

143

(*d*) any period immediately following the end, as a result of the death of the insured, of any period falling within any of paragraphs (*a*) to (*c*) above;

and in this subsection 'the relevant part of the policy' means so much of it as relates to insurance against one or more risks mentioned in subsection (3) above.

(5) For the purposes of subsection (2)(*d*) above provisions relating to a qualifying risk are of a qualifying type if they are of such a description that their inclusion in any policy of insurance containing provisions relating only to a comparable risk would (apart from any reinsurance) involve the possibility for the insurer that a significant loss might be sustained on the amounts payable by way of premiums in respect of the risk, taken together with any return on the investment of those amounts.

(6) An annual payment shall not be exempt from income tax under this section if it is paid in accordance with a contract the whole or any part of any premiums under which have qualified for relief for the purposes of income tax by being deductible either—

(*a*) in the computation of the insured's income from any source; or
(*b*) from the insured's income.

(7) Where a person takes out any insurance policy wholly or partly for the benefit of another and that other person pays or contributes to the payment of the premiums under that policy, then to the extent only that the benefits under the policy are attributable, on a just and reasonable apportionment, to the payments or contributions made by that other person—

(*a*) that other person shall be treated for the purposes of this section and section 580B as the insured in relation to that policy;
(*b*) this section shall have effect in relation to those benefits, so far as comprised in payments to that other person or his spouse, as if the reference in subsection (1)(*a*) above to Case III of Schedule D included a reference to Schedule E; and
(*c*) subsection (6) above shall have effect as if the references to the premiums under the policy were references only to the payments or contributions made by that other person in respect of the premiums.

(8) Where—

(*a*) payments are made to or in respect of any person ('the beneficiary') under any insurance policy ('the individual policy'),
(*b*) the rights under the individual policy in accordance with which the payments are made superseded, with effect from the time when another policy ('the employer's policy') ceased to apply to that person, any rights conferred under that other policy,
(*c*) the employer's policy is or was a policy entered into wholly or partly for the benefit of persons holding office or employment under any person ('the employer') against risks falling within subsection (3)(*a*) above,
(*d*) the individual policy is one entered into in pursuance of, or in accordance with, any provisions contained in the employer's policy, and
(*e*) the beneficiary has ceased to hold office or employment under the employer as a consequence of the occurrence of anything insured against by so much of the employer's policy as related to risks falling within subsection (3)(*a*) above,

this section shall have effect as if the employer's policy and the individual policy were one policy.

(9) In the preceding provisions of this section references to the insured, in relation to any insurance policy, include references to—

(*a*) the insured's spouse; and

(*b*) in the case of a policy entered into wholly or partly for purposes connected with the meeting of liabilities arising from an actual or proposed transaction identified in the policy, any person on whom any of those liabilities will fall jointly with the insured or his spouse.

(10) References in this section and section 580B to insurance against a risk include references to any insurance for the provision (otherwise than by way of indemnity) of any benefits against that risk, and references to what is insured against by a policy shall be construed accordingly.

580B   Meaning of 'self-contained' for the purposes of s 580A

(1) For the purposes of section 580A the provisions of an insurance policy by which insurance is provided against a qualifying risk are self-contained unless subsection (2) or (3) below applies to the provisions of that policy so far as they relate to that risk; but, in determining whether either of those subsections so applies, regard shall be had to all the persons for whose benefit insurance is provided by that policy against that risk.

(2) This subsection applies to the provisions of an insurance policy so far as they relate to a qualifying risk if—

(*a*) that insurance policy contains provision for the payment of benefits other than those relating to that risk;

(*b*) the terms of the policy so far as they relate to that risk, or the manner in which effect is given to those terms, would have been significantly different if the only benefits under the policy had been those relating to that risk; and

(*c*) that difference is not one relating exclusively to the fact that the amount of benefits receivable by or in respect of any person under the policy is applied for reducing the amount of other benefits payable to or in respect of that person under the policy.

(3) This subsection applies to the provisions of an insurance policy ('the relevant policy') so far as they relate to a qualifying risk if—

(*a*) the insured under that policy is, or has been, the insured under one or more other policies;

(*b*) that other policy, or each of those other policies, is in force or has been in force at a time when the relevant policy was in force or at the time immediately before the relevant policy was entered into;

(*c*) the terms of the relevant policy so far as relating to that risk, or the manner in which effect is given to those terms, would have been significantly different if the other policy or policies had not been entered into; and

(*d*) that difference is not one relating exclusively to the fact that the amount of benefits receivable by or in respect of any person under the other policy, or any of the other policies, is applied for reducing the amount of benefits payable to or in respect of that person under the relevant policy.

(4) In subsections (2)(*b*) and (3)(*c*) above the references to the terms of a policy so far as they relate to a risk include references to the terms fixing any amount payable by way of premium or otherwise in respect of insurance against that risk.''

145

(2) This section has effect for the year 1996–97 and subsequent years of assessment in relation to—

(*a*) any payment which under the policy in question falls to be paid at any time on or after 6th April 1996; and

(*b*) any payment not falling within paragraph (*a*) above in relation to which the conditions mentioned in subsection (3)(*a*) and (*b*) below are satisfied.

(3) This section shall also be deemed to have had effect for earlier years of assessment in relation to any payment in relation to which the following conditions are satisfied, that is to say—

(*a*) the payment was made under a policy in relation to which the requirements of subsection (4) below were fulfilled; and

(*b*) the policy in question provided for the right to annual payments under the policy to cease when all the liabilities in question were discharged.

(4) The requirements of this subsection are fulfilled in relation to any policy if—

(*a*) the only or main purpose of the insurance under the policy was to secure that the insured would be able to meet (in whole or in part) liabilities that would or might arise from any transaction;

(*b*) the policy expressly identified the transaction or, as the case may be, all the transactions (whether actual or proposed) by reference to which the insurance was taken out; and

(*c*) none of the transactions which would or might give rise to the liabilities mentioned in paragraph (*a*) above could be one entered into after any of the circumstances insured against arose.

(5) In subsection (4) above "transaction" includes any arrangements for the provision of credit or for the supply of services to residential premises.

BACKGROUND NOTE

This measure introduces a wide-ranging exemption from tax for regular payments under insurance policies providing benefits in the event of accident, sickness, disability, infirmity or unemployment. The intention to bring forward legislation exempting regular payments under certain mortgage protection policies was announced on 2 May 1995, followed on 4 May 1995 by the announcement of a wider review covering other analogous insurance benefits. The new exemption extends not only to the mortgage protection policies originally mentioned, but also to permanent health insurance (currently the subject of a partial, concessional, exemption), credit insurance and certain types of long-term care insurance. Benefits received under group policies taken out by employers to cover sick pay will also be exempt insofar as they reflect contributions made by the employee.

SUBSECTION (1): THE EXEMPTION

This subsection inserts in TA 1988 new ss 580A and 580B.

TA 1988 s 580A.

Subsections (1)–(6) set out the scope of the exemption.

Subsection (1) restricts the exemption to annual payments under an insurance policy which would otherwise be within the charge to tax under Case III of Schedule D and to similar payments within Case V of Schedule D. The exemption does not affect the taxation of lump sums which are not annual payments, nor does it apply to sums received other than under an insurance policy. The term "insurance policy" is not defined and must be assumed to bear its ordinary meeting of a document which is evidence of a contract of insurance. The inclusion of payments chargeable under Case V ensures that the exemption is available in respect of amounts received under policies issued outside the UK by a non-resident insurer, for example where an EC insurer does business with UK residents on a services basis, or where the beneficiary has been working overseas but returns to the UK following the event giving rise to the payment of benefits.

As the benefits in question are removed from the charge to tax there is no requirement to deduct tax from them (TA 1988 s 394 no longer applies).

Subsections (2)–(5) set out a number of conditions all of which have to be met for the exemption to apply. These are—

(*a*) the insurance must be partly or wholly against a "qualifying risk", which is defined, by sub-s (3), as either a risk that the insured will be affected by the onset or deterioration of a condition resulting from illness, infirmity or disability, or the risk of unemployment (including the cessation of self-employment);

(*b*) the terms of the policy providing cover against the risk in question must be "self-contained", as defined in new s 580B;

(*c*) the policy must only provide benefits for a period throughout which one of a number of "conditions of payment" are satisfied; these conditions, which are set out in sub-s (4), are—

(i) the insured continues to suffer from the illness etc insured against (including convalescence or rehabilitation);

(ii) the insured is out of work in the circumstances covered by the policy;

(iii) the insured's income (excluding the policy benefits) is reduced on account of the circumstances insured against;

(iv) the period immediately following the death of the insured in a period within (i)–(iii) (this allows the exemption to continue in respect of benefits paid to a surviving spouse or dependant);

(*d*) the terms of the policy covering the risk in question must at all times have been of a "qualifying type", as defined in sub-s (5), that is, they must expose the insurer to the risk of a significant underwriting loss in relation to the aggregate of the premiums charged and the investment return therefrom; for this purpose the transfer of risk by way of reinsurance is ignored, and the test is to be applied to the individual policy so that, implicitly, the elimination of risk to the insurer by the aggregation of a sufficient number of similar contingent risks is also disregarded; this last condition denies the exemption to what might in essence be savings type policies (see Official Report, Standing Committee E, 22 February 1996, col 452).

The various conditions set out in the legislation relate for the most part to the contingency triggering the payment rather than the financial loss which the policy benefits are intended to alleviate. It appears that the exemption will be available in, and indeed is intended to cover, a wide variety of cases such as mortgage payment protection, permanent health insurance, some types of credit insurance and certain forms of long-term care insurance (see Revenue Budget Press Release REV 6, 28 November 1995, "Tax exemption for sickness or unemployment insurance payments"). The exemption does not extend to annuities purchased to fund residential nursing care, except where some form of disability is the condition of and occasion of payment, or to annuities purchased as part of the structured settlement of damages for personal injury. Payments under the latter are separately exempted by TA 1988 ss 329AA and 329AB (inserted by s 150 of FA 1996 and replacing TA 1988 s 329A).

Subsection (6) denies the exemption where the premiums under the policy have been relieved either as a deduction in computing the insured's income or as a relief against that income, thus preventing effective double relief.

Subsections (7)–(9) extend the relief in certain circumstances to payments under policies taken out in favour of other persons than the insured and to payments made to the insured's spouse, but not to payments made under policies taken out in respect of a child of the insured (see Official Report, Standing Committee E, 22 February 1996, col 448).

Subsection (7) extends the exemption to the part of the benefits attributable to contributions by the beneficiary where the policy, which would otherwise be within the scope of the exemption, is taken out by a person other than the beneficiary. The exemption applies to payments to a spouse of the beneficiary, and to payments which would otherwise be within Schedule E (because they are related to an office or employment).

Where an employee ceases to be employed as a result of illness, disability etc, sub-s (8) extends the exemption to payments under a policy which replaces cover previously afforded against the same risks by a policy taken out by the employer (this situation could arise where responsibility for employees losing their job on health grounds is assumed by pension fund trustees).

Subsection (9) extends the exemption to benefits paid to an insured's spouse or, where the policy covers liabilities arising from a specific transaction, benefits paid to any person jointly liable with the insured or the insured's spouse. This extension is likely to be in point in the case of certain credit insurance policies.

Finally, sub-s (10) makes clear that benefits paid in connection with a specified risk are within the scope of the exemption even if they do not indemnify the insured against a measured financial loss. Policies covering accident and sickness benefits commonly provide specified benefits in respect of particular conditions or injuries. The benefits may exceed, or fall short of, pure indemnity, or the actual financial loss may be difficult or impossible to quantify. Such policies are not strictly policies of indemnity, but are said to be in respect of "valued losses", that is, losses on which a value has been placed for the purposes of the insurance.

TA 1988 s 580B.

This section provides the meaning of "self-contained" needed to interpret the condition in s 580A(2)(*a*). It does so by setting out the types of policy which are not "self-contained" for the purposes of the previous section. Subsection (1) makes it clear that in the case of a group policy its eligibility must be determined by reference to the risks covered in respect of all the persons who may benefit under the policy.

Subsection (2) excludes from the category of "self-contained" policies any policy which provides benefits other than those relating to the qualifying risk (defined in s 580A(3)); or whose terms as regards the qualifying risk would have been significantly different if it had been confined to the qualifying risk; and the difference is not related to the operation of an overall limit on the benefits payable under different heads to the person concerned. This provision appears to be intended to prevent the exemption being obtained in respect of savings related benefits paid under a hybrid policy, where the sickness or disability trigger is in some way artificial.

Subsection (3) similarly excludes from exemption benefits paid under a policy where the terms are significantly affected by the simultaneous existence of another policy in favour of the same insured, otherwise than by the operation of an overall limit on benefits paid under the policies in question.

Subsection (4) makes it clear that in this section the terms of an insurance policy include the amount of the premiums as well as the amount or level of benefits provided under the policy.

SUBSECTIONS (2)–(5): COMMENCEMENT AND TRANSITION
Under sub-s (2) the exemption applies to payments made at any time on or after 6 April 1996, whenever the policy was issued and whether or not benefits are already in payment on that date, and also retrospectively to certain payments made before that date provided the policy meets all of the following conditions, which are set out in sub-ss (3) and (4)—

(*a*) the policy provided for annual payments to cease once the liabilities covered by the policy were discharged;
(*b*) the only or main purpose of the policy was to secure payment of liabilities under transaction(s) specified in the policy;
(*c*) the transaction(s) in question could not be entered into after the occurrence of the event or condition triggering payment.

The intention of this provision is to provide retrospective exemption for payments to meet existing commitments, for example mortgage repayments. Subsection (5) makes it clear that the term transaction includes arrangements for the provision of credit or the supply of services to the insured's home.

144   Vocational training

(1) Section 32 of the Finance Act 1991 (vocational training relief) shall be amended in accordance with the following provisions of this section.

(2) In subsection (1) (application of section) for paragraph (*ca*) (individual has attained school leaving age etc at time of paying for the course) there shall be substituted—

"(*ca*) at the time the payment is made, the individual—

(i) in a case where the qualifying course of vocational training is such a course by virtue only of paragraph (*b*) of subsection (10) below, has attained the age of thirty, or
(ii) in any other case, has attained school-leaving age and, if under the age of nineteen, is not a person who is being provided with full-time education at a school,".

(3) For subsection (10) (meaning of "qualifying course of vocational training") there shall be substituted—

"(10) In this section 'qualifying course of vocational training' means—

(*a*) any programme of activity capable of counting towards a qualification—

(i) accredited as a National Vocational Qualification by the National Council for Vocational Qualifications; or
(ii) accredited as a Scottish Vocational Qualification by the Scottish Vocational Education Council; or

(*b*) any course of training which—

(i) satisfies the conditions set out in the paragraphs of section 589(1) of the Taxes Act 1988 (qualifying courses of training etc),

(ii) requires participation on a full-time or substantially full-time basis, and

(iii) extends for a period which consists of or includes four consecutive weeks,

but treating any time devoted to study in connection with the course as time devoted to the practical application of skills or knowledge.''

(4) This section applies to payments made on or after 6th May 1996.

GENERAL NOTE

Under FA 1991 s 32, vocational training relief (VTR) is available for individuals paying for employment-related courses capable of counting towards a National Vocational Qualification (NVQ) or Scottish Vocational Qualification (SVQ). Individuals qualifying for VTR pay fees to the course provider net of basic rate tax, which the course provider can then reclaim from the Revenue.

EXTENSION OF VTR

The range of courses qualifying for VTR is now extended to most full-time courses of between four weeks and one year which are aimed at retraining for gainful employment, whether there is a link with NVQs or SVQs or not, but only for trainees aged 30 and over. It is intended that those undergoing specialised courses, such as MBAs, should benefit in particular. By making the new rules refer back to TA 1988 s 589, the intention is to put those funding their own retraining on an equal footing to those whose retraining is paid for by their employers or former employers, to whom the latter section applies.

Younger trainees remain subject to the existing rules, so their courses will still need to be geared to an NVQ or SVQ.

THE DETAIL

A "qualifying course of vocational training" within the meaning of FA 1991 s 32 is now either—

(*a*) any programme of activity capable of counting towards an NVQ or SVQ (FA 1991 s 32(10)(*a*), as substituted by s 144(3)); or

(*b*) any course of training satisfying the conditions in TA 1988 s 589(1), requiring participation on a full-time or substantially full-time basis, and extending for a period including or consisting of four consecutive weeks (FA 1991 s 32(10)(*b*), as substituted by s 144(3)).

Where a course satisfies only the requirements of para (*b*) above, the trainee must have attained the age of 30 at the time the payment is made (FA 1991 s 32(1)(*ca*)(i), as substituted by s 144(2)).

TRAINING COURSES UNDER TA 1988 s 589

The courses that will now qualify for VTR when undertaken by trainees aged 30 and over are defined by reference to TA 1988 s 589, which, together with TA 1988 s 588, provides that there shall be no Schedule E charge on employees or former employees whose fees for such courses, aimed at retraining, are paid by their employer or former employer.

The conditions in TA 1988 s 589(1) are that the course—

(*a*) must provide training "designed to impart or improve skills or knowledge" relevant and intended for use in any gainful employment (or self-employment);

(*b*) must be entirely devoted to teaching or practical application of those skills or that knowledge; and

(*c*) must not exceed one year and take place entirely within the UK.

In applying these conditions to VTR, any study time spent in connection with the course is treated as time devoted to the practical application of the skills or knowledge (FA 1991 s 32(10), as substituted by s 144(3)).

TAKING EFFECT

The new rules apply to payments made after 5 May 1996.

See also Budget Press Release REV 11, 28 November 1995, "Extension of vocational training relief".

145   Personal reliefs for non-resident EEA nationals

(1) In section 278(2)(*a*) of the Taxes Act 1988 (exclusion of non-residents from entitlement to personal reliefs not to apply to Commonwealth citizens or

citizens of the Republic of Ireland), for "a citizen of the Republic of Ireland" there shall be substituted "an EEA national".

(2) After subsection (8) of that section (claims to be made to the Board) there shall be added the following subsection—

"(9) In this section 'EEA national' means a national of any State, other than the United Kingdom, which is a Contracting Party to the Agreement on the European Economic Area signed at Oporto on 2nd May 1992, as adjusted by the Protocol signed at Brussels on 17th March 1993."

(3) This section has effect for the year 1996–97 and subsequent years of assessment.

GENERAL NOTE

In general, the availability of personal allowances under TA 1988 Part VII Chapter I is limited to individuals who are UK resident (TA 1988 s 278(1)). There are two main exceptions to this rule: a non-resident may be entitled to claim personal allowances either because he falls within one of the classes of individual delineated in s 278(2) or because under the terms of the relevant double taxation treaty concluded by the UK, he is a resident of the other contracting state and the relevant article of the treaty confers entitlement.

TA 1988 s 278(2) confers entitlement on, inter alia, Irish and Commonwealth citizens and residents of the Isle of Man or of the Channel Islands. As for double taxation treaties, it is chiefly the UK's older treaties that make personal allowances available. Newer treaties tend expressly to exclude entitlement. The treaties still in force that do confer entitlement (to individuals who are, for the purposes of the treaty, residents of the treaty partner) are those with—

Austria	Mauritius
Belgium	Myanmar
Faroe Islands	Namibia
Fiji	Netherlands
Finland	Norway
France	Portugal
Germany	Singapore
Greece	South Africa
Indonesia	Swaziland
Ireland	Switzerland
Kenya	Zambia
Luxembourg	

In addition, the treaty with Germany allows German nationals (whether or not resident in Germany) to claim UK personal allowances. It should be noted, however, that many treaties deny personal allowances where the income of the claimant taxable in the UK consists solely of dividends, interest or royalties.

EXTENSION OF PERSONAL ALLOWANCES TO EEA NATIONALS

This section extends entitlement to personal allowances (reliefs) under TA 1988 Part VII Chapter I to nationals of the other member states of the European Economic Area (EEA), as from the year of assessment 1996–97.

The EEA consists of the 15 member states of the European Union, plus the EFTA countries of Iceland, Liechtenstein and Norway. Switzerland, the remaining member of EFTA, is not a member state of the EEA. The countries involved, other than the UK, are thus—

Austria	Italy
Belgium	Liechtenstein
Denmark	Luxembourg
Finland	Netherlands
France	Norway
Germany	Portugal
Greece	Spain
Iceland	Sweden
Ireland	

It will be noted that several of these have double taxation treaties with the UK that confer entitlement to UK personal allowances on their residents (as defined in the treaty). The new rules do not affect that entitlement, but extend it as a matter of UK domestic law to nationals of those countries, whether or not they are at the relevant time resident in that country for treaty purposes.

See also Budget Press Release REV 9, 28 November 1995, "Personal allowances for non-residents".

146   Exemptions for charities

(1) Section 505(1) of the Taxes Act 1988 (exemptions for charities) shall be amended as follows.

(2) For paragraph (*a*) (rents etc) there shall be substituted the following paragraph—

"(*a*) exemption from tax under Schedules A and D in respect of any profits or gains arising in respect of rents or other receipts from an estate, interest or right in or over any land (whether situated in the United Kingdom or elsewhere) to the extent that the profits or gains—

(i) arise in respect of rents or receipts from an estate, interest or right vested in any person for charitable purposes; and
(ii) are applied to charitable purposes only;".

(3) For sub-paragraph (ii) of paragraph (*c*) (yearly interest and annual payments) there shall be substituted the following sub-paragraphs—

"(ii) from tax under Case III of Schedule D,
(iia) from tax under Case IV or V of Schedule D in respect of income equivalent to income chargeable under Case III of that Schedule but arising from securities or other possessions outside the United Kingdom,
(iib) from tax under Case V of Schedule D in respect of income consisting in any such dividend or other distribution of a company not resident in the United Kingdom as would be chargeable to tax under Schedule F if the company were so resident, and".

(4) In paragraph (*e*) (trading profits), after "by a charity" there shall be inserted "(whether in the United Kingdom or elsewhere)".

(5) This section has effect—

(*a*) for the purposes of income tax, for the year 1996–97 and subsequent years of assessment; and
(*b*) for the purposes of corporation tax, in relation to accounting periods ending after 31st March 1996.

GENERAL NOTE
This section is a tidying-up measure, amending TA 1988 s 505 (which confers exemption from income tax on certain income of a charity) by enacting an extra-statutory concession (B9) and making certain other amendments.

ENACTMENT OF EXTRA-STATUTORY CONCESSION B9
Exemption for the investment income of a charity assessable under Schedule D has been restricted, by statute, to yearly interest and other annual payments (s 505(1)(*c*)(ii)). Until now, this exemption has been supplemented by Extra-statutory Concession B9, which extends the exemption to bank interest of whatever nature, interest and dividends payable gross by a building society, profits from discounting transactions chargeable under Schedule D Case III, and to "other overseas income—mainly rents and bank interest".

Subsections (2)–(4), by substituting s 505(1)(*a*) and s 505(1)(*c*)(ii), and inserting s 505(1)(*c*)(iia) and (iib), replace Extra-statutory Concession B9.

Subsections (3) exempts the income of a charity from tax under Schedule D Case III generally, and from tax under Schedule D Case IV or V where the income would be chargeable under Schedule D Case III if it arose in the UK. It also exempts income, otherwise assessable under Schedule D Case V, in the form of dividends and other distributions of a non-resident company, which would be taxable under Schedule F if the distributing company were UK resident.

It remains a condition for exemption that the income be applicable and applied for charitable purposes only.

TRADES CARRIED ON ABROAD
Subsection (4) makes it explicit that the exemption from tax under Schedule D for trading income of a charity (s 505(1)(*e*)) applies to a trade carried on abroad as it does to a trade carried on in the UK, under the existing conditions.

Subsection (2) substitutes a new s 505(1)(a), which exempts rents and other income from land of a charity from tax under Schedules A and D, subject to the usual conditions. It stipulates explicitly that the land in question may be situated elsewhere than in the UK and generally simplifies the wording of the existing s 505(1)(a).

TAKING EFFECT
These changes take effect from the year of assessment 1996–97 for the purposes of income tax and with respect to accounting periods ending after 31 March 1996 for the purposes of corporation tax.

See also Budget Press Release REV 10, 28 November 1995, "Charities: higher limit for payroll giving".

147   Withdrawal of relief for Class 4 contributions

(1) In section 617 of the Taxes Act 1988 (social security benefits and contributions), subsection (5) (relief for Class 4 contributions) shall cease to have effect.

(2) In consequence of the provision made by subsection (1) above, in paragraph 3(2) of Schedule 2 to—

(a) the Social Security Contributions and Benefits Act 1992, and
(b) the Social Security Contributions and Benefits (Northern Ireland) Act 1992,

the words "(e) section 617(5) (relief for Class 4 contributions);" shall be omitted.

(3) This section shall have effect in relation to the year 1996–97 and subsequent years of assessment.

GENERAL NOTE
Ostensibly as a simplification measure for the coming of self-assessment, the income tax relief for 50 per cent of a self-employed individual's Class 4 contributions (introduced in 1984 and given under TA 1988 s 617(5)) is withdrawn entirely as from 1996–97. As a *quid pro quo*, the rate of Class 4 National Insurance is reduced from 7.3 per cent to 6 per cent, also with effect from 1996–97. The latter measure does not, of course, appear in the Finance Act but has been enacted by statutory instrument (see the Social Security (Contributions) (Rerating and National Insurance Fund Payments) Order 1996, SI 1996/597, art 5).

Amendments consequential on the withdrawal of the income tax relief are made to the Social Security Contributions and Benefits Act 1992 and the Social Security Contributions and Benefits (Northern Ireland) Act 1992.

Although the changes are intended to be broadly revenue neutral, there are inevitably winners and losers. Since the relief under TA 1988 s 617 is given by deduction, higher rate taxpayers lose most.

Without the changes, the maximum Class 4 NIC payable in 1996–97 would have been—
$(£23,660 - £6,860) \times 7.3\% = £1,226.40$

The maximum relief under TA 1988 s 617(5) would thus have been—
$(£1,226 \div 2) \times 40\% = £245.20$

The maximum Class 4 NIC saving from the rate reduction on the other hand is—
$£16,800 \times 1.3\% = £218.40$

The maximum loss to the higher rate payer is thus £26.80 (hence the 50p per week cited by Budget Press Release REV 25).

A basic rate payer paying the maximum Class 4 NIC will still gain £218.40 but lose—
$(£1,226 \div 2) \times 24\% = £147.12$,
an overall gain of £71.28 (or £1.37 a week; the maximum £1.25 per week quoted in the Press Release was apparently computed using a basic rate of 25 per cent).

148   Mis-sold personal pensions etc

(1) Income tax shall not be chargeable on any payment falling within subsection (3) or (5) below.

(2) Receipt of a payment falling within subsection (3) below shall not be regarded for the purposes of capital gains tax as the disposal of an asset.

(3) A payment falls within this subsection if it is a capital sum by way of compensation for loss suffered, or reasonably likely to be suffered, by a person in a case where that person, or some other person, acting in reliance on bad investment advice at least some of which was given during the period beginning with 29th April 1988 and ending with 30th June 1994,—

(*a*) has, while eligible, or reasonably likely to become eligible, to be a member of an occupational pension scheme, instead become a member of a personal pension scheme or entered into a retirement annuity contract;

(*b*) has ceased to be a member of, or to pay contributions to, an occupational pension scheme and has instead become a member of a personal pension scheme or entered into a retirement annuity contract;

(*c*) has transferred to a personal pension scheme accrued rights of his under an occupational pension scheme; or

(*d*) has ceased to be a member of an occupational pension scheme and has instead (by virtue of such a provision as is mentioned in section 591(2)(*g*) of the Taxes Act 1988) entered into arrangements for securing relevant benefits by means of an annuity contract.

(4) A payment chargeable to income tax apart from subsection (1) above may nevertheless be regarded as a capital sum for the purpose of determining whether it falls within subsection (3) above.

(5) A payment falls within this subsection if and to the extent that it is a payment of interest, on the whole or any part of a capital sum such as is mentioned in subsection (3) above, for a period ending on or before the earliest date on which a determination (whether or not subsequently varied on an appeal or in any other proceedings) of the amount of the particular capital sum in question is made, whether by agreement or by a decision of—

(*a*) a court, tribunal or commissioner,

(*b*) an arbitrator or (in Scotland) arbiter, or

(*c*) any other person appointed for the purpose.

(6) In this section—

"bad investment advice" means investment advice in respect of which an action against the person who gave it has been, or may be, brought—

(*a*) in or for negligence;

(*b*) for breach of contract;

(*c*) by reason of a breach of a fiduciary obligation; or

(*d*) by reason of a contravention which is actionable under section 62 of the Financial Services Act 1986;

"investment advice" means advice such as is mentioned in paragraph 15 of Schedule 1 to the Financial Services Act 1986;

"occupational pension scheme" means—

(*a*) a scheme approved, or being considered for approval, under Chapter I of Part XIV of the Taxes Act 1988 (retirement benefit schemes);

(*b*) a relevant statutory scheme, as defined in section 611A(1) of that Act; or

(*c*) a fund to which section 608 of that Act applies (superannuation funds approved before 6th April 1980 etc);

"personal pension scheme" has the meaning given by section 630(1) of the Taxes Act 1988;

"relevant benefits" has the meaning given by section 612(1) of the Taxes Act 1988;

"retirement annuity contract" means a contract made before 1st July 1988 and approved by the Board under or by virtue of any provision of Chapter III of Part XIV of the Taxes Act 1988.

(7) This section shall have effect, and be taken always to have had effect, in relation to any payment falling within subsection (3) or (5) above, whether made before or after the passing of this Act.

GENERAL NOTE

The Securities and Investments Board (SIB) commissioned reports on practices within the Financial Services Industry relating to individuals who had taken out personal pensions. Their findings caused some alarm within the Life and Pensions Industry and attracted considerable media attention. Consequently, all members of self-regulatory organisations are having to review individual pension contracts likely to be affected. Where it is agreed that bad advice was given as a result of which a person has suffered or is likely to suffer a loss, this clause will exempt any compensation payment from income tax or capital gains tax.

PERSONS AFFECTED

Broadly there are three categories where bad advice may have been given as a result of which an individual may suffer a loss. Firstly, individuals who were eligible to join their employer's pension scheme but were advised not to do so and took out a personal pension instead. Secondly, individuals who were members of their employer's pension scheme but who were advised to opt out in favour of a personal pension. Thirdly, individuals who had transferred their accrued pension rights from an employer's pension scheme (usually after the employment had ceased) into either a personal pension scheme or a buy-out annuity contract under TA 1988 s 591(2)(g) (commonly referred to as a s 32 policy).

In order to be exempt from tax on the compensation payment, the bad investment advice must have been given during the period from 29 April 1988 to 30 June 1994.

ELIGIBLE PAYMENTS

Payments which will be exempt from income tax and CGT are—

(a) a capital sum by way of compensation for a loss suffered, or reasonably likely to be suffered as a result of bad investment advice;
(b) interest on a capital sum compensation payment accruing up to the earliest date on which the compensation payment is determined (any interest accruing after that date would be subject to income tax in the normal manner).

COMPENSATION PAYMENTS: ALTERNATIVE TREATMENTS

Where an individual transferred his deferred pension rights from an occupational scheme into a personal pension or annuity contract, some occupational pension scheme trustees have indicated willingness to allow the individual's pension rights to be transferred back into the occupational scheme. If the amount transferred back in includes any compensation for loss suffered during the intervening period, the whole of the resultant pension will be taxable in the normal manner.

If it is agreed that the compensation payment is added to an existing individual policy arrangement, eg personal pension, the resultant pension would also be taxable in the normal manner.

Where individuals are compensated directly for any loss suffered or reasonably likely to be suffered, the capital sum and any additional eligible interest will be tax free. The amount received ought to be reinvested in a tax efficient investment vehicle.

If it is agreed that the capital sum compensation together with eligible interest is to be paid into a tax approved pension scheme, any further interest (arising after the date of determination of the compensation award) should be received directly by the individual (and not paid into the tax approved pension scheme) because this extra element of interest will be taxable upon the individual.

This section will have effect in relation to qualifying compensation payments, whether made before or after the date of Royal Assent.

149 Annual payments in residuary cases

(1) Section 347A of the Taxes Act 1988 (annual payments not a charge on the income of a payer) shall apply to any payment made on or after 6th April 1996—

(a) in pursuance of any obligation which falls within section 36(4)(a) of the Finance Act 1988 (existing obligations under certain court orders), and
(b) for the benefit, maintenance or education of a person (whether or not

the person to whom the payment is made) who attained the age of 21 before 6th April 1994,

as if that obligation were not an existing obligation within the definition contained in section 36(4) of the Finance Act 1988.

(2) Subsection (1) above does not apply to any payment to which section 38 of the Finance Act 1988 (treatment of certain maintenance payments under existing obligations) applies.

GENERAL NOTE

Special rules for maintenance payments for persons over the age of 21 were introduced with effect from March 1988. For court orders or binding agreements made before 14 March 1988, if maintenance payments continued after the child reached the age of 21, the payer was eligible for tax relief on the full amount, even where these payments continued after the child's 21st birthday.

As originally drafted in the Finance Bill, this section would have affected all payments made after 5 April 1996 to or for the benefit of the adult child of the payer, who reached the age of 21 before 6 April 1994. The payment would no longer have been treated as a charge on the payer's income, nor as taxable income of the recipient.

The Bill was amended (sub-s (2)) to ensure that the new rules do not apply to maintenance payments to separated or divorced spouses under the FA 1988 s 38 transitional rules (existing obligations). Such maintenance payments can therefore continue to be treated as a charge on the payer's income.

150 Income tax exemption for periodical payments of damages and compensation for personal injury

(1) The sections set out in Schedule 26 to this Act shall be inserted after section 329 of the Taxes Act 1988.

(2) The first of those sections supersedes sections 329A and 329B inserted by the Finance Act 1995 and applies to payments received after the passing of this Act irrespective of when the agreement or order referred to in that section was made or took effect.

(3) Subsections (1) and (2) of the second of those sections supersede section 329C inserted by the Criminal Injuries Compensation Act 1995 and apply to payments received after the passing of that Act.

(4) The repeal of sections 329A and 329B does not affect the operation of those sections in relation to payments received before the passing of this Act.

GENERAL NOTE

This section introduces Sch 26, which extends the income tax relief available where there is a structured settlement in a personal injury case.

Taxation of benefits

151 Benefits under pilot schemes

(1) The Treasury may by order make provision for the Income Tax Acts to have effect in relation to any amount of benefit payable by virtue of a Government pilot scheme as if it was, as they think fit, either—

(*a*) wholly or partly exempt from income tax and, accordingly, to be disregarded in computing the amount of any receipts brought into account for income tax purposes; or

(*b*) to the extent specified in the order, to be brought into account for the purposes of income tax as income of a description so specified or as a receipt of a description so specified.

(2) The Treasury may by order provide for any amount of benefit payable by virtue of a Government pilot scheme to be left out of account, to the extent specified in the order, in the determination for the purposes of section 153 of

the Capital Allowances Act 1990 (subsidies etc) of how far any expenditure has been or is to be met directly or indirectly by the Crown or by an authority or person other than the person actually incurring it.

(3) In this section "Government pilot scheme" means any arrangements (whether or not contained in a scheme) which—

(*a*) are made, under any enactment or otherwise, by the Secretary of State or any Northern Ireland department;

(*b*) make provision for or about the payment of amounts of benefit either—

(i) for purposes that are similar to those for which any social security or comparable benefit is payable; or

(ii) for purposes connected with the carrying out of any functions of the Secretary of State or any such department in relation to employment or training for employment;

(*c*) are arrangements relating to a temporary experimental period; and

(*d*) are made wholly or partly for the purpose of facilitating a decision as to whether, or to what extent, it is desirable for provision to be made on a permanent basis for or in relation to any benefit.

(4) In subsection (3)(*b*) above the reference to making provision for or about the payment of amounts of benefit for purposes that are similar to those for which any social security or comparable benefit is payable shall include a reference to making provision by virtue of which there is a modification of the conditions of entitlement to, or the conditions for the payment of, an existing social security or comparable benefit.

(5) An order under this section may—

(*a*) make different provision for different cases, and

(*b*) contain such incidental, supplemental, consequential and transitional provision (including provision modifying provision made by or under the Income Tax Acts) as the Treasury may think fit.

(6) In this section "benefit" includes any allowance, grant or other amount the whole or any part of which is payable directly or indirectly out of public funds.

(7) The power to make an order under this section—

(*a*) shall be exercisable for the year 1996–97 and subsequent years of assessment; and

(*b*) so far as exercisable for the year 1996–97, shall be exercisable in relation to benefits, allowances and other amounts paid at times on or after 6th April 1996 but before the making of the order.

(8) The Treasury shall not make an order under this section containing any such provision as is mentioned in subsection (1)(*b*) above unless a draft of the order has been laid before, and approved by a resolution of, the House of Commons.

GENERAL NOTE

This section relates to pilot trials of new social security benefits or work incentive payments. The taxation status of such new benefits under existing legislation may be unclear and, in order to provide the necessary flexibility, their tax treatment is to be defined by secondary legislation.

The Treasury is given power to provide by order that a pilot scheme benefit is either wholly or partly exempt from income tax, or wholly or partly chargeable to income tax (sub-s (1)). Such an order may also specify that a pilot scheme benefit is to be left out of account in determining, for the purposes of capital allowances, whether expenditure has been met by a subsidy (sub-s (2)). An order to the effect that a benefit is wholly or partly taxable is subject to approval by a resolution of the House of Commons (sub-s (8)).

This provision may apply not only to trial of a new benefit, but also to experimental amendment of the conditions applicable to an existing benefit (sub-s (4)).

Under sub-s (7), the power to make an order has effect for 1996–97 and subsequent years of assessment. As regards 1996–97, an order may apply retrospectively to benefits paid after 5 April 1996 but before the making of the order.

152   Jobfinder's grant

(1) The Income Tax Acts shall have effect, and be deemed always to have had effect, as if jobfinder's grant were exempt from income tax and, accordingly, were to be disregarded in computing the amount of any receipts brought into account for income tax purposes.

(2) In this section "jobfinder's grant" means grant paid under that name by virtue of arrangements made in pursuance of section 2 of the Employment and Training Act 1973 or section 1 of the Employment and Training Act (Northern Ireland) 1950 (arrangements for assisting persons to select, train for, obtain or retain employment).

GENERAL NOTE
Jobfinder's grant is available, subject to the applicable conditions, to the long-term unemployed. It is intended to help with the costs of starting work again.

Under this section, jobfinder's grant is exempted from income tax. The exemption applies from the introduction of the grant in April 1995.

Investments

153   Foreign income dividends

Schedule 27 to this Act (which makes provision relating to foreign income dividends) shall have effect.

GENERAL NOTE
This section incorporates the provisions of Sch 27. The effect of Sch 27 is to amend the code for foreign income dividends that was enacted by FA 1994 Sch 16. This includes amendments to the legislation relating to international headquarters of companies within TA 1988 ss 246S–246Y.

154   FOTRA securities

(1) The modifications which, under section 60 of the Finance Act 1940, may be made for the purposes of any issue of securities to the conditions about tax exemption specified in section 22 of the Finance (No 2) Act 1931 shall include a modification by virtue of which the tax exemption contained in any condition of the issue applies, as respects capital, irrespective of where the person with the beneficial ownership of the securities is domiciled.

(2) Subject to subsections (3) to (5) below, nothing in the Tax Acts shall impose any charge to tax on any person in respect of so much of any profits or gains arising from a FOTRA security, or from any loan relationship represented by a FOTRA security, as is expressed to be exempt from tax in the tax exemption condition applying to that security.

(3) Exemption from tax shall not be conferred by virtue of subsection (2) above in relation to any security unless the requirements imposed as respects that exemption by the conditions with which the security is issued (including any requirement as to the making of a claim) are complied with.

(4) The tax exemption condition of a FOTRA security shall not be taken to confer any exemption from any charge to tax imposed by virtue of the provisions of Chapter IA of Part XV or Chapter III of Part XVII of the Taxes Act 1988 (anti-avoidance provisions for residents etc).

(5) Nothing in this section shall entitle any person to any repayment of tax

which he has not claimed within the time limit which would be applicable under the Tax Acts (apart from this section) to a claim for the repayment of that tax.

(6) A person with the beneficial ownership of a FOTRA security who would, by virtue of this section, be exempt from tax in respect of some or all of the profits and gains arising from that security, or from any loan relationship represented by it, shall not be entitled for the purposes of income tax or corporation tax to bring into account any amount—

(*a*) in respect of changes in the value of that security;
(*b*) as expenses or disbursements incurred in, or in connection with, the holding of the security or any transaction relating to the security; or
(*c*) as a debit given, in respect of any loan relationship represented by that security, by any provision of Chapter II of this Part of this Act in respect of such a relationship.

(7) Schedule 28 to this Act (which contains amendments consequential on the provisions of this section) shall have effect.

(8) References in this section to a FOTRA security are references to—

(*a*) any security issued with such a condition about exemption from taxation as is authorised in relation to its issue by virtue of section 22 of the Finance (No 2) Act 1931; or
(*b*) any $3\frac{1}{2}$% War Loan 1952 Or After which was issued with a condition authorised by virtue of section 47 of the Finance (No 2) Act 1915;

and references, in relation to such a security, to the tax exemption condition shall be construed accordingly.

(9) This section and Schedule 28 to this Act shall have effect—

(*a*) for the purposes of income tax, for the year 1996–97 and subsequent years of assessment; and
(*b*) for the purposes of corporation tax, for accounting periods ending after 31st March 1996.

GENERAL NOTE
   This section makes amendments to the Treasury's power to issue FOTRA gilts and introduces Sch 28.
   FOTRA gilts are those which may be issued under terms which provide that they are "free of tax to residents abroad". FOTRA gilts includes 3.5% War Loan Stock 1952 for this purpose.
   The Treasury's powers are modified so that the exemption can be applied to capital irrespective of where the person beneficially owning the gilt is domiciled.
   There is to be no tax charge under the Tax Acts on any capital profit or gain from a FOTRA security on any person, provided that the relevant requirements under the conditions of issue are met, including any necessary claims. The exemption does not apply to certain anti-avoidance provisions (Chapter IA Part XV (settlements) and Chapter III Part XVII (transfers of assets abroad)) and does not entitle any person to a repayment if he does not make the claim within the relevant time.
   This section also provides that such a person shall not be entitled to any deduction for a loss on the security, expenses in connection with the security or any debit under Chapter II of the Act in respect of a loan relationship represented by the security.
   The section is applicable for income tax purposes for accounting periods ending after 31 March 1996 and for income tax purposes for the year 1996–97.

155   Directions for payment without deduction of tax

After section 51 of the Taxes Act 1988 there shall be inserted the following section—

"51AA   Commencement of direction under section 50 or 51

A direction under section 50 or 51 that any security shall be deemed to have been issued subject to the condition that the interest thereon shall be paid without deduction of tax may provide that the direction is to have effect in relation only to payments of interest made on or after such date as may be specified in the direction."

GENERAL NOTE
   This section introduces new s 51AA into TA 1988, which provides that interest on certain gilts may be paid gross from certain specified dates.
   It is planned to introduce a gilt strips market. The Bank of England issued a paper on the development of a gilt strips market parallel to the May 1995 Revenue consultative document on gilts and bonds. The stripping of a gilt causes the entitlements to payment of future interest and repayment of principal to be separated and allows them to be held separately. This is beneficial in that it allows holders of gilts to structure their holdings so that they match their future cash flow requirements more closely. The stripped gilt can be reconstituted into its original form.
   For the market to work efficiently, interest must be paid gross and so the powers in TA 1988 ss 50–51 are to be used to allow gross payment of interest on the "strippable gilts". This is being implemented by new s 51AA allowing the exempting provisions to apply for interest payments on or after the date of direction. This will allow existing gilts to be specified as "strippable".

156   Paying and collecting agents etc

Schedule 29 to this Act (which amends the rules relating to paying and collecting agents) shall have effect.

GENERAL NOTE
   This section introduces Sch 29, which sets out a new scheme for the collection of tax on public revenue dividends (such as interest on gilts) and foreign dividends or interest. The change is consequent on the new rules for corporate debt (see FA 1996 ss 80–105), the abolition of Schedule C and the repeal of TA 1988 s 123 and Sch 3 (see FA 1996 s 79 and Sch 7).

157   Stock lending fees

(1) After section 129A of the Taxes Act 1988 (interest on cash collateral paid in connection with stock lending arrangements) there shall be inserted the following section—

"129B   Stock lending fees

(1) The income which, as income deriving from investments of a description specified in any of the relevant provisions, is eligible for relief from tax by virtue of that provision shall be taken to include any relevant stock lending fee.

(2) For the purposes of this section the relevant provisions are sections 592(2), 608(2)(*a*), 613(4), 614(3), 620(6) and 643(2).

(3) In this section 'relevant stock lending fee', in relation to investments of any description, means any amount, in the nature of a fee, which is payable in connection with an approved stock lending arrangement relating to investments which, but for any transfer under the arrangement, would be investments of that description.

(4) In this section 'approved stock lending arrangement' has the same meaning as in Schedule 5A."

(2) This section has effect in relation to any arrangements entered into on or after 2nd January 1996.

GENERAL NOTE
Approved pension arrangements, such as exempt approved occupational schemes, personal pension plans and retirement annuity schemes, enjoy a general exemption from tax on their investment income.

This section extends the exemption to stock lending fees which relate to qualifying invest-ments, provided that the stock lending arrangement concerned is within TA 1988 s 129 and TCGA 1992 s 271(9). The exemption is achieved by the insertion of a new s 129B in TA 1988.

The section has effect with regard to stock lending arrangements entered into after 1 January 1996. The commencement date for the section has been set to coincide with the introduction of the new open gilt repo market on 2 January 1996 (see Budget Press Release, 28 November 1995, "Financial markets", *Simon's Weekly Tax Intelligence* 1995, p 1875). Further connected changes are being introduced by regulation to take effect at the same time—these will exempt manufactured payments and profits from repo transactions in the hands of approved pension schemes. Extra-statutory Concession C19, which exempts certain manufactured payments (but not stock lending fees) received by approved pension funds, will be withdrawn (see Budget Press Release, 28 November 1995, "Manufactured payments and profits from repo transactions—exempt funds and insured pension business", *Simon's Weekly Tax Intelligence* 1995, p 1876).

158 Transfers on death under the accrued income scheme

(1) In section 710(5) of the Taxes Act 1988 (meaning of "transfer" in sections 711 to 728), after "or otherwise" there shall be inserted ", but—

> (*a*) does not include the vesting of securities in a person's personal representatives on his death; and".

(2) Subsection (1) of section 721 of that Act (transfer of securities on death) shall cease to have effect.

(3) For subsection (2) of that section (transfers by personal representatives to legatees) there shall be substituted—

> "(2) Where—
>> (*a*) an individual who is entitled to securities dies, and
>> (*b*) in the interest period in which the individual died, the securities are transferred by his personal representatives to a legatee,
>
> section 713 shall not apply to the transfer."

(4) Subsection (4) of that section (interest period treated as ending with death) shall cease to have effect.

(5) This section has effect as respects deaths on or after 6th April 1996.

GENERAL NOTE
This section provides for the exclusion of transfers on death to a personal representative from the accrued income scheme.

It does so by amending the definition of "transfer" within TA 1988 s 710(5) and causes TA 1988 s 721(1) to cease to apply. It causes the transfers from a personal legatee to a personal representative within the interest period in which the owner died to be outside of the scope of TA 1988 s 713(2).

It applies to deaths on or after 6 April 1996.

159 Manufactured payments, repos, etc

(1) Sections 729, 737A(2)(*b*) and 786(4) of the Taxes Act 1988 (provisions applying to sale and repurchase agreements) shall cease to have effect except in relation to cases where the initial agreement to sell or transfer the securities or other property was made before the appointed day.

(2) In section 737 of that Act—

> (*a*) in subsection (5) (manufactured dividends paid to UK residents by non-residents), for the words from "a person resident in the United Kingdom" to "the United Kingdom recipient shall" there shall be substituted "a United Kingdom recipient, that recipient shall"; and
> (*b*) after that subsection there shall be inserted the following subsection—

"(5AAA) For the purposes of subsection (5) above a person who receives a manufactured dividend is a United Kingdom recipient if—

(*a*) he is resident in the United Kingdom; or
(*b*) he is not so resident but receives that dividend for the purposes of a trade carried on through a branch or agency in the United Kingdom."

(3) In section 737C of that Act (deemed manufactured payments), the following subsection shall be inserted after subsection (11A) in relation to cases where the initial agreement to sell the securities is made on or after the appointed day, that is to say—

"(11B) The preceding provisions of this section shall have effect in cases where paragraph 2, 3 or 4 of Schedule 23A would apply by virtue of section 737A(5) but for paragraph 5 of that Schedule as they have effect in a case where the paragraph in question is not disapplied by paragraph 5; and where—

(*a*) the gross amount of the deemed manufactured interest, or
(*b*) the gross amount of the deemed manufactured overseas dividend,

falls to be calculated in such a case under subsection (8) or (11) above, it shall be so calculated by reference to the provisions of paragraph 3 or 4 of Schedule 23A that would have applied but for paragraph 5 of that Schedule."

(4) In sub-paragraph (3) of paragraph 4 of Schedule 23A to that Act (manufactured overseas dividends paid to UK residents by non-residents), for the words from "a person resident in the United Kingdom" to "the United Kingdom recipient shall" there shall be substituted "a United Kingdom recipient, that recipient shall".

(5) After that sub-paragraph there shall be inserted the following sub-paragraphs—

"(3A) For the purposes of sub-paragraph (3) above a person who receives a manufactured overseas dividend is a United Kingdom recipient if—

(*a*) he is resident in the United Kingdom; or
(*b*) he is not so resident but receives that dividend for the purposes of a trade carried on through a branch or agency in the United Kingdom.

(3B) Dividend manufacturing regulations may make provision, in relation to cases falling within sub-paragraph (3) above, for the amount of tax required under that sub-paragraph to be taken to be reduced, to such extent and for such purposes as may be determined under the regulations, by reference to amounts of overseas tax charged on, or in respect of—

(*a*) the making of the manufactured overseas dividend; or
(*b*) the overseas dividend of which the manufactured overseas dividend is representative."

(6) In sub-paragraph (7) of paragraph 4 of that Schedule (regulations for off-setting), for the words from "against" to "and account" in the words after paragraph (*b*) there shall be substituted "in accordance with the regulations and to the prescribed extent, amounts falling within paragraph (*a*) of sub-paragraph (7AA) below against the sums falling within paragraph (*b*) of that sub-paragraph, and to account"; and after that sub-paragraph there shall be inserted the following sub-paragraph—

"(7AA) Those amounts and sums are—

(*a*) amounts of overseas tax in respect of overseas dividends received by him in that chargeable period, amounts of overseas tax charged on, or in

161

respect of, the making of manufactured overseas dividends so received by him and amounts deducted under sub-paragraph (2) above from any such manufactured overseas dividends; and

(*b*) the sums due from him on account of the amounts deducted by him under sub-paragraph (2) above from the manufactured overseas dividends paid by him in that chargeable period.''

(7) In sub-paragraph (1) of paragraph 8 of that Schedule (power to modify provisions of Schedule)—

(*a*) before the "or" at the end of paragraph (*a*) there shall be inserted—

"(*aa*) such persons who receive, or become entitled to receive, manufactured dividends, manufactured interest or manufactured overseas dividends as may be prescribed,"

and

(*b*) in the words after paragraph (*b*), for "paragraph 2, 3 or 4 above" there shall be substituted "paragraphs 2 to 5 above".

(8) After sub-paragraph (1) of paragraph 8 of that Schedule there shall be inserted the following sub-paragraph—

"(1A) Dividend manufacturing regulations may provide, in relation to prescribed cases where a person makes or receives the payment of any amount representative of an overseas dividend, or is treated for any purposes of this Schedule or such regulations as a person making or receiving such a payment—

(*a*) for any entitlement of that person to claim relief under Part XVIII to be extinguished or reduced to such extent as may be found under the regulations; and

(*b*) for the adjustment, by reference to any provision having effect under the law of a territory outside the United Kingdom, of any amount falling to be taken, for any prescribed purposes of the Tax Acts or the 1992 Act, to be the amount paid or payable by or to any person in respect of any sale, repurchase or other transfer of the overseas securities to which the payment relates.''

(9) Subsections (2), (4) and (5) above have effect—

(*a*) for the purposes of corporation tax, in relation to accounting periods ending after 31st March 1996; and

(*b*) for the purposes of income tax, in relation to the year 1996–97 and subsequent years of assessment.

(10) In this section "the appointed day" means such day as the Treasury may by order appoint, and different days may be appointed under this subsection for different purposes.

GENERAL NOTE

The amendments effected by this section are as follows—

(*a*) rationalisation of provisions relating to sale and repurchase of securities (sub-ss (1) and (3));
(*b*) a change to the rules which apply when a manufactured dividend is paid by a non-resident to a person who is resident in the UK (sub-ss (2), (4) and (5));
(*c*) modification of the power to make regulations in relation to overseas dividends (sub-ss (6) and (8)); and
(*d*) insertion of an additional power to make regulations in relation to recipients of manufactured payments (sub-s (7)).

The alteration of the power to make regulations in relation to overseas dividends is connected with the intended introduction of simpler rules for the deduction of tax from manufactured overseas dividends (see Budget Press Release, 28 November 1995, "Financial markets", *Simon's Weekly Tax Intelligence* 1995, p 1875).

SALE AND REPURCHASE OF SECURITIES

This change relates to three provisions which are concerned with agreements for the sale and repurchase of securities—TA 1988 s 729, s 737A and s 786(4). The aim of all three provisions is to prevent the avoidance of liability to tax on dividends or interest paid in respect of the securities which have been transferred. In the case of TA 1988 s 729, this is achieved by deeming the dividends or interest to be the income of the transferor; TA 1988 s 786(4) provides that the transferor is to be chargeable to tax on an amount equal to any income arising; and TA 1988 s 737A deems a manufactured payment to be made to the transferor, so that the rules relating to manufactured payments then come into play (TA 1988 s 737 and Sch 23A), generally resulting in an assumed payment to the transferor of a dividend, interest, or an annual payment.

Under sub-s (1), the situation is to be rationalised by the repeal of TA 1988 ss 729 and 786(4). This will apply to cases where the initial agreement to transfer the securities or other property is made on or after the day to be appointed under sub-s (10). It may be noted here that TA 1988 s 786(4) does not apply only to transfers of securities, but to any income producing assets which are transferred in connection with a loan or credit.

Where TA 1988 s 737A applies, the amount of the deemed manufactured payment, and the corresponding adjustment to the repurchase price for the purposes of TA 1988 s 730A, are specified by TA 1988 s 737C, by reference to TA 1988 s 737 and Sch 23A paras 2–4. Because TA 1988 Sch 23A para 5 applies in place of s 737 and Sch 23A paras 2–4 in specified circumstances, it is necessary to ensure that TA 1988 s 737A operates satisfactorily in such a case. Thus, sub-s (3) provides for a modification to TA 1988 s 737C so that, where Sch 23A paras 2–4 are disapplied by para 5, those paragraphs are nevertheless assumed to apply for the purposes of s 737C.

MANUFACTURED DIVIDEND PAID BY A NON-RESIDENT

Where a manufactured payment is made by a non-resident, otherwise than in the course of a trade carried on through a UK branch, the rules applicable to manufactured payments apply differently. Generally, if the recipient of such a payment is resident in the UK, that person is liable to account for the tax which a UK resident dividend manufacturer would have had to pay in respect of the manufactured dividend. However, the recipient of the payment has not previously been chargeable with this tax if he could show that the dividend manufacturer was entitled to payment of the dividend either—

(*a*) as the registered holder of the securities; or
(*b*) from a transferor or transferee of the securities, who was entitled to payment of the dividend as the registered holder of the securities.

This section amends the above rules by removing the exemption which was previously available to the recipient by reference to (*a*) and (*b*) above. The charge will also apply not only to UK resident recipients, but also to non-residents who receive the manufactured dividend for the purposes of a trade carried on through a UK branch.

The change is effected by sub-ss (2), (4) and (5), through amendments to TA 1988 s 737 (in relation to cases other than a manufactured overseas dividend or a manufactured dividend which is representative of a foreign income dividend) and to TA 1988 Sch 23A para 4 (in relation to manufactured overseas dividends). As regards a dividend which is representative of a foreign income dividend, there is generally no corresponding liability of a UK dividend manufacturer to account for tax, as a result of Sch 23A, para 2(6).

There is also provision for regulations to be made in relation to the tax chargeable on recipients of manufactured overseas dividends, to take account of overseas tax.

This change has effect for accounting periods ending after 31 March 1996, and for 1996-97 and subsequent years of assessment (sub-s (9)).

REGULATIONS RELATING TO OVERSEAS DIVIDENDS

There is an amendment to the power to make regulations with regard to the set off by an overseas dividend manufacturer of tax suffered by him against the tax due from him under the rules for manufactured dividends (sub-s (6)). As a result of the change, it will be possible for regulations to provide for the set off against tax due under TA 1988 Sch 23A para 4(2) of overseas tax charged by reference to the making of manufactured overseas dividends which are received by him.

A further amendment to the power to make regulations in relation to manufactured overseas dividends is covered by sub-s (8). This relates to a case where a person either pays or receives, or is deemed to pay or receive, an amount which represents an overseas dividend. First, it will be possible for the regulations to amend the entitlement of the person concerned to double tax relief. Second, regulations may also require an adjustment, by reference to any provision of an overseas country, of the figure taken for UK tax purposes as the amount payable in respect of any sale, repurchase or other transfer of the overseas securities concerned.

REGULATIONS IN RELATION TO RECIPIENTS OF MANUFACTURED PAYMENTS

Under TA 1988 Sch 23A para 8(1), regulations may provide for manufactured payments and the payment manufacturers to be treated otherwise than as specified in Sch 23A paras 2–4. That subparagraph is amended so that the regulations may also affect the treatment of the recipients of manufactured payments. Sch 23A para 5 (Dividends and interest passing through the market) is also included in the paragraphs whose operation may be amended by the regulations (sub-s (7)).

160 Investments in housing

Schedule 30 to this Act (which makes provision conferring relief from corporation tax on companies that invest in housing) shall have effect.

GENERAL NOTE
This section introduces Sch 30, which contains provisions for an extension of the permitted investments of approved investment trust companies. As a result of the change, such companies will be able to invest in certain categories of residential property to be let on assured tenancies. Net rental income accruing to an investment trust in respect of such housing will be taxed at the small companies' rate of corporation tax, and the normal exemption of investment trusts from tax on capital gains will apply to their disposals of the properties.

161 Venture capital trusts: control of companies etc

(1) Schedule 28B to the Taxes Act 1988 (venture capital trusts: meaning of qualifying holdings) shall have effect, and be deemed always to have had effect, subject to the amendments in subsections (2) and (3) below.

(2) In paragraph 9 (requirements as to subsidiaries etc of the relevant company), the following shall be omitted—

(*a*) in sub-paragraph (1), the words "subject to sub-paragraph (*a*) below"; and

(*b*) sub-paragraph (2).

(3) In paragraph 13 (interpretation), for sub-paragraphs (2) and (3) ("connected" and "control" to be construed in accordance with sections 839 and 416(2) to (6)) there shall be substituted the following sub-paragraphs—

"(2) For the purposes of paragraphs 5(2) and 9 above, the question whether a person controls a company shall be determined in accordance with subsections (2) to (6) of section 416 with the modification given by sub-paragraph (3) below.

(3) The modification is that, in determining whether a person controls a company, there shall be disregarded—

(*a*) his or any other person's possession of, or entitlement to acquire, relevant fixed-rate preference shares of the company; and

(*b*) his or any other person's possession of, or entitlement to acquire, rights as a loan creditor of the company.

(4) Section 839 shall apply for the purposes of this Schedule, but as if the reference in subsection (8) to section 416 were a reference to subsections (2) to (6) of section 416 with the modification given by sub-paragraph (3) above.

(5) For the purposes of sub-paragraph (3) above—

(*a*) 'relevant fixed-rate preferences shares' are fixed-rate preference shares that do not for the time being carry voting rights; and

(*b*) 'fixed-rate preference shares' has the same meaning as in section 95."

GENERAL NOTE
Introduced in FA 1995 as a new form of tax advantaged investment vehicle, aimed at attracting investment into small and medium-sized unquoted companies, venture capital trusts ("VCT") have been very slow to take off. The Inland Revenue Press Release of 4 March 1996, referring to the amendments discussed below, points to only £40 million of investment in VCTs so far.

THE AMENDMENTS
This section provides retrospective amendments to the legislation inserted as TA 1988 Sch 28B by FA 1995 Sch 14. These provisions are deemed to have always had effect and are putting into

legislation an extra-statutory concession which has been operated since September 1995. That had followed on from consultations with the industry after the enactment of the original legislation. The Government, in the words of the 4 March 1996 Press Release, have "accepted that certain types of business could have difficulty in structuring their financing in accordance with the rules of the VCT scheme on the control of companies".

For the purposes of the control test in Sch 28B paras 5(2) and 9, non-voting fixed rate preference shares and loans, including those invested in or lent to the target company by persons other than the VCT, are to be disregarded for the test. This removes a restriction which could have prevented VCTs from investing in a target company with others under co-investment arrangements.

Where the fixed rate preference shares have a contingent right to vote under defined circumstances in the future, the shares will continue to be disregarded for this test until the contingency vests and the shares have become voting shares.

Fixed rate preference shares for this purpose are defined in TA 1988 s 95(5) as shares offering only a fixed amount or rate of return (such return together with any sum payable on redemption not exceeding a reasonable commercial rate of return) and the shares are not convertible into another class of share or security.

Insurance policies

162   Qualifying life insurance policies: certification

(1) Section 55 of the Finance Act 1995 (removal of certification requirements for qualifying policies with respect to any time on or after 5th May 1996 etc) shall have effect—

(*a*) with the substitution for "5th May 1996", wherever occurring, of "the appointed date"; and

(*b*) with the addition of the following subsection after subsection (8)—

"(9) In this section "the appointed date" means such date as may be specified for the purpose in an order made by the Board."

(2) In Schedule 15 to the Taxes Act 1988 (qualifying policies) paragraphs 24(2A) and 25(2) shall have effect with the substitution for "5th May 1996" of "the appointed date for the purposes of section 55 of the Finance Act 1995 (removal of certification requirements)".

GENERAL NOTE
This section defers the coming into force of FA 1995 s 55 which, as originally enacted, was to remove the certification requirement from 5 May 1966 onwards. Changes in the rules relating to qualifying policies, and to other aspects of the taxation of policy holders, were expected to come into force on that date, but their introduction has been deferred to allow time for further consultation. The present intention is that draft legislation should be published in the Spring of 1996 (Revenue Press Release, 8 November 1995, "Taxation of life assurance policyholders"). As a result of the amendment the removal of the certification requirement will take effect from an appointed day.

Insurance companies

163   Life assurance business losses

Schedule 31 to this Act, which makes provision about losses arising to insurance companies in the carrying on of life assurance business, shall have effect.

GENERAL NOTE
This section introduces Sch 31 containing provisions amending the treatment of losses incurred in life assurance business.

164   Limits on relief for expenses

(1) For subsections (2) to (5) of section 76 of the Taxes Act 1988 there shall be substituted the following subsections—

"(2) Where, in the case of any such company, the amount mentioned in paragraph (*a*) of subsection (2A) below exceeds for any accounting period the amount mentioned in paragraph (*b*) of that subsection, the amount which by virtue of this section is to be deductible by way of management expenses for that period shall be equal to the basic deduction for that period reduced by the amount of the excess.

(2A) Those amounts are—

(*a*) the amount which would be the profits of the company's life assurance business for that period if computed in accordance with the provisions applicable to Case I of Schedule D and adjusted in respect of losses; and
(*b*) the amount (including any negative amount) produced by deducting the following aggregate amount from the company's relevant income for that period from its life assurance business, that is to say, the aggregate of—

(i) the basic deduction,
(ii) any non-trading deficit on the company's loan relationships which is produced for that period in relation to that business by a separate computation under paragraph 2 of Schedule 11 to the Finance Act 1996,
(iii) any amount which in pursuance of a claim under paragraph 4(3) of that Schedule is carried back to that period and (in accordance with paragraph 4(5) of that Schedule) applied in reducing profits of the company for that period, and
(iv) any charges on income for that period so far as they consist in annuities or other annual payments that are referable to the company's life assurance business and, if they are not annuities, are payable by the company wholly or partly in satisfaction of claims under insurance policies.

(2B) For the purposes of subsection (2A) above a company's relevant income for any accounting period from its life assurance business is the sum of the following—

(*a*) the income and gains of the company's life assurance business for that accounting period; and
(*b*) the relevant franked investment income of the company for that period so far as it arises from assets held for the purposes of that business and is not included in the income and gains mentioned in paragraph (*a*) above.

(2C) The adjustment in respect of losses that is to be made for any accounting period under paragraph (*a*) of subsection (2A) above is a deduction of the amount equal to the unused part of the sum which—

(*a*) by reference to computations made in respect of the company's life assurance business in accordance with the provisions applicable to Case I of Schedule D, and
(*b*) disregarding section 434A(2),

would fall, in the case of the company, to be set off under section 393 against the company's income for that period.

(2D) For the purposes of subsection (2C) above, an amount is unused to the extent that it has not been taken into account for any previous accounting period in determining the amount by reference to which the following question was answered, namely, the question whether, and by how much, the amount deductible by virtue of this section by way of management expenses was less than the basic deduction.

(5) Subject to paragraph 4(11) to (13) of Schedule 11 to the Finance Act 1996, where the basic deduction for any period exceeds the amount which for that period is to be deductible by virtue of this section by way of management expenses, the amount to be carried forward by virtue of section 75(3) (including the amount to be so carried forward for the purpose of computing the amount of the basic deduction for any period) shall be increased by the amount of the excess."

(2) In subsection (8) of that section—

(*a*) after the definition of "authorised person" there shall be inserted the following definition—

"'basic deduction', in relation to an accounting period of an insurance company, means the amount which, by virtue of this section, would be deductible by way of management expenses for that period but for subsection (2) above;"

and

(*b*) after the definition of "recognised self-regulating organisation" there shall be inserted the following definition—

"'relevant franked investment income', in relation to any insurance company, means any franked investment income of the company in so far as it is not income the tax credits comprised in which may be claimed by the company under section 438(4) or 441A(7);".

(3) In paragraph 5 of Schedule 19AC to the Taxes Act 1988 (modification of section 76)—

(*a*) in sub-paragraph (1), in the subsection (6B) treated as inserted in section 76, for "their" there shall be substituted "its" and the words "and subsections (2) and (3)(*b*) above" shall be omitted; and

(*b*) after that sub-paragraph there shall be inserted the following sub-paragraph—

"(1A) In section 76 references to franked investment income shall be treated as being references to UK distribution income within the meaning of paragraph 5B of this Schedule."

(4) In section 56(4) of the Taxes Act 1988 (which contains a reference to the computation required by section 76(2) of that Act), for "by" there shall be substituted "for the purposes of".

(5) Subject to subsection (6) below, this section has effect in relation to accounting periods beginning on or after 1st January 1996.

(6) Notwithstanding anything in the previous provisions of this section, section 76 of the Taxes Act 1988 has effect in relation to accounting periods beginning on or after 1st January 1996—

(*a*) as if the reference in subsection (2D) of that section to a previous accounting period included a reference to an accounting period beginning before that date, and

(*b*) in relation to such a previous accounting period, as if the references—

(i) to the amount deductible by virtue of this section, and
(ii) to the basic deduction,

were to be construed by reference to whatever provisions had effect in

167

relation to that previous period for purposes corresponding to those of that section as amended by this section.

BACKGROUND NOTE

Most insurance companies carrying on life insurance business are assessed not on their trading profits, in respect of such business, but on investment income and gains, in order to charge to tax the investment return accruing for the benefit of policy holders. A minimum tax rule, known as the *notional Case I* rule, is applied to ensure that the company does not pay less tax than it would if it were assessed under Schedule D Case I.

This section repeals the old *notional Case I* rule in TA 1988 s 76(2)–(5) and substitutes what is intended to be a much clearer provision in place of the current obscure language. The proposed rule operates by comparing two amounts, (*a*) the amount of the (notional) Case I assessment and (*b*) the income less the "basic amount" of expenses, that is, the net expenses which would be available for relief but for the operation of the Case I rule. It should be noted that the restriction of expenses by reference to a Case I figure only applies to life insurance business which is assessed on the *income less expenses* basis, and not to business which is actually assessed Case I, either under the Revenue option or because it is pure reinsurance business (which may only be assessed Case I following TA 1988 s 439A inserted by FA 1995 Sch 8 para 26). The rules affecting the Case I computation itself are unchanged, so that franked investment income may be included under the provision in TA 1988 s 434(1)(*b*),.and the special rules in FA 1989 ss 82–83A continue to apply.

The new rule will apply to post-1937 capital redemption business as well as life insurance, following the introduction, in s 168 and Sch 33, of statutory relief for the management expenses of that class of business.

THE NEW NOTIONAL CASE I RULE

Subsection (1).

This substitutes new sub-ss (2)–(5) for the repealed provisions in TA 1988 s 76(2)–(5).

The new sub-ss (2) and (2A) provide that where (*a*) the (notional) Case I figure (adjusted for losses) exceeds (*b*) the "relevant income" less the aggregate of the "basic deduction" for management expenses, amounts set off in respect of a non-trading deficit under the new loan relationships legislation (including amounts brought back from a later accounting period under the provisions of Sch 11 para 4(3)–(5)), and certain charges, then the relief to be given in respect of expenses of management is to be the "basic deduction" less the excess of (*a*) over (*b*). The calculation of the non-trading deficit is made under the provisions in Sch 11 para 2 of this Act. The charges which are deductible are annuities and annual payments referable to life insurance business and, in the case of annual payments other than annuities, are payable in satisfaction of claims under insurance policies (changes in the treatment of annual payments are made in s 165 of this Act). The effect of the new measure is to give a figure of *income less expenses* equal to or greater than the Case I figure, which is the object of the current legislation.

New sub-s (2B) defines "relevant income" as the sum of (*a*) income and gains referable to life insurance business and (*b*) franked investment income arising from assets held for the purposes of that business, insofar as not within (*a*).

New sub-s (2C) specifies the losses which are to be taken into account in adjusting the Case I figure used in the comparison described above. They are "unused losses" arising from categories of life insurance business which are assessed under Case I rules (pension business, overseas life assurance business and life reinsurance business) insofar as they would be available for setting against income but for the restriction in TA 1988 s 434A(2). The ban on setting Case VI losses in respect of these categories of business against Case VI profits from another source (TA 1988 ss 436(4), 439B(4) and 441(5) disapplying s 396) is not affected, the adjustment in respect of the unused losses applying only to the calculation of any Case I restriction of relief for expenses of management.

New sub-s (2D) defines "unused losses" as losses not taken into account in any previous period in calculating the Case I restriction of expenses.

New sub-s (5) provides that where the "basic deduction" for expenses of management, adjusted for amounts carried back in respect of loan relationship deficits, exceeds the amount actually allowable the excess is to be carried forward.

Subsection (2).

This inserts in TA 1988 s 76 definitions of "basic deduction" (the amount of relievable expenses before any restriction) and "relevant franked investment income" (excluding income the tax credits of which are repayable under the provisions relating to pension business or overseas life assurance business).

Subsection (3).

This makes consequential changes to TA 1988 Sch 19AC (modification of general provisions in respect of overseas life insurance companies) and sub-s (4) makes a minor amendment to a cross reference.

COMMENCEMENT AND TRANSITION

Subsection (5).
The new rules are to take effect for accounting periods beginning after 31 December 1995.

Subsection (6).
Continuity of relief is ensured by extending the references in new sub-s (2D) to the "basic deduction" and the amounts allowable for relief under the new provisions to the equivalent amounts for accounting periods ending before 1 January 1996. Expenses of management unrelieved for any such previous periods, whether because of insufficiency of income or the operation of the old *notional Case I* rule, may therefore be taken into account in making the comparison prescribed by the new rules.

165   Annual payments under insurance policies: deductions

(1) In section 337 of the Taxes Act 1988 (deductions in computing income), the following subsections shall be inserted after subsection (2)—

"(2A) In computing any profits or losses of a company in accordance with the provisions of this Act applicable to Case I of Schedule D, subsection (2)(*b*) above shall not prevent the deduction of any annuity or other annual payment which is payable by a company wholly or partly in satisfaction of any claim under an insurance policy in relation to which the company is the insurer.

(2B) The reference in subsection (2A) above to an annuity payable wholly or partly in satisfaction of a claim under an insurance policy shall be taken, in relation to an insurance company (within the meaning of Chapter I of Part XII), to include a reference to every annuity payable by that company; and the references in sections 338(2) and 434B(2) to an annuity paid wholly or partly as mentioned in subsection (2A) above shall be construed accordingly."

(2) In section 338(2) of that Act, in the words after paragraph (*b*) (payments which are not charges on income), after "corporation tax" there shall be inserted "nor any annuity or other annual payment which (without being so deductible) is paid wholly or partly as mentioned in section 337(2A)".

(3) In section 434B of that Act (treatment of interest and annuities in the case of insurance companies), subsection (1) shall cease to have effect; and in subsection (2), for the words from the beginning to "mentioned in subsection (1) above" there shall be substituted—

"(2) Nothing in section 337(2A) or 338(2) shall be construed as preventing any annuity or other annual payment which is paid wholly or partly as mentioned in section 337(2A)".

(4) Subject to subsection (5) below, this section has effect in relation to accounting periods beginning on or after 1st January 1996.

(5) In relation to any accounting period beginning on or after 1st January 1996 but ending before 1st April 1996, this section shall have effect as if any reference in provisions inserted by this section to an annuity payable or paid by an insurance company included a reference to any such interest as was mentioned in section 434B(1) of the Taxes Act 1988 before its repeal by virtue of this section.

BACKGROUND NOTE
This section alters the treatment of certain annual payments made by insurance companies. Their treatment for the most part as charges on income gives rise to a number of anomalies where in economic terms they are trade expenses rather than payments out of commercial profits. The problems caused by the non-deductibility of annuities in the notional Case I computation of a life insurance company were remedied by TA 1988 s 434B, inserted by FA 1995 Sch 8. It appears that the review of the taxation of the recipients of certain annual payments, resulting in the changes

made by s 143, has highlighted the similar anomalies which have existed for some time in the non-life field. In particular, the treatment of permanent health annuities has been the subject of confusion, partly because the majority of payments under such policies are covered by the Revenue Extra-statutory Concession A83.

This section provides for relief to be given in all cases as a trading expense in Case I computations (including notional Case I and Case VI).

THE NEW RULES
Subsection (1) inserts in TA 1988 s 337 new sub-s (2A) and (2B) which apply only to insurance companies. The new sub-s (2A) disapplies the prohibition in sub-s (2) on the deduction of annuities and annual payments insofar as they are payable wholly or partly in settlement of a claim under an insurance policy. Subsection (2B) makes it clear that in the case of an insurance company authorised to carry on business in the UK (including EC and EEA companies) any annuity is to be regarded as within the new sub-s (2A). The legislation applies to all forms of annuity and so includes annuities payable under permanent health contracts and purchased life annuities. It will cover an annuity paid under a structured settlement of a claim for personal injury either by the general insurer (where the liability is self-funded) or purchased from a life insurance company, but not where the annuity is paid by a person other than an insurance company (for the treatment of this type of annuity in the hands of the annuitant, see TA 1988 ss 329A and 329B).

Subsection (2) makes the corresponding and opposite amendment to TA 1988 s 338(2), providing that annuities and annual payments within the new s 337(2A) are not charges.

Subsection (3) repeals TA 1988 s 434B(1), which is replaced by the wider provision of the new s 337(2A) and, by the new treatment of interest payable in s 99 and Sch 11, makes a consequential amendment to s 434B(2).

COMMENCEMENT AND TRANSITION
Subsection (4) brings the new provisions into effect for accounting periods beginning after 31 December 1995. Subsection (5) provides, in the exceptional case of an accounting period beginning and ending between 1 January and 31 March 1996, both dates inclusive, for the deduction of interest referable to a company's life insurance business.

166 Equalisation reserves

Schedule 32 to this Act (which makes provision about the tax treatment of equalisation reserves maintained by insurance companies) shall have effect.

GENERAL NOTE
This section introduces Sch 32 which contains the primary legislation governing transfers made to or from the equalisation reserves which will have to be maintained by general insurance companies in respect of certain types of business, together with regulation making powers.

167 Industrial assurance business

(1) In section 432 of the Taxes Act 1988, subsection (2) (industrial assurance business treated as separate business for the purposes of Chapter I of Part XII) shall cease to have effect.

(2) In section 432A(2) of the Taxes Act 1988, for paragraphs (*d*) and (*e*) (different categories of basic life assurance and general annuity business, including and not including industrial assurance business), there shall be substituted the following paragraph—

"(*d*) basic life assurance and general annuity business; and".

(3) In section 86 of the Finance Act 1989 (spreading of relief for acquisition expenses)—

(*a*) in subsection (1)(*a*), for "in respect of industrial life assurance business carried on by the company" there shall be substituted "for persons who collect premiums from house to house"; and

(*b*) in subsection (2), for "in respect of industrial life assurance business" there shall be substituted "for persons who collect premiums from house to house".

(4) In section 832 of the Taxes Act 1988 (interpretation), in the definition of "industrial assurance business" for "has" there shall be substituted "means

any such business carried on before the day appointed for the coming into force of section 167(4) of the Finance Act 1996 as was industrial assurance business within''.

(5) In Schedule 14 to the Taxes Act 1988 (ancillary provisions about relief in respect of life assurance premiums), in paragraph 8, at the beginning of sub-paragraph (4) (policy which is varied so as to increase benefits, etc to be treated as issued after 13th March 1984) there shall be inserted ''Subject to sub-paragraph (8) below,''.

(6) After sub-paragraph (7) of that paragraph there shall be inserted the following sub-paragraph—

''(8) Sub-paragraph (4) above does not apply in the case of a variation so as to increase the benefits secured, if the variation is made—

(*a*) on or after such day as the Board may by order appoint, and
(*b*) in consideration of a change in the method of payment of premiums from collection by a person collecting premiums from house to house to payment by a different method.''

(7) In Schedule 15 to the Taxes Act 1988 (qualifying policies)—

(*a*) in paragraph 1(6) (calculation of amount included in premiums of whole life and term insurances in respect of their payment otherwise than annually), for ''and if the policy is issued in the course of an industrial assurance business,'' there shall be substituted ''and if the policy provides for payment otherwise than annually without providing for the amount of the premiums if they are paid annually,''; and
(*b*) in paragraph 2(2) (the equivalent calculation for endowment assurances), for ''issued in the course of an industrial assurance business'', there shall be substituted ''that provides for the payment of premiums otherwise than annually without providing for the amount of the premiums if they are paid annually,''.

(8) After paragraph 8 of that Schedule there shall be inserted the following paragraph—

''**8A.**—(1) Paragraphs 7 and 8 above shall have effect in relation to any policy issued on or after the appointed day as if the references to the issue of a policy in the course of an industrial assurance business were references to the issue of a policy by any company in a case in which—

(*a*) the company, before that day and in the course of such a business, issued any policy which was a qualifying policy by virtue of either of those paragraphs; and
(*b*) the policies which on 28th November 1995 were being offered by the company as available to be issued included policies of the same description as the policy issued on or after the appointed day.

(2) In this paragraph 'the appointed day' means such day as the Board may by order appoint.''

(9) In paragraph 18(3) of that Schedule (certain variations of a policy not to affect whether policy is a qualifying policy), after paragraph (*b*) there shall be inserted ''or

(*c*) any variation so as to increase the benefits secured or reduce the premiums payable which is effected—

(i) on or after such day as the Board may by order appoint, and
(ii) in consideration of a change in the method of payment of premiums

171

from collection by a person collecting premiums from house to house to payment by a different method.''

(10) Subsections (1) to (3) above have effect in relation to accounting periods beginning on or after 1st January 1996.

(11) Subsection (4) above shall come into force on such day as the Board may by order appoint.

(12) Subsection (7) above shall have effect in relation to policies issued on or after such day as the Board may by order appoint.

BACKGROUND NOTE

The changes made by this section, and the associated repeals, reflect a proposed change in the regulatory provisions following which industrial assurance business and ordinary life insurance business will cease to be treated as different categories of business and the Industrial Assurance Acts will be repealed (the repeal, and consequential changes to the regulatory provisions, are to be effected by a Treasury Order, under the Deregulation and Contracting-Out Act 1994, which is expected to be made in the summer of 1996).

The conduct of industrial assurance business is regulated by the Industrial Assurance Act 1923 and the Industrial Assurance and Friendly Societies Act 1948. The business is characterised by the collection of premiums in cash from the policy holder's home, at intervals of less than two months and often weekly (Industrial Assurance Act 1923 s 1), and the issue of premium receipt books in which the payment of premiums is recorded (Industrial Assurance and Friendly Societies Act 1948 s 8). A company which carries on both industrial assurance business and ordinary life business must maintain separate records of and separate funds in respect of each kind of business (Insurance Companies Act 1982 ss 28–29). Because of the much higher expenses of industrial assurance business separate tax computations have been required since 1923 (currently by TA 1988 s 432), and for the same reason the rules for identifying qualifying life policies contain special provisions taking account of the characteristics of industrial life policies.

In recent years the amount of industrial assurance business written by both insurance companies and friendly societies has significantly declined (by more than 46 per cent between 1975 and 1993) for a number of reasons, including high costs and the increased use of bank accounts and direct debit facilities (see Treasury consultation document issued 27 June 1995, ''Review of the Industrial Assurance Acts''). Following the repeal of the Industrial Assurance Acts policy holders will, if they wish, be able to switch to more convenient ways of paying premiums and insurers will be able to modernise the way they carry on the business (Treasury press release of 14 November 1995, ''Re-vamp for door-to-door assurance'').

The tax measures reflect the expected changes in the regulatory legislation. As industrial assurance business will cease to exist as an identifiable category of life insurance business separate corporation tax computations will no longer be needed for periods beginning on or after 1 January 1966 (whether or not the deregulation provisions take effect for any such period). Similarly, from a day to be appointed, the appropriate changes are made to the rules for premium relief and qualifying policies, in particular providing for continuity of reliefs and qualifying status where policy holders switch to a different method of payment.

AMENDMENTS TO CORPORATION TAX PROVISIONS

Subsection (1) removes the requirement, in TA 1988 s 432(2), that industrial assurance business shall be treated as a separate business from any other category of life insurance business. It follows that a separate *income less expenses* computation, involving the segregation of the management expenses and a separate *notional Case I* computation, will no longer need to be made and the figures relating to the two categories of business will be merged (it is anticipated that they will no longer be separately accounted for in the regulatory return made to the DTI).

Subsection (2) makes the corresponding change to TA 1988 s 432A(2) which sets out the categories of business for which income and gains have to be separately identified.

Subsection (3) retains the special treatment for commissions in respect of business that was previously industrial business, insofar as the insurer continues to have the premiums collected from the policy holder's home. Such commissions will still be excluded from the spreading provisions of FA 1989 s 86.

DEFINITION OF INDUSTRIAL ASSURANCE BUSINESS

Subsection (4) amends the definition of industrial assurance business in TA 1988 s 832 to reflect the repeal of the Industrial Assurance Acts and in such a way as to retain an effective definition for the purpose of distinguishing existing business after the repeal.

AMENDMENTS TO INCOME TAX PROVISIONS

Subsections (5) and (6) allow continuity of the tax relief for premiums where a pre-13 March 1984 policy is varied after the appointed day so as to provide an increase in the benefits under the policy which reflects a change in the method of payment of the premiums away from home collection (an increase in benefits would otherwise result in withdrawal of the relief in respect of premiums paid after the variation). This provision allows a company which ends home collection to pass on to the policy holders concerned the benefit of the cost savings therefrom.

Subsections (7)–(9) amend TA 1988 Sch 15 (which contains the rules for determining whether or not a policy is a qualifying policy for tax purposes).

Subsection (7) amends the 75 per cent rule in Sch 15 paras 1 and 2 to retain the 10 per cent disregard where the policy provides for premiums to be paid other than annually, with the result that policies which would previously have been written as industrial assurance policies will continue to benefit from the relaxation in the 75 per cent rule which reflects the heavier expense ratio of such business. This provision applies only to policies where an annual premium is not included in the terms of the policy, and not to policies which for example provide for payment of an annual premium by quarterly or monthly instalments.

Subsection (8) inserts a new para 8A which continues the benefit of special rules applicable to certain old-style industrial assurance policies to similar policies issued after the appointed day provided that such policies had actually been issued by the insurer before the appointed day and were available for issue on 28 November 1995 (Budget Day). The policies concerned secure payments at intervals, rather than a single lump sum.

Subsectoin (9) amends Sch 15 para 18 so as to disregard a variation, made after the appointed day, in the terms of a policy in order to reflect the ending of home collection, enabling the cost benefit of the change to be passed on to the policy holder.

COMMENCEMENT

Subsections (10)–(11) provide for commencement—

(*a*) for periods beginning on or after 1 January 1996 in respect of the corporation tax provisions;
(*b*) by reference to an appointed day in respect of the income tax provisions (the day to be appointed is the day on which the measures deregulating the conduct of industrial assurance business come into force—see Revenue Press Release of 14 November 1995, "Industrial assurance business").

168   Capital redemption business

(1) For subsection (3) of section 458 of the Taxes Act 1988 (meaning of capital redemption business) there shall be substituted the following subsection—

"(3) In this section 'capital redemption business' means any business in so far as it—

(*a*) is insurance business for the purposes of the Insurance Companies Act 1982, but not life assurance business; and

(*b*) consists in effecting on the basis of actuarial calculations, and carrying out, contracts under which, in return for one or more fixed payments, a sum or series of sums of a specified amount become payable at a future time or over a period."

(2) Schedule 33 to this Act (which makes provision for the application of the I minus E basis of charging tax to companies carrying on capital redemption business) shall have effect.

(3) In Chapter I of Part XII of the Taxes Act 1988, after section 458 (capital redemption business) there shall be inserted the following section—

"458A   Capital redemption business: power to apply life assurance provisions

(1) The Treasury may by regulations provide for the life assurance provisions of the Corporation Tax Acts to have effect in relation to companies carrying on capital redemption business as if capital redemption business were, or were a category of, life assurance business.

(2) Regulations under this section may provide that the provisions applied

by the regulations are to have effect as respects capital redemption business with such modifications and exceptions as may be provided for in the regulations.

(3) Regulations under this section may—

(*a*) make different provision for different cases;
(*b*) include such incidental, supplemental, consequential and transitional provision (including provision modifying provisions of the Corporation Tax Acts other than the life assurance provisions) as the Treasury consider appropriate; and
(*c*) include retrospective provision.

(4) In this section references to the life assurance provisions of the Corporation Tax Acts are references to the following—

(*a*) the provisions of this Chapter so far as they relate to life assurance business or companies carrying on such business; and
(*b*) any other provisions of the Corporation Tax Acts making separate provision by reference to whether or not the business of a company is or includes life assurance business or any category of insurance business that includes life assurance business.

(5) In this section 'capital redemption business' has the same meaning as in section 458.''

(4) In section 539(3) of that Act, in the definition of ''capital redemption policy'' for ''insurance'' there shall be substituted ''contract''.

(5) In section 553(10) of that Act, in paragraph (*a*) of the definition of ''new offshore capital redemption policy'', for ''an insurance'' there shall be substituted ''a contract''.

(6) Subsection (1) above shall have effect as respects accounting periods ending on or after the day appointed under section 199 of the Finance Act 1994 for the purposes of Chapter III of Part IV of that Act (self-assessment management provisions), and subsections (4) and (5) above shall have effect as respects contracts effected on or after that day.

BACKGROUND NOTE
   Capital redemption is a class of long-term business (Class VI of Sch 1 of the Insurance Companies Act 1982) traditionally carried on by life insurance companies. Although arguably not insurance at all it is treated as insurance for regulatory purposes by the Insurance Companies Acts 1982 s 95. Very little such business is now written, but it was at one time more important and included what was known as investment bond business, much of which was reclassified as life insurance business as a result of the decision in *Joseph v Law Integrity Insurance Co Ltd* [1916] 2 Ch 581. Nowadays the business consists mainly of sinking fund business, which provides a lump sum to meet a future liability such as lease redemption, and contracts for annuities certain (annuities which continue for a specified period, irrespective of the death of the annuitant).
   Capital redemption was not affected by the segregation of life insurance business introduced in 1915 and consequently continued to be assessed on a Case I basis. Because the deduction of actuarial liabilities combined with the exclusion of franked investment income led to the creation of artificial losses FA 1937 introduced the segregation of this type of business and provided for the inclusion of franked investment income in computing losses. This measure, which only applied to post-1937 business, paved the way for assessment of the investment income, and later the chargeable gains, referable to the business. The current legislation, which has changed little since 1937, is to be found in TA 1988 s 458. It does not provide any relief for expenses of management, but these are customarily given by concession, subject to a notional Case I restriction.
   The new legislation provides a statutory basis for relief for expenses, and regulation making powers to enable the life insurance provisions to be adapted to give a comprehensive code for the taxation of this type of business. The need to move from a concessional to a statutory basis is in part dictated by the introduction of self-assessment.

DEFINITION, EXPENSES RELIEF AND REGULATIONS

Subsection (1) substitutes a new definition of capital redemption business for the one presently in TA 1988 s 458(3). The old definition repeated the one originally to be found in the Insurance Companies Act 1974, but dropped from the regulatory legislation on the implementation in 1981 of the EC First Life Assurance Directive of 5 March 1979 (79/267/EEC). The new definition is based on that in Article 1.2 of the First Life Directive.

Subsection (2) introduces Sch 33 which makes provision for the application of the *income less expenses* basis to capital redemption business.

Subsection (3) inserts in TA 1988 a new s 458A allowing the Treasury to make regulations for the application to capital redemption business of legislation which applies to life insurance.

Subsections (4) and (5) alter the wording of TA 1988 ss 539(3) and 553(10) to remove any uncertainty due to the use of the word "insurance".

COMMENCEMENT

Subsection (6) provides for the definition in new s 458(3) to take effect for accounting periods ending on or after the appointed day for the application of the self-assessment provisions to corporation tax, and for the altered wording in TA 1988 ss 539 and 553 to apply to contracts made on or after that day.

No amendments are made to TA 1988 s 458(4), so the new provisions do not apply to pre-1938 capital redemption business. Such business, the amounts of which are negligible, will continue to be assessed under the provisions of Case I.

169   Provisional repayments in connection with pension business

(1) Schedule 19AB to the Taxes Act 1988 (pension business: payments on account of tax credits and deducted tax) shall be amended in accordance with the provisions of Part I of Schedule 34 to this Act.

(2) Schedule 19AC to the Taxes Act 1988 (modification of that Act in relation to overseas life insurance companies) shall be amended in accordance with the provisions of Part II of Schedule 34 to this Act.

(3) The amendments made by Schedule 34 to this Act shall have effect in relation to provisional repayment periods, within the meaning of Schedule 19AB to the Taxes Act 1988, falling in accounting periods ending on or after the day appointed under section 199 of the Finance Act 1994 for the purposes of Chapter III of Part IV of that Act (self-assessment management provisions).

GENERAL NOTE

This section introduces Sch 34, which modifies the rules in TA 1988 Sch 19AB (and their modification in Sch 19AC as regards overseas life insurance companies) which give companies carrying on pension business a statutory right to provisional repayments of income tax and payments of tax credit in respect of income referable to that business. The existing provisions were introduced by FA 1991 and took effect for accounting periods beginning after 1 October 1992. The rules are being changed to make them fit with self-assessment procedures, and the changes will take effect for provisional repayment periods (the periods in respect of which provisional repayments are made) in accounting periods ending on or after the day appointed for the commencement of the corporation tax self-assessment provisions.

170   Time for amending and enquiring into returns

(1) After section 11AB of the Taxes Management Act 1970 there shall be inserted the following sections—

"11AC   Modifications of sections 11AA and 11AB in relation to non-annual accounting of general insurance business

(1) This section applies in any case where a company carrying on insurance business in any period delivers a return for that period under section 11 of this Act which is based wholly or partly on accounts which the company is required or permitted to draw up using the method described in paragraph 52 of Schedule 9A to the Companies Act 1985 (accounting for general insurance business on a non-annual basis).

(2) Where this section applies, section 11AA(2) of this Act shall have effect as if after paragraph (*b*) there were added ''and

(*c1*) where a company has delivered a return which is based wholly or partly on accounts drawn up as mentioned in section 11AC(1) of this Act, then, at any time before the end of the period of twelve months beginning with the date on which any particular technical provision constituted in the case of those accounts as described in paragraph 52 of Schedule 9A to the Companies Act 1985 is replaced as described in sub-paragraph (4) of that paragraph, the company may by notice to an officer of the Board so amend its self-assessment as to give effect to any amendments to the return—

(i) which arise from the replacement of that technical provision, and
(ii) which the company has notified to such an officer.''

(3) Where this section applies, section 11AB of this Act shall have effect—

(*a*) as if in subsection (1)(*b*) after ''subsection (2)(*b*)'' there were inserted ''or (*c1*)''; and
(*b*) as if in subsection (2) for the words from ''is'' to the end of paragraph (*b*) there were substituted—

''(*a1*) in the case of a return (whenever delivered) which is based wholly or partly on accounts drawn up as mentioned in section 11AC(1) of this Act, is whichever of the following periods ends the later, that is to say—

(i) the period of two years beginning with the date (or, if there is more than one such date, the latest date) on which any technical provision constituted in the case of those accounts as described in paragraph 52 of Schedule 9A to the Companies Act 1985 is replaced as mentioned in sub-paragraph (4) of that paragraph; or
(ii) the period ending with the quarter day next following the first anniversary of the day on which the return was delivered; and

(*b1*) in the case of an amendment of such a return—

(i) if the amendment is made on or before the filing date, is the period of twelve months beginning with that date; or
(ii) if the amendment is made after that date, is the period ending with the quarter day next following the first anniversary of the day on which the amendment was made;''.

11AD Modifications of sections 11AA and 11AB for insurance companies with non-annual actuarial investigations

(1) This section applies in any case where a return under section 11 of this Act is delivered by an insurance company which is permitted by an order under section 68 of the Insurance Companies Act 1982 to cause investigations to be made into its financial condition less frequently than is required by section 18 of that Act.

(2) Where this section applies, section 11AA(2) of this Act shall have effect as if, after paragraph (*b*), there were added ''and

(*c2*) where a company falling within section 11AD(1) of this Act has delivered a return for any period, then, at any time before the end of the period of twelve months beginning with the date as at which the relevant investigation is carried out, that is to say—

(i) if the return is for a period as at the end of which there is carried out an investigation under section 18 of the Insurance Companies Act 1982 into the financial condition of the company, that investigation, or

(ii) if the return is not for such a period, the first such investigation to be made into the financial condition of the company as at the end of a subsequent period,

the company may by notice to an officer of the Board so amend its self-assessment as to give effect to any amendments to its return which arise from that investigation and which the company has notified to such an officer.''

(3) Where this section applies, section 11AB of this Act shall have effect—

(*a*) as if in subsection (1)(*b*) after "subsection (2)(*b*)" there were inserted "or (*c2*)"; and

(*b*) as if in subsection (2) for the words from "is" to the end of paragraph (*b*) there were substituted—

"(*a2*) in the case of a return delivered at any time by a company falling within section 11AD(1) of this Act, is the period of two years beginning with the date as at which the relevant investigation, as defined in section 11AA(2)(*c2*) of this Act, is carried out; and

(*b2*) in the case of an amendment of such a return—

(i) if the amendment is made on or before the filing date, is the period of twelve months beginning with that date; or

(ii) if the amendment is made after that date, is the period ending with the quarter day next following the first anniversary of the day on which the amendment was made;''.

11AE   Modifications of sections 11AA and 11AB for friendly societies with non–annual actuarial investigations

(1) This section applies in any case where a return under section 11 of this Act is delivered by a friendly society which is required by section 47 of the Friendly Societies Act 1992 to cause an investigation to be made into its financial condition at least once in every period of three years.

(2) Where this section applies, section 11AA(2) of this Act shall have effect as if, after paragraph (*b*), there were added "and

(*c3*) where a friendly society falling within section 11AE(1) of this Act has delivered a return for any period, then, at any time before the end of the period of fifteen months beginning with the date as at which the relevant investigation is carried out, that is to say—

(i) if the return is for a period as at the end of which there is carried out an investigation under section 47 of the Friendly Societies Act 1992 into the financial condition of the society, that investigation, or

(ii) if the return is not for such a period, the first such investigation to be made into the financial condition of the society as at the end of a subsequent period,

the society may by notice to an officer of the Board so amend its self-assessment as to give effect to any amendments to its return which arise from that investigation and which the company has notified to such an officer.''

(3) Where this section applies, section 11AB of this Act shall have effect—

(*a*) as if in subsection (1)(*b*) after "subsection (2)(*b*)" there were inserted "or (*c3*)"; and

(b) as if in subsection (2) for the words from "is" to the end of paragraph (b) there were substituted—

"(a3) in the case of a return delivered at any time by a friendly society falling within section 11AE(1) of this Act, is the period of twenty seven months beginning with the date as at which the relevant investigation, as defined in section 11AA(2)(c3) of this Act, is carried out; and
(b3) in the case of an amendment of such a return—

(i) if the amendment is made on or before the filing date, is the period of twelve months beginning with that date; or
(ii) if the amendment is made after that date, is the period ending with the quarter day next following the first anniversary of the day on which the amendment was made;".

(2) The amendment made by subsection (1) above shall have effect as respects accounting periods ending on or after the day appointed under section 199 of the Finance Act 1994 for the purposes of Chapter III of Part IV of that Act (self-assessment management provisions).

INTRODUCTION
Some insurance companies and friendly societies draw up accounts on a non-annual basis, that is, they do not strike a balance of profit in respect of current business until they draw up accounts for a later year, or do so only at intervals greater than one year. Such concerns are not able to make complete returns under the self-assessment procedures within the ordinary time limits. The new legislation makes special provision for—

(a) general insurers accounting on a non-annual basis in accordance with the Companies Act 1985 Sch 9A para 52 (non-annual accounting is commonly used for marine, aviation and transport business, and always for certain types of reinsurance);
(b) companies carrying on long-term business which are allowed, by an order made under the Insurance Companies Act 1982 s 68, to make an actuarial valuation at intervals greater than one year;
(c) friendly societies which are required by the Friendly Societies Act 1992 s 47 to make an actuarial valuation once in every three years (the larger societies are required to make annual valuations).

MODIFICATION OF TMA 1970 ss 11AA AND 11AB
Subsection (1) inserts in TMA 1970 new ss 11AC–11AE which make special provision for returns, under the new self-assessment procedures, by the concerns identified above.

TMA 1970 s 11AC
Subsections (1) and (2) modify TMA 1970 s 11AA(2) so that a company accounting on an non-annual basis may amend its self-assessment at any time within 12 months of the date on which it closes the underwriting account (that is, it strikes a profit in respect of the underwriting for the year in question) by the substitution of a calculated technical provision for the balance brought forward.
Subsection (3) makes a corresponding modification to s 11AB allowing Revenue enquiries regarding the return to be made within the later of two years from the closing of the underwriting account or the end of the period ending with the quarter day next following the first anniversary of the amendment of the return.

TMA 1970 s 11AD
Subsections (1) and (2) similarly modify TMA 1970 s 11AA(2) so that a company accounting for its long-term business on the basis of actuarial valuations made at intervals greater than one year may amend its self-assessment at any time within 12 months of the end of the accounting period for which the valuation is made.
Subsection (3) makes a corresponding modification to s 11AB allowing Revenue enquiries regarding the return to be made within the later of two years from the date as at which the valuation is made or the end of the period ending with the quarter day next following the first anniversary of the amendment of the return.

TMA 1970 s 11AE
Subsections (1) and (2) again modify TMA 1970 s 11AA(2) so that a friendly society making actuarial valuations at intervals of three years may amend its return at any time within 15 months from the date as at which the valuation is made.

Subsection (3) makes a corresponding modification to s 11AB allowing Revenue enquiries regarding the return to be made within the later of 27 months from the date at which the valuation is made or the end of the period ending with the quarter day next following the first anniversary of the amendment of the return.

COMMENCEMENT
Subsection (2) provides for the modifications to take effect for accounting periods ending on or after the day appointed for the coming into effect of the corporation tax self-assessment provisions.

Friendly societies

171   Life or endowment business

(1) In section 466 of the Taxes Act 1988 (interpretation of Chapter II of Part XII) for subsection (1) (meaning of "life or endowment business") there shall be substituted—

"(1) In this Chapter "life or endowment business" means, subject to subsections (1A) and (1B) below,—

(*a*) any business within Class I, II or III of Head A of Schedule 2 to the Friendly Societies Act 1992;
(*b*) pension business;
(*c*) any other life assurance business;
(*d*) any business within Class IV of Head A of that Schedule, if—

(i) the contract is one made before 1st September 1996; or
(ii) the contract is one made on or after 1st September 1996 and the effecting and carrying out of the contract also constitutes business within Class I, II or III of Head A of that Schedule.

(1A) Life or endowment business does not include the issue, in respect of a contract made before 1st September 1996, of a policy affording provision for sickness or other infirmity (whether bodily or mental), unless—

(*a*) the policy also affords assurance for a gross sum independent of sickness or other infirmity;
(*b*) not less than 60 per cent of the amount of the premiums is attributable to the provision afforded during sickness or other infirmity; and
(*c*) there is no bonus or addition which may be declared or accrue upon the assurance of the gross sum.

(1B) Life or endowment business does not include the assurance of any annuity the consideration for which consists of sums obtainable on the maturity, or on the surrender, of any other policy of assurance issued by the friendly society, being a policy of assurance forming part of the tax exempt life or endowment business of the friendly society."

(2) In subsection (2) of that section (other definitions) there shall be inserted at the appropriate places—

(*a*) "'insurance company' shall be construed in accordance with section 431;"; and
(*b*) "'long term business' shall be construed in accordance with section 431;".

(3) In section 266 of that Act (life assurance premium relief) in subsection (6) (deduction from total income where relief given for part of certain payments to friendly societies) after paragraph (*b*) there shall be inserted "and

(*c*) the insurance or contract is not excluded by subsection (6A) below,".

(4) After that subsection there shall be inserted—

"(6A) For the purposes of subsection (6)(*c*) above, an insurance or contract is excluded by this subsection if it is made on or after 1st September 1996 and affords provisions for sickness or other infirmity (whether bodily or mental), unless—

(*a*) it also affords assurance for a gross sum independent of sickness or other infirmity;

(*b*) not less than 60 per cent of the amount of the premiums is attributable to the provision afforded during sickness or other infirmity; and

(*c*) there is no bonus or addition which may be declared or accrue upon the assurance of the gross sum."

(5) In section 463(1) of that Act (Corporation Tax Acts to apply to friendly societies' life or endowment business as they apply to insurance companies' mutual life business) after "mutual life assurance business" there shall be inserted "(or other long term business)".

(6) The amendment made by subsection (5) above shall have effect in relation to accounting periods ending on or after 1st September 1996.

GENERAL NOTE
Societies created since 1 June 1973 (new societies) are exempt from tax on life or endowment business in respect of premiums up to £270 a year. The definition of "life or endowment business", for the purposes of the Taxes Acts, has historically included a policy which covers both life and sickness risks only if certain conditions were satisfied. One of these conditions has been that the sickness cost should be at least 60 per cent of the total premium (TA 1988 s 466(1) prior to amendment). This requirement has produced difficulties for new societies, and has been removed in respect of contracts made on or after 1 September 1996, provided that the contract would otherwise qualify as life or endowment business (TA 1988 s 466(1), (1A), (1B)). Similar amendment is made to the provisions dealing with life assurance premium relief (TA 1988s 266(6)). Other amendments include the importation, into TA 1988 s 466(2), of the definitions of "insurance company" and "long-term business" from TA 1988 s 431.

Personal pension schemes

172   Return of contributions on or after death of member

(1) In section 633(1) of the Taxes Act 1988 (Board not to approve a personal pension scheme which makes provision for any benefit other than those specified in paragraphs (*a*) to (*e*)) in paragraph (*e*) (payment on or after the death of a member of a lump sum satisfying the conditions in section 637A) for the words following "a lump sum" there shall be substituted "with respect to which the conditions in section 637A (return of contributions) are satisfied".

(2) For section 637A of that Act (return of contributions on or after death of member) there shall be substituted—

"637A   Return of contributions on or after death of member

(1) The lump sum payable under the arrangements in question (or, where two or more lump sums are so payable, those lump sums taken together) must represent no more than the return of contributions together with reasonable interest on contributions or bonuses out of profits, after allowing for—

(*a*) any income withdrawals, and

(*b*) any purchases of annuities such as are mentioned in section 636.

To the extent that contributions are invested in units under a unit trust scheme, the lump sum (or lump sums) may represent the sale or redemption price of the units.

(2) A lump sum must be payable only if, in the case of the arrangements in question,—

(*a*) no such annuity as is mentioned in section 634 has been purchased by the member;

(*b*) no such annuity as is mentioned in section 636 has been purchased in respect of the relevant interest; and

(*c*) no election in accordance with subsection (5)(*a*) of section 636 has been made in respect of the relevant interest.

(3) Where the member's death occurs after the date which is his pension date in relation to the arrangements in question, a lump sum must not be payable more than two years after the death unless, in the case of that lump sum, the person entitled to such an annuity as is mentioned in section 636 in respect of the relevant interest—

(*a*) has elected in accordance with section 636A to defer the purchase of an annuity; and

(*b*) has died during the period of deferral.

(4) In this section "the relevant interest" means the interest, under the arrangements in question, of the person to whom or at whose direction the payment in question is made, except where there are two or more such interests, in which case it means that one of them in respect of which the payment is made.

(5) Where, under the arrangements in question, there is a succession of interests, any reference in subsection (2) or (3) above to the relevant interest includes a reference to any interest (other than that of the member) in relation to which the relevant interest is a successive interest."

(3) This section—

(*a*) has effect in relation to approvals, of schemes or amendments, given under Chapter IV of Part XIV of the Taxes Act 1988 (personal pension schemes) after the passing of this Act; and

(*b*) does not affect any approval previously given.

GENERAL NOTE

FA 1995 introduced the new concept of income drawdown for personal pensions. This enables the member to draw income (within limits) out of a personal pension and defer the purchase of an annuity to age 75 at the latest. If the member dies during the deferral period, a surviving spouse or dependant can continue to make income withdrawals, or buy an annuity. A third option exercisable within two years of the member's death, is to take the fund in cash subject to a 35 per cent tax charge.

If the surviving spouse or dependant opted to make income withdrawals and then dies more than two years after the date of the original member, the balance of the fund would be retained by the provider (eg insurance company). This anomaly was the subject of much lobbying.

This section will now ensure that where a surviving spouse or dependant opts for income withdrawals and subsequently dies before buying an annuity, the remaining pension fund may pass as a lump sum to the survivor's heirs irrespective of the time lapsed since the original member's death, but subject of course to the 35 per cent tax charge.

TRANSFERS FROM OCCUPATIONAL PENSION SCHEMES

It should not be assumed that all personal pensions will automatically qualify for this new treatment. Where a transfer has been made from an occupational pension scheme into a personal pension and the member subsequently dies, the amount payable in the form of lump sum is limited to 25 per cent of the pension fund, with the balance of 75 per cent being used to provide dependants' pensions (Personal Pension Schemes (Transfer Payments) Regulations, SI 1998/1014, para 8(2)(*b*).) The purpose of this restriction was to prevent people increasing their tax free cash by transferring from occupational into personal schemes. Following the introduction of s 172, if death now occurs during income drawdown from a personal pension and the balance of the fund is to pass as a lump sum, the 35 per cent tax charge to be applied would make redundant the original reason for the 25 per cent rule appropriate to occupational scheme transfers.

While maintaining that the 25 per cent rule persists, it is understood that the Inland Revenue Pension Schemes Office intends to review the Transfer Payments Regulations and the future applicability of the 25 per cent lump sum rule.

Participators in close companies

173   Loans to participators etc

(1) Section 419 of the Taxes Act 1988 (loans to participators etc) shall be amended in accordance with subsections (2) to (4) below.

(2) For subsection (3) (time when tax becomes due) there shall be substituted the following subsection—

"(3) Tax due by virtue of this section in relation to any loan or advance shall be due and payable on the day following the expiry of nine months from the end of the accounting period in which the loan or advance was made."

(3) After subsection (4) (relief in respect of repayment) there shall be inserted the following subsection—

"(4A) Where the repayment of the whole or any part of a loan or advance occurs on or after the day on which tax by virtue of this section becomes due in relation to that loan or advance, relief in respect of the repayment shall not be given under subsection (4) above at any time before the expiry of nine months from the end of the accounting period in which the repayment occurred."

(4) In subsection (6) (application to loans and advances to certain companies who are participators etc), the words "and to a company not resident in the United Kingdom" shall be omitted.

(5) In section 826(4) of that Act (interest on repayment of tax by virtue of section 419), for paragraph (*a*) there shall be substituted the following paragraph—

"(*a*) the date when the entitlement to relief in respect of the repayment accrued, that is to say—

(i) where the repayment of the loan or advance (or part thereof) occurred on or after the day mentioned in section 419(4A), the date nine months after the end of that accounting period; and
(ii) in any other case, the date nine months after the end of the accounting period in which the loan or advance was made;

or".

(6) This section has effect in relation to any loan or advance made in an accounting period ending on or after 31st March 1996.

GENERAL NOTE
   Significant elements of the "close company" legislation were abolished in 1989, however, two of the elements of that legislation which have remained in place have now been amended. These are—

(*a*) legislation (contained in TA 1988 s 419) which treats loans made by a close company to a participator or to an associate of a participator as if they were quasi-dividends and therefore requires the company making the loan to account for an amount of tax equivalent to ACT on the loan principal; and
(*b*) legislation (contained in TCGA 1992 s 13) which seeks to prevent advantage being taken of the territorial nature of the UK capital gains legislation by a UK resident close company arranging to realise capital gains via overseas resident subsidiary companies and not distributing the gains up to the UK parent company (where the distribution would be chargeable to tax).

   A close company is defined (in TA 1988 s 414) as, broadly, a UK resident company which is owned by its directors or by five or fewer participators and their associates.

BACKGROUND NOTE
   TA 1988 s 419 works on the basis that when a loan is made to a participator in a close company or to his associate (both these terms are defined in TA 1988 s 417), the company becomes liable to

account for an amount of tax equal to the ACT rate for the accounting period in which the advance was made, applied to the principal of the loan. When the participator repays the loan, the tax paid over (on making the loan) becomes repayable to the company. Essentially, this makes the tax on the loan an enforced deposit made by the company to the Exchequer.

In respect of accounting periods which ended before 30 September 1993 (the appointed day for the commencement of "pay and file"), there was no immediate obligation on a company to pay over the ACT equivalent amount on making a loan to a participator, merely a general obligation to report the loan and to wait for the Revenue to issue an assessment. They would do so in the full amount of the loan and would take no account of repayments made in the meantime and the ACT equivalent amount would be due and payable within 14 days of the date on which the assessment was issued. When the loan was repaid, the company could claim a tax refund (within six years of the repayment of the loan).

In respect of accounting periods which ended after 30 September 1993 the need for the Revenue to assess the company was removed and the company had an obligation to report the loan and to account for the ACT equivalent amount within 14 days of the end of the accounting period. Interest is chargeable on late payments of tax but interest on tax overpaid is also provided for (under TA 1988 s 826(4)).

Unfortunately it has been found in practice that the time gap between the end of the accounting period and 14 days thereafter is too short and this provision had become a compliance nightmare for both taxpayers and the Revenue. The Budget Press Release (REV 27) admits that "The application of these rules is a common cause of error in the tax computations of close companies. Moreover, the rules do not fit easily with those proposed for paying corporation tax under self assessment."

SUBSECTION (2) AMENDING TA 1988 s 419(3)
The main effect of this amendment is to extend the gap between the end of the accounting period to the due date for tax from 14 days to 9 months (thus aligning it with the due date for corporation tax on the company's profits). The present requirement that tax becomes chargeable whether or not the loan has been repaid is removed and, under the amended regime, where a loan is repaid prior to the due date for paying the tax on the loan no tax will become chargeable.

SUBSECTION (3) INSERTING A NEW TA 1988 s 419(4a)
The due date for refunds of tax in respect of repayments of such loans is also extended to 9 months after the end of the accounting period. If the repayment of the loan occurred after the due date for tax on the original loan, the due date for the tax refund will be 9 months after the end of the accounting period in which the repayment of the loan took place. Tax refunds will not be automatic but will still require a claim to be made by the company.

SUBSECTION (4) AMENDING TA 1988 s 419(6)
Under the prior legislation, in order to cover unusual arrangements under which loans may be routed via third parties so that in the absence of legislation to the contrary they might avoid the charge to tax, certain transactions by companies not resident in the UK involved in the arrangements may be deemed to form part of the making of the loan to a participator. The amendment removes companies not resident in the UK from the ambit of this wider definition.

SUBSECTION (5) AMENDING TA 1988 s 826(4)
Interest on tax overpaid is available where tax is refundable on a repayment of a loan. Where the loan was repaid after the due date (ie 9 months after the end of the accounting period), interest will become payable from the date 9 months after the end of the accounting period in which the repayment was made. Thus, for example, if a loan was made in the year to 31 December 1996 and repaid in the accounting period to 31 December 1998, interest will only be payable from 1 October 1999. Where the loan is repaid after the end of the accounting period but before the due date of the tax, interest will be payable from the due date to the actual date of the tax refund.

SUBSECTION (6)
This legislation was the subject of consultation prior to the Budget and the Budget Press Release (REV 27) reports that the main comment arising from the responses to the consultative document was that the changes should take effect as soon as possible. This request has been met by advancing the effective date of the amendment to apply to loans made in accounting periods ending on or after 31 March 1996.

174 Attribution of gains to participators in non-resident companies

(1) Section 13 of the Taxation of Chargeable Gains Act 1992 (attribution of gains to members of non-resident companies) shall be amended in accordance with subsections (2) to (9) below.

(2) In subsection (2) (persons subject to charge on gain to company), for "holds shares" there shall be substituted "is a participator".

(3) For subsections (3) and (4) (part of gain attributed to person subject to charge) there shall be substituted the following subsections—

"(3) That part shall be equal to the proportion of the gain that corresponds to the extent of the participator's interest as a participator in the company.

(4) Subsection (2) above shall not apply in the case of any participator in the company to which the gain accrues where the aggregate amount falling under that subsection to be apportioned to him and to persons connected with him does not exceed one twentieth of the gain.".

(4) In subsection (5), paragraph (*a*) (section not to apply where gain distributed within two years) shall be omitted; and after that subsection there shall be inserted the following subsection—

"(5A) Where—

(*a*) any amount of capital gains tax is paid by a person in pursuance of subsection (2) above, and
(*b*) an amount in respect of the chargeable gain is distributed (either by way of dividend or distribution of capital or on the dissolution of the company) within 2 years from the time when the chargeable gain accrued to the company,

that amount of tax (so far as neither reimbursed by the company nor applied as a deduction under subsection (7) below) shall be applied for reducing or extinguishing any liability of that person to income tax in respect of the distribution or (in the case of a distribution falling to be treated as a disposal on which a chargeable gain accrues to that person) to any capital gains tax in respect of the distribution."

(5) In subsection (7) (deduction of tax paid in computing gain on shares in the company)—

(*a*) for "not reimbursed by the company)" there shall be inserted "neither reimbursed by the company nor applied under subsection (5A) above for reducing any liability to tax)"; and
(*b*) for "the shares by reference to which the tax is paid" there shall be substituted "any asset representing his interest as a participator in the company."

(6) After subsection (7) there shall be inserted the following subsection—

"(7A) In ascertaining for the purposes of subsection (5A) or (7) above the amount of capital gains tax or income tax chargeable on any person for any year on or in respect of any chargeable gain or distribution—

(*a*) any such distribution as is mentioned in subsection (5A)(*b*) above and falls to be treated as income of that person for that year shall be regarded as forming the highest part of the income on which he is chargeable to tax for the year;
(*b*) any gain accruing in that year on the disposal by that person of any asset representing his interest as a participator in the company shall be regarded as forming the highest part of the gains on which he is chargeable to tax for that year;
(*c*) where any such distribution as is mentioned in subsection (5A)(*b*) above falls to be treated as a disposal on which a gain accrues on which that person is so chargeable, that gain shall be regarded as forming the

next highest part of the gains on which he is so chargeable, after any gains falling within paragraph (*b*) above; and

(*d*) any gain treated as accruing to that person in that year by virtue of subsection (2) above shall be regarded as the next highest part of the gains on which he is so chargeable, after any gains falling within paragraph (*c*) above.''

(7) In subsection (9) (cases where person charged is a company)—

(*a*) for "the person owning any of the shares in the company" there shall be substituted "a person who is a participator in the company"; and

(*b*) for the words from "to the shares" onwards there shall be substituted "to the participating company's interest as a participator in the company to which the gain accrues shall be further apportioned among the participators in the participating company according to the extent of their respective interests as participators, and subsection (2) above shall apply to them accordingly in relation to the amounts further apportioned, and so on through any number of companies.''

(8) In subsection (10) (application to trustees), for "owning shares in the company" there shall be substituted "who are participators in the company, or in any company amongst the participators in which the gain is apportioned under subsection (9) above,''.

(9) After subsection (11) there shall be inserted the following subsections—

''(12) In this section 'participator', in relation to a company, has the meaning given by section 417(1) of the Taxes Act for the purposes of Part XI of that Act (close companies).

(13) In this section—

(*a*) references to a person's interest as a participator in a company are references to the interest in the company which is represented by all the factors by reference to which he falls to be treated as such a participator; and

(*b*) references to the extent of such an interest are references to the proportion of the interests as participators of all the participators in the company (including any who are not resident or ordinarily resident in the United Kingdom) which on a just and reasonable apportionment is represented by that interest.

(14) For the purposes of this section, where—

(*a*) the interest of any person in a company is wholly or partly represented by an interest which he has under any settlement ("his beneficial interest"), and

(*b*) his beneficial interest is the factor, or one of the factors, by reference to which that person would be treated (apart from this subsection) as having an interest as a participator in that company,

the interest as a participator in that company which would be that person's shall be deemed, to the extent that it is represented by his beneficial interest, to be an interest of the trustees of the settlement (and not of that person), and references in this section, in relation to a company, to a participator shall be construed accordingly.

(15) Any appeal under section 31 of the Management Act involving any question as to the extent for the purposes of this section of a person's interest as a participator in a company shall be to the Special Commissioners.''

185

(10) In paragraph 1(3) of Schedule 5 to the Taxation of Chargeable Gains Act 1992 (application of section 86 to section 13 gains)—

(*a*) in paragraph (*a*), for "hold shares in a company which originate" there shall be substituted "are participators in a company in respect of property which originates";

(*b*) in paragraph (*b*), for "the shares" there shall be substituted "so much of their interest as participators as arises from that property"; and

(*c*) at the end there shall be added—

"Subsections (12) and (13) of section 13 shall apply for the purposes of this sub-paragraph as they apply for the purposes of that section."

(11) This section applies to gains accruing on or after 28th November 1995.

GENERAL NOTE

TCGA 1992 s 13 works by attributing to the UK resident shareholder (either corporate or individual) capital gains realised by a non-resident company, which, if it were UK resident, would have been a "close company". The legislation permits the attribution process to look through multiple layers of ownership. At present the attributable proportion of the gain (at each level of ownership) is ascertained by looking at the share of assets the shareholder would be entitled to on a winding up of the company taken at the date of the disposal.

The main thrust of s 174 is to replace this definition of ownership (by reference to entitlement on a winding up) with one which more closely represents the economic interests of the UK resident shareholders in the underlying capital gain. The Budget Press Release (REV 36) referred to fears of increasing avoidance of this legislation by devices which minimise the UK shareholder's entitlement on a winding up of the non-resident company only at the relevant time. Indeed, the Press Release pointed to a potential Exchequer loss in excess of £30 million and rising, in the absence of these amendments.

Gains on certain assets are ignored for this purpose. These are either gains on tangible assets or currency or debts used in a trade carried on overseas or on assets used in a business which is chargeable to UK taxation or gains which have been realised in circumstances which would allow for a tax free transaction had they been realised by a UK resident. Losses are only attributed so as to relieve attributed gains realised in the same accounting period.

No assessment is made in respect of an attributed gain where the shareholder's interest is less than five per cent (for this purpose, ownership interests are not aggregated with shareholdings by associates) or where the terms of a double taxation treaty between the UK and the country of residence of the non-resident company prevent such a charge to tax. In the case of a UK resident individual shareholder, no assessment can be made if they are not also a UK domiciled person.

Double tax credit relief is allowed against the UK tax payable on a TCGA 1992 s 13 assessment and the creditable foreign taxes suffered on the gain are attributed to the UK resident shareholder on the same basis as the gain itself was attributed.

THE AMENDMENTS

The amended legislation will apply to all relevant disposals after 28 November 1995.

PARTICIPATORS' INTERESTS

The change in definition of the UK resident shareholder's interest is accomplished by replacing all references in TCGA 1992 s 13 to a person "owning shares in the [non-resident] company" with references to a "participator". The definition of "participator" is imported into the section from TA 1988 s 417(1) and is then further amplified. The s 417 definition of "participator" is extremely widely drawn and includes both existing and contingent interests in the shares of the non-resident company. It recognises such interests by reference to entitlement to surplus assets in a winding up of the company or by reference to dividend or voting rights. It will also recognise the interests of loan creditors of the company.

In the attribution process, the participator's interest in the non-resident company realising the gain is to be derived by looking through all levels of intermediate holdings (including, where relevant, holdings via trusts) and at all interests in the shares, including those of non-resident participators, in the company. The apportionment process is subject to an overriding criterion that it must achieve a just and reasonable result.

The opportunity has been taken to introduce drafting which clarifies the attribution process where multiple layers of ownership are involved (s 174(7)(*b*) amending s 13(9)).

SUBSEQUENT DISTRIBUTIONS

Under the prior legislation assessments made under TCGA 1992 s 13 were required to be discharged if, within two years of the date on which the gain in question was realised, the gain is distributed to the UK (either by way of a dividend, distribution of capital or on a winding up of the overseas company). The uncertainty caused by such a system does not sit too well with "pay and file" and s 174(4) inserts a new s 13(5A) under which the s 13 assessment is now treated as final but the tax charged on the assessment is to be available as a credit against tax on subsequent distributions. Insofar as the tax cannot be absorbed as a credit it will remain available as allowable base cost on a subsequent sale of the interest in the non-resident company.

To facilitate this, s 174(6) inserts a new s 13(7A) which sets out the hierarchy of identification rules for income and capital gains attributable to the participator's interest in the non-resident close company as elements of the participator's total income. These are—

(*a*) The distribution is to be treated as the highest part of total income (new s 13(7A)(a)).

(*b*) Any gain realised by the person on a subsequent disposal of an interest in the non-resident company is to be treated as the highest part of his capital gains (eg, in allocating losses or the annual exemption) (new s 13(7A)(*b*)).

(*c*) If the subsequent distribution falls to be taxed as a capital gain, that will form the next highest part of the person's capital gains (new s 13(7A)(*c*)).

(*d*) Lastly, any s 13 assessable gains of the year will form the next highest part of the capital gains (new s 13(7A)(*d*)). By elimination, if there are no subsequent distributions or realisations of the interest in the non-resident company in the year in which the s 13 gain accrues, that will form the highest part of any capital gains in that year.

(*e*) Any tax which could not be absorbed as credit against tax on a subsequent distribution, can be treated as allowable base cost in calculating the gain on a subsequent capital gains disposal of the person's interest in the company (s 174(5) amending s 13(7)).

If the tax charged on the s 13 assessment is reimbursed by the non-resident company, that will not be treated as taxable income of the participator, however, it will mean that such tax is not available as a credit (on a subsequent distribution) or as allowable base cost (on a subsequent sale of the interest).

EXAMPLE

1995–96		
Section 13 assessable amount		£250,000
Tax thereon @ 40%	£100,000	
Less: attributable foreign tax credit	(10,000)	
	£ 90,000	
1996–97		
Distribution received		£150,000
Tax thereon @ 40%	£60,000	
Less: withholding tax	(7,500)	
	52,500	
Less: s 13 tax credit from 1995–96	(52,500)	
	£ —	
1998–99		
Capital gain on sale of interest		£60,000
Less: s 13 tax treated as base cost (ignoring indexation)		(37,500)
Chargeable gain		£22,500

It is important to note that where the amount attributed to the UK company under s 13 is covered to any extent by reliefs (eg, losses) and, therefore, no tax is charged or the tax charged is reduced, no deemed amount of tax credit is available against a subsequent distribution or as base cost on a subsequent sale of the interest. Similarly, because the apportionment process does not necessarily follow the legal chain of ownership, frequently the subsequent distribution or even the person to whom it will be made will not necessarily match the amount assessed under s 13, wasting part or all of any tax credit. Such anomalies are not addressed by the legislation.

Cancellation of tax advantages

175   Transactions in certain securities

(1) In section 704 of the Taxes Act 1988 (which relates to the cancellation of tax advantages and specifies the circumstances mentioned in section 703(1)) in paragraph D(2)(*b*) (companies which do not satisfy the conditions there specified with respect to their shares or stocks) for "are authorised to be dealt in on the Stock Exchange, and are so dealt in (regularly or from time to time)"

there shall be substituted "are listed in the Official List of the Stock Exchange, and are dealt in on the Stock Exchange regularly or from time to time".

(2) The reference in paragraph D(2)(*b*) of section 704 of the Taxes Act 1988 to being listed in the Official List of the Stock Exchange and being dealt in on the Stock Exchange regularly or from time to time shall be taken to include a reference to being dealt in on the Unlisted Securities Market regularly or from time to time, but this subsection is subject to subsection (3) below.

(3) Subsection (2) above—

(*a*) so far as relating to sub-paragraph (2) of paragraph D of section 704 of the Taxes Act 1988 as it applies for the purposes of sub-paragraph (1) of that paragraph or paragraph E of that section, shall not have effect where the relevant transaction takes place after the date on which the Unlisted Securities Market closes;

(*b*) so far as relating to paragraph D of that section as it applies for the purposes of section 210(3) or 211(2) of that Act (which relate to bonus issues following, and other matters to be treated or not treated as, repayment of share capital) shall not have effect—

(i) in the case of section 210(3), in relation to share capital issued after that date; or

(ii) in the case of section 211(2), in relation to distributions made after that date.

(4) Except as provided by subsection (3) above, this section—

(*a*) so far as relating to sub-paragraph (2) of paragraph D of section 704 of the Taxes Act 1988 as it applies for the purposes of sub-paragraph (1) of that paragraph or paragraph E of that section, shall have effect where the relevant transaction takes place after the passing of this Act; and

(*b*) so far as relating to paragraph D of that section as it applies for the purposes of section 210(3) or 211(2) of that Act, shall have effect—

(i) in the case of section 210(3), in relation to share capital issued after the passing of this Act; or

(ii) in the case of section 211(2), in relation to distributions made after the passing of this Act.

(5) In this section "the relevant transaction" means—

(*a*) the transaction in securities mentioned in paragraph (*b*) of section 703(1) of the Taxes Act 1988, or

(*b*) the first of the two or more such transactions mentioned in that paragraph,

as the case may be.

GENERAL NOTE

The purpose of this section is to modify the definition of companies falling within para D(2)(*b*) of TA 1988 s 704 (broadly, unquoted companies). The modification is required by recent changes to the structure of the London Stock Exchange. Hitherto, companies whose shares have been traded off-market, for instance under the "Rule 4.2" facility, have generally fallen within para D(2)(*b*). However, the new Alternative Investment Market will include some companies which would previously have fallen within para D(2)(*b*) and would cease to do so as a result of joining that market. The change in the legislation will restore the previous position.

TA 1988 s 704 prescribes the circumstances in which the provisions of TA 1988 s 703 (cancellation of tax advantages from certain transactions in securities) are capable of applying. The definition of companies falling within para D is relevant for the purposes of both para D and para E. The definition is also relevant for certain purposes of TA 1988 ss 210 and 211 (bonus issues and repayments of share capital).

By virtue of this section, the companies to which para D of TA 1988 s 704 applies are—

(*a*) any company under the control of not more than five persons; and

(*b*) any other company which does not satisfy the conditions that its shares or stocks or some class thereof (disregarding debenture stock, preferred shares or preferred stock), are listed in the Official List of the Stock Exchange, and are dealt in on the Stock Exchange regularly or from time to time;

so, however, that para D does not apply to a company under the control (as defined) of one or more companies to which para D does not apply.

Hitherto, the relevant shares or stocks to which sub-para (*b*) referred were those which were authorised to be dealt in on the Stock Exchange and were so dealt in regularly or from time to time.

This section has effect for the purposes of paras D and E of TA 1988 s 704 where the relevant transaction (as defined) takes effect after the passing of the Act. It has effect for the purposes of TA 1988 s 210(3) in relation to share capital issued after the passing of the Act and for the purposes of TA 1988 s 211(2) in relation to distributions made after the passing of the Act.

UNLISTED SECURITIES MARKET
Until the Unlisted Securities Market closes, the reference in para D(2)(*b*) of TA 1988 s 704 to being listed in the Official List of the Stock Exchange and being dealt in on the Stock Exchange regularly or from time to time is to be taken to include a reference to being dealt in on the Unlisted Securities Market regularly or from time to time. Precise transitional provisions are set out.

Chargeable gains: reliefs

176 Retirement relief: age limits

(1) In each of sections 163 and 164 of, and paragraph 5 of Schedule 6 to, the Taxation of Chargeable Gains Act 1992 (retirement relief), for "the age of 55", wherever occurring, there shall be substituted "the age of 50".

(2) The amendments made by this section shall apply in relation to disposals on or after 28th November 1995.

GENERAL NOTE
This section brings down the age limit for retirement relief. It applies to disposals on or after 28 November 1995 (sub-s (2)).

Hitherto retirement relief has applied automatically once the taxpayer has reached the age of 55, provided the various conditions in TCGA 1992 ss 163, 164 and Sch 6 are satisfied. Younger individuals only attracted relief if they could show ill health and made a claim. The effect of the present section is to bring the age limit for automatic relief down to 50. In appropriate cases younger people can still make ill-health claims.

177 Reinvestment relief on disposal of qualifying corporate bond

Section 164A of the Taxation of Chargeable Gains Act 1992 (reinvestment relief) shall have effect, and be deemed always to have had effect, as if the following subsections were inserted after subsection (2)—

"(2A) Where the chargeable gain referred to in subsection (1)(*a*) above is one which (apart from this section) would be deemed to accrue by virtue of section 116(10)(*b*)—

(*a*) any reduction falling to be made by virtue of subsection (2)(*a*) above shall be treated as one made in the consideration mentioned in section 116(10)(*a*), instead of in the consideration for the disposal of the asset disposed of; but

(*b*) if the disposal on which that gain is deemed to accrue is a disposal of only part of the new asset, it shall be assumed, for the purpose only of making a reduction affecting the amount of that gain—

(i) that the disposal is a disposal of the whole of a new asset,

(ii) that the gain accruing on that disposal relates to an old asset consisting in the corresponding part of what was in fact the old asset, and

(iii) that the corresponding part of the consideration deemed to be given for what was in fact the old asset is taken to be the consideration by reference to which the amount of that gain is computed;

and in this subsection 'new asset' and 'old asset' have the same meanings as in section 116.

(2B) Where a chargeable gain accrues in accordance with subsection (12) of section 116, this Chapter shall have effect—

(*a*) as if that gain were a gain accruing on the disposal of an asset; and

(*b*) in relation to that deemed disposal, as if references in this Chapter to the consideration for the disposal were references to the sum of money falling, apart from this Chapter, to be used in computing the gain accruing under that subsection.''

GENERAL NOTE
Reinvestment relief applies where a chargeable gain accrues to an individual on the disposal of an asset (TCGA 1992 s 164A(1)(*a*)). Where it applies, a reduction is made under s 164A(2) in ''the consideration for the disposal of the asset disposed of''. These rules have caused uncertainty in relation to qualifying corporate bonds acquired on paper for paper exchanges within TCGA 1992 s 135.

Under TCGA 1992 s 116(10)(*a*), the exchange is not treated as a disposal, but the gain that would have accrued is computed, and it is deemed to accrue when the bond is disposed of. Initially the Revenue took the view that reinvestment relief was available if the bonds were disposed of, and the reinvestment effected, within three years of the exchange. Subsequently they were advised that the relief was not available at all (see Inland Revenue Press Release 27 September 1995). The reason appears to have been that under s 116, the consideration received on the disposal of the bonds is not treated as received either for the disposal of the bonds or for that of the original shares.

The present section ensures that reinvestment relief applies on all disposals of bonds received on an exchange, regardless of when the exchange took place. It does this by inserting new sub-s (2A) to s 164A. Subsection (2A)(*a*) deems any reduction made under s 14A(2) to be made in the consideration treated as given under s 116(10)(*a*) for the shares given up on the exchange. This then causes the gain held over to be reduced, and so achieves the desired reduction in the gain coming into charge on the disposal of the bonds. Subsection (2A)(*b*) provides for appropriate apportionments where only part or some of the bonds are disposed of.

The present section also inserts sub-s (2B) into s 164. This deals with the position where the shareholder receives a sum of money as well as bonds on the exchange. Under s 116(12) a proportion of the gain corresponding to the money is deemed to accrue at the time of the exchange. However under s 116 no disposal is treated as taking place, and so that gain too would not be eligible for reinvestment relief. Sub-section (2B) cures this defect by deeming the gain represented by the money to have accrued on a disposal.

The changes effected by this section are deemed always to have had effect. The new s 164A(2A) was published as draft legislation on 15 November 1995 (Inland Revenue Press Release 15 November 1995).

Special cases

178   Sub-contractors in the construction industry

(1) In section 566 of the Taxes Act 1988 (powers to make regulations in connection with the provisions relating to sub-contractors in the construction industry), after subsection (2) there shall be inserted the following subsection—

''(2A) The Board may by regulations make provision—

(*a*) for the issue of documents (to be known as 'registration cards') to persons who are parties, as sub-contractors, to any contract relating to construction operations or who are likely to become such parties;

(*b*) for a registration card to contain all such information about the person to whom it is issued as may be required, for the purposes of any regulations under this section, by a person making payments under any such contract;

(*c*) for a registration card to take such form and to be valid for such period as may be prescribed by the regulations;

(*d*) for the renewal, replacement or cancellation of a registration card;

(*e*) for requiring the surrender of a registration card in such circumstances as may be specified in the regulations;

(*f*) for requiring the production of a registration card to such persons and in such circumstances as may be so specified;

(*g*) for requiring any person who—

(i) makes or is proposing to make payments to which section 559 applies, and

(ii) is a person to whom a registration card has to be produced under the regulations,

to take steps that ensure that it is produced to him and that he has an opportunity of inspecting it for the purpose of checking that it is a valid registration card issued to the person required to produce it.

(2B) A person who fails to comply with an obligation imposed on him by virtue of subsection (2A)(*g*) above shall be liable to a penalty not exceeding £3,000.

(2C) Subject to subsection (2D) below, where—

(*a*) a person who is a party to a contract relating to any construction operations ('the contractor') makes or is proposing to make payments to which section 559 applies,

(*b*) the contractor is required by regulations under this section to make statements about another party to the contract ('the sub-contractor') in any return, certificate or other document,

(*c*) a registration card containing the information to be stated should have been produced, in accordance with any such regulations, to the contractor, and

(*d*) the statements made in the return, certificate or other document, so far as relating to matters the information about which should have been obtainable from the card, are inaccurate or incomplete in any material respect,

the contractor shall be liable to a penalty not exceeding £3,000.

(2D) A person shall not be liable to a penalty under subsection (2C) above if—

(*a*) a valid registration card issued to the sub-contractor, or a document which the contractor had reasonable grounds for believing to be such a card, was produced to the contractor and inspected by him before the statements in question were made; and

(*b*) the contractor took all such steps as were reasonable, in addition to the inspection of that card, for ensuring that the statements were accurate and complete.

(2E) A person liable to a penalty under subsection (2C) above shall not, by reason only of the matters in respect of which he is liable to a penalty under that subsection, be liable to any further penalty under section 98 of the Management Act.

(2F) Regulations under this section may make different provision for different cases.''

(2) In the second column of the Table in section 98 of the Taxes Management Act 1970 (penalties in respect of certain information provisions), for the entry

relating to regulations under section 566(1) and (2) of the Taxes Act 1988 there shall be substituted the following entry—

"regulations under section 566(1), (2) or (2A);".

GENERAL NOTE
Regulations are to be introduced requiring all subcontractors who do not have an exemption certificate (714 certificate) to obtain a registration card. The registration card will show the sub-contractor's name and photograph, tax reference and National Insurance number. Any contractor making a payment to a sub-contractor who does not hold a valid 714 certificate must inspect the new registration card before making the payment. This requirement is additional to the requirement to deduct tax from the payment. If the contractor fails to inspect the card, he is liable to a penalty not exceeding £3,000. There is a similar penalty for incorrect returns of such payments. It is not clear what the contractor should do if the subcontractor fails to produce a card. Presumably there are two possibilities: to defer payment until the card is produced or to treat the subcontractor as an employee (which may be technically incorrect).
These new rules will come into force on an appointed day, which will not be before August 1998.

179 Roll-over relief in respect of ships

Schedule 35 to this Act (which amends sections 33A to 33F of the Capital Allowances Act 1990) shall have effect.

GENERAL NOTE
This section introduces Sch 35, which extends the relief contained in CAA 1990 ss 33A–33F in respect of deferment of a balancing charge on disposal of a ship. The amendment allows the relief to apply where the disposal of the old ship and the acquisition of the new ship are undertaken by different members of a 75 per cent group of companies.

180 Scientific research expenditure: oil licences

(1) The Capital Allowances Act 1990 shall have effect, and be deemed always to have had effect, with the following sections inserted after section 138 (assets ceasing to belong to traders)—

"138A Disposal of oil licences etc

(1) For the purposes of section 138 where—

(*a*) a person ('the transferor') disposes of any interest in an oil licence to another ('the transferee'), and
(*b*) part of the value of that interest is attributable to any allowable exploration expenditure incurred by the transferor,

that disposal shall be deemed (subject to section 138B) to be a disposal by which an asset representing the allowable exploration expenditure to which that part of the value is attributable ceases to belong to the transferor.

(2) Section 138 shall have effect in relation to the disposal of an interest in an oil licence, to the extent that the disposal is treated by virtue of subsection (1) above as a disposal of an asset representing allowable exploration expenditure, as if the disposal value of the asset were an amount equal to such part of the transferee's expenditure on acquiring the interest as it is just and reasonable to attribute to the part of the value of that interest that is attributable to the allowable exploration expenditure.

(3) In this section and section 138B references to allowable exploration expenditure are references to any allowable scientific research expenditure of a capital nature incurred on mineral exploration and access.

(4) In this section and section 138B—

'foreign oil concession' means any right to search for or win overseas petroleum, being a right conferred or exercisable (whether or not by virtue of a licence) in relation to a particular area;

'interest' in relation to an oil licence, includes, where there is an agreement which—

(*a*) relates to oil from the whole or any part of the area to which the licence applies, and

(*b*) was made before the extraction of the oil to which it relates,

any entitlement under that agreement to, or to a share of, either that oil or the proceeds of its sale;

'mineral exploration and access' has the same meaning as in Part IV;

'oil'—

(*a*) except in relation to a UK licence, means any petroleum (within the meaning of the Petroleum (Production) Act 1934); and

(*b*) in relation to such a licence, has the same meaning as in Part I of the Oil Taxation Act 1975;

'oil licence' means any UK licence or foreign oil concession;

'overseas petroleum' means any petroleum that exists in its natural condition at a place to which neither the Petroleum (Production) Act 1934 nor the Petroleum (Production) Act (Northern Ireland) 1964 applies;

'petroleum' has the same meaning as in the Petroleum (Production) Act 1934; and

'UK licence' means a licence within the meaning of Part I of the Oil Taxation Act 1975.

138B   Disposal of oil licences: election for alternative tax treatment

(1) Subsections (2) and (3) below apply where—

(*a*) a person ('the transferor') disposes of any interest in an oil licence to another ('the transferee') during the transitional period;

(*b*) part of the value of the interest is attributable to allowable exploration expenditure incurred by the transferor; and

(*c*) an election is made in accordance with this section specifying an amount as the amount to be treated as so attributable.

(2) Section 138 shall have effect in relation to the disposal as if—

(*a*) the disposal were a disposal by which an asset representing the allowable exploration expenditure ceases to belong to the transferor; and

(*b*) the disposal value of that asset were an amount equal to the amount specified in the election.

(3) For the purposes of Part IV, the amount of any expenditure incurred—

(*a*) by the transferee in acquiring the interest from the transferor, or

(*b*) by any person subsequently acquiring the interest (or an interest deriving from the interest),

which is taken to be attributable to expenditure incurred, before the disposal to the transferee, on mineral exploration and access shall be the lesser of the amount specified in the election and the amount which, apart from this subsection, would be taken to be so attributable.

(4) An election—

(*a*) shall be made by notice to the Board given by the transferor; and (*b*) subject to subsection (5) below, shall not have effect unless a copy of it is served on the transferee and the transferee consents to it.

(5) If the Special Commissioners are satisfied—

(*a*) that the disposal was made under or in pursuance of an agreement entered into by the transferor and the transferee on the mutual understanding that a quantified (or quantifiable) part of the value of the interest disposed of was attributable to allowable exploration expenditure, and
(*b*) that the part quantified in accordance with that understanding and the amount specified in the election are the same,

they may dispense with the need for the transferee to consent to the election.

(6) Any question falling to be determined by the Special Commissioners under subsection (5) above shall be determined by them in like manner as if it were an appeal; but both the transferor and the transferee shall be entitled to appear and be heard by those Commissioners or to make representations to them in writing.

(7) Subject to subsection (8) below, an election may specify any amount, including a nil amount, as the amount to be treated as mentioned in subsection (1)(*c*) above.

(8) Where—

(*a*) a return has been made for a chargeable period of the transferor, and
(*b*) the return includes, at the time when it is made, an amount which, disregarding the provisions of this section, would be treated under section 138 as a trading receipt accruing in that period,

the election must not specify an amount less than the amount included in the return unless the Board agrees the lesser amount in question.

(9) An election made in accordance with this section—

(*a*) is irrevocable; and
(*b*) shall not be varied after it is made.

(10) For the purposes of this section a disposal is a disposal made during the transitional period if it is one made—

(*a*) before 13th September 1995; or
(*b*) on or after that date in pursuance of any obligation to make the disposal which, immediately before that date, was an unconditional obligation.

(11) For the purposes of subsection (10) above, the fact that a third party who is not connected with the transferor or the transferee may, by exercising any right or withholding any permission, prevent the fulfilment of an obligation does not prevent the obligation from being treated as unconditional.

(12) In subsection (11) above the reference to a third party is a reference to any person, body, government or public authority, whether within or outside the United Kingdom; and section 839 of the principal Act (connected persons) applies for the purposes of that subsection.

(13) All such assessments and adjustments of assessments shall be made as may be necessary to give effect to this section.''

(2) Section 151(1) of the Capital Allowances Act 1990 (procedure on apportionments under Parts I, III to VI and Part VIII) shall have effect, and

be deemed always to have had effect, as if for "VI" there were substituted "VII".

(3) In section 118 of the Capital Allowances Act 1990 (mineral extraction licences in the case of assets formerly owned by non-traders), the existing provisions shall become subsection (1) of that section and the following subsection shall be inserted after that subsection—

"(2) Section 138A shall have effect for the purposes of subsection (1) above in relation to expenditure on mineral exploration and access as it has effect for the purposes of section 138 in relation to allowable scientific research expenditure of a capital nature."

(4) Subsection (3) above applies in relation to any sale taking place on or after 13th September 1995.

(5) In any case to which enactments re-enacted in the Capital Allowances Act 1990 apply instead of that Act, this section shall have effect as if it required amendments equivalent to those made by subsections (1) and (2) above to have effect, and be deemed always to have had effect, in relation to those enactments.

GENERAL NOTE

CAA 1990 s 138 imposes a balancing charge where an asset representing allowable scientific research expenditure ceases to belong to the trader who incurred the expenditure. The amount of the charge is treated as a trading receipt. It is now provided that the disposal of an interest in an oil licence is deemed to be the disposal of an asset representing such expenditure where part of the value is attributable to allowable exploration expenditure incurred by the transferor. The disposal consideration is apportioned on a just and reasonable basis to the allowable expenditure and to other factors (new s 138A). This provision is deemed always to have had effect. The normal procedure for dealing with apportionments applies (s 151).

However, in relation to disposals occurring before 13 September 1995, or under an unconditional obligation entered into before that date, the transferor may, with the consent of the transferee, elect that the disposal value to be brought into account under s 138 should be an amount specified in the notice of election. That same amount, or the actual acquisition cost if less, will be deemed to be the transferee's acquisition cost. The election must be sent to the Board. If the transferee refuses consent, the matter may be referred to the Special Commissioners who have power to validate the election without the transferee's consent (new s 138B). An election under these provisions is irrevocable and it may not be varied once made.

Where the transferor did not carry on a trade, the transferee may claim allowances under s 118 if the transfer takes place on or after 13 September 1995.

181 Overseas petroleum

(1) In subsection (1) of section 196 of the Taxation of Chargeable Gains Act 1992 (interpretation of sections 194 and 195), for "licence" there shall be substituted "UK licence".

(2) After subsection (1) of section 196 of that Act there shall be inserted the following subsection—

"(1A) For the purposes of section 194 a licence other than a UK licence relates to an undeveloped area at any time if, at that time—

(*a*) no development has actually taken place in any part of the licensed area; and
(*b*) no condition for the carrying out of development anywhere in that area has been satisfied—

(i) by the grant of any consent by the authorities of a country or territory exercising jurisdiction in relation to the area; or
(ii) by the approval or service on the licensee, by any such authorities, of any programme of development.";

and in subsection (2) of that section for "subsection (1) above" there shall be substituted "subsections (1) and (1A) above".

(3) For subsection (5) of section 196 of that Act there shall be substituted the following subsections—

"(5) In sections 194 and 195 and this section—

'foreign oil concession' means any right to search for or win overseas petroleum, being a right conferred or exercisable (whether or not by virtue of a licence) in relation to a particular area;

'interest' in relation to a licence, includes, where there is an agreement which—

(*a*) relates to oil from the whole or any part of the licensed area, and
(*b*) was made before the extraction of the oil to which it relates,

any entitlement under that agreement to, or to a share of, either that oil or the proceeds of its sale;

'licence' means any UK licence or foreign oil concession;
'licensed area' (subject to subsection (4) above)—

(*a*) in relation to a UK licence, has the same meaning as in Part I of the Oil Taxation Act 1975; and
(*b*) in relation to a foreign oil concession, means the area to which the concession applies;

'licensee'—

(*a*) in relation to a UK licence, has the same meaning as in Part I of the Oil Taxation Act 1975; and
(*b*) in relation to a foreign oil concession, means the person with the concession or any person having an interest in it;

'oil'—

(*a*) except in relation to a UK licence, means any petroleum (within the meaning of the Petroleum (Production) Act 1934); and
(*b*) in relation to such a licence, has the same meaning as in Part I of the Oil Taxation Act 1975;

'overseas petroleum' means any oil that exists in its natural condition at a place to which neither the Petroleum (Production) Act 1934 nor the Petroleum (Production) Act (Northern Ireland) 1964 applies; and
'UK licence' means a licence within the meaning of Part I of the Oil Taxation Act 1975.

(5A) References in sections 194 and 195 to a part disposal of a licence shall include references to the disposal of any interest in a licence."

(4) Subsections (1) to (3) above shall have effect in relation to any disposal on or after 13th September 1995 and subsection (3) shall also have effect, and be deemed always to have had effect, for the construction of section 195 of the Taxation of Chargeable Gains Act 1992 in its application to disposals before that date.

(5) Where enactments re-enacted in the Taxation of Chargeable Gains Act 1992 apply, instead of that Act, in the case of any disposal before 13th September 1995, this section shall have effect as if it required amendments equivalent to those made by subsection (3) above to have effect, and be deemed always to have had effect, for the construction of any enactment corresponding to section 195 of that Act.

GENERAL NOTE
TCGA 1992 s 194 sets out special rules for computing the gains and losses arising on disposals of oil licences relating to undeveloped areas. It is now provided that a foreign licence relates to an undeveloped area if no development has taken place in any part of the licensed area and no condition for carrying out development in the area has been satisfied by the grant of consent or approval of a development programme by the relevant authority (new s 196(1A)). This rule applies to disposals on or after 13 September 1995. As far as the deduction of allowable expenditure under s 38 is concerned, it is deemed always to have had effect.

A part disposal is defined to include the disposal of any interest in a licence and there are various other definitions of terms.

182   Controlled foreign companies

Schedule 36 to this Act (which contains amendments of Chapter IV of Part XVII of the Taxes Act 1988) shall have effect in relation to accounting periods of a controlled foreign company, within the meaning of that Chapter, beginning on or after 28th November 1995.

GENERAL NOTE
This section introduces Sch 36, which amends TA 1988 s 747A, and Schs 24 and 25.

PART V

183   Rate bands

(1) For the Table in Schedule 1 to the Inheritance Tax Act 1984 there shall be substituted—

TABLE OF RATES OF TAX

Portion of value		Rate of tax
Lower limit	Upper limit	Per cent
£	£	
0	200,000	Nil
200,000	—	40

(2) Subsection (1) above shall apply to any chargeable transfer made on or after 6th April 1996; and section 8 of that Act (indexation of rate bands) shall not have effect as respects any difference between the retail prices index for the month of September 1994 and that for the month of September 1995.

GENERAL NOTE

The Conservative Government have been reducing the impact of IHT for many years, and in his Budget Speech on 28 November 1995 the Chancellor of the Exchequer said that it is their objective to abolish IHT as soon as it can be afforded. Meanwhile, this Finance Act makes substantial reductions in the tax, through a large increase in the threshold in this section and the extension of 100 per cent business relief to all unquoted shares in s 184. The increase made by this section in the IHT threshold to £200,000, for occasions of IHT charge after 5 April 1996, is a major reduction in the tax (the present threshold is £154,000). If the threshold was left to be uprated for inflation by the indexation provisions of IHTA 1984 s 8, the increase would be to £160,000 only, as has already been specified as from 6 April 1996 by the Inheritance Tax (Indexation) Order 1995 (SI 1995/3032) made under s 8. This Order has no effect: see s 183(2) for the express exclusion of s 8 in relation the tax year 1996–97. In the Budget Press Release of 28 November 1995, "Inheritance tax—big increase in threshold" it was stated that this increase in the threshold will remove 7,500 estates from IHT in 1996–97, with the total paying it in that fiscal year estimated at 15,000, ie about 1 in 45 of all death estates. This is the biggest change in the rate structure since the change made in March 1988 from five rate bands (with 60 per cent as the highest) to a wide nil rate band and a single flat rate of 40 per cent.

184   Business property relief

(1) The Inheritance Tax Act 1984 shall be amended as follows.

(2) In section 105(1) (relevant business property for the purposes of business property relief)—

(a) in paragraph (b) (unquoted shares and securities attracting 100 per cent relief where they gave the transferor control of a company)—

(i) the words "shares in or" shall be omitted; and
(ii) for the words "shares or securities owned by the transferor" there shall be substituted "securities owned by the transferor and any unquoted shares so owned";

(b) for paragraph (bb) (unquoted shares attracting 100 per cent relief in other cases) there shall be substituted the following paragraph—

"(bb) any unquoted shares in a company;"

and

(*c*) paragraph (*c*) (unquoted shares attracting 50 per cent relief) shall be omitted.

(3) In section 107(4) (replacement of property with unquoted shares), for the words from the beginning to "such shares" there shall be substituted—

"(4) Without prejudice to subsection (1) above, where any shares falling within section 105(1)(*bb*) above which are".

(4) In section 113A(3A)(*b*) (which contains a reference to shares and securities falling within paragraph (*b*) of section 105(1)), after "(*b*)" there shall be inserted "or (*bb*)".

(5) For the removal of any doubt, the following subsection shall be inserted in section 113A (provisions applying to business property relief where there is a transfer within seven years of death) after subsection (7)—

"(7A) The provisions of this Chapter for the reduction of value transferred shall be disregarded in any determination for the purposes of this section of whether there is a potentially exempt or chargeable transfer in any case."

(6) This section—

(*a*) so far is it inserts a new subsection (7A) in section 113A, has effect in relation to any transfer of value on or after 28th November 1995; and

(*b*) so far as it makes any other provision, has effect—

(i) in relation to any transfer of value on or after 6th April 1996, and
(ii) for the purposes of any charge to tax by reason of an event occurring on or after 6th April 1996, in relation to transfers of value before that date.

GENERAL NOTE

Relief from CTT for various kinds of business property, including certain unquoted shares or securities in trading companies, was originally introduced in 1976. After 26 October 1977 the rates of relief for unquoted shareholdings in trading companies consisted of 50 per cent relief for controlling unquoted holdings of shares or securities, and 20 per cent relief for non-controlling unquoted holdings of shares (the rate of relief for the latter was raised to 30 per cent from 15 March 1983) if various conditions as to period of ownership and type of business etc were fulfilled (see *Simon's Direct Tax Service* I7.121–I7.142). From 16 March 1987 the higher, 50 per cent, rate of relief was extended to holdings of shares (but not securities) with less than control of the company but controlling more than 25 per cent of the votes.

One justification for the differential rates of relief as between these different categories of shareholding was that there was a higher rate of relief where the holding would be valued on a higher per-unit basis as a result of the transferor's degree of voting control of the company. Where the holding was a minority one the lower rate of relief might, in a rough and ready way, be balanced by the lower per-unit valuation. This approximate equilibrium was upset by the introduction, for transfers after 9 March 1992, of a higher rate of relief of 100 per cent (ie for unquoted controlling holdings of shares or securities or unquoted shareholdings controlling more than 25 per cent of the votes) and a lower rate of relief of 50 per cent (ie for other holdings of unquoted shares). After this, a transfer of a holding not controlling more than 25 per cent of the votes, even allowing for a lower per-unit value than a larger holding of the same shares, would give rise, in some cases, to a substantial IHT charge while a transfer of a holding with more than 25 per cent of the votes might well give rise to no IHT charge at all. However, this section, for transfers after 5 April 1996, puts all unquoted holdings of shares on the same footing by extending 100 per cent relief to all holdings of unquoted shares in trading companies.

EXTENSION OF 100 PER CENT RELIEF

This extension of 100 per cent relief is principally effected by sub-s (2). After the amendments made by sub-s (2) there will be two categories of unquoted company share or security qualifying for business property relief in relation to a transfer of value—

(*a*) unquoted securities (eg loan stock) which by themselves or together with other such securities and any unquoted shares owned by the transferor gave him control of the company (IHTA 1984 s 105(1)(b) as amended by sub-s (2)(a));
(*b*) any unquoted shares (IHTA 1984 s 105(1)(bb) as substituted by sub-s (2)(b)).

The first of these preserves the existing position as regards relief in relation to unquoted securities (as opposed to shares) which are or form part of a controlling holding. Fifty per cent relief on controlling holdings of quoted shares or securities remains unaltered (IHTA 1984 s 105(1)(*cc*)). Unlisted Securities Market and Alternative Investment Market shares are unquoted shares for the purposes of the relief (see IHTA 1984 s 105(1ZA)).

REPLACEMENT PROPERTY

Subsection (3) of this section was added at the Report stage, and is a welcome liberalisation of the rules for unquoted shares which are replacement property. To qualify for IHT business relief on a transfer of business property, the transferor must have owned the property throughout the two years preceding the transfer (IHTA 1984 s 106), unless it replaced other business property (of any of the kinds which can qualify for business relief) and the transferor owned the replaced property and the replacement property for periods which together amount to two years out of the preceding five year (IHTA 1984 s 107(1)). However, before the amendment made to IHTA 1984 s 107(4) by sub-s (3) of this section, IHTA 1984 s 107(4) prevented this principal provision concerning replacement property (ie IHTA 1984 s 107(1) from applying to non-controlling holdings of unquoted shares, and only allowed such holdings which replaced other property within the two years before the transfer to qualify for relief where they represented other shareholdings as a result of capital reconstructions, amalgamations etc. The amendment to IHTA 1984 s 107(4) made by sub-s (3) both preserves the existing application of IHTA 1984 s 107(1) to *controlling* unquoted holdings, and makes it apply also to all non-controlling unquoted shareholdings, while retaining the alternative of the share-identification rules under s 107(4) being also available. The main practical consequence of the extension of s 107(1) to non-controlling holdings of unquoted shares is that where a partnership's or sole trader's business has been incorporated, with the former partners or proprietor receiving unquoted shares in a company in return for their or his transfers of the business to that company, it will be possible for the former partners or proprietor to count the period of their or his direct ownership of the business before incorporation towards the two-year ownership qualification even where they or he have a non-controlling shareholding in the company.

CONSEQUENTIAL PROVISIONS

Subsection (4) makes a technical change to the clawback rules (see below) so that clawback will not occur in relation to unquoted shares or securities which qualify for business property relief at the time of a lifetime transfer, provided that the transferee retains them until the transferor's or his own earlier death, and they remain unquoted, without having to satisfy the more stringent requirement of IHTA 1984 s 113A(3)(*b*) of being relevant business property immediately before the transferor's (or transferee's own earlier) death.

Part VI of Sch 41 to this Act contains consequential repeals of IHTA 1984 ss 105(1A), (1B), (2A), and 109A, which all related to the former 100 per cent relief category of shares controlling more than 25 per cent of the votes but with less than control.

COMMENCEMENT

The commencement provisions for these changes have two features of particular interest. Subsection (6)(*b*)(i) states that they apply in relation to any transfer of value after 5 April 1996, and sub-s (6)(*b*)(ii) makes it clear that they will also apply in relation to transfers of value on or before that date for the purposes of any charge to tax occurring after it. The latter provision relates primarily to a case where someone dies after 5 April 1996 having made a lifetime transfer on or before that date but within seven years before his death. If the value transferred was attributable to, eg, non-voting unquoted shares, and there has been no clawback of relief under IHTA 1984 s 113A (see below), the rate of any available relief for the purposes of calculating any IHT charge arising from his death will be 100 per cent. The Revenue's interpretation of the commencement provision for the introduction of 100 per cent relief in FA 1992 (FA 1992 Sch 14 para 8) was to a similar effect, but it was not so clear that the wording of that commencement provision had that effect. A further consequence of this commencement provision is that it seems to apply this section's enlargement of business relief for unquoted shares to any lifetime transfer made before 6 April 1996 and within seven years before a subsequent transfer made by the same transferor after 5 April 1996 (such as the deemed transfer on the transferor's death after 5 April 1996 and within seven years), for the purposes of determining the value of the pre-6 April 1996 transfer to be taken into account as part of the transferor's cumulation of previous transfers when calculating the IHT on the later transfer. It should also be noted that this commencement provision applies to the extension of the replacement property rules (see s 184(3) and above) as well as to the extension of 100 per cent relief on unquoted shareholdings.

The other point concerning sub-s (6)(*b*) is that it is only stated to apply to transfers of value after the specified date, and not, as commencement provisions have done in the past, to transfers of value or other events occurring after a specified date. It is arguable that the more restricted formula means that the changes to business property relief do not apply by virtue of it to occasions of IHT charges on settled property not subject to an interest in possession; these are deemed to be chargeable transfers under IHTA 1984 s 2(3), but not deemed to be transfers of value by

IHTA 1984 s 3. This is probably not an intended result of this wording. This point is only relevant to occasions of IHT charge occurring in the fairly short period between 6 April 1996 and the date of the Royal Assent to the Act. The amendments to the business relief rules in IHTA 1984 made by this Act will apply to all occasions of IHT charge occurring after this Act is passed, including those relating to discretionary trusts: IHTA 1984 s 103(1) provides that "transfer of value" in IHTA 1984 Part V Chapter I (ie the business relief chapter) includes occasions of IHT charge on settled property with no interest in possession. There does not seem to be anything to cause this extended definition in IHTA 1984 s 103(1) to relate to the references to transfers of value in the commencement provisions in sub-s (6) of this section.

The clawback rules in IHTA 1984 s 113A relate to any potentially exempt or immediately chargeable lifetime transfer of value where the transferor dies within seven years of the transfer and some or all of the property comprised in the transfer qualified for IHT business property relief at the time of the transfer. They have the effect that the transferee must have retained the business property until the transferor's (or his own earlier) death, and the property must have retained some or all of its character as business property, for the business property relief to be available when it comes to determining the amount of IHT or additional IHT payable as a result of the death of the transferor. IHTA 1984 s 113B allows a degree of replacement of business property by other business property between the transfer and the death. There are similar rules in IHTA 1984 ss 124A and 124B for clawback of agricultural property relief.

After 100 per cent business and agricultural property relief were introduced in 1992 it became apparent that there was a puzzle about the interaction of 100 per cent business (and agricultural) property relief and the clawback rules. If the value transferred by a lifetime transfer of value was reduced to nil or a very small amount by 100 per cent business or agricultural property relief, it was arguable that the clawback rules could not apply on the transferor's subsequent death within seven years of the transfer, even if the property had been, eg sold by the transferee, either on the grounds that a reduction in the value transferred to nil by virtue of the relief meant that there was no potentially exempt or chargeable transfer, or on the grounds that the reduction in value by virtue of the relief brought the transfer within the exemption for small gifts under IHTA 1984 s 20. For details of the argument see Derek Robinson "Icing on the Cake: How to make £250 Go a Long Way" *Private Client Business*, 1992 Issue, p 7, and Richard Wallington "Business and Agricultural Property Relief" *Tax Journal*, No 197, 28 January 1993, p 8 (which is supplemented by correspondence in ibid, No 199, 11 February 1993, p 5).

This point was arguable either way, but sub-s (5) resolves it for transfers after 27 November 1995 (see sub-s (6)(*a*) for the commencement date) by making clear that clawback can occur where a lifetime transfer is initially reduced to a low or nil value by 100 per cent business property relief. It does this by providing that the relief is disregarded when determining whether there is a potentially exempt transfer or chargeable transfer to which IHTA 1984 s 113A applies in the first place. Section 185(4) makes the same provision in relation to agricultural property relief clawback.

185 Agricultural property relief

(1) Chapter II of Part V of the Inheritance Tax Act 1984 (agricultural property) shall be amended as follows.

(2) In section 116 (relief for transfers of agricultural property) after subsection (5) there shall be inserted—

"(5A) Where, in consequence of the death on or after 1st September 1995 of the tenant or, as the case may be, the last surviving tenant of any property, the tenancy—

(*a*) becomes vested in a person, as a result of his being a person beneficially entitled under the deceased tenant's will or other testamentary writing or on his intestacy, and
(*b*) is or becomes binding on the landlord and that person as landlord and tenant respectively,

subsection (2)(*c*) above shall have effect as if the tenancy so vested had been a tenancy beginning on the date of the death.

(5B) Where in consequence of the death on or after 1st September 1995 of the tenant or, as the case may be, the last surviving tenant of any property, a tenancy of the property or of any property comprising the whole or part of it—

(*a*) is obtained by a person under or by virtue of an enactment, or

(*b*) is granted to a person in circumstances such that he is already entitled under or by virtue of an enactment to obtain such a tenancy, but one which takes effect on a later date, or

(*c*) is granted to a person who is or has become the only or only remaining applicant, or the only or only remaining person eligible to apply, under a particular enactment for such a tenancy in the particular case,

subsection (2)(*c*) above shall have effect as if the tenancy so obtained or granted had been a tenancy beginning on the date of the death.

(5C) Subsection (5B) above does not apply in relation to property situate in Scotland.

(5D) If, in a case where the transferor dies on or after 1st September 1995,—

(*a*) the tenant of any property has, before the death, given notice of intention to retire in favour of a new tenant, and

(*b*) the tenant's retirement in favour of the new tenant takes place after the death but not more than thirty months after the giving of the notice,

subsection (2)(*c*) above shall have effect as if the tenancy granted or assigned to the new tenant had been a tenancy beginning immediately before the transfer of value which the transferor is treated by section 4(1) above as making immediately before his death.

(5E) In subsection (5D) above and this subsection—

'the new tenant' means—

(*a*) the person or persons identified in a notice of intention to retire in favour of a new tenant as the person or persons who it is desired should become the tenant of the property to which that notice relates; or

(*b*) the survivor or survivors of the persons so identified, whether alone or with any other person or persons;

'notice of intention to retire in favour of a new tenant' means, in the case of any property, a notice or other written intimation given to the landlord by the tenant, or (in the case of a joint tenancy or tenancy in common) all of the tenants, of the property indicating, in whatever terms, his or their wish that one or more persons identified in the notice or intimation should become the tenant of the property;

'the retiring tenant's tenancy' means the tenancy of the person or persons giving the notice of intention to retire in favour of a new tenant;

'the tenant's retirement in favour of the new tenant' means—

(*a*) the assignment, or (in Scotland) assignation, of the retiring tenant's tenancy to the new tenant in circumstances such that the tenancy is or becomes binding on the landlord and the new tenant as landlord and tenant respectively; or

(*b*) the grant of a tenancy of the property which is the subject of the retiring tenant's tenancy, or of any property comprising the whole or part of that property, to the new tenant and the acceptance of that tenancy by him;

and, except in Scotland, 'grant' and 'acceptance' in paragraph (*b*) above respectively include the deemed grant, and the deemed acceptance, of a tenancy under or by virtue of any enactment.''

(3) In consequence of subsection (2) above, subsection (2A) of that section (which made, in relation to Scotland, provision which is superseded by the subsection (5A) inserted by subsection (2) above) shall cease to have effect.

(4) For the removal of any doubt, the following subsection shall be inserted in section 124A (provisions applying to agricultural property relief where there is a transfer within seven years of death) after subsection (7)—

"(7A) The provisions of this Chapter for the reduction of value transferred shall be disregarded in any determination for the purposes of this section of whether there is a potentially exempt or chargeable transfer in any case."

(5) Subsection (2) above—

(*a*) so far as relating to subsections (5A) to (5C) of section 116 of the Inheritance Tax Act 1984, has effect in any case where the death of the tenant or, as the case may be, the sole surviving tenant, occurs on or after 1st September 1995; and

(*b*) so far as relating to subsections (5D) and (5E) of that section, has effect in any case where the death of the transferor occurs on or after 1st September 1995.

(6) Subsection (3) above has effect in any case where the death of the tenant or, as the case may be, the sole surviving tenant, occurs on or after 1st September 1995.

(7) Subsection (4) above has effect in relation to any transfer of value on or after 28th November 1995.

EXTENSION OF 100 PER CENT RELIEF ON TENANTED LAND

It will be recalled that as a result of the amendments to agricultural relief made by FA 1995 there can be 100 per cent agricultural relief where agricultural land which qualifies for the relief is subject to a tenancy commencing after 31 August 1995 (IHTA 1984 s 116(2)(*c*)). The Revenue subsequently confirmed that this applies even where that tenancy is granted pursuant to statutory succession rights arising on the death of a tenant. Subsection (2) of this section broadens the scope of this relief where one tenant succeeds another after 31 August 1995. It adds three new categories qualifying for 100 per cent relief, in the new IHTA 1984 s 116(5A), (5B) and (5D).

The new IHTA 1984 s 116(5A) extends 100 per cent relief to cases where, after 31 August 1995, a tenant dies and another person succeeds to the same tenancy (ie without a new tenancy being granted). There would not be 100 per cent relief in such a case without this provision, where the tenancy commenced before 1 September 1995 (because it would not be a tenancy beginning after 31 August 1995), except that a slightly more limited provision to a similar effect was made for Scotland only by the existing s 116(2A) (repealed by sub-s (3) as it is superseded by the new s 116(5A)). Section 116(5A) is not confined to Scotland, but is of greatest relevance to Scotland. One other effect of the new s 116(5A) which is worth noting is its treatment of the deemed new tenancy as commencing on the death of the tenant, so that if the owner of the land subject to the tenancy dies or gives away the land after the tenant's death and before the successor tenant has taken over the tenancy, the 100 per cent relief is available.

The new IHTA 1984 s 116(5B) does not apply to Scotland (see s 116(5C)), and has the effect of bringing forward the date on which the 100 per cent relief becomes available where there is a statutory succession to a tenancy in consequence of the death of a tenant after 31 August 1995. Statutory successions to tenancies in England and Wales normally take effect by the grant of a new tenancy, and so the land subject to a succession occurring after 31 August 1995 would qualify under the existing rules for 100 per cent relief, but only as from the grant of the tenancy. The main point of the new s 116(5B) seems to be to treat the successor's tenancy as beginning at the date of the death of the tenant whom he has succeeded, so that if the owner of the land dies after the death of the tenant but before the successor has been granted a new tenancy, the relief is still at the rate of 100 per cent.

The new IHTA 1984 s 116(5D), supplemented by the definitions in s 116(5E), confers 100 per cent relief where the owner of tenanted agricultural property dies after 31 August 1995 and after a notice of intention to retire in favour of a new tenant has been given by an existing tenant of the land, and the owner's death is before the retirement of the tenant in favour of a new tenant has taken effect, provided that such retirement takes place within 30 months after the notice. This provision treats the tenancy granted to or assigned to the new tenant as commencing immediately before the death of the owner of the land, so that 100 per cent relief is available. This has two effects. First, in a case of retirement where a new tenancy is granted after 31 August 1995, 100 per cent relief is available in the event of the death of the owner of the land after the notice of retirement has been given but before the grant of the tenancy, which it would not be under the existing provisions (ie 100 per cent relief would only be available as from the grant of the new tenancy). Second, where the successor to the retiring tenant receives an assignment or (in Scotland) assignation of the existing tenancy (and it is a tenancy which began before 1 September 1995), it will be treated as a tenancy beginning after 31 August 1995 and enable the land to qualify for 100 per cent relief, *but only in the limited circumstances of an assignment after the death of the owner of the land pursuant to a notice of retirement given before it.* There seems to be an anomaly here; if a tenant has retired and already assigned the existing tenancy (being one which began before 1 September 1995) to a new tenant before the owner's death, the rate of relief will apparently still be only 50 per cent.

Subsections (5) and (6) provide for these provisions to operate in relation to relevant events occurring after 31 August 1995.

CLARIFICATION OF CLAWBACK RULES

Subsection (4) makes the same provision for the agricultural property relief clawback rules as s 184(5) makes for the business property relief clawback rules. See the notes on s 184(5), above.

PART VI

STAMP DUTY AND STAMP DUTY RESERVE TAX

Stamp duty

186 Transfers of securities to members of electronic transfer systems etc

(1) Stamp duty shall not be chargeable on an instrument effecting a transfer of securities if the transferee is a member of an electronic transfer system and the instrument is in a form which will, in accordance with the rules of the system, ensure that the securities are changed from being held in certificated form to being held in uncertificated form so that title to them may become transferable by means of the system.

(2) In this section—

"certificated form" has the same meaning as in the relevant regulations;
"electronic transfer system" means a system and procedures which, in accordance with the relevant regulations, enable title to securities to be evidenced and transferred without a written instrument;
"member", in relation to an electronic transfer system, means a person who is permitted by the operator of the system to transfer by means of the system title to securities held by him in uncertificated form;
"operator" means a person approved by the Treasury under the relevant regulations as operator of an electronic transfer system;
"the relevant regulations" means regulations under section 207 of the Companies Act 1989 (transfer without written instrument);
"securities" means stock or marketable securities;
"uncertificated form" has the same meaning as it has in the relevant regulations.

(3) This section applies in relation to instruments executed on or after 1st July 1996.

(4) This section shall be construed as one with the Stamp Act 1891.

BACKGROUND NOTE
The proposed system for paperless transfers of shares ("CREST") is expected to start operation in 1996. Stamp duty is a tax on instruments but the whole basis of the CREST system is that changes in title or ownership of securities within the CREST system will be made electronically. Accordingly SDRT will be charged on agreements to transfer securities within the system rather than stamp duty. The changes made by ss 186–196 facilitate the application of SDRT to such transfers.

GENERAL NOTE
Although there are some exceptions from the charge to stamp duty of 50p per instrument on a conveyance or transfer otherwise than on sale (eg the exemption under FA 1976 s 127 of transfers to a stock exchange nominee), in order that transfers made to a person preparatory to "dematerialisation" of the shares in question do not attract such charges sub-s (1) provides an exemption. The requirements are that the transferee is a member of an electronic transfer system and the transfer is in a form which will ensure that the securities become held in uncertificated form.

DEFINITIONS
Subsection (2) provides that "certificated form" and "uncertificated form" shall have the same meaning as in "the relevant regulations", ie those made under CA 1989 s 207. It also defines "electronic transfer system", (ie CREST); a "member", ie a person permitted by the "operator" (also defined) to transfer securities in uncertificated form; and defines "securities" as stock or marketable securities. Since sub-s (4) provides for the section being construed as one with SA 1891, the definition of "stock" and "marketable securities" in SA 1891 s 122(1) should apply.

COMMENCEMENT
Subsection (3) causes the exemption to be available in respect of instruments executed after 30 June 1996.

Stamp duty reserve tax

187 Territorial scope of the tax

(1) In section 86 of the Finance Act 1986 (introduction) after subsection (3) there shall be added—

"(4) Stamp duty reserve tax shall be chargeable in accordance with the provisions of this Part of this Act—

(*a*) whether the agreement, transfer, issue or appropriation in question is made or effected in the United Kingdom or elsewhere, and
(*b*) whether or not any party is resident or situate in any part of the United Kingdom."

(2) The amendment made by subsection (1) above shall have effect—

(*a*) in relation to an agreement, if—

(i) the agreement is conditional and the condition is satisfied on or after 1st July 1996; or
(ii) the agreement is not conditional and is made on or after that date; and

(*b*) in relation to a transfer, issue or appropriation made or effected on or after that date.

GENERAL NOTE
By long-standing practice SDRT has not been applied to agreements to transfer chargeable securities made between persons not resident in the UK where the transaction is carried out abroad: see para 2.10 of the Revenue SDRT Notes for Guidance. Prior to dematerialisation of securities under CREST the non-application of SDRT would in many cases have been irrelevant as subsequent transfers of the UK shares would have attracted stamp duty in any event. However, there could have been a significant reduction in revenue if overseas persons' agreements to transfer dematerialised securities had not attracted SDRT. Budget Press Release IR 19, 28 November 1995, states that "recent legal advice . . . suggests that the agreements are chargeable . . . [and] the legislation will be amended . . .".

Accordingly sub-s (1) introduces a new FA 1986 s 86(4) confirming that SDRT is due whether or not the agreement, transfer, issue or appropriation (in the latter two cases in connection with depositary receipt or clearance systems) is made or carried out in the UK and whether or not *any* party thereto is a UK resident. Under the Stamp Duty Reserve Tax Regulations 1986, SI 1986/1711, "accountable persons" rather than the person liable to the tax can be liable to account for the tax.

COMMENCEMENT
The change applies to agreements to transfer chargeable securities which are made after 30 June 1996 or, if made before 1 July 1996, become unconditional on or after that date and to all transfers, issues or appropriations on or after 1 July 1996.

188 Removal of the two month period

(1) In section 87 of the Finance Act 1986 (the principal charge) in subsection (2) (tax charged on the expiry of the period of two months beginning with the relevant day unless the first and second conditions are fulfilled before that period expires) the following shall be omitted—

(*a*) the words "the expiry of the period of two months beginning with", and
(*b*) the words from "unless" to the end.

(2) In section 88 of that Act (special cases) in subsection (1) (which provides for instruments on which stamp duty is not chargeable by virtue of certain

enactments to be disregarded for the purposes of section 87(4) and (5)) before paragraph (*a*) there shall be inserted—

> "(*aa*) section 65(1) of the Finance Act 1963 (renounceable letters of allotment etc),
> (*ab*) section 14(1) of the Finance Act (Northern Ireland) 1963 (renounceable letters of allotment etc),".

(3) Subsections (2) and (3) of that section (which are superseded by subsection (2) above) shall cease to have effect.

(4) In section 92(1) of that Act (repayment or cancellation of tax where the conditions in section 87(4) and (5) are shown to have been fulfilled after the expiry of the period of two months beginning with the relevant day but before the expiry of six years so beginning)—

> (*a*) for "after the expiry of the period of two months (beginning with the relevant day, as defined in section 87(3))" there shall be substituted "on or after the relevant day (as defined in section 87(3))"; and
> (*b*) for "(so beginning)" there shall be substituted "(beginning with that day)".

(5) The amendments made by this section shall have effect in relation to an agreement to transfer securities if—

> (*a*) the agreement is conditional and the condition is satisfied on or after 1st July 1996; or
> (*b*) the agreement is not conditional and is made on or after that date.

BACKGROUND NOTE
   At the time SDRT was introduced stamp duty was the principal tax on transfers of shares (and other "chargeable securities"). Accordingly in many cases where a chargeable agreement to transfer shares arose shortly thereafter stamp duty was paid (in order to be able to put the transferee on the register of members, a transferee would want the transfer stamped in view of the fine potentially payable were a registrar to amend the register of members without a stamped transfer—see SA 1891 s 17). Hence FA 1986 s 87(2) provides for a two-month period between the agreement being made or, if later, becoming unconditional and a charge arising. If in that time a duly stamped instrument satisfying the requirements of FA 1986 s 87(4) and (5) is executed no SDRT charge arises (and there are refund/cancellation procedures if SDRT has been accounted for/become due and any stamp duty on a transfer of the chargeable securities agreed to be transferred has been paid). In view of the introduction of the CREST system under which stamp duty will never be payable on transfers of dematerialised securities, the Revenue have taken the opportunity to remove the two month "waiting period". As regards transfers of non-dematerialised chargeable securities, stamp duty may still be paid (cancelling out the SDRT liability) before the accountable date: if not refunds of SDRT should be available.

GENERAL NOTE
   Subsection (1) amends FA 1986 s 87(2) so that the charge arises on, not two months after, the relevant date.

RENOUNCEABLE LETTERS OF ALLOTMENT
   Certain letters of allotment remain exempt from stamp duty and so there was no need to provide a two-month "waiting period" before making the agreements to transfer chargeable securities effected by renunciation of such letters: this was achieved by FA 1986 s 88(2) and (3). The effect of the amendment to FA 1986 s 88(1) made by sub-s (2) is that potentially dutiable letters of allotment can be ignored in computing whether a SDRT charge arises.
   Accordingly there is no longer need for s 88(2) and (3), which accelerated the SDRT charge for exempt (from stamp duty) letters of allotment and sub-s (3) repeals these subsections.

CANCELLATION OF LIABILITY/REFUND OF TAX
   Subsection (4) makes amendments, consequential upon the removal of the two-month waiting period, to FA 1986 s 92(1).

COMMENCEMENT
   By sub-s (5) the amendments apply to agreements made on or after 1 July 1996 or, if made earlier, which become unconditional after 30 June 1996.

189   Transfers to members of electronic transfer systems etc

(1) In section 88 of the Finance Act 1986 (special cases) after subsection (1) there shall be inserted—

"(1A) An instrument on which stamp duty is not chargeable by virtue of section 186 of the Finance Act 1996 (transfers of securities to members of electronic transfer systems etc) shall be disregarded in construing section 87(4) and (5) above unless—

(*a*) the transfer is made by a stock exchange nominee; and
(*b*) the maximum stamp duty chargeable on the instrument, apart from section 186 of the Finance Act 1996, would be 50p;

and in this subsection 'stock exchange nominee' means a person designated for the purposes of section 127 of the Finance Act 1976 as a nominee of The Stock Exchange by an order made by the Secretary of State under subsection (5) of that section."

(2) This section has effect in relation to an agreement to transfer securities if an instrument is executed on or after 1st July 1996 in pursuance of the agreement.

GENERAL NOTE
In order that s 186 did not provide an opportunity for beneficial interests in chargeable securities to be transferred without attracting either an SDRT or stamp duty charge sub-s (1) amends FA 1986 s 88. It inserts a new s 88(1A) enabling an SDRT charge to arise in relation to agreement preceding any transfer exempt under s 186 unless the transfer is made by a "stock exchange nominee" designated under FA 1976 s 127 (ie SEPON Limited) and the charge to stamp duty would otherwise have been 50p (ie the transfer was not a "conveyance on sale").

COMMENCEMENT
It applies to agreements to transfer chargeable securities, whenever made, if the exempt (by virtue of s 186) transfer is made after 30 June 1996.

190   Transfers between associated bodies

(1) In section 88 of the Finance Act 1986 (special cases) after subsection (1A) there shall be inserted—

"(1B) An instrument on which stamp duty is not chargeable by virtue of section 42 of the Finance Act 1930 or section 11 of the Finance Act (Northern Ireland) 1954 (transfer between associated bodies corporate) shall be disregarded in construing section 87(4) and (5) above in any case where—

(*a*) the property mentioned in section 42(2)(*a*) of the Finance Act 1930 or, as the case may be, section 11(2)(*a*) of the Finance Act (Northern Ireland) 1954 consists of chargeable securities of any particular kind acquired in the period of two years ending with the day on which the instrument was executed; and
(*b*) the body corporate from which the conveyance or transfer there mentioned is effected acquired the chargeable securities—

(i) in a transaction which was given effect by an instrument of transfer on which stamp duty was not chargeable by virtue of section 81 above;
(ii) in pursuance of an agreement to transfer securities as regards which section 87 above did not apply by virtue of section 89 above; or
(iii) in circumstances with regard to which the charge to stamp duty or stamp duty reserve tax was treated as not arising by virtue of regulations under section 116 or 117 of the Finance Act 1991."

(2) At the end of that section there shall be added—

"(4) For the purposes of subsection (1B) above, if the securities mentioned in paragraph (*a*) of that subsection cannot (apart from this subsection) be identified, securities shall be taken as follows, that is to say, securities of the same kind acquired later in the period of two years there mentioned (and not taken under this subsection for the purposes of any earlier instrument) shall be taken before securities acquired earlier in that period.

(5) If, in a case where subsection (4) above applies, some, but not all, of the securities taken in accordance with that subsection were acquired as mentioned in paragraph (*b*) of subsection (1B) above by the body corporate mentioned in that paragraph, the stamp duty reserve tax chargeable under section 87 above by virtue of subsection (1B) above shall not exceed the tax that would have been so chargeable had the agreement to transfer the securities related only to such of the securities so taken as were so acquired.

(6) Where a person enters into an agreement for securities to be transferred to him or his nominee, the securities shall be treated for the purposes of subsections (1B)(*a*) and (4) above as acquired by that person at the time when he enters into the agreement, unless the agreement is conditional, in which case they shall be taken to be acquired by him when the condition is satisfied.''

(3) This section has effect where the instrument on which stamp duty is not chargeable by virtue of section 42 of the Finance Act 1930 or section 11 of the Finance Act (Northern Ireland) 1954 is executed on or after 4th January 1996 in pursuance of an agreement to transfer securities made on or after that date.

BACKGROUND NOTE

FA 1930 s 42 and FA (NI) 1954 s 11 (its Northern Ireland equivalent) provide an exemption from stamp duty for transfers between associated companies; broadly, companies in a 75 per cent ordinary share capital relationship with each other or a common parent company.

Relief from ad valorem stamp duty is available in respect of transfers, pursuant to a stock lending transaction, *to* a market maker: FA 1986 s 81. Equivalent relief from SDRT in respect of the agreement preceding such transfers, and also certain other agreements involving brokers and dealers, is available under FA 1986 s 89. FA 1991 ss 116 and 117 enable regulations providing for relief from stamp duty and SDRT to be made, principally benefiting LIFFE equity options market-makers: Stamp Duty Reserve Tax (Investment Exchanges and Clearing Houses) Regulations 1992, SI 1992/570.

GENERAL NOTE

Subsection (1) inserts in FA 1986 s 88 a new sub-s (1B) which provides that in determining whether an instrument transferring all the chargeable securities to which an agreement relates has been entered into, transfers adjudicated free from duty under FA 1930 s 42 (or its Northern Ireland equivalent) are to be ignored. (Were it not for new sub-s (1B) the conditions of s 87(4) and (5) would have been satisfied so no liability would arise or, if SDRT had been paid, it could be recovered under s 92.)

These are transfers of ''chargeable securities of any particular kind'' acquired within two years of the date on which the exempt transfer was executed where the transferor had obtained the securities without being liable to ad valorem duty or SDRT by virtue of relief under FA 1986 ss 81 or 89 or FA 1991 ss 116 or 117.

IDENTIFICATION OF SECURITIES, PARTIAL RELIEF AND TIMING

Subsection (2) inserts three additional subsections into FA 1986 s 88. New sub-s (4) provides that where, probably because of fungibility, securities transferred under one of the relieving provisions cannot be identified, securities acquired later in the two-year period shall be treated as transferred pursuant to the instrument adjudicated free of duty before those acquired earlier in the period: ie a ''LIFO basis''.

New sub-s (5) effectively enables relief from SDRT to apply to such shares or other securities agreed to be transferred to the transferee as were not acquired within the two-year period.

New sub-s (6) provides that securities are to be treated as having been acquired by the transferor when he entered into an agreement for their transfer to him or his nominee unless the agreement was conditional, in which case their acquisition by him is treated as occurring when the agreement becomes unconditional.

209

COMMENCEMENT
The removal of relief from SDRT applies to instruments adjudicated free of duty executed after
3 January 1996 pursuant to agreements to transfer securities made after that date.

191 Stock lending and collateral security arrangements

(1) After section 89A of the Finance Act 1986 (exceptions from section 87 for public issues) there shall be inserted—

"89B Section 87: exceptions for stock lending and collateral security arrangements

(1) Where a person (P) has contracted to sell chargeable securities of a particular kind in the ordinary course of his business as a market maker in chargeable securities of that kind and, to enable him to fulfil the contract, he enters into an arrangement under which—

(*a*) another person (Q) is to transfer chargeable securities to P or his nominee, and

(*b*) in return, chargeable securities of the same kind and amount are to be transferred (whether or not by P or his nominee) to Q or his nominee,

section 87 above shall not apply as regards an agreement to transfer chargeable securities which is made for the purpose of performing the obligation to transfer chargeable securities described in paragraph (*a*) or (*b*) above.

(2) Where the arrangement mentioned in subsection (1) above is also one under which—

(*a*) an amount of chargeable securities of some other kind is to be transferred by P or his nominee to Q or his nominee by way of security for the performance of the obligation described in paragraph (*b*) of that subsection, and

(*b*) on performance of that obligation, the securities mentioned in paragraph (*a*) above, or chargeable securities of the same kind and amount as those securities, are to be transferred to P or his nominee,

section 87 above shall also not apply as regards an agreement to transfer chargeable securities which is made for the purpose of performing the obligation to transfer chargeable securities described in paragraph (*a*) or (*b*) above.

(3) Where, to enable Q to make the transfer to P or his nominee which is mentioned in paragraph (*a*) of subsection (1) above, Q enters into an arrangement under which—

(*a*) another person (R) is to transfer chargeable securities to Q or his nominee, and,

(*b*) in return, chargeable securities of the same kind and amount are to be transferred (whether or not by Q or his nominee) to R or his nominee,

section 87 above shall not apply as regards an agreement to transfer chargeable securities which is made for the purpose of performing the obligation to transfer chargeable securities described in paragraph (*a*) or (*b*) above.

(4) Where the arrangement mentioned in subsection (3) above is also one under which—

(*a*) an amount of chargeable securities of some other kind is to be transferred by Q or his nominee to R or his nominee by way of security for the performance of the obligation described in paragraph (*b*) of that subsection, and

(*b*) on performance of that obligation, the securities mentioned in paragraph (*a*) above, or chargeable securities of the same kind and amount as those securities, are to be transferred to Q or his nominee,

section 87 above shall also not apply as regards an agreement to transfer chargeable securities which is made for the purpose of performing the obligation to transfer chargeable securities described in paragraph (*a*) or (*b*) above.

(5) For the purposes of this section a person is a market maker in chargeable securities of a particular kind if he—

(*a*) holds himself out at all normal times in compliance with the rules of The Stock Exchange as willing to buy and sell chargeable securities of that kind at a price specified by him, and

(*b*) is recognised as doing so by The Stock Exchange.

(6) The Treasury may by regulations provide that for subsection (5) above (as it has effect for the time being) there shall be substituted a subsection containing a different definition of a market maker for the purposes of this section.

(7) Regulations under subsection (6) above shall apply in relation to any agreement to transfer chargeable securities in pursuance of an arrangement entered into on or after such day after 1st July 1996 as is specified in the regulations.

(8) The power to make regulations under subsection (6) above shall be exercisable by statutory instrument subject to annulment in pursuance of a resolution of the House of Commons.''

(2) This section applies in relation to agreements to transfer chargeable securities in pursuance of an arrangement entered into on or after 1st July 1996.

BACKGROUND NOTE

Stock lending transactions (ie transactions whereby A transfers securities to B to enable B to perform his obligations to C on terms that in due course B will transfer similar securities to A technically involve transfers and "retransfers" potentially liable to stamp duty and/or SDRT. Over the years various reliefs (eg FA 1986 s 82 in relation to stamp duty) or concessional practices (eg those referred to under Inland Revenue Press Release, 2 October 1995) have grown up. The increased emphasis on SDRT under the CREST regime and changes to relevant Stock Exchange rules on stock lending provide an opportunity to codify these.

GENERAL NOTE

Accordingly, sub-s (1) inserts a new s 89B in FA 1986. New s 89B(1) provides for relief where a market maker (P) who had contracted to sell chargeable securities in the ordinary course of its market-making business has had to borrow, in order to fulfil that contract, chargeable securities from a lender (Q). More precisely no SDRT charge under FA 1986 s 87 will arise on agreements by Q to transfer chargeable securities to P or his nominee or on agreements (whether or not involving P or his nominee) to transfer chargeable securities of the same kind or amount to Q or his nominee ("repayment of the borrowing").

COLLATERAL (1)

Where, under s 89B(1) arrangements, chargeable securities of some other kind ("the collateral"), are to be transferred by P or his nominee to Q or his nominee as security for the obligation to procure or effect repayment of the "borrowing", and that obligation having been performed those chargeable securities (or other securities of the same kind or amount) are to be transferred to P (or his nominee), new s 89B(2) exempts from SDRT agreements to transfer or retransfer the collateral.

211

In s 89B(1) circumstances if the lender (Q) in turn needs to borrow from a third party lender (R) to enable him to transfer appropriate securities to the market maker (P) or his nominee, new s 89B(3) provides SDRT will not apply to Q's agreement with R for the transfer of securities to Q or his nominee and that Q would itself (or through its nominee) transfer, or procure the transfer of, appropriate chargeable securities "back" to R (or its nominee).

COLLATERAL (2)
Section 89B(4) provides that where—

(*a*) there is tripartite lending of the type described in s 89B(3); and
(*b*) securities of a different kind to those agreed to be sold by P (and lent by R to Q) are to be transferred by Q (or his nominee) to R (or his nominee) as security for Q's obligation to deliver, or procure delivery of, an appropriate number of chargeable securities to R;

no SDRT charges will apply to the agreements to transfer chargeable securities to R in satisfaction of Q's obligation to deliver such collateral to R and to retransfer the collateral (or procure the transfer of similar securities) to Q.

DEFINITION
New s 89B(5) contains an identical definition of market maker as is contained in FA 1986s 89(3)(*a*), and s 89B(6) contains an identical power (enabling a different definition of market maker to be substituted) to that in s 89(6) as regards agreements entered into after 30 June 1996.

COMMENCEMENT
These relieving provisions apply to post-30 June 1996 agreements: s 191(2).

192   Repayment or cancellation of tax

(1) In consequence of section 188(1) above, subsections (4), (5) and (8) of section 87 of the Finance Act 1986 (exemption from stamp duty reserve tax where an instrument is executed etc) shall cease to have effect.

(2) In section 88 of that Act (which provides for instruments on which stamp duty is not chargeable by virtue of certain enactments to be disregarded for the purposes of section 87(4) and (5)) in subsections (1), (1A) and (1B) for "section 87(4) and (5) above" there shall be substituted "section 92(1A) and (1B) below".

(3) In section 92 of that Act (repayment or cancellation of tax) in subsection (1) (which refers to the conditions in section 87(4) and (5))—

(*a*) for "section 87(4) and (5)" there shall be substituted "subsections (1A) and (1B) below"; and
(*b*) for "the following provisions of this section shall apply" there shall be substituted "subsections (2) to (4A) of this section shall apply".

(4) After that subsection, there shall be inserted—

"(1A) The first condition is that an instrument is (or instruments are) executed in pursuance of the agreement and the instrument transfers (or the instruments between them transfer) to B or, as the case may be, to his nominee all the chargeable securities to which the agreement relates.

(1B) The second condition is that the instrument (or each instrument) transferring the chargeable securities to which the agreement relates is duly stamped in accordance with the enactments relating to stamp duty if it is an instrument which, under those enactments, is chargeable with stamp duty or otherwise required to be stamped."

(5) At the end of that section there shall be added—

"(6) In this section 'the enactments relating to stamp duty' means the Stamp Act 1891 and any enactment which amends or is required to be construed together with that Act."

(6) The amendments made by this section shall have effect in relation to an agreement to transfer securities if—

(*a*) the agreement is conditional and the condition is satisfied on or after 1st July 1996; or

(*b*) the agreement is not conditional and is made on or after that date.

GENERAL NOTE

Notwithstanding the changes made by, inter alia, s 188, which have the effect of removing the two-month waiting period, sub-s (1) repeals FA 1986 s 87(4), (5) and (8). Subsection (4) then re-enacts in identical language s 87(4) and (5) as new s 92(1A) and (1B); sub-s (4) re-enacts sub-s (8) in identical language as new s 92(6). Subsections (2) and (3) make appropriate amendments to ss 88 and 92(1).

COMMENCEMENT

The changes apply to agreements made after 30 June 1996 or, if made on or before that date, agreements which become unconditional after that date.

193 Depositary receipts

(1) Section 93 of the Finance Act 1986 (depositary receipts) shall be amended in accordance with the following provisions of this section.

(2) In subsection (1) (charge to stamp duty reserve tax where certain things are done in pursuance of an arrangement) in paragraph (*b*) (transfer or issue to, or appropriation by, a person falling within subsection (3))—

(*a*) after "transferred or issued to" there shall be inserted "the person mentioned in paragraph (*a*) above or"; and

(*b*) for "such a person" there shall be substituted "the person mentioned in paragraph (*a*) above or a person falling within subsection (3) below".

(3) In subsection (6) (payment by instalments) in paragraph (*d*) (instrument received by person falling within subsection (3)) for "subsection (3)" there shall be substituted "subsection (2) or (3)".

(4) This section has effect—

(*a*) so far as relating to the charge to tax under section 93(1) of the Finance Act 1986, where securities are transferred, issued or appropriated on or after 1st July 1996 (whenever the arrangement was made);

(*b*) so far as relating to the charge to tax under section 93(10) of that Act, in relation to instalments payable on or after 1st July 1996.

BACKGROUND NOTE

Depositary receipts ("DRs") are documents which represent the holders' entitlement (after payment of the DR issuer's/operator's costs) to have transferred to them a number of underlying shares or other chargeable securities. The current SDRT legislation (FA 1986 ss 93–95) envisage the issuer of the DRs being distinct from the holder of the underlying securities which "back" the DRs.

GENERAL NOTE

This section amends the circumstances in which a charge can arise under FA 1986 s 93 to include where the holder of the underlying securities is the same as the issuer of the DRs (and makes consequential amendments to s 93(6) which deals with instalment arrangements).

COMMENCEMENT

The amendments made by this section apply to issues, transfers or appropriation of chargeable securities after 30 June 1996 whether or not made pursuant to arrangements made on or before that date. Subsection (4) causes the amendments to apply to payments of instalments payable after 30 June 1996 in respect of chargeable securities issued or transferred (whether before, on or after that date) on terms providing for payments of instalments and interim certificates pending full payment.

194　Rates of charge expressed as percentages

(1)　In section 87 of the Finance Act 1986, in subsection (6) (which specifies the rate at which stamp duty reserve tax under that section is charged) for "50p for every £100 or part of £100" there shall be substituted "0.5 per cent."

(2)　In section 93 of that Act (depositary receipts)—

(*a*)　in subsection (4) (rate of charge) for "£1.50 for every £100 or part of £100" there shall be substituted "1.5 per cent";

(*b*)　in subsection (5) (which applies subsection (4) with modifications in certain cases where the securities are transferred by a chargeable instrument) for the words from "as if '£1.50' read" onwards there shall be substituted "as if '1.5 per cent' read '1 per cent'"; and

(*c*)　in subsection (10) (payment in instalments etc) in paragraph (*b*), for "£1.50 for every £100 or part of £100" there shall be substituted "1.5 per cent of the amount".

(3)　Section 94(8) of that Act (which defines "the day of The Stock Exchange reforms" for the purposes of section 93(5) and which becomes unnecessary in consequence of the amendment made by subsection (2)(*b*) above) shall be omitted.

(4)　In section 96 of that Act (clearance services)—

(*a*)　in subsection (2) (rate of charge) for "£1.50 for every £100 or part of £100" there shall be substituted "1.5 per cent";

(*b*)　in subsection (3) (which applies subsection (2) with modifications in certain cases where the securities are transferred by a chargeable instrument) for the words from "as if '£1.50' read" onwards there shall be substituted "as if '1.5 per cent' read '1 per cent'"; and

(*c*)　in subsection (8) (payment in instalments etc) in paragraph (*b*), for "£1.50 for every £100 or part of £100" there shall be substituted "1.5 per cent of the amount".

(5)　Section 96(12) of that Act (which defines "the day of The Stock Exchange reforms" for the purposes of subsection (3) and which becomes unnecessary in consequence of the amendment made by subsection (4)(*b*) above) shall be omitted.

(6)　In section 99 of that Act (interpretation) after subsection (12) there shall be added—

"(13)　Where the calculation of any tax in accordance with the provisions of this Part results in an amount which is not a multiple of one penny, the amount so calculated shall be rounded to the nearest penny, taking any ½p as nearest to the next whole penny above."

(7)　Subsections (1) to (5) above have effect in accordance with the following provisions of this subsection, that is to say—

(*a*)　in relation to the charge to tax under section 87 of the Finance Act 1986, subsection (1) above applies where—

(i)　the agreement to transfer is conditional and the condition is satisfied on or after 1st July 1996; or

(ii)　the agreement is not conditional and is made on or after 1st July 1996;

(*b*)　in relation to the charge to tax under section 93(1) of that Act, paragraphs (*a*) and (*b*) of subsection (2) above apply where securities are transferred, issued or appropriated on or after 1st July 1996 (whenever the arrangement was made) and subsection (3) above has effect accordingly;

(*c*)　in relation to the charge to tax under section 93(10) of that Act, paragraph (*c*) of subsection (2) above applies in relation to instalments payable on or after 1st July 1996;

(*d*) in relation to the charge to tax under section 96(1) of that Act, paragraphs (*a*) and (*b*) of subsection (4) above apply where securities are transferred or issued on or after 1st July 1996 (whenever the arrangement was made) and subsection (5) above has effect accordingly;

(*e*) in relation to the charge to tax under section 96(8) of that Act, paragraph (*c*) of subsection (4) above applies in relation to instalments payable on or after 1st July 1996.

BACKGROUND NOTE
When SDRT was introduced the rate at which it was payable, whether at the basic rate or at the higher rate applicable to depository receipt arrangements, and clearance services, was based on the stamp duty model of bands of consideration. This section amends the SDRT legislation so that the charge is a simple percentage of the consideration.

GENERAL NOTE
Accordingly sub-s (1) amends the SDRT basic charge to 0.5 per cent; sub-s (2) amends the rate generally applicable to DR arrangements (including instalment arrangements) to 1.5 per cent and the relief (effectively where stamp duty on a purchase has previously been paid) to 1 per cent; and sub-s (4) makes similar amendments to the clearance services charges in ss 96 and 97.

SERVICES CHARGES IN SS 96 AND 97
Repeals
Subsections (3) and (5) respectively repeal spent references to "Big Bang" in FA 1986 s 94(8) and s 96(12).

Rounding
Subsection (6) adds a new s 89(13) which provides that where the relevant percentage rate applicable to the consideration or value attributed to the chargeable securities results in a fraction of a penny it should be rounded to the nearest penny, ½p being rounded up.

Commencement
Subsection (7) provides for the changes made by sub-ss (1)–(5) to apply—

(*a*) to agreements to transfer made after 30 June 1996 or which become unconditional after that date;

(*b*) to transfers, issues or appropriations attracting the higher rate charges made on or after 1 July 1996; and

(*c*) to instalments payable after 30 June 1996.

195 Regulations concerning administration: sub-delegation to the Board

In section 98 of the Finance Act 1986 (Treasury regulations with respect to administration etc) after subsection (1) there shall be inserted—

"(1A) The power conferred on the Treasury by subsection (1) above includes power to make provision conferring or imposing on the Board functions which involve the exercise of a discretion."

GENERAL NOTE
This section amends FA 1986 s 98 to enable the Treasury under its existing regulation-making powers to confer on, or require the Board of Inland Revenue to carry out, functions which require a discretion to be exercised.

Clearance services

196 Election by operator for alternative system of charge

(1) In section 70 of the Finance Act 1986 (clearance services) in subsection (1) (which, subject to subsection (9), makes provision with respect to stamp duty on transfers into clearance services) after "Subject to subsection (9)" there shall be inserted "and section 97A".

(2) In section 96 of that Act (clearance services) in subsection (1) (which, subject to subsection (5) and section 97, provides for stamp duty reserve tax to be chargeable on transfers into clearance services) for "section 97" there shall be substituted "sections 97 and 97A".

(3) After section 97 of that Act (exceptions) there shall be inserted—

"97A Clearance services: election for alternative system of charge

(1) A person whose business is or includes the provision of clearance services for the purchase and sale of chargeable securities or relevant securities (an 'operator') may, with the approval of the Board, elect that stamp duty and stamp duty reserve tax shall be chargeable in accordance with this section in connection with those clearance services.

(2) An election under subsection (1) above—

(*a*) shall come into force on such date as may be notified to the operator by the Board in giving their approval; and
(*b*) shall continue in force unless and until it is terminated in accordance with the following provisions of this section.

(3) If and so long as an election under subsection (1) above is in force, stamp duty or stamp duty reserve tax (as the case may require) shall, in connection with the clearance services to which the election relates, be chargeable in relation to—

(*a*) a transfer or issue falling within section 70(1) or 96(1) above,
(*b*) an agreement falling within section 90(4) above by virtue of section 96(1) above, or
(*c*) an agreement falling within section 90(5) above,

as it would be chargeable apart from sections 70, 90(4) and (5) and 96 above.

(4) Where stamp duty or stamp duty reserve tax is chargeable by virtue of subsection (3) above in relation to a transfer, issue or agreement, sections 70, 90(4) and (5) and 96 above shall not have effect in relation to that transfer, issue or agreement.

(5) Nothing in subsection (3) or (4) above affects the application of section 70 or 96 above in relation to a transfer falling within section 70(1) or 96(1) above by the operator or his nominee to, or to a nominee of, another operator in relation to whom no election under subsection (1) above is for the time being in force.

(6) The Board may require the operator, as a condition of the approval of his election under subsection (1) above, to make and maintain such arrangements as they may consider satisfactory—

(*a*) for the collection of stamp duty reserve tax chargeable in accordance with this section, and
(*b*) for complying, or securing compliance, with the provisions of this Part and of regulations under section 98 below, so far as relating to such tax.

(7) Where the operator is not resident in the United Kingdom and has no branch or agency in the United Kingdom, the Board may require him, as a condition of the approval of his election under subsection (1) above, to appoint and, so long as the election remains in force, maintain a tax representative.

(8) A person shall not be an operator's tax representative under this section unless that person—

(*a*) has a business establishment in the United Kingdom, and
(*b*) is approved by the Board.

(9) A person who is at any time an operator's tax representative under this section—

(*a*) shall be entitled to act on the operator's behalf for the purposes of stamp duty and stamp duty reserve tax in connection with the clearance services to which the operator's election under subsection (1) above relates,
(*b*) shall secure (where appropriate by acting on the operator's behalf) the operator's compliance with and discharge of the obligations and liabilities to which the operator is subject, in connection with the clearance services to which the operator's election under subsection (1) above relates, by virtue of legislation relating to stamp duty or stamp duty reserve tax (including obligations and liabilities arising before he became the operator's tax representative), and
(*c*) shall be personally liable in respect of any failure to secure the operator's compliance with or discharge of any such obligation or liability, and in respect of anything done for purposes connected with acting on the operator's behalf,

as if the obligations and liabilities imposed on the operator were imposed jointly and severally on the tax representative and the operator.

(10) An election under subsection (1) above may be terminated—

(*a*) by not less than thirty days' notice given by the operator to the Board or by the Board to the operator; or
(*b*) if there is or has been a breach of a condition of the approval of the election imposed by virtue of subsection (6) or (7) above, by a notice—

(i) given by the Board to the operator,
(ii) taking effect on the giving of the notice or at such later time as may be specified in the notice, and
(iii) stating that it is given by reason of the breach of condition.

(11) Where an election under subsection (1) above is terminated, section 96 above shall have effect as if chargeable securities of the same amounts and kinds as are, immediately before the termination, held by the operator or his nominee in connection with the provision of the clearance services, had, immediately after the termination, been transferred to the operator or, as the case may be, to the nominee by a transfer falling within subsection (1) of that section.

(12) In this section 'relevant securities' has the same meaning as in section 70 above.''

(4) Section 97(2) of that Act (no charge to tax under section 96 on transfers to a stock exchange nominee or to, or to a nominee of, a recognised investment exchange or recognised clearing house) shall not have effect in relation to any transfer effected on or after 1st July 1996.

(5) In section 99(10) of that Act (interpretation of "chargeable securities" in sections 93, 94 and 96) for "and 96" there shall be substituted "96 and 97A''.

(6) Subsections (1), (2), (3) and (5) above shall come into force on 1st July 1996.

BACKGROUND NOTE

Currently the higher rate charge of SDRT in respect of clearance services envisages a one-off charge when chargeable securities are issued or transferred to the provider (or a nominee) of such services. Thereafter generally transfers of interests in the securities held within a clearance service can take place without a further charge to stamp duty or SDRT arising. Subsection (3) introduces a new s 97A into FA 1986 enabling the one-off entry charge to be avoided on the basis that the ordinary 0.5 per cent SDRT charge would apply to transfers of securities made within the system.

GENERAL NOTE

Subsection (1) amends FA 1986 s 70 (the stamp duty charge on transfers into clearance services) in effect to preclude the stamp duty charge arising where the operator has entered into an agreement under new s 97A. Subsection (2) makes similar amendments to the basic clearance service SDRT charge contained in s 96.

THE ELECTIVE REGIME

New s 97A(1) enables the operator of the clearance service to elect, with the Revenue's approval, for charges to arise in accordance with s 97A(3): s 97A(2) provides that an election operates from the date notified by the Revenue until determined in accordance with sub-s (10). Under s 97A(6) the Revenue as a pre-condition of approval of an election may require the operator to make and maintain arrangements satisfactory to the Revenue for collection of SDRT and UK compliance. As a further precondition if the operator is neither UK resident nor has a UK branch or agency, the Revenue may acquire appointment, and retention (while the election remains in force), of a tax representative: see new s 97A(7). Only persons approved by the Revenue with a UK business establishment may be an operator's tax representative: see news 97A(8).

Section 97A(10) provides that an election may be terminated by the Board of Inland Revenue either—

(*a*) where there has been a breach of a s 97A(6) or (7) condition, provided that the notice terminating the election states that it is because of the breach, either immediately or at a later specified time; or

(*b*) seemingly without a reason being given, provided at least 30 days notice is given to the operator.

The operator may terminate the election again on giving not less than 30 days notice to the Board.

THE CHARGING BASIS

Under s 97A(3) if an election is in force the stamp duty or SDRT charge that would otherwise arise absent FA 1986 s 70, s 90(4) and (5) and s 96 would apply to—

(*a*) a transfer of relevant securities of a company incorporated in the UK to the operator of the clearance service (or other persons mentioned in s 70(6)–(8));

(*b*) a transfer or issue of chargeable securities to the operator of the clearance services;

(*c*) an agreement to transfer chargeable securities held within a clearance service (where, absent the s 97A election, no charge would have arisen because of s 90(4)); or

(*d*) an agreement to transfer certain securities to nominees or agents of clearance service operators (where, absent the s 97A election, no charge would have arisen because of s 90(5) and (6)).

Accordingly while the election is in force s 70, 90(4) and (5), and s 96 do not apply to such transfers, issues or agreements: new s 97A(4). Further any transfer by the clearance service operator (or its nominee) to, or to a nominee of, another operator which does not benefit from a current s 97A(1) election remains chargeable in the usual way.

New s 97A(11) provides for an exit charge where an election has been terminated: accordingly, immediately after the election ceasing to have effect there is a notional transfer of chargeable securities of the same kind and amount as were held immediately prior to its termination, liable to the ordinary s 96(1) charge.

DEFINITIONS

The stamp duty definition of "relevant securities" (see s 72(1)) applying for s 70 also applies for s 97A: see s 97A(12). Subsection (5) amends the definition of "chargeable securities" applicable to, inter alia, s 96 consequential upon the introduction of s 97A.

REPEALS AND COMMENCEMENT

Consequent upon SDRT being the primary tax for dematerialised securities, sub-s (4) removes the exemption from the higher rate SDRT charge in respect of clearance services contained in FA 1986 s 97(2) in respect of post-30 June 1996 transfers.

The amendments contained in sub-ss (1), (2) and (5) and the new s 97A introduced by sub-s (3) apply from 1 July 1996.

PART VII

MISCELLANEOUS AND SUPPLEMENTAL

Miscellaneous: indirect taxation

197 Setting of rates of interest

(1) The rate of interest applicable for the purposes of an enactment to which this section applies shall be the rate which for the purposes of that enactment is provided for by regulations made by the Treasury under this section.

(2) This section applies to—

(*a*) paragraphs 7 and 9 of Schedule 6 to the Finance Act 1994 (interest payable to or by the Commissioners of Customs and Excise in connection with air passenger duty);

(*b*) paragraphs 21 and 22 of Schedule 7 to that Act (interest on amounts of insurance premium tax and on amounts payable by the Commissioners in respect of that tax);

(*c*) sections 74 and 78 of the Value Added Tax Act 1994 (interest on VAT recovered or recoverable by assessment and interest payable in cases of official error); and

(*d*) paragraphs 26 and 29 of Schedule 5 to this Act (interest payable to or by the Commissioners in connection with landfill tax).

(3) Regulations under this section may—

(*a*) make different provision for different enactments or for different purposes of the same enactment,

(*b*) either themselves specify a rate of interest for the purposes of an enactment or make provision for any such rate to be determined, and to change from time to time, by reference to such rate or the average of such rates as may be referred to in the regulations,

(*c*) provide for rates to be reduced below, or increased above, what they otherwise would be by specified amounts or by reference to specified formulae,

(*d*) provide for rates arrived at by reference to averages or formulae to be rounded up or down,

(*e*) provide for circumstances in which changes of rates of interest are or are not to take place, and

(*f*) provide that changes of rates are to have effect for periods beginning on or after a day determined in accordance with the regulations in relation to interest running from before that day, as well as in relation to interest running from, or from after, that day.

(4) The power to make regulations under this section shall be exercisable by statutory instrument subject to annulment in pursuance of a resolution of the House of Commons.

(5) Where—

(*a*) regulations under this section provide, without specifying the rate determined in accordance with the regulations, for a new method of determining the rate applicable for the purposes of any enactment, or

(*b*) the rate which, in accordance with regulations under this section, is the rate applicable for the purposes of any enactment changes otherwise than by virtue of the making of regulations specifying a new rate,

the Commissioners of Customs and Excise shall make an order specifying the new rate and the day from which, in accordance with the regulations, it has effect.

(6) The words "the rate applicable under section 197 of the Finance Act 1996" shall be substituted—

(*a*) for the words "the specified rate" in each of paragraphs 7(1) and (3) and 9(1) of Schedule 6 to the Finance Act 1994 (air passenger duty);

(*b*) for the words "the prescribed rate" in each of sub-paragraphs (1) and (3) of paragraph 21 of Schedule 7 to that Act (insurance premium tax);

(*c*) for the words from "such rate" onwards in sub-paragraph (2) of paragraph 22 of that Schedule; and

(*d*) in the Value Added Tax Act 1994—

(i) for the words "the prescribed rate" in each of subsections (1), (2) and (4) of section 74, and

(ii) for the words from "such rates" onwards in subsection (3) of section 78.

(7) Subsections (1) and (6) above shall have effect for periods beginning on or after such day as the Treasury may by order made by statutory instrument appoint and shall have effect in relation to interest running from before that day, as well as in relation to interest running from, or from after, that day; and different days may be appointed under this subsection for different purposes.

GENERAL NOTE
The Treasury is given power to make regulations determining the rates of interest payable to or by Customs and Excise in the following circumstances—

(*a*) interest on Air Passenger Duty;
(*b*) interest on Insurance Premium Tax;
(*c*) interest on VAT recovered or recoverable by assessment and interest payable in cases of official error.

These provisions replace the existing provisions for determining the rates of interest for the taxes concerned. They will apply from a date to be appointed by statutory instrument.

Miscellaneous: direct taxation

198 Banks

Schedule 37 to this Act (which re-defines "bank" for certain purposes, and makes related amendments) shall have effect.

GENERAL NOTE
This section introduces Sch 37 which defines the term "bank" for various tax purposes.

199 Quotation or listing of securities

Schedule 38 to this Act (which contains amendments of enactments referring to the quotation or listing of securities) shall have effect.

GENERAL NOTE
This section introduces Sch 38 which substitutes the word "listed" for the word "quoted" at various places in IHTA 1984 and in TCGA 1992, and also in the provisions relating to the territorial extension of the charge to income tax, CGT and corporation tax (see FA 1973 s 38(2)(*c*)).

200 Domicile for tax purposes of overseas electors

(1) In determining—

(*a*) for the purposes of inheritance tax, income tax or capital gains tax where a person is domiciled at any time on or after 6th April 1996, or

(*b*) for the purposes of section 267(1)(*a*) of the Inheritance Tax Act 1984 (deemed UK domicile for three years after ceasing to be so domiciled) where a person was domiciled at any time on or after 6th April 1993,

there shall be disregarded any relevant action taken by that person (whether before, on or after that date) in connection with electoral rights.

(2) Relevant action is taken by a person in connection with electoral rights where—

(*a*) he does anything with a view to, or in connection with, being registered as an overseas elector; or

(*b*) when registered as an overseas elector, he votes in any election at which he is entitled to vote by virtue of being so registered.

(3) For the purposes of this section, a person is registered as an overseas elector if he is—

(*a*) registered in any register mentioned in section 12(1) of the Representation of the People Act 1983 (right to be registered of persons entitled to vote at parliamentary elections) on account of any entitlement to vote conferred on him by section 1 of the Representation of the People Act 1985 (extension of parliamentary franchise to certain non-resident British citizens); or

(*b*) registered under section 3 of that Act 1985 (certain non-resident peers entitled to vote at European Parliamentary elections).

(4) Nothing in subsection (1) above prevents regard being had, in determining the domicile of a person at any time, to any relevant action taken by him in connection with electoral rights if—

(*a*) his domicile at that time falls to be determined for the purpose of ascertaining his or any other person's liability to any of the taxes mentioned in subsection (1)(*a*) above; and

(*b*) the person whose liability is being ascertained wishes regard to be had to that action;

and a person's domicile determined in accordance with any such wishes shall be taken to have been so determined for the purpose only of ascertaining the liability in question.

GENERAL NOTE
    With effect from 6 April 1996, the fact that an individual is registered on the UK electoral roll as an overseas voter does not affect his domicile status for income tax, CGT or IHT purposes unless he wishes it to be taken into account. The same rule applies in determining whether an individual ceased to be domiciled in the UK on or after 6 April 1993, for the purposes of the continuing three year domicile rule under IHTA 1984 s 267(1)(*a*).

201 Enactment of Inland Revenue concessions

Schedule 39 to this Act has effect for the purpose of enacting certain extra-statutory concessions relating to income tax, corporation tax, capital gains tax, and stamp duty.

GENERAL NOTE
    This section introduces Sch 39 which enacts the following ESCs—

B19	Capital allowances for buildings: balancing charge after cessation of trade
B28	Leased cars costing over £12,000—rebate of hire charges
B39	Contributions to overseas pension schemes
D19, D1	Replacement of buildings destroyed
D28	Assets of negligible value
D43	Settled property
D48	Retirement relief
D36	Relief for irrecoverable loans to traders (including QCBs)
G1, G2	Stamp allowance on lost or spoiled documents

Miscellaneous: other matters

202 Gilt stripping

(1) In section 47 of the Finance Act 1942 (Treasury regulations with respect to the transfer and registration of Government stock), after paragraph (*bb*) of subsection (1) there shall be inserted the following paragraphs—

"(*bc*) for the exchange of any such stock and bonds (whenever issued) for strips thereof;
(*bd*) for exchanges by which such strips (whether deriving from the same security or from different securities) are consolidated into a single security of a description so specified;".

(2) After subsection (1A) of that section (transfer of deceased persons' stocks and bonds) there shall be inserted the following subsections—

"(1B) In this section 'strip', in relation to any stock or bond, means a security issued under the National Loans Act 1968 which—

(*a*) is issued for the purpose of representing the right to, or of securing—

(i) a payment corresponding to a payment of interest or principal remaining to be made under the stock or bond, or
(ii) two or more payments each corresponding to a different payment remaining to be so made;

(*b*) is issued in conjunction with the issue of one or more other securities which, together with that security, represent the right to, or secure, payments corresponding to every payment remaining to be made under the stock or bond; and
(*c*) is not itself a security that represents the right to, or secures, payments corresponding to a part of every payment so remaining.

(1C) For the purposes of subsection (1B) of this section, where the balance has been struck for a dividend on any stock or bond, any payment to be made in respect of that dividend shall, at times falling after that balance has been struck, be treated as not being a payment remaining to be made under the stock or bond.

(1D) Without prejudice to the generality of the powers conferred by the preceding provisions of this section (but subject to subsection (1E) of this section), regulations made by virtue of paragraph (*bc*) or (*bd*) of subsection (1) of this section may—

(*a*) provide, for the purpose of authorising the making of exchanges, for any stock or bonds to be treated as issued on such terms as may be specified in the regulations;
(*b*) contain such provision as the Treasury think fit about the circumstances in which and the conditions subject to which exchanges may be effected; and
(*c*) contain any such provision as could be contained in rules made under section 14(3) of the National Loans Act 1968 (Treasury rules as to exchange of securities).

(1E) Regulations made by virtue of subsection (1)(*bc*) or (*bd*) of this section shall not make provision for the exchange of any stock or bonds, or of any strips, in any cases other than those where the exchange is at the request of the holder or in accordance with an order made by a court.

(1F) Regulations under this section may make different provision for different cases and contain such exceptions and exclusions as the Treasury think fit; and the powers of the Treasury to make regulations under this section are without prejudice to any of their powers under the National Loans Act 1968."

(3) After section 2 of the National Debt (Stockholders Relief) Act 1892 (date for striking balance for a dividend on stock) there shall be inserted the following section—

"2A   Payment of dividend on stock stripped after balance struck

(1) Where—

(a) any stock is exchanged for strips of that stock, and
(b) that exchange takes place after the balance has been struck for a dividend on that stock but before the day on which that dividend is payable,

any person who would have been entitled to that dividend but for the exchange shall remain entitled to that dividend notwithstanding the exchange.

(2) The Treasury may by order made by statutory instrument provide that for the purposes of this section and section 47(1C) of the Finance Act 1942, the balance for any dividend on any stock is to be deemed to be struck at a time which, by such a period as is specified in the order, precedes the time when the balance is actually struck.

(3) A period specified in an order under subsection (2) above shall not exceed 7 days; and an order made under that subsection may make different provision for different cases.

(4) In this section 'strip', in relation to any stock, has the meaning given by section 47 of the Finance Act 1942."

(4) In section 16 of the National Loans Act 1968 (supplemental provisions as to national debt), after subsection (4) there shall be inserted the following subsection—

"(4A) In subsections (3) and (4) above the references to stock or registered bonds issued under this Act include references to a strip (within the meaning of section 47 of the Finance Act 1942) of any stock or bond (whether the stock or bond is issued under this Act or otherwise)."

(5) The Treasury may by regulations make provision for securing that enactments and subordinate legislation which—

(a) apply in relation to government securities or to any description of such securities, or
(b) for any other purpose refer (in whatever terms) to such securities or to any description of them,

have effect with such modifications as the Treasury may think appropriate in consequence of the making of any provision or arrangements for, or in connection with, the issue or transfer of strips of government securities or the consolidation of such strips into other securities.

(6) Regulations under subsection (5) above may—

(a) impose a charge to income tax, corporation tax, capital gains tax, inheritance tax, stamp duty or stamp duty reserve tax;
(b) include provision applying generally to, or to any description of, enactments or subordinate legislation;
(c) make different provision for different cases; and

(*d*) contain such incidental, supplemental, consequential and transitional provision as the Treasury think appropriate.

(7) The power to make regulations under subsection (5) above shall be exercisable by statutory instrument subject to annulment in pursuance of a resolution of the House of Commons.

(8) Schedule 40 to this Act (which makes provision in relation to strips for taxation purposes) shall have effect.

(9) The enactments that may be modified by regulations under this section shall include section 95 above and the enactments contained in Schedule 40 to this Act.

(10) In this section—

"government securities" means any securities included in Part I of Schedule 11 to the Finance Act 1942;
"modifications" includes amendments, additions and omissions; and
"subordinate legislation" has the same meaning as in the Interpretation Act 1978;

and expressions used in this section and in section 47 of the Finance Act 1942 have the same meanings in this section as in that section.

GENERAL NOTE
The Treasury is given power to make regulations to facilitate the exchange of gilts in their present form for stripped versions of the same gilts. This involves issuing separate securities representing the principal and the interest elements of the gilt. Each security may then be dealt in independently of the other. Separate coupons may be issued in respect of each payment of interest. The regulations may also include provisions relating to the taxation of such "strips".

The section also introduces Sch 40 which amends the Accrued Income Scheme rules to deal with the exchanges referred to above.

203 Modification of the Agriculture Act 1993

(1) Part I of Schedule 2 to the Agriculture Act 1993 (taxation provisions applying to the reorganisation of the milk marketing boards) shall have effect, and be deemed always to have had effect, in accordance with subsections (2) to (4) below where—

(*a*) any approved scheme has made provision as to the functions of a milk marketing board in the period after the transfers taking effect on the vesting day under section 11 of that Act;
(*b*) regulations have been made by virtue of section 14(2) of that Act (provision following re-organisation) for giving effect to that provision; and
(*c*) a transaction is or has been entered into by that board in pursuance of any obligation under those regulations to carry out those functions so far as they relate to a subsidiary of the board.

(2) For the purposes of that Part of that Schedule—

(*a*) anything done by way of entering into the transaction, or for the purpose of carrying it out, shall be deemed to have been done under and in accordance with the scheme; and
(*b*) the terms and other provisions having effect in relation to that transaction by virtue of anything contained in, or anything done in exercise of powers conferred by, any regulations under section 14(2) of the Agriculture Act 1993 shall be deemed to be terms for which the scheme provided or, as the case may be, to be provisions of the scheme.

(3) Sub-paragraph (1) of paragraph 16 of Schedule 2 to the Agriculture Act 1993 (distributions) shall have effect, and be deemed always to have had effect,

in a case where the terms and provisions mentioned in subsection (2)(*b*) above involved or involve—

(*a*) the issue or transfer of any shares in, or securities of, any body,
(*b*) the conferring of any right to a distribution out of the assets of any body,
(*c*) the conferring of any right to, or to acquire, shares in any body, or
(*d*) the transfer to any person of any property or rights of a milk marketing board, or of the subsidiary of such a board,

as if the references to the vesting day in paragraphs (*a*), (*c*), (*d*) and (*e*) of that sub-paragraph were references to the day on which the winding up of the board is completed.

(4) Sub-paragraph (4) of paragraph 31 of Schedule 2 to the Agriculture Act 1993 (condition to be satisfied if body to be qualifying body by virtue of sub-paragraph (1)(*c*)) shall have effect, and be deemed always to have had effect, as if—

(*a*) the reference, in relation to a company, to 90 per cent. of its ordinary share capital were a reference to 70 per cent. of its ordinary share capital; and
(*b*) the references to shares having been issued to any person included references to their having been allotted to that person.

(5) Paragraph 1 of Schedule 2 to the Agriculture Act 1993 (tax continuity with successor bodies) shall have effect, and be deemed to have had effect, in relation to any relevant transfer after 31st December 1995 to a society registered under the Industrial and Provident Societies Act 1965 of—

(*a*) a trade, or part of a trade, of a milk marketing board, or
(*b*) any property, rights or liabilities of such a board,

as it has effect in relation to any transfer under section 11 of that Act to a qualifying body.

(6) Paragraphs 16, 20, 25, 26, 28 and 29 of Schedule 2 to the Agriculture Act 1993 shall have effect, and be deemed to have had effect, in relation to any relevant transfer after 31st December 1995 of assets of a milk marketing board to a society registered under the Industrial and Provident Societies Act 1965 as if—

(*a*) the terms and other provisions of the transaction for effecting the transfer were contained in an approved scheme;
(*b*) the society were a relevant successor of that board; and
(*c*) references in those paragraphs to the vesting day were references to the day on which the winding up of the board is completed.

(7) For the purposes of subsections (5) and (6) above, a transfer of anything to a society registered under the Industrial and Provident Societies Act 1965 is a relevant transfer if—

(*a*) it is a transfer in pursuance of regulations made by virtue of section 14(2) of the Agriculture Act 1993;
(*b*) it is not a transfer of shares in a subsidiary of a milk marketing board; and
(*c*) the condition mentioned in sub-paragraph (5) of paragraph 31 of Schedule 2 to that Act would have been met in relation to that society if the provision made as to the persons to whom the membership of the society is open were contained in an approved scheme providing for the transfer.

(8) Paragraph 20 of Schedule 2 to the Agriculture Act 1993 (treatment of

acquisition of certain shares and securities) shall not apply, and shall be deemed never to have applied, in relation to the acquisition of any security after 31st December 1995 if the indebtedness acknowledged by that security does not fall, for the purposes of the Taxation of Chargeable Gains Act 1992, to be treated as a debt on a security (as defined in section 132 of that Act of 1992).

(9) For the purposes of Chapter II of Part IV of this Act, so far as it has effect for any accounting period ending after 31st March 1996 in relation to any creditor relationship represented by a debenture issued on or after 31st December 1995, paragraph 25 of Schedule 2 to the Agriculture Act 1993 shall have effect as if sub-paragraph (2)(*a*) of that paragraph (deemed consideration for issue of debenture issued under approved scheme) were omitted.

(10) For the purposes of the Taxation of Chargeable Gains Act 1992, where any debenture to which paragraph 25 of Schedule 2 to the Agriculture Act 1993 applies has been or is issued at any time after 31st December 1995, the indebtedness acknowledged by that debenture shall be deemed (where that would not otherwise be the case) to be, and always to have been, a debt on a security (as defined in section 132 of that Act of 1992).

(11) Expressions used in this section and in Part I of the Agriculture Act 1993 have the same meanings in this section as in that Part.

GENERAL NOTE
  This section amends the taxation provisions relating to the reorganisation of the milk marketing boards.

Supplemental

204 Interpretation
In this Act "the Taxes Act 1988" means the Income and Corporation Taxes Act 1988.

205 Repeals
(1) The enactments mentioned in Schedule 41 to this Act (which include spent provisions) are hereby repealed to the extent specified in the third column of that Schedule.

(2) The repeals specified in that Schedule have effect subject to the commencement provisions and savings contained in, or referred to, in the notes set out in that Schedule.

206 Short title
This Act may be cited as the Finance Act 1996.

SCHEDULES

SCHEDULE 3   Section 26

VALUE ADDED TAX: FISCAL AND OTHER WAREHOUSING

1 In subsection (1) of section 6 of the Value Added Tax Act 1994, for the words "section 18" there shall be substituted the words "sections 18, 18B and 18C".

GENERAL NOTE
    This paragraph amends VATA 1994 s 6(1). It provides that the time of supply rules in s 6 do not apply to supplies within ss 18B(2) and 18C(3) (as to which see para 5 below).

2 In subsection (1) of section 7 of the Value Added Tax Act 1994, for the words "sections 14 and 18" there shall be substituted the words "sections 14, 18 and 18B".

GENERAL NOTE
    This paragraph amends VATA 1994 s 7(1). It provides that the place of supply rules in s 7 do not apply to supplies within s 18B(2) (as to which see para 5 below).

3 In subsection (1) of section 12 of the Value Added Tax Act 1994, for the words "section 18" there shall be substituted "sections 18 and 18B".

GENERAL NOTE
    This paragraph amends VATA 1994 s 12(1). It provides that the time of acquisition rules in s 12 do not apply to acquisitions within s 18B(1) (as to which see para 5 below).

4 In subsection (1) of section 13 of the Value Added Tax Act 1994, for the words "section 18" there shall be substituted "sections 18 and 18B".

GENERAL NOTE
    This paragraph amends VATA 1994 s 13(1). It provides that the place of acquisition rules in s 13 do not apply to acquisitions within s 18B(1) (as to which see para 5 below).

5 The following sections shall be inserted in the Value Added Tax Act 1994 after section 18—

"18A Fiscal warehousing

(1) The Commissioners may, if it appears to them proper, upon application approve any registered person as a fiscal warehousekeeper; and such approval shall be subject to such conditions as they shall impose.

(2) Subject to those conditions and to regulations made under section 18F such a person shall be entitled to keep a fiscal warehouse.

(3) 'Fiscal warehouse' means such place in the United Kingdom in the occupation or under the control of the fiscal warehousekeeper, not being retail premises, as he shall notify to the Commissioners in writing; and such a place shall become a fiscal warehouse on receipt by the Commissioners of that notification or on the date stated in it as the date from which it is to have effect, whichever is the later, and, subject to subsection (6) below, shall remain a fiscal warehouse so long as it is in the occupation or under the control of the fiscal warehousekeeper or until he shall notify the Commissioners in writing that it is to cease to be a fiscal warehouse.

(4) The Commissioners may in considering an application by a person to be a fiscal warehousekeeper take into account any matter which they consider relevant, and may without prejudice to the generality of that provision take into account all or any one or more of the following—

(a) his record of compliance and ability to comply with the requirements of this Act and regulations made hereunder;

(b) his record of compliance and ability to comply with the requirements of the

227

fiscal warehousekeeper of warehousing or fiscally warehousing the goods) the person to whom the supply is made gives the supplier a certificate, in such a form as the Commissioners may by regulations specify, that the services are so performed;

(*d*) the supply of services would (apart from this section) be taxable and not zero-rated; and

(*e*) the supplier issues to the person to whom the supply is made an invoice of such a description as the Commissioners may by regulations prescribe,

his supply shall be zero-rated.

(2) If a supply of services is zero-rated under subsection (1) above ('the zero-rated supply of services') then, unless there is a supply of the goods in question the material time for which is—

(*a*) while the goods are subject to a warehousing or fiscal warehousing regime, and

(*b*) after the material time for the zero-rated supply of services,

subsection (3) below shall apply.

(3) Where this subsection applies—

(*a*) a supply of services identical to the zero-rated supply of services shall be treated for the purposes of this Act as being, at the time the goods are removed from the warehousing or fiscal warehousing regime or (if earlier) at the duty point, both made (for the purposes of his business) to the person to whom the zero-rated supply of services was actually made and made by him in the course or furtherance of his business,

(*b*) that supply shall have the same value as the zero-rated supply of services,

(*c*) that supply shall be a taxable (and not a zero-rated) supply, and

(*d*) VAT shall be charged on that supply even if the person treated as making it is not a taxable person.

(4) In this section 'specified services' means—

(*a*) services of an occupier of a warehouse or a fiscal warehousekeeper of keeping the goods in question in a warehousing or fiscal warehousing regime;

(*b*) in relation to goods subject to a warehousing regime, services of carrying out on the goods operations which are permitted to be carried out under Community customs provisions or warehousing regulations as the case may be; and

(*c*) in relation to goods subject to a fiscal warehousing regime, services of carrying out on the goods any physical operations (other than any prohibited by regulations made under section 18F), for example, and without prejudice to the generality of the foregoing words, preservation and repacking operations.

18D Removal from warehousing: accountability

(1) This section applies to any supply to which section 18B(4) or section 18C(3) applies (supply treated as taking place on removal or duty point) and any acquisition to which section 18B(5) applies (acquisition treated as taking place on removal where acquirer not a taxable person).

(2) Any VAT payable on the supply or acquisition shall (subject to any regulations under subsection (3) below) be paid—

(*a*) at the time when the supply or acquisition is treated as taking place under the section in question; and

(*b*) by the person by whom the goods are removed or, as the case may be, together with the excise duty, by the person who is required to pay that duty.

(3) The Commissioners may by regulations make provision for enabling a taxable person to pay the VAT he is required to pay by virtue of subsection (2) above at a time later than that provided by that subsection; and they may make different provisions for different descriptions of taxable persons and for different descriptions of goods and services.

18E Deficiency in fiscally warehoused goods

(1) This section applies where goods have been subject to a fiscal warehousing regime and, before being lawfully removed from the fiscal warehouse, they are found to be missing or deficient.

(2) In any case where this section applies, unless it is shown to the satisfaction of the Commissioners that the absence of or deficiency in the goods can be accounted for by natural waste or other legitimate cause, the Commissioners may require the fiscal warehousekeeper to pay immediately in respect of the missing goods or of the whole or any part of the deficiency, as they see fit, the VAT that would have been chargeable.

(3) In subsection (2) 'VAT that would have been chargeable' means VAT that would have been chargeable on a supply of the missing goods, or the amount of goods by which the goods are deficient, taking place at the time immediately before the absence arose or the deficiency occurred, if the value of that supply were the open market value; but where that time cannot be ascertained to the Commissioners' satisfaction, that VAT shall be the greater of the amounts of VAT which would have been chargeable on a supply of those goods—

(*a*) if the value of that supply were the highest open market value during the period (the relevant period) commencing when the goods were placed in the fiscal warehousing regime and ending when the absence or deficiency came to the notice of the Commissioners, or

(*b*) if the rate of VAT chargeable on that supply were the highest rate chargeable on a supply of such goods during the relevant period and the value of that supply were the highest open market value while that rate prevailed.

(4) This section has effect without prejudice to any penalty incurred under any other provision of this Act or regulations made under it.

18F Sections 18A to 18E: supplementary

(1) In sections 18A to 18E and this section—

'duty point' has the meaning given by section 18(6);
'eligible goods' has the meaning given by section 18B(6);
'fiscal warehouse' means a place notified to the Commissioners under section 18A(3) and from which such status has not been withdrawn;
'fiscal warehousekeeper' means a person approved under section 18A(1);
'material time'—

(*a*) in relation to any acquisition or supply the time of which is determined in accordance with regulations under section 6(14) or 12(3), means such time as may be prescribed for the purpose of this section by those regulations;

(*b*) in relation to any other acquisition, means the time when the goods reach the destination to which they are despatched from the member State in question;

(*c*) in relation to any other supply of goods, means the time when the supply would be treated as taking place in accordance with subsection (2) of section 6 if paragraph (*c*) of that subsection were omitted; and

(*d*) in relation to any other supply of services, means the time when the services are performed;

'warehouse', except in the expression 'fiscal warehouse', has the meaning given by section 18(6);
'warehousing regulations' has the same meaning as in the Management Act.

(2) Any reference in sections 18A to 18E or this section to goods being subject to a fiscal warehousing regime is, subject to any regulations made under subsection (8)(*e*) below, a reference to eligible goods being kept in a fiscal warehouse or being transferred between fiscal warehouses in accordance with such regulations; and any reference to the removal of goods from a fiscal warehousing regime shall be construed accordingly.

(3) Subject to subsection (2) above, any reference in sections 18C and 18D to goods

being subject to a warehousing regime or to the removal of goods from a warehousing regime shall have the same meaning as in section 18(7).

(4) Where as a result of an operation on eligible goods subject to a fiscal warehousing regime they change their nature but the resulting goods are also eligible goods, the provisions of sections 18B to 18E and this section shall apply as if the resulting goods were the original goods.

(5) Where as a result of an operation on eligible goods subject to a fiscal warehousing regime they cease to be eligible goods, on their ceasing to be so sections 18B to 18E shall apply as if they had at that time been removed from the fiscal warehousing regime; and for that purpose the proprietor of the goods shall be treated as if he were the person removing them.

(6) Where—

(a) any person ceases to be a fiscal warehousekeeper; or
(b) any premises cease to have fiscal warehouse status,

sections 18B to 18E and this section shall apply as if the goods of which he is the fiscal warehousekeeper, or the goods in the fiscal warehouse, as the case may be, had at that time been removed from the fiscal warehousing regime; and for that purpose the proprietor of the goods shall be treated as if he were the person removing them.

(7) The Commissioners may make regulations governing the deposit, keeping, securing and treatment of goods in a fiscal warehouse, and the removal of goods from a fiscal warehouse.

(8) Regulations may, without prejudice to the generality of subsection (7) above, include provisions—

(a) in relation to—

(i) goods which are, have been or are to be subject to a fiscal warehousing regime,
(ii) other goods which are, have been or are to be kept in fiscal warehouses,
(iii) fiscal warehouse premises, and
(iv) fiscal warehousekeepers and their businesses,

as to the keeping, preservation and production of records and the furnishing of returns and information by fiscal warehousekeepers and any other persons;

(b) requiring goods deposited in a fiscal warehouse to be produced to or made available for inspection by an authorised person on request by him;
(c) prohibiting the carrying out on fiscally warehoused goods of such operations as they may prescribe;
(d) regulating the transfer of goods from one fiscal warehouse to another;
(e) concerning goods which, though kept in a fiscal warehouse, are not eligible goods or are not intended by a relevant person to be goods in respect of which reliefs are to be enjoyed under sections 18A to 18E and this section;
(f) prohibiting the fiscal warehousekeeper from allowing goods to be removed from the fiscal warehousing regime without payment of any VAT payable under section 18D on or by reference to that removal and, if in breach of that prohibition he allows goods to be so removed, making him liable for the VAT jointly and severally with the remover,

and may contain such incidental or supplementary provisions as the Commissioners think necessary or expedient.

(9) Regulations may make different provision for different cases, including different provision for different fiscal warehousekeepers or descriptions of fiscal warehousekeeper, for fiscal warehouses of different descriptions or for goods of different classes or descriptions or of the same class or description in different circumstances."

GENERAL NOTE
This paragraph inserts new VATA 1994 ss 18A–18F, which set out the administrative provisions relating to fiscal warehouses and the taxation of both warehoused goods and services relating to them.

VATA 1994 s 18A

A "fiscal warehouse" is a place in the UK other than retail premises which is occupied or controlled by a fiscal warehousekeeper and has been notified by him to the Commissioners. The place becomes a fiscal warehouse from the date when the Commissioners receive the notification or from such later date as may be specified therein. The place remains a fiscal warehouse while it continues to be occupied or controlled by the fiscal warehousekeeper. It ceases to be a fiscal warehouse if the fiscal warehousekeeper notifies the Commissioners to that effect in writing or the Commissioners withdraw fiscal warehouse status from the premises by a written notice (s 18A(3), (6)(c), (8)).

The Commissioners may approve any registered person (including a body corporate included in a group registration) as a fiscal warehousekeeper (s 18A(1) and (9)). A written application must be made in the prescribed manner (s 18A(7)). In considering an application, the Commissioners may take into account any matter which they consider relevant and, in particular, the matters listed in s 18A(4)(a)–(f) (s 18A(4)). An approved person remains a fiscal warehousekeeper until he ceases to be a registered person, he notifies the Commissioners in writing that he is to cease being a fiscal warehousekeeper or the Commissioners withdraw their approval by a written notice (s 18A(5), (6)(b), (8)).

The Commissioners may impose conditions (s 18A(1)). They may subsequently impose additional conditions, and vary or revoke conditions previously imposed, by a written notice (s 18A(6)(a), (8)).

An approved person is entitled to keep a fiscal warehouse (s 18A(2)).

VATA 1994 s 18B

The charge to VAT is modified in relation to supplies and acquisitions of "eligible goods" subject to a fiscal warehousing regime. Goods of a description within VATA 1994 Sch 5A (as to which see para 18 below) are "eligible goods" for this purpose if (in the case of imported goods) any import duties and VAT payable on importation have been paid or deferred and (in the case of goods subject to excise duty) any excise duty has been paid or deferred (s 18B(6)).

An acquisition of eligible goods is within the modified charge if (s 18B(1), (7))—

(a) the goods are subject to a fiscal warehousing regime at the material time of acquisition and the acquirer prepares and keeps a certificate to this effect in the prescribed form; or

(b) the goods are placed within a fiscal warehousing regime after the material time of acquisition but before the material time of the supply (if any) which next follows and the acquirer prepares and keeps a certificate in the prescribed form that he will cause this condition to be met.

A supply of eligible goods under something other than a retail transaction is within the modified charge if (s 18B(2), (7))—

(a) the goods are subject to a fiscal warehousing regime at the material time of supply; or

(b) the goods are placed within a fiscal warehousing regime after the material time of supply but before the material time of the supply (if any) which next follows and the recipient of the supply gives the supplier a certificate in the prescribed form that he will cause this condition to be met.

A supply or acquisition within the modified charge is treated as taking place outside the UK (so that it is not charged to VAT) if the material time for any subsequent supply of the goods will occur while they remain subject to the fiscal warehousing regime (s 18B(3), (7))). If this condition is not met, the supply or acquisition is treated as taking place in the UK when the goods are removed from the fiscal warehousing regime (s 18B(4)). It seems clear that VAT is chargeable if the goods are liable to VAT at a positive rate and the supply or acquisition is made by a taxable person. It is specifically provided that VAT is also chargeable if the supply or acquisition is made by a person who is not a taxable person, but would be but for the fact that such supplies and acquisitions are disregarded in determining liability to registration (as to which see paras 13–15 below (s 18B(5))). For payment of the VAT chargeable, see s 18D below.

VATA 1994 Sch 5A (inserted by para 18 below) may be varied by order (s 18B(8)).

For the material time of supply or acquisition, see VATA 1994 s 18F(1) below. For the meaning of "fiscal warehousing regime", see s 18F(2) below. For incorrect certificates prepared or given for the purposes of this section, see para 8 below.

VATA 1994 s 18C

This section applies both to warehousing regimes (as to which see VATA 1994 s 18(7)) and fiscal warehousing regimes (as to which see s 18F(2) below). It makes provision for the zero-rating of a supply of "specified services" and for a subsequent self-supply of those services by the recipient. "Specified services" for this purpose comprise the services of keeping goods in a warehousing or fiscal warehousing regime and carrying our permitted operations on goods subject to such a regime (s 18C(4)).

A supply of specified services (referred to as "the zero-rated supply of services") is zero-rated if (s 18C(1))—

(*a*) the service is supplied by a taxable person;
(*b*) it is wholly performed on, or in relation to, goods subject to a warehousing or fiscal warehousing regime;
(*c*) (if it comprises carrying out operations on goods) the recipient of the supply gives the supplier a certificate in the prescribed form that the services are wholly performed on goods subject to a warehousing or fiscal warehousing regime;
(*d*) the supply would be chargeable to VAT at a positive rate but for this provision; and
(*e*) the supplier issues an invoice in the prescribed form to the recipient of the supply.

The recipient of the zero-rated supply of services is deemed both to make and receive an identical supply of services unless (s 18C(2), (3)(*a*))—

(*a*) the goods to which the services relate are supplied; and
(*b*) the material time for the supply of goods (as to which see s 18F(1) below) is while the goods are subject to a warehousing or fiscal warehousing regime and after the material time for the zero-rated supply of services (as to which see ibid).

The time of supply is the earlier of (s 18C(3)(*a*))—

(*a*) the time when the goods are removed from the warehousing or fiscal warehousing regime; and
(*b*) the duty point (as defined in s 18F(1)).

The value of the supply is the same value as the zero-rated supply of services (s 18C(3)(*b*)). The supply is chargeable to VAT at a positive rate (s 18C(3)(*c*)). This applies whether or not the recipient of the zero-rated supply of services is a taxable person (s 18C(3)(*d*)). For payment of the VAT chargeable, see s 18D below.

For incorrect certificates given for the purpose of this section, see para 8 below.

VATA 1994 s 18D
This section deals with payment of VAT on (s 18D(1))—

(*a*) a supply chargeable under s 18B(4) above made by a taxable person;
(*b*) a supply or acquisition chargeable under s 18B(4), (5) above made by a non-taxable person; and
(*c*) a self-supply chargeable under s 18C(3) above made by a taxable or non-taxable person.

Any VAT payable on the supply, self-supply or acquisition must be paid at the time when the supply or acquisition is treated as taking place (ie the time stated in ss 18B(4) and 18C(3)(*a*)) (s 18D(2)(*a*)). The VAT must be paid by the person removing the goods or by the person required to pay excise duty on the removal (s 18D(2)(*b*)). A later time may be prescribed by regulations (s 18D(3)). No regulations have been made to date.

VATA 1994 s 18E
The Commissioners may require a fiscal warehousekeeper (as to which see s 18F(1) below) to pay VAT in respect of goods found to be missing or deficient while subject to a fiscal warehousing regime (s 18E(1), (2)). The VAT payable is determined by reference to the open market value of the missing or deficient goods immediately before the absence arose or the deficiency occurred. If the time when the absence arose or the deficiency occurred is unclear, VAT is payable by reference to the highest open market value for the "relevant period" or (if the rate of VAT changed during the relevant period and this produces a higher value) the highest open market value for the period during which the highest rate of VAT prevailed. The "relevant period" commences when the goods were placed in the fiscal warehousing regime and ends when the absence or deficiency came to the Commissioners' notice (s 18E(3)).
No payment of VAT is required if the Commissioners are satisfied that the absence or deficiency can be accounted for by natural waste or other legitimate cause (s 18E(2)).

VATA 1994 s 18F
The terms "duty point", "eligible goods", "fiscal warehouse", "fiscal warehousekeeper", "material time", "warehouse", "warehousing regulations", "goods subject to a fiscal warehousing regime", "goods subject to a warehousing regime" and "removal of goods from a warehousing regime" are defined (s 18F(1)–(3)).
An operation on eligible goods subject to a fiscal warehousing regime may change their nature. If the resulting goods are also eligible goods, ss 18B–18E above apply as if the resulting goods were the original goods. If not, ss 18B–18E above apply as if the goods had been removed from a fiscal warehouse by the proprietor of the goods (s 18F(4), (5)).
For the purposes of ss 18B–18F, goods in a fiscal warehouse are deemed to have been removed therefrom by the proprietor of the goods if the fiscal warehousekeeper ceases to be approved or the premises cease to have fiscal warehouse status (s 18F(6)).
The Commissioners are given wide powers to make regulations in respect of fiscal warehouses (s 18F(7)–(9)). No regulations have been made to date.

6 In subsection (1) of section 20 of the Value Added Tax Act 1994, there shall be inserted at the beginning the words "Subject to section 18C,".

GENERAL NOTE
This paragraph amends VATA 1994 s 20(1). It provides that the rules for valuing acquisitions in s 20 do not apply to a charge to VAT under s 18C (as to which see para 5 above). The purpose of this amendment is unclear given that the charge to VAT under s 18C is a self-supply of services.

7 In section 30 of the Value Added Tax Act 1994 the following subsection shall be added after subsection (8)—

"(8A) Regulations may provide for the zero-rating of supplies of goods, or of such goods as may be specified in regulations, in cases where—

(*a*) the Commissioners are satisfied that the supply in question involves both—

(i) the removal of the goods from a fiscal warehousing regime within the meaning of section 18F(2); and

(ii) their being placed in a warehousing regime in another member State, or in such member State or States as may be prescribed, where that regime is established by provisions of the law of that member State corresponding, in relation to that member State, to the provisions of sections 18A and 18B; and

(*b*) such other conditions, if any, as may be specified in the regulations or the Commissioners may impose are fulfilled.",

and in subsection (10) for the words "subsection (8) or (9)" there shall be substituted the words "subsection (8), (8A) or (9)" and for the words "subsection (6), (8) or (9)", there shall be substituted the words "subsection (6), (8), (8A) or (9)".

GENERAL NOTE
This paragraph inserts a new VATA 1994 s 30(8A), and makes a corresponding amendment to s 30(10). The Commissioners may make regulations zero-rating goods removed from a fiscal warehousing regime to an equivalent regime in another EC member state.

8 (1) Section 62 of the Value Added Tax Act 1994 shall be amended as follows.

(2) In paragraph (*a*) of subsection (1), after the words "a person" there shall be inserted the words "by whom one or more acquisitions or", the words "or" at the end of sub-paragraph (i) and "and" at the end of sub-paragraph (ii) shall be omitted and the following additional sub-paragraphs shall be inserted—

"(iii) prepares a certificate in accordance with section 18B(1)(*d*) or gives a supplier a certificate in accordance with section 18B(2)(*d*); or

(iv) gives the supplier a certificate in accordance with section 18C(1)(*c*); and".

(3) In the passage following paragraph (*b*) of subsection (1) and in subsections (3) and (4), after the word "giving" wherever it appears there shall be inserted the words "or preparing".

(4) In subsection (3) after the words "gave" and "given" there shall be inserted in each case the words "or prepared".

GENERAL NOTE
This paragraph amends VATA 1994 s 62(1), (3), (4). A person acquiring, or receiving a supply of, goods is liable to a penalty under s 62 if he prepares an incorrect certificate under s 18B(1)(*d*) or gives an incorrect certificate under ss 18B(2)(*d*) or 18C(1)(*c*). For ss 18B and 18C, see para 5 above.

9 In subsection (1) of section 69 of the Value added Tax Act 1994 after paragraph (*f*) the following shall be added—

"; or
(*g*) section 18A in the form of a condition imposed by the Commissioners under subsection (1) or (6) of that section,".

GENERAL NOTE
This paragraph inserts a new VATA 1994 s 69(1)(*g*). A fiscal warehousekeeper is liable to a penalty under s 69 if he fails to comply with a condition imposed by the Commissioners under s 18A(1) or (6) (as inserted by para 5 above) in relation to his approval as such.

10 In section 73 of the Value Added Tax Act 1994 the following subsections shall be added after subsection (7)—

"(7A) Where a fiscal warehousekeeper has failed to pay VAT required by the Commissioners under section 18E(2), the Commissioners may assess to the best of their judgment the amount of that VAT due from him and notify it to him.

(7B) Where it appears to the Commissioners that goods have been removed from a warehouse or fiscal warehouse without payment of the VAT payable under section 18(4) or section 18D on that removal, they may assess to the best of their judgment the amount of VAT due from the person removing the goods or other person liable and notify it to him."

GENERAL NOTE
This paragraph inserts a new VATA 1994 s 73(7A) and (7B). It allows the Commissioners to assess VAT due from a fiscal warehousekeeper in respect of missing or deficient goods (as to which see s 18E(2), as inserted by para 5 above) and VAT due when goods are removed from a warehouse (as to which see s 18(4)) or fiscal warehouse (as to which see s 18D, as inserted by para 5 above).

11 In sections 73(9) and 76(5) of the Value Added Tax Act 1994 for the words "or (7)" there shall be substituted ", (7), (7A) or (7B)".

GENERAL NOTE
This paragraph amends VATA 1994 ss 73(9) and 76(5) as a consequence of para 10 above.

12 In section 83 of the Value Added Tax Act 1994 the following paragraph shall be added after paragraph (*d*)—

"(*da*) a decision of the Commissioners under section 18A—

(i) as to whether or not a person is to be approved as a fiscal warehousekeeper or the conditions from time to time subject to which he is so approved;
(ii) for the withdrawal of any such approval; or
(iii) for the withdrawal of fiscal warehouse status from any premises;",

and in paragraph (*p*)(ii) for "subsection (7)" there shall be substituted "subsections (7), (7A) or (7B)".

GENERAL NOTE
This paragraph inserts a new VATA 1994 s 83(*da*). An appeal lies to a VAT and Duties Tribunal against a decision of the Commissioners under s 18A (as inserted by para 5 above) in relation to approval of a fiscal warehousekeeper, conditions imposed by the Commissioners in relation to such an approval, withdrawal of such an approval and withdrawal of fiscal warehouse status from any premises.
This paragraph also amends VATA 1994 s 83(*p*)(ii) as a consequence of para 10 above.

13 In paragraph 1 of Schedule 1 to the Value Added Tax Act 1994, the following sub-paragraph shall be added after sub-paragraph (8)—

"(9) In determining the value of a person's supplies for the purposes of sub-paragraph (1) or (2) above, supplies to which section 18B(4) (last acquisition or supply of goods before removal from fiscal warehousing) applies and supplies treated as made by him under section 18C(3) (self-supply of services on removal of goods from warehousing) shall be disregarded.".

GENERAL NOTE
This paragraph inserts a new VATA 1994 Sch 1 para 1(9). An acquisition or supply under s 18B(4) (as to which see para 5 above) and a self-supply of services under s 18C(3) (as to which see para 5 above) are disregarded in determining whether a person is liable to registration under Sch 1 para 1(1), (2).

14 In paragraph 1 of Schedule 2 to the Value Added Tax Act 1994, the following sub-paragraph shall be added after sub-paragraph (6)—

"(7) For the purposes of sub-paragraphs (1) and (2) above supplies to which section 18B(4) (last acquisition or supply of goods before removal from fiscal warehousing) applies shall be disregarded.".

GENERAL NOTE
This paragraph inserts a new VATA 1994 Sch 2 para 1(7). An acquisition or supply under s 18B(4) (as to which see para 5 above) is disregarded in determining whether a person is liable to registration under Sch 2 para 1(1), (2).

15 In paragraph 1 of Schedule 3 to the Value Added Tax Act 1994, the following sub-paragraph shall be added after sub-paragraph (5)—

"(6) In determining the value of a persons acquisitions for the purposes of sub-paragraph (1) or (2) above, acquisitions to which section 18(B)(4) (last acquisition or supply of goods before removal from fiscal warehousing) applies shall be disregarded.".

GENERAL NOTE
This paragraph inserts a new VATA 1994 Sch 3 para 1(6). An acquisition or supply under s 18B(4) (as to which see para 5 above) is disregarded in determining whether a person is liable to registration under Sch 3 para 1(1), (2).

16 In paragraph 8(1) of Schedule 11 to the Value Added Tax Act 1994 after the words "another member State" there shall be inserted the words ", or in the possession of a fiscal warehousekeeper,".

GENERAL NOTE
This paragraph amends VATA 1994 Sch 11 para 8(1). An authorised person may take samples of goods in the possession of a fiscal warehousekeeper in order to protect the revenue against fraud or mistake. For fiscal warehousekeepers, see VATA 1994 s 18A (as inserted by para 5 above).

17 In paragraph 10(2) of Schedule 11 to the Value Added Tax Act 1994, after the words "on those premises" there shall be inserted the words ", or that any premises are used as a fiscal warehouse,".

GENERAL NOTE
This paragraph amends VATA 1994 Sch 11 para 10(2). An authorised person may enter and inspect premises used as a fiscal warehouse and inspect any goods found there. For premises used as a fiscal warehouse, see VATA 1994 s 18A (as inserted by para 5 above).

18 The following Schedule shall be added to the Value Added Tax Act 1994—

"SCHEDULE 5A

GOODS ELIGIBLE TO BE FISCALLY WAREHOUSED

Description of goods	*Combined nomenclature code of the European Communities*
Tin	8001
Copper	7402
	7403
	7405
	7408
Zinc	7901
Nickel	7502
Aluminium	7601
Lead	7801
Indium	ex 811291
	ex 811299

237

Description of goods	Combined nomenclature code of the European Communities
Cereals	1001 to 1005
	1006: unprocessed rice only
	1007 to 1008
Oil seeds and oleaginous fruit	1201 to 1207
Coconuts, Brazil nuts and cashew nuts	0801
Other nuts	0502
Olives	071120
Grains and seeds (including soya beans)	1201 to 1207
Coffee, not roasted	0901 11 00
	0901 12 00
Tea	0902
Cocoa beans, whole or broken, raw or roasted	1801
Raw sugar	1701 11
	1701 12
Rubber, in primary forms or in plates, sheets or strip	4001
	4002
Wool	5101
Chemicals in bulk	Chapters 28 and 29
Mineral oils (including propane and butane; also including crude petroleum oils)	2709
	2710
	2711 12
	2711 13
Silver	7106
Platinum (palladium, rhodium)	7110 11 00
	7110 21 00
	7110 31 00
Potatoes	0701
Vegetable oils and fats and their fractions, whether or not refined, but not chemically modified	1507 to 1515"

GENERAL NOTE
    This paragraph inserts a new VATA 1994 Sch 5A. This sets out the description of goods treated as eligible goods for the purpose of s 18B(6)(*a*) (as to which see para 5 above). For the power to vary Sch 5A, see VATA 1994 s 18B(8) (as inserted by para 5 above).

SCHEDULE 4

Section 31

VALUE ADDED TAX: ANTI-AVOIDANCE PROVISIONS

GENERAL NOTE

This Schedule and s 31(2) insert a new VATA 1994 Sch 9A. The new Sch 9A supersedes VATA 1994 s 43(1A) (which is repealed by s 31(5)) as the Commissioners' countermeasure against tax avoidance schemes which "through manipulation of the grouping rules, seek to recover VAT (as input tax) in circumstances where it would not normally be recoverable" (Budget Notice 129/ 95 para 1). It has particular application to "entry schemes" and "exit schemes".

A typical entry scheme involves X (a leasing company) acting in concert with Y (a company wishing to use goods or services subject to VAT which it cannot recover). X and Y are *not* members of the same VAT group. X purchases an asset (recovering the associated VAT) and leases it to Y. X then joins the VAT group of which Y is a member. Alternatively, X transfers his business as a going concern to Z (a member of the same VAT group as Y) so that Z now leases the asset to Y. The supply by X to Z is outside the scope of VAT by virtue of VAT (Special Provisions) Order 1995, SI 1995/1268 art 5(1)–(3). Periodic payments under the leasing contracts are so staged that the greater part falls due when X and Y (or Y and Z) are members of the same VAT group so that the related supplies are disregarded under VATA 1994 s 43(1)(a).

A typical exit scheme involves X (a central purchasing company) acting in concert with Y (a company wishing to use goods or services subject to VAT which it cannot recover). X and Y are members of the same VAT group. X enters into a contract to supply goods or services to Y. Y makes a substantial prepayment and the related supply made by X is disregarded under VATA 1994 s 43(1)(a). X then leaves the VAT group, purchases the goods or services from a third party (recovering the associated VAT in full) and supplies them to Y. Y pays the balance of the contract price and the related supply made by X is charged to VAT.

The new Sch 9A enables the Commissioners to counteract these schemes by making a direction that X, Y or Z are deemed to be, or not to be, members of a VAT group from a specified date (so that no intra-group supply is disregarded) or that an intra-group supply between X, Y or Z is not disregarded. Future transactions affected by the direction are dealt with on that basis. If the direction affects past transactions, any VAT due is recovered by assessing the person served with the direction. The effect on past transactions is limited by providing that a direction can be made only if a specified part of the scheme (referred to as a "relevant event") takes place after 28 November 1995.

POWER TO GIVE DIRECTIONS

The Commissioners may give a direction if—

(*a*) either of the following events (referred to as a "relevant event") has occurred after 28 November 1995 (Sch 9A paras 1(1)(*a*), (2) and 4(2), (3)(*a*))—

(i) a body corporate has joined or left a VAT group, or
(ii) a body corporate has entered into a transaction;

(*b*) a taxable supply (referred to as "the undercharged supply") has been, will be or may be made (Sch 9A para 1(1)(*b*), (3)(*a*));
(*c*) the undercharged supply is chargeable to VAT at something other than its full value (Sch 9A para 1(1)(*b*), (3)(*a*)), ie the amount which (having regard to any direction made under VATA 1994 Sch 6 para 1 for a supply to be valued at open market value) would be the full value of the supply for the purpose of the charge to VAT if the supply were not wholly or partly disregarded under VATA 1994 s 43(1)(*a*) (so as to be outside the scope of VAT) by virtue of the fact that both the supplier and the recipient of the supply were members of the same VAT group (Sch 9A para 1(9));
(*d*) all or part of theundercharged supply is chargeable to VAT at a positive rate (Sch 9A para 1(1)(*b*), (3)(*b*));
(*e*) any of the following events (referred to as a "tax advantage") flows from the undercharged supply—

(i) VAT is attributable to all or part of the undercharged supply so that the supplier becomes entitled to input tax credit in respect of it (Sch 9A para 1(1)(*b*), (3)(*c*), (4)(*a*),
(ii) the supplier becomes entitled to input tax credit for VAT on goods or services used by him in making all or part of the undercharged supply whether or not the VAT was attributable to that supply or part when the entitlement to credit arose (Sch 9A para 1(1)(*b*), (3)(*c*), (4)(*a*), (5)), or
(iii) the recipient become entitled to a repayment of VAT charged on the undercharged supply in accordance with the VAT Regulations, SI 1995/2518, regs 173–184 (if he is an EC trader) or regs 185–197 (if he is a third country trader) (Sch 9A para 1(1)(*b*), (3)(*c*), (4)(*b*)); and

(*f*) the conditions in heads (*b*)–(*e*) are met only because the event in head (*a*) has occurred (Sch 9A para 1(1)(*c*)).

The transaction entered into by a body corporate under head (*a*)(ii) above may be a supply. If so, no direction may be made unless and until the body corporate has entered into another transaction which is also a supply. Moreover, a direction may be made only if the conditions in heads (*b*)–(*f*) are met in relation to both transactions (Sch 9A para 1(1)(*d*)).

A supply of the assets of a business is treated as neither a supply of goods nor a supply of services (so as to be outside the scope of VAT) if all or part of the business is transferred as a going concern and stated conditions are met (see the VAT (Special Provisions) Order 1995, SI 1995/1268, art 5(1)–(3)). If the supply is so treated, the transferor and transferee of the business (or part), together with the transferor(s) of all previous transfers of the same business (or part) where the supply of the assets was also so treated, are regarded as the same person in determining whether VAT is attributable to a supply of the assets for the purposes of head (*e*)(i) or (ii) above (Sch 9A, para 1(6), (7)). Thus, if A purchases an asset which passes to D following successive going concern transfers by A to B, B to C and C to D, A, B, C and D are regarded as the same person.

A person may supply a right to goods or services, or supply goods or services by virtue of such a right. If so, the supply of the right and the supply of the goods or services are regarded as different parts of a single supply for the purposes of head (*e*)(i)–(iii) above (Sch 9A para 1(8)). The supply of a right for this purpose includes both the supply of any right, option or priority with respect to the supply of goods or services and the supply of an interest deriving from any right to goods or services (Sch 9A para 1(10)).

The Commissioners may not give a direction if they are satisfied that the relevant event in head (*a*) above has as its main purpose (or each of its main purposes) a genuine commercial purpose unconnected with the undercharged supply in head (*b*) above (Sch 9A para 2).

FORM AND EFFECT OF A DIRECTION
The Commissioners may give either of the following directions (Sch 9A para 3(1))—

(*a*) a direction relating to all or part of a supply of goods or services made by one body corporate to another ; or
(*b*) a direction relating to a particular body corporate.

A direction under head (*a*) requires VATA 1994 s 43(1)(*a*) to be disregarded to the extent specified in the direction. In consequence, the supply or part is chargeable to VAT whether or not the bodies were members of the same VAT group at the time of supply (Sch 9A para 3(2)). The direction can apply to any supply or part made after 31 March 1973 (Sch 9A para 4(3)(*b*)). The direction is given to the person who made the supply, the representative member of the VAT group or which that person was a member at the time of supply, or any receiver, liquidator or representative acting in relation to either person (Sch 9A paras 5(1), 7(2)).

A direction under head (*b*) requires it to be assumed that membership of a VAT group has been varied for a specified period in a specified manner. Thus, the body corporate may be deemed to be a member of any VAT group of which it is entitled to be a member for the relevant period, or deemed not to be a member of a VAT group or particular VAT group. The period may commence at any time after 31 March 1973 (Sch 9A paras 3(3), 4(3)(*b*)). The direction may specify which body corporate is deemed to be the representative member of the varied VAT group at specified times or for specified periods (Sch 9A para 3(5)). The direction is given to the body corporate, the representative member of which the body is, was or is deemed to be or have been, a member, or any receiver, liquidator or representative acting in relation to either person (Sch 9A paras 5(2), 7(2)).

A direction may be made even if the foregoing consequences would have followed had the Commissioners made a different decision under VATA 1994 s 43(4), (5), (5A) in connection with the VAT group concerned (Sch 9A para 3(8)).

Insofar as the assumptions specified in a direction relate to times on or after the day when the direction is given, a person must give effect to those assumptions when complying with his obligations under the VAT legislation (eg in deciding whether or not an intra-group supply is disregarded under VATA 1994 s 43(1)(*a*)). Insofar as the assumptions relate to earlier times, the Commissioners may give effect to them by making an assessment under Sch 9A para 6 (Sch 9A para 3(4)).

MAKING, VARYING AND WITHDRAWING DIRECTIONS
A direction is given by a notice in writing which specifies the relevant event by reference to which it is given (Sch 9A para 5(3), (4)). It must be given within six years of the time when the relevant event in Sch 9A para 1(1)(*a*) occurred of, if later, within six years of the time when the entitlement to input tax credit or repayment of VAT in Sch 9A para 1(4) arose (Sch 9A para 4(1), (4)).

The effect of a direction may be varied by giving another direction (Sch 9A para 3(6)).

A direction may be withdrawn at any time by giving written notice to the person to whom the direction was given or to any receiver, liquidator or representative acting in relation to him (Sch 9A paras 3(7), 7(2)).

ASSESSMENT OF TAX

A "relevant person" is the person to whom a direction is given or the representative member (or assumed representative member) of the VAT group (or assumed VAT group) of which that person was (or was assumed to have been) a member at the time when an assumption is required to be made in accordance with a direction (Sch 9A para 6(11)).

The Commissioners may make an assessment if, as a result of a direction, a relevant person would have been liable to an amount of VAT (referred to as "unpaid tax") before the direction was given by applying the assumptions specified in the direction (Sch 9A para 6(1)). The amount assessed is the unpaid tax of (if lower) the amount which, to the Commissioners, appears to be the amount of the "actual revenue loss" (Sch 9A para 6(1), (3)).

"Unpaid tax" is the aggregate of (Sch 9A para 6(2))—

(*a*) the additional output tax which would have been due from a relevant person at the end of a prescribed accounting period ending before the direction was given by applying the assumptions specified in the direction;
(*b*) the amount by which a relevant person's entitlement to input tax would have been reduced at the end of a prescribed accounting period ending before the direction was given by applying the assumptions specified in the direction; and
(*c*) the amount by which a relevant person's entitlement to a repayment under the VAT Regulations 1995, SI 1995/2518, regs 173–197 would have been reduced by applying the assumptions specified in the direction.

The "actual revenue loss" is the amount of unpaid tax less the aggregate of every increased entitlement to input tax credit, or repayment under the 1995 Regulations, which would have been due to anyone by applying the assumptions specified in the direction (Sch 9A para 6(4)).

The amount concerned must be assessed to the Commissioners' best judgement (Sch 9A para 6(1), (3)). It must be notified to the relevant person, or to any receiver, liquidator or representative acting in relation to him (Sch 9A paras 6(1), 7(2)). An assessment may be notified by incorporating it in the notice by which the direction is given (Sch 9A para 6(5)).

An assessment must be made no later than the first anniversary of the day on which the direction was given. However, no assessment may be made if the direction has been withdrawn (Sch 9A para 6(6)).

An assessment may be withdrawn or reduced (Sch 9A para 6(8)). The amount (or reduced amount) assessed is deemed to be an amount of VAT due from the person assessed and is recovered accordingly (as to which see VATA 1994 Sch 11 para 5(1)) from that person or from the representative member of the VAT group of which that person is a member. If two or more persons are liable in respect of the amount (or reduced amount) assessed, they are treated as jointly and severally liable for that amount (Sch 9A para 6(7)).

The Commissioners may make a supplementary assessment in accordance with VATA 1994 s 77(6) (Sch 9A para 6(9)).

INTEREST

VAT assessed under Sch 9A para 6(1), (3) carries interest under VATA 1994 s 74 in the same manner as VAT assessed under s 73. However, s 74(1) applies so that interest runs from the date when the VAT assessment was notified until the date when it is paid (Sch 9A para 6(9)). Moreover, contrary to s 74(3), the maximum period for which interest runs under s 74(1), (2) is the two-year period ending on the day when the interest assessment is made (Sch 9A para 6(10)).

Interest is assessed in accordance with VATA 1994 s 76(1), (7)–(10) and 77(6). The remaining provisions of ss 76, 77 do not apply. Interest may be assessed for an unlimited period in accordance with s 76(7), (8) if the VAT assessment has not been paid by the day specified in s 76(7) (*a*) (Sch 9A para 6(10)).

The following is the Schedule which shall be inserted after Schedule 9 to the Value Added Tax Act 1994—

"SCHEDULE 9A

ANTI-AVOIDANCE PROVISIONS: GROUPS

Power to give directions

1 (1) Subject to paragraph 2 below, the Commissioners may give a direction under this Schedule if in any case—

(*a*) a relevant event has occurred;

(*b*) the condition specified in sub-paragraph (3) below is fulfilled;

(*c*) the condition would not be fulfilled apart from the occurrence of that event; and

(*d*) in the case of an event falling within sub-paragraph (2)(*b*) below, the transaction in question is not a supply which is the only supply by reference to which the case falls within paragraphs (*a*) to (*c*) above.

(2) For the purposes of this Schedule, a relevant event occurs when a body corporate—

(*a*) begins to be, or ceases to be, treated as a member of a group; or

(*b*) enters into any transaction.

(3) The condition mentioned in sub-paragraph (1) above is that—

(*a*) there has been, or will or may be, a taxable supply on which VAT has been, or will or may be, charged otherwise than by reference to the supply's full value;

(*b*) there is at least a part of the supply which is not or, as the case may be, would not be zero-rated; and

(*c*) the charging of VAT on the supply otherwise than by reference to its full value gives rise or, as the case may be, would give rise to a tax advantage.

(4) For the purposes of this paragraph the charging of VAT on a supply ("the undercharged supply") otherwise than by reference to its full value shall be taken to give rise to a tax advantage if, and only if, a person has become entitled—

(*a*) to credit for input tax allowable as attributable to that supply or any part of it, or

(*b*) in accordance with regulations under section 39, to any repayment in respect of that supply or any part of it.

(5) The cases where a person shall be taken for the purposes of sub-paragraph (4) above to have become entitled to a credit for input tax allowable as attributable to the undercharged supply, or to a part of it, shall include any case where—

(*a*) a person has become entitled to a credit for any input tax on the supply to him, or the acquisition or importation by him, of any goods or services; and

(*b*) whatever the supplies to which the credit was treated as attributable when the entitlement to it arose, those goods or services are used by him in making the undercharged supply, or a part of it.

(6) For the purposes of sub-paragraphs (4) and (5) above where—

(*a*) there is a supply of any of the assets of a business of a person ("the transferor") to a person to whom the whole or any part of that business is transferred as a going concern ("the transferee"), and

(*b*) that supply is treated, in accordance with an order under section 5(3), as being neither a supply of goods nor a supply of services,

the question, so far as it falls to be determined by reference to those assets, whether a credit for input tax to which any person has become entitled is one allowable as attributable to the whole or any part of a supply shall be determined as if the transferor and the transferee were the same person.

(7) Where, in a case to which sub-paragraph (6) above applies, the transferor himself acquired any of the assets in question by way of a supply falling within paragraphs (*a*) and (*b*) of that sub-paragraph, that sub-paragraph shall have the effect, as respects the assets so acquired, of requiring the person from whom those assets were acquired to be treated for the purposes of sub-paragraphs (4) and (5) above as the same person as the transferor and the transferee, and so on in the case of any number of successive supplies falling within those paragraphs.

(8) For the purposes of this paragraph any question—

(*a*) whether any credit for input tax to which a person has become entitled was, or is to be taken to have been, a credit allowable as attributable to the whole or any part of a supply, or

242

(*b*) whether any repayment is a repayment in respect of the whole or any part of a supply,

shall be determined, in relation to a supply of a right to goods or services or to a supply of goods or services by virtue of such a right, as if the supply of the right and supplies made by virtue of the right were a single supply of which the supply of the right and each of those supplies constituted different parts.

(9) References in this paragraph to the full value of a supply are references to the full value of a supply is a reference to the amount which (having regard to any direction under paragraph 1 of Schedule 6) would be the full value of that supply for the purposes of the charge to VAT if that supply were not a supply falling to be disregarded, to any extent, in pursuance of section 43(1)(*a*).

(10) References in this paragraph to the supply of a right to goods or services includes references to the supply of any right, option or priority with respect to the supply of goods or services, and to the supply of an interest deriving from any right to goods or services.

Restrictions on giving directions

2 The Commissioners shall not give a direction under this Schedule by reference to a relevant event if they are satisfied that—

(*a*) the change in the treatment of the body corporate, or
(*b*) the transaction in question,

had as its main purpose or, as the case may be, as each of its main purposes a genuine commercial purpose unconnected with the fulfilment of the condition specified in paragraph 1(3) above.

Form of directions under Schedule

3 (1) The directions that may be given by the Commissioners under this Schedule are either—

(*a*) a direction relating to any supply of goods or services that has been made, in whole or in part, by one body corporate to another; or
(*b*) a direction relating to a particular body corporate.

(2) A direction under this Schedule relating to a supply shall require it to be assumed (where it would not otherwise be the case) that, to the extent described in the direction, the supply was not a supply falling to be disregarded in pursuance of section 43(1)(*a*).

(3) A direction under this Schedule relating to a body corporate shall require it to be assumed (where it would not otherwise be the case) that, for such period (comprising times before the giving of the direction or times afterwards or both) as may be described in the direction, the body corporate—

(*a*) did not fall to be treated, or is not to be treated, as a member of a group, or of a particular group so described; or
(*b*) fell to be treated, or is to be treated, as a member of any group so described of which, for that period, it was or is eligible to be a member.

(4) Where a direction under this Schedule requires any assumptions to be made, then—

(*a*) so far as the assumptions relate to times on or after the day on which the direction is given, this Act shall have effect in relation to such times in accordance with those assumptions; and
(*b*) paragraph 6 below shall apply for giving effect to those assumptions in so far as they relate to earlier times.

(5) A direction falling within sub-paragraph (3)(*b*) above may identify in relation to any times or period the body corporate which is to be assumed to have been, or to be, the representative member of the group at those times or for that period.

(6) A direction under this Schedule may vary the effect of a previous direction under this Schedule.

(7) The Commissioners may at any time, by notice in writing to the person to whom it was given, withdraw a direction under this Schedule.

(8) The refusal or non-refusal by the Commissioners of an application under section 43 shall not prejudice the power of the Commissioners to give a direction under this Schedule requiring any case to be assumed to be what it would have been had the application not been refused or, as the case may be, had it been refused.

Time limit on directions

4 (1) A direction under this Schedule shall not be given more than six years after whichever is the later of—

(*a*) the occurrence of the relevant event by reference to which it is given; and
(*b*) the time when the relevant entitlement arose.

(2) A direction under this Schedule shall not be given by reference to a relevant event occurring on or before 28th November 1995.

(3) Subject to sub-paragraphs (1) and (2) above, a direction under this Schedule—

(*a*) may be given by reference to a relevant event occurring before the coming into force of this Schedule; and
(*b*) may require assumptions to be made in relation to times (including times before 29th November 1995) falling before the occurrence of the relevant event by reference to which the direction is given, or before the relevant entitlement arose.

(4) For the purposes of this paragraph the reference, in relation to the giving of a direction, to the relevant entitlement is a reference to the entitlement by reference to which the requirements of paragraph 1(4) above are taken to be satisfied for the purposes of that direction.

Manner of giving directions

5 (1) A direction under this Schedule relating to a supply may be given to—

(*a*) the person who made the supply to which the direction relates; or
(*b*) any body corporate which, at the time when the direction is given, is the representative member of a group of which that person was treated as being a member at the time of the supply.

(2) A direction under this Schedule relating to a body corporate ('the relevant body') may be given to that body or to any body corporate which at the time when the direction is given is, or in pursuance of the direction is to be treated as, the representative member of a group of which the relevant body—

(*a*) is treated as being a member;
(*b*) was treated as being a member at a time to which the direction relates; or
(*c*) is to be treated as being, or having been, a member at any such time.

(3) A direction given to any person under this Schedule shall be given to him by notice in writing.

(4) A direction under this Schedule must specify the relevant event by reference to which it is given.

Assessment in consequence of a direction

6 (1) Subject to sub-paragraph (3) below, where—

(*a*) a direction is given under this Schedule, and
(*b*) there is an amount of VAT ('the unpaid tax') for which a relevant person would have been liable before the giving of the direction if the facts had accorded with the assumptions specified in the direction,

the Commissioners may, to the best of their judgment, assess the amount of unpaid tax as tax due from the person to whom the direction was given or another relevant person and notify their assessment to that person.

(2) In sub-paragraph (1) above the reference to an amount of VAT for which a person would, on particular assumptions, have been liable before the giving of a direction under this Schedule is a reference to the aggregate of the following—

(*a*) any amount of output tax which, on those assumptions but not otherwise, would have been due from a relevant person at the end of a prescribed accounting period ending before the giving of the direction;

(*b*) the amount of any credit for input tax to which a relevant person is treated as having been entitled at the end of such an accounting period but to which he would not have been entitled on those assumptions; and

(*c*) the amount of any repayment of tax made to a relevant person in accordance with regulations under section 39 but to which he would not have been entitled on those assumptions.

(3) Where any assessment falls to be made under this paragraph in a case in which the Commissioners are satisfied that the actual revenue loss is less than the unpaid tax, the total amount to be assessed under this paragraph shall not exceed what appears to them, to the best of their judgement, to be the amount of that loss.

(4) For the purposes of the making of an assessment under this paragraph in relation to any direction, the actual revenue loss shall be taken to be equal to the amount of the unpaid tax less the amount given by aggregating the amounts of every entitlement—

(*a*) to credit for input tax, or

(*b*) to a repayment in accordance with regulations under section 39,

which (whether as an entitlement of the person in relation to whom the assessment is made or as an entitlement of any other person) would have arisen in the assumptions contained in the direction, but not otherwise.

(5) An assessment under this paragraph relating to a direction may be notified to the person to whom that direction is given by being incorporated in the same notice as that direction.

(6) An assessment under this paragraph shall not be made more than one year after the day on which the direction to which it relates was given or in the case of any direction that has been withdrawn.

(7) Where an amount has been assessed on any person under this paragraph and notified to him—

(*a*) that amount shall be deemed (subject to the provisions of this Act as to appeals) to be an amount of VAT due from him;

(*b*) that amount may be recovered accordingly, either from that person or, in the case of a body corporate that is for the time being treated as a member of a group, from the representative member of that group; and

(*c*) to the extent that more than one person is liable by virtue of any assessment under this paragraph in respect of the same amount of unpaid tax, those persons shall be treated as jointly and severally liable for that amount.

(8) Sub-paragraph (7) above does not have effect if or to the extent that the assessment in question has been withdrawn or reduced.

(9) Sections 74 and 77(6) apply in relation to assessments under this paragraph as they apply in relation to assessments under section 73 but as if the reference in subsection (1) of section 74 to the reckonable date were a reference to the date on which the assessment is notified.

(10) Where by virtue of sub-paragraph (9) above any person is liable to interest under section 74—

(*a*) section 76 shall have effect in relation to that liability with the omission of subsections (2) to (6); and

(*b*) section 77, except subsection (6), shall not apply to an assessment of the amount due by way of interest;

and (without prejudice to the power to make assessments for interest for later periods) the interest to which any assessment made under section 76 by virtue of paragraph (*a*) above may relate shall be confined to interest for a period of no more than two years ending with the time when the assessment to interest is made.

(11) In this paragraph 'a relevant person', in relation to a direction, means—

(*a*) the person to whom the direction is given;

(*b*) the body corporate which was the representative member of any group of which that person was treated as being, or in pursuance of the direction is to be treated as having been, a member at a time to which the assumption specified in the direction relates; or

(*c*) any body corporate which, in pursuance of the direction, is to be treated as having been the representative member of such a group.

Interpretation of Schedule etc

7 (1) References in this Schedule to being treated as a member of a group and to being eligible to be treated as a member of a group shall be construed in accordance with section 43.

(2) For the purposes of this Schedule the giving of any notice or notification to any receiver, liquidator or person otherwise acting in a representative capacity in relation to another shall be treated as the giving of a notice or, as the case may be, notification to the person in relation to whom he so acts.''

SCHEDULE 5

Section 60

LANDFILL TAX

GENERAL NOTE
 Landfill tax is charged on disposals of waste material made at landfill sites on or after 1 October 1996 (see ss 39–40). The new tax is administered by the Commissioners of Customs and Excise. This Schedule contains provisions for enforcement and recovery of landfill tax and additional administrative provisions. The enforcement provisions are broadly modelled on the corresponding VAT provisions and are described only in outline in the notes on each paragraph below.

PART I

INFORMATION

General

1 (1) Every person who is concerned (in whatever capacity) with any landfill disposal shall furnish to the Commissioners such information relating to the disposal as the Commissioners may reasonably require.

(2) The information mentioned in sub-paragraph (1) above shall be furnished within such time and in such form as the Commissioners may reasonably require.

GENERAL NOTE
 The Commissioners have a general power to require information from any person concerned in a landfill disposal (see s 70).

Records

2 (1) Regulations may require registrable persons to make records.

(2) Regulations under sub-paragraph (1) above may be framed by reference to such records as may be stipulated in any notice published by the Commissioners in pursuance of the regulations and not withdrawn by a further notice.

(3) Regulations may—

(*a*) require registrable persons to presume records of a prescribed description (whether or not the records are required to be made in pursuance of regulations) for such period not exceeding six years as may be specified in the regulations;
(*b*) authorise the Commissioners to direct that any such records need only be preserved for a shorter period than that specified in the regulations;
(*c*) authorise a direction to be made so as to apply generally or in such cases as the Commissioners may stipulate.

(4) Any duty under regulations to preserve records may be discharged by the preservation of the information contained in them by such means as the Commissioners may approve; and where that information is so preserved a copy of any document forming part of the records shall (subject to the following provisions of this paragraph) be admissible in evidence in any proceedings, whether civil or criminal, to the same extent as the records themselves.

(5) The Commissioners may, as a condition of approving under sub-paragraph (4) above any means of preserving information contained in any records, impose such reasonable requirements as appear to them necessary for securing that the information will be as readily available to them as if the records themselves had been preserved.

(6) A statement contained in a document produced by a computer shall not by virtue of sub-paragraph (4) above be admissible in evidence—

(*a*) in criminal proceedings in England and Wales, except in accordance with sections 69 and 70 of the Police and Criminal Evidence Act 1984 and Part II of the Criminal Justice Act 1988;
(*b*) in civil proceedings in Scotland, except in accordance with sections 5 and 6 of the Civil Evidence (Scotland) Act 1988;

247

(*c*) in criminal proceedings in Scotland, except in accordance with Schedule 8 to the Criminal Procedure (Scotland) Act 1995;
(*d*) in civil proceedings in Northern Ireland, except in accordance with sections 2 and 3 of the Civil Evidence Act (Northern Ireland) 1971;
(*e*) in criminal proceedings in Northern Ireland, except in accordance with Article 68 of the Police and Criminal Evidence (Northern Ireland) Order 1989 and Part II of the Criminal Justice (Evidence, Etc) (Northern Ireland) Order 1988.

(7) In the case of civil proceedings in England and Wales to which sections 5 and 6 of the Civil Evidence Act 1968 apply, a statement contained in a document produced by a computer shall not be admissible in evidence by virtue of sub-paragraph (4) above except in accordance with those sections.

GENERAL NOTE
Registrable persons (see s 47) are required to keep and preserve records. The record-keeping requirements will be set out in regulations to be made by the Commissioners. The records to be preserved may include documents arising in the normal course of business, such as waste transfer notes and invoices, as well as records specifically required for the purposes of landfill tax (para 2(3)(*a*), HC Official Report, 28 March 1996, col 1181).

Documents

3 (1) Every person who is concerned (in whatever capacity) with any landfill disposal shall upon demand made by an authorised person produce or cause to be produced for inspection by that person any documents relating to the disposal.

(2) Where, by virtue of sub-paragraph (1) above, an authorised person has power to require the production of any documents from any person, he shall have the like power to require production of the documents concerned from any other person who appears to the authorised person to be in possession of them; but where any such other person claims a lien on any document produced by him, the production shall be without prejudice to the lien.

(3) The documents mentioned in sub-paragraphs (1) and (2) above shall be produced—

(*a*) at such place as the authorised person may reasonably require, and
(*b*) at such time as the authorised person may reasonably require.

(4) An authorised person may take copies of, or make extracts from, any document produced under sub-paragraph (1) or (2) above.

(5) If it appears to him to be necessary to do so, an authorised person may, at a reasonable time and for a reasonable period, remove any document produced under sub-paragraph (1) or (2) above and shall, on request, provide a receipt for any document so removed; and where a lien is claimed on a document produced under sub-paragraph (2) above the removal of the document under this sub-paragraph shall not be regarded as breaking the lien.

(6) Where a document removed by an authorised person under sub-paragraph (5) above is reasonably required for any purpose he shall, as soon as practicable, provide a copy of the document, free of charge, to the person by whom it was produced or caused to be produced.

(7) Where any documents removed under the powers conferred by this paragraph are lost or damaged the Commissioners shall be liable to compensate their owner for any expenses reasonably incurred by him in replacing or repairing the documents.

GENERAL NOTE
A person authorised by the Commissioners may demand to see, and make copies of, any documents relating to a landfill disposal. He can require production of the documents by any person concerned in the landfill disposal and anyone else who appears to have possession of such documents. He may also keep the documents for a reasonable period.

PART II
POWERS

Entry and inspection

4 For the purpose of exercising any powers under this Part of this Act an authorised person may at any reasonable time enter and inspect premises used in connection with the carrying on of a business.

GENERAL NOTE
 A person authorised by the Commissioners has power to enter and inspect business premises at any reasonable time.

Entry and search

5 (1) Where—

(*a*) a justice of the peace is satisfied on information on oath that there is reasonable ground for suspecting that a fraud offence which appears to be of a serious nature is being, has been or is about to be committed on any premises or that evidence of the commission of such an offence is to be found there, or
(*b*) in Scotland a justice, within the meaning of section 307 of the Criminal Procedure (Scotland) Act 1995, is satisfied by evidence on oath as mentioned in paragraph (*a*) above,

he may issue a warrant in writing authorising any authorised person to enter those premises, if necessary by force, at any time within one month from the time of the issue of the warrant and search them.

(2) A person who enters the premises under the authority of the warrant may—

(*a*) take with him such other persons as appear to him to be necessary;
(*b*) seize and remove any documents or other things whatsoever found on the premises which he has reasonable cause to believe may be required as evidence for the purposes of proceedings in respect of a fraud offence which appears to him to be of a serious nature;
(*c*) search or cause to be searched any person found on the premises whom he has reasonable cause to believe to be in possession of any such documents or other things;

but no woman or girl shall be searched except by a woman.

(3) The powers conferred by a warrant under this paragraph shall not be exercisable—

(*a*) by more than such number of authorised persons as may be specified in the warrant,
(*b*) outside such times of day as may be so specified, or
(*c*) if the warrant so provides, otherwise than in the presence of a constable in uniform.

(4) An authorised person seeking to exercise the powers conferred by a warrant under this paragraph or, if there is more than one such authorised person, that one of them who is in charge of the search shall provide a copy of the warrant endorsed with his name as follows—

(*a*) if the occupier of the premises concerned is present at the time the search is to begin, the copy shall be supplied to the occupier;
(*b*) if at that time the occupier is not present but a person who appears to the authorised person to be in charge of the premises is present, the copy shall be supplied to that person;
(*c*) if neither paragraph (*a*) nor paragraph (*b*) above applies, the copy shall be left in a prominent place on the premises.

(5) In this paragraph "a fraud offence" means an offence under any provision of paragraph 15(1) to (5) below.

GENERAL NOTE

On the authority of a warrant issued by a justice of the peace, a person authorised by the Commissioners may enter and search premises, seize and remove documents and other evidence, and search anyone on the premises who is believed to be in possession of such evidence. These powers relate to the investigation of fraud offences, ie criminal offences of landfill tax evasion or furnishing false documents or information for landfill tax purposes (see para 15(1)–(5)).

Arrest

6 (1) Where an authorised person has reasonable grounds for suspecting that a fraud offence has been committed he may arrest anyone whom he has reasonable grounds for suspecting to be guilty of the offence.

(2) In this paragraph "a fraud offence" means an offence under any provision of paragraph 15(1) to (5) below.

GENERAL NOTE

A person authorised by the Commissioners has the power to arrest anyone who he has reasonable grounds for suspecting has committed a fraud offence, ie landfill tax evasion or furnishing false documents or information for landfill tax purposes (see para 15(1)–(5)).

Order for access to recorded information etc

7 (1) Where, on an application by an authorised person, a justice of the peace or, in Scotland, a justice (within the meaning of section 307 of the Criminal Procedure (Scotland) Act 1995) is satisfied that there are reasonable grounds for believing—

(*a*) that an offence in connection with tax is being, has been or is about to be committed, and

(*b*) that any recorded information (including any document of any nature whatsoever) which may be required as evidence for the purpose of any proceedings in respect of such an offence is in the possession of any person,

he may make an order under this paragraph.

(2) An order under this paragraph is an order that the person who appears to the justice to be in possession of the recorded information to which the application relates shall—

(*a*) give an authorised person access to it, and

(*b*) permit an authorised person to remove and take away any of it which he reasonably considers necessary,

not later than the end of the period of 7 days beginning with the date of the order or the end of such longer period as the order may specify.

(3) The reference in sub-paragraph (2)(*a*) above to giving an authorised person access to the recorded information to which the application relates includes a reference to permitting the authorised person to take copies of it or to make extracts from it.

(4) Where the recorded information consists of information contained in a computer, an order under this paragraph shall have effect as an order to produce the information in a form in which it is visible and legible and, if the authorised person wishes to remove it, in a form in which it can be removed.

(5) This paragraph is without prejudice to paragraphs 3 to 5 above.

GENERAL NOTE

A person authorised by the Commissioners can apply to a justice of the peace for an order allowing him access to any recorded information required as evidence in proceedings in respect of a landfill tax offence.

Removal of documents etc

8 (1) An authorised person who removes anything in the exercise of a power conferred by or under paragraph 5 or 7 above shall, if so requested by a person showing himself—

(*a*) to be the occupier of premises from which it was removed, or

(*b*) to have had custody or control of it immediately before the removal, provide that person with a record of what he removed.

(2) The authorised person shall provide the record within a reasonable time from the making of the request for it.

(3) Subject to sub-paragraph (7) below, if a request for permission to be allowed access to anything which—

(*a*) has been removed by an authorised person, and
(*b*) is retained by the Commissioners for the purposes of investigating an offence,

is made to the officer in overall charge of the investigation by a person who had custody or control of the thing immediately before it was so removed or by someone acting on behalf of such a person, the officer shall allow the person who made the request access to it under the supervision of an authorised person.

(4) Subject to sub-paragraph (7) below, if a request for a photograph or copy of any such thing is made to the officer in overall charge of the investigation by a person who had custody or control of the thing immediately before it was so removed, or by someone acting on behalf of such a person, the officer shall—

(*a*) allow the person who made the request access to it under the supervision of an authorised person for the purpose of photographing it or copying it, or
(*b*) photograph or copy it, or cause it to be photographed or copied.

(5) Subject to sub-paragraph (7) below, where anything is photographed or copied under sub-paragraph (4)(*b*) above the officer shall supply the photograph or copy, or cause it to be supplied, to the person who made the request.

(6) The photograph or copy shall be supplied within a reasonable time from the making of the request.

(7) There is no duty under this paragraph to allow access to, or to supply a photograph or copy of, anything if the officer in overall charge of the investigation for the purposes of which it was removed has reasonable grounds for believing that to do so would prejudice—

(*a*) that investigation,
(*b*) the investigation of an offence other than the offence for the purposes of the investigation of which the thing was removed, or
(*c*) any criminal proceedings which may be brought as a result of the investigation of which he is in charge or any such investigation as is mentioned in paragraph (*b*) above.

(8) Any reference in this paragraph to the officer in overall charge of the investigation is a reference to the person whose name and address are endorsed on the warrant concerned as being the officer so in charge.

GENERAL NOTE
See note to para 9.

9 (1) Where, on an application made as mentioned in sub-paragraph (2) below, the appropriate judicial authority is satisfied that a person has failed to comply with a requirement imposed by paragraph 8 above, the authority may order that person to comply with the requirement within such time and in such manner as may be specified in the order.

(2) An application under sub-paragraph (1) above shall be made—

(*a*) in the case of a failure to comply with any of the requirements imposed by sub-paragraphs (1) and (2) of paragraph 8 above, by the occupier of the premises from which the thing in question was removed or by the person who had custody or control of it immediately before it was so removed, and
(*b*) in any other case, by the person who had such custody or control.

(3) In this paragraph "the appropriate judicial authority" means—

(*a*) in England and Wales, a magistrates' court;
(*b*) in Scotland, the sheriff;

(*c*) in Northern Ireland, a court of summary jurisdiction, as defined in Article 2(2)(*a*) of the Magistrates' Court (Northern Ireland) Order 1981.

(4) In England and Wales and Northern Ireland, an application for an order under this paragraph shall be made by way of complaint; and sections 21 and 42(2) of the Interpretation Act (Northern Ireland) 1954 shall apply as if any reference in those provisions to any enactment included a reference to this paragraph.

GENERAL NOTE

The Commissioners must provide on request a record of any documents or other things removed under these powers and (unless this would prejudice their investigations) allow supervised access to them, including the making of copies or photographs (para 8). If these requirements are not complied with, the person who previously had custody of the things removed, or from whose premises they were removed, may apply to a magistrates' court (or, in Scotland, the sheriff) for an order specifying what must be done to comply and a time limit for doing it (para 9).

Power to take samples

10 (1) An authorised person, if it appears to him necessary for the protection of the revenue against mistake or fraud, may at any time take, from material which he has reasonable cause to believe is intended to be, is being, or has been disposed of as waste by way of landfill, such samples as he may require with a view to determining how the material ought to be or to have been treated for the purposes of tax.

(2) Any sample taken under this paragraph shall be disposed of in such manner as the Commissioners may direct.

GENERAL NOTE

A person authorised by the Commissioners may take samples of material believed to be waste intended for landfill disposal. The samples must be required in order to determine the landfill tax treatment of the material.

PART III
RECOVERY

General

11 Tax due from any person shall be recoverable as a debt due to the Crown.

GENERAL NOTE

Landfill tax due is recoverable as a debt due to the Crown.

Preferential and preferred debts

12 (1) In the Insolvency Act 1986, in section 386(1) (preferential debts) the words "landfill tax", shall be inserted after "insurance premium tax", and in Schedule 6 (categories of preferential debts) the following paragraph shall be inserted after paragraph 3A—

"**3B** Any landfill tax which is referable to the period of 6 months next before the relevant date (which period is referred to below as the '6-month period').

For the purposes of this paragraph—

(*a*) where the whole of the accounting period to which any landfill tax is attributable falls within the 6-month period, the whole amount of that tax is referable to that period; and

(*b*) in any other case the amount of any landfill tax which is referable to the 6-month period is the proportion of the tax which is equal to such proportion (if any) of the accounting period in question as falls within the 6-month period;

and references here to accounting periods shall be construed in accordance with Part III of the Finance Act 1996."

(2) In the Bankruptcy (Scotland) Act 1985, Schedule 3 (preferred debts) shall be amended as mentioned in sub-paragraphs (3) and (4) below.

(3) In paragraph 2 the following sub-paragraph shall be inserted after sub-paragraph (1A)

"(1B) Any landfill tax which is referable to the period of six months next before the relevant date."

(4) The following shall be inserted after paragraph 8A—

"Periods to which landfill tax referable

8B (1) For the purpose of paragraph 2(1B) of Part I of this Schedule—

(*a*) where the whole of the accounting period to which any landfill tax is attributable falls within the period of six months next before the relevant date ('the relevant period'), the whole amount of that tax shall be referable to the relevant period; and

(*b*) in any other case the amount of any landfill tax which shall be referable to the relevant period shall be the proportion of the tax which is equal to such proportion (if any) of the accounting period in question as falls within the relevant period.

(2) In sub-paragraph (1) above 'accounting period' shall be construed in accordance with Part III of the Finance Act 1996."

(5) In the Insolvency (Northern Ireland) Order 1989, in Article 346(1) (preferential debts) the words "landfill tax" shall be inserted after "insurance premium tax" and in Schedule 4 (categories of preferential debts) the following paragraph shall be inserted after paragraph 3A—

"3B Any landfill tax which is referable to the period of 6 months next before the relevant date (which period is referred to below as 'the 6-month period').

For the purposes of this paragraph—

(*a*) where the whole of the accounting period to which any landfill tax is attributable falls within the 6-month period, the whole amount of that tax is referable to that period; and

(*b*) in any other case the amount of any landfill tax which is referable to the 6-month period is the proportion of the tax which is equal to such proportion (if any) of the accounting period in question as falls within the 6-month period;

and references here to accounting periods shall be construed in accordance with Part III of the Finance Act 1996."

GENERAL NOTE
Landfill tax is a preferential debt in insolvency insofar as it is referable to a six-month period up to the relevant date under the insolvency legislation. This covers tax for accounting periods falling wholly within that period and a proportion of the tax for accounting periods falling partly within it.

Distress and diligence

13 (1) Regulations may make provision in respect of England and Wales and Northern Ireland—

(*a*) for authorising distress to be levied on the goods and chattels of any person refusing or neglecting to pay any tax due from him or any amount recoverable as if it were tax due from him;

(*b*) for the disposal of any goods or chattels on which distress is levied in pursuance of the regulations;

(*c*) for the imposition and recovery of costs, charges, expenses and fees in connection with anything done under the regulations.

(2) In respect of Scotland, where any tax or any amount recoverable as if it were tax is due and has not been paid, the sheriff, on an application by the Commissioners accompanied by a certificate by the Commissioners—

(*a*) stating that none of the persons specified in the application has paid the tax or other sum due from him, (*b*) stating that payment of the amount due from each such person has been demanded from him, and

(*c*) specifying the amount due from and unpaid by each such person,

shall grant a summary warrant in a form prescribed by act of sederunt authorising the recovery, by any of the diligences mentioned in sub-paragraph (3) below, of the amount remaining due and unpaid.

(3) The diligences referred to in sub-paragraph (2) above are—

(*a*) a poinding and sale in accordance with Schedule 5 to the Debtors (Scotland) Act 1987;

(*b*) an earnings arrestment;

(*c*) an arrestment and action of forthcoming or sale.

(4) Subject to sub-paragraph (5) below and without prejudice to paragraphs 25 to 34 of Schedule 5 to the Debtors (Scotland) Act 1987 (expenses of poinding and sale) the sheriff officer's fees, together with the outlays necessarily incurred by him, in connection with the execution of a summary warrant shall be chargeable against the debtor.

(5) No fee shall be chargeable by the sheriff officer against the debtor for collecting, and accounting to the Commissioners for, sums paid to him by the debtor in respect of the amount owing.

(6) Regulations may make provision for anything which the Commissioners may do under sub-paragraphs (2) to (5) above to be done by an officer of the Commissioners holding such rank as the regulations may specify.

GENERAL NOTE
Landfill tax may be recovered by distraint on goods or chattels in England and Wales and in Northern Ireland. Details are to be set out in regulations made by the Commissioners.
In Scotland the tax may be recovered by poinding and sale and other diligences.

Recovery of overpaid tax

14 (1) Where a person has paid an amount to the Commissioners by way of tax which was not tax due to them, they shall be liable to repay the amount to him.

(2) The Commissioners shall only be liable to repay an amount under this paragraph on a claim being made for the purpose.

(3) It shall be a defence, in relation to a claim under this paragraph, that repayment of an amount would unjustly enrich the claimant.

(4) No amount may be claimed under this paragraph after the expiry of six years from the date on which it was paid.

(5) A claim under this paragraph shall be made in such form and manner and shall be supported by such documentary evidence as may be prescribed by regulations.

(6) Except as provided by this paragraph, the Commissioners shall not be liable to repay an amount paid to them by way of tax by virtue of the fact that it was not tax due to them.

GENERAL NOTE
Overpaid tax must be repaid on a claim by the taxpayer unless the claimant would be unjustly enriched by the repayment. The claim for repayment must be made within six years of the date on which the tax was paid. The form and manner of claiming landfill tax repayments are to be prescribed by regulations made by the Commissioners.

PART IV

CRIMINAL PENALTIES

Criminal offences

15 (1) A person is guilty of an offence if—

(*a*) being a registrable person, he is knowingly concerned in, or in the taking of steps with a view to, the fraudulent evasion of tax by him or another registrable person, or (*b*) not being a registrable person, he is knowingly concerned in, or in the taking of steps with a view to, the fraudulent evasion of tax by a registrable person.

(2) Any reference in sub-paragraph (1) above to the evasion of tax includes a reference to the obtaining of a payment under regulations under section 51(2)(*c*) or (*d*) or (*f*) of this Act.

(3) A person is guilty of an offence if with the requisite intent—

(*a*) he produces, furnishes or sends, or causes to be produced, furnished or sent, for the purposes of this Part of this Act any document which is false in a material particular, or

(*b*) he otherwise makes use for those purposes of such a document;

and the requisite intent is intent to deceive or to secure that a machine will respond to the document as if it were a true document.

(4) A person is guilty of an offence if in furnishing any information for the purposes of this Part of this Act he makes a statement which he knows to be false in a material particular or recklessly makes a statement which is false in a material particular.

(5) A person is guilty of an offence by virtue of this sub-paragraph if his conduct during any specified period must have involved the commission by him of one or more offences under the preceding provisions of this paragraph; and the preceding provisions of this sub-paragraph apply whether or not the particulars of that offence or those offences are known.

(6) A person is guilty of an offence if—

(*a*) he enters into a taxable landfill contract, or

(*b*) he makes arrangements for other persons to enter into such a contract,

with reason to believe that tax in respect of the disposal concerned will be evaded.

(7) A person is guilty of an offence if he carries out taxable activities without giving security (or further security) he has been required to give under paragraph 31 below.

(8) For the purposes of this paragraph a taxable landfill contract is a contract under which there is to be a taxable disposal.

GENERAL NOTE

The following criminal offences are created in connection with landfill tax—

(*a*) being knowingly concerned in, or taking steps with a view to, fraudulent evasion of tax (including obtaining payment in respect of credits) by a registrable person (sub-paras (1)–(2));

(*b*) producing or making use of a materially false document with intent to deceive (sub-para (3));

(*c*) knowingly or recklessly making a materially false statement (sub-para (4));

(*d*) conduct which must have involved commission of one or more of the above offences (sub-para (5));

(*e*) making or arranging a taxable landfill contract with reason to believe that tax in respect of the disposal will be evaded (sub-para (6));

(*f*) where security for tax has been required (see para 31), carrying out taxable activities (see s 69) without giving the required security.

The penalties for the fraud offences ((*a*)–(*d*) above) may comprise a financial penalty and/or a term of imprisonment. Financial penalties may be imposed for the other two offences. The maximum penalties are set out in para 16.

Criminal penalties

16 (1) A person guilty of an offence under paragraph 15(1) above is liable—

(*a*) on summary conviction, to a penalty of the statutory maximum or of three times the amount of the tax, whichever is the greater, or to imprisonment for a term not exceeding six months or to both;

(*b*) on conviction on indictment, to a penalty of any amount or to imprisonment for a term not exceeding seven years or to both.

(2) The reference in sub-paragraph (1) above to the amount of the tax shall be construed, in relation to tax itself or a payment falling within paragraphs 15(2) above, as a reference to the aggregate of—

(*a*) the amount (if any) falsely claimed by way of credit, and

(*b*) the amount (if any) by which the gross amount of tax was falsely understated.

(3) A person guilty of an offence under paragraph 15(3) or (4) above is liable—

(*a*) on summary conviction, to a penalty of the statutory maximum (or, where sub-paragraph (4) below applies, to the alternative penalty there specified if it is greater) or to imprisonment for a term not exceeding six months or to both;

(*b*) on conviction on indictment, to a penalty of any amount or to imprisonment for a term not exceeding seven years or to both.

(4) Where—

(*a*) the document referred to in paragraph 15(3) above is a return required under this Part of this Act, or

(*b*) the information referred to in paragraph 15(4) above is contained in or otherwise relevant to such a return,

the alternative penalty is a penalty equal to three times the aggregate of the amount (if any) falsely claimed by way of credit and the amount (if any) by which the gross amount of tax was understated.

(5) A person guilty of an offence under paragraph 15(5) above is liable—

(*a*) on summary conviction, to a penalty of the statutory maximum (or, if greater, three times the amount of any tax that was or was intended to be evaded by his conduct) or to imprisonment for a term not exceeding six months or to both;

(*b*) on conviction on indictment, to a penalty of any amount or to imprisonment for a term not exceeding seven years or to both;

and paragraph 15(2) and sub-paragraph (2) above shall apply for the purposes of this sub-paragraph as they apply respectively for the purposes of paragraph 15(1) and sub-paragraph (1) above.

(6) A person guilty of an offence under paragraph 15(6) above is liable on summary conviction to a penalty of level 5 on the standard scale or three times the amount of the tax, whichever is the greater.

(7) A person guilty of an offence under paragraph 15(7) above is liable on summary conviction to a penalty of level 5 on the standard scale.

(8) In this paragraph—

(*a*) "credit" means credit for which provision is made by regulations under section 51 of this Act;

(*b*) "the gross amount of tax" means the total amount of tax due before taking into account any deduction for which provision is made by regulations under section 51(2) of this Act.

GENERAL NOTE
This paragraph specifies the maximum penalties for the criminal offences created by para 15. The "statutory maximum" for penalties imposed on summary conviction (see Interpretation Act 1978 Sch 1) was increased to £5,000 with effect from 1 October 1992. The "standard scale" refers to the scale of financial penalties for summary offences (see Interpretation Act 1978 Sch 1). Level 5 on the standard scale was also set at £5,000 with effect from 1 October 1992.

Criminal proceedings etc

17 Sections 145 to 155 of the Customs and Excise Management Act 1979 (proceedings for offences, mitigation of penalties and certain other matters) shall apply in relation to offences under paragraph 15 above and penalties imposed under paragraph 16 above as they apply in relation to offences and penalties under the customs and excise Acts as defined in that Act.

GENERAL NOTE
The general provisions for proceedings relating to customs and excise offences are extended to landfill tax offences. These provisions deal with the initiation of proceedings, service of process, time limits, place of trial, enforcement of penalties, mitigation of penalties, evidence and conduct of the proceedings.

PART V

CIVIL PENALTIES

Evasion

18 (1) Where—

(a) for the purpose of evading tax, a registrable person does any act or omits to take any action, and

(b) his conduct involves dishonesty (whether or not it is such as to give rise to criminal liability),

he is liable to a penalty equal to the amount of tax evaded, or (as the case may be) sought to be evaded, by his conduct; but this is subject to sub-paragraph (7) below.

(2) The reference in sub-paragraph (1)(a) above to evading tax includes a reference to obtaining a payment under regulations under section 51(2)(c) or (d) or (f) of this Act in circumstances where the person concerned is not entitled to the sum.

(3) The reference in sub-paragraph (1) above to the amount of tax evaded or sought to be evaded is a reference to the aggregate of—

(a) the amount (if any) falsely claimed by way of credit, and

(b) the amount (if any) by which the gross amount of tax was falsely understated.

(4) In this paragraph—

(a) "credit" means credit for which provision is made by regulations under section 45 of this Act;

(b) "the gross amount of tax" means the total amount of tax due before taking into account any deduction for which provision is made by regulations under section 45(2) of this Act.

(5) Statements made or documents produced by or on behalf of a person shall not be inadmissible in any such proceedings as are mentioned in sub-paragraph (6) below by reason only that it has been drawn to his attention—

(a) that, in relation to tax, the Commissioners may assess an amount due by way of a civil penalty instead of instituting criminal proceedings and, though no undertaking can be given as to whether the Commissioners will make such an assessment in the case of any person, it is their practice to be influenced by the fact that a person has made a full confession of any dishonest conduct to which he has been a party and has given full facilities for investigation, and

(b) that the Commissioners or, on appeal, an appeal tribunal have power under paragraph 25 below to reduce a penalty under this paragraph,

and that he was or may have been induced thereby to make the statements or produce the documents.

(6) The proceedings referred to in sub-paragraph (5) above are—

(a) any criminal proceedings against the person concerned in respect of any offence in connection with or in relation to tax, and

(b) any proceedings against him for the recovery of any sum due from him in connection with or in relation to tax.

(7) Where, by reason of conduct falling within sub-paragraph (1) above, a person is convicted of an offence (whether under this Part of this Act or otherwise) that conduct shall not also give rise to liability to a penalty under this paragraph.

GENERAL NOTE

Where a registrable person makes any act or omission for the purpose of evading landfill tax (or obtaining payment of credits to which he is not entitled) and his conduct involves dishonesty, he is liable to a tax-related penalty (sub-paras (1)–(4)). No civil penalty is incurred if the same conduct has formed the basis of a criminal conviction (sub-para (7)).

19 (1) Where it appears to the Commissioners—

(a) that a body corporate is liable to a penalty under paragraph 18 above, and (*b*) that the conduct giving rise to that penalty is, in whole or in part, attributable to the dishonesty of a person who is, or at the material time was, a director or managing officer of the body corporate (a named officer),

the Commissioners may serve a notice under this paragraph on the body corporate and on the named officer.

(2) A notice under this paragraph shall state—

(*a*) the amount of the penalty referred to in sub-paragraph (1)(*a*) above (the basic penalty), and
(*b*) that the Commissioners propose, in accordance with this paragraph, to recover from the named officer such portion (which may be the whole) of the basic penalty as is specified in the notice.

(3) Where a notice is served under this paragraph, the portion of the basic penalty specified in the notice shall be recoverable from the named officer as if he were personally liable under paragraph 18 above to a penalty which corresponds to that portion; and the amount of that penalty may be assessed and notified to him accordingly under paragraph 32 below.

(4) Where a notice is served under this paragraph—

(*a*) the amount which, under paragraph 32 below, may be assessed as the amount due by way of penalty from the body corporate shall be only so much (if any) of the basic penalty as is not assessed on and notified to a named officer by virtue of sub-paragraph (3) above, and
(*b*) the body corporate shall be treated as discharged from liability for so much of the basic penalty as is so assessed and notified.

(5) No appeal shall lie against a notice under this paragraph as such but—

(*a*) where a body corporate is assessed as mentioned in sub-paragraph (4)(*a*) above, the body corporate may require a review of the Commissioners' decision as to its liability to a penalty and as to the amount of the basic penalty as if it were specified in the assessment;
(*b*) where an assessment is made on a named officer by virtue of sub-paragraph (3) above, the named officer may require a review of the Commissioners' decision that the conduct of the body corporate referred to in sub-paragraph (1)(*b*) above is, in whole or in part, attributable to his dishonesty and of their decision as to the portion of the penalty which the Commissioners propose to recover from him;
(*c*) sections 49 and 50 of this Act shall apply accordingly.

(6) In this paragraph a "managing officer", in relation to a body corporate, means any manager, secretary or other similar officer of the body corporate or any person purporting to act in any such capacity or as a director; and where affairs of a body corporate are managed by its members, this paragraph shall apply in relation to the conduct of a member in connection with his functions of management as if he were a director of the body corporate.

GENERAL NOTE
A landfill tax evasion penalty (under para 18 above) imposed on a company may by notice be apportioned to a named director or managing officer of the company where the conduct giving rise to the penalty is attributable to the dishonesty of that officer.

Misdeclaration or neglect

20 (1) Where, for an accounting period—

(*a*) a return is made which understates a persons liability to tax or overstates his entitlement to credit, or
(*b*) an assessment is made which understates a person's liability to tax and, at the end of the period of 30 days beginning on the date of the assessment, he has not taken all such steps as are reasonable to draw the understatement to the attention of the Commissioners,

the person concerned is liable, subject to sub-paragraphs (3) and (4) below, to a penalty equal to 5 per cent. of the amount of the understatement of liability or (as the case may be) overstatement of entitlement.

(2) Where—

(*a*) a return for an accounting period overstates or understates to any extent a person's liability to tax or his entitlement to credit, and
(*b*) that return is corrected, in such circumstances and in accordance with such conditions as may be prescribed by regulations, by a return for a later accounting period which understates or overstates, to the corresponding extent, that liability or entitlement,

it shall be assumed for the purposes of this paragraph that the statement made by each such return is a correct statement for the accounting period to which the return relates.

(3) Conduct falling within sub-paragraph (1) above shall not give rise to liability to a penalty under this paragraph if the person concerned furnishes full information with respect to the inaccuracy concerned to the Commissioners—

(*a*) at a time when he has no reason to believe that enquiries are being made by the Commissioners into his affairs, so far as they relate to tax, and
(*b*) in such form and manner as may be prescribed by regulations or specified by the Commissioners in accordance with provision made by regulations.

(4) Where, by reason of conduct falling within sub-paragraph (1) above—

(*a*) a person is convicted of an offence (whether under this Part of this Act or otherwise), or
(*b*) a person is assessed to a penalty under paragraph 18 above,

that conduct shall not also give rise to liability to a penalty under this paragraph.

(5) In this paragraph "credit" means credit for which provision is made by regulations under section 51 of this Act.

GENERAL NOTE
A penalty for misdeclaration or neglect is incurred where tax is understated or entitlement to credit is overstated on a person's landfill tax return, or where he fails to inform the Commissioners that an assessment understates his tax liability. The penalty is 5 per cent of the tax or credit at issue (sub-para (1)).

The penalty may be avoided by voluntary disclosure of the inaccuracy in the return or assessment at a time when the taxpayer has no reason to believe that he is the subject of landfill tax enquiries by the Commissioners. The Commissioners may by regulations prescribe the form and manner in which such voluntary disclosures are to be made (sub-para (3)). No misdeclaration or neglect penalty can be imposed on the basis of conduct for which a person has been convicted of a criminal offence or has been assessed to a civil penalty for tax evasion (under para 18).

A return may be corrected in a return for a later accounting period. The Commissioners may make regulations to provide for this. Where such a correction is made, both returns are treated as correct for their respective accounting periods (sub-para (2)).

Registration

21 (1) A person who fails to comply with section 47(3) of this Act is liable to a penalty equal to 5 per cent of the relevant tax or, if it is greater or the circumstances are such that there is no relevant tax, to a penalty of £250; but this is subject to sub-paragraph (4) below.

(2) In sub-paragraph (1) above "relevant tax" means the tax (if any) for which the person concerned is liable for the period which—

(*a*) begins on the date with effect from which he is, in accordance with section 47 of this Act, required to be registered, and
(*b*) ends on the date on which the Commissioners received notification of, or otherwise became aware of, his liability to be registered.

(3) A person who fails to comply with section 47(4) of this Act is liable to a penalty of £250.

(4) Where, by reason of conduct falling within sub-paragraph (1) above—

(*a*) a person is convicted of an offence (whether under this Part of this Act or otherwise), or

(*b*) a person is assessed to a penalty under paragraph 18 above,

that conduct shall not also give rise to liability to a penalty under this paragraph.

GENERAL NOTE

A person who is not registered for landfill tax and fails to notify the Commissioners of his intention to carry out taxable activities (see ss 47(3), 69) is liable to a penalty of the greater of £250 or 5 per cent of any tax for which he is liable up to the time when the Commissioners become aware of his liability to register. There is no liability to such a penalty if the failure forms the basis of a criminal conviction or an assessment of a civil penalty for tax evasion (under para 18). Failure to notify the Commissioners when a person ceases to have the intention to carry out taxable activities (see s 47(4)) incurs a penalty of £250.

Information

22   (1) If a person—

(*a*) fails to comply with any provision of paragraph 1 or 3 above, or

(*b*) fails to make records as required by any provision of regulations made under paragraph 2 above,

he is liable to a penalty of £250; but this is subject to sub-paragraph (4) below.

(2) Where—

(*a*) a penalty (an initial penalty) is imposed on a person under sub-paragraph (1) above, and

(*b*) the failure which led to the initial penalty continues after its imposition,

he is (subject to sub-paragraph (4) below) liable to a further penalty of £20 for each day during which (or any part of which) the failure continues after the day on which the initial penalty was imposed.

(3) A person who fails to preserve records in compliance with any provision of regulations made under paragraph 2 above (read with that paragraph and any direction given under the regulations) is liable to a penalty of £250; but this is subject to sub-paragraph (4) below.

(4) Where by reason of a failure falling within sub-paragraph (1) or (3) above—

(*a*) a person is convicted of an offence (whether under this Part of this Act or otherwise), or

(*b*) a person is assessed to a penalty under paragraph 18 above,

that failure shall not also give rise to liability to a penalty under this paragraph.

GENERAL NOTE

Failure to supply information or produce documents required by a person authorised by the Commissioners (paras 1, 3), or to keep the necessary records (para 2), incurs an initial penalty of £250 and a continuing penalty of £20 per day while the failure continues. Failure to preserve records as required by the regulations will also incur a penalty of £250. These penalties do not apply if the failure forms the basis of a criminal conviction or an assessment of a civil penalty for tax evasion (under para 18).

Breach of regulations

23   (1) Where regulations made under this Part of this Act impose a requirement on any person, they may provide that if the person fails to comply with the requirement he shall be liable to a penalty of £250; but this is subject to sub-paragraphs (2) and (3) below.

(2) Where by reason of any conduct—

(*a*) a person is convicted of an offence (whether under this Part of this Act or otherwise), or

(*b*) a person is assessed to a penalty under paragraph 18 above,

that conduct shall not also give rise to liability to a penalty under the regulations.

(3) Sub-paragraph (1) above does not apply to any failure mentioned in paragraph 22 above.

GENERAL NOTE
Failure to comply with any other requirement imposed by regulations made by the Commissioners incurs a penalty of £250. Again this penalty does not apply if the failure forms the basis of a criminal conviction or an assessment of a civil penalty for tax evasion (under para 18).

Walking possession agreements

24 (1) This paragraph applies where—

(*a*) in accordance with regulations under paragraph 13(1) above a distress is authorised to be levied on the goods and chattels of a person (a person in default) who has refused or neglected to pay any tax due from him or any amount recoverable as if it were tax due from him, and
(*b*) the person levying the distress and the person in default have entered into a walking possession agreement.

(2) For the purposes of this paragraph a walking possession agreement is an agreement under which, in consideration of the property distrained upon being allowed to remain in the custody of the person in default and of the delaying of its sale, the person in default—

(*a*) acknowledges that the property specified in the agreement is under distraint and held in walking possession, and
(*b*) undertakes that, except with the consent of the Commissioners and subject to such conditions as they may impose, he will not remove or allow the removal of any of the specified property from the premises named in the agreement.

(3) If the person in default is in breach of the undertaking contained in a walking possession agreement, he is liable to a penalty equal to half of the tax or other amount referred to in sub-paragraph (1)(*a*) above.

(4) This paragraph does not extend to Scotland.

GENERAL NOTE
Where goods and chattels on which distress has been levied (in England and Wales) for recovery of landfill tax (under para 13) are left in possession of the debtor under a walking possession agreement, a penalty of half the tax or amount recoverable is imposed for breach of any undertaking in the agreement.

Mitigation of penalties

25 (1) Where a person is liable to a penalty under this Part of this Schedule the Commissioners or, on appeal, an appeal tribunal may reduce the penalty to such amount (including nil) as they think proper.

(2) Where the person concerned satisfies the Commissioners or, on appeal, an appeal tribunal that there is a reasonable excuse for any breach, failure or other conduct, that is a factor which (among other things) may be taken into account under sub-paragraph (1) above.

(3) In the case of a penalty reduced by the Commissioners under sub-paragraph (1) above an appeal tribunal, on an appeal relating to the penalty, may cancel the whole or any part of the reduction made by the Commissioners.

GENERAL NOTE
The Commissioners or an appeal tribunal can reduce a civil penalty to take account of mitigating factors, including any reasonable excuse for the conduct giving rise to the penalty. The penalty may be reduced to nil. On appeal the tribunal may cancel all or part of any reduction allowed by the Commissioners.
For the first year of operation of landfill tax, the Commissioners will take a lenient view of genuine errors resulting from unfamiliarity with, or misunderstanding of, the landfill tax provisions. Penalties will not be imposed for a first offence unless deliberate evasion or manipulation is suspected (HC Official Report, Standing Committee E, 8 February 1996, col 200, *Simon's Weekly Tax Intelligence* 1996, p 307).

PART VI

INTEREST

Interest on under-declared tax

26 (1) Sub-paragraph (2) below applies where—

(*a*) under section 50(1) of this Act the Commissioners assess an amount of tax due from a registrable person for an accounting period and notify it to him, and

(*b*) the assessment is made on the basis that the amount (the additional amount) is due from him in addition to any amount shown in a return made in relation to the accounting period.

(2) The additional amount shall carry interest for the period which—

(*a*) begins with the day after that on which the person is required by provision made under section 49 of this Act to pay tax due from him for the accounting period, and

(*b*) ends with the day before the relevant day.

(3) For the purposes of sub-paragraph (2) above the relevant day is the earlier of—

(*a*) the day on which the assessment is notified to the person;

(*b*) the day on which the additional amount is paid.

(4) Sub-paragraph (5) below applies where under section 50(2) of this Act the Commissioners assess an amount as being tax due from a registrable person for an accounting period and notify it to him.

(5) The amount shall carry interest for the period which—

(*a*) begins with the day after that on which the person is required by provision made under section 49 of this Act to pay tax due from him for the accounting period, and

(*b*) ends with the day before the relevant day.

(6) For the purposes of sub-paragraph (5) above the relevant day is the earlier of—

(*a*) the day on which the assessment is notified to the person;

(*b*) the day on which the amount is paid.

(7) Interest under this paragraph shall be payable at the rate applicable under section 197 of this Act.

(8) Interest under this paragraph shall be paid without any deduction of income tax.

(9) Sub-paragraph (10) below applies where—

(*a*) an amount carries interest under this paragraph (or would do so apart from that sub-paragraph), and

(*b*) all or part of the amount turns out not to be due.

(10) In such a case—

(*a*) the amount or part (as the case may be) shall not carry interest under this paragraph and shall be treated as never having done so, and

(*b*) all such adjustments as are reasonable shall be made, including adjustments by way of repayment by the Commissioners where appropriate.

GENERAL NOTE

Where landfill tax assessed for an accounting period to the best of the Commissioners' judgment (see s 50(1)) supplements tax shown in a return made for the period, interest is payable on the tax assessed. The interest runs from the due date for the accounting period up to the date on which the assessment is notified or, if earlier, the date of payment (sub-paras (1)–(3)).

An assessment to recover overpaid credit (see s 50(2)) also carries interest from the due date for the accounting period up to the date on which the assessment is notified or, if earlier, the date of payment (sub-paras (4)–(5)).

The rate of interest will be set by statutory instrument (see s 197). Interest on landfill tax assessments is payable without deduction of income tax. The interest is remitted where all or part of the amount assessed is later found not to be due.

Interest on unpaid tax etc

27 (1) Sub-paragraph (2) below applies where—

(*a*) a registrable person makes a return under provision made under section 49 of this Act (whether or not he makes it at the time required by such provision), and

(*b*) the return shows that an amount of tax is due from him for the accounting period in relation to which the return is made.

(2) The amount shall carry interest for the period which—

(*a*) begins with the day after that on which the person is required by provision made under section 49 of this Act to pay tax due from him for the accounting period, and

(*b*) ends with the day before that on which the amount is paid.

(3) Sub-paragraph (4) below applies where—

(*a*) under section 50(1) of this Act the Commissioners assess an amount of tax due from a registrable person for an accounting period and notify it to him, and

(*b*) the assessment is made on the basis that no return required by provision made under section 49 of this Act has been made by the person in relation to the accounting period.

(4) The amount shall carry interest for the period which—

(*a*) begins with the day after that on which the person is required by provision made under section 49 of this Act to pay tax due from him for the accounting period, and

(*b*) ends with the day before that on which the amount is paid.

(5) Sub-paragraph (6) below applies where—

(*a*) under section 50(1) of this Act the Commissioners assess an amount of tax due from a registrable person for an accounting period and notify it to him, and

(*b*) the assessment (the supplementary assessment) is made on the basis that the amount (the additional amount) is due from him in addition to any amount shown in a return, or in any previous assessment, made in relation to the accounting period.

(6) The additional amount shall carry interest for the period which—

(*a*) begins with the day on which the supplementary assessment is notified to the person, and

(*b*) ends with the day before that on which the additional amount is paid.

(7) Sub-paragraph (8) below applies where under section 50(2) of this Act the Commissioners assess an amount as being tax due from a registrable person for an accounting period and notify it to him.

(8) The amount shall carry interest for the period which—

(*a*) begins with the day on which the assessment is notified to the person, and

(*b*) ends with the day before that on which the amount is paid.

(9) Sub-paragraph (10) below applies where under paragraph 32 below the Commissioners—

(*a*) assess an amount due from a person by way of penalty under Part V of this Schedule and notify it to him, or

(*b*) assess an amount due from a person by way of interest under paragraph 26 above and notify it to him.

(10) The amount shall carry interest for the period which—

(*a*) begins with the day on which the assessment is notified to the person, and

(*b*) ends with the day before that on which the amount is paid.

(11) Interest under this paragraph shall be compound interest calculated—

(*a*) at the penalty rate, and

(*b*) with monthly rests;

and the penalty rate is the rate found by taking the rate at which interest is payable under paragraph 26 above and adding 10 percentage points to that rate.

(12) Interest under this paragraph shall be paid without any deduction of income tax.

(13) Where—

(*a*) the Commissioners assess and notify an amount as mentioned in sub-paragraph (5)(*a*) or (7) or (9)(*a*) or (*b*) above,

(*b*) they also specify a date for the purposes of this sub-paragraph, and
(*c*) the amount concerned is paid on or before that date,

the amount shall not carry interest by virtue of sub-paragraph (6) or (8) or (10) above (as the case may be).

(14) Sub-paragraph (15) below applies where—

(*a*) an amount carries interest under this paragraph (or would do so apart from that sub-paragraph), and
(*b*) all or part of the amount turns out not to be due.

(15) In such a case—

(*a*) the amount or part (as the case may be) shall not carry interest under this paragraph and shall be treated as never having done so, and
(*b*) all such adjustments as are reasonable shall be made, including adjustments by way of repayment by the Commissioners where appropriate.

GENERAL NOTE
Compound interest (calculated with monthly rests) at a penalty rate, 10 per cent higher than the normal rate (sub-para (11)), is payable on the following—

(*a*) tax shown as due on a return unpaid after the due date (sub-paras (1)–(2));
(*b*) an assessment to the best of the Commissioners' judgment (see s 50(1)) made in the absence of a return (sub-paras (3)–(4));
(*c*) a supplementary assessment for an accounting period (sub-paras (5)–(6));
(*d*) an assessment to recover overpaid credits for an accounting period (sub-paras (7)–(8));
(*e*) civil penalties and ordinary interest assessed as due (sub-paras (9)–(10)).

In cases (*c*), (*d*), or (*e*) above, no penalty interest is due if the amount outstanding is paid by the date specified by the Commissioners (sub para (13)).
The interest is payable without deduction of income tax (sub-para (12)) and is remitted where all or part of the amount on which the interest was charged is later found not to be due (sub-paras (14)–(15)).

28 (1) Where a person is liable to pay interest under paragraph 27 above the Commissioners or, on appeal, an appeal tribunal may reduce the amount payable to such amount (including nil) as they think proper.

(2) Where the person concerned satisfies the Commissioners or, on appeal, an appeal tribunal that there is a reasonable excuse for the conduct giving rise to the liability to pay interest, that is a factor which (among other things) may be taken into account under sub-paragraph (1) above.

(3) In the case of interest reduced by the Commissioners under sub-paragraph (1) above an appeal tribunal, on an appeal relating to the interest, may cancel the whole or any part of the reduction made by the Commissioners.

GENERAL NOTE
Interest at the penalty rate (under para 27 above) may be reduced by the Commissioners or an appeal tribunal to take account of mitigating factors, including any reasonable excuse for the conduct giving rise to liability for the interest. The interest may be reduced to nil. On appeal the tribunal may cancel all or part of any reduction allowed by the Commissioners.
For the first year of operation of landfill tax, the Commissioners will take a lenient view of genuine errors resulting from unfamiliarity with, or misunderstanding of, the landfill tax provisions. Penalties will not be imposed for a first offence unless deliberate evasion or manipulation is suspected (HC Official Report, Standing Committee E, 8 February 1996, col 200, *Simon's Weekly Tax Intelligence* 1996, p 307).

Interest payable by Commissioners

29 (1) Where, due to an error on the part of the Commissioners, a person—

(*a*) has paid to them by way of tax an amount which was not tax due and which they are in consequence liable to repay to him,
(*b*) has failed to claim payment of an amount to the payment of which he was entitled in pursuance of provision made under section 51(2)(*c*) or (*d*) or (*f*) of this Act, or

(*c*) has suffered delay in receiving payment of an amount due to him from them in connection with tax,

then, if and to the extent that they would not be liable to do so apart from this paragraph, they shall (subject to the following provisions of this paragraph) pay interest to him on that amount for the applicable period.

(2) The applicable period, in a case falling within sub-paragraph (1)(*a*) above, is the period—

(*a*) beginning with the date on which the payment is received by the Commissioners, and
(*b*) ending with the date on which they authorise payment of the amount on which the interest is payable.

(3) The applicable period, in a case falling within sub-paragraph (1)(*b*) or (*c*) above, is the period—

(*a*) beginning with the date on which, apart from the error, the Commissioners might reasonably have been expected to authorise payment of the amount on which the interest is payable, and
(*b*) ending with the date on which they in fact authorise payment of that amount.

(4) In determining the applicable period for the purposes of this paragraph, there shall be left out of account any period referable to the raising and answering of any reasonable enquiry relating to any matter giving rise to, or otherwise connected with, the person's entitlement to interest under this paragraph.

(5) In determining for the purposes of sub-paragraph (4) above whether any period is referable to the raising and answering of such an enquiry as is there mentioned, there shall be taken to be so referable any period which begins with the date on which the Commissioners first consider it necessary to make such an enquiry and ends with the date on which the Commissioners—

(*a*) satisfy themselves that they have received a complete answer to the enquiry, or
(*b*) determine not to make the enquiry or (if they have made it) not to pursue it further;

but excluding so much of that period as may be prescribed by regulations.

(6) For the purposes of sub-paragraph (5) above it is immaterial—

(*a*) whether any enquiry is in fact made;
(*b*) whether any enquiry is or might have been made of the person referred to in sub-paragraph (1) above or of an authorised person or of some other person.

(7) The Commissioners shall only be liable to pay interest under this paragraph on a claim made in writing for that purpose.

(8) No claim shall be made under this paragraph after the expiry of six years from the date on which the claimant discovered the error or could with reasonable diligence have discovered it.

(9) Any reference in this paragraph to receiving a payment from the Commissioners includes a reference to the discharge, by way of set-off, of their liability to make it.

(10) Interest under this paragraph shall be payable at the rate applicable under section 197 of this Act.

GENERAL NOTE
The Commissioners are liable to pay interest at the normal rate (see para 26 and s 197) where due to their error tax is overpaid, credit not claimed, or payment is delayed (sub-paras (1), (10)). Such interest must be claimed in writing within six years from the date by which the claimant discovered, or with reasonable diligence could have discovered, the Commissioners' error (sub-paras (7)–(8)).
The interest period runs from the date the Commissioners receive the overpayment, or might reasonably have been expected to authorise payment of the amount due to the taxpayer, and ends on the date when payment (or set-off) is actually authorised by them (sub-paras (2)–(3), (9)); but no interest is due for periods referable to raising and answering reasonable enquiries (sub-paras (4)–(6)).

30 (1) Where—

(*a*) any interest is payable by the Commissioners to a person on a sum due to him under this Part of this Act, and

(*b*) he is a person to whom regulations under section 51 of this Act apply,

the interest shall be treated as an amount to which he is entitled by way of credit in pursuance of the regulations.

(2) Sub-paragraph (1) above shall be disregarded for the purpose of determining a person's entitlement to interest or the amount of interest to which he is entitled.

GENERAL NOTE
Interest payable by the Commissioners is treated as an amount to which the claimant is entitled by way of credit.

PART VII
MISCELLANEOUS

Security for tax

31 Where it appears to the Commissioners requisite to do so for the protection of the revenue they may require a registrable person, as a condition of his carrying out taxable activities, to give security (or further security) of such amount and in such manner as they may determine for the payment of any tax which is or may become due from him.

GENERAL NOTE
For protection of the Revenue the Commissioners may require a registrable person (see s 47) to give security as a condition of carrying out taxable activities (see s 69).

Assessments to penalties etc

32 (1) Where a person is liable—

(*a*) to a penalty under Part V of this Schedule, or

(*b*) for interest under paragraph 26 or 27 above,

the Commissioners may, subject to sub-paragraph (2) below, assess the amount due by way of penalty or interest (as the case may be) and notify it to him accordingly; and the fact that any conduct giving rise to a penalty under Part V of this Schedule may have ceased before an assessment is made under this paragraph shall not affect the power of the Commissioners to make such an assessment.

(2) In the case of the penalties and interest referred to in the following paragraphs of this sub-paragraph, the assessment under this paragraph shall be of an amount due in respect of the accounting period which in the paragraph concerned is referred to as the relevant period—

(*a*) in the case of a penalty under paragraph 18 above relating to the evasion of tax, and in the case of interest under paragraph 27 above on an amount due by way of such a penalty, the relevant period is the accounting period for which the tax evaded was due;

(*b*) in the case of a penalty under paragraph 18 above relating to the obtaining of a payment under regulations under section 51(2)(*c*) or (*d*) or (*f*) of this Act, and in the case of interest under paragraph 27 above on an amount due by way of such a penalty, the relevant period is the accounting period in respect of which the payment was obtained;

(*c*) in the case of interest under paragraph 26 above, and in the case of interest under paragraph 27 above on an amount due by way of interest under paragraph 26 above, the relevant period is the accounting period in respect of which the tax was due;

(*d*) in the case of interest under paragraph 27 above on an amount of tax, the relevant period is the accounting period in respect of which the tax was due.

(3) In a case where the amount of any penalty or interest falls to be calculated by reference to tax which was not paid at the time it should have been and that tax cannot be readily attributed to any one or more accounting periods, it shall be treated for the

purposes of this Part of this Act as tax due for such period or periods as the Commissioners may determine to the best of their judgment and notify to the person liable for the tax and penalty or interest.

(4) Where a person is assessed under this paragraph to an amount due by way of any penalty or interest falling within sub-paragraph (2) above and is also assessed under subsection (1) or (2) of section 50 of this Act for the accounting period which is the relevant period under sub-paragraph (2) above, the assessments may be combined and notified to him as one assessment, but the amount of the penalty or interest shall be separately identified in the notice.

(5) Sub-paragraph (6) below applies in the case of an amount due by way of interest under paragraph 27 above.

(6) Where this sub-paragraph applies in the case of an amount—

(*a*) a notice of assessment under this paragraph shall specify a date, being not later than the date of the notice, to which the amount of interest which is assessed is calculated, and

(*b*) if the interest continues to accrue after that date, a further assessment or further assessments may be made under this paragraph in respect of amounts which so accrue.

(7) If, within such period as may be notified by the Commissioners to the person liable for the interest under paragraph 27 above, the amount referred to in paragraph 27(2), (4), (6), (8) or (10) above (as the case may be) is paid, it shall be treated for the purposes of paragraph 27 above as paid on the date specified as mentioned in sub-paragraph (6)(*a*) above.

(8) Where an amount has been assessed and notified to any person under this paragraph it shall be recoverable as if it were tax due from him unless, or except to the extent that, the assessment has subsequently been withdrawn or reduced.

(9) Subsection (8) of section 44 of this Act shall apply for the purposes of this paragraph as it applies for the purposes of that section.

GENERAL NOTE

The Commissioners may issue assessments of amounts due in respect of penalties or interest. Once assessed and notified to the taxpayer, the amount is recoverable as tax, except insofar as the assessment is withdrawn or reduced (s 50(7), sub-para (8)). Notification to a person acting in a representative capacity is notice to the taxpayer (s 50(8), sub-para (9)).

The amount assessed is attributed to a relevant accounting period (sub-paras (2)–(3)). Penalty or interest assessments can be combined with assessments to tax or overpaid credit for the same accounting period and notified together as one assessment, provided the amount of the penalty or interest is separately identified (sub-para (4)). A notice of assessment in respect of interest at the penalty rate (see para 27) must state the date to which the interest has been calculated; interest accruing after that date may be the subject of further assessments (sub-paras (5)–(7)).

Assessments: time limits

33 (1) Subject to the following provisions of this paragraph, an assessment under—

(*a*) any provision of section 50 of this Act, or
(*b*) paragraph 32 above,

shall not be made more than six years after the end of the accounting period concerned or, in the case of an assessment under paragraph 32 above of an amount due by way of a penalty which is not a penalty referred to in sub-paragraph (2) of that paragraph, six years after the event giving rise to the penalty.

(2) Subject to sub-paragraph (5) below, an assessment under paragraph 32 above of—

(*a*) an amount due by way of any penalty referred to in sub-paragraph (2) of that paragraph, or
(*b*) an amount due by way of interest,

may be made at any time before the expiry of the period of two years beginning with the time when the amount of tax due for the accounting period concerned has been finally determined.

(3) In relation to an assessment under paragraph 32 above, any reference in sub-paragraph (1) or (2) above to the accounting period concerned is a reference to that period which, in the case of the penalty or interest concerned, is the relevant period referred to in sub-paragraph (2) of that paragraph.

(4) Subject to sub-paragraph (5) below, if tax has been lost—

(*a*) as a result of conduct falling within paragraph 18(1) above or for which a person has been convicted of fraud, or

(*b*) in circumstances giving rise to liability to a penalty under paragraph 21 above,

an assessment may be made as if, in sub-paragraph (1) above, each reference to six years were a reference to twenty years.

(5) Where after a person's death the Commissioners propose to assess an amount as due by reason of some conduct of the deceased—

(*a*) the assessment shall not be made more than three years after the death, and

(*b*) if the circumstances are as set out in sub-paragraph (4) above, the modification of sub-paragraph (1) above contained in that sub-paragraph shall not apply but any assessment which (from the point of view of time limits) could have been made immediately after the death may be made at any time within three years after it.

GENERAL NOTE

Assessments of landfill tax, overpaid credit, or penalties or interest must generally be made within six years after the end of the accounting period. For some penalty assessments the six-year period runs from the event giving rise to the penalty (sub-para (1)). The six-year period is increased to 20 years where tax is lost by evasion for which a person has been convicted of fraud or by a person's failure to notify an intention to carry out taxable activities (sub-para (4)).

The normal time limit for penalty and interest assessments is two years commencing on the date when the tax due for the relevant accounting period is finally determined (sub-paras (2)–(3)).

Where the person whose conduct gave rise to liability to penalties or interest has died, the assessment cannot be made more than three years after the death. The extended 20-year time limit does not apply; but if the assessment would have been in time immediately after the death, it can be made at any time within three years after the death (sub-para (5)).

Supplementary assessments

34 If, otherwise than in circumstances falling within subsection (5)(*b*) of section 50 of this Act, it appears to the Commissioners that the amount which ought to have been assessed in an assessment under any provision of that section or under paragraph 32 above exceeds the amount which was so assessed, then—

(*a*) under the like provision as that assessment was made, and

(*b*) on or before the last day on which that assessment could have been made,

the Commissioners may make a supplementary assessment of the amount of the excess and shall notify the person concerned accordingly.

GENERAL NOTE

Assessments of landfill tax, overpaid credit, penalties or interest may be augmented by supplementary assessments made within the time limits for the original assessment. This is subject to the Commissioners' power to make a new assessment within one year after getting evidence of facts sufficient to justify it (see s 50(5)).

Disclosure of information

35 (1) Notwithstanding any obligation not to disclose information that would otherwise apply, the Commissioners may disclose information to—

(*a*) the Secretary of State,

(*b*) the Environment Agency,

(*c*) the Scottish Environment Protection Agency,

(*d*) the Department of the Environment for Northern Ireland,

(*e*) a district council in Northern Ireland, or

(*f*) an authorised officer of any person (a principal) mentioned in paragraphs (*a*) to (*e*) above, for the purpose of assisting the principal concerned in the performance of the principal's duties.

(2) Notwithstanding any such obligation as is mentioned in sub-paragraph (1) above, any person mentioned in sub-paragraph (1)(*a*) to (*f*) above may disclose information to the Commissioners or to an authorised officer of the Commissioners for the purpose of assisting the Commissioners in the performance of duties in relation to tax.

(3) Information that has been disclosed to a person by virtue of this paragraph shall not be disclosed by him except—

(*a*) to another person to whom (instead of him) disclosure could by virtue of this paragraph have been made, or
(*b*) for the purpose of any proceedings connected with the operation of any provision of, or made under, any enactment in relation to the environment or to tax.

(4) References in the preceding provisions of this paragraph to an authorised officer of any person (the principal) are to any person who has been designated by the principal as a person to and by whom information may be disclosed by virtue of this paragraph.

(5) The Secretary of State shall notify the Commissioners in writing of the name of any person designated by the Secretary of State under sub-paragraph (4) above.

(6) No charge may be made for a disclosure made by virtue of this paragraph.

GENERAL NOTE
Information may be exchanged between the Commissioners and specified government departments and agencies.

The register: publication

36 (1) The Commissioners may publish, by such means as they think fit, information which—

(*a*) is derived from the register kept under section 47 of this Act, and
(*b*) falls within any of the descriptions set out below.

(2) The descriptions are—

(*a*) the names of registered persons;
(*b*) the addresses of any sites or other premises at which they carry on business;
(*c*) the registration numbers assigned to them in the register;
(*d*) the fact (where it is the case) that the registered person is a body corporate which under section 59 of this Act is treated as a member of a group;
(*e*) the names of the other bodies corporate treated under that section as members of the group;
(*f*) the addresses of any sites or other premises at which those other bodies carry on business.

(3) Information may be published in accordance with this paragraph notwithstanding any obligation not to disclose the information that would otherwise apply.

GENERAL NOTE
The Commissioners may publish the names and business addresses of persons registered for landfill tax, their registration numbers and information about group registrations.

Evidence by certificate etc

37 (1) A certificate of the Commissioners—

(*a*) that a person was or was not at any time registered under section 47 of this Act,
(*b*) that any return required by regulations made under section 49 of this Act has not been made or had not been made at any time, or
(*c*) that any tax shown as due in a return made in pursuance of regulations made under section 49 of this Act, or in an assessment made under section 50 of this Act, has not been paid,

shall be sufficient evidence of that fact until the contrary is proved.

(2) A photograph of any document furnished to the Commissioners for the purposes of

this Part of this Act and certified by them to be such a photograph shall be admissible in any proceedings, whether civil or criminal, to the same extent as the document itself.

(3) Any document purporting to be a certificate under sub-paragraph (1) or (2) above shall be taken to be such a certificate until the contrary is proved.

GENERAL NOTE
A certificate by the Commissioners is prima facie evidence as to—

(*a*) whether a person was registered for landfill tax at any time;
(*b*) whether a return had been made; and
(*c*) whether tax payable on a return or assessment had been paid.

Photocopy documents certified by the Commissioners are admissible in evidence to the same extent as the original documents.

Service of notices etc

38 Any notice, notification or requirement to be served on, given to or made of any person for the purposes of this Part of this Act may be served, given or made by sending it by post in a letter addressed to that person at his last or usual residence or place of business.

GENERAL NOTE
See note to para 39.

39 (1) This paragraph applies to directions, specifications and conditions which the Commissioners or an authorised person may give or impose under any provision of this Part.

(2) A direction, specification or condition given or imposed by the Commissioners may be withdrawn or varied by them.

(3) A direction, specification or condition given or imposed by an authorised person may be withdrawn or varied by him or by another authorised person.

(4) No direction, specification or condition shall have effect as regards any person it is intended to affect unless—

(*a*) a notice containing it is served on him, or
(*b*) other reasonable steps are taken with a view to bringing it to his attention.

(5) No withdrawal or variation of a direction, specification or condition shall have effect as regards any person the withdrawal or variation is intended to affect unless—

(*a*) a notice containing the withdrawal or variation is served on him, or
(*b*) other reasonable steps are taken with a view to bringing the withdrawal or variation to his attention.

GENERAL NOTE
Directions, specifications and conditions issued by the Commissioners and their authorised officers may be withdrawn or varied (sub-paras (1)–(3)). Notification to a person is necessary before a direction, specification or condition, or the withdrawal or variation, has effect in relation to him. Notification may be given by serving a notice or taking other reasonable steps to bring the matter to his attention (sub-paras (4)–(5)).
Notices, notifications and requirements under the landfill tax legislation may be served on any person by post to his last or usual residence or place of business (para 38).

No deduction of penalties or interest

40 In section 827 of the Taxes Act 1988 (no deduction for penalties etc) the following subsection shall be inserted after subsection (1B)—

"(1C) Where a person is liable to make a payment by way of—

(*a*) penalty under Part V of Schedule 4 to the Finance Act 1996 (landfill tax), or
(*b*) interest under paragraph 26 or 27 of that Schedule,

the payment shall not be allowed as a deduction in computing any income, profits or losses for any tax purposes."

GENERAL NOTE
Penalties and interest in respect of landfill tax are not deductible in computing income, profits or losses for tax purposes (TA 1988 s 827(1C)).

Destination of receipts

41 All money and securities for money collected or received for or on account of the tax shall—

(*a*) if collected or received in Great Britain, be placed to the general account of the Commissioners kept at the Bank of England under section 17 of the Customs and Excise Management Act 1979;
(*b*) if collected or received in Northern Ireland, be paid into the Consolidated Fund of the United Kingdom in such manner as the Treasury may direct.

Set-off of amounts

42 (1) Regulations may make provision in relation to any case where—

(*a*) a person is under a duty to pay to the Commissioners at any time an amount or amounts in respect of landfill tax, and
(*b*) the Commissioners are under a duty to pay to that person at the same time an amount or amounts in respect of any tax (or taxes) under their care and management.

(2) The regulations may provide that if the total of the amount or amounts mentioned in sub-paragraph (1)(*a*) above exceeds the total of the amount or amounts mentioned in sub-paragraph (1)(*b*) above, the latter shall be set off against the former.

(3) The regulations may provide that if the total of the amount or amounts mentioned in sub-paragraph (1)(*b*) above exceeds the total of the amount or amounts mentioned in sub-paragraph (1)(*a*) above, the Commissioners may set off the latter in paying the former.

(4) The regulations may provide that if the total of the amount or amounts mentioned in sub-paragraph (1)(*a*) above is the same as the total of the amount or amounts mentioned in sub-paragraph (1)(*b*) above no payment need be made in respect of the former or the latter.

(5) The regulations may include provision treating any duty to pay mentioned in sub-paragraph (1) above as discharged accordingly.

(6) References in sub-paragraph (1) above to an amount in respect of a particular tax include references not only to an amount of tax itself but also to other amounts such as interest and penalty.

(7) In this paragraph "tax" includes "duty".

GENERAL NOTE
The Commissioners may provide by regulations for set-off of amounts due in respect of landfill tax against amounts in respect of landfill tax or any other taxes or duties under their care and management. The regulations may allow amounts in respect of landfill tax due from the taxpayer to be set against amounts payable to him by the Commissioners in respect of that or any other such taxes.

43 (1) Regulations may make provision in relation to any case where—

(*a*) a person is under a duty to pay to the Commissioners at any time an amount or amounts in respect of any tax (or taxes) under their care and management, and
(*b*) the Commissioners are under a duty to pay to that person at the same time an amount or amounts in respect of landfill tax.

(2) The regulations may provide that if the total of the amount or amounts mentioned in sub-paragraph (1)(*a*) above exceeds the total of the amount or amounts mentioned in sub-paragraph (1)(*b*) above, the latter shall be set off against the former.

(3) The regulations may provide that if the total of the amount or amounts mentioned in sub-paragraph (1)(*b*) above exceeds the total of the amount or amounts mentioned in sub-paragraph (1)(*a*) above, the Commissioners may set off the latter in paying the former.

(4) The regulations may provide that if the total of the amount or amounts mentioned in sub-paragraph (1)(*a*) above is the same as the total of the amount or amounts mentioned in sub-paragraph (1)(*b*) above no payment need be made in respect of the former or the latter.

(5) The regulations may include provision treating any duty to pay mentioned in sub-paragraph (1) above as discharged accordingly.

(6) References in sub-paragraph (1) above to an amount in respect of a particular tax include references not only to an amount of tax itself but also to other amounts such as interest and penalty.

(7) In this paragraph "tax" includes "duty".

GENERAL NOTE
This paragraph is the converse of para 42 and allows regulations to be made to enable amounts due from the taxpayer in respect of other taxes to be set off against payments due to him in respect of landfill tax.

Amounts shown as tax on invoices

44 (1) Where—

(*a*) a registrable person issues an invoice showing an amount as tax chargeable on an event, and
(*b*) no tax is in fact chargeable on the event,

an amount equal to the amount shown as tax shall be recoverable from the person as a debt due to the Crown.

(2) Where—

(*a*) a registrable person issues an invoice showing an amount as tax chargeable on a taxable disposal, and
(*b*) the amount shown as tax exceeds the amount of tax in fact chargeable on the disposal,

an amount equal to the excess shall be recoverable from the person as a debt due to the Crown.

(3) References in this paragraph to an invoice are to any invoice, whether or not it is a landfill invoice within the meaning of section 61 of this Act.

GENERAL NOTE
If a registrable person issues an invoice showing tax which is not chargeable or exceeds the amount chargeable, the amount wrongly shown as tax, or the excess, is recoverable from him as a debt due to the Crown. This applies whether or not the invoice qualifies a landfill invoice (see s 61).

Adjustment of contracts

45 (1) This paragraph applies where—

(*a*) material undergoes a landfill disposal,
(*b*) a payment falls to be made under a disposal contract relating to the material, and
(*c*) after the making of the contract there is a change in the tax chargeable on the landfill disposal.

(2) In such a case the amount of the payment mentioned in sub-paragraph (1)(*b*) above shall be adjusted, unless the disposal contract otherwise provides, so as to reflect the tax chargeable on the landfill disposal.

(3) For the purposes of this paragraph a disposal contract relating to material is a contract providing for the disposal of the material, and it is immaterial—

(*a*) when the contract was made;
(*b*) whether the contract also provides for other matters;
(*c*) whether the contract provides for a method of disposal and (if it does) what method it provides for.

(4) The reference in sub-paragraph (1) above to a change in the tax chargeable is a reference to a change—

(*a*) to or from no tax being chargeable, or
(*b*) in the amount of tax chargeable.

GENERAL NOTE
A contract for the disposal of waste material by landfill is varied if it was made prior to a change in the landfill tax chargeable on the disposal, eg where the contract was made before the introduction of the tax was announced or before a change in the rates of landfill tax.
Payments under the contract are automatically adjusted to reflect the landfill tax actually chargeable on the disposal.
An adjustment under this paragraph can, however, be excluded by express provision in the contract (sub-para (2)).

46 (1) This paragraph applies where—

(*a*) work is carried out under a construction contract,
(*b*) as a result of the work, material undergoes a landfill disposal,
(*c*) the contract makes no provision as to the disposal of such material, and
(*d*) the contract was made on or before 29th November 1994 (when the proposal to create tax was announced).

(2) In such a case the amount of any payment which falls to be made—

(*a*) under the construction contract, and
(*b*) in respect of the work,

shall be adjusted, unless the contract otherwise provides, so as to reflect the tax (if any) chargeable on the disposal.

(3) For the purposes of this paragraph a construction contract is a contract under which all or any of the following work is to be carried out—

(*a*) the preparation of a site;
(*b*) demolition;
(*c*) building;
(*d*) civil engineering.

GENERAL NOTE
The introduction of landfill tax was first announced on 29 November 1994 (see *Simon's Tax Intelligence* 1994, Budget Issue, p 1554).
Special provision is made for the adjustment of payments under construction contracts involving site preparation, demolition, building, or civil engineering works (sub-para (3)).
The adjustment applies where waste material is disposed of by landfill as a result of work carried out under a construction contract made before 30 November 1994 if the contract did not provide for the disposal of the material. Payments in respect of that work are automatically adjusted to reflect the landfill tax chargeable on the disposal.
An adjustment under this paragraph is, however, excluded if the contract contained an express provision to the contrary (sub-para (2)).

Adjustment of rent etc

47 (1) This paragraph applies where—

(*a*) an agreement with regard to any sum payable in respect of the use of land (whether the sum is called rent or royalty or otherwise) provides that the amount of the sum is to be calculated by reference to the turnover of a business,
(*b*) the agreement was made on or before 29th November 1994 (when the proposal to create tax was announced), and
(*c*) the circumstances are such that (had the agreement been made after that date) it can reasonably be expected that it would have provided that tax be ignored in calculating the turnover.

(2) In such a case the agreement shall be taken to provide that tax be ignored in calculating the turnover.

GENERAL NOTE

The introduction of landfill tax was first announced on 29 November 1994 (see *Simon's Tax Intelligence* 1994, Budget Issue, p 1554).

Special provision is made with regard to certain payments in respect of the use of land. This applies to payments, whether expressed to be rent, royalties or otherwise, which are determined by reference to turnover under the terms of an agreement made before 30 November 1994. In such cases there is an implied term that any landfill tax is to be ignored in calculating the turnover provided the parties could reasonably be expected to have agreed such a provision if the payment terms had been decided after the introduction of the tax was announced.

SCHEDULE 6   Section 73

TAXATION OF SAVINGS AT THE LOWER RATE

GENERAL NOTE

Section 73 inserts a new section, TA 1988 s 1A. The effect of that section, together with supplementary amendments made by this Schedule, is to abolish the basic rate charge on certain savings income of individuals, personal representatives and trustees of interest in possession trusts. Such income is therefore subject to income tax at the lower rate only with effect from the year 1996–97 (except, in the case of individuals, to the extent that it exceeds the higher rate threshold, see s 73 above). This Schedule contains also consequential amendments relating to the charge at the lower rate on savings income.

The Taxes Management Act 1970 (c 9)

1 In section 86 of the Taxes Management Act 1970 (interest on tax assessed in addition to deducted tax etc), so far as it has effect without the substitutions made by paragraph 23 of Schedule 19 to the Finance Act 1994 and section 110 of the Finance Act 1995, in subsection (2)(*b*) after "the basic rate" there shall be inserted "or the lower rate".

GENERAL NOTE

This paragraph amends TMA 1970 s 86, which charges interest on tax paid late. The amendment ensures that, for 1996–97 and subsequent years, the section will apply to tax charged by assessment in respect of income which has been paid subject to deduction (or deemed deduction) of tax at the lower rate (eg to assessments on higher rate taxpayers in respect of bank or building society interest).

The Taxes Act 1988

2 In section 4(2) of the Taxes Act 1988 (meaning of "relevant year of assessment" for the purposes of deductions etc), for "subsection (1) above" there shall be substituted "this section".

GENERAL NOTE

TA 1988 s 4(2) provides that the "relevant year of assessment" for the purpose of determining the appropriate rate of deduction for payments made subject to deduction of basic rate tax at source, is the year in which the payment is due, for amounts paid wholly out of profits etc brought into charge to tax, and the year in which the payment is made, for other amounts. This paragraph extends that provision to payments made subject to the deduction of tax at the lower rate after 5 April 1996.

3 In section 5(4) of that Act (time when tax in addition to deducted tax etc becomes due), after "basic rate" there shall be inserted "or the lower rate".

GENERAL NOTE

Where additional tax is assessed in respect of income paid subject to deduction of basic rate income tax, the due date for payment of the additional tax is 1 ecember following the end of the year to which the assessment relates (TA 1988 s 5(4)). This paragraph extends this provision to assessments for additional tax in respect of income paid after 5 April 1996 subject to deduction of income tax at the lower rate.

4 (1) Subject to sub-paragraph (2) below, in subsection (1)(*b*) of section 51B of that Act (periodic returns of tax on gilts), for "basic rate" there shall be substituted "lower rate".

(2) Sub-paragraph (1) above has effect for the purposes only of the exercise on or after the day on which this Act is passed of the Treasury's power to make regulations under that section; but that power may be exercised on or after that day for the purpose of making provision, with retrospective effect, on the basis that the assumption to be applied in relation to all payments made on or after 6th April 1996 was an assumption that such payments bear tax at the lower rate.

TA 1988 ss 51A and 51B introduced a new scheme, which came into force with effect from 2 January 1996, under which interest on certain gilts is payable gross. TA 1988 s 51B provides for regulations to be made under which certain recipients of payments of gross interest may be required to make quarterly returns of those payments and the amounts of tax for which the recipient is accountable on them, assuming that the payments bear interest at the basic rate of tax (TA 1988 s 51(1)(*b*)).

This paragraph amends that provision so that the regulations can be amended, after the date of Royal Assent to the 1996 Finance Bill, to provide for income tax to be accounted for at the lower rate of tax in respect of payments after 5 April 1996. (In practice, recipients accounting for tax between 6 April 1996 and the date on which the amended regulations come into force will be permitted to apply the lower rate during that period in order to avoid the need for retrospective adjustments: Inland Revenue Press Release, 11 December 1995, *Simon's Weekly Tax Intelligence* 1995, p 2044).

5 In paragraph (*c*) of section 246D(2) of that Act (application of section 207A to certain foreign income dividends), for the words from "as income" to the end of the paragraph there shall be substituted "(without prejudice to paragraph (*a*) above) as if it were income to which section 1A applies;".

GENERAL NOTE
TA 1988 s 246D(2)(*c*) applies TA 1988 s 207A to ensure that foreign income dividends received by an individual are taxed in the same way as other dividends, ie they are chargeable to income tax only at the lower rate and, to the extent that the recipient's income exceeds the basic rate limit, at the higher rate. As a result of the extension of this treatment of Schedule F income to savings income with effect from the year 1996–97, the provisions of TA 1988 s 207A are superseded by the new TA 1988 s 1A (inserted by s 73 above). Consequently, this paragraph replaces the reference to TA 1988 s 207A with a reference to TA 1988 s 1A.

6 In section 249(4)(*c*) of that Act (application of section 207A), for the words from "as income" to "but" there shall be substituted "(without prejudice to paragraph (*a*) above) as if it were income to which section 1A applies, but".

GENERAL NOTE
TA 1988 s 249(4)(*c*) applies TA 1988 s 207A to ensure that stock dividends received by an individual are taxed in the same way as other dividends chargeable under Schedule F, ie they are chargeable to income tax only at the lower rate and, to the extent that the recipient's income exceeds the basic rate limit, at the higher rate. As a result of the extension of this treatment of Schedule F income to savings income with effect from the year 1996–97, the provisions of TA 1988 s 207A are superseded by the new TA 1988 s 1A (inserted by s 73 above). Consequently, this paragraph replaces the reference to TA 1988 s 207A with a reference to TA 1988 s 1A.

7 (1) In subsection (2)(*b*)(ii) of section 326B of that Act (loss of exemption for TESSAs), for the words from "basic rate on" to the end of the sub-paragraph there shall be substituted "applicable rate on any interest or bonus paid on the account before that time;".

(2) After subsection (2) of that section there shall be inserted the following subsection—

"(2A) In subsection (2)(*b*)(ii) above 'the applicable rate' means—

(*a*) in the case of interest or bonus paid before 6th April 1996, the basic rate for the year of assessment in which the payment was made; and

(*b*) in any other case, the lower rate for the year of assessment in which it was made."

(3) This paragraph has effect as respects withdrawals on or after 6th April 1996.

GENERAL NOTE
TA 1988 s 326B(2)(*b*) provides that the exemption of interest and bonuses paid in respect of a TESSA (tax exempt special savings account) is lost if, at any point during the five-year period from the date on which it is opened, withdrawals from the account exceed the amount of the interest and bonuses paid up to the date of the withdrawal, less tax on those amounts at the basic rate. This paragraph amends that provision to reflect the fact that interest and bonuses paid after 5 April 1996 would be subject to deduction of tax at the lower rate.

8 In section 350 of that Act (charge to tax where payments made subject to deduction), in subsection (1) for "basic rate" there shall be substituted "applicable rate"; and after that subsection there shall be inserted the following subsection—

"(1A) In subsection (1) above 'the applicable rate' means the rate which is applicable to the payment under section 4."

GENERAL NOTE
TA 1988 s 350(1) provides for an assessment to be raised to recover tax at the basic rate from a person who has made an annual payment subject to deduction of tax, to the extent that the payment was not made wholly out of profits or gains charged to income tax. To take account of the fact that certain annual payments of interest etc made after 5 April 1996 are payable subject to deduction of tax at the lower rate, this paragraph amends s 350(1) to provide (by reference to TA 1988 s 4 as amended by s 73) that the assessment may be made to recover tax at the lower rate or the basic rate as applicable.

9 In section 421(1)(c) of that Act (application of section 207A), for the words from "as income" to "but" there shall be substituted "(without prejudice to paragraph (b) above) as if it were income to which section 1A applies, but".

GENERAL NOTE
TA 1988 s 421(1)(c) applies TA 1988 s 207A so that, on the release of a loan made by a close company, the amount released is treated in the hands of the person to whom it was lent in the same way as dividends chargeable under Schedule F, ie it is chargeable to income tax only at the lower rate and, to the extent that the recipient's income exceeds the basic rate limit, at the higher rate. As a result of the extension of this treatment of Schedule F income to savings income with effect from the year 1996–97, the provisions of TA 1988 s 207A are superseded by the new TA 1988 s 1A (inserted by s 73 above). Consequently, this paragraph replaces the reference to TA 1988 s 207A with a reference to TA 1988 s 1A.

10 (1) In section 468 of that Act (authorised unit trusts to be subject to corporation tax), the following subsection shall be inserted after subsection 1—

"(1A) In relation to any authorised unit trust the rate of corporation tax for the financial year 1996 and subsequent financial years shall be deemed to be the rate at which income tax at the lower rate is charged for the year of assessment which begins on 6th April in the financial year concerned."

(2) Sub-paragraph (1) above has effect in relation to any accounting period ending after 31st March 1996.

(3) Sections 468E and 468EE of that Act (rate of corporation tax on authorised unit trusts) shall not apply in relation to any accounting period ending after 31st March 1996 except so far as those sections relate to the financial year 1995.

GENERAL NOTE
Hitherto, the rate of corporation tax applicable to most authorised unit trusts has been equal to the basic rate of income tax (TA 1988 s 468E), although certain authorised unit trusts could claim to be taxed instead at a rate equivalent to the lower rate of income tax (TA 1988 s 468EE).
This paragraph repeals TA 1988 ss 468E and 468EE with effect for accounting periods ending after 31 March 1996 (except to the extent that they relate to the financial year 1995). It provides instead for the corporation tax rate applicable to all authorised unit trusts to be equal to the lower rate of income tax, with effect for accounting periods ending after 31 March 1996 (TA 1988 s 468(1A) inserted by sub-paras (1), (2)).

11 (1) In section 468L of that Act (interest distributions), after subsection (1) there shall be inserted the following subsection—

"(1A) For the purposes of this Chapter no amount shall be shown as so available unless the authorised unit trust in question satisfies the qualifying investments test throughout the distribution period."

(2) After subsection (7) of that section there shall be inserted the following subsections—

"(8) For the purposes of this section an authorised unit trust satisfies the qualifying investments test throughout a distribution period ('the relevant period') if at all times in that period, the market value of the qualifying investments exceeds 60 per cent. of the market value of all the investments of that trust.

277

(9) Subject to subsection (13) below, in this section 'qualifying investments', in relation to an authorised unit trust, means the investments of that trust which are of any of the following descriptions—

(a) money placed at interest;
(b) securities;
(c) shares in a building society;
(d) qualifying entitlements to a share in the investments of another authorised unit trust.

(10) For the purposes of subsection (9) above an entitlement to a share in the investments of another authorised unit trust is a qualifying entitlement at any time in the relevant period if, and only if, the other authorised unit trust would itself (on the relevant assumption) satisfy the qualifying investments test throughout that period.

(11) For the purposes of subsection (10) above the relevant assumption is that the only investments of the other authorised unit trust which are to be regarded as qualifying investments are those falling within paragraphs (a) to (c) of subsection (9) above.

(12) In this section 'security' does not include shares in a company; and references in this section to investments of an authorised unit trust are references to investments subject to the trusts of that authorised unit trust but do not include references to cash awaiting investment.

(13) The Treasury may by order amend subsection (9) above so as to extend or restrict the descriptions of investments of an authorised unit trust that are qualifying investments.

(14) An order made by the Treasury under subsection (13) above may—

(a) make different provision for different cases; and
(b) contain such incidental, supplemental, consequential and transitional provision as the Treasury may think fit;

and, without prejudice to the generality of paragraph (b) above, such an order may make such incidental modifications of subsection (11) above as the Treasury may think fit."

(3) This paragraph has effect in relation to distribution periods ending on or after 1st April 1996.

GENERAL NOTE
With effect for distribution periods ending after 31 March 1996, an authorised unit trust will only be entitled to pay an interest distribution where it satisfies a "qualifying investments test" throughout the distribution period (TA 1988 s 468L(1A) inserted by sub-paras (1), (3)).

The test is that, at all times during the distribution period, the market value of the trust's qualifying investments exceeds 60 per cent of the market value of all the investments held by the trust (excluding cash awaiting investment) (TA 1988 s 468L(8), (12) inserted by sub-para (2)).

For this purpose, "qualifying investments" comprise money placed at interest, securities (excluding shares in a company), shares in a building society and qualifying entitlements to a share in the investments of another authorised unit trust. (A "qualifying entitlement" exists where, throughout the relevant distribution period, over 60 per cent of the investments of the other unit trust comprise money placed at interest, securities and shares in building societies.) The list of qualifying investments may be amended by Treasury order (TA 1988 s 468L(9)–(13) inserted by sub-para (2).)

12 In section 469(2) of that Act (taxation of income of unauthorised unit trusts), after the words "unit holders)", in the first place where they occur, there shall be inserted "and, in the case of income to which section 1A applies, chargeable to income tax at the basic rate, instead of at the lower rate".

GENERAL NOTE
The amendment made by this paragraph provides for trustees of unauthorised unit trusts to be charged at the basic rate, rather than the lower rate, on all income within the scope of the new TA 1988 s 1A (broadly, interest etc chargeable under Schedule D Case III, distributions chargeable

under Schedule F and equivalent foreign income chargeable under Schedule D Cases IV and V, see s 73).

The amendment has effect for the year 1996–97 and subsequent years of assessment (see para 28 below). It will only actually change the tax treatment of certain distributions from UK companies, which are at present charged at the lower rate; all other types of income are presently charged at the basic rate on the trustees, so such income will continue to be subject to the same treatment.

13 In sections 549(2), 686(1), 699(2) and 819(2) of that Act (which refer to income tax being chargeable at the lower rate in accordance with section 207A), for "section 207A" there shall be substituted "section 1A".

GENERAL NOTE

As TA 1988 s 207A, which set out the lower rate charge on UK dividend income received by individuals, is superseded by the new TA 1988 s 1A, which extends that treatment to other savings income with effect from 1996–97 (see s 73), this paragraph makes consequential amendments, substituting references to s 1A for references to s 207A in the definitions of excess liability in TA 1988 s 549(2) (relief for losses or deficiencies occurring on the final termination of a life policy or life annuity contract) and s 699(2) (relief for inheritance tax attributable to income accruing before a person's death and included in the total income of a beneficiary with an absolute interest in the residue of the estate).

A similar substitution is made in TA 1988 s 686(1) (charge on certain income of discretionary trusts at the special rate applicable to trusts, instead of at the basic or lower rates) and s 819(2) (construction of provisions for the payment of amounts free of income tax other than surtax).

14 (1) In paragraph (*a*)(i) of subsection (2) of section 582 of that Act (funding bonds), for "basic" there shall be substituted "applicable".

(2) After that subsection there shall be inserted the following subsection—

"(2A) In subsection (2) above 'the applicable rate', in relation to a year of assessment, means whichever of the basic rate and the lower rate for that year is the rate at which the person by or through whom the bonds are issued would have had to deduct income tax from the amount of interest in question if that amount had been actually paid by or through him."

GENERAL NOTE

TA 1988 s 582 provides for funding bonds issued in respect of interest on certain debts to be treated for tax purposes as if they were payments of interest. If the person issuing the bonds would be required to deduct tax at source from an actual payment of interest, he must retain bonds equal in value to tax at the basic rate on the deemed interest payment.

In consequence of the abolition of the basic rate charge on such interest payments from 1996–97 (see s 73), this paragraph amends s 582 to require the retention of bonds equal in value to the "appropriate" rate of tax on the deemed interest payment, ie the lower or basic rate as applicable.

15 In section 686 of that Act (liability to additional rate in the case of trustees of discretionary trusts), after subsection (2A) there shall be inserted the following subsection—

"(2B) For the purposes of subsection (2A) above where the income tax borne by any income arising to trustees is limited in accordance with section 128 of the Finance Act 1995 (limit on income chargeable on non-residents), the income arising to the trustees which shall be taken not to bear tax by reason wholly or partly of their not having been resident in the United Kingdom shall include so much of any income arising to them as—

(*a*) is excluded income within the meaning of that section; and

(*b*) is not income which is treated for the purposes of subsection (1)(*b*) of that section as income the tax on which is deducted at source."

GENERAL NOTE

FA 1995 s 128 limits the UK income tax liability of non-residents in respect of most investment income to the amount of any tax deducted at source (effectively making statutory the Revenue practice under Concession B13).

TA 1988 s 686(2A) provides that where part of the income arising to the trustees of a discretionary trust in a year of assessment does not bear income tax because the trustees were not resident in that year (or were treated as non-resident under a double taxation agreement), a corresponding proportion of the trustees' management expenses which would otherwise be chargeable to income are disregarded.

This paragraph provides (by inserting a new TA 1988 s 686(2B) that income treated as excluded income under FA 1995 s 128 but which has borne deduction of tax at source is not to be treated as income which has not borne tax for the purposes of TA 1988 s 686(2A). There will therefore be no restriction on the set-off of management expenses in respect of such income.

16 In Part XV of that Act (settlements), at the end of Chapter IC there shall be inserted the following Chapter—

"CHAPTER ID

TRUST MANAGEMENT EXPENSES

689A   Disregard of expenses where beneficiary non-resident

(1) This section applies where—

(*a*) there is income ('the distributed income') arising to trustees in any year of assessment which (before being distributed) is income of a person ('the beneficiary') other than the trustees;

(*b*) the trustees have any expenses in that year ('the management expenses') which are properly chargeable to that income or would be so chargeable but for any express provisions of the trust; and

(*c*) the beneficiary is not liable to income tax on an amount of the distributed income ('the untaxed income') by reason wholly or partly of—

(i) his not having been resident in the United Kingdom, or

(ii) his being deemed under any arrangements under section 788, or any arrangements having effect by virtue of that section, to have been resident in a territory outside the United Kingdom.

(2) Where this section applies, there shall be disregarded in computing the income of the beneficiary for the purposes of the Income Tax Acts such part of the management expenses as bears the same proportion to all those expenses as the untaxed income bears to the distributed income.

(3) For the purpose of computing the proportion mentioned in subsection (2) above, the amounts of the distributed income and of the untaxed income shall not, in either case, include so much (if any) of the income as is equal to the amount of income tax, or of any foreign tax, chargeable on the trustees (by way of deduction or otherwise) in respect of that income.

(4) In subsection (3) above, 'foreign tax' means any tax which is—

(*a*) of a similar character to income tax; and

(*b*) imposed by the laws of a territory outside the United Kingdom.

(5) For the purposes of this section, where the income tax chargeable on any person is limited in accordance with section 128 of the Finance Act 1995 (limit on income chargeable on non-residents), the income of that person on which he is not liable to tax by reason of not having been resident in the United Kingdom shall be taken to include so much of any income of his as—

(*a*) is excluded income within the meaning of that section; and

(*b*) is not income which is treated for the purposes of subsection (1)(*b*) of that section as income the tax on which is deducted at source.

689B   Order in which expenses to be set against income

(1) The expenses of any trustees in any year of assessment, so far as they are properly chargeable to income (or would be so chargeable but for any express provisions of the trust), shall be treated—

(*a*) as set against so much (if any) of any income as is income falling within subsection (2) or (3) below before being set against other income; and

(*b*) as set against so much (if any) of any income as is income falling within subsection (2) below before being set against income falling within subsection (3) below.

(2) Income falls within this subsection if it is—

(*a*) so much of the income of the trustees as is income the amount or value of which is determined in accordance with section 233(1A);

(*b*) income which is treated as having arisen to the trustees by virtue of section 246D(4) or 249(6); or

(*c*) income which is treated as received by the trustees by virtue of section 421(1)(*a*).

(3) Income falls within this subsection if it is income to which section 1A applies but which does not fall within subsection (2) above.

(4) This section has effect—

(*a*) subject to sections 686(2A) and 689A, but

(*b*) notwithstanding anything in section 1A(5) and (6).''

GENERAL NOTE

This paragraph inserts a new Chapter ID (consisting of two sections, ss 689A and 689B) in TA 1988 Part XV (settlements).

The new Chapter provides for the partial disallowance of trust management expenses attributable to income which (before distribution) is income of a beneficiary rather than the trustees, where part of that income does not bear UK income tax because the beneficiary is not UK resident (or is treated as non-resident under the terms of a double taxation agreement) (TA 1988 s 689A(1)).

In those circumstances a proportion of those management expenses equal to the proportion of the income belonging to the beneficiary which does not bear UK income tax is disregarded in computing the beneficiary's income for tax purposes (TA 1988 s 689A(2)). In computing the relevant proportion, there is excluded (both from the amount of the beneficiary's income and the amount of untaxed income) an amount equal to any income tax and any foreign tax chargeable on the trustees in respect of the income (TA 1988 s 689A(3)). Only foreign tax "of a similar character to income tax" is taken into account for this purpose (TA 1988 s 689A(4)).

FA 1995 s 128 limits the UK income tax liability of non-residents in respect of most investment income to the amount of any tax deducted at source (effectively making statutory the Revenue practice under Concession B13). However, income treated as excluded income under FA 1995 s 128 but which has borne deduction of tax at source is not to be treated as income which has not borne tax for the purposes of the new TA 1988 s 689A. There will therefore be no restriction on the set-off of management expenses in respect of such income (TA 1988 s 689A(5)).

The new TA 1988 s 689B prescribes the order in which trust management expenses chargeable to income are to be set off against that income.

The first category of income against which the expenses are to be set comprises—

(*a*) any of the following income chargeable at the special rate applicable to discretionary trusts (under TA 1988 s 686): qualifying distributions of UK companies (in respect of which the trustees are not entitled to a tax credit by reason of their residence status: TA 1988 s 233(1A)), foreign income dividends (TA 1988 s 246D(4)) and stock dividends (TA 1988 s 249(6));

(*b*) and amounts assessable in respect of released or written-off loans from close companies (TA 1988 s 421(1)(*a*)).

The next category of income against which expenses may be set is investment income within the scope of the new TA 1988 s 1A (broadly, interest etc chargeable under Schedule D Case III, distributions chargeable under Schedule F and equivalent foreign income chargeable under Schedule D Cases IV and V, see s 73), but excluding any income within the first category above.

Finally, expenses may be set against any income outside the categories set out above.

These set-off provisions are subject to the provisions which expressly disallow a proportion of expenses equivalent to the proportion of any trust income which does not bear UK income tax because the trustees, or the beneficiary entitled to the income, are non-resident or deemed to be non-resident under a double taxation agreement (TA 1988 ss 686(2A), 689A).

17 In section 698A of that Act (taxation at the lower rate of the income of beneficiaries)—

(*a*) in subsection (1), for the words from "section 207A" to the end there shall be substituted "section 1A shall have effect as if that income were income to which that section applies."; and

(*b*) in subsection (2), for the words from "section 207A" to the end there shall be substituted "section 1A shall have effect as if the payment made to the trustee were income of the trustee to which that section applies."

GENERAL NOTE
TA 1988 s 698A applies the provisions for the lower rate charge in respect of UK dividends (TA 1988 s 207A) to income received by the beneficiary of an estate which is treated as having borne income tax at the lower rate. With effect from the year 1996–97, TA 1988 s 207A is superseded by the new TA 1988 s 1A, which abolishes the basic rate charge in respect of most savings income. This paragraph simply substitutes references to s 1A for those to s 207A.

18 (1) In subsection (1) of section 737 of that Act (deductions from manufactured payments), after "shall apply" there shall be inserted "(subject to subsection (1A) below)", and for subsection (1A) of that section there shall be substituted the following subsection—

"(1A) The deduction of tax which is deemed to have been made under subsection (1) above shall be taken to have been made at the lower rate as if the deemed annual payment were income to which section 1A applied; and—

(*a*) the reference to the applicable rate in subsection (1) of section 350, so far as it has effect by virtue of subsection (1) above, and
(*b*) Schedule 16, so far as it so has effect,

shall be construed accordingly."

(2) This paragraph has effect in relation to payments on or after 6th April 1996.

GENERAL NOTE
Where, under a contract for the transfer of shares, stock or other securities, one of the parties (the dividend manufacturer) is required to pay the other an amount representing a dividend or a periodical payment of interest on the securities, the dividend manufacturer is required to account to the Revenue for tax on the payment. At present, where the manufactured payment represents a dividend which would be chargeable under Schedule F in the hands of an individual recipient, the manufacturer is required to account for tax at the lower rate on the grossed up amount of the payment; in respect of other payments the manufacturer is required to account for tax at the basic rate as if the payment were an annual payment made after deduction of tax at source (TA 1988 s 737(1), (1A)).
This paragraph substitutes a new TA 1988 s 737(1A) which provides that, in respect of all manufactured payments made after 5 April 1996, the manufacturer is required to account for tax on the basis that the payment was an annual payment made subject to deduction of tax at source at the lower rate.

19 In section 737C(6) of that Act (computation of amount of deemed manufactured interest), for "basic" there shall be substituted "lower".

GENERAL NOTE
In consequence of the amendment made by para 18 above, this paragraph amends the provisions relating to deemed manufactured payments in connection with agreements to sell and repurchase securities. The amendment provides for the amount of tax deemed to have been deducted from the payment of deemed manufactured interest to be calculated at the lower, rather than the basic, rate on the gross amount of the payment.

20 In section 743(1) of that Act (supplemental provisions relating to transfers of assets abroad)—

(*a*) after the words "the basic rate", in the first place where they occur, there shall be inserted "or the lower rate"; and
(*b*) for "income that has borne tax at the basic rate", there shall be substituted "any income to the extent that it has borne tax at that rate".

GENERAL NOTE
Where, as a result of a transfer of assets abroad, income becomes payable to a person who is not resident or not domiciled in the UK, an income tax charge may arise where either the transferor has power to enjoy any income of a non-resident or non-domiciled person or the transferor becomes entitled to receive a capital sum in connection with the transfer or an associated operation (TA 1988 s 739).
However, income which has borne UK income tax at the basic rate (by deduction at source or

otherwise) will not be charged again at the basic rate on the transferor, although it will still be chargeable at the higher rate if applicable (TA 1988 s 743(1)).

Since, with effect from 1996–97, most investment income subject to deduction of tax at source will suffer deduction at the lower rate rather than the basic rate of tax, this paragraph substitutes references to the lower rate for the references to the basic rate in TA 1988 s 743(1).

21   In section 789(2) of that Act (old double taxation relief agreements), for "to bear income tax at the basic rate" there shall be substituted "—

(*a*) to bear income tax at the basic rate or, where that income is income to which section 1A applies, at the lower rate; and

(*b*)".

GENERAL NOTE

TA 1988 s 789(2) states that double taxation arrangements made before 30 March 1971 which provide for the exemption of any income from surtax are to be construed as if they provided for such income to bear income tax at the basic rate and to be disregarded in computing total income.

In the light of the new rules abolishing the basic rate charge on certain savings income with effect from 1996–97 (TA 1988 s 1A, see s 73), this paragraph amends TA 1988 s 789(2) to provide for such agreements to be construed, in so far as they relate to savings income within s 1A, as providing for that income to bear income tax at the lower rate.

22   In paragraph (*a*) of section 821(1) of that Act (under-deductions from payments made before passing of annual Act to be charged under Case VI of Schedule D), for the words from "under Schedule D in respect" to the end of the paragraph there shall be substituted "under Case III of Schedule D in respect of those payments; and".

GENERAL NOTE

TA 1988 s 821(1) provides for the recovery of tax which should have been deducted from or charged on half-yearly or quarterly payments in respect of interest, dividends etc, where the payments were made before the rates of tax for the relevant year of assessment were fixed and either no tax was deducted or charged, or tax was charged or deducted at a different rate from that ultimately fixed.

The section provides for amounts undercharged or underdeducted to be charged under Schedule D Case VI (TA 1988 s 821(1)(*a*)). This paragraph amends that provision to provide for the charge to be made under Schedule D Case III with effect for the year 1996–97 and subsequent years of assessment (see para 28 below).

23   In section 822(1) of that Act (over-deductions from interest on loan capital etc made before the passing of annual Act where basic rate for the year is lower than in the previous year), for "basic rate lower" there shall be substituted "lower rate less".

GENERAL NOTE

TA 1988 s 822 provides for adjustments in certain cases where a company has made interest payments on its securities subject to deduction of income tax at the basic rate applying for the previous year of assessment and the basic rate is reduced for the year in which the payment is made.

Since such payments are to be made subject to deduction of tax at the lower rate with effect from 1996–97 (see s 73), this paragraph substitutes a reference to the lower rate for the reference to the basic rate in s 822.

24   In section 835(6)(*a*) of that Act (estimating total income), after "basic rate" there shall be inserted "or the lower rate".

GENERAL NOTE

TA 1988 s 835(6) provides that, in estimating a person's total income, any income charged with income tax by way of deduction at the basic rate in force for a particular year of assessment is deemed to be income of that year.

In the light of the new rules providing for certain savings income to be subject to deduction at source at the lower rate from 1996–97, this paragraph extends s 835(6) to make similar provision in relation to income charged with income tax by way of deduction at the lower rate in force for any year of assessment.

25   (1) In Schedule 3 to that Act (public revenue dividends etc) —

(*a*) in paragraph 1(*c*), for "basic" there shall be substituted "lower";

(*b*) in paragraph 6A—

(i) in sub-paragraph (1), for "applicable" there shall be substituted "lower"; and

(ii) sub-paragraph (4) shall cease to have effect.

(2) This paragraph has effect in relation to payments made on or after 6th April 1996 and before the day on which this Act is passed.

GENERAL NOTE

This paragraph amends the provisions contained in TA 1988 Sch 3 for the deduction and payment of tax by paying and collecting agents in respect of public revenue dividends, foreign dividends and coupons, to reflect the fact that such payments after 5 April 1996 are to be made subject to deduction of tax at the lower rate rather than the basic rate.

TA 1988 Sch 3 is repealed by FA 1996 Sch 7 para 27 subject to transitional provisions which apply until FA 1996 is passed (Sch 7 paras 33–35, see below). This paragraph therefore only applies for payments made before the date on which FA 1996 is passed.

The Finance Act 1989 (c 26)

26 (1) In section 88(1) of the Finance Act 1989 (rate of corporation tax on policy holders' fraction of profits to be equal to the basic rate), after "subsection (2)" there shall be inserted "and section 88A below".

(2) After section 88 of that Act there shall be inserted the following section—

"88A Lower corporation tax rate on certain insurance company profits

(1) Subject to subsection (2) below, in the case of a company carrying on basic life assurance and general annuity business, the rate of corporation tax chargeable for any financial year on so much of the company's BLAGAB profits for any accounting period as represents the company's lower rate income for the period shall be deemed to be the rate at which income tax at the lower rate is charged for the year of assessment which begins on 6th April in the financial year concerned.

(2) Subsection (1) above does not apply in relation to profits charged under Case I of Schedule D.

(3) In this section, references to a company's lower rate income for any accounting period are references to so much of the income and gains of its basic life assurance and general annuity business for the period as consists in income of any of the following descriptions—

(*a*) income falling within paragraph (*a*) of Case III of Schedule D, as that Case applies for the purposes of corporation tax;

(*b*) purchased life annuities to which section 656 of the Taxes Act 1988 applies or to which that section would apply but for section 657(2)(*a*) of that Act;

(*c*) any such dividends or other distributions of a company not resident in the United Kingdom as would be chargeable under Schedule F if the company were resident in the United Kingdom;

(*d*) so much of—

(i) any dividend distribution (within the meaning of section 468J of the Taxes Act 1988), or

(ii) any foreign income distribution (within the meaning of section 468K of that Act),

as is deemed by subsection (2) of section 468Q of that Act (or by that subsection as applied by section 468R(2) of that Act) to be an annual payment.

(4) Where for any period—

(*a*) an insurance company's basic life assurance and general annuity business is mutual business,

(*b*) the policy holders' share of the company's relevant profits is equal to all those profits, or

(*c*) the policy holders' share of the company's relevant profits is more than the company's BLAGAB profits,

the amount to be taken for the purposes of this section as the amount of the company's BLAGAB profits for that period representing its lower rate income for that period shall be the amount equal to the applicable proportion of its BLAGAB profits.

(5) Where subsection (4) above does not apply in the case of an insurance company for any period, the amount to be taken for the purposes of this section as the amount of the company's BLAGAB profits for the period representing its lower rate income for that period shall be the amount produced by multiplying the following, that is to say—

(*a*) the applicable proportion of those profits; and
(*b*) the fraction given by dividing the policy holders' share of the relevant profits of the company for the period by its BLAGAB profits for that period.

(6) For the purposes of this section the applicable proportion of a company's BLAGAB profits for any period is the amount which bears the same proportion to those profits as the aggregate amount of the company's lower rate income for that period bears to the total income and gains for that period of the company's basic life assurance and general annuity business.

(7) For the purposes of this section, the BLAGAB profits of a company for an accounting period are the income and gains of the company's basic life assurance and general annuity business reduced by the aggregate amount of—

(*a*) any non-trading deficit on the company's loan relationships,
(*b*) expenses of management falling to be deducted under section 76 of the Taxes Act 1988, and
(*c*) charges on income,

so far as referable to the company's basic life assurance and general annuity business.

(8) Section 88(3) above applies for the purposes of this section as it applies for the purposes of section 88(1) above."

(3) In section 89 of that Act (meaning of "policy holders' share" of profits), in subsection (1)—

(*a*) for "section 88" there shall be substituted "sections 88 and 88A";
(*b*) after "life assurance business" there shall be inserted "or, as the case may be, basic life assurance and general annuity business"; and
(*c*) for "the business" there shall be substituted "its life assurance business";

and in subsection (2), in each of paragraphs (*b*) and (*c*), for "the business" there shall be substituted "the company's life assurance business".

(4) This paragraph shall have effect for the financial year 1996 and subsequent financial years.

GENERAL NOTE
Life insurance companies taxed on the income less expenses basis are subject to corporation tax at a reduced rate on the part of the taxable amount which represents the return to the policy holders. In a mutual insurance company, which has no shareholders, all profits are deemed to be held for the benefit of policy holders, so the whole of the taxable amount is charged at the reduced rate. The reduced rate is currently equal to the basic rate of income tax (FA 1989 s 88).

This paragraph inserts a new section, FA 1989 s 88A, which broadly provides that, for the financial year 1996 and subsequent years, the part of the policy holders' share of the taxable amount which is derived from "lower rate income" (broadly equivalent to savings income within the scope of the new TA 1988 s 1A, see s 73) will be subject to corporation tax at a rate equal to the lower rate of income tax (FA 1989 s 88A(1), (4)–(8)). The definition of "policy holders' share" in FA 1989 s 89 is applied for the purposes of the new provisions (FA 1989 s 89(9) inserted by sub-para (3)).

The provision only applies to profits charged on the income less expenses basis (ie, not under Schedule D Case I) (FA 1989 s 88A(2)).

"Lower rate income" comprises so much of the income and gains of a company's basic life assurance and general annuity business as consists of (FA 1989 s 88A(3))—

(*a*) annual profits or gains arising from loan relationships which are chargeable under Schedule D Case III para (*a*) (see FA 1996 Sch 14 para 5);
(*b*) purchased life annuities within TA 1988 s 656 (or annuities which would be within that

section but for the fact that they would (apart from s 656) be treated as consisting to any extent of the payment or repayment of a capital sum);

(*c*) distributions of non-resident companies which would be chargeable under Schedule F if the company was UK resident; and

(*d*) so much of any dividend distribution or foreign income distribution, as defined in the legislation relating to foreign income dividends (TA 1988 ss 468J, 468K) as is deemed by that legislation (TA 1988 s 468Q(2)) to be an annual payment.

For any period in which an insurance company's basic life assurance and general annuity business (BLAGAB) is mutual business, or in which the policy holders' share of the company's "relevant profits" (see below) equals those profits or exceeds the company's BLAGAB profits, the proportion of those profits representing the company's lower rate income is equal to the proportion which the aggregate amount of the company's lower rate income for the period in question bears to the total income and gains of its basic life assurance and general annuity business for that period (FA 1989 s 88A(4), (6)).

For any other accounting period, the amount of BLAGAB profits representing the company's lower rate income is found by multiplying together—

(*a*) the proportion which the aggregate amount of the company's lower rate income for the period in question bears to the total income and gains of its basic life assurance and general annuity business for that period; and

(*b*) the proportion (expressed as a fraction) which the policy holders' share of the company's "relevant" profits (see below) for the period bears to the whole amount of its BLAGAB profits for the period (FA 1989 s 88A(5), (6)).

For the purposes of the calculations above, a company's BLAGAB profits for an accounting period are taken to be the income and gains of its basic life assurance and general annuity business as reduced by any non-trading deficit on its loan relationships, management expenses (deductible under TA 1988 s 76) and charges on income, which are referable to that business (FA 1989 s 88A(7)).

A company's "relevant profits" for an accounting period are the income and gains of its life assurance business less any deductible management expenses and charges on income referable to that business (FA 1989 s 88(3) applied by s 88A(8)).

The Taxation of Chargeable Gains Act 1992 (c 12)

27 In section 4(3A) of the Taxation of Chargeable Gains Act 1992 (disregard of income chargeable at lower rate in accordance with section 207A of the Taxes Act 1988), for "section 207A" there shall be substituted "section 1A".

GENERAL NOTE

For 1988–89 and later years, individuals are chargeable to capital gains tax at the income tax rates which would apply if the chargeable gains were the top slice of their income. For the purpose of calculating the extent to which capital gains are chargeable at the higher rate, certain adjustments are made to the amount of the taxpayer's total income which must be set against the lower and basic rate bands. One of the adjustments required is that distributions received from UK resident companies which are chargeable at the lower rate (or would be so chargeable if they were not chargeable at the higher rate) in accordance with TA 1988 s 207A, are to be disregarded. With effect from the year 1996–97, the income to be disregarded is extended to include all savings income within the scope of the new TA 1988 s 1A (see s 73).

Commencement of Schedule

28 Subject to any express provisions as to commencement that are contained in the preceding provisions of this Schedule, this Schedule has effect for the year 1996–97 and subsequent years of assessment.

SCHEDULE 7

TRANSFER OF CHARGE UNDER SCHEDULE C TO SCHEDULE D

GENERAL NOTE

In the light of the abolition of the charge to tax under Schedule C (see s 79 above), this Schedule provides for income previously charged under Schedule C to be charged to income tax under Schedule D Cases III, IV and V. (Different provision is made in relation to corporation tax: see Sch 14 para 5.)

The Schedule also makes a number of consequential amendments, some of which are applicable for both income and corporation tax purposes.

The Schedule has effect for the year 1996–97 and subsequent years of assessment for income tax purposes and for accounting periods ending after 31 March 1996 in respect of corporation tax (in line with the effective date for the abolition of Schedule C by s 79). However, this is subject to transitional provisions which preserve certain requirements on paying and collecting agents to deduct and account for tax in respect of periods up to the date on which FA 1996 is passed.

Amendments of the Taxes Act 1988

1 The Taxes Act 1988 shall be amended in accordance with paragraphs 2 to 28 below.

2 In section 1(1) (the charge to income tax), for "Schedules A, C, D, E and F" there shall be substituted "Schedules A, D, E and F".

GENERAL NOTE

This paragraph amends TA 1988 s 1(1), which sets out the charge to income tax, by removing the reference to Schedule C.

3 Section 17 (Schedule C) shall be omitted.

GENERAL NOTE

This paragraph repeals TA 1988 s 17, which sets out the charge to tax under Schedule C.

4 (1) In section 18 (Schedule D), in subsection (1), in paragraph (*b*) of Schedule D, for "not charged under Schedule A, C or E" there shall be substituted "not charged under Schedule A or E".

(2) In subsection (3) of that section—

(*a*) in Case III, in paragraph (*c*) for the words from "except income charged under Schedule C" to the end of the paragraph there shall be substituted "from securities which is payable out of the public revenue of the United Kingdom or Northern Ireland";

(*b*) in Case IV, the words "except such income as is charged under Schedule C" shall be omitted; and

(*c*) in Case VI, for "Schedule A, C or E" there shall be substituted "Schedule A or E".

(3) Immediately before subsection (4) of section 18, there shall be inserted the following subsections—

"(3B) The references in Case IV of Schedule D to income arising from securities out of the United Kingdom, and in Case V of Schedule D to income arising from possessions out of the United Kingdom, shall be taken, in the case of relevant foreign holdings, to include references to the following—

(*a*) any proceeds of such a sale or other realisation of coupons for foreign dividends as is effected by a bank in the United Kingdom which pays the proceeds over or carries them into an account;

(*b*) any proceeds of a sale of such coupons to a dealer in coupons in the United Kingdom by a person who is not a bank or another dealer in coupons.

(3C) In this section 'relevant foreign holdings' means—

(*a*) any securities issued by or on behalf of a government or a public or local authority in a country outside the United Kingdom; or (*b*) any shares or securities issued by or on behalf of a body of persons not resident in the United Kingdom;

and 'securities' here includes loan stock and similar securities.

(3D) In this section 'foreign dividends' means—

(*a*) in relation to relevant foreign holdings falling within subsection (3C)(*a*) above, interest or annual payments payable out of the revenue of the government or authority in question; and

(*b*) in relation to relevant foreign holdings falling within subsection (3C)(*b*) above, any dividends, interest or annual payments payable in respect of the holdings in question.

(3E) In this section—

(*a*) 'bank' has the meaning given by section 840A; and

(*b*) references to coupons include, in relation to any foreign dividends, warrants for and bills of exchange purporting to be drawn or made in payment of those dividends."

(4) In subsection (5) of that section, for "Part IV contains" there shall be substituted "Parts III and IV contain".

GENERAL NOTE

This paragraph transfers to Schedule D sources of income which were previously charged under Schedule C. The amendments made by this paragraph apply only for income tax purposes. (For corporation tax, all income formerly charged under Schedule C will be charged under Schedule D Case III, which is expanded, for the purposes of corporation tax only, to include all profits and gains arising from non-trading loan relationships, including income hitherto charged under Case IV or V: see TA 1988 s 18(3A) inserted by FA 1996 Sch 14 para 5).

All income from securities payable out of the public revenue of the UK or Northern Ireland is to be charged under Schedule D Case III (sub-para (2)(*a*)).

All income from securities outside the UK will be charged to income tax (but not corporation tax, see above) under Schedule D Case IV (sub-para (2)(*b*)).

All income from possessions outside the UK (other than emoluments of an office or employment) will be charged to income tax (but not corporation tax, see above) under Schedule D Case V.

The income from securities or possessions chargeable under Case IV or V respectively includes, in respect of securities issued by a foreign government or a foreign public or local authority, or shares or securities issued by any non-resident body of persons ("relevant foreign holdings")—

(*a*) proceeds from the realisation of coupons for foreign dividends by a UK bank which pays over the proceeds or keeps them in an account;

(*b*) proceeds from the sale of coupons for foreign dividends to a UK dealer in coupons by a person other than a bank or another dealer (TA 1988 s 18(3B), (3C) inserted by sub-para (3)).

"Foreign dividends" include interest or annual payments payable out of the revenue of the relevant foreign government or authority or dividends, interest or annual payments payable in respect of the shares or securities issued by the relevant non-resident body (TA 1988 s 18(3D) inserted by sub-para (3)).

"Coupons" include warrants for and bills of exchange purporting to be drawn or made in payment of foreign dividends (TA 1988 s 18(3E) inserted by sub-para (3)).

The term "bank" is defined in TA 1988 s 840A (inserted by FA 1996 Sch 37 para 1, see below) (TA 1988 s 18(3E) inserted by sub-para (3)).

5 In section 19(1), in paragraph 2 of Schedule E, for the words "under Schedule C" there shall be substituted "under paragraph (*c*) of Case III of Schedule D".

GENERAL NOTE

This paragraph makes a consequential amendment to the Schedule E charging provisions to reflect the fact that all annuities and pensions payable out of the public revenue of the UK or Northern Ireland are charged to income tax under Schedule D Case III following the abolition of the charge under Schedule C with effect from the year 1996–97.

6 For the heading to Part III there shall be substituted the following heading—

"GOVERNMENT SECURITIES"

GENERAL NOTE
See note to para. 12.

7   Section 44 (mode of charge of tax under Schedule C) shall be omitted.

GENERAL NOTE
See note to para 12.

8   Section 45 (interpretation of Part III) shall be omitted.

GENERAL NOTE
See note to para 12.

9   Section 48 (securities of foreign states) shall be omitted.

GENERAL NOTE
See note to para 12.

10   In section 49 (stock and dividends in name of Treasury etc), after subsection (2) there shall be inserted the following subsection—

"(3) In this section 'dividends' means any interest, public annuities, dividends or shares of annuities."

GENERAL NOTE
See note to para 12.

11   In sections 50(1) and 51A(1) (which provide for interest on certain securities to be paid without deduction of tax), the words "but shall be chargeable to tax under Case III of Schedule D" shall in each case be omitted.

GENERAL NOTE
See note to para 12.

12   Section 52 (taxation of interest on converted securities and interest which becomes subject to deduction) shall be omitted.

GENERAL NOTE
Paragraphs 6–12 amend TA 1988 Part III (ss 44–52), which hitherto contained provisions relating to the charge under Schedule C and general provisions about government securities.
Provisions relating specifically to the charge under Schedule C are repealed and consequential amendments are made to other provisions.
Paragraph 6 amends the heading of Part III to remove the reference to Schedule C.
Paragraph 7 repeals TA 1988 s 44, which specified the persons responsible for the deduction and payment of tax in respect of the various types of income chargeable under Schedule C.
Paragraph 8 repeals TA 1988 s 45, which contained definitions for the purposes of the Schedule C charge. (Definitions relevant for the charge under Schedule D are re-enacted in TA 1988 ss 18 and 49(3).)
Paragraph 9 repeals TA 1988 s 48, which exempted from the charge under Schedule C certain interest, public annuities, dividends, shares of annuities and proceeds from the realisation of coupons where the person entitled to the income was not resident in the UK.
Paragraph 10 re-enacts for the purposes of TA 1988 s 49 (exemption from tax on stocks or dividends transferred to accounts in the books of the Bank of England in the name of the Treasury or the National Debt Commissioners) the definition of "dividends" previously contained in TA 1988 s 45 (repealed by para 8 above).
Paragraph 11 makes consequential amendments to TA 1988 s 50(1) (payment of interest on certain UK government securities without deduction of tax) and s 51A(1) (payment of interest on certain gilt-edged securities without deduction of tax).
Paragraph 12 repeals TA 1988 s 52 (election for relief where a double charge arose on the conversion of certain government securities or on an application by the taxpayer (under TA 1988 s 50(2)) for income tax to be deducted at source from interest on securities where such interest had previously been paid gross (by virtue of TA 1988 s 50(1)). (A double charge could have arisen on the conversion of securities where interest on the original security was paid gross and assessed

under Schedule D Case III on the preceding year basis, but interest on the substituted security was charged by deduction at source on the current year basis.)

13   Section 123 (foreign dividends) shall be omitted.

GENERAL NOTE
   Paragraph 13 repeals TA 1988 s 123, which provided for the taxation of foreign dividends derived from coupons paid or collected by a UK agent or sold to a UK dealer. The term "foreign dividends" for the purposes of this section covered interest, dividends and other annual payments payable out of or in respect of the stocks, funds, shares or securities of a non-resident body of persons. Such payments were charged under Schedule D but the machinery rules of Schedule C applied. They are now brought within the scope of Schedule D Cases IV and V by TA 1988 s 18(3B)–(3E) inserted by para 4 above.

14   In section 24—

   (*a*) in subsection (6) (definitions in connection with quoted Eurobonds), the definitions of "recognised clearing system" and "relevant foreign securities", and the word "and" immediately preceding those definitions, and
   (*b*) subsection (7),

shall be omitted.

GENERAL NOTE
   Paragraph 14 repeals the definition of "recognised clearing system" in TA 1988 s 124(6) (interest on quoted Eurobonds); the term is now defined in a new TA 1988 s 841A inserted by para 26 (see below).

15   In section 322(1) (consular officers and employees), the words "and he shall be treated as not resident in the United Kingdom for the purposes of sections 48 and 123(4)" shall be omitted.

GENERAL NOTE
   This paragraph makes a consequential amendment to TA 1988 s 322(1) (income tax exemptions for foreign consular officers and employees), deleting the references to the exemptions for non-residents in respect of income from overseas public revenue dividends and foreign dividends under TA 1988 ss 48 and 123 (which were repealed by paras 9 and 13 above respectively).

16   In section 398 (transactions in deposits with and without certificates or in debts), in paragraph (*b*), the words "C or" shall be omitted.

GENERAL NOTE
   This paragraph removes the reference to Schedule C in TA 1988 s 398 (set-off of losses on transactions in certificates of deposits against interest chargeable under Schedule C or D).

17   In section 468M(4) (meaning of "eligible income" in connection with interest distributions of authorised unit trusts), for paragraphs (*c*) to (*e*) there shall be substituted the following paragraph—

   "(*cc*)   any foreign dividends (as defined by section 18(3D)) and any proceeds falling within section 18(3B)(*a*) or (*b*);"

GENERAL NOTE
   TA 1988 s 468M(4) sets out the categories of income ("eligible income") which may be distributed by authorised unit trusts without deduction of withholding tax to non-resident unit holders. These categories of income included interest earned as overseas public revenue dividends payable in the UK or Northern Ireland, the coupon amount realised where such interest was not received but was included in the sale proceeds of the security (hitherto taxable under Schedule C) and interest, dividends etc on overseas securities which were previously taxable under TA 1988 s 123. As all such income is subject to income tax under Schedule D with effect from the year 1996–97 (see para 4 above), this paragraph substitutes a reference to the new charging provisions and definitions (TA 1988 s 18(3)–(3E)).

18   In section 474 (treatment of tax-free income), subsections (1) and (3) shall be omitted.

GENERAL NOTE
TA 1988 s 484(1) excluded banking, insurance and securities businesses carried on in the UK by non-residents from the exemptions for non-residents under TA 1988 s 48 (in respect of income from securities of foreign states) and s 123(4) (in respect of foreign dividends). Following the repeal of both provisions (by paras 9 and 13 above respectively) with effect from the year 1996–97 (for income tax purposes) and for accounting periods ending after 31 March 1996 (for corporation tax purposes), s 484(1) is no longer necessary and is therefore repealed by this paragraph.

19 (1) In section 505 (exemptions for charities), in subsection (1), in paragraph (*c*), sub-paragraph (i) shall be omitted.

(2) For paragraph (*d*) of that subsection there shall be substituted the following paragraph—

"(*d*) exemption from tax under Schedule D in respect of public revenue dividends on securities which are in the name of trustees, to the extent that the dividends are applicable and applied only for the repair of—

(i) any cathedral, college, church or chapel, or
(ii) any building used only for the purposes of divine worship;".

(3) After that subsection there shall be inserted the following subsection—

"(1A) In subsection (1)(*d*) above 'public revenue dividends' means—

(*a*) income from securities which is payable out of the public revenue of the United Kingdom or Northern Ireland;
(*b*) income from securities issued by or on behalf of a government or a public or local authority in a country outside the United Kingdom."

GENERAL NOTE
This paragraph deletes references to tax under Schedule C from the list of exemptions which charities may claim. An exemption from tax under Schedule D in respect of UK and overseas public revenue dividends is substituted for the former exemption from tax under Schedule C in respect of equivalent income from securities held in the name of trustees, to the extent that the dividends are applicable and applied for the repair of buildings used for worship.

20 (1) In section 512 (exemption from income tax for Atomic Energy Authority and National Radiological Protection Board)—

(*a*) in subsection (1)(*a*), for "Schedules A and C" there shall be substituted "Schedule A"; and
(*b*) in subsection (1)(*b*), after "annual payment" there shall be inserted "or in respect of public revenue dividends".

(2) After subsection (2) of that section there shall be inserted the following subsection—

"(3) In subsection (1) above 'public revenue dividends' means—

(*a*) income from securities which is payable out of the public revenue of the United Kingdom or Northern Ireland;
(*b*) income from securities issued by or on behalf of a government or a public or local authority in a country outside the United Kingdom."

GENERAL NOTE
This paragraph deletes the reference to tax under Schedule C from the list of exemptions which the Atomic Energy Authority and the National Radiological Protection Board may claim. An exemption from tax under Schedule D in respect of UK and overseas public revenue dividends is substituted for the former exemption from tax under Schedule C in respect of equivalent income.

21 (1) In section 516 (government securities held by non-resident central banks), in subsection (1), for "dividends (within the meaning of Schedule C) paid out of the public revenue of the United Kingdom where they are" there shall be substituted "income from securities which is payable out of the public revenue of the United Kingdom and which is".

(2) In subsection (2) of that section, for "such dividends" there shall be substituted "such income".

This paragraph amends the wording of the exemption for non-resident central banks from tax on dividends etc paid out of the UK public revenue to reflect the fact that such income is henceforth chargeable under Schedule D rather than Schedule C.

22 In section 582A (designated international organisations), subsection (3) shall be omitted.

TA 1988 s 582A exempts designated international organisations from the requirement to deduct and account to the Revenue for tax at the basic rate on certain payments of rent, dividends, annual interest and other annual payments.

The exemptions include an exemption in TA 1988 s 582A(3) from the requirement to deduct and account for tax on interest, dividends and other annual payments paid to a UK resident through a UK bank or other paying agent in respect of stock, funds, shares and securities of a non-resident organisation: such payments are treated as being excluded from the definition of "foreign dividends" for the purposes of TA 1988 s 123.

The provisions of TA 1988 s 123 for the deduction of tax at source from such income are repealed by para 13 above, and accordingly TA 1988 s 582A(3) is no longer necessary and is repealed by this paragraph.

23 In section 730 (transfers of income arising from securities)—

(a) in subsections (2), (4)(b) and (6), for "under Schedule C or under section 123(3)", and

(b) in subsection (8), for "under Schedule C or section 123(3)",

there shall in each case be substituted "by virtue of section 18(3B)".

TA 1988 s 730 provides that where, in any chargeable period, the owner of any securities transfers or sells the right to receive any interest payable in respect of the securities without selling or transferring the securities themselves, then the interest is deemed to be his income for tax purposes and not any other person's. The owner is subject to tax under Schedule D Case VI in respect of the interest unless he can show that the proceeds of the sale etc of the right to receive the interest have been charged to tax under Schedule C or under TA 1988 s 123(3).

In consequence of the abolition of Schedule C and the repeal of TA 1988 s 123 (see para 13 above), and the transfer of income formerly chargeable under Schedule C to Schedule D (TA 1988 s 18), this paragraph substitutes references to TA 1988 s 18(3B) for references in TA 1988s 730 to Schedule C and TA 1988 s 123(3).

24 In section 828(2) (orders and regulations not required to be made by statutory instrument), for "section 124(6) or 841(1)(b) or paragraph 15(4) of Schedule 3" there shall be substituted "section 841(1)(b) or 841A".

TA 1988 s 828(2) provides that certain orders do not need to be made by statutory instrument. These include orders under TA 1988 s 124(6) (designating recognised clearing systems) and under Sch 3 para 15(4) (specifying the information requirements for the relief from the duty to deduct UK income tax from payments of interest, dividends etc out of the public revenue of the Republic of Ireland to a person in the UK).

With effect from the year 1996–97, the power to make orders designating recognised clearing systems has been re-enacted in TA 1988 s 841A (see para 26 below) and the provisions of TA 1988 Sch 3 providing the machinery for the collection of income tax under Schedule C have been repealed (see para 27 below).

This paragraph accordingly makes consequential amendments, substituting a reference to TA 1988 s 841A for the reference to TA 1988 s 124(6) in TA 1988 s 828(2) and deleting the reference to Sch 3 para 15(4).

25 In section 832(1) (interpretation of the Tax Acts), the definition of "recognised clearing system" shall be omitted.

This paragraph repeals the definition of "recognised clearing system" in TA 1988 s 832(1), which referred to TA 1988 s 124(6). The definition in the latter provision has been re-enacted in TA 1988 s 841A, see para 26 below.

26 After section 841 there shall be inserted the following section—

"841A Recognised clearing systems

(1) In the Tax Acts, 'recognised clearing system' means any system for clearing—

    (*a*) quoted Eurobonds (as defined by section 124), or
    (*b*) relevant foreign holdings (as defined by section 18(3C)),

which is for the time being designated for the purposes of this section as a recognised clearing system by an order made by the Board.

(2) An order under this section—

    (*a*) may contain such transitional and other supplemental provision as appears to the Board to be necessary or expedient; and
    (*b*) may be varied or revoked by a subsequent order."

GENERAL NOTE
    This paragraph inserts a new section, TA 1988 s 841A, which contains the definition of "recognised clearing system" (formerly defined in TA 1988 s 124(6)).
    A recognised clearing system is defined as a system for clearing quoted Eurobonds or relevant foreign holdings, which is designated as a recognised clearing system by an order made by the Board. Any such order may contain transitional or supplementary provisions and may be varied or revoked by a subsequent order.
    A quoted Eurobond is defined (in TA 1988 s 124(6)) as a security issued by a company which is quoted on a recognised stock exchange, is in bearer form and carries a right to interest.
    Relevant foreign holdings are defined (in TA 1988 s 18(3C) inserted by para 4 above) as securities issued by a foreign government or a foreign public or local authority, or shares or securities issued by any non-resident body of persons.

27 Schedule 3 (machinery for payment of income tax under Schedule C and, in certain cases, Schedule D) shall be omitted.

GENERAL NOTE
    This paragraph repeals TA 1988 Sch 3, which sets out the provisions under which paying and collecting agents have hitherto been required to deduct and account for tax in respect of public revenue dividends, foreign dividends and proceeds of coupons chargeable under Schedule C or Schedule D. However, the repeal is subject to transitional provisions covering the period up to the date on which FA 1996 is passed; see under paras 33–35 below.

28 (1) In Schedule 23A (manufactured dividends and interest), in paragraph 1(1) (definitions)—

    (*a*) in paragraph (*b*) of the definition of "overseas securities", and
    (*b*) in the definition of "United Kingdom securities",

for "Eurobonds held in a recognised clearing system, within the meaning of section 124," there shall be substituted "Eurobonds (as defined by section 124) held in a recognised clearing system".

(2) In paragraph 4(8) of that Schedule, for paragraphs (*a*) to (*d*) there shall be substituted the following paragraphs—

    "(*b*) a foreign dividend (as defined by section 18(3D)), or
    (*c*) interest on a quoted Eurobond (as defined by section 124) held in a recognised clearing system,".

GENERAL NOTE
    This paragraph makes consequential amendments to TA 1988 Sch 23A, which sets out the detailed provisions for accounting for tax on manufactured dividends and interest. The amendments take account of the transfer of the definition of "recognised clearing system" to TA 1988 s 841A (see para 26 above) and the repeal of TA 1988 s 123 (see para 13 above).

Other amendments

29 In the Table in section 98 of the Taxes Management Act 1970 (penalties in respect of certain information provisions—

(*a*) in the first column, the entry relating to paragraph 13(1) of Schedule 3 to the Taxes Act 1988, and

(*b*) in the second column, the entry relating to paragraph 6C of that Schedule,

shall be omitted.

GENERAL NOTE

In consequence of the repeal of the provisions of TA 1988 Sch 3, which provided the machinery for the collection of income tax under Schedule C (see para 27 above), this paragraph deletes the entries in the table of penalties in TMA 1970 s 98 relating to failures by paying and collecting agents to make records available (TA 1988 Sch 3 para 13(1)) or to make returns (Sch 3 para 6C) in respect of payments of public revenue dividends, foreign dividends and proceeds of coupons.

30 In section 178(2)(*m*) of the Finance Act 1989 (provisions to which power to set rates of interest applies), the words "and paragraph 6B of Schedule 3 to" shall be omitted.

GENERAL NOTE

In consequence of the repeal of the provisions of TA 1988 Sch 3, which provided the machinery for the collection of income tax under Schedule C (see para 27 above), this paragraph deletes the provision in FA 1989 s 178(2)(*m*) for setting the rate of interest on late remissions of tax deducted by paying and collecting agents from public revenue dividends, foreign dividends and proceeds of coupons.

31 In section 128 of the Finance Act 1995 (limit on income chargeable on non-residents: income tax), in subsection (3)(*a*), the words "Schedule C," shall be omitted.

GENERAL NOTE

FA 1995 s 128 limits the UK tax liability of non-residents (except as regards Schedule A income and income from a trade or profession carried on in the UK) to tax deducted at source. It achieves this partly by taking out of charge "excluded income" (except to the extent that such income has been taxed by deduction at source). In consequence of the abolition of Schedule C, this paragraph deletes the reference to income chargeable under Schedule C from the list of excluded income in FA 1995 s 128(3).

Commencement, etc

32 Subject to paragraphs 33 and 34 below, this Schedule has effect—

(*a*) for the purposes of income tax, for the year 1996–97 and subsequent years of assessment;

(*b*) for the purposes of corporation tax, for accounting periods ending after 31st March 1996.

GENERAL NOTE

This paragraph provides for the amendments made by Sch 7 to have effect for the year 1996–97 and subsequent years of assessment for income tax purposes and for accounting periods ending after 31 March 1996 in respect of corporation tax (in line with the effective date for the abolition of Schedule C by s 79). However, this is subject to transitional provisions contained in paras 33–35 below.

Position of paying and collecting agents

33 (1) Subject to the following provisions of this paragraph and paragraph 34 below—

(*a*) nothing in section 79 of this Act or this Schedule shall affect the obligations of any person under Schedule 3, in relation to times to which this paragraph applies, to set apart, retain or pay any amount of tax; and

(*b*) Schedule 3 shall have effect accordingly in relation to amounts set apart, retained or paid in pursuance of those obligations.

(2) The repeal of Schedule 3 shall not affect the operation of paragraph 6B of that Schedule in relation to any amount—

(*a*) which became due and payable in relation to a transaction occurring before the day on which this Act was passed; but

(*b*) which remains unpaid at any time on or after that day.

(3) The Board may by regulations make provision with respect to returns to be made for the quarter which includes both times before the day on which this Act was passed and times on and after that day.

(4) Regulations under sub-paragraph (3) above may, in particular, provide that section 98 of the Taxes Management Act 1970 shall have effect as if it included a reference in the second column of the Table to any specified provision of the regulations.

(5) In this paragraph "Schedule 3" means Schedule 3 to the Taxes Act 1988.

GENERAL NOTE
See note to para 35.

Position of taxpayers

34   (1) Transitional payments of tax made on a person's behalf in relation to times to which this paragraph applies shall be treated as made only for the purpose of being applied in the discharge of that person's liability to tax charged under Schedule D.

(2) If a transitional payment of tax has been made on a person's behalf but it appears to the Board that—

(*a*) that person was not liable to tax, or
(*b*) the sum paid exceeded his liability,

the Board shall make or allow such repayments, adjustments or set-offs against unpaid tax as they think appropriate.

(3) In this paragraph "transitional payment of tax" means a payment to which paragraph 33 above applies.

GENERAL NOTE
See note to para 35.

Times to which paragraphs 33 and 34 apply

35   Paragraphs 33 and 34 above apply in relation to times falling—

(*a*) within a year of assessment or an accounting period mentioned in paragraph 32 above, but
(*b*) before the day on which this Act was passed.

GENERAL NOTE
These paragraphs make transitional provisions in respect of income tax for the period from 6 April 1996 to the date on which FA 1996 is passed; and in respect of corporation tax for the period from the beginning of any company's accounting period which spans or begins after 31 March 1996 to the date on which FA 1996 is passed (para 35).
   The repeal of TA 1988 Sch 3 (machinery under which paying and collecting agents are required to deduct and account for tax on public revenue dividends etc) by para 27 above does not affect the obligation to deduct, retain or pay any amount of tax in respect of this transitional period (para 33(1)).
   It also does not affect the interest charge (under TA 1988 Sch 3 para 6B) in respect of tax due on transactions occurring before the date on which FA 1996 is passed but not paid over to the Revenue by the paying or collecting agent by that date (para 33(2)).
   The Board may make provision by regulations in respect of paying and collecting agents' returns for the quarter spanning the date on which FA 1996 is passed; such regulations may authorise the charging of penalties under TMA 1970 s 98 in respect of failures to provide any information or documents required (para 33(3), (4)).
   Transitional payments of tax made on a taxpayer's behalf under the above provisions are to be treated as made only for the purpose of satisfying the taxpayer's liability to tax under Schedule D. To the extent that such payments appear to exceed the taxpayer's liability, the Board may allow any repayment, adjustment or set-off that they consider to be appropriate (para 34).

Section 83

SCHEDULE 8

LOAN RELATIONSHIPS: CLAIMS RELATING TO DEFICITS

GENERAL NOTE

This Schedule provides further guidance on the relief available under s 83 for non-trading deficits.

Claim to set off deficit against other profits for the deficit period

1 (1) This paragraph applies where a claim is made under section 83(2)(*a*) of this Act for the whole or any part of the deficit to be set off against profits of any description for the deficit period.

(2) Subject to the following provisions of this paragraph—

(*a*) the amount to which the claim relates shall be set off against the profits of the company for the deficit period that are identified in the claim; and

(*b*) those profits shall be treated as reduced accordingly.

(3) Any reduction by virtue of sub-paragraph (2) above shall be made—

(*a*) after relief has been given for any loss incurred in a trade in an earlier accounting period; and

(*b*) before any relief is given against profits for that period either—

(i) under section 393A(1) of the Taxes Act 1988 (trading losses set against profits for the same or preceding accounting periods); or

(ii) by virtue of any claim made, in respect of a deficit for a subsequent period, under section 83(2)(*c*) of this Act.

(4) Relief shall not be given by virtue of a claim under section 83(2) (*a*) of this Act against any ring fence profits of the company within the meaning of Chapter V of Part XII of the Taxes Act 1988 (petroleum extraction activities).

GENERAL NOTE

This paragraph applies to claims under s 83(2)(*a*) for a non-trading deficit to be set off against any other profits of the deficit period and provides the sequence in which relief is to be given.

The claim must specify the profits against which the deficit may be set off. Such claim may be for the whole or part of the loss and it is to be affected after the set-off of trading losses carried forward from earlier periods. The loss is utilised in priority to a trading loss of the deficit period (under TA 1988 s 393A(1)) and any non-trading credits carried back from subsequent periods (under s 83(2)(*c*) above). It cannot be set off against ring fence profits from petroleum extraction activities.

Claim to treat deficit as eligible for group relief

2 (1) This paragraph applies where the company makes a claim under section 83(2)(*b*) of this Act for the whole or any part of the deficit to be treated as eligible for group relief.

(2) The amount to which the claim relates shall be treated as if, for the purposes of subsection (1) of section 403 of the Taxes Act 1988 (group relief for trades)—

(*a*) it were a loss incurred in the deficit period by a company carrying on a trade; and

(*b*) the exclusions in subsection (2) of that section did not apply.

GENERAL NOTE

This paragraph applies to claims under s 83(2)(*b*) for a non-trading deficit to be group relieved.

The paragraph was amended as the Bill passed through Parliament. Originally, the amount claimed was to be treated as a charge on income of the deficit period for the purposes of TA 1988 s 403(7) which restricted the amount available for relief to the excess of the non-trading deficit over the surrendering company's profits of the period (or for an oil company the excess of its non oil profits by reason of TA 1988 s 494 which is effective for the purposes of s 403(7)).

As amended para 2 provides that the non-trading deficit is treated as a trading loss for the purposes of TA 1988 s 403(1). Further, s 403(2) (which limits relief under s 403(1) for certain trades with Schedule D Case V under s 393A(3) and for certain farming and market gardening trades under s 397) is disapplied.

Claim to carry back deficit to previous accounting periods

3 (1) This paragraph applies where a claim is made under section 83(2)(*c*) of this Act for the whole or any part of the deficit to be carried back to be set off against profits for earlier accounting periods.

(2) The claim shall have effect only if it relates to an amount that is equal to whichever is smaller of the following amounts, that is to say—

(*a*) so much of that deficit as is neither—

(i) an amount in relation to which a claim is made under subsection (2)(*a*) or (*b*) of section 83 of this Act, nor
(ii) an amount excluded by virtue of subsection (4) of that section from the amounts in relation to which claims may be made under subsection (2) of that section;

and

(*b*) the total amount of the profits available for relief under this paragraph.

(3) Where the claim has effect, the amount to which the claim relates shall be set off against the profits available for relief under this paragraph—

(*a*) by treating those profits as reduced accordingly; and
(*b*) to the extent that those profits are profits for more than one accounting period, by applying the relief to profits for a later period before setting off any remainder of the amount to which the claim relates against profits for an earlier period.

(4) Subject to sub-paragraph (5) below, the profits available for relief under this paragraph are the amounts which, for accounting periods ending within the permitted period, would be taken—

(*a*) apart from any relief under this paragraph, and
(*b*) after the giving of every relief which under sub-paragraph (6) below falls to be given in priority to relief under this paragraph,

to be chargeable under Case III of Schedule D as profits and gains arising from the company's loan relationships.

(5) Where any accounting period begins before the beginning of the permitted period but ends in the course of it—

(*a*) any amount chargeable in respect of that accounting period under Case III of Schedule D as profits and gains of the company's loan relationships shall be apportioned according to the proportions of the accounting period falling before and after the beginning of the permitted period; and
(*b*) the amount attributable, on that apportionment, to before the beginning of the permitted period shall not be available for relief under this paragraph.

(6) The reliefs which fall to be given in priority to relief under this paragraph in respect of any loss are—

(*a*) any relief in respect of a loss or deficit incurred or treated as incurred in an accounting period before the deficit period;
(*b*) any relief under section 338 of the Taxes Act 1988 (charges on income) in respect of payments made wholly and exclusively for the purposes of a trade;
(*c*) where the company is an investment company for the purposes of Part IV of that Act—

(i) any allowance under section 28 of the Capital Allowances Act 1990 (machinery and plant of investment companies);
(ii) any deduction in respect of management expenses under section 75 of the Taxes Act 1988; and
(iii) any relief under section 338 of the Taxes Act 1988 in respect of payments made wholly and exclusively for the purposes of its business;

(*d*) any relief under section 393A of the Taxes Act 1988 (trading losses set against profits of the same or any preceding accounting periods); and
(*e*) any relief in pursuance of a claim under section 83(2)(*a*) or (*b*) of this Act.

(7) In this paragraph "the permitted period" means the period of three years immediately preceding the beginning of the deficit period so far as that three year period falls after 31st March 1996.

GENERAL NOTE

This paragraph provides the rules for the carry back of non-trading deficits under s 83(2)(c). The amount claimed is limited to the lesser of—

(a) the amount of deficit left after the claims under s 83(2)(a) and (b) and excluding any deficit carried forward from earlier periods;
(b) the amount of "profits available for relief".

The "profits available for relief" are the company's Schedule D Case III profits from loan relationships for accounting periods within the "permitted period". For this purpose, the following reliefs are given in priority, to determine the profits available for relief—

(a) carried forward loss of deficits;
(b) charges on income made wholly and exclusively for the purposes of a trade relieved under TA 1988 s 338;
(c) for investment companies, capital allowances on plant and machinery, expenses of management and charges on income made wholly and exclusively in the course of its business;
(d) trading losses set off against profits of the same or preceding periods; and
(e) claims under s 83(2)(a) and (b).

The permitted period is three years immediately preceding the deficit period. The carry back is on a LIFO basis and in any event cannot go back to or before 31 March 1996. Where an accounting period straddles the opening of the three-year period sub-s (5) provides for the Schedule D Case III income to be apportioned.

Claim to carry forward deficit to next accounting period

4 (1) This paragraph applies where a claim is made under section 83(2)(d) of this Act for the whole or any part of the deficit to be carried forward and set against non-trading profits for the next accounting period.

(2) The amount to which the claim relates shall be set off against the non-trading profits of the company for the accounting period immediately following the deficit period, and those profits shall be treated as reduced accordingly.

(3) In this paragraph "non-trading profits", in relation to a company, means so much of any profits of the company (of whatever description) as do not consist in trading income for the purposes of section 393A of the Taxes Act 1988 (setting-off of trading losses against profits of the same or an earlier period).

GENERAL NOTE

This paragraph applies to claims under s 83(2)(d) for the carry forward of non-trading deficit against non-trading profits of the next accounting period.

The amount claimed is set off against the company's non-trading profits of the accounting period immediately following the deficit period. For this purpose non-trading profits are any profits of the company which are not trading income for the purposes of TA 1988 s 393A(a), (b) as "the total income which falls or would fall to be included in respect of the trade in the total profits of the company".

Construction of Schedule

5 In this Schedule "the deficit" and "the deficit period" shall be construed by reference to section 83(1) of this Act.

GENERAL NOTE

This paragraph provides for the definitions of "deficit period" and "the deficit" contained in s 83(1) to apply.

SCHEDULE 9

LOAN RELATIONSHIPS: SPECIAL COMPUTATIONAL PROVISIONS

GENERAL NOTE
This Schedule is introduced by s 84 and provides guidance on a range of computational issues.

Distributions

1 The credits and debits to be brought into account for the purposes of this Chapter shall not include any credits or debits relating to any amount falling, when paid, to be treated as a distribution.

GENERAL NOTE
This paragraph excludes any amount treated as a distribution (TA 1988 s 209) from being a debit or credit. Where only part of an amount is treated as a distribution, the balance will still be capable of being interest on a loan relationship.

Late interest

2 (1) This paragraph applies for the purpose of bringing debits into account for the purposes of this Chapter in respect of a debtor relationship of a company where an authorised accruals basis of accounting is used as respects that relationship in pursuance of section 87 of this Act.

(2) If—

(*a*) interest payable under that relationship is not paid within the period of twelve months following the end of the accounting period in which it would (apart from this paragraph) be treated as accruing, and
(*b*) credits representing the full amount of the interest are not for any accounting period brought into account for the purposes of this Chapter in respect of the corresponding creditor relationship,

then debits relating to that interest shall be brought into account on the assumption that the interest does not accrue until it is paid.

GENERAL NOTE
This paragraph provides for a deviation from the authorised accounting method where there is a delay in the payment of the interest.
Where an authorised basis of accounting is used by reason of s 87 (connected parties) but the interest has not been paid within 12 months of the end of the accounting period in which it is recognised, the interest will only be deductible on a paid basis.

Options etc

3 (1) This paragraph applies for determining the credits and debits to be brought into account for any accounting period in accordance with an authorised accruals basis of accounting, where—

(*a*) the answer to the question whether any amount will become due under a loan relationship after the end of that period,
(*b*) the amount which will become due under a loan relationship after the end of that period, or
(*c*) the time after the end of that period when an amount will become due under a loan relationship,

depends on the exercise of an option by a party to the relationship or an associate of his, or is otherwise under the control of such a party or an associate of his.

(2) It shall be assumed that the party or his associate will exercise his power to determine whether and on what date any amount will become due in the manner which (apart from taxation) appears, as at the end of the accounting period in question, to be the most advantageous to that party.

(3) In this paragraph "associate" has the meaning given for the purposes of Part XI of the Taxes Act 1988 by section 417(3) and (4) of that Act.

GENERAL NOTE

This paragraph provides the manner in which debits and credits are to be determined for an accounting period when an authorised accruals basis is used, but where there is a contingency upon which the outcome must be determined.

The paragraph applies where there is an option which may be exercised by a party to the relationship or an associate (as defined by TA 1988 s 417(3) and (4)) which affects—

(*a*) whether any amount will become due after the end of the period;
(*b*) the amount which will become due after the end of the period; or
(*c*) the time after the end of the period when an amount will become due.

Similarly, the paragraph applies where there is not an option, but the issue is otherwise under the control of the party or associate.

It is assumed that the party or the associate will exercise its power in the manner which "appears" to be the most advantageous to it (disregarding taxation) at the end of the relevant accounting period.

Foreign exchange gains and losses

4 (1) The credits and debits to be brought into account for the purposes of this Chapter shall be computed disregarding so much of any authorised accounting method as, by requiring the translation or conversion of amounts from one currency into another, has the effect that credits and debits produced by that method include sums in which profits, gains or losses arising from fluctuations in the value of a currency are to any extent represented.

(2) This paragraph is without prejudice to the provisions of Chapter II of Part II of the Finance Act 1993 (exchange gains and losses).

GENERAL NOTE

This paragraph provides for foreign exchange differences arising from an authorised accounting method affecting the calculation of debits and credits.

It provides that any amounts arising from exchange fluctuations are to be disregarded from the calculation of the debits and credits. Such amounts remain subject to the provisions of FA 1993.

Bad debt etc

5 (1) In determining the credits and debits to be brought into account in accordance with an accruals basis of accounting, a departure from the assumption in the case of the creditor relationships of a company that every amount payable under those relationships will be paid in full as it becomes due shall be allowed (subject to paragraph 6 below) to the extent only that—

(*a*) a debt is a bad debt;
(*b*) a doubtful debt is estimated to be bad; or
(*c*) a liability to pay any amount is released.

(2) Such a departure shall be made only where the accounting arrangements allowing the departure also require appropriate adjustments, in the form of credits, to be made if the whole or any part of an amount taken or estimated to represent an amount of bad debt is paid or otherwise ceases to be an amount in respect of which such a departure is allowed.

(3) Where—

(*a*) a liability to pay any amount under a debtor relationship of a company is released, and
(*b*) the release takes place in an accounting period for which an authorised accruals basis of accounting is used as respects that relationship,

no credit in respect of the release shall be required to be brought into account in the case of that company if the release is part of a relevant arrangement or compromise (within the meaning given by section 74(2) of the Taxes Act 1988) or the relationship is one as respects which section 87 of this Act requires the use of an authorised accruals basis of accounting.

GENERAL NOTE
This paragraph provides for bad debt relief when using an authorised accruals basis of accounting.

It is necessary to assume that amounts payable to the creditor will be paid when they become due, except, subject to para 6 below—

(*a*) if the debt is bad;
(*b*) if a doubtful debt is estimated to be bad; or
(*c*) the liability to pay is released.

This is dependent upon the accounting method requiring an adjusting credit if the circumstances change. There is an exception to this in that a credit need not be brought into account if the accruals basis is being used and there is a release as part of a relevant arrangement or compromise under TA 1988 s 74(2) (eg a voluntary arrangement under the Insolvency Act 1986) or the relationship is one to which s 79 applies so as to require the use of an accruals basis.

Bad debt etc where parties have a connection

6 (1) This paragraph applies where for any accounting period section 87 of this Act requires an authorised accruals basis of accounting to be used as respects a creditor relationship of a company.

(2) The credits and debits which for that period are to be brought into account for the purposes of this Chapter in accordance with that accounting method shall be computed subject to sub-paragraphs (3) to (6) below.

(3) The assumption that every amount payable under the relationship will be paid in full shall be applied as if no departure from that assumption were authorised by virtue of paragraph 5 above except where it is allowed by sub-paragraph (4) below.

(4) A departure from that assumption shall be allowed in relation to a liability to pay any amount to the company ("the creditor company") under the creditor relationship where—

(*a*) in consideration of, or of any entitlement to, any shares forming part of the ordinary share capital of the company on whom the liability would otherwise have fallen, the creditor company treats the liability as discharged; and
(*b*) the condition specified in sub-paragraph (5) below is satisfied.

(5) That condition is that there would be no connection between the two companies for the accounting period in which that consideration is given if the question whether there is such a connection for that period fell to be determined, in accordance with section 87 of this Act, by reference only to times before the creditor company acquired possession of, or any entitlement to, the shares in question.

(6) Where the company ceases in the accounting period in question to be a party to the relationship—

(*a*) the debits brought into account for that period in respect of that relationship shall not (subject to sub-paragraph (7) below) be more than they would have been had the company not ceased to be a party to the relationship; and
(*b*) the credits brought into account for that period in respect of the relationship shall not (subject to that sub-paragraph) be less than they would have been in those circumstances.

(7) In determining for the purposes of sub-paragraph (6) above the debits and credits that would have been brought into account if a company had not ceased to be a party to a loan relationship, no account shall be taken of any amounts that would have accrued at times after it ceased to be a party to the relationship.

GENERAL NOTE
This paragraph provides further guidance on bad debts where the debtor and creditor are "connected" and s 87 requires an authorised accruals basis to be used.

The paragraph provides that the credits and debits are to follow the authorised accruals basis, as if para 5 above did not apply unless sub-para (4) applies. Subparagraph (4) applies where the creditor company treats the liability as discharged in consideration (or entitlement to) ordinary shares of the debtor company, provided that the companies were not connected under s 87 at times before the creditor company acquired possession of, or entitlement to, the shares. (For this purpose connected refers to the parties being or having been companies under common control, or one in the control of the other, within the previous two years.)

Where the creditor ceases to be party to a connected loan relationship, the debits brought into accounts shall not be more than (and any credits shall not be less than) if the loan relationship had continued. This calculation ignores any debits or credits which would have accrued after the cessation.

Writing-off of government investments

7 (1) Where any government investment in a company is written off by the release of a liability to pay any amount under a debtor relationship of the company, no credit shall be required, in the case of that company, to be brought into account for the purposes of this Chapter in respect of that release.

(2) Subsections (7) and (8) of section 400 of the Taxes Act 1988 shall apply, as they apply for the purposes of that section, for construing the reference in sub-paragraph (1) above to the writing-off of a government investment.

GENERAL NOTE

This paragraph deals with the release of a government investment in a company.

It provides that no credit is required to be brought into account in such circumstances. For this purpose writing off of a government debt is as defined in TA 1988 s 400(7) and (8).

Restriction on writing off overseas sovereign debt etc

8 (1) This paragraph applies for the purposes of the use, as respects any loan relationship of a company and in conformity with paragraph 5 above, of an authorised accruals basis of accounting.

(2) Where the company is one to which a relevant overseas debt is owed, the debits and credits to be brought into account on that basis for the purposes of this Chapter shall be determined, for any accounting period of the company, on the assumption that it is not permissible for more than the relevant percentage of the debt to be estimated to be bad.

(3) For the purposes of this paragraph the relevant percentage of a debt for any accounting period of a company is (subject to sub-paragraph (4) below) such percentage (which may be zero) as may be determined, by reference to the position at the end of the relevant period of account, in accordance with regulations made by the Treasury.

(4) Where, apart from this sub-paragraph, the relevant percentage of a debt for any accounting period is more than the adjusted base percentage of that debt for that period, the relevant percentage of the debt for that period shall be taken to be equal to its adjusted base percentage for that period.

(5) For the purposes of this paragraph the adjusted base percentage of a debt for any accounting period shall be calculated by—

(*a*) taking the percentage which, in accordance with section 88B of the Taxes Act 1988 and any regulations made under that section, was or (assuming the debt to have been a debt of the company at the end of the base period) would have been the base percentage for that debt; and

(*b*) increasing that base percentage by five percentage points for every complete year (except the first) between—

(i) the time by reference to which the base percentage was, or would have been, determined, and

(ii) the end of the relevant period of account.

(6) In this paragraph "the relevant period of account", in relation to any accounting period of a company, means the period of account ending with that accounting period or, if a period of account does not end with that accounting period, the last period of account of the company to end before the end of that accounting period.

(7) In this paragraph "relevant overseas debt" means any debt which—

(*a*) satisfies one of the conditions specified in sub-paragraph (8) below; but

(*b*) is neither interest on a debt nor a debt which represents the consideration for the provision of goods or services.

(8) Those conditions are—

(*a*) that the debt is owed by an overseas State authority; or
(*b*) that payment of the debt is guaranteed by an overseas State authority; or
(*c*) that the debt is estimated to be bad for the purposes of this Chapter wholly or mainly because due payment is or may be prevented, restricted or subjected to conditions—

(i) by virtue of any law of a State or other territory outside the United Kingdom or any act of an overseas State authority; or
(ii) under any agreement entered into in consequence or anticipation of such a law or act.

(9) In this paragraph "overseas State authority" means—

(*a*) a State or other territory outside the United Kingdom;
(*b*) the government of such a State or territory;
(*c*) the central bank or other monetary authority of such a State or territory;
(*d*) a public or local authority in such a State or territory; or
(*e*) a body controlled by such a State, territory, government, bank or authority;

and for this purpose "controlled" shall be construed in accordance with section 840 of the Taxes Act 1988.

(10) The Treasury shall not make any regulations under this paragraph unless a draft of them has been laid before and approved by a resolution of the House of Commons.

GENERAL NOTE
This paragraph imposes certain additional restrictions on relief for bad debts on "relevant overseas debt" where an authorised accruals basis is used in place of TA 1988 ss 88A and 88B. (These are supplemented by further restrictions in para 9 below.)
In a similar fashion to TA 1988 s 88A, a "relevant overseas debt" is a debt which is not interest nor a debt in consideration for goods or services provided and is—

(*a*) owed, or the payment of which is guaranteed, by an "overseas State authority"; or
(*b*) which is estimated to be bad wholly or mainly because there are restrictions preventing payment (or subjecting conditions) because of the law of a state or other non-UK territory or act of an "overseas State authority". This extends to any agreement as a result of, or in anticipation of, such a law or act.

An "overseas State authority" is defined by sub-para (9).
The relief available for such a debt which is estimated to be bad is limited to the "relevant percentage", which may be zero and is to be set by Treasury regulations (approved by a resolution of the House of Commons) by reference to the position at the end of the "relevant period of account" (as defined by sub-para (6)). This amount is restricted so that it cannot exceed the "adjusted base percentage" which is the base percentage of the debt (under TA 1988 s 88B and associated regulations) and increasing it by 5 per cent for each subsequent year.

Further restriction on bringing into account losses on overseas sovereign debt etc

9 (1) This paragraph applies where—

(*a*) for an accounting period in which a company ceases to be a party to a loan relationship ("the loss period") any amount falls for the purposes of this Chapter to be brought into account in respect of that relationship in accordance with an authorised accruals basis of accounting;
(*b*) by the bringing into account of that amount in that period a loss incurred in connection with a relevant overseas debt falling within sub-paragraph (2) below is treated for the purposes of this Chapter as arising in that period;
(*c*) the amount of the loss is greater than 5 per cent. of the debt; and
(*d*) the loss is not one incurred on a disposal of the debt to an overseas State authority in a case in which the State or territory by reference to which it is an overseas State authority is the same as that by reference to which the debt is a relevant overseas debt.

(2) A relevant overseas debt falls within this sub-paragraph if—

(*a*) a deduction has been made in respect of the debt in accordance with section 74(1)(*j*) of the Taxes Act 1988 for any period of account of the company ending before 1st April 1996;

(b) any debit relating to the debt has been brought into account for the purposes of this Chapter in accordance with so much of any authorised accruals basis of accounting as relates to the matters mentioned in paragraph 5(1)(a) to (c) above; or

(c) the debt is one acquired by the company on or after 20th March 1990 for a consideration greater than the price which it might reasonably have been expected to fetch on a sale in the open market at the time of acquisition.

(3) Where this paragraph applies, the amounts brought into account for the purposes of this Chapter in the loss period shall be such as to secure that only so much of the loss as does not exceed 5 per cent. of the debt is treated for the purposes of this Chapter as arising in the loss period; but sub-paragraph (4) below applies as respects further parts of that loss until the loss is exhausted.

(4) A part of the loss may, in accordance with sub-paragraph (5) below, be brought into account for the purposes of this Chapter in the form of a debit for any accounting period after the loss period ("a subsequent period").

(5) The amount of the debit brought into account under sub-paragraph (4) above for any subsequent period shall not exceed such amount as, together with any parts of the loss which for earlier periods have been represented by—

(a) the amount of the loss treated as arising in the loss period in accordance with sub-paragraph (3) above, or

(b) debits brought into account in accordance with this sub-paragraph,

is equal to 5 per cent of the debt for each complete year that has elapsed between the beginning of the loss period and the end of the subsequent period.

(6) In this paragraph "overseas State authority" and "relevant overseas debt" have the same meanings as in paragraph 8 above.

(7) References in this paragraph to a loss do not include so much of any loss as falls to be disregarded for the purposes of this Chapter by virtue of paragraph 10 below or to any loss incurred before 1st April 1996.

GENERAL NOTE
This paragraph introduces further restrictions in respect of "relevant overseas debts", but on disposal. It replaces TA 1988 s 88C where losses arise after 1 April 1996.

The provisions apply to losses incurred where the company, using an authorised accruals basis, ceases to be party to certain "relevant overseas debt", where the loss exceeds 5 per cent of the debt. The "relevant overseas debt" is one—

(a) where a deduction has been claimed for bad debt relief under TA 1988 s 74(1)(j) for an accounting period ending before 1 April 1996;

(b) where a debit has been brought into account under the bad debt provisions of para 5(1) (a)–(c) above; or

(c) where the debt was acquired on or after 20 March 1990 (the effective date for s 88C) for a consideration greater than the then market value.

Where the paragraph applies, the relief is spread with a maximum amount of 5 per cent of the debt allowed each year.

Imported losses etc

10 (1) This paragraph applies in the case of a company ("the chargeable company") for an accounting period ("the loss period") where—

(a) an authorised accruals basis of accounting is used as respects a loan relationship of that company for the loss period;

(b) in accordance with that basis of accounting there is an amount which would fall (apart from this paragraph) to be brought into account for the purposes of this Chapter in respect of that relationship;

(c) by the bringing into account of that amount in that period a loss incurred in connection with that loan relationship would be treated for the purposes of this Chapter as arising in that period; and

(d) that loss is referable in whole or in part to a time when the relationship was not subject to United Kingdom taxation.

(2) The amounts brought into account for the purposes of this Chapter in the loss period shall be such as to secure that no part of the loss that is referable to a time when the relationship was not subject to United Kingdom taxation shall be treated for the purposes of this Chapter as arising in the loss period or any other accounting period of the chargeable company.

(3) For the purposes of this paragraph a loss is referable to a time when a relationship is not subject to United Kingdom taxation to the extent that, at the time to which the loss is referable, the chargeable company would not have been chargeable to tax in the United Kingdom on any profits or gains arising from the relationship.

(4) Sub-paragraph (3) above shall have effect where the chargeable company was not a party to the relationship at the time to which the loss is referable as if the reference to that company were a reference to the person who at that time was in the same position as respects the relationship as is subsequently held by the chargeable company.

GENERAL NOTE
This paragraph restricts relief available under an authorised accruals basis to prevent losses being recognised which relate to periods when the loan relationship was outside the scope of UK tax.

For this purpose, the loss is referable to a period when the loan relationship is outside the scope of UK tax if the chargeable company would not have been subject to tax on any profit or gain arising from the loan relationship. This applies even where the chargeable company itself was not party to the loan relationship, but the person who was party would not have been so chargeable.

Transactions not at arm's length

11 (1) Subject to sub-paragraphs (2) and (3) below, where—

(a) debits or credits in respect of a loan relationship of a company fall to be brought into account for the purposes of this Chapter in accordance with an authorised accounting method,

(b) those debits or credits relate to amounts arising from, or incurred for the purposes of, a related transaction, and

(c) that transaction is not a transaction at arm's length,

the debits or credits given by that method shall be determined on the assumption that the transaction was entered into on the terms on which it would have been entered into between independent persons.

(2) Sub-paragraph (1) above shall not apply to debits arising from the acquisition of rights under a loan relationship where those rights are acquired for less than market value.

(3) Sub-paragraph (1) above does not apply—

(a) in the case of any related transaction between two companies that are members of the same group; or

(b) in relation to a member of a group of companies, in the case of any transaction which is part of a series of transactions having the same effect as a related transaction between two members of the same group.

(4) In this paragraph "related transaction" has the same meaning as in section 84 of this Act.

(5) Section 170 of the Taxation of Chargeable Gains Act 1992 (groups etc) shall apply for the interpretation of this paragraph as it applies for the interpretation of sections 171 to 181 of that Act.

GENERAL NOTE
This paragraph provides for the application of arm's length terms to transactions not at arm's length.

It applies where an authorised accruals basis is used and debits and credits arise from (or are incurred for the purposes) of a "related transaction", which is not at arm's length. Where it applies, the debits and credits are determined as if it had been a transaction between independent persons.

The paragraph does not apply to—

(a) debits arising from the acquisition of rights for less than market value;

(*b*) related transactions between two group companies (as defined in TCGA 1992 s 170); and
(*c*) a series of transactions having the same effect as (*b*).

"Related transaction" is as defined in s 84.

Continuity of treatment: groups etc

12 (1) Subject to paragraph 15 below, this paragraph applies where, as a result of—

(*a*) a related transaction between two members of the same group of companies,
(*b*) a series of transactions having the same effect as a related transaction between two companies each of which has been a member of the same group at any time in the course of that series of transactions,
(*c*) the transfer between two companies of the whole or part of the long term business of any insurance company in accordance with a scheme sanctioned by a court under Part I of Schedule 2C to the Insurance Companies Act 1982, or
(*d*) any transfer between two companies which is a qualifying overseas transfer within the meaning of paragraph 4A of Schedule 19AC to the Taxes Act 1988 (transfer of business of overseas life insurance company),

one of those companies ("the transferee company") directly or indirectly replaces the other ("the transferor company") as a party to a loan relationship.

(2) The credits and debits to be brought into account for the purposes of this Chapter in the case of the two companies shall be determined as follows—

(*a*) the transaction, or series of transactions, by virtue of which the replacement takes place shall be disregarded except for the purpose of identifying the company in whose case any debit or credit not relating to that transaction, or those transactions, is to be brought into account; and
(*b*) the transferor company and the transferee company shall be deemed (except for that purpose) to be the same company.

(3) This paragraph does not apply by virtue of sub-paragraph (1)(*a*) or (*b*) above in relation to any transfer of an asset, or of any rights under or interest in an asset, where the asset was within one of the categories set out in section 440(4)(*a*) to (*e*) of the Taxes Act 1988 (assets held for certain categories of long term business) either immediately before the transfer or immediately afterwards.

(4) This paragraph does not apply by virtue of sub-paragraph (1)(*c*) or (*d*) above in relation to any transfer of an asset, or of any rights under or interest in an asset, where—

(*a*) the asset was within one of the categories set out in section 440(4) of the Taxes Act 1988 immediately before the transfer; and
(*b*) is not within that category immediately afterwards.

(5) For the purposes of sub-paragraph (4) above, where one of the companies is an overseas life insurance company an asset shall be taken to be within the same category both immediately before the transfer and immediately afterwards if it—

(*a*) was within one category immediately before the transfer; and
(*b*) is within the corresponding category immediately afterwards.

(6) References in this paragraph to one company replacing another as a party to a loan relationship shall include references to a company becoming a party to any loan relationship under which its rights are equivalent to those of the other company under a loan relationship of which that other company has previously ceased to be a party.

(7) For the purposes of sub-paragraph (6) above a person's rights under a loan relationship are equivalent to rights under another such relationship if they entitle the holder of an asset representing the relationship—

(*a*) to the same rights against the same persons as to capital, interest and dividends, and
(*b*) to the same remedies for the enforcement of those rights,

notwithstanding any difference in the total nominal amounts of the assets, in the form in which they are held or in the manner in which they can be transferred.

(8) Sub-paragraphs (4) and (5) of paragraph 11 above have effect for the purposes of this paragraph as they have effect for the purposes of that paragraph.

(9) In this paragraph "overseas life insurance company" has the same meaning as in Chapter I of Part XII of the Taxes Act 1988.

GENERAL NOTE
This paragraph deals with transfers of loans where one group company directly or indirectly replaces another group company as a party to a loan relationship.
The paragraph applies where such an event happens as a result of—

(a) a "related transaction" (as defined by s 84) between two group companies (as defined by TCGA 1992 s 170);
(b) a series of transactions having the same effect as (a), where the two companies were members of the same group at some time during the course of the series of transactions; or
(c) where there is a transfer of long-term insurance business sanctioned by the court or by a regulatory authority or court in another EEA state.

Replacement for this purpose includes the situation where one loan relationship is ceased and a company becomes party to a loan relationship with equivalent rights. The rights are equivalent if the holder of an asset representing the loan relationship is entitled to the same rights against the same persons as to capital, interest and dividends and for enforcement of those rights.
The transfer is to be disregarded for all purposes except that the transferee company becomes entitled to any debits and credits not relating to the transaction (ie the remaining debits and credits).
The paragraph does apply [by virtue of (a) or (b) above] where the asset is transferred into or out of the long-term business fund of an insurance company (under TA 1988 s 440(4)(a) to (e)). Similarly, the paragraph does not apply [by virtue of (c) above] where the asset is held by the transferor company for one category of business [set out in TA 1988 s 440(4)] and by the transferee company for another and this exception also applies where any of the parties is an overseas life insurance company (as defined in TA 1988 s 431(2)).

Loan relationships for unallowable purposes

13 (1) Where in any accounting period a loan relationship of a company has an unallowable purpose, the debits which, for that period fall, in the case of that company, to be brought into account for purposes of this Chapter shall not include so much of the debits given by the authorised accounting method used as respects that relationship as, on a just and reasonable apportionment, is attributable to the unallowable purpose.

(2) For the purposes of this paragraph a loan relationship of a company shall be taken to have an unallowable purpose in an accounting period where the purposes for which, at times during that period, the company—

(a) is a party to the relationship, or
(b) enters into transactions which are related transactions by reference to that relationship,

include a purpose ("the unallowable purpose") which is not amongst the business or other commercial purposes of the company.

(3) For the purposes of this paragraph the business and other commercial purposes of a company do not include the purposes of any part of its activities in respect of which it is not within the charge to corporation tax.

(4) For the purposes of this paragraph, where one of the purposes for which a company—

(a) is a party to a loan relationship at any time, or
(b) enters into a transaction which is a related transaction by reference to any loan relationship of the company,

is a tax avoidance purpose, that purpose shall be taken to be a business or other commercial purpose of the company only where it is not the main purpose, or one of the main purposes, for which the company is a party to the relationship at that time or, as the case may be, for which the company enters into that transaction.

(5) The reference in sub-paragraph (4) above to a tax avoidance purpose is a reference to any purpose that consists in securing a tax advantage (whether for the company or any other person).

(6) In this paragraph—

"related transaction" has the same meaning as in section 84 of this Act; and

"tax advantage" has the same meaning as in Chapter I of Part XVII of the Taxes Act 1988 (tax avoidance).

GENERAL NOTE

This paragraph excludes reliefs for any debits arising from "unallowable" loan relationships.

The paragraph was subject to significant amendment during the Standing Committee debate.

A loan relationship has an "unallowable purpose" in an accounting period if, during the period, the purposes for which the company is party to the relationship or enters into related transactions (as defined by s 84), include one which is not amongst the business or other commercial purposes of the company. The business or other commercial purposes do not include any part of its activities which are outside the charge to corporation tax.

Where one of the purposes is a tax avoidance purpose, it will only be taken to be a business or other commercial purpose if it is not the main, or one of the main purposes for the company then being a party to the relationship or for entering into the transaction. For this purpose, tax avoidance purpose refers to securing a tax advantage, as defined by TA 1988 s 709, whether for the company or some other person.

The amount of the debits to be attributed to the unallowable purposes shall be made on a just and reasonable basis.

Debits and credits treated as relating to capital expenditure

14 (1) This paragraph applies where any debit or credit given by an authorised accounting method for any accounting period in respect of a loan relationship of a company is allowed by normal accountancy practice to be treated, in the accounts of the company, as an amount brought into account in determining the value of a fixed capital asset or project.

(2) Notwithstanding the application to it of the treatment allowed by normal accountancy practice, the debit or credit shall be brought into account for the purposes of corporation tax, for the accounting period for which it is given, in the same way as a debit or credit which, in accordance with normal accountancy practice, is brought into account in determining the company's profit or loss for that period.

GENERAL NOTE

This paragraph provides for the treatment of interest (debit or credit) which is capitalised in valuing a fixed capital asset or project under normal accountancy practice.

Such interest is to be recognised for tax purposes, for the accounting period in which it is "given", in the same way as a debit or credit is recognised in the company's profit and loss account in accordance with normal accountancy practice.

Repo transactions and stock-lending

15 (1) In determining the debits and credits to be brought into account for the purposes of this Chapter in respect of any loan relationship, it shall be assumed that a disposal or acquisition to which this paragraph applies is not a related transaction for the purposes of section 84 of this Act.

(2) This paragraph applies to any such disposal or acquisition of rights or liabilities under the relationship as is made in pursuance of any repo or stock-lending arrangements.

(3) In this paragraph "repo or stock-lending arrangements" means any arrangements consisting in or involving an agreement or series of agreements under which provision is made—

(a) for the transfer from one person to another of any rights under that relationship; and

(b) for the transferor, or a person connected with him, subsequently to be or become entitled, or required—

(i) to have the same or equivalent rights transferred to him; or

(ii) to have rights in respect of benefits accruing in respect of that relationship on redemption.

(4) For the purposes of sub-paragraph (3) above rights under a loan relationship are

equivalent to rights under another such relationship if they entitle the holder of an asset representing the relationship—

(*a*) to the same rights against the same persons as to capital, interest and dividends, and

(*b*) to the same remedies for the enforcement of those rights,

notwithstanding any difference in the total nominal amounts of the assets, in the form in which they are held or in the manner in which they can be transferred.

(5) Nothing in this paragraph shall prevent any redemption or discharge of rights or liabilities under a loan relationship to which any repo or stock-lending arrangements relate from being treated for the purposes of this Chapter as a related transaction (within the meaning of section 84 of this Act).

(6) This paragraph is without prejudice to section 730A(2) and (6) of the Taxes Act 1988 (deemed payments of loan interest in the case of the sale and repurchase of securities).

(7) Section 839 of the Taxes Act 1988 (connected persons) applies for the purposes of this paragraph.

GENERAL NOTE
This paragraph provides that certain transactions will not be treated as "related transactions" under s 84 and are therefore disregarded.

The paragraph applies to disposals and acquisitions under "repo or stock lending arrangements". Repos are agreements whereby one party sells, for instance, a security and at the same time agrees to buy it back at a future date for a predetermined price. A stock loan is an agreement whereby one party will lend securities to another person, typically secured in some way, eg by cash or other securities (see also TA 1988 s 129). Both types of transactions are critical to the operation of the financial markets. Typically normal accountancy practice does not regard an asset subject to such arrangements as having been transferred between the parties but instead reflects the economic rather than legal ownership of the asset.

Under para 15 "repo or stock lending arrangements" are any arrangements under an agreement or series of agreements where the rights under a loan relationship are transferred to a person and the transferor or a connected person (as defined under TA 1988 s 839) is entitled or required to have the same or equivalent rights transferred to him. It also applies where the transferor's rights or entitlement relate to the benefits accruing on redemption of the rights (eg a repo to maturity). The rights are equivalent if the holder of an asset representing the loan relationship is entitled to the same rights against the same persons as to capital, interest and dividends and for enforcement of those rights, although there may be differences in the nominal amounts, or in the holding or transfer of the assets.

The paragraph does not prevent the operation of TA 1988, s 730A(2) and (6), which cause the price differential on sales and repurchases of securities to be treated as interest.

A redemption or discharge of rights or liabilities under a loan relationship to which a repo or stock loan relate can still be a "related transaction".

Imputed interest

16 (1) This paragraph applies where, in pursuance of sections 770 to 772 of the Taxes Act 1988 (transactions at an undervalue or overvalue), as those sections have effect by virtue of section 773(4) of that Act, any amount falls to be treated as interest payable under a loan relationship of a company.

(2) Those sections shall have effect, notwithstanding the provisions of any authorised accounting method, so as to require credits or debits relating to the deemed interest to be brought into account for the purposes of this Chapter to the same extent as they would be in the case of an actual amount of interest accruing or becoming due and payable under the loan relationship in question.

GENERAL NOTE
This paragraph provides for the provisions of the Finance Act 1996 to apply to interest imputed under an existing loan relationship as a result of a transfer pricing adjustment under TA 1988 ss 770–772.

The position of interest arising where there is no existing deemed loan relationship is covered by s 100.

Discounted securities where companies have a connection

17 (1) This paragraph applies as respects any accounting period ("the relevant period") where—

(*a*) a debtor relationship of a company ("the issuing company") is represented by a relevant discounted security issued by that company;

(*b*) the benefit of that security is available to another company at any time in that period;

(*c*) for that period there is a connection between the issuing company and the other company; and

(*d*) credits representing the full amount of the discount that is referable to that period are not for any accounting period brought into account for the purposes of this Chapter in respect of the corresponding creditor relationship.

(2) The debits falling in the case of the issuing company to be brought into account for the purposes of this Chapter in respect of the loan relationship shall be adjusted so that every debit relating to the amount of the discount that is referable to the relevant period is brought into account for the accounting period in which the security is redeemed, instead of for the relevant period.

(3) References in this paragraph to the amount of the discount that is referable to the relevant period are references to the amount relating to the difference between—

(*a*) the issue price of the security, and

(*b*) the amount payable on redemption,

which (apart from this paragraph) would for the relevant period be brought into account for the purposes of this Chapter in the case of the issuing company.

(4) In this paragraph "relevant discounted security" has the same meaning as in Schedule 13 to this Act; and the provisions of that Schedule shall apply for the purposes of this paragraph for determining the difference between the issue price of a security and the amount payable on redemption as they apply for the purposes of paragraph 3(3) of that Schedule.

(5) For the purposes of this paragraph there is a connection between one company and another for the relevant period if (subject to the following provisions of this paragraph)—

(*a*) there is a time in that period, or in the period of two years before the beginning of that period, when one of the companies has had control of the other; or

(*b*) there is a time in that period, or in those two years, when both the companies have been under the control of the same person.

(6) Two companies which have at any time been under the control of the same person shall not, by virtue of that fact, be taken for the purposes of this paragraph to be companies between whom there is a connection if the person was the Crown, a Minister of the Crown, a government department, a Northern Ireland department, a foreign sovereign power or an international organisation.

(7) Section 88 of this Act shall apply for the purposes of this paragraph in the case of a debtor relationship of a company represented by a relevant discounted security as it would apply for the purposes of section 87 of this Act in the case of the corresponding creditor relationship of the company holding that security and, accordingly, as if—

(*a*) the reference to section 87 of this Act in section 88(4)(*b*) were a reference to this paragraph; and

(*b*) section 88(5) were omitted.

(8) For the purposes of this paragraph the benefit of a security is available to a company if—

(*a*) that security, or any entitlement to rights attached to it, is beneficially owned by that company; or

(*b*) that company is indirectly entitled, by reference to a series of loan transactions, to the benefit of any rights attached to the security.

(9) Subsections (2) to (6) of section 416 of the Taxes Act 1988 (meaning of "control")

shall apply for the purposes of this paragraph as they apply for the purposes of Part XI of that Act.

GENERAL NOTE
This paragraph applies to any accounting period (the "relevant accounting period") where the loan is a "relevant discounted security" and the parties are connected, providing that the issuer does not get relief until maturity.

The paragraph applies where a "relevant discounted security" has been issued and the benefit of it is at any time in that period "available to a company" "connected" with the issuing company. In these circumstances, where credits representing the full amount of the discount referable to that relevant period are not brought into account for any accounting period by the creditor company the discount may only be recognised at redemption. For this purpose, the amount which is referable to the relevant period is the element of the difference between the issue and redemption price, which would otherwise have been recognised under Chapter II by the issuing company.

"Relevant discounted security" is as defined in Sch 13 and the provisions of that Schedule apply in determining the amount of the discount.

The benefit of a security is "available to a company" if the security or any rights attached to it are beneficially owned by the company or the company is indirectly entitled to the benefits of those rights by reference to a series of loan transactions.

Two companies are "connected" at any time if one has the control of the other or both are under control of the same person during the relevant period. The test is extended to periods within the previous two years before the beginning of the accounting period in question. Control is as defined by TA 1988 s 416(2)–(6). However, two companies are not connected if the controlling person was the Crown, a Minister of the Crown, a government department, a Northern Ireland department, a foreign sovereign power or international organisation. Section 88, which provides exemptions from the connected party provisions of s 87, applies for the purposes of para 17 as if the reference to s 87 in s 88(4) and as if s 88 were omitted.

Discounted securities of close companies

18 (1) This paragraph applies for any accounting period where—

(*a*) a debtor relationship of a close company is represented by a relevant discounted security issued by the company; and

(*b*) at any time in or before that period that security has been beneficially owned by a person who at the time was—

(i) a participator in the company;
(ii) an associate of such a participator; or
(iii) a company of which such a participator has control.

(2) The debits falling in the case of the company to be brought into account for the purposes of this Chapter in respect of the loan relationship shall be adjusted so that no amount is brought into account in respect of the difference between—

(*a*) the issue price of the security, and
(*b*) the amount payable on redemption,

for any accounting period before that in which the security is redeemed.

(3) In this paragraph "relevant discounted security" has the same meaning as in Schedule 13 to this Act; and the provisions of that Schedule shall apply for the purposes of this paragraph for determining the difference between the issue price of a security and the amount payable on redemption as they apply for the purposes of paragraph 3(3) of that Schedule.

(4) In this paragraph—

"associate" has the meaning given in section 417(3) and (4) of the Taxes Act 1988;
"control" shall be construed in accordance with section 416(2) to (6) of that Act; and
"participator" means a person who, by virtue of section 417 of that Act, is a participator in the company for the purposes of Part XI of that Act, other than a person who is a participator for those purposes by virtue only of his holding a relevant discounted security issued by the company.

(5) In determining whether a person who carries on a business of banking is a participator in a company for the purposes of this paragraph, there shall be disregarded any securities of the company acquired by him in the ordinary course of his business.

GENERAL NOTE

This paragraph applies where the loan is a "relevant discounted security" and it is issued by a close company, providing that the issuer does not get relief until maturity in certain situations.

The paragraph applies where such a security has been beneficially owned by a "participator", or his "associate" or a company which is under the "control" of such a participator. In these circumstances the discount is not recognised until maturity.

"Relevant discounted security" is as defined in Sch 13 and the provisions of that Schedule apply in determining the amount of the discount.

"Participator" is as defined in TA 1988 s 417, other than a person who would be a participator only because of its holding of the relevant discounted security. Securities acquired by a bank in the ordinary course of its banking business shall be disregarded for the purposes of determining whether it is a participator.

"Associate" is as defined in TA 1988 s 417(3) and (4) and "control" as in s 416(2)–(6).

SCHEDULE 10
Section 98

LOAN RELATIONSHIPS: COLLECTIVE INVESTMENT SCHEMES

BACKGROUND NOTE

UK collective investment schemes are tax advantaged in various ways. This has meant that the basis of taxing the profits and gains arising out of their loan relationships, which applies generally to companies chargeable to tax in the UK, is unlikely to be appropriate if those tax advantages are to be maintained and special bases have had to be carved out from the basic regime—

(*a*) investment trusts and venture capital trusts are to be subject to a modified accruals basis (and may not use the ordinary "accruals" or the "mark-to-market" basis);

(*b*) authorised unit trusts (and unauthorised unit trusts) will not be subject to the loan relationships legislation; and

(*c*) in respect of the calculation of their UK equivalent profit, distributing offshore funds are to be treated in the same way as authorised unit trusts and effectively exempted from this legislation.

However, investors in certain authorised unit trusts and offshore funds (essentially those which are invested as to 60 per cent or more of their gross investment value in debt instruments) will find that their investment returns are subject to the loan relationships legislation.

Investment trusts

1 (1) This paragraph applies for the purposes of the application of this Chapter in relation to investment trusts and venture capital trusts.

(2) If the Treasury by order approve the use of an accounting method for the creditor relationships of investment trusts or venture capital trusts—

(*a*) that method, instead of any method for which section 85 of this Act provides, shall be used as respects the creditor relationships of the trusts for which it is approved; and

(*b*) this Chapter shall have effect (subject to the provisions of the order) as if the accounting method were, for the purposes for which it is approved, an authorised accruals basis of accounting.

(3) Where an approval is given under this paragraph, it must be an approval of one of the following—

(*a*) the use of an accruals basis of accounting appearing to the Treasury to be recognised by normal accounting practice for use in the case of investment trusts;

(*b*) the use, with such modifications as may be provided for in the order, of an accruals basis of accounting appearing to them to be so recognised; or

(*c*) the use, with such modifications as may be so provided for, of an accounting method which, apart from the order, would be an authorised accruals basis of accounting.

(4) An order under this paragraph may provide for any approval of the use (with or without modifications) of a basis of accounting recognised by normal accounting practice to have effect in relation to accounting periods beginning before the time as from which the use of that method is recognised and before the making of the order.

GENERAL NOTE

Authorised investment trust companies ("AITC") and venture capital trusts ("VCT") are subject to tax on their income but, providing that they continue to meet all of the qualifying conditions of TA 1988 s 842, are exempt from tax on their capital gains. Broadly, both AITCs and VCTs are subject to the loan relationships legislation but neither of the two alternative bases of accounting referred to in FA 1996 s 85 (the "accruals basis" and the "mark-to-market" basis) are to apply to them. Instead, a special authorised accruals basis of accounting will apply.

This authorised basis will follow the normal accounting bases which apply to AITCs (and VCTs), as set out in the Statement of Recommended Practice ("the SORP") issued in January 1996 by the Association of Investment Trust Companies. The SORP provides for an acceptable modified version of the accruals basis which will apply to holdings of securities and other debt instruments. Any profits or losses not recognised as accounting income on this accruals basis will be treated as capital (and therefore not subject to tax).

The s 842(1)(*a*), "income derived wholly or mainly from shares" test can be met since the approved accounting basis will be defining the accrued income derived from loan relationships as

313

income from shares or securities. Some problems might have been anticipated from the requirement in s 842(1)(*d*), the prohibition against distributing capital surplus. However, since the SORP provides that all of the return on debt instruments accounted for as accounting income on this modified basis is, by definition, income and all other amounts are, by definition, capital, there should not be any need to breach this condition. The condition in s 842(1)(*e*), the retention test, should also provide no difficulties if the SORP is followed since there will be no distortions between the amount of the accounting profit and the measure of profit for tax purposes.

Authorised unit trusts

2 (1) The provisions of this Chapter so far as they relate to the creditor relationships of a company shall not apply for the purposes of corporation tax in computing the profits or losses of an authorised unit trust.

(2) For the purposes of corporation tax the profits and gains, and losses, that are to be taken to arise from the creditor relationships of an authorised unit trust shall be computed—

(*a*) in accordance with the provisions applicable, in the case of unauthorised unit trusts, for the purposes of income tax; and
(*b*) as if the provisions so applicable had effect in relation to an accounting period of an authorised unit trust as they have effect, in the case of unauthorised unit trusts, in relation to a year of assessment.

(3) In relation to the first accounting period of any authorised unit trust to end after 31st March 1996, the reference in sub-paragraph (2)(*a*) above to the provisions applicable for the purposes of income tax is a reference to the provisions so applicable for the year 1996–97.

(4) In this paragraph "unauthorised unit trust" means the trustees of any unit trust scheme which is not an authorised unit trust but is a unit trust scheme for the purposes of section 469 of the Taxes Act 1988.

GENERAL NOTE
Authorised unit trusts will be kept entirely outside this legislation and income and gains arising from loan relationships will be taxed in the same way as before. That is: the income will continue to be taxed on a receipts basis, while capital gains and losses will continue to be exempt from tax.

Distributing offshore funds

3 (1) For the purposes of paragraph 5(1) of Schedule 27 to the Taxes Act 1988 (computation of UK equivalent profit), the assumptions to be made in determining what, for any period, would be the total profits of an offshore fund are to include an assumption that paragraph 2 above applies in the case of that offshore fund as it applies in the case of any authorised unit trust.

GENERAL NOTE
In calculating whether or not an offshore fund will meet the UK equivalent profits tests and, therefore, can be a distributing offshore fund—in this case that it has distributed at least 85 per cent of the equivalent UK taxable profits of the accounting period—the calculation is to be made on the footing that the provisions of the new loan relationships legislation do not apply.

Company holdings in unit trusts and offshore funds

4 (1) This paragraph applies for the purposes of corporation tax in relation to any company where—

(*a*) at any time in an accounting period that company holds any of the following ("a relevant holding"), that is to say, any rights under a unit trust scheme or any relevant interests in an offshore fund; and
(*b*) there is a time in that period when that scheme or fund fails to satisfy the non-qualifying investments test.

(2) The Corporation Tax Acts shall have effect for that accounting period in accordance with sub-paragraphs (3) and (4) below as if the relevant holding were rights under a creditor relationship of the company.

(3) An accruals basis of accounting shall not be used for the purposes of this Chapter as respects the company's relevant holdings.

(4) The authorised mark to market basis of accounting used for any accounting period as respects a relevant holding shall not be taken, for the purposes of this Chapter, to require the bringing into account of any credit relating to any distributions of an authorised unit trust which become due and payable in that period other than interest distributions within the meaning of section 468L(3) of the Taxes Act 1988.

GENERAL NOTE
 If at any time during an accounting period a company holds shares or units in an offshore fund or an authorised unit trust and that investment vehicle has failed the 60 per cent test described at para 6 below, the holding will be treated as a "creditor relationship". However, an authorised accruals basis of accounting is not to be applied. A mark-to-market basis can apply but dividend or foreign income distributions of an authorised unit trust are not required to be brought into account in the calculation of the return.
 Put more simply, if the mark-to-market basis is not adopted by the corporate unit-holder, the return brought into account will be any interest distribution received from an authorised unit trust and any distribution received from an offshore fund which has failed the 60 per cent test. If a mark-to-market basis is adopted, the return will consist of any uplift in value over the accounting period plus any interest distribution received from an authorised unit trust and any distribution received from an offshore fund (which has failed the 60 per cent test). Dividend distributions and foreign income distributions will continue to be treated as such and will remain outside the loan relationships regime.

Holding becoming or ceasing to be paragraph 4 holding

5 (1) Section 116 of the 1992 Act (reorganisations etc involving qualifying corporate bonds) shall have effect in accordance with the assumptions for which this paragraph provides if—

(*a*) a relevant holding is held by a company both at the end of one accounting period and at the beginning of the next; and
(*b*) paragraph 4 above applies to that holding for one of those periods but not for the other.

(2) Where—

(*a*) the accounting period for which paragraph 4 above applies to the relevant holding is the second of the periods mentioned in sub-paragraph (1) above, and
(*b*) the first of those periods is not a period ending on 31st March 1996 or a period at the end of which there is deemed under section 212 of the 1992 Act to have been a disposal of the relevant holding,

the holding shall be assumed to have become a holding to which paragraph 4 above applies for the second of those periods in consequence of the occurrence, at the end of the first period, of a transaction such as is mentioned in section 116(1) of that Act.

(3) In relation to the transaction that is deemed to have occurred as mentioned in sub-paragraph (2) above—

(*a*) the relevant holding immediately before the beginning of the second accounting period shall be assumed to be the old asset for the purposes of section 116 of the 1992 Act; and
(*b*) the relevant holding immediately after the beginning of that period shall be assumed for those purposes to be the new asset.

(4) Where the accounting period for which paragraph 4 above applies to the relevant holding is the first of the periods mentioned in sub-paragraph (1) above, then, for the purposes of the 1992 Act—

(*a*) the holding shall be assumed to have become a holding to which paragraph 4 above does not apply for the second of those periods in consequence of the occurrence at the beginning of the second of those periods of a transaction such as is mentioned in section 116(1) of that Act;
(*b*) the relevant holding immediately before the beginning of that second period shall

be assumed, in relation to that transaction, to be the old asset for the purposes of section 116 of the 1992 Act; and

(*c*) the relevant holding immediately after the beginning of that period shall be assumed, in relation to that transaction, to be the new asset for those purposes.

(5) In this paragraph "the 1992 Act" means the Taxation of Chargeable Gains Act 1992.

GENERAL NOTE
See note to para 6.

Opening valuation of paragraph 4 holding

6 Where—

(*a*) paragraph 5(2) above applies in the case of any relevant holding of a company, and

(*b*) for the purpose of bringing amounts into account for the purposes of this Chapter on the mark to market basis used for that period in pursuance of paragraph 4 above, an opening valuation of the holding falls to be made as at the beginning of that period,

the value of that asset at the beginning of that period shall be taken for the purpose of the opening valuation to be equal to whatever, in relation to a disposal immediately before the end of the previous accounting period, would have been taken to be the market value of the holding for the purposes of the Taxation of Chargeable Gains Act 1992.

GENERAL NOTE
The Finance Bill, as originally drafted, provided for no transitional rules where authorised unit trusts or offshore funds move into or out of meeting or failing to meet the 60 per cent test. Paragraphs 5 and 6 are amendments requested by the Association of British Insurers. Under this, a holding in a fund which previously met the test during one accounting period, but fails it during the next, is deemed to have the reorganisation provisions of TCGA 1992 s 116 applied to it. This is of particular relevance where the unit-holder uses the mark-to-market basis. The holding is brought in at the beginning of the accounting period during which it failed the test at its open market value (arrived at the end of the previous period).
For the purposes of para 4, the TA 1988 s 759(1) definition of an offshore fund is extended to include schemes which would have met the definition except that they do not qualify as collective investment schemes under the Financial Services Act 1986.

Meaning of offshore funds

7 (1) For the purposes of paragraph 4 above an interest is a relevant interest in an offshore fund if—

(*a*) it is a material interest in an offshore fund for the purposes of Chapter V of Part XVII of the Taxes Act 1988; or

(*b*) it would be such an interest if the assumption mentioned in sub-paragraph (2) below were made.

(2) That assumption is that the unit trust schemes and arrangements referred to in paragraphs (*b*) and (*c*) of subsection (1) of section 759 of the Taxes Act 1988 are not limited to those which are also collective investment schemes.

GENERAL NOTE
The Treasury may make orders for any purposes of this Schedule, in particular to introduce further rules to extend or reduce the categories of qualifying investments and also to provide any transitional measures thought necessary.

Non-qualifying investments test

8 (1) For the purposes of paragraph 4 above a unit trust scheme or offshore fund fails to satisfy the non-qualifying investments test at any time when the market value of the qualifying investments exceeds 60 per cent. of the market value of all the investments of the scheme or fund.

(2) Subject to sub-paragraph (8) below, in this paragraph "qualifying investments", in

relation to a unit trust scheme or offshore fund, means investments of the scheme or fund which are of any of the following descriptions—

(*a*) money placed at interest;
(*b*) securities;
(*c*) shares in a building society;
(*d*) qualifying holdings in a unit trust scheme or an offshore fund.

(3) For the purposes of sub-paragraph (2) above a holding in a unit trust scheme or offshore fund is a qualifying holding at any time if—

(*a*) at that time, or
(*b*) at any other time in the same accounting period,

that scheme or fund would itself fail (even on the relevant assumption) to satisfy the non-qualifying investments test.

(4) For the purposes of sub-paragraph (3) above the relevant assumption is that investments of the scheme or fund are qualifying investments in relation to that scheme or fund only if they fall within paragraphs (*a*) to (*c*) of sub-paragraph (2) above.

(5) References in this paragraph to investments of a unit trust scheme or offshore fund are references, as the case may be—

(*a*) to investments subject to the trusts of the scheme, or
(*b*) to assets of the fund,

but in neither case do they include references to cash awaiting investment.

(6) References in this paragraph to a holding—

(*a*) in relation to a unit trust scheme, are references to an entitlement to a share in the investments of the scheme; and
(*b*) in relation to an offshore fund, are references to shares in any company by which that fund is constituted or any entitlement to a share in the investments of the fund.

(7) In this paragraph "security" does not include shares in a company.

(8) The Treasury may by order amend this paragraph so as to extend or restrict the descriptions of investments of a unit trust scheme or offshore fund that are qualifying investments for the purposes of this paragraph.

GENERAL NOTE
FA 1994 introduced a new corporation tax rate, equal to the lower rate of income tax (20 per cent), for unit trusts not invested in debt instruments and deposits as to more than 60 per cent of their assets by market value. Where the 60 per cent test could not be met, the corporation tax rate remained 25 per cent. FA 1996 s 73 and Sch 6 paras 10 and 11 provide amendments to TA 1988 s 468 etc in respect of accounting periods of authorised unit trusts ending after 31 March 1996, under which the income of all authorised unit trusts will be subject to tax at the 20 per cent rate. However, the amendments also restrict the unit trust's ability to pay interest distributions so that, effectively, only unit trusts which meet the 60 per cent test can pay them.
    This 60 per cent test has been adapted for use in determining whether the holder of shares or units in an offshore fund or in an authorised unit trust holds an asset which is to be treated as a "creditor relationship" (as defined in FA 1996 s 81). If more than 60 per cent by market value of a fund's investment consists of qualifying investments (as defined below), the investment in the fund will need to be treated as a creditor relationship.
    Qualifying investments comprise the following:

(*a*) money placed at interest;
(*b*) securities (ie instruments other than shares in a company, but including secured or unsecured loan stock, issued by any Government or public or local authority or any company);
(*c*) shares in a building society; or
(*d*) any investment in an authorised unit trust which itself invests more than 60 per cent by market value (excluding uninvested cash) in such assets.

Cash temporarily deposited awaiting reinvestment is not included within qualifying investments and in most equity based authorised unit trusts, all of their cash will come within this category. Property funds and derivatives funds will also be able to meet the 60 per cent test since real property and futures and options are not qualifying investments.
    In determining whether the underlying investments in funds into which the fund has invested will be qualifying investments only assets in categories (*a*) to (*c*) need to be considered.

Powers to make orders

9 (1) An order made by the Treasury under any provision of this Schedule may—

(*a*) make different provision for different cases; and

(*b*) contain such incidental, supplemental, consequential and transitional provision as the Treasury may think fit.

(2) Without prejudice to the generality of sub-paragraph (1) above, an order under paragraph 8(8) above may make such incidental modifications of paragraph 8(4) above as the Treasury may think fit.

SCHEDULE 11 Section 99

LOAN RELATIONSHIPS: SPECIAL PROVISIONS FOR INSURERS

PART I

INSURANCE COMPANIES

I minus E basis

1 (1) Nothing in this Chapter shall be construed as preventing profits and gains arising from loan relationships of an insurance company from being included, where—

   (*a*) the relationship is referable to any life assurance business or capital redemption business carried on by the company, and

   (*b*) that business is business in respect of which the I minus E basis is applied,

in profits and gains on which the company is chargeable to tax in accordance with that basis.

(2) Where, for any accounting period, the I minus E basis is applied in respect of any life assurance business or capital redemption business carried on by an insurance company, the effect of applying that basis shall be—

   (*a*) that none of the credits or debits falling for the purposes of this Chapter to be brought into account in respect of loan relationships of the company that are referable to that business shall be brought into account as mentioned in section 82(2) of this Act; but

   (*b*) that (subject to the following provisions of this Schedule) all those credits and debits shall, instead, be brought into account, in applying that basis to that business, as non-trading credits or, as the case may be, non-trading debits;

and the reference in paragraph 2(1) below to non-trading credits and non-trading debits shall be construed accordingly.

Rules for different categories of business

2 (1) Where an insurance company carries on basic life assurance and general annuity business or capital redemption business or both of them, a separate computation, using only the non-trading credits and non-trading debits referable to the business in question, shall be made for the purposes of this Chapter in relation to that business or, as the case may be, in relation to each of them.

(2) References in any enactment to the computation of any profits of an insurance company in accordance with the provisions of the Taxes Act 1988 applicable to Case I of Schedule D shall have effect as if those provisions included the provisions of this Chapter but, in accordance with sub-paragraph (3) below, only to the extent that they relate to the bringing into account in accordance with section 82(2) of this Act of credits and debits in respect of a company's debtor relationships.

(3) Where an insurance company carries on—

   (*a*) life assurance business or any category of life assurance business, or

   (*b*) capital redemption business,

the credits and debits referable to that business, or category of business, that are given by this Chapter in respect of creditor relationships of the company shall be disregarded for the purposes of any computations falling to be made, in relation to that business or category of business, in accordance with provisions applicable to Case I of Schedule D.

(4) Accordingly (and notwithstanding section 80(5) of this Act), the amounts which are to be brought into account in any computations such as are mentioned in sub-paragraph (3) above shall be determined under the provisions applicable apart from this Chapter.

(5) To the extent that any profits of an insurance company in respect of any business or category of business fall to be computed in accordance with provisions applicable to Case I of Schedule D the credits and debits referable to that business or category of business that fall to be disregarded under sub-paragraph (3) above shall also be disregarded in any computations falling to be made for the purposes of this Chapter otherwise than in accordance with sub-paragraph (1) above.

GENERAL NOTE

This paragraph provides for the common situation where a company carries on different categories of insurance business subject to separate computational rules.

Subparagraph (1) provides that a separate computation or computations should be made in respect of the non-trading credits or debits referable to basic life assurance and general annuity business or capital redemption business, mirroring the requirements of TA 1988 ss 432(1) and 458.

Subparagraph (2) imports into the Case I rules for insurance companies (notional Case I computations for basic life assurance and general annuity business and capital redemption and Case VI for other categories of business) the principle, in s 82(2), that credits and debits in respect of loan relationships should be taxed as trading receipts and expenses, but only insofar as they apply to debtor relationships, in effect the equivalent of interest paid. Subparagraphs (3)–(5) disapply the special provisions of Part IV Chapter II except insofar as they apply, after the adaptations made by paras 1 and 2(1), to the *I minus E* computations in respect of basic life assurance and general annuity business and capital redemption business. This avoids a possible conflict between two sets of figures. The treatment of trading credits and debits in the principal legislation is to follow the way they are accounted for under one of two "authorised accounting methods", which are the accruals basis or a mark-to-market basis (ss 84–86). In the Case I computations for a life insurance company, however, whether made for notional, actual or Case VI purposes, the legislation already contains special rules, in FA 1989 ss 83 and 83A, which derive the figures for assessment from those in the return made for regulatory purposes (the DTI return in the case of a UK company or a non-resident company other than an EC or EEA company). The disapplication of the new rules for trading credits and debits in respect of creditor relationships allows the provisions of FA 1989 to operate in the ordinary way.

Apportionments

3 Where—

(*a*) any creditor relationship of an insurance company is represented by an asset which is an asset of a fund of the company or is linked to any category of insurance business, and

(*b*) any question arises for the purposes of the Corporation Tax Acts as to the extent to which credits or debits given for the purposes of this Chapter in respect of that relationship are referable to any category of the company's long term business,

section 432A of the Taxes Act 1988 (apportionment of insurance companies' income) shall have effect in relation to the credits and debits so given in respect of that relationship as it has effect in relation to the income arising from an asset.

GENERAL NOTE

The provisions of TA 1988 s 432A are applied to determine how credits and debits from loan relationships are to be attributed to different categories of insurance business. The attribution is made by reference to the asset giving rise to the credit or debit, so that where the asset is part of the overseas life assurance fund the credit or debit will be attributed to overseas life assurance business, where the asset is linked to another category of business the credit or debit will be attributed to that category, and in other cases the amount in question will be apportioned in accordance with the rules in TA 1988 s 432A(5)–(8).

Treatment of deficit

4 (1) Where, in the case of any insurance company, a non-trading deficit on its loan relationships is produced for any accounting period ("the deficit period") by any separate computation made under paragraph 2 above for—

　(*a*)　basic life assurance and general annuity business, or

　(*b*)　capital redemption business,

the following provisions of this paragraph shall apply in relation to that deficit, instead of section 83 of, and Schedule 8 to, this Act.

(2) On a claim made by the company in relation to the whole or any part of the deficit—

　(*a*)　the amount to which the claim relates shall be set off against any net income and gains of the deficit period referable to the relevant category of business and arising or accruing otherwise than in respect of loan relationships; and

　(*b*)　the amount of the net income and gains against which it is set off shall be treated as reduced accordingly;

and any such reductions shall be made before any deduction by virtue of section 76 of the Taxes Act 1988 of any expenses of management.

(3) Subject to the following provisions of this paragraph, on a claim made by the company in relation to the whole or any part of so much (if any) of the deficit as exceeds the amount of the net income and gains for the deficit period that are referred to in sub-paragraph (2)(*a*) above, the amount to which the claim relates shall be—

　(*a*)　carried back to the three immediately preceding accounting periods; and

　(*b*)　in accordance with sub-paragraph (5) below, set against the eligible profits of the company for those periods.

(4) If the whole or any amount of the deficit is not set off under sub-paragraph (2) or (3) above, so much of it as is not set off shall be—

　(*a*)　carried forward to the accounting period immediately following the deficit period; and

　(*b*)　treated for the purposes of the Corporation Tax Acts (including the following provisions of this paragraph) as an amount to be included in the company's expenses of management for the period following the deficit period.

(5) Subject to sub-paragraph (6) below, where, in pursuance of a claim under sub-paragraph (3) above, any amount falls to be carried back to be set off against the eligible profits of the company for the three accounting periods preceding the deficit period, that amount shall be set off against those profits as follows, that is to say—

　(*a*)　the amount shall be applied, up to the limit for the first set-off period, in reducing the company's eligible profit for that period;

　(*b*)　any remainder of that amount after the limit for the first set-off period is reached shall be applied, up to the limit for the second set-off period, in reducing the company's eligible profit for the second set-off period; and

　(*c*)　any remainder of that amount after the limit for the second set-off period has been reached shall be applied, up to the limit for third set-off period, in reducing the company's eligible profit for the third set-off period.

(6) No reduction shall be made in pursuance of any such claim in a company's eligible profit for any accounting period ending before 1st April 1996.

(7) For the purposes of this paragraph the eligible profit of the company for an accounting period is the amount (if any) which, in pursuance of any separate computation made for that period for the relevant category of business, is chargeable to tax for that period under Case III of Schedule D as profits and gains arising from the company's loan relationships.

(8) For the purpose of this paragraph—

　(*a*)　the first set-off period is the accounting period immediately preceding the deficit period, (*b*) the second set-off period is the accounting period immediately preceding the first set-off period, and

(*c*) the third set-off period is the accounting period immediately preceding the second set-off period, and

(*d*) the limit for a set-off period is the amount equal to the adjusted amount of the company's eligible profit for that period.

(9) In sub-paragraph (8) above, the reference to the adjusted amount of a company's eligible profit for a set-off period is a reference to so much (if any) of the company's eligible profit for that period as remains after reducing it by an amount equal to the unused part of the relevant deductions for that period.

(10) For the purposes of sub-paragraph (9) above the unused part of the relevant deductions for any set-off period is the amount (if any) by which the aggregate of—

(*a*) so much of the amount of any deductions for the set-off period by virtue of section 76 of the Taxes Act 1988 as is referable to the relevant category of business, and

(*b*) so much of the aggregate of the deductions made in the case of the company in respect of charges on income for that period as is so referable,

exceeds the aggregate of the amounts referable to the relevant category of business that could for that period be applied in making deductions by virtue of that section, or in respect of charges on income, if the eligible profit of the company for that period were disregarded.

(11) In sub-paragraph (10) above, the references, in relation to a claim under sub-paragraph (3) above ("the relevant claim"), to deductions by virtue of section 76 of the Taxes Act 1988 for a set-off period are references to the deductions by way of management expenses that would have fallen to be made by virtue of that section for that period if—

(*a*) no account were taken of either—

(i) the relevant claim; or

(ii) any claim under sub-paragraph (3) above relating to a deficit for an accounting period after the deficit period;

but

(*b*) there were made all such adjustments required by virtue of any sum having been carried back to that set-off period—

(i) under the Corporation Tax Acts, but

(ii) otherwise than in pursuance of the relevant claim or of any other such claim as is mentioned in paragraph (*a*) above.

(12) Where—

(*a*) in pursuance of a claim under sub-paragraph (3) above any amount is set-off against the eligible profit of a company for any set-off period, and

(*b*) there is a section 76(5) amount for that period which is attributable to that claim,

that section 76(5) amount shall not be carried forward by virtue of section 75(3) of the Taxes Act 1988 but, if that set-off period is the first or second set-off period, sub-paragraph (13) below shall apply to that amount instead.

(13) Where this sub-paragraph applies to a section 76(5) amount for any set-off period, the amount available in accordance with sub-paragraph (5) above to be carried back from that set-off period to be set off against eligible profits of previous set-off periods (or, as the case may be, against the eligible profit of the previous set-off period) shall be treated as increased by an amount equal to the amount to which this sub-paragraph applies.

(14) In relation to any claim under sub-paragraph (3) above, the amount which for any set-off period is, for the purposes of this paragraph, to be taken to be the section 76(5) amount attributable to that claim is the amount (if any) by which the amount specified in paragraph (*a*) below is exceeded by the amount specified in paragraph (*b*) below, that is to say—

(*a*) the amount that would have fallen to be carried forward by virtue of section 75(3) of the Taxes Act 1988 if the claim had not been made; and

(*b*) the amount which, after the making of the claim, would have fallen to be carried forward to a subsequent period by virtue of section 75(3) of that Act if sub-paragraphs (12) and (13) above, so far as they relate to that claim, were to be disregarded.

(15) A claim for the purposes of sub-paragraph (2) or (3) above must be made within the period of two years immediately following the end of the deficit period or within such further period as the Board may allow.

(16) In this paragraph—

"net income and gains" has the meaning given by subsection (1) of section 76 of the Taxes Act 1988; and

"the relevant category of business", in relation to a deficit, means the category of business in relation to which the deficit was produced.

GENERAL NOTE
Subparagraph (1) introduces special rules for relieving a non-trading deficit from loan relationships referable to basic life assurance and general annuity business or capital redemption business, in place of the rules in s 83 and Sch 8.

Subparagraphs (2)–(4) provide that the company may claim to set the whole or any part of the deficit against other net income and gains attributable to the category of business in question, the set-off being made before relief for expenses of management, and to set the whole or part of any unrelieved deficit against the eligible profits of the three immediately preceding accounting periods. Where the whole of the deficit is not so used any balance is included in management expenses for the subsequent period.

Subparagraphs (5)–(14) set out the detailed rules for implementing a claim to carry back an unrelieved deficit.

The deficit is to be set first against the profits of the latest of the three years of the carry-back period, any amount unrelieved being set against profits of the preceding year, and so on (sub-paras (5) and (8)). No relief may be given for any accounting period ending before 1 April 1996 (sub-para (6)).

The profits eligible for relief are the amount of the Case III assessment in respect of loan relationships referable to the category of business in question (sub-para (7)). The set-off is however limited (sub-paras (7)(*d*) and (8)) to an amount equal to the eligible profits less the excess of management expenses and charges actually deducted over the amount thereof which would have been deducted if the elibible profit for that period had been disregarded (sub-paras (9) and (10)). In calculating the amounts in question, the effect of the claim in respect of the deficit under consideration, or of any later deficit, is to be disregarded, but account is to be taken of any reliefs carried back under other provisions (sub-para (11)).

Subparagraphs (12)–(14) provide for the situation where the carry-back claim results in disallowance of management expenses under the *Notional Case I* provisions of TA 1988 s 76(2). The amount which would otherwise be carried forward under TA 1988 s 76(5) is added to the deficit carried back to an earlier set-off period.

Subparagraph (15) provides that claims in respect of a set-off against other income and gains under sub-para (2) or to carry back under sub-para (3) are to be made within two years of the end of the deficit period. The Board of Inland Revenue is given discretion to extend the time limit.

Subparagraph (16) ensures that the computations for each category of business are kept separate, and defines "net income and gains" as the income and gains after all other reliefs apart from expenses of management.

Election for accruals basis for long term business assets

5 (1) Subject to sub-paragraphs (3) to (6) below, sub-paragraph (2) below applies for any accounting period to so much of any creditor relationship of an insurance company as—

(*a*) for the whole or any part of that period is an asset within one of the categories set out in section 440(4)(*d*) and (*e*) of the Taxes Act 1988 (assets held for certain categories of long term business); and

(*b*) is an asset in relation to which an election under this paragraph is made by the company for that period.

(2) Where—

(*a*) this sub-paragraph applies for any accounting period to any asset, and (*b*) apart from this paragraph, a mark to market basis of accounting would have had to be used for the purposes of this Chapter as respects that asset for the whole or any part of that period,

this Chapter shall have effect as if an authorised accruals basis of accounting had to be used for the purposes of this Chapter as respects that asset for that period or part.

(3) Sub-paragraph (2) above shall not apply to any holding to which paragraph 4(3) of Schedule 10 to this Act applies.

(4) An election under this paragraph shall not be made except by notice in writing given to an officer of the Board not more than three months after the end of the accounting period to which the election relates.

(5) An election under this paragraph shall be irrevocable, and shall not be varied, once it has been made.

(6) An election shall not be made under this paragraph for any accounting period ending after 31st March 1998.

(7) The Treasury may, if they think fit, by order—

(*a*) amend sub-paragraph (6) above to substitute a later date for the date for the time being specified in that sub-paragraph; or
(*b*) repeal that sub-paragraph.

GENERAL NOTE
Subparagraphs (1) and (2) allow insurers carrying on long-term business to elect to be taxed on an accruals basis where the legislation in ss 85 and 86 would otherwise require the company to account for tax on a mark-to-market basis (because that basis is used in the accounts). The reason for this provision, which is transitory in nature, is that insurers are expected to adopt an accruals basis of accounting in accordance with a Statement of Recommended Practice which is presently in course of preparation.
The provision applies only to assets which are solely linked to basic life assurance and general annuity business and other assets of the long-term business fund which are not solely linked to other categories of long-term business (sub-para (1)(*a*) applying TA 1988 s 440(4)(*d*) and (*e*)). The company may elect for this treatment in respect of specific assets and not others (sub-para (1)(*b*)), but may not use the accruals basis in respect of certain holdings in unit trusts and offshore funds (sub-para (3) applying Sch 10 para 4(3)).
An election for accruals basis treatment under this paragraph, which is irrevocable, must be made within three months of the end of the accounting period (sub-paras (4) and (5)). No elections may be made for accounting periods ending after 31 March 1988, but that limit may be extended or removed by Treasury Order (sub-paras (6) and (7)).

Interpretation of Part I

6 In this Part of this Schedule—

"basic life assurance and general annuity business" and "long term business" have the same meanings as in Chapter I of Part XII of the Taxes Act 1988;
"capital redemption business" means any capital redemption business, within the meaning of section 458 of that Act, which is business to which that section applies;
"the I minus E basis" means the basis commonly so called (under which a company carrying on life assurance business or capital redemption business is charged to tax on that business otherwise than under Case I of Schedule D);
"life assurance business" includes any annuity business within the meaning of Chapter I of Part XII of that Act.

GENERAL NOTE
This paragraph imports definitions from the principal legislation relating to insurance companies, in TA 1988 Part XII Chapter I.

PART II

CORPORATE MEMBERS OF LLOYD'S

7 (1) This Chapter does not apply as respects any loan relationship of a corporate member of Lloyd's in so far as rights or liabilities making up that relationship, or any securities representing them, are—

(*a*) assets forming part of that member's premiums trust fund; or

(*b*) liabilities attached to that fund.

(2) Section 230 of the Finance Act 1994 (interpretation of provisions applying to corporate members of Lloyd's) shall apply for the purposes of this paragraph as it applies for the purposes of Chapter V of Part IV of that Act.

GENERAL NOTE

The principal legislation does not apply to a corporate member of Lloyd's, insofar as the loan relationships are referable to the member's premiums trust fund (as defined by FA 1994 s 230). Under the special rules applying to premiums, trust funds assets are already taxed on the equivalent of a mark-to-market basis. The principal legislation on loan relationships only applies to companies so individual members of Lloyd's are not affected.

SCHEDULE 12

MEANING OF DEBT CONTRACT OR OPTION

GENERAL NOTE

This Schedule, which is introduced by s 101, provides a new s 150A to FA 1994, which defines "debt contract" and "debt option". Section 101 provides for the treatment of such debt contracts and options within the loan relationship and financial instrument regimes.

Section 150A(1) defines a "debt contract" as a contract—

(*a*) which is not an interest rate contract or option or currency contract or option (which are the terms used to define those financial instruments currently within the financial instrument regime and are contained in FA 1994 ss 149 and 150);

(*b*) which provides that a "qualifying company" is entitled to, or subject to a duty to, become a party to a loan relationship (whether conditionally or not); and

(*c*) which provides only for transfers of money or money's worth falling within sub-s (5) of this section or FA 1994 s 151 (which are those payments which are not "qualifying payments" but may be made under a "qualifying contract" without jeopardising the contract's status) as amended by s 101(4) (this ignores any payments due under the loan relationship itself).

Payments falling within sub-s (5) are payments of—

(*a*) an amount representing the price for becoming party to the loan relationship;

(*b*) an amount determined by reference to the value at any time of the money debt in question;

(*c*) a settlement amount determined by reference to the difference at specified times between (*a*) and (*b*) above.

A company is treated as entitled to, or subject to a duty to, become subject to a loan relationship if the entitlement or duty relates to an "equivalent relationship" or relates to making one or more of the payments falling within sub-s (5). This applies equally to an entitlement or a duty to become treated as a person with rights and liabilities corresponding to those of a party to a loan relationship.

A contract will also be a debt contract if—

(*a*) it is not a debt contract under sub-s (1), nor an interest rate contract or option nor a currency contract or option;

(*b*) it provides that a "qualifying company" is entitled, or subject to a duty to, become treated as a person with rights and liabilities corresponding to a party to a loan relationship (whether conditionally or not); and

(*c*) it provides only for transfers of money or money's worth falling within sub-s (6) of this section or FA 1994 s 151 (as noted above).

Payments falling within sub-s (6) are settlement payments determined by reference to the difference at specified times between—

(*a*) the price for becoming so treated; and

(*b*) the value of the money debt in question.

A "debt option" is defined as an option to enter not a "debt contract" or an option to enter into such an option, provided that the only transfers of money or money's worth for which it provides are payments within FA 1994 s 151 (which are those payments which are not "qualifying payments" but may be made under a "qualifying contract" without jeopardising the contract's status).

Where a contract contains provisions which would constitute a debt contract or option and also other provisions unrelated to the "debt contract or option", the part representing the "debt contract or option" is treated as a separate contract. The other contents of the contract may be attributed to the separate contract on a just and reasonable basis and this apportionment extends to payments of money or money's worth which cannot be attributed directly.

Loan relationships do not include convertible securities within s 92, nor those linked to the value of chargeable assets within s 93. Otherwise, the definitions contained in the loan relationship provisions of apply in this section.

Where there is a transfer of money's worth relating to a debt contract or option which has a value of any amount, it is treated as a payment of that amount for the purposes of the section and FA 1994 s 151.

The section inserted after section 150 of the Finance Act 1994 by section 101(3) of this Act is as follows—

"150A Debt contracts and options

(1) A contract is a debt contract for the purposes of this Chapter if, not being an interest rate contract or option or a currency contract or option—

(*a*) it is a contract under which, whether unconditionally or subject to conditions being fulfilled, a qualifying company has any entitlement, or is subject to any duty, to become a party to a loan relationship; and

(*b*) the only transfers of money or money's worth for which the contract provides (apart from those that will be made under the loan relationship) are payments falling within subsection (5) below and payments falling within section 151 below.

(2) A contract is also a debt contract for the purposes of this Chapter if, not being a debt contract by virtue of subsection (1) above or an interest rate contract or option or a currency contract or option—

(*a*) it is a contract under which, whether unconditionally or subject to conditions being fulfilled, a qualifying company has any entitlement, or is subject to any duty, to become treated as a person with rights and liabilities corresponding to those of a party to a loan relationship; and

(*b*) the only transfers of money or money's worth for which the contract provides are payments falling within subsection (6) below and payments falling within section 151 below.

(3) In this section references to an entitlement to become a party to a loan relationship, or to a duty to become such a party, shall be taken to include references, in relation to a specified loan relationship, to either of the following, namely—

(*a*) an entitlement or, as the case may be, a duty to become a party to an equivalent relationship; and

(*b*) an entitlement or, as the case may be, a duty relating to the making of any one or more such payments as fall within subsection (5) below.

(4) Subsection (3) above shall apply in relation to references in this section to an entitlement or a duty to become treated as a person with rights and liabilities corresponding to those of a party to a loan relationship as it applies to references to an entitlement or, as the case may be, a duty to become such a party.

(5) The payments falling within this subsection are—

(*a*) a payment of an amount representing the price for becoming a party to the relationship;

(*b*) a payment of an amount determined by reference to the value at any time of the money debt by reference to which the relationship subsists;

(*c*) a settlement payment of an amount determined by reference to the difference at specified times between—

(i) the price for becoming a party to the relationship; and

(ii) the value of the money debt by reference to which the relationship subsists, or (if the relationship were in existence) would subsist.

(6) A payment falls within this subsection if it is a settlement payment of an amount determined by reference to the difference at specified times between—

(*a*) the price for becoming treated as a person with rights and liabilties corresponding to those of a party to a relationship; and

(*b*) the value of the money debt by reference to which the relationship subsists or (if the relationship existed) would subsist.

(7) Each of the following, namely—

(*a*) an option to enter into a contract which would be a debt contract, and

(*b*) an option to enter into such an option,

is a debt option for the purposes of this Chapter if the only transfers of money or money's worth for which the option provides are payments falling within section 151 below.

(8) For the purposes of this Chapter where any contract contains both—

(*a*) provisions under which, whether unconditionally or subject to conditions being fulfilled, a qualifying company has any entitlement, or is subject to any duty, to become a party to a loan relationship, and

(b) any provisions that have effect otherwise than for the purposes of or in relation to the provisions conferring that entitlement or imposing that duty,

the provisions mentioned in paragraph (a) above, together with the other contents of that contract so far as they are attributable on a just and reasonable basis to the provisions mentioned in that paragraph, shall be treated as a separate contract.

(9) For the purposes of this Chapter where—

(a) any attribution of the contents of a contract falls to be made between provisions falling within paragraph (a) of subsection (8) above and provisions falling within paragraph (b) of that subsection, and

(b) that contract provides for the making of any payment constituting a transfer of money or money's worth which cannot be attributed to the provisions falling within only one of those paragraphs,

that payment shall be treated as apportioned between the provisions falling within each of those paragraphs in such manner as may be just and reasonable.

(10) Expressions used in this section and in Chapter II of Part IV of the Finance Act 1996 have the same meanings in this section as in that Chapter; but references in this section to a loan relationship do not include—

(a) any loan relationship represented by an asset to which section 92 of that Act (convertible securities) applies; or

(b) any loan relationship to which section 93 of that Act (securities indexed to chargeable assets) applies.

(11) For the purposes of this section and, so far as it relates to a debt contract or option, of section 151 below the transfer of money's worth having a value of any amount shall be treated as the payment of that amount.''

SCHEDULE 13   Section 102

DISCOUNTED SECURITIES: INCOME TAX PROVISIONS

GENERAL NOTE
This Schedule is introduced by s 102 and provides for the income tax treatment of discounted securities on their transfer or redemption.

Charge to tax on realised profit comprised in discount

1 (1) Where a person realises the profit from the discount on a relevant discounted security, he shall be charged to income tax on that profit under Case III of Schedule D or, where the profit arises from a security out of the United Kingdom, under Case IV of that Schedule.

(2) For the purposes of this Schedule a person realises the profit from the discount on a relevant discounted security where—

(*a*) he transfers such a security or becomes entitled, as the person holding the security, to any payment on its redemption; and

(*b*) the amount payable on the transfer or redemption exceeds the amount paid by that person in respect of his acquisition of the security.

(3) For the purposes of this Schedule the profit shall be taken—

(*a*) to be equal to the amount of the excess reduced by the amount of any relevant costs; and

(*b*) to arise, for the purposes of income tax, in the year of assessment in which the transfer or redemption takes place.

(4) In this paragraph "relevant costs", in relation to a security that is transferred or redeemed, are all the following costs—

(*a*) the costs incurred in connection with the acquisition of the security by the person making the transfer or, as the case may be, the person entitled to a payment on the redemption; and

(*b*) the costs incurred by that person, in connection with the transfer or redemption of the security;

and for the purposes of this Schedule costs falling within paragraph (*a*) above shall not be regarded as amounts paid in respect of the acquisition of a security.

GENERAL NOTE
This paragraph provides that income tax shall be chargeable on profits realised from "relevant discounted securities" under Schedule D Case III, or Case IV where it is a non UK security.
Paragraph 3 below defines a "relevant discounted security".
Realisation of the profit arises in the year of transfer or redemption and the profit is the proceeds of transfer or redemption, less the amount paid on acquisition and "relevant costs". The "relevant costs" are those incurred on the acquisition, transfer or redemption, although acquisition costs are not regarded as amounts paid on acquisition.

Realised losses on discounted securities

2 (1) Subject to the following provisions of this Schedule, where—

(*a*) a person sustains a loss in any year of assessment from the discount on a relevant discounted security, and

(*b*) makes a claim for the purposes of this paragraph before the end of twelve months from the 31st January next following that year of assessment,

that person shall be entitled to relief from income tax on an amount of the claimant's income for that year equal to the amount of the loss.

(2) For the purposes of this Schedule a person sustains a loss from the discount on a relevant discounted security where—

(*a*) he transfers such a security or becomes entitled, as the person holding the security, to any payment on its redemption; and (*b*) the amount paid by that person in respect of his acquisition of the security exceeds the amount payable on the transfer or redemption.

(3) For the purposes of this Schedule the loss shall be taken—

(*a*) to be equal to the amount of the excess increased by the amount of any relevant costs; and

(*b*) to be sustained for the purposes of this Schedule in the year of assessment in which the transfer or redemption takes place.

(4) Sub-paragraph (4) of paragraph 1 above applies for the purposes of this paragraph as it applies for the purposes of that paragraph.

GENERAL NOTE

This paragraph provides relief for losses sustained on "relevant discounted securities" in a year of assessment.

The relief must be claimed within 12 months from the 31 January next following that year of assessment and is available against the claimant's income for the year equal to the amount of the loss. The loss is sustained in the year of transfer or redemption of the security and is calculated in the same manner as a profit in para 1 above.

Meaning of "relevant discounted security"

3 (1) Subject to sub-paragraph (2) and paragraph 14(1) below, in this Schedule "relevant discounted security" means any security which (whenever issued) is such that—

(*a*) taking the security as at the time of its issue, and

(*b*) assuming redemption in accordance with its terms,

the amount payable on redemption is an amount involving a deep gain or might be an amount which would involve such a gain.

(2) The following are not relevant discounted securities for the purposes of this Schedule—

(*a*) shares in a company;

(*b*) gilt-edged securities that are not strips;

(*c*) excluded indexed securities;

(*d*) life assurance policies;

(*e*) capital redemption policies (within the meaning of Chapter II of Part XIII of the Taxes Act 1988); and

(*f*) subject to paragraph 10 below, securities issued (at whatever time) under the same prospectus as other securities which have been issued previously but (disregarding that paragraph) are not themselves relevant discounted securities.

(3) For the purposes of this Schedule the amount payable on redemption of a security involves a deep gain if—

(*a*) the issue price is less than the amount so payable; and

(*b*) the amount by which it is less represents more than the relevant percentage of the amount so payable.

(4) In this paragraph "the relevant percentage", in relation to the amount payable on redemption of a security, means—

(*a*) the percentage figure equal, in a case where the period between the date of issue and the date of redemption is less than thirty years, to one half of the number of years between those dates; and

(*b*) in any other case, 15 per cent.;

and for the purposes of this paragraph the fraction of a year to be used for the purposes of paragraph (*a*) above in a case where the period mentioned in that paragraph is not a number of complete years shall be calculated by treating each complete month, and any remaining part of a month, in that period as one twelfth of a year.

(5) References in this paragraph to redemption—

(*a*) do not include references to any redemption which may be made before maturity otherwise than at the option of the holder of the security; but (*b*) in the case of a security that is capable of redemption at the option of the holder before maturity, shall have effect as references to the earliest occasion on which the holder of the security may require the security to be redeemed.

(6) For the purposes of this paragraph the amount payable on redemption shall not be taken to include any amount payable on that occasion by way of interest.

GENERAL NOTE
This paragraph defines a "relevant discounted security".
A relevant discounted security is one where the amount payable on redemption would, or might, constitute a "deep gain", taking the security at issue and assuming redemption in accordance with its terms.
Gilt strips are specifically included (see para 14(1) below) but the following are specifically excluded from the definition—

(*a*) shares in a company;
(*b*) gilt-edged securities other than strips;
(*c*) excluded indexed securities (see para 13);
(*d*) life assurance policies;
(*e*) capital redemption policies; and
(*f*) securities issued under the same prospectus as other securities which have been issued previously and which are not relevant discounted security. This applies regardless of when the securities are issued after those previously issued, but is subject to para 10 below.

A "deep gain" arises if the issue price is less than the amount payable on redemption by the "relevant percentage" of that amount. The "relevant percentage" is one half per cent for each year between issue and redemption and, where there is a fraction of a year, each month and part month is treated as one twelfth of a year. The "relevant percentage" is 15 per cent, in the case of securities where the period between issue and redemption is thirty years or more. This is similar to the definition of deep gains previously contained in FA 1989 Sch 11. Interest payable on redemption is excluded from the calculation.
Redemption does not include redemptions before maturity unless they are at the option of the holder of the security, in which case redemption is assumed to take place at the earliest opportunity.

Meaning of "transfer"

4 (1) Subject to sub-paragraph (2) below, in this Schedule references to a transfer, in relation to a security, are references to any transfer of the security by way of sale, exchange, gift or otherwise.

(2) Where an individual who is entitled to a relevant discounted security dies, then for the purposes of this Schedule—

(*a*) he shall be treated as making a transfer of the security immediately before his death;
(*b*) he shall be treated as obtaining in respect of the transfer an amount equal to the market value of the security at the time of the transfer; and
(*c*) his personal representatives shall be treated as acquiring the security for that amount on his death.

(3) For the purposes of this Schedule a transfer or acquisition of a security made in pursuance of an agreement shall be deemed to take place at the time when the agreement is made, if the person to whom the transfer is made, or who makes the acquisition, becomes entitled to the security at that time.

(4) If an agreement is conditional, whether on the exercise of an option or otherwise, it shall be taken for the purposes of this paragraph to be made when the condition is satisfied (whether by the exercise of the option or otherwise).

(5) This paragraph is without prejudice to paragraph 14(2) to (4) below.

GENERAL NOTE
This paragraph provides for when there is a "transfer" of a security.
A "transfer" is any transfer by way of sale, exchange, gift or otherwise.
The time of transfer or acquisition of a security under an agreement is the time of making the agreement where the transferee or acquirer becomes entitled to it. Where the agreement is conditional (by option or otherwise) the time of making the contract is deemed to be when the condition is satisfied.

On death the individual is treated as transferring his security for market value immediately before his death and his personal representatives as acquiring it on his death.

The paragraph is subject to para 14(2) and (4) which deals with gilt strips.

Redemption to include conversion

5 (1) This paragraph applies where a relevant discounted security is extinguished by being converted, in pursuance of rights conferred by the security, into shares in a company or into any other securities (including other relevant discounted securities).

(2) For the purposes of this Schedule the conversion shall be deemed—

(*a*) to constitute the redemption of the security which is extinguished; and

(*b*) to involve a payment on redemption of an amount equal to whatever, at the time of the conversion, is the market value of the shares or other securities into which the security in question is converted.

(3) This paragraph does not apply to an exchange to which paragraph 14 below applies.

GENERAL NOTE

This paragraph provides that the conversion of a security may be treated as a disposal.

It applies where the conversion is into shares in a company or into any other securities (including relevant discounted securities) in pursuance of rights conferred by the security. The redemption proceeds are deemed to be the market value of the securities acquired.

The paragraph does not apply to exchanges under para 14, which deals with gilt strips.

Trustees and personal representatives

6 (1) Where, on a transfer or redemption of a security by trustees, an amount is treated as income chargeable to tax by virtue of this Schedule—

(*a*) that amount shall be taken for the purposes of Chapters IA and IB of Part XV of the Taxes Act 1988 (settlements: liability of settlor etc) to be income arising—

(i) under the settlement of which the trustees are trustees; and

(ii) from that security;

(*b*) that amount shall be taken for the purposes of Chapter IC of Part XV of that Act (settlements: liability of trustees) to be income arising to the trustees; and

(*c*) to the extent that tax on that amount is charged on the trustees, the rate at which it is chargeable shall be taken (where it would not otherwise be the case) to be the rate applicable to trusts for the year of assessment in which the transfer or redemption is made.

(2) Where the trustees are trustees of a scheme to which section 469 of the Taxes Act 1988 (unauthorised unit trusts) applies, sub-paragraph (1) above shall not apply if or to the extent that the amount is treated as income in the accounts of the scheme.

(3) Without prejudice to paragraph 12 below, paragraphs 1(1) and 2(1) above do not apply in the case of—

(*a*) any transfer of a security for the time being held under a settlement the trustees of which are not resident in the United Kingdom; or

(*b*) any redemption of a security which is so held immediately before its redemption.

(4) Relief shall not be given to trustees under paragraph 2 above except from income tax on income chargeable under paragraph 1 above.

(5) Sub-paragraph (6) below applies where, in the case of any trustees, the amount mentioned in paragraph (*a*) below exceeds in any year of assessment the amount mentioned in paragraph (*b*) below, that is to say—

(*a*) the aggregate amount of the losses in respect of which relief from income tax may be given to the trustees for that year under paragraph 2 above (including any amount treated as such a loss by virtue of that sub-paragraph); and

(*b*) the income of those trustees chargeable for that year to tax under paragraph 1 above.

(6) Subject to paragraph 7(2) below, the excess shall for the purposes of this Schedule be—

(*a*) carried forward to the immediately following year of assessment; and
(*b*) in relation to the year to which it is carried forward, treated as if it were a loss sustained in that year by the trustees from a discount on a relevant discounted security.

(7) Where a relevant discounted security is transferred by personal representatives to a legatee, they shall be treated for the purposes of this Schedule as obtaining in respect of the transfer an amount equal to the market value of the security at the time of the transfer.

(8) In this paragraph "legatee" includes any person taking (whether beneficially or as trustee) under a testamentary disposition or on an intestacy or partial intestacy, including any person taking by virtue of an appropriation by the personal representatives in or towards satisfaction of a legacy or other interest or share in the deceased's property.

GENERAL NOTE
This paragraph sets out the taxation of amounts treated as income from relevant discounted securities held by trustees and personal representatives.
The paragraph provides that income chargeable under this Schedule on the transfer or redemption of securities by trustees will be—

(*a*) where Chapters IA and IB of TA 1988 Part XV apply as arising under a settlement, causing the income to be taxed as if it belonged to the settlor;
(*b*) where Chapter IC applies to be income arising to the trustees and chargeable at the rate applicable to trusts for the year in which the transfer or redemption occurs.

The paragraph does not apply to an unauthorised unit trust under TA 1988 s 469, where the income is recognised in its accounts.
Paragraphs 1(1) and 2(1) apply where there is a transfer of securities by non-UK resident trustees or which are held by them immediately before redemption.
Losses under para 2 may only be relieved against income under para 1. Where the losses exceed income for any year the excess is carried forward and treated as a loss of the following year.
Where a relevant discounted security is transferred by a personal representative to a legatee, the transfer is deemed to take place at the then market value. "Legatee" is defined by sub-para (8).

Treatment of losses where income exempt

7 (1) Where—

(*a*) on the transfer or redemption of any relevant discounted security, a loss is sustained from the discount on that security, and
(*b*) if the person sustaining that loss had realised a profit from that discount on that transfer or redemption, the profit would have been an exempt profit for the year of assessment in which the loss is sustained,

relief shall not be given to that person under paragraph 2 above in respect of that loss except from income tax on income chargeable for that year under paragraph 1 above.

(2) No part of any loss to which sub-paragraph (1) above applies shall be carried forward under paragraph 6(6) above.

(3) The reference in sub-paragraph (1) above to an exempt profit for a year of assessment is a reference to any income for that year which—

(*a*) is eligible for relief from tax by virtue of section 505(1) of the Taxes Act 1988, or would be so eligible but for section 505(3) of that Act (charities); or
(*b*) is eligible for relief from tax by virtue of section 592(2), 608(2)(*a*), 613(4), 614(2), (3), (4) or (5), 620(6) or 643(2) of that Act (pension scheme funds etc).

(4) Where a loss to which sub-paragraph (1) above applies is sustained in a case in which the profit mentioned in paragraph (*b*) of that sub-paragraph would be eligible for relief under section 592(2) of the Taxes Act 1988—

(*a*) relief shall be given under paragraph 2 above in accordance with sub-paragraph (1) above before any computation is made under paragraph 7 of Schedule 22 to that Act, and
(*b*) that paragraph 7 shall have effect, accordingly, so that the amount of income to

which the specified percentage is applied by virtue of sub-paragraph (3)(*a*) of that paragraph is reduced by the amount of the relief.

GENERAL NOTE

This paragraph restricts losses arising under para 2 where a profit from the relevant discounted security would have been exempt from tax for that year for charities and pension funds.

Such a loss may only be used against income chargeable under para 1 in that year and the loss is not available for carry forward by the trustees under para 6(6).

Charities and pension funds are as described in sub-para (3), and sub-para (4) provides for relief for exempt approved schemes under TA 1988 s 592(2).

Transfers between connected persons

8 (1) This paragraph applies where a relevant discounted security is transferred from one person to another and they are connected with each other.

(2) For the purposes of this Schedule—

(*a*) the person making the transfer shall be treated as obtaining in respect of it an amount equal to the market value of the security at the time of the transfer; and

(*b*) the person to whom the transfer is made shall be treated as paying in respect of his acquisition of the security an amount equal to that market value.

(3) Section 839 of the Taxes Act 1988 (connected persons) shall apply for the purposes of this paragraph.

GENERAL NOTE

This paragraph provides for the valuation of transfer of a relevant discounted security between connected persons.

It provides that the transfer, for both transferee and transferor, shall be deemed to be at the market value of the relevant discounted security at the time of the transfer.

TA 1988 s 839 provides the definition of connected persons.

Other transactions deemed to be at market value

9 (1) This paragraph applies where a relevant discounted security is transferred from one person to another in a case in which—

(*a*) the transfer is made for a consideration which consists of or includes consideration not in money or money's worth; or

(*b*) the transfer is made otherwise than by way of a bargain made at arm's length.

(2) For the purposes of this Schedule—

(*a*) the person making the transfer shall be treated as obtaining in respect of it an amount equal to the market value of the security at the time of the transfer, and

(*b*) the person to whom the transfer is made shall be treated as paying in respect of his acquisition of the security an amount equal to that market value.

GENERAL NOTE

This paragraph provides that market value shall be deemed to apply to certain transfers of a relevant discounted security.

It applies to a transfer of a relevant discounted security—

(*a*) for a consideration consisting or including consideration not in money or money's worth; or

(*b*) which is not at arm's length.

The paragraph provides that the transfer, for both transferee and transferor, shall be deemed to be at the market value of the relevant discounted security at the time of transfer.

Issue of securities in separate tranches

10 (1) In a case where—

(*a*) none of the securities issued on the occasion of the original issue of securities under a particular prospectus would be a relevant discounted security apart from this paragraph,

(*b*) some of the securities subsequently issued under the prospectus would be relevant discounted securities apart from paragraph 3(2)(*f*) above, and

(*c*) there is a time (whether before, at or after the beginning of the year 1996–97) when the aggregate nominal value as at that time of the securities falling within paragraph (*b*) above exceeds the aggregate nominal value as at that time of the securities which have been issued under the prospectus and do not fall within that paragraph,

sub-paragraph (2) below shall apply in relation to every security which has been or is issued under the prospectus at any time (whether before, at or after the time mentioned in paragraph (*c*) above).

(2) As regards any event occurring in relation to the security after the time mentioned in sub-paragraph (1)(*c*) above, this Schedule shall have effect as if the security—

   (*a*) were a relevant discounted security; and
   (*b*) had been acquired as such (whatever the time of its acquisition).

(3) For the purposes of sub-paragraph (2) above events, in relation to a security, include anything constituting a transfer, redemption or acquisition for the purposes of this Schedule.

GENERAL NOTE
This paragraph deals with securities issued in tranches.
Paragraph 3(2)(*f*) above provides that "relevant discounted securities" does not include securities issued under the same prospectus as other securities which have been issued previously and which are not relevant discounted security. However, the definition is subject to para 10.
This paragraph applies where—

(*a*) none of the securities issued originally would be a relevant discounted security apart from this paragraph;
(*b*) some of the securities issued subsequently would be relevant discounted securities apart from para 3(2)(*f*); and
(*c*) there is a time (whether before or after the introduction of the changes introduced by the Schedule) when the aggregate nominal value of the securities under (*b*) exceeds that for the securities under (*a*).

Any "event" arising after the time in (*c*) will have effect as if all securities issued (or to be issued at any time) under the prospectus were relevant discounted securities and had been acquired as such. An "event" for this purpose is any transfer, redemption or acquisition for the purposes of the Schedule.

Accrued income scheme

11 In a case where—

   (*a*) paragraph 1 or 2 above applies on the transfer of any security, and
   (*b*) apart from this paragraph, the transfer would be a transfer for the purposes of sections 710 to 728 of the Taxes Act 1988,

the transfer shall be treated as if it were not a transfer for those purposes.

GENERAL NOTE
This paragraph provides for the accrued income scheme to be disapplied to transfers of a relevant discounted security.

Assets transferred abroad

12 For the purposes of sections 739 and 740 of the Taxes Act 1988 (prevention of avoidance of tax by transfer of assets abroad), where a person resident or domiciled outside the United Kingdom realises a profit from the discount on a relevant discounted security, that profit shall be taken to be income of that person.

GENERAL NOTE
This paragraph causes the anti-avoidance provisions of TA 1988 ss 739–740 to apply.
Where a person resident or domiciled outside of the UK realises a profit from the discount on a relevant discounted security, it is treated as his income for the purposes of these sections.

Excluded indexed securities

13 (1) For the purposes of this Schedule a security is an excluded indexed security if the amount payable on redemption is linked to the value of chargeable assets.

(2) For the purposes of this paragraph an amount is linked to the value of chargeable assets if, in pursuance of any provision having effect for the purposes of the security, it is equal to an amount determined by applying a relevant percentage change in the value of chargeable assets to the amount for which the security was issued.

(3) In sub-paragraph (2) above the reference to a relevant percentage change in the value of chargeable assets is a reference to the amount of the percentage change (if any) over the relevant period in the value of chargeable assets of any particular description or in any index of the value of any such assets.

(4) In sub-paragraph (3) above "the relevant period" means—

(*a*) the period between the time of the issue of the security and its redemption; or
(*b*) any other period in which almost all of that period is comprised and which differs from that period exclusively for purposes connected with giving effect to a valuation in relation to rights or liabilities under the security.

(5) If—

(*a*) there is a provision which, in the case of the amount payable on the redemption of any security, falls within sub-paragraph (2) above,
(*b*) that provision is made subject to any other provision applying to the determination of that amount,
(*c*) that other provision is to the effect only that that amount must not be less than a specified percentage of the amount for which the security is issued, and
(*d*) the specified percentage is not more than 10 per cent,

that other provision shall be disregarded in determining for the purposes of this paragraph whether the amount payable on redemption is linked to the value of chargeable assets.

(6) For the purposes of this paragraph an asset is a chargeable asset in relation to any security if any gain accruing to a person on a disposal of that asset would, on the assumptions specified in sub-paragraph (7) below, be a chargeable gain for the purposes of the Taxation of Chargeable Gains Act 1992.

(7) Those assumptions are—

(*a*) where it is not otherwise the case, that the asset is an asset of the person in question and that that person does not have the benefit of any exemption conferred by section 100 of that Act of 1992 (exemption for authorised unit trusts etc);
(*b*) that the asset is not one the disposal of which by that person would fall to be treated for the purposes of income tax as a disposal in the course of a trade, profession or vocation carried on by that person; and
(*c*) that chargeable gains that might accrue under section 116(10) of that Act are to be disregarded.

(8) For the purposes of this paragraph neither—

(*a*) the retail prices index, nor
(*b*) any similar general index of prices published by the government of any territory or by the agent of any such government,

shall be taken to be an index of the value of chargeable assets.

GENERAL NOTE
This paragraph defines "excluded indexed securities" which are not relevant discounted securities by virtue of para 3(2)(*c*) above.

An excluded indexed security is a security where the amount payable on redemption is linked to the value of chargeable assets.

A "chargeable asset" for this purpose is an asset in relation to any security if a gain on its disposal on or after 1 April 1996 would be a chargeable gain under TCGA 1992 assuming that—

(*a*) the asset is an asset of the person (if it is not) and that exemption under TCGA 1992 s 100 (exemption for authorised unit trusts etc) is not applicable;
(*b*) a disposal of the asset would not be a disposal for income tax purposes, in the course of a trade, profession or vocation carried on by that person; and
(*c*) the deferral provisions of TCGA 1992 s 116(10) did not apply.

Under sub-para (2) an amount is "linked to the value" of a chargeable asset if, in pursuance of any provision having effect for the purposes of the security, it is determined by applying a "relevant percentage change in the value of chargeable assets" to the amount for which the security was originally issued. This is modified where there is a provision falling within sub-para (2), which is subject to any "other provision" applying to determining the redemption amount. Where the "other provision" provides that the redemption amount must not be less than the issue amount by up to and including 10 per cent the "other provision" is to be disregarded in determining whether the amount payable on redemption is linked to the value of the chargeable asset.

For this purpose, the "relevant percentage change in the value of chargeable assets" is the percentage change in the "relevant period" in the value of any chargeable assets. This also includes changes in value of an index of the value of such assets, but such index excludes the RPI and any similar general index of prices published by the government of any territory of by the agent of any such government.

The "relevant period" is the time between the issue and redemption of the security or such other period in which "almost all" of that period is comprised, where it differs exclusively to effecting the valuation of the rights or liabilities under the security.

Gilt strips

14 (1) Every strip is a relevant discounted security for the purposes of this Schedule.

(2) For the purposes of this Schedule, where a person exchanges a gilt-edged security for strips of that security, the person who receives the strips in the exchange shall be deemed to have paid, in respect of his acquisition of each strip, the amount which bears the same proportion to the market value of the security as is borne by the market value of the strip to the aggregate of the market values of all the strips received in exchange for the security.

(3) For the purposes of this Schedule, where strips are consolidated into a single gilt-edged security by being exchanged by any person for that security, each of the strips shall be deemed to have been redeemed at the time of the exchange by the payment to that person of the amount equal to its market value.

(4) A person who holds a strip on the 5th April in any year of assessment, and who (apart from this sub-paragraph) does not transfer or redeem it on that day, shall be deemed for the purposes of this Schedule—

(*a*) to have transferred that strip on that day;

(*b*) to have received in respect of that transfer an amount equal to the strip's market value on that day; and

(*c*) to have re-acquired the strip on the next day on payment of an amount equal to the amount for which it is deemed to have been disposed of on the previous day;

and the deemed transfer and re-acquisition shall be assumed for the purposes of paragraphs 1 and 2 above to be transactions in connection with which no relevant costs are incurred.

(5) Without prejudice to the generality of any power conferred by section 187 of this Act, the Treasury may by regulations provide that this Schedule is to have effect with such modifications as they may think fit in relation to any relevant discounted security which is a strip.

(6) Regulations made by the Treasury under this paragraph may—

(*a*) make provision for the purposes of sub-paragraphs (2) to (4) above as to the manner of determining the market value at any time of any security;

(*b*) make different provision for different cases; and

(*c*) contain such incidental, supplemental, consequential and transitional provision as the Treasury may think fit.

(7) References in sub-paragraphs (2) and (3) above to the market value of a security given or received in exchange for another are references to its market value at the time of the exchange.

GENERAL NOTE

This paragraph deals with the taxation of gilt strips and effectively causes a mark-to-market basis of taxation to apply each 5 April.

The paragraph provides that every gilt strip is a relevant discounted security. The term "strip" is defined by FA 1942 s 47. The Bank of England issued a parallel paper to the May 1995 Inland

Revenue consultative document on the development of a gilt strips market. The stripping of a gilt causes the entitlements to payment of future interest and repayment of principal to be separated and allows them to be held separately. This is beneficial in that it allows holders of gilts to structure their holdings so that they more closely match their future cash flow requirements. The stripped gilt can be reconstituted into its original form.

Where a person exchanges a gilt for strips of that security, the amount paid for each strip needs to be determined. For the purposes of Sch 13, this is done by allocating the market value of the gilt to the strips and this is done for any particular strip in proportion to the market value of that strip to the aggregate value of the strips.

Where the gilt is reconstituted, each of the strips is deemed to have been redeemed for the payment of its market value at the time of the exchange.

For these purposes market value is that at the time of the exchange.

Where a person holds a strip on any 5 April, he will be deemed to have transferred the strip on 5 April for market value and re-acquired it on the next day for the same amount. For the purposes of paras 1 and 2 above it will be assumed there will be no relevant costs.

The Treasury may make regulations to provide that the Schedule shall have effect to any relevant discounted security which is a gilt as they think fit. Specifically the regulations make provision for the manner of determining market value of the gilts and these may make different provisions for different cases and contain associated provisions as the Treasury thinks fit.

General interpretation

15 (1) In this Schedule—

"deep gain" shall be construed in accordance with paragraph 3(3) above;

"excluded indexed security" has the meaning given by paragraph 13 above;

"market value" (except in paragraph 14 above) has the same meaning as in the Taxation of Chargeable Gains Act 1992;

"relevant discounted security" has the meaning given by paragraphs 3 and 14(1) above;

"strip" means anything which, within the meaning of section 47 of the Finance Act 1942, is a strip of a gilt-edged security.

(2) Where a person, having acquired and transferred any security, subsequently re-acquires it, references in this Schedule to his acquisition of the security shall have effect, in relation to—

(*a*) the transfer by him of that security, or

(*b*) the redemption of the security in a case where he becomes entitled to any amount on its redemption,

as references to his most recent acquisition of the security before the transfer or redemption in question.

GENERAL NOTE

This paragraph provides definitions and general interpretation provisions.

It provides that "market value" is as provided by TCGA 1992. In addition it provides that where a person acquires a security, disposes of it and then re-acquires it, that on a transfer by him or the redemption of the security the term acquisition shall relate to the most recent acquisition.

Application of Schedule for income tax purposes only

16 (1) This Schedule does not apply for the purposes of corporation tax.

(2) Sub-paragraph (1) above is without prejudice to any enactment not contained in this Schedule by virtue of which the definition of a relevant discounted security, or any other provision of this Schedule, is applied for the purposes of corporation tax.

GENERAL NOTE

This paragraph provides that the Schedule does not apply for corporation tax purposes, although the term "relevant discounted security" which is defined in the Schedule (or any other provision of it) may be applied for the purposes of corporation tax.

SCHEDULE 14

LOAN RELATIONSHIPS: MINOR AND CONSEQUENTIAL AMENDMENTS

GENERAL NOTE

This Schedule makes consequential amendments to existing corporation tax and income tax legislation as a result of the legislation contained in Chapter II of the Finance Act 1996 ("Chapter II") in respect of loan relationships and is introduced by s 104.

The Taxes Management Act 1970 (c 9)

1 (1) In subsection (4A) of section 87A of the Taxes Management Act 1970 (interest on overdue corporation tax)—

(*a*) in paragraph (*a*), for the words from "a relievable amount" to the end of the paragraph there shall be substituted "a non-trading deficit on the company's loan relationships,"; and

(*b*) in paragraph (*b*), for the words from "subsection (5)" to "subsection (10) of that section)" there shall be substituted "section 83(2)(*c*) of the Finance Act 1996 or paragraph 4(3) of Schedule 11 to that Act the whole or part of the deficit for the later period is set off against profits".

(2) In subsection (4B) of that section, for the words "section 131(5) or (6) of the Finance Act 1993", in each place where they occur, there shall be substituted "section 83(2)(*c*) of the Finance Act 1996 or paragraph 4(3) of Schedule 11 to that Act".

GENERAL NOTE

This paragraph provides for consequential amendments to TMA 1970.

The Inheritance Tax Act 1984 (c 51)

2 (1) In section 174(1)(*b*) of the Inheritance Tax Act 1984 (unpaid tax relating to deep discount securities deemed to be transferred on death), for the words from "paragraph 4" onwards there shall be substituted "Schedule 13 to the Finance Act 1996 (discounted securities) on a transfer which is treated as taking place by virtue of paragraph 4(2) of that Schedule."

(2) This paragraph applies in relation to deaths on or after 6th April 1996.

GENERAL NOTE

This paragraph provides for consequential amendments to IHTA 1984 in relation to deaths on or after 6 April 1996.

The Airports Act 1986 (c 31)

3 In section 77 of the Airports Act 1986 (taxation provisions), for subsection (3) there shall be substituted the following subsection—

"(3) For the purposes of Part VI of the Income and Corporation Taxes Act 1988 (company distributions) and Chapter II of Part IV of the Finance Act 1996 (loan relationships), any debentures of the company issued in pursuance of section 4 shall be treated as having been issued for new consideration equal to the principal sum payable under the debenture."

GENERAL NOTE

This paragraph provides for consequential amendments to the Airports Act 1986.

The Gas Act 1986 (c 44)

4 In section 60 of the Gas Act 1986 (taxation provisions), for subsection (3) there shall be substituted the following subsection—

"(3) For the purposes of Part VI of the Income and Corporation Taxes Act 1988 (company distributions) and Chapter II of Part IV of the Finance Act 1996 (loan relationships), any debentures issued in pursuance of section 51 above shall be treated as having been issued for new consideration equal to the principal sum payable under the debenture."

This paragraph provides for consequential amendments to the Gas Act 1986.

The Taxes Act 1988

5 In section 18 of the Taxes Act 1988 (Schedule D), the following subsection shall be inserted after subsection (3)—

"(3A) For the purposes of corporation tax subsection (3) above shall have effect as if the following Case were substituted for Cases III and IV, that is to say—

'Case III: tax in respect of—
     (*a*) profits and gains which, as profits and gains arising from loan relationships, are to be treated as chargeable under this Case by virtue of Chapter II of Part IV of the Finance Act 1996;
     (*b*) any annuity or other annual payment which—
         (i) is payable (whether inside or outside the United Kingdom and whether annually or at shorter or longer intervals) in respect of anything other than a loan relationship; and
         (ii) is not a payment chargeable under Schedule A;
     (*c*) any discount arising otherwise than in respect of a loan relationship;'

and as if Case V did not include tax in respect of any income falling within paragraph (*a*) of the substituted Case III."

This paragraph provides for foreign sourced loan relationships previously assessable under Schedule D Case IV to be assessable under Case III for the purposes of corporation tax.

It inserts a new sub-s (3A) into TA 1988 s 18 which provides that tax on income assessable in respect of loan relationships under Schedule D Case III is to be excluded from Case V.

6 In section 56 of that Act (transactions in deposits with or without certificates or in debts), after subsection (4) there shall be inserted the following subsections—

"(4A) This section and section 56A shall not apply for the purposes of corporation tax except in relation to rights in existence before 1st April 1996.

(4B) For the purposes of corporation tax, where any profits or gains arising from the disposal or exercise of a right in existence before 1st April 1996 are, or (if there were any) would be, chargeable under this section, nothing in Chapter II of Part IV of the Finance Act 1996 (loan relationships) shall require any amount relating to that disposal, or to the exercise of that right, to be brought into account for the purposes of that Chapter."

This paragraph provides for the taxation of transactions in deposits with or without certificates.

It provides that TA 1988 ss 56 and 56A which apply to such transactions, assessing profits under Schedule D Case VI, will cease to apply except for rights in existence before 1 April 1996, when the existing rules and not Chapter II will apply.

7 In section 70(3) of that Act (extension of Cases IV and V of Schedule D to non-resident companies), for "Cases IV and V" there shall be substituted "Cases III and V".

This paragraph is consequential on para 5.

8 In section 75 of that Act (expenses of management), after subsection (1) there shall be inserted the following subsection—

"(1A) The expenses of management of a company shall not include any expenses in relation to which a debit falls to be brought into account for the purposes of Chapter

II of Part IV of the Finance Act 1996 (loan relationships) in computing the amount from which sums disbursed as expenses of management are deductible."

GENERAL NOTE
This paragraph excludes expenses relieved as debits under Chapter II from the definition of expenses of management under TA 1988 s 75.

9 In section 77 of that Act (incidental costs of obtaining loan finance), after subsection (7) there shall be inserted the following subsection—

"(8) This section shall not apply for the purposes of corporation tax."

GENERAL NOTE
This paragraph provides that TA 1988 s 77 will not apply for the purposes of corporation tax as the relevant expenses will now be relieved under Chapter II.

10 (1) Section 78 of that Act (discounted bills of exchange) shall cease to have effect except in relation to bills of exchange drawn before 1st April 1996.

(2) Where any bill so drawn is paid on or after 1st April 1996—

(*a*) the amount which subsection (2) of that section provides to be treated as a deduction against total profits and as a charge on income shall (instead of being so treated) be brought into account for the purposes of this Chapter as a non-trading debit; and

(*b*) that amount shall be the only amount brought into account for the purposes of this Chapter in respect of the discount in question.

GENERAL NOTE
This paragraph provides for the treatment of discounted bills of exchange within TA 1988 s 78.
Section 78 will cease to have effect for bills drawn on or after 1 April 1996. Where bills drawn before this date are paid on or after that date, relief will be given for the amount allowed under s 78(2) only as a non-trading debit under Chapter II.

11 (1) In section 209 of that Act (meaning of "distribution"), after subsection (3) there shall be inserted the following subsection—

"(3A) Where any security of a company is issued at a premium representing new consideration—

(*a*) the references in subsection (2)(*d*), (*da*) and (*e*) above to so much of any distribution as represents, or is an amount representing, the principal secured by a security shall be construed, in relation to a distribution in respect of the security issued at a premium, as references to the aggregate of—

(i) so much of the distribution as represents, or is an amount representing, that principal, and
(ii) so much of it as represents, or is an amount representing, the premium;

and

(*b*) the reference in subsection (2)(*d*) above to so much of any distribution as represents a reasonable commercial return for the use of the principal secured by a security shall be construed, in relation to a distribution in respect of the security issued at a premium, as a reference to the aggregate of—

(i) so much of the distribution as represents a reasonable commercial return for the use of that principal, and
(ii) so much of it as (when regard is had to the extent to which distributions represent the premium) represents a reasonable commercial return for the use of the premium."

(2) Sub-paragraph (1) above does not apply to distributions made before 1st April 1996.

GENERAL NOTE
This paragraph provides for amendments to TA 1988 s 209 which provides the meaning of "distribution", which is effective for distributions made on or after 1 April 1996.

It inserts a new sub-s (3A) into s 209 and relates to securities issued at a premium representing new consideration.

First, it provides that references in s 209(2)(*d*), (*da*) and (*e*) to the amount of a distribution which represents the principal secured, shall be the sum of the amounts representing the principal and the premium. Each of these subsections provides that amounts representing a return of such principal will not be treated as a distribution.

Second, it provides that references in s 209(2)(*d*) to the amount of a distribution which represents a reasonable commercial return for the use of the principal secured by a security shall be the sum of the amounts representing such a return for the use of the principal and the premium. Section 209(2)(*d*) provides that amounts representing a reasonable commercial return for the use of such principal will be treated as a distribution.

12 (1) In subsection (2) of section 242 of that Act (set off of losses against surplus franked investment income), for paragraph (*f*) there shall be substituted—

"(*f*) the setting of amounts against profits in pursuance of a claim under, section 83 of the Finance Act 1996 (non-trading deficits on loan relationships) or paragraph 4 of Schedule 11 to that Act (deficits of insurance companies)."

(2) In subsection (8) of that section, for paragraph (*e*) there shall be substituted the following paragraph—

"(*e*) if and so far as the purpose for which the claim is made is the setting of an amount against profits in pursuance of a claim under—

(i) section 83 of the Finance Act 1996 (non-trading deficits on loan relationships), or

(ii) paragraph 4 of Schedule 11 to that Act (deficits of insurance companies),

the time limit that by virtue of subsection (6) of that section or sub-paragraph (15) of that paragraph would be applicable to such a claim."

GENERAL NOTE
This paragraph amends TA 1988 s 242(2)(*f*) (which allows non-trading foreign exchange losses under FA 1993 s 131(4) to be set off against surplus franked investment income) to be amended to allow a non-trading deficit (including that of an insurance company) in the same way. It should be noted that the non-trading foreign exchange losses are now given under Chapter II (see Sch 14 para 68 below).

13 (1) In subsection (4) of section 247 of that Act (payments between companies), for "for corporation tax charges on income of the payer company" there shall be substituted "deductible payments in relation to the payer company for the purposes of corporation tax".

(2) After that subsection there shall be inserted the following subsection—

"(4A) The reference in subsection (4) above to a payment which is a deductible payment in relation to a company for the purposes of corporation tax is a reference to any payment which is—

(*a*) a charge on income of that company for those purposes; or

(*b*) a payment of interest in relation to which a debit falls to be brought into account in the case of that company for the purposes of Chapter II of Part IV of the Finance Act 1996 (loan relationships)."

GENERAL NOTE
This paragraph provides for payments of interest which give rise to debits under Chapter II to be subject to the group income provisions of TA 1988 s 247.

14 (1) In subsection (2)(*b*) of section 337 of that Act (deduction of yearly interest etc in computing income), for "yearly interest, annuity or other annual payment" there shall be substituted "annuity or other annual payment which is not interest".

(2) Subsection (3) of that section (deduction of yearly interest payable to a bank) shall cease to have effect.

GENERAL NOTE
This paragraph amends TA 1988 s 337 so that it will no longer prevent yearly interest other than that paid to a UK bank within s 337(3), from being deductible in computing profits from any source, but see para 15 below.

15   After section 337 of that Act there shall be inserted the following section—

"337A   Interest payable by companies

No deduction shall be made in respect of interest in computing a company's income from any source except in accordance with Chapter II of Part IV of the Finance Act 1996 (loan relationships)."

GENERAL NOTE
This paragraph inserts a new s 337A into TA 1988 which provides that no interest shall be deductible in computing a company's income from any source other than interest within Chapter II.

16   (1) Section 338 of that Act (charges on income) shall be amended as follows.

(2) In subsection (3)—

(*a*) in paragraph (*a*), for the words from "any yearly interest" to "annual payment" there shall be substituted "any annuity or annual payment payable otherwise than in respect of any of the company's loan relationships"; and
(*b*) the words from "and" at the end of paragraph (*a*) to the end of the subsection shall be omitted.

(3) In subsection (4), paragraphs (*b*) and (*c*) shall be omitted.

(4) In subsection (5)(*a*), the words ", not being interest," shall be omitted.

(5) Subsection (6) shall cease to have effect.

GENERAL NOTE
This paragraph excludes yearly interest in respect of loan relationships from the provisions allowing relief for charges on income.

17   Sections 338A, 340 and 341 of that Act (charges on income to include certain loans to buy land, provisions relating to interest payable to non-residents and provisions relating to payments between related companies) shall cease to have effect.

GENERAL NOTE
This paragraph provides that TA 1988 ss 338A, 340 and 341 cease to have effect.

18   In section 349(2) of that Act (deductions from interest payments), after "Schedule D" there shall be inserted "(as that Schedule has effect apart from the modification made for the purposes of corporation tax by section 18(3A))".

GENERAL NOTE
This paragraph provides that withholding tax under TA 1988 s 349 will only apply to payments of yearly interest which are UK sourced.

19   In section 400 of that Act (writing-off of government investment), after subsection (9) of that section there shall be inserted the following subsection—

"(9) Nothing in section 80(5) of the Finance Act 1996 (matters to be brought into account in the case of loan relationships only under Chapter II of Part IV of that Act) shall be construed as preventing this section from applying where a government investment in a body corporate is written off by the extinguishment, in whole or in part, of any liability under a loan relationship."

GENERAL NOTE
This paragraph makes amendment to TA 1988 s 400, which provides that where any amount of a government investment in a company is written off, its losses brought forward shall be reduced by the amount of the write-off.
The paragraph inserts a new sub-s (9) which provides that s 80(5) (which provides that the

provisions of Chapter II shall be the only basis of subjecting profits and losses from loan relationships to corporation tax unless otherwise provided) will not prevent the operation of TA 1988 s 400.

20 (1) In section 401 of that Act (relief for pre-trading expenditure), after subsection (1) there shall be inserted the following subsections—

"(1AA) Subsection (1) above shall not apply to any expenditure in relation to which any debit falls, or (but for subsection (1AB) below) would fall, to be brought into account for the purposes of Chapter II of Part IV of the Finance Act 1996 (loan relationships).

(1AB) Where, in the case of any company—

(*a*) a non-trading debit is given for any accounting period for the purposes of Chapter II of Part IV of the Finance Act 1996 (loan relationships), and
(*b*) an election for the purposes of this section is made by that company with respect to that debit within the period of 2 years beginning with the end of that accounting period,

that debit shall not be brought into account for the purposes of that Chapter as a non-trading debit for that period, but subsection (1AC) below shall apply instead.

(1AC) If a company—

(*a*) begins to carry on a trade within the period of seven years after the end of the accounting period for which a non-trading debit is given for the purposes of Chapter II of Part IV of the Finance Act 1996 (loan relationships),
(*b*) that debit is such that, if it had been given for the accounting period in which the company begins to carry on that trade, it would have been brought into account by reference to that trade in accordance with section 82(2) of that Act (trading debits and credits), and
(*c*) an election is or has been made with respect to that debit under subsection (1AB) above,

that debit shall be treated for the purposes of that Chapter as if it were a debit for the accounting period in which the company begins to carry on the trade and shall be brought into account for that period in accordance with section 82(2) of that Act."

(2) Subsection (1A) of that section shall cease to have effect.

GENERAL NOTE
This paragraph provides that the existing rules allowing relief for pre-trading funding costs incurred within seven years of commencement of trading under TA 1988 s 401 are amended so as to apply to debits under Chapter II.

21 (1) In subsection (6) of section 404 of that Act (dual resident trading companies treated as investing companies)—

(*a*) in paragraph (*a*), after sub-paragraph (i) there shall be inserted the following sub-paragraph—

"(ia) making payments in relation to which, being payments under loan relationships, any debits fall to be brought into account for the purposes of Chapter II of Part IV of the Finance Act 1996;"

(*b*) in paragraph (*c*)(i), for "amount" there shall be substituted "aggregate of the debits relating to interest on the company's debtor relationships that fall to be brought into account for the purposes of Chapter II of Part IV of the Finance Act 1996 and the amounts";
(*c*) in paragraph (*c*)(ii), for "those charges include" there shall be substituted "that aggregate includes"; and
(*d*) in paragraph (*c*)(iii), for "the paying of those charges" there shall be substituted "the payment by the company of interest under its debtor relationships and of amounts treated as charges on income".

(2) After that subsection there shall be inserted the following subsection—

"(7) In this section 'debtor relationship' has the same meaning as in Chapter II of Part IV of the Finance Act 1996."

GENERAL NOTE
This paragraph amends TA 1988 s 404, which restricts group relief available in respect of certain dual resident companies so that the restriction applies to debits under Chapter II in the same way as it applied previously to interest.

22 (1) In subsection (1)(*b*) of section 407 of that Act (relationship between group relief and other relief), after "338(1)" there shall be inserted "of this Act or by virtue of section 83 of, or paragraph 4 of Schedule 11 to, the Finance Act 1996 (non-trading deficits)".

(2) In subsection (2) of that section, for paragraph (*c*) and the words after that paragraph there shall be substituted the following paragraph—

"(*c*) relief in pursuance of a claim under section 83(2) of, or paragraph 4 of Schedule 11 to, the Finance Act 1996 (non-trading deficits) in respect of any deficit for a deficit period after the accounting period the profits of which are being computed."

GENERAL NOTE
This paragraph provides that for the purposes of TA 1988 s 407, which orders the set off of different reliefs, will apply in the same way to non-trading deficits under Chapter II as it did to interest which would have been a charge on income.
The amendment in the manner of giving foreign exchange losses as non-trading deficits (provided by para 69 below) is also recognised in defining "relief derived from a subsequent accounting period".

23 (1) Where this Chapter has effect in relation to any accounting period in relation to which section 434A of that Act (computation of losses and limitation on relief) has effect without any of the amendments made by paragraph 2 of Schedule 31 to this Act, subsection (2) of that section of that Act shall have effect in relation to that period with the following amendments, that is to say—

(*a*) in paragraph (*b*), for "amount of interest and annuities treated as charges" there shall be substituted "aggregate amount treated as a charge", and at the end there shall be inserted "and"; and
(*b*) after that paragraph there shall be inserted the following paragraph—

"(*c*) any relevant non-trading deficit for that period on the company's debtor relationships."

(2) After that subsection there shall be inserted the following subsection—

"(2A) The reference in subsection (2)(*c*) above to a relevant non-trading deficit for any period on a company's debtor relationships is a reference to the non-trading deficit on the company's loan relationships which would be produced by any separate computation made under paragraph 2 of Schedule 11 to the Finance Act 1996 for the company's basic life assurance and general annuity business if credits and debits given in respect of the company's creditor relationships (within the meaning of Chapter II of Part IV of that Act) were disregarded."

(3) In subsection (3) of that section (losses not allowable against policy holders' share of relevant profits), for the words from "under" to the end of paragraph (*b*) there shall be substituted—

"(*a*) under Chapter II (loss relief) or Chapter IV (group relief) of Part X, or
(*b*) in respect of any amount representing a non-trading deficit on the company's loan relationships that has been computed otherwise than by reference to debits and credits referable to that business,".

GENERAL NOTE
This and the following two paragraphs make a number of minor amendments to the special provisions relating to insurance companies.
Paragraph 23 amends TA 1988 s 434A, which prevents double relief for losses and ring-fences policy holders' income and gains, to fit with the new treatment of loan relationships.
Subparagraph (1) removes from s 434A(2)(*b*) the reference to interest and replaces it with a new

sub-s (2)(*c*) referring to a non-trading deficit on debtor relationships (the equivalent of interest payable). This amendment applies only to accounting periods which are not affected by the new provisions governing the calculation of and relief for losses (TA 1988 s 434A as amended by Sch 31 para 2 of this Act).

Subparagraph (2) inserts a new s 434A(2A) which makes it clear that the non-trading deficit in new sub-s (2)(*c*) is to be calculated independently of amounts relating to creditor relationships.

Subparagraph (3) amends s 434A(3) to refer to non-trading deficits instead of non-trading losses on interest rate and currency contracts. The losses referable to the interest rate and currency contracts are in future to be assimilated with the deficits on loan relationships instead of with FOREX losses (see paras 71 and 74 of this Schedule amending FA 1994 s 160 and Sch 18). The losses and deficits which are not referable to an insurance company's life business may not be set against the share of profits referable to policy holders.

24   Where this Chapter has effect in relation to any accounting period in relation to which section 434B of that Act (treatment of interest and annuities in the case of insurance companies) has effect without the amendments made by section 165 of this Act, that section of that Act shall have effect in relation to that period as if the words "interest or", in each place where they occur, were omitted.

GENERAL NOTE
This is a transitional provision dealing with the different commencement dates for s 165 and the provisions relating to loan relationships. Where the latter come into operation before the changes in TA 1988 s 434B made by s 165 the references to interest in s 434B are to be omitted, in order to prevent double relief.

25   In section 440 of that Act (transfer of assets between categories of business of insurance companies), after subsection (2) there shall be inserted the following subsection—

"(2A) Where under subsection (1) or (2) above there is a deemed disposal and re-acquisition of any asset representing a loan relationship of a company, any authorised accounting method used as respects that asset for the purposes of Chapter II of Part IV of the Finance Act 1996 shall be applied as respects that asset as if the asset that is deemed to be disposed of and the asset that is deemed to be re-acquired were different assets."

GENERAL NOTE
A new TA 1988 s 440(2A) allows differing (authorised) accounting methods to continue undisturbed in respect of assets transferred between different categories of business carried on by an insurance company, or in the case of transfers between companies, under the Insurance Companies Act 1982 Sch 2C Part I, where there is continuity of tax treatment.

26   In section 468L(5) of that Act (interest distributions), for the words from the beginning to "complied with" there shall be substituted "Nothing in subsection (2) above or Chapter II of Part IV of the Finance Act 1996 (loan relationships) shall require any amount relating to an interest distribution to be brought into account for the purposes of that Chapter otherwise than by virtue of paragraph 4(4) of Schedule 10 to that Act; but the interest distributions of an authorised unit trust for a distribution period".

GENERAL NOTE
This paragraph provides that in general, interest distributions by unit trusts are to be ignored for the purposes of this legislation. (The one exception is that interest distributions by any unit trust which fails the non-qualifying investments test in Sch 10 para 8 are required to be brought into account in valuing a company's holding in that trust.) However, the interest distributions continue to be allowed under TA 1988 s 468L as a deduction against the profits of an authorised unit trust for its accounting period in which the distribution period ends.

27   (1) In subsection (2) of section 475 of that Act (relief in relation to tax free Treasury securities in respect of borrowed money), for paragraph (*b*) there shall be substituted the following paragraph—

"(*b*) shall not be brought into account by way of any debit given for the purposes of Chapter II of Part IV of the Finance Act 1996 (loan relationships)."

(2) In subsection (4) of that section, for the words from "and is not" onwards there shall be substituted "or to be brought into account by way of a debit given for the purposes of Chapter II of Part IV of the Finance Act 1996 (loan relationships)."

GENERAL NOTE
This paragraph provides that TA 1988 s 475 is to be amended so as to prevent relief for debits under Chapter II in the prescribed circumstances. Section 475 prevents relief for the funding cost of UK branches of foreign companies, associated with the acquisition of FOTRA gilts, which give rise to exempt income in the hands of non-UK resident companies.

28 (1) In subsection (3) of section 477A of that Act (building societies: regulations for deducting tax), for paragraph (*a*) there shall be substituted the following paragraphs—

"(*a*) liability to pay the dividends or interest shall be treated for the purposes of Chapter II of Part IV of the Finance Act 1996 as a liability arising under a loan relationship of the building society;
(*aa*) if the dividends or interest are payable to a company, they shall be treated for those purposes as payable to that company in pursuance of a right arising under a loan relationship of that company;".

(2) Subsections (3A) to (3C) of that section shall cease to have effect.

GENERAL NOTE
This paragraph amends the power to make regulations for building societies under TA 1988 s 477A to take account of the loan relationships legislation.

29 Sections 484 and 485 of that Act (savings banks: exemption from tax) shall cease to have effect.

GENERAL NOTE
This paragraph repeals the specific exemption for savings banks under TA 1988 ss 484, 485. Following the introduction of the legislation on loan relationships, it is no longer necessary.

30 In section 486 of that Act (industrial and provident societies)—

(*a*) in subsection (1), for the words from "and, subject to subsection (7)" onwards there shall be substituted "but interest payable by such a society (whether as share interest or loan interest) shall be treated for the purposes of corporation tax as interest under a loan relationship of the society."; and
(*b*) in subsection (7), for the words from "not be deductible" onwards there shall be substituted "not be brought into account in that period for the purposes of Chapter II of Part IV of the Finance Act 1996 (loan relationships)."

GENERAL NOTE
This paragraph amends the treatment of share interest or loan interest payable by a registered industrial and provident society or by certain forms of co-operative to take account of the loan relationships legislation.

31 (1) In subsection (1) of section 487 of that Act (credit unions), for paragraph (*b*) there shall be substituted the following paragraph—

"(*b*) no credits shall be brought into account for the purposes of Chapter II of Part IV of the Finance Act 1996 in respect of any loan relationship of a credit union as respects which a member of the union stands in the position of a debtor as respects the debt in question."

(2) In subsection (3) of that section—

(*a*) for "No share interest, loan interest or annuity or other annual payment" there shall be substituted "An annuity or other annual payment (not being a payment of share interest or loan interest) which is"; and
(*b*) after "shall" there shall be inserted "not".

(3) After that subsection there shall be inserted the following subsection—

"(3A) No debits shall be brought into account for the purposes of Chapter II of Part

IV of the Finance Act 1996 in respect of any loan relationship of a credit union as respects which a member of the union stands in the position of a creditor as respects the debt in question."

GENERAL NOTE
This paragraph amends the tax treatment of credit unions to take account of the loan relationships legislation.

32 (1) In subsection (1) of section 494 of that Act (charges on income and ring fence profits), after "Section 338" there shall be inserted "of this Act and Chapter II of Part IV of the Finance Act 1996 (loan relationships)".

(2) For the first sentence of subsection (2) of that section there shall be substituted the following—

"(2) Debits shall not be brought into account for the purposes of Chapter II of Part IV of the Finance Act 1996 in respect of any loan relationship of a company in any manner that results in a reduction of what would otherwise be the company's ring fence profits except—

(*a*) to the extent that the loan relationship is in respect of money borrowed by the company which has been—

(i) used to meet expenditure incurred by the company in carrying on oil extraction activities or in acquiring oil rights otherwise than from a connected person; or
(ii) appropriated to meeting expenditure to be so incurred by the company;

(*b*) in the case of debits falling to be brought into account by virtue of subsection (4) of section 84 of that Act in respect of a loan relationship that has not been entered into, to the extent that the relationship would have been one entered into for the purpose of borrowing money to be used or appropriated as mentioned in paragraph (*a*) above;
(*c*) in the case of debits in respect of a loan relationship deemed to exist for the purposes of section 100 of that Act, to the extent that the payment of interest under that relationship is expenditure incurred as mentioned in sub-paragraph (i) of paragraph (*a*) above; and
(*d*) in the case of debits in respect of a debtor relationship of the company which is a creditor relationship of a company associated with the company, to the extent that (subject always to paragraph (*a*) above) the debit does not exceed what, having regard to—

(i) all the terms on which the money was borrowed, and
(ii) the standing of the borrower,

would be the debit representing a reasonable commercial rate of return on the money borrowed.

In this subsection 'debtor relationship' and 'creditor relationship' have the same meanings as in Chapter II of Part IV of the Finance Act 1996, and references to a loan relationship, in relation to the borrowing of money, do not include references to any loan relationship deemed to exist for the purposes of section 100 of that Act."

(3) After subsection (2) of that section there shall be inserted the following subsection—

"(2A) Where any debit—

(*a*) falls to be brought into account for the purposes of Chapter II of Part IV of the Finance Act 1996 in respect of any loan relationship of a company, but
(*b*) in accordance with subsection (2) above cannot be brought into account in a manner that results in any reduction of what would otherwise be the company's ring fence profits,

then (notwithstanding anything in section 82(2) of that Act) that debit shall be brought into account for those purposes as a non-trading debit."

(4) For subsection (4) of that section (charges on income), there shall be substituted the following subsections—

"(4) Subsection (7) of section 403 shall have effect as if the reference in that subsection to the profits of the surrendering company for an accounting period did not include the relevant part of the company's ring fence profits for that period.

(5) For the purpose of subsection (4) above the relevant part of a company's ring fence profits for an accounting period are—

(*a*) if for that period—

(i) there are no charges on income paid by the company that are allowable under section 338, or

(ii) the only charges on income so allowable are charges to which subsection (3) above applies,

all the company's ring fence profits; and

(*b*) in any other case, so much of its ring fence profits as exceeds the amount of the charges on income paid by the company as are so allowable for that period and are not charges to which subsection (3) above applies."

GENERAL NOTE

This paragraph amends the provisions concerning the extent of relief for charges on income against ring fence profits derived from oil extraction activities or oil rights to take account of the loan relationships legislation. Debits which may not be set against the company's ring fence profits are treated as non-trading debits under this legislation, even where they are derived from a trading activity. The basis for restricting group relief in respect of charges exceeding the company's profits is expressed in a different way.

33 In section 587A of that Act (extra return on new issues of securities), in subsection (1), after paragraph (*e*) there shall be inserted the following—

"but this section shall not apply for the purposes of corporation tax, except where the issue of the new securities was before 1st April 1996."

GENERAL NOTE

This paragraph extends the exemption for certain overseas pension funds to profit realised from a relevant discounted security within Sch 13 para 1.

34 In section 614 of that Act (exemptions and reliefs in respect of income from certain pension funds etc), after subsection (2) of that section there shall be inserted the following subsection—

"(2A) The reference in subsection (2) above to interest on sums forming part of a fund include references to any amount which is treated as income by virtue of paragraph 1 of Schedule 13 to the Finance Act 1996 (relevant discounted securities) and derives from any investment forming part of that fund."

GENERAL NOTE

This paragraph provides that, for corporation tax, TA 1988 s 587A only applies to issues of "new securities" which are issued before 1 April 1996.

Section 587A deals with securities which are issued in tranches, where a subsequent tranche of "new securities" is issued, when there is accrued interest on existing securities which has not yet been paid. It provides that the "extra return" payable on the new securities is not deductible for tax purposes by the issuer.

35 In section 687(3) of that Act (payments under discretionary trusts), after paragraph (j) there shall be inserted the following paragraph—

"(*k*) the amount of any tax on an amount which is treated as income of the trustees by virtue of paragraph 1 of Schedule 12 to the Finance Act 1996 and is charged to tax at the rate applicable to trusts by virtue of paragraph 6 of that Schedule."

GENERAL NOTE

This paragraph ensures that tax charged on discount profits made by trustees of discretionary trusts is credited against the tax due under TA 1988 s 687 on discretionary payments made to beneficiaries.

36 In section 710 of that Act (interpretation of sections 711 to 728), after subsection (1) there shall be inserted the following subsection—

"(1A) Sections 711 to 728 shall not apply for the purposes of corporation tax except as respects transfers of securities taking place before 1st April 1996."

GENERAL NOTE
This paragraph amends s 710 so as to provide that the accrued income scheme (TA 1988 ss 711–728) will not apply for corporation tax purposes except for transfers taking place before 1 April 1996.

37 In section 730A of that Act (treatment of price differential on repos) the following subsections shall be substituted for subsection (6)—

"(6) For the purposes of Chapter II of Part IV of the Finance Act 1996 (loan relationships)—

(*a*) interest deemed by virtue of subsection (2) above to be paid or received by any company shall be deemed to be interest under a loan relationship; and
(*b*) the debits and credits falling to be brought into account for the purposes of that Chapter so far as they relate to the deemed interest shall be those given by the use in relation to the deemed interest of an authorised accruals basis of accounting.

(6A) Any question whether debits or credits brought into account in accordance with subsection (6) above in relation to any company—

(*a*) are to be brought into account under section 82(2) of the Finance Act 1996 (trading loan relationships), or
(*b*) are to be treated as non-trading debits or credits,

shall be determined (subject to Schedule 11 to that Act (insurance companies)) according to the extent (if any) to which the company is a party to the repurchase in the course of activities forming an integral part of a trade carried on by the company."

GENERAL NOTE
This paragraph amends TA 1988 s 730A so that the price differential on a repo (or other agreement covered by that section) which is characterised as interest, will be treated as interest paid under a loan relationship. The issue of whether the resulting debits and credits are trading or non-trading will be subject to the same rules as in Chapter II.

38 In section 737(5A) of that Act (relief in respect of manufactured dividends), after "a manufactured dividend" there shall be inserted "that is not manufactured interest to which section 97 of the Finance Act 1996 applies".

GENERAL NOTE
This paragraph amends TA 1988 s 737(5A) and excludes manufactured payments within s 97 from its effect. Section 737(5A) prevents relief for amounts of income tax withheld from manufactured payments in certain circumstances.

39 (1) For subsections (10) and (11) of section 768B of that Act (change in ownership of investment companies), there shall be substituted the following subsection—

"(10) Part IV of Schedule 28A shall have effect for the purpose of restricting, in a case where this section applies, the debits to be brought into account for the purposes of Chapter II of Part IV of the Finance Act 1996 (loan relationships) in respect of the company's loan relationships."

(2) In subsection (13) of that section (modified application of section 768(6)), after "company's total profits" there shall be inserted ", or the debits to be brought into account for the purposes of Chapter II of Part IV of the Finance Act 1996 in the case of a company in respect of its loan relationships,".

GENERAL NOTE
This paragraph provides for amendment to TA 1988 s 768B, which restricts the deductibility of expenses generally, and causes the application of TA 1988 Sch 28A, in prescribed circumstances

when there is a change in ownership of an investment company. The paragraph causes Sch 28A to apply to debits under Chapter II so as to restrict relief in the prescribed circumstances.

40 For subsections (9) and (10) of section 768C of that Act there shall be substituted the following subsection—

"(9) Part IV of Schedule 28A shall have effect for the purpose of restricting, in a case where this section applies, the debits to be brought into account for the purposes of Chapter II of Part IV of the Finance Act 1996 (loan relationships) in respect of the relevant company's loan relationships."

GENERAL NOTE
The paragraph provides for amendments to TA 1988 s 768C which restricts the deductibility of expenses and causes the application of TA 1988 Sch 28A, in prescribed circumstances when there is a change in ownership of an investment company and there is a transfer of an asset from a group company. The paragraph causes Sch 28A to apply to debits under Chapter II so as to restrict relief in the prescribed circumstances.

41 In section 795 of that Act (computation of income subject to foreign tax), after subsection (3) there shall be inserted the following subsection—

"(4) Subsections (2) and (3) above have effect for the purposes of corporation tax notwithstanding anything in section 80(5) of the Finance Act 1996 (matters to be brought into account in the case of loan relationships only under Chapter II of Part IV of that Act)."

GENERAL NOTE
The paragraph amends TA 1988 s 795, which deals with the computation of income subject to foreign tax. An additional subparagraph is inserted into s 795, which provides that s 795(2) and (3) shall have effect disregarding s 80(5). Section 80(5) provides that where amounts are brought into account under Chapter II, they shall be the only amounts recognised for corporation tax purposes unless otherwise provided.

42 (1) In section 797 of that Act (limits on credit for foreign tax in the case of corporation tax), after subsection (3) there shall be inserted the following subsections—

"(3A) Where, in a case to which section 797A does not apply, a company has a non-trading deficit on its loan relationships for the relevant accounting period, then for the purposes of subsection (3) above that deficit shall be treated, to the extent that it is an amount to which a claim under—

(*a*) subsection (2)(*a*) of section 83 of the Finance Act 1996 (deficit set against current year profits), or
(*b*) paragraph 4(2) of Schedule 11 to that Act (set-off of deficits in the case of insurance companies),

relates, as an amount that can in that period be set against profits of any description but can be allocated in accordance with subsection (3) above only to the profits against which it is set off in pursuance of the claim.

(3B) For the purposes of subsection (3) above, where—

(*a*) section 797A does not apply in the case of any company, and
(*b*) any amount is carried forward to the relevant accounting period in pursuance of a claim under subsection (2)(*d*) of section 83 of the Finance Act 1996 or in accordance with subsection (3) of that section,

then that amount must be allocated to non-trading profits of the company for that period (so far as they are sufficient for the purpose) and cannot be allocated to any other profits."

(2) After subsection (5) of that section there shall be inserted the following subsection—

"(6) In this section 'non-trading profits' has the same meaning as in paragraph 4 of Schedule 8 to the Finance Act 1996."

GENERAL NOTE

This paragraph provides amendment to TA 1988 s 797.

Section 797 provides that the amount of foreign tax that may be credited under arrangements against UK corporation tax is limited to the UK tax on the relevant income or gains.

Subsection (3) provides that if the company has charges on income that are available for relief against profits of more than one description, the company may choose the allocation. This allows the company to maximise the use of the foreign tax credits by allocating charges against the relevant income or gains last.

This paragraph introduces new sub-s (3A) which applies where a company has a non-trading deficit for the relevant accounting period and s 797A (which is introduced by para 43 below) does not apply. It causes any part of the deficit claimed for set off against other current year profits under s 83(2)(*a*) or Sch 11 para 4(2) to be allocated under s 797(3) in the same way.

The paragraph introduces new sub-s (3B) which provides further guidance in the operation of sub-s (3). It applies where a company sets off a non-trading deficit brought forward unders 83(3) or under a claim under s 83(2)(*d*) and s 797A does not apply. For the purposes of sub-s (3), the amount so set off must be allocated only to non-trading profits for that period.

Non-trading profits is as defined in Sch 8 para 4.

43   After section 797 of that Act there shall be inserted the following section—

"797A   Foreign tax on interest brought into account as a non-trading credit

(1)   This section applies for the purposes of any arrangements where, in the case of any company—

(*a*)   any non-trading credit relating to an amount of interest is brought into account for the purposes of Chapter II of Part IV of the Finance Act 1996 (loan relationships) for any accounting period ('the applicable accounting period'); and

(*b*)   there is in respect of that amount an amount of foreign tax for which, under the arrangements, credit is allowable against United Kingdom tax computed by reference to that interest.

(2)   It shall be assumed that tax chargeable under paragraph (*a*) of Case III of Schedule D on the profits and gains arising for the applicable accounting period from the company's loan relationships falls to be computed on the actual amount of its non-trading credits for that period, and without any deduction in respect of non-trading debits.

(3)   Section 797(3) shall have effect (subject to subsection (7) below) as if—

(*a*)   there were for the applicable accounting period an amount equal to the adjusted amount of the non-trading debits falling to be brought into account by being set against profits of the company for that period of any description; and

(*b*)   different parts of that amount might be set against different profits.

(4)   For the purposes of this section, the adjusted amount of a company's non-trading debits for any accounting period is the amount equal, in the case of that company, to the aggregate of the non-trading debits given for that period for the purposes of Chapter II of Part IV of the Finance Act 1996 (loan relationships) less the aggregate of the amounts specified in subsection (5) below.

(5)   Those amounts are—

(*a*)   so much of any non-trading deficit for the applicable accounting period as is an amount to which a claim under subsection (2)(*b*), (*c*) or (*d*) of section 83 of the Finance Act 1996 or paragraph 4(3) of Schedule 11 to that Act (group relief and transfer to previous or subsequent period of deficits) relates;

(*b*)   so much of any non-trading deficit for that period as falls to be carried forward to a subsequent period in accordance with subsection (3) of that section or paragraph 4(4) of that Schedule; and

(*c*)   any amount carried forward to the applicable accounting period in pursuance of a claim under section 83(2)(*d*) of that Act.

(6)   Section 797(3) shall have effect as if any amount specified in subsection (5)(*c*) above were an amount capable of being allocated only to any non-trading profits of the company.

(7) Where—

(*a*) the company has a non-trading deficit for the applicable accounting period,
(*b*) the amount of that deficit exceeds the aggregate of the amounts specified in subsection (5) above, and
(*c*) in pursuance of a claim under—

(i) subsection (2)(*a*) of section 83 of the Finance Act 1996 (deficit set against current year profits), or
(ii) paragraph 4(2) of Schedule 11 to that Act (set-off of deficits in the case of insurance companies),

the excess falls to be set off against profits of any description,

section 797(3) shall have effect as if non-trading debits of the company which in aggregate are equal to the amount of the excess were required to be allocated to the profits against which they are set off in pursuance of the claim.

(8) In this section 'non-trading profits' has the same meaning as in paragraph 4 of Schedule 8 to the Finance Act 1996.''

GENERAL NOTE
This paragraph introduces a new section, s 797A into TA 1988 which provides for foreign tax suffered on interest assessable as a non-trading credit.

The section applies where any non-trading credit is brought into account for any ''applicable accounting period'' and there is foreign tax for which, under arrangements, credit is allowable against UK tax by reference to that interest.

The section amends TA 1988 s 797. Section 797 provides that the amount of foreign tax that may be credited against UK corporation tax is limited to the UK tax on the relevant income or gains. Subsection (3) provides that if the company has charges on income that are available for relief against profits of more than one description, the company may choose the allocation. This allows the company to maximise the use of the foreign tax credits by allocating the charges against the relevant income or gains last.

Section 797A assumes that tax under Schedule D Case III (as amended by Sch 14 para 5 above) will be chargeable on the actual amount of the non-trading credits for the applicable accounting period from the company's loan relationships without deduction of any non-trading debits.

Further s 797A provides that s 797(3) shall have effect for the applicable accounting period, as if the ''adjusted amount of the non-trading debits'' were available for set off against profits of any description of that period and that the amount could be allocated against different profits. For this purpose, ''adjusted amount of the non-trading debits'' is the aggregate of the company's non-trading debits for the period less the aggregate of the following non-trading debits—

(*a*) those, for the applicable accounting period, which are group relieved under s 83(2)(*b*) or carried back under s 83(2)(*c*) or carried forward against non-trading profits for the next accounting period under s 83(2)(*d*) or, for insurance companies carried back under Sch 11 para 4(3);
(*b*) those which are carried forward under s 83(3) or Sch 11 para 4(3); and
(*c*) those which are carried forward to the applicable accounting period under a claim under s 83(2)(*d*).

Section 797A provides that in the operation of TA 1988 s 797(3)—

(i) the amount noted at (*c*) above shall, for the purposes of s 797(3), only be allocated against non-trading profits as defined in Sch 8 para 4(3);
(ii) the allocation under s 797(3) is further prescribed where the company has claimed under s 83(2)(*a*) (or Sch 11 para 4(2)) for the excess of its non-trading deficit for the applicable accounting period to be set off against profits of any description of the deficit period. The allocation under s 797(3) will follow this claim to the extent that the amount of the claim exceeds the aggregate of the non-trading debits listed at (*a*) to (*c*) above.

44 (1) In section 798 of that Act (interest on certain overseas loans), after subsection (2) there shall be inserted the following subsection—

''(2A) For the purposes of corporation tax, this section shall apply only where the expenditure referred to in subsection (1)(*b*) above falls, in the case of the lender, to be brought into account for the purposes of Chapter II of Part IV of the Finance Act 1996 (loan relationships) in accordance with section 82(2) of that Act (trading debits and credits).''

(2) After subsection (3) of that section (deemed increase of interest) there shall be inserted the following subsection—

"(3A) Subsection (3) above has effect for the purposes of corporation tax notwithstanding anything in section 80(5) of the Finance Act 1996 (matters to be brought into account in the case of loan relationships only under Chapter II of Part IV of that Act)."

GENERAL NOTE

This paragraph amends TA 1988 s 798 which restricts the amount of foreign tax credit available on certain overseas loans. Section 798 provides that relief for foreign tax in the prescribed circumstances is limited to UK tax on that income after financial expenditure in relation to the loan.

The paragraph introduces new sub-s (2A) which makes it clear that, for corporation tax purposes, the section only applies where the expenditure which is deductible in computing the profits on the foreign loan interest is brought into account under s 82(2) as a trading debit.

The paragraph further introduces new sub-s (3A) which provides that sub-s (3) (which deals with spared tax and increases the assessable income) is not precluded from operation by s 80(5). Section 80(5) provides that where amounts are brought into account under Chapter II, they shall be the only amounts recognised for corporation tax purposes unless otherwise provided.

45 In section 807 of that Act (sale of securities with or without accrued interest), after subsection (5) there shall be inserted the following subsection—

"(6) This section does not apply for the purposes of corporation tax."

GENERAL NOTE

This paragraph provides that TA 1988 s 807 does not apply for corporation tax purposes.

46 After section 807 of that Act there shall be inserted the following section—

"807A Disposals and acquisitions of company loan relationships with or without interest

(1) This Part shall have effect for the purposes of corporation tax in relation to any company as if tax falling within subsection (2) below were to be disregarded.

(2) Tax falls within this subsection in relation to a company to the extent that it is—

(*a*) tax under the law of a territory outside the United Kingdom; and
(*b*) is attributable, on a just and reasonable apportionment, to interest accruing under a loan relationship at a time when the company is not a party to the relationship.

(3) Subject to subsections (1), (4) and (5) of this section, where—

(*a*) any non-trading credit relating to an amount of interest under a loan relationship is brought into account for the purposes of Chapter II of Part IV of the Finance Act 1996 (loan relationships) in the case of any company,
(*b*) that amount falls, as a result of any related transaction, to be paid to a person other than the company, and
(*c*) had the company been entitled, at the time of that transaction, to receive a payment of an amount of interest equal to the amount of interest to which the non-trading credit relates, the company would have been liable in respect of the amount of interest received to an amount of tax under the law of a territory outside the United Kingdom,

credit for that amount of tax shall be allowable under section 790(4) as if that amount of tax were an amount of tax paid under the law of that territory in respect of the amount of interest to which the non-trading credit relates.

(4) Subsection (3) above does not apply in the case of a credit brought into account in accordance with paragraph 1(2) of Schedule 11 to the Finance Act 1996 (the I minus E basis).

(5) The Treasury may by regulations provide for subsection (3) above to apply—

(*a*) in the case of trading credits as well as in the case of non-trading credits;
(*b*) in the case of any credit ("an insurance credit") in the case of which, by virtue of subsection (4) above, it would not otherwise apply.

(6) Regulations under subsection (5) above may—

(*a*) provide for subsection (3) above to apply in the case of trading credit or an insurance credit only if the circumstances are such as may be described in the regulations;
(*b*) provide for subsection (3) above to apply, in cases where it applies by virtue of any such regulations, subject to such exceptions, adaptations or other modifications as may be specified in the regulations;
(*c*) make different provision for different cases; and
(*d*) contain such incidental, supplemental, consequential and transitional provision as the Treasury think fit.

(7) In this section

'related transaction' has the same meaning as in section 84 of the Finance Act 1996, and
'trading credit' means any credit falling to be brought into account for the purposes of Chapter II of Part IV of the Finance Act 1996 (loan relationships) in accordance with section 82(2) of that Act."

GENERAL NOTE
This paragraph introduces new TA 1988 s 807A for the purposes of corporation tax.
First, under sub-s (1) TA 1988 Part XVIII is to be disapplied on a "just and reasonable apportionment" for foreign tax attributable to income accruing on a loan relationship at a time when the company is not party to it.
Second, under sub-s (3) it provides for unilateral relief under s 790(4)—

(*a*) where a non-trading credit is brought into account by a company;
(*b*) that amount is paid to another person as a result of a related transaction (as defined ins 84(5); and
(*c*) the company would have suffered foreign tax on a receipt of the relevant interest.

Subsection (3) does not apply where Sch 11 para 1(2) applies and is subject to sub-s (1). Further, the Treasury may provide regulations for sub-s (3) to apply in the case of trading credits (as defined by s 82(2)) and in the case of "insurance credits" (as otherwise precluded by Sch 11 para 1(2) as well.
The circumstances and manner in which the regulations apply may be prescribed and the regulations may distinguish different cases and make associated (including transitional) provisions.

47 In section 811 of that Act (deduction of foreign tax where no credit available), after subsection (2) there shall be inserted the following subsection—

"(3) This section has effect for the purposes of corporation tax notwithstanding anything in section 80(5) of the Finance Act 1996 (matters to be brought into account in the case of loan relationships only under Chapter II of Part IV of that Act)."

GENERAL NOTE
This paragraph introduces new sub-s (3) into TA 1988 s 811 for the purposes of corporation tax.
Section 811 allows a deduction for foreign tax where no credit is available. Subsection (3) will apply notwithstanding s 80(5). Section 80(5) provides that where amounts are brought into account under Chapter II, they shall be the only amounts recognised for corporation tax purposes unless otherwise provided.

48 (1) In subsection (7C) of section 826 of that Act (interest on tax overpaid)—

(*a*) in paragraph (*a*), for the words from "a relievable amount" to the end of the paragraph there shall be substituted "a non-trading deficit on the company's loan relationships,";
(*b*) in paragraph (*b*), for the words from "subsection (5)" to "subsection (10) of that section)" there shall be substituted "section 83(2)(*c*) of the Finance Act 1996 or paragraph 4(3) of Schedule 11 to that Act the whole or part of the deficit for the later period is set off against profits"; and
(*c*) in the words after paragraph (*c*), for "subsection (5) or (6) (as the case may be) of

that section" there shall be substituted "section 83(2)(c) of that Act or, as the case may be, paragraph 4(3) of Schedule 11 to that Act".

(2) In subsection (7CA) of that section, for the words "section 131(5) or (6) of the Finance Act 1993", in each place where they occur, there shall be substituted "section 83(2)(c) of the Finance Act 1996 or paragraph 4(3) of Schedule 11 to that Act".

GENERAL NOTE
This paragraph provides amendment to TA 1988 s 826(7C). It provides that where tax is repaid for an earlier period as a result of a non-trading deficit being carried back under s 83(2)(c) or Sch 11 para 4(3), interest runs from the current date and not when the tax was paid. It also amends s 826(7CA) to reflect the changes to the manner of gaining relief for non-trading foreign exchange losses (see para 69 below).

49 In subsection (1) of section 834 of that Act (definitions for the purposes of the Corporation Tax Acts), after the definition of "group relief" there shall be inserted the following definitions—

"'loan relationship' has the same meaning as it has for the purpose of Chapter II of Part IV of the Finance Act 1996;
'non-trading deficit', in relation to a company's loan relationships, shall be construed in accordance with section 82 of the Finance Act 1996."

GENERAL NOTE
This paragraph imports definitions of "loan relationship" and "non-trading deficit" into TA 1988 s 834 (interpretation).

50 Schedule 4 to that Act (deep discount securities) shall cease to have effect.

GENERAL NOTE
This paragraph repeals the deep discount provisions of TA 1988 Sch 4.

51 In paragraph 5B(2) of Schedule 19AC to that Act (overseas life companies), the following paragraph shall be inserted after paragraph (*d*)—

"(*e*) the setting of amounts against profits under, or in pursuance of a claim under, paragraph 4 of Schedule 11 to the Finance Act 1996 (loan relationships of insurance companies)."

GENERAL NOTE
This paragraph permits an overseas life insurance company to set a non-trading deficit within Sch 11 para 4 against UK distribution income.

52 (1) Schedule 23A to that Act (manufactured payments) shall be amended as follows.

(2) In paragraph 3 (manufactured interest on UK securities), after sub-paragraph (4) there shall be inserted the following sub-paragraph—

"(5) Without prejudice to section 97 of the Finance Act 1996 (manufactured interest), the references in this paragraph to all the purposes of the Tax Acts do not include the purposes of Chapter II of Part IV of that Act (loan relationships)."

(3) In paragraph 3A(3) (gilt-edged securities)—

(*a*) for "Sub-paragraph (4)" there shall be substituted "Sub-paragraphs (4) and (5)"; and
(*b*) for "it applies" there shall be substituted "they apply".

(4) In paragraph 4 (manufactured interest on overseas dividends), after sub-paragraph (8) there shall be inserted the following sub-paragraph—

"(9) Without prejudice to section 97 of the Finance Act 1996 (manufactured interest), the references in this paragraph to all the purposes of the Tax Acts do not include the purposes of Chapter II of Part IV of that Act (loan relationships)."

(5) In paragraph 5 (dividends and interest passing through the market), in sub-paragraphs (2)(*b*) and (4)(*b*), at the end there shall be inserted, in each case, "and shall

also be treated, in the case of interest the recipient of which is a company, as if for the purposes of Chapter II of Part IV of the Finance Act 1996 it were interest under a loan relationship to which the company is a party".

(6) In paragraph 6 (unapproved manufactured payments) sub-paragraphs (3), (4), (6) and (7) shall cease to have effect.

(7) In paragraph 7 (irregular manufactured payments), after sub-paragraph (1) there shall be inserted the following sub-paragraph—

"(1A) Sub-paragraph (1) above does not apply in the case of the amount of any manufactured interest or manufactured overseas dividend which falls in accordance with section 91 of the Finance Act 1996 to be treated for the purposes of Chapter II of Part IV of that Act as interest under a loan relationship."

GENERAL NOTE
This paragraph amends TA 1988 Sch 23A, which provides for the treatment of manufactured dividends.
First, it is provided that Chapter II is to take precedence over Sch 23A paras 3 (UK securities), 3A (UK gilts within TA 1988 s 51A) and 4 (overseas securities).
Second, it amends Sch 23A para 5(2)(b) and (4)(b), which caused interest which is "passed on" to be the income of the recipient (or subsequent recipient as appropriate) and not that of the manufacturer. For corporation tax purposes, para 52 treats the interest passed on as arising under a loan relationship to which the recipient company is party.
Third, it causes para 6, which restricts "relief" and limits the use of income tax and foreign tax suffered for "unapproved manufactured payments", to cease to have effect in respect of overseas securities and UK securities.
Finally, it disapplies Sch 23A para 7(1) (which deals with irregular manufactured payments) in respect of manufactured interest and manufactured overseas dividends which are treated within s 97 as interest under a loan relationship.

53 In Schedule 26 to that Act (controlled foreign companies), in paragraph 1(3), the word "and" shall be inserted at the end of paragraph (*e*), and after that paragraph there shall be inserted the following paragraph—

"(*f*) any non-trading deficit on its loan relationships."

GENERAL NOTE
This paragraph makes consequential amendment to TA 1988 Sch 26 to include any non-trading deficit within the meaning of "relevant allowance" in para 1(3).

54 (1) In paragraph 6 of Schedule 28A to that Act (amounts in issue for the purposes of section 768B of that Act), after sub-paragraph (*d*) there shall be inserted the following sub-paragraphs—

"(*da*) the amount (if any) of the adjusted Case III profits and gains or non-trading deficit of the company for that accounting period;
(*db*) the amount of any non-trading debit (other than one within sub-paragraph (*dc*) or (*dd*) below) that falls to be brought into account for that accounting period for the purposes of Chapter II of Part IV of the Finance Act 1996 (loan relationships) in respect of any debtor relationship of the company;
(*dc*) the amount of any non-trading debit given for that accounting period by section 83(3) of the Finance Act 1996 (carried forward deficit not set off against profits);
(*dd*) the amount of any non-trading debit given for that accounting period by paragraph 13 of Schedule 15 to the Finance Act 1996 (transitional adjustment for past interest) in respect of any debtor relationship of the company;".

(2) In Part II of that Schedule, after paragraph 6 there shall be inserted the following paragraph—

"**6A** For the purposes of paragraph 6(*da*) above, the amount for any accounting period of the adjusted Case III profits and gains or non-trading deficit of a company is the amount which, as the case may be, would be—

(*a*) the amount of the profits and gains chargeable under Case III of Schedule D as profits and gains arising from the company's loan relationships, or (*b*) the amount of the company's non-trading deficit on those relationships for that period,

if, in computing that amount, amounts for that period falling within paragraph 6(*db*) to (*dd*) above were disregarded.''

(3) In paragraph 7(1) of that Schedule (apportionment for the purposes of section 768B)—

(*a*) in paragraph (*b*), after ''in paragraph 6(*c*) above,'' there shall be inserted ''or in the case of the non-trading debit mentioned in paragraph 6(*dc*) above,'';

(*b*) in paragraph (*c*), after ''6(*d*)'' there shall be inserted, ''(*da*)''; and

(*c*) after paragraph (*c*) there shall be inserted the following paragraphs—

''(*d*) in the case of any such debit as—

(i) is mentioned in paragraph 6(*db*) above,

(ii) falls to be brought into account for the purposes of Chapter II of Part IV of the Finance Act 1996 in accordance with an authorised accruals basis of accounting, and

(iii) so falls to be brought into account otherwise than on the assumption, specified in paragraph 2(2) of Schedule 9 to that Act, that the interest to which it relates does not accrue until it is paid,

by reference to the time of accrual of the amount to which the debit relates;

(*e*) in the case of any such debit as—

(i) is mentioned in paragraph 6(*db*) above,

(ii) falls to be brought into account for the purposes of Chapter II of Part IV of the Finance Act 1996 in accordance with an authorised accruals basis of accounting, and

(iii) so falls to be brought into account on the assumption mentioned in paragraph (*d*)(iii) above,

by apportioning the whole amount of the debit to the first part of the accounting period being divided;

(*f*) in the case of any such debit as is mentioned in paragraph 6(*dd*) above, by apportioning the whole amount of the debit to the first part of the accounting period being divided.''

(4) For Part IV of that Schedule (excess overdue interest) there shall be substituted the following Part—

''PART IV

DISALLOWED DEBITS

9 (1) This paragraph has effect in a case to which section 768B applies for determining the debits to be brought into account for the purposes of Chapter II of Part IV of the Finance Act 1996 (loan relationships) for—

(*a*) the accounting period beginning immediately after the change in the ownership of the company; and

(*b*) any subsequent accounting period.

(2) The debits so brought into account shall not include the debits falling within paragraph 11 below to the extent (if at all) that the aggregate of—

(*a*) the amount of those debits, and

(*b*) the amount of any debits falling within that paragraph which have been brought into account for the purposes of that Chapter for any previous accounting period ending after the change in the ownership,

exceeds the profits for the accounting period ending with the change in the ownership.

(3) The reference in sub-paragraph (2) above to the profits is a reference to profits after making all deductions and giving all reliefs that for the purposes of corporation tax are made or given against the profits, including deductions and reliefs which under any provision are treated as reducing them for those purposes.

10 (1) This paragraph has effect in a case to which section 768C applies for determining the debits to be brought into account for the purposes of Chapter II of Part IV of the Finance Act 1996 (loan relationships) for—

(*a*) the accounting period beginning immediately after the change in the ownership of the relevant company; and

(*b*) any subsequent accounting period.

(2) The debits so brought into account for any such accounting period shall not include the debits falling within paragraph 11 below to the extent (if at all) that the amount of those debits exceeds the modified total profits for the accounting period.

(3) The reference in sub-paragraph (2) above to the modified total profits for an accounting period is a reference to the total profits for that period—

(*a*) reduced, if that period is the period in which the relevant gain accrues, by an amount equal to the amount of the total profits for that period which represents the relevant gain; and

(*b*) after making all deductions and giving all reliefs that for the purposes of corporation tax are made or given against the profits, including deductions and reliefs which under any provision are treated as reducing them for those purposes, other than any reduction by virtue of paragraph 1(2) of Schedule 8 to the Finance Act 1996.

(4) Where by virtue of sub-paragraph (2) above a debit is to any extent not brought into account for an accounting period, that debit may (to that extent) be brought into account for the next accounting period, but this is subject to the application of sub-paragraphs (1) to (3) above to that next accounting period.

11 (1) A debit falls within this paragraph if it is a non-trading debit which—

(*a*) falls to be brought into account for the purposes of Chapter II of Part IV of the Finance Act 1996 in accordance with an authorised accruals basis of accounting;

(*b*) so falls to be brought into account on the assumption, specified in sub-paragraph (2) of paragraph 2 of Schedule 9 to that Act, that the interest to which it relates does not accrue until it is paid; and

(*c*) apart from that sub-paragraph, would have fallen to be brought into account for those purposes for an accounting period ending before or with the change in the ownership of the company or, as the case may be, the relevant company.

(2) The debits that fall within this paragraph also include—

(*a*) any non-trading debit given by section 83(3) of the Finance Act 1996 (carried forward deficit from previous period not set off against non-trading profits of current period) for the post-change accounting period;

(*b*) any non-trading debit given by paragraph 13 of Schedule 15 to the Finance Act 1996 (transitional adjustment for past interest) in respect of any debtor relationship of the company or, as the case may be, the relevant company.

(3) The debits that fall within this paragraph also include any non-trading debit which—

(*a*) is not such a debit as is mentioned in sub-paragraph (1) or (2) above;

(*b*) is a debit in respect of a debtor relationship of the company or, as the case may be, the relevant company;

(*c*) falls to be brought into account for the purposes of Chapter II of Part IV of the Finance Act 1996 in accordance with an authorised accruals basis of accounting; and

(*d*) relates to an amount that accrued before the change in the ownership of that company.

(4) In this paragraph 'post-change accounting period' means the accounting period beginning immediately after the change in the ownership of the company or, as the case may be, the relevant company.

12 Expressions used both in this Part of this Schedule and in Chapter II of Part IV of the Finance Act 1996 have the same meanings in this Part of this Schedule as in that Chapter.''

(5) In paragraph 13(1) of that Schedule (amounts in issue for the purposes of section 768C of that Act), after paragraph (*e*) there shall be inserted the following paragraphs—

"(*ea*) the amount (if any) of the adjusted Case III profits and gains or non-trading deficit of the company for that accounting period;

(*eb*) the amount of any non-trading debit (other than one within paragraph (*ec*) or (*ed*) below) that falls to be brought into account for that accounting period for the purposes of Chapter II of Part IV of the Finance Act 1996 (loan relationships) in respect of any debtor relationship of the company;

(*ec*) the amount of any non-trading debit given for that accounting period by section 83(3) of the Finance Act 1996 (carried forward deficit not set off against profits);

(*ed*) the amount of any non-trading debit given for that accounting period by paragraph 13 of Schedule 15 to the Finance Act 1996 (transitional adjustment for past interest) in respect of any debtor relationship of the company;".

(6) In Part V of that Schedule, after paragraph 13 there shall be inserted the following paragraph—

"**13A** Paragraph 6A above shall apply for the purposes of paragraph 13(1)(*ea*) above as it applies for the purposes of paragraph 6(*da*) above."

(7) In paragraph 16(1) of that Schedule (apportionment for the purposes of section 768C)—

(*a*) in paragraph (*b*), after "in paragraph 13(1)(*d*) above," there shall be inserted "or in the case of the non-trading debit mentioned in paragraph 13(1)(*ec*) above,";

(*b*) in paragraph (*c*), after "13(1)(*e*)" there shall be inserted ", (*ea*)"; and

(*c*) after paragraph (*c*) there shall be inserted the following paragraphs—

"(*d*) in the case of any such debit as—

(i) is mentioned in paragraph 13(1)(*eb*) above,

(ii) falls to be brought into account for the purposes of Chapter II of Part IV of the Finance Act 1996 in accordance with an authorised accruals basis of accounting, and

(iii) so falls to be brought into account otherwise than on the assumption, specified in paragraph 2(2) of Schedule 9 to that Act, that the interest to which it relates does not accrue until it is paid,

by reference to the time of accrual of the amount to which the debit relates;

(*e*) in the case of any such debit as—

(i) is mentioned in paragraph 13(1)(*eb*) above,

(ii) falls to be brought into account for the purposes of Chapter II of Part IV of the Finance Act 1996 in accordance with an authorised accruals basis of accounting, and

(iii) so falls to be brought into account on the assumption mentioned in paragraph (*d*)(iii) above, by apportioning the whole amount of the debit to the first part of the accounting period being divided;

(*f*) in the case of any such debit as is mentioned in paragraph 13(1)(*ed*) above, by apportioning the whole amount of the debit to the first part of the accounting period being divided."

GENERAL NOTE
This paragraph provides consequential amendments to Sch 28A, which deals with changes in ownership of investment companies and provides for the potential restriction in carrying forward management expenses.

The British Steel Act 1988 (c 35)

55 In section 11 of the British Steel Act 1988 (taxation provisions), for subsection (7) there shall be substituted the following subsection—

"(7) For the purposes of Part VI of the Income and Corporation Taxes Act 1988 (company distributions) and Chapter II of Part IV of the Finance Act 1996 (loan relationships), any debentures issued in pursuance of section 3 above shall be treated as having been issued for new consideration equal to the principal sum payable under the debenture.''

GENERAL NOTE
This paragraph amends the British Steel Act 1988 s 11 to provide that debentures issued under that Act are treated for the purposes of distributions and loan relationships as issued for new consideration equal to the principal sum payable.

The Finance Act 1989 (c 26)

56 In section 88(3) of the Finance Act 1989 (relevant profits of company), the following paragraph shall be inserted before paragraph (*a*)—

''(*aa*) amounts falling in respect of any non-trading deficits on the company's loan relationships to be brought into account in that period in accordance with paragraph 4 of Schedule 11 to the Finance Act 1996.''.

GENERAL NOTE
FA 1989 ss 88 and 89 apply a special rate of tax to the profits of a company carrying on life insurance business insofar as they accrue for the benefit of policy holders. The policy holders' share is calculated by deducting from the life business net income and gains the amount which would be assessed if the business were being taxed under Case I rules. The amendment to s 88(3) ensures that non-trading deficits, including deficits carried forward or back under the provisions of Sch 11 para 4(2) or (3), are deducted from income, profits and gains in making the calculation, thus preventing excessive rate relief.

57 Schedule 11 to that Act (deep gain securities) shall cease to have effect.

GENERAL NOTE
This paragraph repeals the deep gain provisions of FA 1989 Sch 11.

The Finance Act 1990 (c 29)

58 Schedule 10 to the Finance Act 1990 (convertible securities) shall cease to have effect.

GENERAL NOTE
This paragraph repeals the ''qualifying convertible securities'' provisions of FA 1990 Sch 10.

The Taxation of Chargeable Gains Act 1992 (c 12)

59 In section 108(1) of the Taxation of Chargeable Gains Act 1992 (meaning of relevant securities), after paragraph (*a*) there shall be inserted the following paragraph—

''(*aa*) qualifying corporate bonds;''.

GENERAL NOTE
This paragraph provides that the definition of ''relevant securities'' within TCGA 1992 s 108(1) (identification provisions) shall include ''qualifying corporate bonds'' (see para 61 below).

60 (1) Section 116 of that Act (reorganisations, conversions and reconstructions) shall be amended as follows.

(2) After subsection (4) there shall be inserted the following subsection—

''(4A) In determining for the purposes of subsections (1) to (4) above, as they apply for the purposes of corporation tax—

(*a*) whether sections 127 to 130 would apply in any case, and
(*b*) what, in a case where they would apply, would constitute the original shares and the new holding,

it shall be assumed that every asset representing a loan relationship of a company is a security within the meaning of section 132.''

(3) After subsection (8) there shall be inserted the following subsection—

''(8A) where subsection (6) above applies for the purposes of corporation tax in a case where the old asset consists of a qualifying corporate bond, Chapter II of Part

IV of the Finance Act 1996 (loan relationships) shall have effect so as to require such debits and credits to be brought into account for the purposes of that Chapter in relation to the relevant transaction as would have been brought into account if the transaction had been a disposal of the old asset at the market value mentioned in that subsection.''

(4) After subsection (15) there shall be inserted the following subsection—

''(16) This section has effect for the purposes of corporation tax notwithstanding anything in section 80(5) of the Finance Act 1996 (matters to be brought into account in the case of loan relationships only under Chapter II of Part IV of that Act).''

GENERAL NOTE

This paragraph amends for corporation tax purposes TCGA 1992 s 116, which deals with reorganisations, conversions and reconstructions within TCGA 1992 ss 127–130 (the reorganis-ation provisions), involving a ''qualifying corporate bond''.

First, it provides that in determining for sub-ss (1)–(4) whether the reorganisation provisions apply an asset representing a loan relationship will be a security within TCGA 1992 s 132.

Second, where an ''old asset'' within s 116(6) consists of a ''qualifying corporate bond'', Chapter II has effect so as to cause a relevant transaction to be treated as a disposal at market value.

Third, s 116 is to have effect regardless of s 80(5). Section 80(5) provides that where amounts are brought into account under Chapter II, they shall be the only amounts recognised for corporation tax purposes unless otherwise provided.

61 (1) In section 117 of that Act (meaning of ''qualifying corporate bond''), before subsection (1) there shall be inserted the following subsection—

''(A1) For the purposes of corporation tax 'qualifying corporate bond' means (subject to sections 117A and 117B below) any asset representing a loan relationship of a company; and for purposes other than those of corporation tax references to a qualifying corporate bond shall be construed in accordance with the following provisions of this section.''

(2) After subsection (2) of that section there shall be inserted the following subsection—

''(2AA) For the purposes of this section 'corporate bond' also includes any asset which is not included in the definition in subsection (1) above and which is a relevant discounted security for the purposes of Schedule 13 to the Finance Act 1996.''

(3) After subsection (6A) of that section there shall be inserted the following subsections—

''(6B) An excluded indexed security issued on or after 6th April 1996 is not a corporate bond for the purposes of this section; and an excluded indexed security issued before that date shall be taken to be such a bond for the purposes of this section only if—

(*a*) it would be so taken apart from this subsection; and
(*b*) the question whether it should be so taken arises for the purposes of section 116(10).

(6C) In subsection (6B) above 'excluded indexed security' has the same meaning as in Schedule 12 to the Finance Act 1996 (relevant discounted securities).''

(4) After subsection (8) of that section there shall be inserted the following subsection—

''(8A) A corporate bond falling within subsection (2AA) above is a qualifying corporate bond whatever its date of issue.''

GENERAL NOTE

This paragraph provides that the definition of ''qualifying corporate bond'' in TCGA 1992 s 117 for the purposes of corporation tax is any asset representing a loan relationship of the company (subject to ss 117A and 117B (see para 62 below)).

The definition of ''corporate bond'' specifically includes any relevant discounted security within Sch 13 which is not within s 117(1) whenever issued.

It further provides that an ''excluded indexed security'' (as defined in Sch 13 para 13) issued on or after 6 April 1996 is not a corporate bond for this purpose. An excluded indexed security issued before 6 April 1996, is a corporate bond for the purposes of s 117 only if it would otherwise have qualified apart from its date of issue and the question arises for the purposes of s 116(10).

62 After section 117 of that Act there shall be inserted the following sections—

"117A   Assets that are not qualifying corporate bonds for corporation tax purposes

(1) An asset to which this section applies is not a qualifying corporate bond for the purposes of corporation tax in relation to any disposal of that asset.

(2) This section applies to any asset representing a loan relationship of a company where—

(*a*) subsection (3) or (4) below applies to the asset; and
(*b*) it is held in exempt circumstances.

(3) This subsection applies to an asset if—

(*a*) the settlement currency of the debt to which it relates is a currency other than sterling; and
(*b*) that debt is not a debt on a security.

(4) This subsection applies to an asset if the debt to which it relates is a debt on a security and is in a foreign currency.

(5) For the purposes of subsection (4) above a debt is a debt in a foreign currency if it is—

(*a*) a debt expressed in a currency other than sterling;
(*b*) a debt the amount of which in sterling falls at any time to be determined by reference to the value at that time of a currency other than sterling; or
(*c*) subject to subsection (6) below, a debt as respects which provision is made for its conversion into, or redemption in, a currency other than sterling.

(6) A debt is not a debt in a foreign currency for those purposes by reason only that provision is made for its redemption on payment of an amount in a currency other than sterling equal, at the rate prevailing at the date of redemption, to a specified amount in sterling.

(7) The provisions specified in subsection (8) below, so far as they require a disposal to be treated as a disposal on which neither a gain nor a loss accrues, shall not apply to any disposal of an asset to which this section applies.

(8) The provisions referred to in subsection (7) above are—

(*a*) sections 139, 140A, 171 and 172 of this Act; and
(*b*) section 486(8) of the Taxes Act.

(9) Paragraph 3 of Schedule 17 to the Finance Act 1993 shall have effect for construing the reference in subsection (2)(*b*) above to exempt circumstances as if references to a currency were references to the debt to which the relationship relates.

(10) In this section 'security' includes a debenture that is deemed to be a security for the purposes of section 251, by virtue of subsection (6) of that section.

117B   Holdings in unit trusts and offshore funds excluded from treatment as qualifying corporate bonds

(1) For the purposes of corporation tax an asset to which this section applies is not a qualifying corporate bond in relation to any disposal of that asset in an accounting period for which that asset falls, under paragraph 4 of Schedule 10 to the Finance Act 1996 (holdings in unit trusts and offshore funds), to be treated as a right under a creditor relationship of a company.

(2) This section applies to an asset which is comprised in a relevant holding (within the meaning of paragraph 4 of Schedule 10 to the Finance Act 1996) if—

(*a*) it is denominated in a currency other than sterling; and
(*b*) it is held in exempt circumstances.

(3) For the purposes of this section—

(*a*) a unit in a unit trust scheme, or

(*b*) a right (other than a share in a company) which constitutes a relevant interest in an offshore fund,

shall be taken to be denominated in a currency other than sterling if the price at which it may be acquired from, or disposed of to, persons concerned in the management of the trust or fund is fixed by those persons in a currency other than sterling.

(4) For the purposes of this section shares constituting a relevant interest in an offshore fund shall be taken to be denominated in a currency other than sterling if their nominal value is expressed in such a currency.

(5) The provisions specified in subsection (6) below, so far as they require a disposal to be treated as a disposal on which neither a gain nor a loss accrues, shall not apply to any disposal in relation to which this section applies.

(6) The provisions referred to in subsection (5) above are—

(*a*) sections 139, 140A, 171 or 172 of this Act; and
(*b*) section 486(8) of the Taxes Act.

(7) Paragraph 3 of Schedule 17 to the Finance Act 1993 shall have effect for construing the reference in subsection (2)(*b*) above to exempt circumstances as if references to a currency were references to the asset in question.

(8) Paragraph 5 of Schedule 10 to the Finance Act 1996 shall apply for construing any reference in this section to a relevant interest in an offshore fund as it applies for the purposes of paragraph 4 of that Schedule.''.

GENERAL NOTE

This paragraph adds new ss 117A, 117B to TCGA 1992, which provide that certain assets are not to be qualifying corporate bonds for corporation tax purposes.

Section 117A applies to any asset held in "exempt circumstances" (as defined in FA 1993 Sch 17 para 3(1)) where the debt to which it relates—

(*a*) is not a debt on a security and its settlement currency is not sterling; or
(*b*) is a debt on a security and is in a foreign currency.

For this purpose a debt is in a foreign currency if it is expressed in a currency other than sterling, or the amount of the debt in sterling at any time is determined by reference to another currency or there is provision for it to be converted or redeemed in another currency (unless it simply allows for redemption in another currency at the then equivalent to sterling).

The provisions of TCGA 1992 ss 139, 140A, 171, 172 and TA 1988 s 486(8) which treat a disposal as being for no gain no loss, do not apply to assets within this section.

Under s 117B, non-sterling holdings in unit trusts and offshore funds which are held in exempt circumstances are excluded from treatment as qualifying corporate bonds where they are treated under FA 1996 Sch 10 para 4 as rights under a creditor relationship. Units in a trust, and rights other than shares in an offshore fund, are taken to be non-sterling where the price for their purchase from or sale to the managers is fixed by the latter in a non-sterling currency. The test for shares is the currency in which their nominal value is expressed. The same no gain, no loss provisions as are referred to in s 117A are disapplied for disposals of assets to which s 117B applies.

63   In section 212 of that Act (annual deemed disposal of holdings of unit trusts), after subsection (2) there shall be inserted the following subsection—

''(2A) Subsection (1) above shall not apply to assets falling by virtue of paragraph 4 of Schedule 9 to the Finance Act 1996 (company holdings in unit trusts) to be treated for the accounting period in question as representing rights under a creditor relationship of the company.''

GENERAL NOTE

This paragraph provides that assets which represent rights under a creditor relationship of the company, and so fall within the loan relationships legislation, are excluded from the annual capital gains deemed disposal by an insurance company of the rights which it holds under authorised unit trusts.

64   In section 251 of that Act (exclusion for debts that are not debts on a security), after subsection (6) there shall be inserted the following subsections—

''(7) Where any instrument specified in subsection (8) below is not a security (as defined in section 132), that instrument shall be deemed to be such a security for the purposes of this section, other than the purposes of determining what is or is not an allowable loss in any case.

(8) The instruments mentioned in subsection (7) above are—

(*a*) any instrument that would fall to be treated for the purposes of this Act as an asset representing a loan relationship of a company if the provisions of sections 92(4) and 93(4) of the Finance Act 1996 (convertible securities and assets linked to the value of chargeable assets) were disregarded; or

(*b*) any instrument which (even apart from those provisions) is not a loan relationship of a company but which would be a relevant discounted security for the purposes of Schedule 13 to that Act if paragraph 3(2)(*c*) of that Schedule (excluded indexed securities) were omitted.''.

GENERAL NOTES

This paragraph amends TCGA 1992 s 251, inter alia, which provides that no chargeable gain accrues on the disposal of a debt by the original creditor unless it is a debt on security as defined by TCGA 1992 s 132.

The paragraph provides that certain instruments which are not debts on security shall be deemed to be so, for the purposes of s 251, other than in determining whether a loss is allowable. The instruments are—

(*a*) those which would be treated as assets representing a loan relationship of a company if the provisions of s 92(4) (convertible securities) and s 93(4) (relationships linked to the value of chargeable assets) were disregarded;

(*b*) those which are not loan relationships but which would be relevant discounted securities for the purposes of Sch 13, but for being excluded indexed securities (Sch 13 paras 3(2)(*c*) and 13).

65 In section 253(3) of that Act (relief for loans to traders), in the words after paragraph (*c*), at the beginning there shall be inserted—

"then, to the extent that that amount is not an amount which, in the case of the claimant, falls to be brought into account as a debit given for the purposes of Chapter II of Part IV of the Finance Act 1996 (loan relationships),''.

GENERAL NOTE

This paragraph provides that a claim under TCGA 1992 s 253(3) for relief for a "qualifying loan" to traders shall exclude any amount for which relief has been given as a debit under Chapter II.

66 In section 254 of that Act (relief for debts on qualifying corporate bonds), in subsection (1)(*c*), after "bond" there shall be inserted "but is not a relevant discounted security for the purposes of Schedule 13 to the Finance Act 1996".

(2) After subsection (12) of that section there shall be inserted the following subsection—

"(13) This section does not apply for the purposes of corporation tax."

GENERAL NOTE

This paragraph amends TCGA 1992 s 254 which gives relief for debts on "qualifying corporate bonds". First, it provides that relevant discounted securities within Sch 13 para 3 are excluded. Second, it provides that s 254 does not apply for corporation tax purposes.

The Finance Act 1993 (c 34)

67 In section 127 of the Finance Act 1993 (accrual of amounts where debts vary), after subsection (1) there shall be inserted the following subsections—

"(1A) For the purposes of this section if, in the case of any debt—

(*a*) an amount in respect of any discount or premium relating to that debt is treated, on an accruals basis of accounting, as accruing at any time for the purposes of Chapter II of Part IV of the Finance Act 1996 (loan relationships), or

(*b*) any such amount would be treated as so accruing if the authorised method of accounting used for those purposes as respects the loan relationship relating to that debt were an accruals basis of accounting, instead of a mark to market basis,

then, for the purposes of this section, there shall be deemed to be such a variation at that time of the nominal amount of the debt outstanding as is specified in subsection (1B) below.

(1B)　That variation is—

(*a*) if the amount mentioned in paragraph (*a*) or (*b*) of subsection (1A) above relates to a discount, a variation that increases the nominal amount of the debt outstanding by the amount so mentioned; and

(*b*) if the amount so mentioned relates to a premium, a variation that decreases the nominal amount of the debt outstanding by the amount so mentioned."

GENERAL NOTE

This paragraph amends FA 1993 s 127, which deals with debts which vary in nominal amount for the purposes of the foreign exchange legislation, by introducing new subsections into s 127.

Subsection (1A) provides that where a discount or premium on a debt is recognised on an accruals basis at any time, or would be if mark-to-market were not used, there will be deemed to be a variation as specified in sub-s (1B). Subsection (1B) provides that the variation amount equals the accrual of the discount or premium.

The effect is to cause exchange differences on a discount or premium to be within the foreign exchange provisions of FA 1993 by treating the discount or premium as a variation.

68　(1)　In subsection (2) of section 129 of that Act (non-trading exchange gains), for the words after paragraph (*b*) there shall be substituted—

"and the rule in section 130(1) below shall apply."

(2)　In subsection (4) of that section (non-trading exchange losses), for the words after paragraph (*b*) there shall be substituted—

"and the rule in section 130(2) below shall apply."

(3)　Subsections (5) and (6) of that section (computation of net exchange gains or net exchange losses) shall cease to have effect.

(4)　In subsection (7)(*b*) of that section (no gain or loss accruing on a right by virtue of a debt to receive income), for "(whether interest, dividend or otherwise)" there shall be substituted "that is not interest falling to be brought into account for the purposes of Chapter II of Part IV of the Finance Act 1996 (loan relationships) as interest accruing, or (according to the authorised method of accounting used) becoming due and payable, in an accounting period ending after 31st March 1996".

GENERAL NOTE

This paragraph amends FA 1993 s 129 which deals with the taxation of non-trading foreign exchange gains and losses.

Subsection (2) is amended so as to cause such a gain to be taxed in accordance with the new s 130 (introduced by para 69 below) rather than the existing ss 130–133. It similarly amends sub-s (4) which deals with such losses.

This paragraph causes s 129(5) and (6), which deal with such gains and losses recognised in the same accounting period, to cease to have effect.

It also amends s 129(7) which excludes a right to receive income (including interest) form the calculation of the foreign exchange gain or loss arising on an asset consisting of a right to settlement under a qualifying debt. The paragraph provides that amounts assessable under Chapter II are similarly excluded.

69　For sections 130 to 133 of that Act (charge to tax of non-trading gains and treatment of losses), there shall be substituted the following section—

"130　Non-trading gains and losses

(1)　Where a company is treated by virtue of section 129 above as receiving any amount in an accounting period, that amount shall be brought into account for that accounting period as if it were a non-trading credit falling for the purposes of Chapter II of Part IV of the Finance Act 1996 (loan relationships) to be brought into account in respect of a loan relationship of the company.

(2)　Where a company is treated by virtue of section 129 above as incurring any loss in an accounting period, the amount of the loss shall be brought into account for that accounting period as if it were a non-trading debit falling for the purposes of Chapter

II of Part IV of the Finance Act 1996 to be brought, into account in respect of a loan relationship of the company.''

GENERAL NOTE
This paragraph replaces FA 1993 ss 130–133, which assess non-trading foreign exchange gains and give relief for such losses with a new s 130.

New s 130 provides that foreign exchange gains will be taxed as non-trading credits under Chapter II (s 82) and such losses will be relieved as non-trading debits (s 83 and Sch 8).

70 (1) For subsection (4) of section 153 of that Act (qualifying assets and liabilities) there shall be substituted the following subsection—

''(4) A right to settlement under a qualifying debt is not a qualifying asset where the company having the right holds an asset representing the debt and that asset is—

(*a*) an asset to which section 92 of the Finance Act 1996 applies (convertible securities); or

(*b*) an asset representing a loan relationship to which section 93 of that Act (relationships linked to the value of chargeable assets) applies.''

(2) Subsection (6) of that section shall cease to have effect.

GENERAL NOTE
This paragraph provides for amendment to FA 1993 s 153, which defines qualifying assets and liabilities.

It replaces sub-s (4) which excludes a right to settlement under a qualifying debt if it is a debt on security and did not represent a normal commercial loan when advanced (excluding deep gain securities). New sub-s (4) provides that such a right is not a qualifying asset where the company having the right holds the representative asset which is a convertible security in s 92 or is a relationship linked to the value of a chargeable asset within s 93.

It also causes sub-s (6), which excludes similar duties to settle under a qualifying debt from being a qualifying liability, to cease to have effect.

71 In section 154 of that Act (definitions connected with assets), after subsection (12) there shall be inserted the following subsection—

''(12A) So much of any asset as consists in a right to receive interest as respects which any sums fall to be brought into account for the purposes of Chapter II of Part IV of the Finance Act 1996 (loan relationships) shall be taken to be an asset to which the company became entitled at the following time (instead of the time for which subsection (12) above provides), that is to say—

(*a*) where the sums fall to be brought into account for the purposes of that Chapter in accordance with an authorised accruals basis of accounting, the time when the interest is taken for those purposes to have accrued, and

(*b*) where the sums fall to be brought into account for the purposes of that Chapter in accordance with an authorised mark to market basis of accounting, the time when the interest is taken for those purposes to have become due and payable.''

GENERAL NOTE
This paragraph amends FA 1993 s 154, which provides definitions connected with assets, by introducing new sub-s (12A).

Subsection (12A) provides that a company becomes entitled to so much of any asset as consists in a right to receive interest within Chapter II, when it is recognised under Chapter II—

(*a*) where an authorised accruals basis is used when it accrues; and

(*b*) where an authorised mark-to-market is used when it becomes due and payable.

72 In section 155 of that Act (definitions connected with liabilities), after subsection (11) there shall be inserted the following subsection—

''(11A) So much of any liability consisting in a liability to pay interest as respects which debits fall to be brought into account for the purposes of Chapter II of Part IV of the Finance Act 1996 (loan relationships) shall be taken to be a liability to which the company became subject at the following time (instead of at the time for which subsection (11) above provides), that is to say—

(*a*) where the debits fall to be brought into account for the purposes of that

Chapter in accordance with an authorised accruals basis of accounting, the time
when the interest is taken for those purposes to have accrued, and

(*b*) where the debits fall to be brought into account for the purposes of that
Chapter in accordance with an authorised mark to market basis of accounting, the
time when the interest is taken for those purposes to have become due and
payable."

GENERAL NOTE

This paragraph amends FA 1993 s 155, which provides definitions connected with liabilities, by
introducing a new sub-s (11A).

Subsection (11A) provides that a company becomes subject to so much of any liability as
consists in a liability to pay interest within Chapter II, when it is recognised under Chapter II—

(*a*) where an authorised accruals basis is used when it accrues; and

(*b*) where an authorised mark-to-market is used when it becomes due and payable.

73   (1) For subsections (5) to (9) of section 159 of that Act (basic valuation where
accrued income scheme applies) there shall be substituted the following subsection—

"(5) Where—

(*a*) a company becomes entitled, on any transfer by virtue of which it becomes a
party to a loan relationship, to a right of settlement under a qualifying debt on a
security, and

(*b*) that transfer is a transfer with accrued interest,

the basic valuation of that right shall be found by taking the consideration for the
company's becoming entitled to the right and then deducting the amount of the
accrued interest the right to which is transferred."

(2) This paragraph does not apply in relation to transfers before 1st April 1996.

GENERAL NOTE

This paragraph amends FA 1993 s 159, which provides for the basic valuation of an asset or
liability for the foreign exchange provisions, by replacing sub-ss (5)–(9) with new sub-s (5) with
effect for transfers after 1 April 1996.

Subsections (5)–(9) provide for the exclusion of amounts recognised under the accrued income
scheme on transfers of a right to settlement under a qualifying debt on a security. New sub-s (5) is
necessary as Sch 14 para 36 causes the accrued income scheme to cease to apply for corporation
tax purposes for transfers on or after 1 April 1996. Subsection (5) simply provides that the
valuation will be after the deduction of accrued interest.

74   In section 167 of that Act (orders and regulations relating to exchange gains and
losses), after subsection (5) there shall be inserted the following subsections—

"(5A) Without prejudice to the generality of any power of the Treasury to amend
regulations made under this Chapter, every such power shall include power to make
such modifications of any regulations so made as the Treasury consider appropriate
in consequence of the provisions of Chapter II of Part IV of the Finance Act 1996
(loan relationships).

(5B) The power to make any such modifications as are mentioned in subsection (5A)
above shall be exercisable so as to apply those modifications in relation to any
accounting period of a company ending on or after 1st April 1996."

GENERAL NOTE

This paragraph amends s 167 which allows the Treasury to make regulations in relation to the
foreign exchange provisions to allow the regulations to be in consequence of Chapter II, provided
the changes are effective for accounting periods ending on or after 1 April 1996.

The Finance Act 1994 (c 9)

75   In section 160 of the Finance Act 1994 (treatment of non-trading profits and losses
on interest rate and currency contracts), for subsections (2) to (4) there shall be
substituted the following subsections—

"(2) Any amount which for the purposes of this section is treated as a non-trading
profit of a company for any accounting period shall be brought into account for that

accounting period as if it were a non-trading credit falling to be brought into account for the purposes of Chapter II of Part IV of the Finance Act 1996 in respect of a loan relationship of the company.

(2A) Any amount which for the purposes of this section is treated as a non-trading loss of a company for any accounting period shall be brought into account for that accounting period as if it were a non-trading debit falling to be brought into account for the purposes of Chapter II of Part IV of the Finance Act 1996 in respect of a loan relationship of the company.''

GENERAL NOTE

This paragraph amends FA 1994 s 160, which provides for the assessment of non-trading gains and relief of non-trading losses arising under financial instruments.

It introduces sub-ss (2) and (2A) to replace sub-ss (2)–(4). Sections 160(2) and (3) provide that non-trading gains will be assessable and non-trading losses will be relieved under the provisions dealing with foreign exchange non-trading gains and losses under FA 1993 s 129–133. Para-graphs 68 and 69 above amend the foreign exchange non-trading gains and losses provisions, by causing such gains to be taxed and such losses to be relieved as non-trading credits and debits under Chapter II. New sub-paras (2) and (2A) have the same effect for non-trading gains and losses from financial instruments, so that they are assessed and relieved under Chapter II.

76 (1) In subsection (9) of section 167 of that Act (factors to be taken into account when adjusting transactions not at arm's length), before the word "and" at the end of paragraph (*b*) there shall be inserted the following paragraph—

"(*ba*) in a case where the qualifying contract is a debt contract or option, the amount of the debt by reference to which any loan relationship that would have been involved would have subsisted, and any terms as to repayment, redemption or interest that, in the case of that debt or any asset representing it, would have been involved;''.

(2) In paragraph (*c*) of that subsection, for "either" there shall be substituted "and such".

GENERAL NOTE

This paragraph amends FA 1994 s 167, which deals with transactions not at arm's length within the financial instruments legislation.

Section 167(9) describes the factors which may be taken into account in applying the section. This paragraph amends sub-s (9) so that these factors include, for a debt contract or option, the amount of the debt (and its repayment, redemption or interest terms), by reference to which any loan relationship would have subsisted.

77 In section 173(5)(*a*) of that Act (references to the purposes of the Chapter), for the words from "subsections (5)" to "losses)" there shall be substituted "Chapter II of Part IV of the Finance Act 1996 (loan relationships), so far as that Chapter is applied by virtue of section 160(2) or (2A) above,''.

GENERAL NOTE

This paragraph amends FA 1994 s 173(5)(*a*) making consequential amendments as a result of para 75.

78 (1) In subsection (1) of section 177 of that Act (interpretation)—

(*a*) in the definition of "commencement day", after the words "commencement day" there shall be inserted "—

(*a*) for the purposes of this Chapter as it has effect in relation to any debt contract or option, means (subject to paragraph 25 of Schedule 15 to the Finance Act 1996) 1st April 1996; and
(*b*) for all other purposes";

and

(*b*) after the definitions of "currency contract" and "currency option" there shall be inserted—

"'debt contract' and 'debt option' shall be construed in accordance with section 150A above;''.

(2) In subsection (2)(*a*) of that section (time when company becomes entitled to a contract), for "or a currency contract or option," there shall be substituted "a currency contract or option or a debt contract or option".

GENERAL NOTE
This paragraph amends the definition of commencement day for the financial instrument provisions. It provides that in respect of any debt contract or option (see FA 1994 s 147A as introduced by s 101 and FA 1994 s 150A as introduced by Sch 12) the commencement day is 1 April 1996 (subject to the transitional provisions in Sch 15 para 25).

79 For paragraphs 1 and 2 of Schedule 18 to that Act (special provision with respect to financial instruments for insurance companies) there shall be substituted the following paragraphs—

"Application of insurance companies provisions relating to loan relationships

1 (1) Part I of Schedule 11 to the Finance Act 1996 (special provision with respect to loan relationships for insurance companies) shall have effect (subject to sub-paragraph (2) below) in relation to qualifying contracts as it has effect in relation to loan relationships which are creditor relationships within the meaning of Chapter II of Part IV of that Act.

(2) That Part of that Schedule shall have effect in its application in relation to qualifying contracts, as if—

(*a*) references to section 82(2) of the Finance Act 1996 were references to section 159 of this Act, and
(*b*) references to credits and debits given by Chapter II of Part IV of that Act in respect of a loan relationship were references, respectively, to the profits and losses deriving from the contract.

1A (1) Where the I minus E basis is applied for any accounting period in respect of the life assurance business or capital redemption business of any insurance company, this Chapter shall have effect for that period in relation to contracts and options held for the purposes of that business as if the words in subsection (10) of section 150A from 'but references' onwards were omitted.

(2) Expressions used in sub-paragraph (1) above and in Part I of Schedule 11 to the Finance Act 1996 have the same meanings in this paragraph as in that Part of that Schedule.''

GENERAL NOTE
FA 1994 Sch 18 provides special computational rules for dealing with profits and losses on interest rate and currency contracts referable to a company's life insurance business. The amendment substitutes the rules now to be found in Sch 11 Part I of this Act, reflecting the assimilation of profits and losses on currency and interest rate contracts to the treatment of profits and deficits on loan relationships (see the amendment to FA 1994 s 160 made by para 75), and adds a reference to capital redemption business to reflect the introduction, in s 168 and Sch 33, of a comprehensive code for the taxation of that class of business.

SCHEDULE 15　　　Section 105

LOAN RELATIONSHIPS: SAVINGS AND TRANSITIONAL PROVISIONS

Schedule 15 is introduced by s 105 and provides the transitional provisions for the legislation contained in Chapter II Finance Act 1996 in respect of loan relationships.

PART I

CORPORATION TAX

Application and interpretation of Part I

1 (1) This Part of this Schedule has effect for the purposes of corporation tax.

(2) In this Part of this Schedule—

"the 1992 Act" means the Taxation of Chargeable Gains Act 1992;

"continuing loan relationship", in relation to any company, means any loan relationship to which the company was a party both immediately before and on 1st April 1996;

"first relevant accounting period", in relation to a company, means the first accounting period of the company to end after 31st March 1996; and

"transitional accounting period", in relation to a company, means any accounting period of the company beginning before and ending on or after 1st April 1996.

(3) Any question as to whether, or to what extent, credits or debits falling to be brought into account for the purposes of this Chapter by virtue of this Part of this Schedule are referable to any category of an insurance company's long term business shall be determined according to any apportionment in relation to the loan relationship in question which is made for the company's first relevant accounting period.

(4) In this Part of this Schedule references to this Chapter include references to any repeals having effect for the purposes of this Chapter.

GENERAL NOTE

This paragraph provides that Part I (paras 1–25) applies for the purposes of corporation tax and defines that for a company—

(*a*) "continuing loan relationship" means any loan relationship to which it is party to immediately before and on 1 April 1996;

(*b*) "first relevant accounting period" means its first accounting period ending after 31 March 1996; and

(*c*) "transitional accounting period" means any accounting period beginning before and ending on or after 1 April 1996.

It provides for an apportionment to determine how debits and credits are referable to any category of an insurance company's long-term business.

Loan relationships terminated before 1st April 1996

2 Subject to paragraph 13(6) below, the amounts which are to be brought into account for the purposes of corporation tax in any transitional accounting period of a company by reference to any loan relationship to which it was a party only at a time before 1st April 1996—

(*a*) shall not be computed in accordance with this Chapter; but

(*b*) shall, instead, be computed as they would be for an accounting period ending on 31st March 1996.

GENERAL NOTE

This paragraph provides that loan relationships ceasing before 1 April 1996 are not subject to the provisions of Chapter II subject to para 12(6) below.

Basic rules for transitional accounting periods

3 (1) This paragraph applies as respects any continuing loan relationship of a company.

(2) In a transitional accounting period an amount accruing before 1st April 1996 in respect of a continuing loan relationship (whether it accrues as a right or liability) shall be brought into account for the purposes of this Chapter in accordance with an authorised accruals basis of accounting only if it is an amount accruing as interest.

(3) In a transitional accounting period an amount becoming due and payable before 1st April 1996 in respect of a continuing loan relationship shall be brought into account for the purposes of this Chapter in accordance with an authorised mark to market basis of accounting only if it is an amount becoming so due and payable as interest.

(4) Except where sub-paragraph (5) below applies and subject to the following provisions of this Part of this Schedule, any opening valuation that is to be made for the purpose of bringing amounts into account for the purposes of this Chapter in a transitional accounting period on a mark to market basis of accounting shall be made as at 1st April 1996, instead of as at any earlier time.

(5) Where any opening valuation is made in accordance with sub-paragraph (4) above for any transitional accounting period—

(*a*) that valuation, and
(*b*) any closing valuation made as at the end of that period for the purposes mentioned in that sub-paragraph,

shall each be made disregarding any amount of interest that has accrued in respect of any part of that period.

(6) This sub-paragraph applies in the case of a continuing loan relationship if, apart from this Chapter—

(*a*) a mark to market basis of accounting would have been used, in the case of the relationship, for the purpose of bringing amounts into account in the transitional accounting period; and
(*b*) on that basis, an opening valuation as respects the relationship would have fallen to be made for that purpose as at a time before 1st April 1996.

(7) Notwithstanding anything in sub-paragraph (2) or (3) above, where—

(*a*) there is an amount that accrued or became due and payable before 1st April 1996 in respect of a continuing loan relationship of a company,
(*b*) that amount is not interest, and
(*c*) that amount would, apart from this Chapter, have been brought into account for the purposes of corporation tax in the accounting period in which it accrued or, as the case may be, became due and payable,

that amount shall be brought into account in that period for the purposes of corporation tax to the same extent as it would have been so brought into account apart from this Chapter and shall not otherwise be brought into account by virtue of the application in relation to times on or after 1st April 1996 of any authorised accounting method.

GENERAL NOTE
This paragraph provides for the treatment of continuing loan relationships.
In a transitional accounting period in which amounts accrue before 1 April 1996, only interest (income or expense) accruing before 1 April 1996 shall be brought into account under Chapter II. Similarly, if an authorised mark-to-market basis is used only interest becoming due and payable before 1 April 1996 is so recognised. Any other amount accruing or becoming due and payable in the transitional accounting period before 1 April 1996, which would otherwise be within Chapter II, will continue to be assessed under the existing tax legislation and will not be brought into account under Chapter II.
Where a mark-to-market basis is used for bringing amounts into account under Chapter II in the transitional accounting period, the opening valuation shall be as at 1 April 1996, unless the company is already using mark-to-market for tax purposes. Where such an opening valuation is made for a transitional accounting period, that valuation and the closing valuation shall disregard any interest that has accrued in respect of any part of the period.

Application of accruals basis to pre-commencement relationships

4 Subject to the following provisions of this Schedule, any question for the purposes of this Chapter as to the amounts which are to be treated (in accordance with an authorised accruals basis of accounting) as accruing to a company on or after 1st April 1996 shall be determined by applying that basis of accounting for determining, first, what amounts had accrued before that date.

GENERAL NOTE
  This paragraph provides that where an authorised accruals basis is used for Chapter II, that basis will be used in determining the amounts accruing before 1 April 1996. This is for the purpose of determining amounts accruing on or after 1 April 1996.

Adjustments in respect of pre-commencement trading relationships

5 (1) This paragraph applies in the case of any continuing loan relationship of a company as respects which any amounts would have been brought into account for the purposes of corporation tax in computing the profits or losses of the company from any trade carried on by it if—

(*a*) the company had ceased to be a party to the relationship on 31st March 1996; and

(*b*) where it is not otherwise the case, an accounting period of the company had ended on that date.

(2) Where there is a difference between—

(*a*) the notional closing value of the relationship as at 31st March 1996, and

(*b*) the adjusted closing value of that relationship as at that date,

that difference shall be brought into account as provided for in paragraph 6 below.

(3) Except where sub-paragraph (4) or (6) below applies, the notional closing value as at 31st March 1996 of a loan relationship of a company shall be taken for the purposes of this paragraph to be the amount which, for the purposes of computing the profits or losses of the company from any trade carried on by it—

(*a*) was as at that date, or

(*b*) had an accounting period of the company ended on that date, would have been,

the amount falling to be brought into account as representing the value of the company's rights or liabilities under the relationship.

(4) Except where sub-paragraph (6) below applies, if no amount is given by sub-paragraph (3) above, the notional closing value as at 31st March 1996 of a loan relationship of a company shall be taken for the purposes of this paragraph to be the amount which, for the purposes of computing the profits or losses of the company from any trade carried on by it, would have been deductible as representing the cost of becoming a party to the relationship if the company had ceased to be a party to the relationship on 31st March 1996.

(5) Except where sub-paragraph (6) below applies, the adjusted closing value of that relationship as at that date shall be taken for the purposes of this paragraph to be the amount which for the purposes of this Chapter is the opening value as at 1st April 1996 of the company's rights and liabilities under the relationship.

(6) For the purposes of this paragraph where the asset representing a loan relationship of a company is a relevant qualifying asset of the company, or the liabilities of the company under the relationship are relevant liabilities—

(*a*) the notional closing value of the relationship as at 31st March 1996 shall be taken for the purposes of this paragraph to be the value given by paragraph 12 below as the notional closing value as at 31st March 1996 of that asset or, as the case may be, of those liabilities; and

(*b*) the adjusted closing value of the relationship as at 31st March 1996 shall be taken for those purposes to be the amount which is as at 1st April 1996 the opening value of the asset or liabilities for the purposes of this Chapter.

(7) For the purposes of this paragraph, where an accruals basis of accounting is used as

respects a loan relationship for the first relevant accounting period of the company, the opening value as at 1st April 1996 of the company's rights and liabilities under the relationship shall be taken to be the value which (disregarding interest) is treated in accordance with paragraph 4 above as having accrued to the company before that date.

(8) In this paragraph—

"attributed amount" means any attributed gain or loss falling to be calculated in accordance with any regulations made under Schedule 16 to the Finance Act 1993 (transitional provisions for exchange gains and losses) which contain any such provision as is mentioned in paragraph 3(1) of that Schedule;

"commencement day", in relation to a company, means its commencement day for the purposes of Chapter II of Part II of the Finance Act 1993;

"market value" has the same meaning as in the 1992 Act;

"relevant liability", in relation to a company, means any liability under a loan relationship the value of which has been determined as at the company's commencement day for the purpose of calculating any attributed amount;

"relevant qualifying asset", in relation to a company, means any qualifying asset for the purposes of Chapter II of Part II of the Finance Act 1993 the value of which has been determined as at the company's commencement day for the purpose of calculating any attributed amount.

GENERAL NOTE

This paragraph provides for continuing loan relationships, which would give rise to a trading assessment, if the loan relationship had ceased on 31 March 1996 and, if this is not the case, the accounting period had ended on 31 March 1996.

It provides for the difference between the "notional closing value" and the "adjusted closing value" of a loan relationship as at 31 March 1996 to be brought into account as required by para 6 below.

The "notional closing value" is the amount that was or would have been taken into account under existing legislation. Where this gives no value, the notional closing value will be the amount that would have been deductible (for computing taxable trading profits or losses), as being the cost of becoming a party to the relationship on that date.

The "adjusted closing value" is the opening value for the purposes of Chapter II at 1 April 1996 of the company's rights and liabilities under the loan relationship. The opening value for mark-to-market accounting is given by para 3 above. Where an authorised accruals basis of accounting is used for the first relevant accounting period the opening value at 1 April 1996 is the value taken as having accrued (excluding interest) to the company before that date in accordance with para 4 above.

However, where the asset representing the loan relationship is a "relevant qualifying asset" or the liabilities under the loan relationship are "relevant liabilities" there are specific valuation provisions. In these cases, the notional closing value is to be given by para 11 below and the adjusted closing value is the opening value for the purposes of Chapter II.

A "relevant qualifying asset" is any asset within the foreign exchange provisions of FA 1993, which has been valued at the company's commencement day (under FA 1993) for the purposes of calculating any "attributed amount". A "relevant liability" is any liability which has been valued at the company's commencement day (under FA 1993) for the purposes of calculating any "attributed amount". An "attributed amount" means any attributed gain or loss calculated in accordance with the transitional provisions of FA 1993 Sch 16 which contain any provision as is mentioned in para 3(1) of that Schedule.

Method of giving effect to paragraph 5 adjustments

6 (1) Subject to sub-paragraph (4) below, the difference mentioned in paragraph 5(2) above shall be brought into account in accordance with sub-paragraph (2) or (3) below in the accounting period in which the company ceases to be a party to the relationship.

(2) If—

(*a*) the relationship is a creditor relationship and the difference consists in an excess of the amount mentioned in paragraph 5(2)(*b*) above over the amount mentioned in paragraph 5(2)(*a*) above, or

(*b*) the relationship is a debtor relationship and the difference consists in an excess of the amount mentioned in paragraph 5(2)(*a*) above over the amount mentioned in paragraph 5(2)(*b*) above, the difference shall be brought into account as a credit given for the purposes of this Chapter for the period mentioned in sub-paragraph (1) above.

(3) In any other case, the difference shall be brought into account as a debit given for the purposes of this Chapter for the period so mentioned.

(4) Where the company, by notice in writing given on or before 30th September 1996 to an officer of the Board, makes an election for the purposes of this sub-paragraph—

(*a*) sub-paragraphs (1) to (3) above shall not apply; and

(*b*) instead, one sixth of every credit and debit which would have fallen, in accordance with those sub-paragraphs, to be brought into account on the relevant assumption shall be brought into account for each year in the period of six years beginning with the company's first relevant accounting period;

and for this purpose ''the relevant assumption'' is that the company had ceased on 1st April 1996 to be a party to every one of its continuing loan relationships to which paragraph 5 above applies.

(5) Where any amount representing a fraction of a credit or debit falls to be brought into account for any year under sub-paragraph (4) above, that amount shall be—

(*a*) apportioned between the accounting periods beginning or ending in that year; and

(*b*) brought into account in the period to which it is allocated in accordance with that apportionment.

(6) An apportionment between accounting periods of an amount to be brought into account under sub-paragraph (4) above for any year shall be made according to how much of the year is included in each period; and, if that year and the accounting period are the same, the apportionment shall be effected by the allocation of the whole amount to that accounting period.

(7) If the company ceases to be within the charge to corporation tax before the end of the six years mentioned in sub-paragraph (4)(*b*) above, the whole amount of the excess, so far as it has not fallen to be brought into account for an earlier accounting period, shall be brought into account as a debit or credit for the accounting period ending when the company ceases to be within that charge.

(8) Where any credit or debit falls to be brought into account under this paragraph for any accounting period for the whole or any part of which the company carries on the trade in question, the credit or debit shall be brought into account under section 82(2) of this Act in relation to that trade; and, in any other case, it shall be brought into account as a non-trading credit or non-trading debit.

GENERAL NOTE

This paragraph provides the rules for recognising for tax purposes the amounts identified under para 5 above.

It provides that the resulting difference is to be brought into account as a debit or credit, as appropriate, when the company ceases to be party to the loan relationship. An election may be made by 30 September 1996 to allow the debit or credit which would arise if the loan relationship ceased on 1 April 1996 to be recognised, one sixth each year for the next six years. The paragraph provides for apportionment of the one sixth attributable to a year to straddling accounting periods.

If the company ceases to be within the charge to tax in that six-year period, any unrecognised amount is brought into account in its accounting period ending when it ceases to be within charge to tax.

The debits and credits will be treated as trading or non-trading debits and credits in accordance with the general rules.

General savings for the taxation of chargeable gains

7 The amendments of the 1992 Act contained in Schedule 13 to this Act and the related repeals made by this Act—

(*a*) so far as they relate to section 253 of the 1992 Act, do not apply to any loan the outstanding amount of principal on which became irrecoverable before 1st April 1996;

(*b*) so far as they relate to section 254 of the 1992 Act, do not apply to any security whose value became negligible before 1st April 1996;

(*c*) so far as they relate to anything else, do not apply in relation to any disposal made, or deemed to be made, before 1st April 1996.

GENERAL NOTE
This paragraph provides that the amendments in Sch 14 and the related repeals do not apply to any disposal, deemed or made before 1 April 1996 or—

(*a*) for TCGA 1992 s 253 in respect of any loan, where the outstanding principal became irrecoverable before 1 April 1996;

(*b*) for TCGA 1992 s 254 in respect of any security whose value was negligible before 1 April 1996.

Transitional provision for chargeable assets held after commencement

8 (1) This paragraph applies where—

(*a*) on 31st March 1996 any company ("the relevant company") held any asset representing, in whole or in part, any loan relationship to which it was a party on that date;

(*b*) the company did not dispose of that asset on that date and does not fall (apart from by virtue of this paragraph) to be treated for the purposes of the 1992 Act as having made a disposal of it on that date;

(*c*) the asset is not one to which section 86 of this Act or paragraph 15 below applies;

(*d*) that asset is not an asset representing a loan relationship to which section 87 of this Act applies;

(*e*) that asset is not a relevant qualifying asset; and

(*f*) a relevant event occurs.

(2) For the purposes of this paragraph a relevant event occurs on the first occasion after 31st March 1996 when the relevant company or any other company falls to be treated for the purposes of the 1992 Act as making a disposal, other than one to which section 139, 140A, 171(1) or 172 of that Act (disposals on which neither a gain nor a loss accrues) applies, of—

(*a*) the asset in question, so far as it has not come to be represented by an asset falling within paragraph (*b*) below, or

(*b*) any such asset as falls to be treated for the purposes of that Act as the same as that asset.

(3) The amount of any chargeable gain or allowable loss which would have been treated as accruing to the relevant company on the assumption—

(*a*) that it had made a disposal of the asset on 31st March 1996, and

(*b*) (so far as relevant for the purpose of computing the amount of that gain or loss) that the disposal had been for a consideration equal to the market value of the asset,

shall be brought into account (subject to the following provisions of this paragraph and to paragraph 9 below) as one accruing to the company ("the chargeable company") which makes the disposal constituting the relevant event, and shall be so brought into account in the accounting period in which that event occurs.

(4) The amount of the deemed chargeable gain or deemed allowable loss falling to be brought into account in accordance with sub-paragraph (3) above shall be treated as reduced by the extent (if any) to which it is, in relation to the company, an amount that already has been, or falls to be, taken into account for the purposes of corporation tax by virtue of the use of any accruals or mark to market basis of accounting—

(*a*) for those purposes;

(*b*) as respects times before 1st April 1996; and

(*c*) in relation to the asset in question.

(5) To the extent that any deemed chargeable gain or deemed allowable loss falling to be brought into account under sub-paragraph (3) above includes any gain or loss deemed to accrue under section 116(10)(*b*) of the 1992 Act (qualifying corporate bonds acquired in a reorganisation etc), that gain or loss shall be deemed to have accrued for the purposes of that sub-paragraph and (without prejudice to its being brought into

account in accordance with that sub-paragraph) shall not be taken accrue again on the occurrence of the relevant event or any subsequent disposal of any asset.

(6) In any case where—

(*a*) the relevant company is one which at any time before 1st April 1996 was not resident in the United Kingdom,

(*b*) the asset was held by the relevant company at such a time, and

(*c*) if the asset had been disposed of at that time and a gain had accrued to the relevant company on that disposal, it would not have been included in the company's chargeable profits by virtue of section 10(3) of the 1992 Act (gain on a disposal by a branch or agency of a non-resident company),

the relevant company shall be deemed for the purposes of sub-paragraph (3) above to have acquired the asset, at market value, on the first day on which any relevant gain would have been included in the company's chargeable profits for the purposes of corporation tax (whether because it is a day on which the company became resident, or the asset became situated, in the United Kingdom or for any other reason).

(7) In sub-paragraph (5) above the reference, in relation to a company, to a relevant gain is a reference to any gain which would have accrued to the company on the following assumptions, that is to say—

(*a*) that the relevant company disposed of the asset on the day in question;

(*b*) that that disposal gave rise to a gain; and

(*c*) that any allowable losses which might have been available for deduction under section 8(1) of, or Schedule 7A to, the 1992 Act were to be disregarded.

(8) In any case where the company acquired the asset on a disposal on which, by virtue of any enactment specified in section 35(3)(*d*) of the 1992 Act, neither a gain nor a loss accrued to the person making the disposal, the reference in sub-paragraph (6) or (7) above to the relevant company includes—

(*a*) a reference to the company from which it acquired the asset; and

(*b*) if that company also acquired the asset on such a disposal, a reference to the company from which the asset was acquired by that company, and so on through any number of such disposals.

(9) In any case where section 176 of the 1992 Act (depreciatory transactions within a group) would have applied in relation to the disposal referred to in sub-paragraph (3) above if that disposal had actually taken place, that section shall apply for the calculation of any deemed allowable loss to be brought into account by virtue of that sub-paragraph.

(10) For the purposes of this paragraph a company that ceases to be within the charge to corporation tax shall be deemed to make a disposal of all its assets at their market value immediately before ceasing to be within that charge.

(11) In this section—

"market value" has the same meaning as in the 1992 Act; and

"relevant qualifying asset" has the same meaning as in paragraph 5 above.

GENERAL NOTE

This paragraph provides for the treatment of an asset representing (in whole or part) a loan relationship to which the "relevant company" is party on 31 March 1996 for the purposes of corporation tax on capital gains.

The paragraph does not apply to assets which are within s 93 (linked to chargeable assets), within s 92 (eg convertible securities), within para 15 below or which are "relevant qualifying assets" (as defined in para 5 above). It may also be replaced by the elective treatment in para 9 below.

It applies where the "relevant company" holds such an asset, does not dispose of it on that date and a "relevant event" occurs. A "relevant event" occurs where the "chargeable company" disposes of the asset (or one treated as the same asset under TCGA 1992) after 31 March 1996. The "chargeable company" is the relevant company or such other company as is treated as making the disposal under TCGA 1992. A disposal for this purpose does not include a disposal at no gain no loss under TCGA 1992 ss 139, 140A, 171(1) or 172.

Sub-paragraph (3) provides that the asset shall be treated as disposed of on 31 March 1996 for the then market value (as defined in TCGA 1992) by the chargeable company on the date of the relevant event. The amount is reduced by any amounts recognised for corporation tax purposes, under a mark-to-market or accruals basis in relation to that asset before 1 April 1996.

An amendment was made at the Standing Committee stage to introduce sub-paragraph (5). It provides that where the deemed chargeable gain or allowable loss under sub-paragraph (3) includes any gain or loss which arises as a result of TCGA 1992 s 116(10)(*b*), the gain or loss is deemed to accrue for the purposes of sub-paragraph (3) and is not taken into account again on the "relevant event" or subsequent disposal. Without the amendment such held over gain under s 116(10) would have been taxed twice.

For non-UK resident companies which held the asset while it was not subject to corporation tax, the calculation assumes that the asset was acquired at market value on the day it became subject to corporation tax. It does however assume that losses available under TCGA 1992 s 8(1) or Sch 7A are disregarded.

Special rules apply for assets held on 31 March 1982 subject to TCGA 1992 s 35(3)(*d*) and for deprecatory group transactions with TCGA 1992 s 176. Where a company ceases to be within the charge to corporation tax it is deemed to make a disposal of all of its assets for the purposes of this chapter.

Election for alternative treatment of amounts specified in paragraph 8

9 (1) Subject to the following provisions of this paragraph, where (apart from this paragraph) any amount representing a deemed allowable loss would fall in the case of any company to be brought into account for any accounting period in accordance with sub-paragraph (3) of paragraph 8 above, the chargeable company may elect for that amount to be brought into account for that period for the purposes of this Chapter, instead of in accordance with that sub-paragraph.

(2) An amount brought into account for the purposes of this Chapter by virtue of an election under this paragraph shall be so brought into account as a debit given for that period for the purposes of this Chapter.

(3) The question whether or not any debit brought into account for any accounting period in accordance with sub-paragraph (2) above is to be brought into account for that period as a non-trading debit shall be determined according to how other credits or debits relating to the loan relationship in question are, or (if there were any) would be, brought into account for that period.

(4) No election shall be made under this paragraph in respect of any deemed allowable loss in any case where the asset in respect of which that loss is deemed to have accrued was one which, as at 1st April 1996, either—

(*a*) fell in accordance with section 127 or 214(9) of the 1992 Act (equation of new holding with previous holding) to be treated as the same as an asset which was not an asset representing a loan relationship; or
(*b*) would have so fallen but for section 116(5) of that Act.

(5) An election shall not be made under this paragraph at any time more than two years after the occurrence of the relevant event by virtue of which the amount to which the election relates would fall to be brought into account in accordance with paragraph 8(3) above.

GENERAL NOTE
This paragraph provides by election an alternative treatment for a deemed allowable loss for an accounting period under para 8.

It provides that the amount shall be treated as a debit under Chapter II for that period. Whether it is a non-trading debit or not is determined by reference to the treatment of other debits and credits from the loan relationship for that period.

The election must be made within two years of the relevant event. No election shall be made for assets within the provisions of TCGA 1992 s 127 or 214(9) (or would have been except for s 116(5)) at 1 April 1996.

Paragraph 10 deals with the opening valuation of chargeable assets held at 31 March 1996, when mark-to-market accounting is to be adopted for the first relevant accounting period.

Its opening valuation at 1 April 1996, will be the market value on a disposal on 31 March 1996 under TCGA 1992.

For this purpose, "chargeable asset" in relation to a company means any asset meeting one of the following conditions—

(*a*) a gain on a disposal of it after 31 March 1996 would have given rise to a chargeable gain; or
(*b*) a chargeable gain or allowable loss would have accrued on a disposal of it on 31 March 1996.

However, if a disposal of the asset on 31 March 1996 would have been regarded as a disposal of a qualifying corporate bond for TCGA 1992, the asset is not a chargeable asset.

Adjustments of opening value for mark to market accounting in the case of chargeable assets

10 (1) Where—

(a) a mark to market basis of accounting is used as respects any loan relationship of a company for the company's first relevant accounting period,

(b) for the purpose of bringing amounts into account for the purposes of this Chapter on that basis, an opening valuation of an asset representing that relationship falls to be made as at 1st April 1996, and

(c) that asset is a chargeable asset held by that company on 31st March 1996,

the value of that asset on 1st April 1996 shall be taken for the purpose of the opening valuation to be equal to whatever, in relation to a disposal on 31st March 1996, would have been taken to be its market value for the purposes of the 1992 Act.

(2) In this paragraph "chargeable asset", in relation to a company, means (subject to sub-paragraph (3) below) any asset in the case of which one of the following conditions is satisfied, that is to say—

(a) a gain accruing to the company on a disposal of that asset on 31st March 1996 would have fallen to be treated in relation to the company as a chargeable gain; or

(b) a chargeable gain or allowable loss would be deemed to have accrued to the company on any disposal of that asset on that date.

(3) An asset is not a chargeable asset for the purposes of this paragraph if (disregarding the provisions of this Chapter) it is an asset any disposal of which on 31st March 1996 would have fallen to be regarded for the purposes of the 1992 Act as a disposal of a qualifying corporate bond.

GENERAL NOTE

This paragraph provides for further adjustments in respect of chargeable assets.

It applies in respect of chargeable assets and assets which would have been chargeable but for the foreign exchange provisions of FA 1993. It provides that overall profits and loss reflect the position before 1 April 1996 under both the capital gains and foreign exchange regimes.

It applies where an authorised accruals basis is used for the first relevant accounting period, the asset or liability is a "relevant" asset or liability and a deemed disposal on 31 March 1996 would not have been recognised as a trading event for tax purposes. The asset or liability is required to be given a notional closing value at 31 March 1996 in accordance with para 12 below. For this purpose "relevant asset" means "chargeable asset" or "relevant qualifying asset". "Relevant qualifying asset" and "relevant liability" are as defined in para 5 above and therefore incorporate the "attributed amount" adjustments in respect of the foreign exchange regime included in the definitions in para 5(8). "Chargeable asset" means one that would have given rise to a capital gain or loss on a deemed disposal on that date. However if a disposal of the asset on 31 March 1996 would have been regarded as a disposal of a qualifying corporate bond for TCGA 1992, the asset is not a chargeable asset.

Other adjustments in the case of chargeable assets etc

11 (1) Where—

(a) an authorised accruals basis of accounting is applied as respects any continuing loan relationship of a company for the company's first relevant accounting period,

(b) an asset representing that relationship is a relevant asset or any liability under it is a relevant liability, and

(c) the relationship is not one as respects which, if the company had ceased to be a party to the relationship on 31st March 1996, any amounts would have been brought into account in computing, for an accounting period ending on or after that date, the profits or losses of the company from any trade carried on by it,

that accounting method shall be taken for the purposes of this Chapter to require the asset or liability to be given a notional closing value as at 31st March 1996 in accordance with paragraph 12 below and the following provisions of this paragraph shall apply if there is any difference in the case of that relationship between the amounts mentioned in sub-paragraph (2) below.

(2) This Chapter shall have effect in accordance with sub-paragraphs (3) and (4) below in relation to any pre-commencement late interest, that is to say, interest which—

    (a) has accrued or become due and payable in an old accounting period, but

    (b) is paid in an accounting period ending on or after 1st April 1996.

(3) Where—

    (a) an amount of pre-commencement late interest under a debtor relationship of a company is paid by that company,

    (b) the amount paid is not interest which, in the case of that company, was brought into account for the purposes of corporation tax for any old accounting period,

    (c) relief would have been allowable in respect of the amount paid if the provisions of this Chapter had not been enacted, and

    (d) the amount paid is not interest in relation to which any debit falls (apart from under this sub-paragraph) to be brought into account for the purposes of this Chapter in case of that company,

debits shall be brought into account for the purposes of this Chapter in the case of that company as if the amount paid were interest accruing, and becoming due and payable, at the time when it is paid.

(4) Where—

    (a) an amount of pre-commencement late interest under a creditor relationship of a company is paid to that company,

    (b) the amount paid is not interest which, in the case of that company, was brought into account for the purposes of corporation tax for any old accounting period,

    (c) the amount paid is not interest in relation to which any credit falls (apart from under this sub-paragraph) to be brought into account for the purposes of this Chapter in the case of that company,

    (d) the amount paid is not an amount of interest which in relation to a transfer before 1st April 1996 was unrealised interest within the meaning of section 716 of the Taxes Act 1988,

credits shall be brought into account for the purposes of this Chapter in the case of that company as if the amount paid were interest accruing, and becoming due and payable, at the time when it is paid.

(5) Where—

    (a) any interest under a debtor relationship of a company was paid by that company at a time on or after 20th December 1995 but during an old accounting period,

    (b) the company was not required to make the payment at or before that time by virtue of any contractual obligation entered into by that company before 20th December 1995, and

    (c) the interest paid is not interest which, if brought into account for the purposes of corporation tax in accordance with an authorised accruals basis of accounting, would fall to be so brought into account in an old accounting period,

the interest paid shall not, in the case of that company, be brought into account for the purposes of corporation tax in any old accounting period.

(6) Where on 1st April 1996 any interest under a loan relationship remains to be paid to or by a company that ceased to be a party to that relationship before that date, this Chapter (including the preceding provisions of this paragraph) shall have effect, so far as relating to interest under a loan relationship, as if the relationship were a continuing loan relationship.

(7) Sub-paragraphs (8) and (9) below apply where the accounting period for which any credits or debits relating to interest under a loan relationship are brought into account for the purposes of this Chapter is determined either—

    (a) in accordance with an accruals basis of accounting, by reference to the time when by virtue of this paragraph that interest is deemed to accrue; or

    (b) in accordance with a mark to market basis of accounting, by reference to the time when by virtue of this paragraph the interest is deemed to become due and payable.

(8) If—

(*a*) at the time when the interest in fact accrued or (as the case may be) when the interest in fact became due and payable, the company was a party to the relationship in question for the purposes of a trade carried on by it, and

(*b*) the credits or debits relating to that interest fall to be brought into account for an accounting period determined as mentioned in sub-paragraph (7) above which is a period for the whole or any part of which that company carries on that trade,

those credits or debits shall be so brought into account under section 82(2) of this Act.

(9) In a case not falling within sub-paragraph (8) above, credits or debits relating to any interest that fall to be brought into account for the purposes of this Chapter for an accounting period determined as mentioned in sub-paragraph (7) above shall be so brought into account as non-trading credits or, as the case may be, non-trading debits.

(10) References in this paragraph to interest under a loan relationship include references to any amounts brought into account for the purposes of corporation tax in accordance with the provisions of section 477A(3) of the Taxes Act 1988 (whether under those provisions as they had effect apart from the amendments made by this Act or under those provisions as amended by this Act).

(11) In this paragraph "old accounting period", in relation to a company, means any accounting period of that company ending before 1st April 1996.

GENERAL NOTE

This paragraph provides transitional rules in respect of interest.

The first provision relates to interest under a loan relationship accruing or becoming due and payable in an accounting period ending on or after 1 April 1996. Where such interest has already been recognised for corporation tax purposes in an "old accounting period" (ie one ending before 1 April 1996) no further recognition under Chapter II will arise.

Second, where interest is not paid in the old accounting period, but is paid on or after 1 April 1996 ("pre-commencement late interest"), special rules apply. Subparagraph (3) provides for a debtor's pre-commencement late interest which was not recognised for corporation tax purposes for any old accounting period, that would not give rise to a debit recognised under Chapter II but would have been allowed under the old tax regime. Such pre-commencement late interest will be treated as accruing or becoming due and payable when it is paid. Subparagraph (4) provides for similar treatment for a creditor's pre-commencement late interest with the additional requirement that the interest was not unrealised interest within TA 1988 s 716.

Third, special provisions apply to any interest under a debtor relationship which was pre-paid on or after 20 December 1995 in an old accounting period during which it would not have been recognised under an authorised accruals basis. (The issue of whether it is pre-paid is determined by reference to any contractual obligation entered into by the company before 20 December 1995.) Such interest is not to be brought into account for corporation tax in any old accounting period.

Fourth, if interest is unpaid at 1 April 1996, but the relevant loan relationship ceased before that date, Chapter II shall apply as if it were a continuing loan relationship.

Fifth, subparagraph (7) relates to any interest which is deemed to accrue or become due or payable in an accounting period for the purposes of this Chapter, by reference to this paragraph. Under subparagraph (8), if the company was party to the particular loan relationship in the course of its trade, both when such interest actually accrued or became due and payable and when it was deemed to under subparagraph (7), then trading assessment under s 82(2) applies. In any other case, non-trading assessment arises.

Transitional in respect of incidental expenses already allowed

14 To the extent that any deduction in respect of any charges or expenses incurred as mentioned in section 84(3) of this Act has been made for the purposes of corporation tax in any accounting period ending before 1st April 1996, those charges or expenses shall not be included in the charges or expenses in relation to which debits may be brought into account for the purposes of this Chapter.

GENERAL NOTE

This paragraph provides that where charges or expenses within s 84(3) (those incurred for the purposes of loan relationships and related transactions) have been allowed in an accounting period ending before 1 April 1996, they will not be allowable under Chapter II.

Holdings of unit trusts etc

15 (1) This paragraph applies to any asset which—

(*a*) is an asset of an insurance company's long term business fund (within the meaning of Chapter I of Part XII of the Taxes Act 1988) both on and immediately after 31st March 1996; and

(b) falls by virtue of paragraph 4 of Schedule 10 to this Act to be treated for a transitional accounting period of the company as representing rights under a creditor relationship of the company.

(2) Sections 212 and 213 of the 1992 Act (annual disposal of holdings of unit trusts etc) shall have effect (without the amendment made by this Chapter) in relation to the assets to which this paragraph applies as if (where it would not otherwise be the case) 31st March 1996 were the last day of an accounting period of the company holding the asset.

(3) Nothing in this Chapter shall prejudice the effect of section 213 of the 1992 Act in relation to any disposal which (whether by virtue of sub-paragraph (2) above or otherwise) is deemed under section 212 of that Act to be made on or before 31st March 1996.

GENERAL NOTE

The gains of an insurance company's holdings in authorised unit trusts and offshore funds, insofar as referable to basic life assurance and general annuity business or capital redemption business, are already taxed on a mark-to-market basis in accordance with the provisions of TCGA 1992 ss 212–214B. Where the holding is in an authorised unit trust which fails the non-qualifying investment test (Sch 10 paras 4 and 8 of this Act) because more than 60 per cent of its investments are interest bearing assets, the income will be within the new provisions relating to loan relationships and TCGA 1992 s 212 will no longer apply (TCGA 1992 s 212(2A) inserted by Sch 14 para 63). This paragraph provides for the transition by means of a deemed disposal on 31 March 1996 of such assets which are held on and immediately after that date. Subparagraph (3) allows amounts spread forward under TCGA 1992 s 213 in respect of assets within the loan relationships rules to be assessed for periods after 31 March 1996 even though the new rules apply from that date.

Bad debt relieved before commencement

16 (1) This paragraph applies where—

(a) an amount becomes, or is to become, due and payable under a creditor relationship of a company in an accounting period ending on or after 1st April 1996, but

(b) by virtue of any of sub-paragraphs (i) to (iii) of section 74(1)(j) of the Taxes Act 1988 (or any enactment re-enacted in those sub-paragraphs), a deduction of an amount representing the whole or any part of the amount payable was authorised to be made, and was made, in computing for the purposes of corporation tax the profits of the company for any accounting period ending before that date.

(2) Subject to sub-paragraph (3) below, nothing in this Chapter shall require it to be assumed for the purposes of this Chapter that any part of the amount to which the deduction relates will be paid in full as it becomes due.

(3) Subject to sub-paragraph (4) below, where—

(a) the deduction relates to an amount payable under a creditor relationship of a company which has been proved or estimated to be a bad debt, but

(b) in an accounting period ending on or after 1st April 1996 the whole or any part of the liability under that relationship to pay that amount is discharged by payment,

this Chapter shall have effect, in the case of that company, as if there were a credit equal to the amount of the payment to be brought into account for the purposes of this Chapter for that period.

(4) Sub-paragraph (3) above does not apply to so much of any payment as is an amount in relation to which a credit falls to be brought into account for the purposes of this Chapter in accordance with paragraph 13(4) above.

GENERAL NOTE

This paragraph applies where bad debt relief has been taken under TA 1988 s 74(1)(j)(i)–(iii) for corporation tax purposes by the creditor, for any accounting period ending before 1 April 1996 and amounts become due and payable in an accounting period ending after that date.

Where relief was obtained on the basis that the debt was proved or estimated to be bad and it is paid (in whole or part) on or after 1 April 1996, the payment will be treated by the creditor as a credit in the period it is paid. This does not however apply if the payment was already recognised as a credit under para 13(4) above. Otherwise, there is no requirement for it to be assumed for the purposes of Chapter II that the amounts in question will be paid as they become due.

Transitional for overseas sovereign debt etc

17 (1) Subject to any regulations under sub-paragraph (4) below and notwithstanding anything in the preceding provisions of this Schedule, the value which for the purposes of this Chapter is to be taken to be the value as at 1st April 1996 of a company's rights under any creditor relationship relating to a relevant overseas debt any part of which falls to be estimated as bad, is the following amount—

(*a*) where the company was not entitled to the debt before the end of its last period of account to end before 1st April 1996, the amount for which the company acquired those rights; and

(*b*) in any other case, the amount of so much of that debt as did not fall, in accordance with section 88B of the Taxes Act 1988, to be estimated as at the end of that period to be bad.

(2) Subject to any regulations under sub-paragraph (4) below, sub-paragraph (3) below shall apply where there is a loss incurred before 1st April 1996 to which section 88C of the Taxes Act 1988 has applied or applies by virtue of paragraph 2 above.

(3) Where, apart from this Chapter, any amount would have been allowed in respect of the loss as a deduction for any accounting period ending after 31st March 1996, that amount shall not be so allowed but shall, instead, be brought into account for the purposes of this Chapter as if it were a debit given for that accounting period by paragraph 9 of Schedule 9 to this Act in respect of a loss incurred on or after 1st April 1996.

(4) The Treasury may by regulations—

(*a*) make such transitional provision as they consider appropriate for purposes connected with the coming into force of paragraphs 8 and 9 of Schedule 9 to this Act and the repeal of sections 88A to 88C of the Taxes Act 1988 (which contained corresponding provisions); and

(*b*) in connection with any such provision, make such modifications of this Schedule (including sub-paragraphs (1) to (3) above) as they consider appropriate;

and regulations made by virtue of this sub-paragraph may have retrospective effect in relation to any accounting periods ending on or after 1st April 1996.

(5) The Treasury shall not make any regulations under sub-paragraph (4) above unless a draft of them has been laid before and approved by a resolution of the House of Commons.

(6) In this paragraph "relevant overseas debt" has the same meaning as in paragraphs 8 and 9 of Schedule 9 to this Act.

GENERAL NOTE

This paragraph provides special transitional provisions in respect of "relevant overseas debt".

"Relevant overseas debt" is subject to the provisions of Sch 9 paras 8 and 9 and is defined in those paragraphs. Relief in respect of such debts is currently subject to the provisions of TA 1988 ss 88A, 88B and 88C.

Paragraph 17 provides for the value as at 1 April 1996, for the purposes of Chapter II, of a company's rights as a creditor under a loan relationship relating to a relevant overseas debt, any part of which is estimated to be bad. It is the acquisition price when the company acquired the debt after the end of its last period of account to end before 1 April 1996. In any other case it will be the amount of the debt which was not bad under TA 1988 s 88B.

Where a loss arises as a result of a disposal prior to 1 April 1996 to which s 88C applies (or would do by virtue of para 2 above) and it would be allowed as a deduction for an accounting period ended after 31 March 1996, the loss shall be allowed under Chapter II. It will be given as a debit under Sch 9 para 9 above as incurred after 1 April 1996.

The Treasury is given power to make regulations to provide for transitional provisions in respect of Sch 9 paras 8 and 9 and ss 88A–88C and to modify para 15. The changes may have retrospective effect to any accounting period ending on or before 1 April 1996. However, the regulations need to be laid before and approved by the House of Commons.

Transitional for accrued income scheme

18 (1) Subject to sub-paragraph (2) below, where, apart from this Chapter, any company would be treated under subsection (2) or (4) section 714 of the Taxes Act 1988 (treatment of deemed sums and reliefs under accrued income scheme)—

(*a*) as receiving any amount at the end of a period beginning before and ending on or after 1st April 1996, or

(*b*) as entitled to any allowance of any amount in such a period,

that amount shall be brought into account as a non-trading credit or, as the case may be, non-trading debit given for the purposes of this Chapter for the company's first relevant accounting period, instead of in accordance with that subsection.

(2) A debit in respect of an allowance relating to a security shall not, in the case of any company, be brought into account for the purposes of this Chapter in accordance with sub-paragraph (1) above if—

(*a*) the security was transferred to that company with accrued interest in a transitional accounting period; and

(*b*) for the purposes of this Chapter an authorised accruals basis of accounting is used for that period as respects the creditor relationship of the company represented by that security.

(3) Where any excess would, apart from this Chapter, be available by virtue of section 103(4) of the Finance Act 1993 (transitional provision in connection with the repeal of section 724(7) of the Taxes Act 1988) to be applied in reducing the annual profits or gains of a company (if any) for its first relevant accounting period, that excess shall be brought into account for the purposes of this Chapter in the case of that company as a non-trading debit for that period.

(4) Subsection (6) of section 807 of the Taxes Act 1988 shall not prevent that section from having effect for an accounting period ending on or after 1st April 1996 in relation to amounts brought into account under this paragraph.

(5) The repeal by this Act of section 63 of the Finance Act 1993 (deemed transfers for the purposes of the accrued income scheme) and of enactments relating to that section shall not apply in relation to relevant days falling before 1st April 1996; but for the purposes of that section and this sub-paragraph 31st March 1996 shall be deemed (where it would not otherwise be so) to be the last day of an accounting period.

GENERAL NOTE
This paragraph provides for transitional provisions in respect of the repeal of the accrued income scheme (AIS).

Subparagraph (1) provides where amounts would have been assessable or relievable under the AIS for a period straddling (or ending on) 1 April 1996 they will instead be allowed as a non-trading credit or debit under Chapter II for the company's first accounting period.

However, sub-para (1) does not apply where the security was transferred to the company with accrued interest in a transitional accounting period and in respect of that security an authorised accruals basis of accounting is used for that period.

Where an overseas life assurance company would be entitled to relief under FA 1993 s 103(4) relief will similarly be allowed. Further, TA 1988 s 807(6) as inserted by Sch 14 para 45 will not prevent s 807 from applying for accounting periods ending on or after 1 April 1996 in respect of amounts recognised under this paragraph, so as to ensure that the double tax provisions continue to apply.

FA 1993 s 63 will continue to apply, despite its repeal, in relation to relevant days before 1 April 1996. 31 March 1996 shall be deemed to be the last day of an accounting period for the purposes of that section and this paragraph.

Deep discount securities

19 (1) This Chapter shall not affect—

(*a*) the application of paragraph 3 of Schedule 4 to the Taxes Act 1988 (charge to tax after acquisition of deep discount securities) in relation to occasions before 1st April 1996;

(*b*) the application of paragraph 4 of that Schedule (charge to tax on disposal of such securities) in relation to any disposal before that date; or (*c*) the application of paragraph 5 of that Schedule (relief in respect of the income element), in accordance (where applicable) with paragraphs 9 and 10 of that Schedule, in relation to income periods ending before that date.

(2) For the purposes of paragraph 5 of Schedule 4 to the Taxes Act 1988 and sub-paragraph (1)(*c*) above every income period current on 31st March 1996 shall be deemed to end on that date.

(3) The repeal by this Act of section 64 of the Finance Act 1993 (deemed transfers in the case of deep discount securities) and of enactments relating to that section shall not apply in relation to relevant times falling before 1st April 1996; but for the purposes of that section and this sub-paragraph 31st March 1996 shall be deemed (where it would not otherwise be so) to be the last day of an accounting period.

(4) Where—

(*a*) a company issued a deep discount security before 1st April 1996 which was not redeemed before that date, and
(*b*) there is a difference between the adjusted issue price of the security as at 31st March 1996 and the adjusted closing value of that security as at that date,

the amount of that difference shall, in the case of that company, be brought into account for the purposes of this Chapter in accordance with sub-paragraph (5) below.

(5) An amount falling to be brought into account for the purposes of this Chapter in accordance with this sub-paragraph shall be brought into account for those purposes for the accounting period in which the security is redeemed—

(*a*) if the adjusted issue price of the security as at 31st March 1996 is greater than the adjusted closing value of the security as at that date, as a non-trading credit; and
(*b*) if the adjusted closing value of the security as at that date is the greater, as a non-trading debit.

(6) Where—

(*a*) a company held a deep discount security on 31st March 1996,
(*b*) the company did not make any disposal of that security on that date,
(*c*) the security is not one in relation to which there is, or is deemed to be, a relevant time on that date for the purposes of section 64 of the Finance Act 1993, and
(*d*) there is an amount which, if the company had made a disposal of that security on that date, would have been treated under paragraph 4 of Schedule 4 to the Taxes Act 1988 as income chargeable to tax under Case III or IV of Schedule D,

that amount shall be brought into account as a non-trading credit given for the purposes of this Chapter for the accounting period mentioned in sub-paragraph (5) below.

(7) Where—

(*a*) a company held a deep discount security on 31st March 1996,
(*b*) the conditions specified in sub-paragraph (6)(*b*) and (*c*) above are satisfied in relation to that security,
(*c*) the security is not as asset falling to be treated as a relevant asset of the company for the purposes of paragraph 11 above, and
(*d*) there is a difference between the adjusted issue price of the security as at 31st March 1996 and the adjusted closing value of that security as at that date,

the amount of that difference (in addition to any amount given by sub-paragraph (6) above) shall, in the case of that company, be brought into account for the purposes of this Chapter in accordance with sub-paragraph (8) below.

(8) An amount falling to be brought into account for the purposes of this Chapter in accordance with this sub-paragraph shall be brought into account for those purposes for the accounting period mentioned in sub-paragraph (9) below—

(*a*) if the adjusted issue price of the security as at 31st March 1996 is greater than the adjusted closing value of the security as at that date, as a non-trading debit; and
(*b*) if the adjusted closing value of the security as at that date is the greater, as a non-trading credit.

(9) That period is the accounting period in which falls whichever is the earliest of the following, that is to say—

(*a*) the earliest day after 31st March 1996 on which, under the terms on which the security was issued, the company holding the security is entitled to require it to be redeemed;

(*b*) the day on which the security is redeemed; and

(*c*) the day on which the company makes a disposal of that security.

(10) The repeal by this Act of the reference in any enactment to, or to any provision of, paragraph 5 of Schedule 4 to the Taxes Act 1988 shall not have effect in relation to amounts treated as paid before 1st April 1996.

(11) For the purposes of this paragraph, in relation to any company—

(*a*) the adjusted issue price of a deep discount security as at 31st March 1996 is whatever for the purposes of Schedule 4 to the Taxes Act 1988 would have been the adjusted issue price for that security for an income period beginning with 1st April 1996; and

(*b*) the adjusted closing value of a security as at 31st March 1996 is the amount which for the purposes of this Chapter is the opening value as at 1st April 1996 if the company's rights and liabilities under the loan relationship of the company that is represented by that security;

and sub-paragraph (7) of paragraph 5 above shall apply for the purposes of this sub-paragraph as it applies for the purposes of that paragraph.

(12) In this paragraph "deep discount security", "disposal" and "income period" have the same meanings as in Schedule 4 to the Taxes Act 1988.

GENERAL NOTE

This paragraph provides for transitional rules in respect of the deep discount securities provisions, which are repealed by Sch 14 para 50.

The charging and relieving provisions of TA 1988 Sch 4 paras 3–5 remain effective for acquisitions, disposals and periods ending before 1 April 1996 respectively and every income period current on 31 March 1996 is deemed to then end. Similarly, the repeal of FA 1993 s 64 is deemed not to be effective to relevant times before 1 April 1996 and 31 March is deemed to be the end of an accounting period for the purposes of that section.

Where a company has issued, but not redeemed, a deep discount security before 1 April 1996 and there is a difference between the adjusted issue price and adjusted closing value at 31 March 1996, the difference is recognised as a non-trading debit or credit as appropriate on redemption.

The adjusted issue price at 31 March 1996 is as established under TA 1988 Sch 4 for an income period beginning 1 April 1996. Similarly, the adjusted closing value at 31 March 1996 is the opening value under Chapter II as at 1 April 1996 (subject to para 5(7) above).

Where a company holds a deep discount security on 31 March 1996 and does not dispose of it on that day and an amount would be chargeable if it did make such a disposal, the amount is taxed as a non-trading credit under Chapter II on the earliest of three events. The three events are the earliest time after 31 March 1996 when the holder may redeem under the terms of issues, the time of redemption or disposal. (The security in question must not be one where there is, or deemed to be, a relevant time under FA 1993 s 64). Further, where a company holds a deep discount security on 31 March 1996 and does not dispose of it on that day and—

(*a*) the security is not a "relevant asset" (ie a "chargeable asset" (para 11(7)) or a "relevant qualifying asset" (para 5(8)),

(*b*) the security is not one where there is, or is deemed to be, a "relevant time" under FA 1993 s 64, and

(*c*) there is a difference between the "adjusted issue price" and the "adjusted closing price" as at 31 March 1996,

the difference is recognised as a non-trading debit or credit as appropriate on the earliest of three events. The three events are the earliest time after 31 March 1996 when the holder may redeem under the terms of issue, the time of redemption or disposal.

The repeal does not affect amounts treated as paid before 1 April 1996. The terms "deep discount securities", "disposal" and "income period" are as defined in Sch 4.

Deep gain securities

20 (1) This Chapter shall not affect the application of paragraph 5 of Schedule 11 to the Finance Act 1989 (charge on deep gain securities) in relation to any transfer or redemption occurring before 1st April 1996.

(2) The repeal by this Act of section 65 of the Finance Act 1993 (deemed transfers in the case of deep gain securities) and of enactments relating to that section shall not apply in relation to relevant days falling before 1st April 1996; but for the purposes of that section and this sub-paragraph 31st March 1996 shall be deemed (where it would not otherwise be so) to be the last day of an accounting period.

(3) Where—

(*a*) a company held a deep gain security on 31st March 1996,

(*b*) the security was not transferred or redeemed by that company on that date,

(*c*) the security is not one in relation to which that date is, or is deemed to be, a relevant day for the purposes of section 65 of the Finance Act 1993, and

(*d*) there is an amount which, if the company had made a transfer of that security on that date, by selling it for its adjusted closing value would have been treated under paragraph 5 of Schedule 11 to the Finance Act 1989 as income chargeable to tax under Case III or IV of Schedule D,

that amount shall be brought into account as a non-trading credit given for the purposes of this Chapter for the accounting period mentioned in sub-paragraph (4) below.

(4) That period is the accounting period in which falls whichever is the earliest of the following, that is to say—

(*a*) the earliest day after 31st March 1996 on which, under the terms on which the security was issued, the company holding the security is entitled to require it to be redeemed;

(*b*) the day on which the security is redeemed; and

(*c*) the day on which the company makes a disposal of that security.

(5) For the purposes of this paragraph the adjusted closing value of a deep gain security held by a company on 31st March 1996 shall be the amount which for the purposes of this Chapter is the opening value as at 1st April 1996 of the company's rights and liabilities under the relationship represented by that security; and sub-paragraph (7) of paragraph 5 above shall apply for the purposes of this sub-paragraph as it applies for the purposes of that paragraph.

(6) In this paragraph "deep gain security" and "transfer" have the same meanings as in Schedule 11 to the Finance Act 1989.

GENERAL NOTE
This paragraph provides for transitional rules in respect of the deep gain securities provisions, which are repealed by Sch 14 para 57.

It provides that transfers and redemptions before 1 April 1996 are not subject to Chapter II. The repeal of FA 1993 s 65 is deemed not to be effective to relevant days before 1 April 1996 and 31 March is deemed to be the end of an accounting period for the purposes of that section.

Where a company holds a deep gain security on 31 March 1996 and it was not transferred or redeemed on that day and an amount would be chargeable if it had sold it on that date for its "adjusted closing value", that amount is taxed as a non-trading credit under Chapter II on the earliest of three events. The three events are the earliest time after 31 March 1996 when the holder may redeem under the terms of issues, the time of redemption or the time of disposal. For this purpose—

(*a*) the security in question must not be one where there is or is deemed to be a relevant time under FA 1993 s 65; and

(*b*) "adjusted closing value" on 31 March 1996, is the "opening value" under Chapter II as at 1 April 1996 (subject to para 5(7) above).

The terms "deep gain securities" and "transfer" are as defined in FA 1989 Sch 11.

Convertible securities

21   (1) This Chapter shall not affect—

(*a*) the application of paragraph 12 of Schedule 10 to the Finance Act 1990 (charge in the case of convertible securities) in relation to any chargeable event occurring before 1st April 1996; or

(*b*) the application of paragraph 25 of that Schedule (relief in the case of convertible securities) in relation to any redemption occurring before that date.

(2) Where—

    (*a*) a company held a qualifying convertible security on 31st March 1996,
    (*b*) that date was not a date on which any chargeable event occurred in relation to that security, and
    (*c*) there is an amount which, if there had been a chargeable event on that date, would have been treated under paragraph 12 of Schedule 10 to the Finance Act 1990 as income chargeable to tax under Case III or IV of Schedule D,

that amount shall be brought into account, in the case of that company, as a non-trading credit given for the purposes of this Chapter for the accounting period mentioned in sub-paragraph (3) below.

(3) That period is the accounting period in which falls whichever is the earliest of the following, that is to say—

    (*a*) the earliest day after 31st March 1996 on which, under the terms on which the security was issued, the company holding the security is entitled to require it to be redeemed;
    (*b*) the day on which the security is redeemed; and
    (*c*) the day on which the company makes a disposal of that security.

(4) Where—

    (*a*) any qualifying convertible security is redeemed, and
    (*b*) that security is one in the case of which any amount falls to be brought into account under sub-paragraph (2) above,

an amount equal to that amount shall be brought into account, in the case of the company that issued the security, as a non-trading debit given for the purposes of this Chapter for the accounting period in which the redemption occurs.

(5) In this paragraph "chargeable event" and "qualifying convertible security" have the same meanings as in Schedule 10 to the Finance Act 1990.

GENERAL NOTE

This paragraph provides for transitional rules in respect of the convertible securities provisions, which are repealed by Sch 14 para 58.

Paragraph 21 provides that charges to tax as a result of chargeable events (FA 1990 Sch 10 para 12) and claims for relief in respect of redemptions (FA 1990 Sch 10 para 25) before 1 April 1996 are not subject to Chapter II.

Under sub-para (2) where a company holds a qualifying convertible security on 31 March 1996 and no chargeable event happened on that day and an amount would be chargeable if such an event happened, the amount is taxed as a non-trading credit under Chapter II on the earliest of three events. The three events are the earliest time after 31 March 1996 when the holder may redeem under the terms of issues, the time of redemption or the time of disposal.

Where a company redeems a qualifying convertible security to which sub-para (2) applies, it will recognise an equal amount as a non-trading debit for the accounting period in which redemption occurs.

The terms "chargeable event" and "qualifying convertible securities" are as defined in FA 1989 Sch 11.

Transitional and savings for Chapter II of Part II of the Finance Act 1993

22 (1) Chapter II of Part II of the Finance Act 1993 (exchange gains and losses) shall have effect in the case of any continuing loan relationship as follows.

(2) Subsection (1A) of section 127 of that Act (deemed variation of debt in respect of amounts accruing in respect of discounts and premiums) shall have effect in relation to the debt by reference to which the continuing loan relationship at any time subsists as if that debt is one to which the company became subject or entitled on 1st April 1996; and, accordingly, that subsection shall require the nominal amount of the debt outstanding to be treated as varied only where the time of the deemed variation is on or after 1st April 1996.

(3) Where section 127 of that Act has effect in relation to any debt by reference to which a continuing loan relationship at any time subsists, it shall so have effect, so far as the debt is one to which the company is deemed by virtue of sub-paragraph (2) above

to have become subject or entitled on 1st April 1996, as if the nominal amount of the debt outstanding on that date were an amount equal to what it would have been if—

(*a*) sub-paragraph (2) above did not apply; and
(*b*) section 127(1A) of the Finance Act 1993 and the provisions to which it refers had always had effect.

(4) The amendment by this Act of section 153(4) of the Finance Act 1993 (assets excluded from being qualifying assets) shall not apply as respects times before 1st April 1996; and, where a company holds an asset immediately before and on 1st April 1996 and that asset is one which falls to be treated as a qualifying asset by virtue of that amendment—

(*a*) the company shall be treated as having become entitled to that asset on that date; and
(*b*) the basic valuation of the asset shall be taken to be its market value on 31st March 1996 (instead of any amount given by section 159 of that Act of 1993);

and in this sub-paragraph "market value" has the same meaning as in the 1992 Act.

(5) The repeal by this Act of section 153(6) of the Finance Act 1993 (liabilities excluded from being qualifying liabilities) shall not have effect as respects times before 1st April 1996; and, where a company is subject to a liability immediately before and on 1st April 1996 and that liability is one which falls to be treated as a qualifying liability by virtue of that repeal, the company shall be treated as having become subject to that liability on that date.

(6) The repeal by this Act of paragraphs 4 to 6 of Schedule 17 to the Finance Act 1993 (exchange gains and losses) shall not have effect in relation to any disposal before 1st April 1996.

GENERAL NOTE
This paragraph provides transitional rules in respect of the foreign exchange provisions of FA 1993 for containing loan relationships.
Subparagraph (2) provides that FA 1993 s 127(1A) (as introduced by Sch 14 para 67 above) only applies to a discount or premium accruing (or deemed to be accrued) after 1 April 1996. It does so by treating the company as becoming subject, or entitled, to the relevant debt on 1 April 1996.
Subparagraph (3) provides that the nominal amount of the debt outstanding at that time was calculated as if sub-para (2) did not apply, but FA 1993 s 127(1A) had always been effective. This causes the discounts or premiums accruing before 1 April 1996 to be taken into account.
Subparagraph (4) provides that the amendment of FA 1993 s 153(4) by Sch 14 para 70(1) above is not effective before 1 April 1996 and causes a company which holds a qualifying asset, straddling that date, to be treated as becoming entitled to it on that date. Further, the basic valuation of the asset shall be its market value (under TCGA 1992) on 31 March 1996, rather than under FA 1993 s 159.
Subparagraph (5) provides that the repeal of FA 1993 s 153(6) by Sch 14 para 70(2) above is not effective before 1 April 1996 and causes the company to be treated as becoming subject to a qualifying liability, which straddles that date, on that date. This provides that the exclusion for qualifying liabilities under FA 1993 s 153(6) is effective until 1 April 1996.
Subparagraph (6) provides that the repeal of FA 1993 Sch 17 paras 4–6 are not effective for disposals before 1 April 1996. (These paragraphs provide for the taxation of certain qualifying assets which would otherwise be within the capital gains regime.)

Carrying back non-trading losses against exchange profits etc

23 (1) Subject to sub-paragraph (2) below, for the purpose of setting any amount against exchange profits for an accounting period beginning before 1st April 1996—

(*a*) a claim may be made under section 131(5) or (6) of the Finance Act 1993 (treatment of exchange gains and losses) in relation to any relievable amount for an accounting period ending on or after 1st April 1996; and
(*b*) the provisions of sections 129 to 133 of that Act shall be deemed to have effect for the purposes of that claim without the amendments made by Schedule 13 to this Act.

(2) If any claim is made by virtue of sub-paragraph (1) above in respect of the relievable amount for an accounting period beginning on or after 1st April 1996, then an amount

equal to the amount to which the claim relates shall be deemed, for the purposes of the computation falling to be made for that accounting period under section 82 of this Act, to be brought into account for that period as a non-trading credit.

(3) The references in this paragraph and paragraph 24 below to provisions of the Finance Act 1993 shall have effect as including references to those sections as applied by the provisions of Chapter II of Part IV of the Finance Act 1994.

(4) Sub-paragraph (3) above is without prejudice to the generality of section 20(2) of the Interpretation Act 1978 (references to other enactments).

GENERAL NOTE
   This paragraph provides for a claim to allow the carry back of non-trading losses against exchange profits of accounting periods beginning before 1 April 1996.
   It applies where such a claim (under FA 1993 s 131(5) or (6)) is made for a relievable amount for an accounting period ended on or after 1 April 1996 and causes FA 1993 ss 129–133 to apply without the amendments contained in Sch 14 above. It prevents the amount carried back from being "double counted" by ensuring relief is not also available under the provisions of Chapter II. It does so by bringing in an equivalent amount as a non-trading credit in the period in which the relievable amount arose.
   Where this paragraph and para 24 below refer to the provisions of FA 1993, they are as applicable by the financial instrument provisions of FA 1994.

Exchange losses etc carried forward from before 1st April 1996

24   Where there is any amount which apart from this Chapter would fall under section 131(12) of the Finance Act 1993 (carrying forward of exchange gains and losses) to be carried forward to an accounting period ending on or after 1st April 1996, that amount shall be treated in relation to that period as an amount carried forward to that period in pursuance of section 83(3) of this Act.

GENERAL NOTE
   This paragraph causes exchange losses carried forward under FA 1993 s 131(12) at 1 April 1996 to be treated as non-trading debits carried forward under the provisions of s 83(3).

Transitional for debt contracts and options to which Chapter II of Part IV of the Finance Act 1994 is applied

25   (1) This paragraph applies in the case of any debt contract or option held by a company both immediately before and on 1st April 1996 if (apart from this Chapter)—

(*a*) the contract or option is an asset in the case of which the following condition is satisfied, that is to say, a gain accruing to the company on a disposal of that asset on 31st March 1996 would have fallen to be treated as a chargeable gain in relation to the company; or
(*b*) had there been a disposal of that asset on 31st March 1996, amounts with respect to it would have fallen to be brought into account for any accounting period beginning before 1st April 1996 in computing any profits or gains of the company from a trade carried on by it.

(2) Chapter II of Part IV of the Finance Act 1994 (provisions relating to certain financial instruments) shall have effect in relation to the debt contract or option as if references in that Chapter to 1st April 1996 were references to the beginning of the company's first relevant accounting period.

(3) For the accounting period mentioned in sub-paragraph (2) above, section 158(2) to (5) of that Act (adjustments for changes of basis of accounting) shall have effect in relation to the debt contract or option as if—

(*a*) any reference to the new basis were a reference to the basis of accounting on which, as regards the contract or option, the company's profit or loss for the accounting period so mentioned is calculated;
(*b*) any reference to being or not being included in amount A for a preceding accounting period were a reference to being or not being taken into account as receipts or increases in value in computing the company's profits or losses for such a period; and
(*c*) any reference to being or not being included in amount B for a preceding

accounting period were a reference to being or not being taken into account as deductions or reductions in value in computing the company's profits or losses for such a period.

(4) Expressions used in this paragraph and in Chapter II of Part IV of the Finance Act 1994 have the same meanings in this paragraph as in that Chapter.

GENERAL NOTE
This paragraph provides transitional rules for debt contracts and options (which are defined by s 101 above) held by a company before and on 1 April 1996.

It applies where such a contract or option, which is an asset and if it had been disposed of on 31 March 1996, a gain would have been assessable as a chargeable gain or trading profit. The financial instrument provisions of FA 1993 then have effect as for the whole of the company's first relevant accounting period and not just from 1 April 1996.

The paragraph provides that in these circumstances the provisions of FA 1994 s 158(2)–(5) (which deal with changes in accounting basis) apply to provide an adjustment in the period in which 31 March 1996 falls.

PART II
INCOME TAX AND CAPITAL GAINS TAX

Application and interpretation of Part II

26 (1) This Part of this Schedule (except paragraph 29) has effect for the purposes of income tax and capital gains tax but not for the purposes of corporation tax.

(2) In this Part of this Schedule—

"the 1992 Act" means the Taxation of Chargeable Gains Act 1992;

"market value" has the same meaning as in the 1992 Act;

"qualifying indexed security" has the meaning given by paragraph 2 of Schedule 11 to the Finance Act 1989; and

"relevant discounted security" has the meaning given for the purposes of Schedule 13 to this Act.

(3) References in this Part of this Schedule to a disposal within marriage are references to any disposal to which section 58 of the 1992 Act applies.

GENERAL NOTE
This paragraph provides that Part II of the Schedule (paras 26–30) apply for the purposes of income tax and capital gains tax and not corporation tax.

It provides definitions and that a "disposal within marriage" is one to which TCGA 1992 s 58 applies.

Qualifying indexed securities

27 (1) This paragraph applies where—

(*a*) on 5th April 1996 any person ("the relevant person") held a qualifying indexed security;

(*b*) that person did not dispose of that security on that date and does not fall (apart from by virtue of this paragraph) to be treated for the purposes of the 1992 Act as having made a disposal of it on that date; and

(*c*) a relevant event occurs.

(2) For the purposes of this paragraph a relevant event occurs on the first occasion after 5th April 1996 when the relevant person, or a person to whom that person has made a disposal of the security within marriage, falls to be treated for the purposes of the 1992 Act as making a disposal (otherwise than within marriage) which is—

(*a*) a disposal of the security in question; or

(*b*) a disposal of any such asset as falls to be treated for the purposes of that Act as the same as that security.

(3) The amount of any chargeable gain or allowable loss which would have been treated as accruing to the relevant person if—

(*a*) he had made a disposal of the asset on 5th April 1996, and

(*b*) that disposal had been for a consideration equal to the market value of the asset,

shall be brought into account as one accruing to the person who makes the disposal constituting the relevant event in the year of assessment in which that event occurs.

GENERAL NOTE

This paragraph provides for transitional provisions for "qualifying indexed securities" (within TCGA 1992 Sch 11 para 2) held on 5 April 1996.

It applies where a person held such a security on 5 April 1996, did not dispose of it (real or deemed under TCGA 1992) and a "relevant event" occurs. A "relevant event" is a disposal of that security (or one which is treated as a disposal under TCGA 1992) after 5 April 1996. The disposal excludes a disposal within marriage but the paragraph applies to a subsequent disposal by the spouse.

The paragraph causes the gain or loss that would have arisen on a market value disposal on 5 April 1996 to be recognised by the person making the disposal on the "relevant event".

28 For the purposes of Schedule 13 to this Act where—

(*a*) a person held a qualifying indexed security both on and immediately after 5th April 1996, and

(*b*) that security is a relevant discounted security,

the amount which that person shall be taken to have paid in respect of his acquisition of that security on or before 5th April 1996 shall be an amount equal to its market value on that date.

GENERAL NOTE

This paragraph provides for the transitional provisions for "qualifying indexed securities" (within TCGA 1992 Sch 11 para 2) which is also a "relevant discounted security" (within TCGA 1992 Sch 12 para 3).

It provides that in Sch 13 above the deemed acquisition price of the security on or before 5 April 1996 will be its market value on that date.

29 For the purposes of paragraph 2 of Schedule 10 to this Act paragraphs 27 and 28 above shall have effect in relation to an authorised unit trust for the first of its accounting periods to end after 31st March 1996 as if references in those paragraphs to 5th April 1996 were references to 31st March 1996.

GENERAL NOTE

This paragraph provides that paras 27 and 28 above apply for authorised unit trusts as if 5 April 1996 read 31 March 1996, for the purposes of TCGA 1992 Sch 9 para 2.

Transitional in relation to qualifying corporate bonds

30 (1) This paragraph applies where—

(*a*) any person holds any asset on and immediately after 5th April 1996;

(*b*) that asset is one which came to be held by that person as a result of a transaction to which section 127 of the 1992 Act applies; and

(*c*) that asset falls from 5th April 1996 to be treated as a relevant discounted security but is neither a qualifying indexed security nor such that it would have fallen to be treated as a qualifying corporate bond in relation to any disposal of it on that date.

(2) Section 116 of the 1992 Act (reorganisations etc involving qualifying corporate bonds) shall have effect as if—

(*a*) there had been a transaction on 5th April 1996 by which the person holding the asset had disposed of it and immediately re-acquired it;

(*b*) the asset re-acquired had been a qualifying corporate bond; and

(*c*) the transaction had been a transaction to which section 127 of the 1992 Act would have applied but for section 116(5) of that Act.

GENERAL NOTE

This paragraph provides transitional provisions for an asset which—

(*a*) from 5 April 1996 is to be treated as a relevant discounted security;

(*b*) is not a qualifying indexed security; and

(c) would not have been treated as a qualifying corporate bond on a disposal after that date.

The paragraph applies where a person holds such an asset on and immediately after 5 April 1996, which was acquired by him under the re-organisation provisions of TCGA 1992 s 127.

It causes TCGA 1992 s 116 to apply as if the asset was disposed and immediately re-acquired as a qualifying corporate bond on 5 April 1996 and TCGA 1992 s 127 would have applied but for s 116(5). This causes the capital gain or loss to 5 April 1996 to be preserved.

Section 114   SCHEDULE 16

SHARE OPTION SCHEMES APPROVED BEFORE PASSING OF
THIS ACT

Preliminary

1 (1) Subject to sub-paragraphs (2) and (3) below, this Schedule applies to any share option scheme approved by the Board before the day on which this Act is passed in consequence of their being satisfied that the scheme fulfils the requirements of Part IV of Schedule 9 to the Taxes Act 1988 (as well as such requirements of Parts I and II of that Schedule as apply in relation to the scheme).

(2) This Schedule shall not apply to a share option scheme if, before the end of 1996, the grantor gives notice to the Board that it is not to apply.

(3) Where a notice is given to the Board under sub-paragraph (2) above, the scheme shall, with effect from the day on which the notice is given, cease to be approved.

GENERAL NOTE

Broadly, this Schedule incorporates into the rules of any scheme approved before the date of Royal Assent the two major restrictions introduced for subsequent schemes by s 114, ie the £30,000 limit on the value of shares over which options may be held, and the prohibition on the use of an exercise price below the market value of the shares at the time of grant. The Schedule does not apply to a scheme if the grantor company gives notice to the Revenue by 31 December 1996 that it is not to apply. In such a case the scheme ceases to be approved, with effect from the day on which the notice is given (para 1). The effect is that the tax reliefs relating to approved schemes will not be available on the subsequent exercise of existing options (TA 1988 s 185(3)), even if they were granted before 17 July 1995.

Limit on aggregate value of options

2 (1) A scheme to which this Schedule applies shall have effect, notwithstanding anything included in it to the contrary, as if it provided that no person shall, on or after the day on which this Act is passed, obtain rights under it which would, at the time they are obtained, cause the aggregate market value of the shares which that person may acquire in pursuance of rights obtained under the scheme or under any other share option scheme, not being a savings related share option scheme, approved under Schedule 9 to the Taxes Act 1988 and established by the grantor or an associated company of the grantor (and not exercised) to exceed or further exceed £30,000.

(2) Sub-paragraph (3) of paragraph 28 of Schedule 9 to the Taxes Act 1988 (market value of shares to be calculated as at time when rights obtained etc) shall have effect for the purposes of sub-paragraph (1) above as it has effect for the purposes of sub-paragraph (1) of that paragraph.

SUBPARAGRAPH (1)

In more detail, a scheme to which the Schedule applies has effect, notwithstanding any contrary provision in its rules, as if it provided that no person should, on or after the date of Royal Assent, be granted options which, at the time of grant, would cause the aggregate market value of the shares which that person could acquire to exceed, or further exceed, £30,000. The shares which a person could acquire, for this purpose, are those he could acquire by the exercise of options under the scheme in question, or under any other Revenue approved share option scheme (other than a savings-related scheme) established by the grantor of that scheme, or by an associated company. Options already exercised are not taken into account.

SUBPARAGRAPH (2)

For this purpose the market value of shares is calculated as at the time of the grant of the option (or at such earlier time or times as may be agreed between the Revenue and the grantor under the legislation dealing with the determination of the exercise price).

Price at which scheme shares may be obtained

3 A scheme to which this Schedule applies shall have effect, notwithstanding anything included in it to the contrary, as if it provided that the price at which scheme shares may be acquired by the exercise of a right obtained, on or after the day on which this

Act is passed, under the scheme must not be manifestly less than the market value of shares of the same class at that time or, if the Board and the grantor agree in writing, at such earlier time or times as may be provided in the agreement.

GENERAL NOTE
    A scheme to which the Schedule applies has effect, notwithstanding any contrary provision in its rules, as if it provided that the exercise price under an option granted on or after the date of Royal Assent should not be manifestly less than the market value of shares of the same class at that time or, if the Revenue and the grantor should so agree in writing, at such earlier time or times as might be provided for in that agreement.

Approval of the Board to alterations

4   For the purposes of paragraph 4 of Schedule 9 to the Taxes Act 1988 (approval not to have effect from the date of any alteration in the scheme unless the Board have approved the alteration) the alterations made by paragraphs 2 and 3 above in any scheme to which this Schedule applies shall be taken to have been approved by the Board before the day on which this Act is passed.

GENERAL NOTE
    Existing legislation requires alterations to a scheme to be approved by the Revenue. The deemed alterations made by this Schedule are treated as having been approved before the date of Royal Assent.

Interpretation

5   (1) Section 187 of the Taxes Act 1988 (interpretation of sections 185 and 186 and Schedules 9 and 10) applies for the purposes of this Schedule as it applies for the purposes of sections 185 and 186 of, and Schedules 9 and 10 to, that Act.

(2) In this Schedule "scheme shares" has the same meaning as in Part IV of Schedule 9 to the Taxes Act 1988.

GENERAL NOTE
    Interpretative provisions in the existing legislation have effect also for the purposes of this Schedule. This would cover the meaning of terms such as "associated company", "grantor", "market value", "scheme", "scheme shares", "savings-related share option scheme", "shares", etc.

Section 128 # SCHEDULE 17

(Inserted as: Schedule 1B to the Taxes Management Act 1970)

CLAIMS FOR RELIEF INVOLVING TWO OR MORE YEARS

This Schedule is inserted as TMA 1970 Sch 1B. It has effect for claims for 1996–97 onwards (s 128(1)).

Preliminary

1 (1) In this Schedule—

(*a*) any reference to a claim includes a reference to an election or notice; and

(*b*) any reference to the amount in which a person is chargeable to tax is a reference to the amount in which he is so chargeable after taking into account any relief or allowance for which a claim is made.

(2) For the purposes of this Schedule, two or more claims to which this Schedule applies which are made by the same person are associated with each other in so far as the same year of assessment is the earlier year in relation to each of those claims.

(3) In sub-paragraph (2) above, any reference to claims to which this Schedule applies includes a reference to amendments and revocations to which paragraph 4 below applies.

GENERAL NOTE

The Schedule applies to elections and notices as well as claims and (in para 4) to amendments and revocations. The amount in which a person is chargeable to tax for a year is the amount after allowing any claim for that year; subsequent paras specify the year for which the claim is made. Where more than one claim is made under this Schedule, and the same year is the earlier year in each claim, such claims are associated claims, eg if losses for years 2 and 3 are both claimed against income of year 1.

Loss relief

2 (1) This paragraph applies where a person makes a claim requiring relief for a loss incurred or treated as incurred, or a payment made, in one year of assessment ("the later year") to be given in an earlier year of assessment ("the earlier year").

(2) Section 42(2) of this Act shall not apply in relation to the claim.

(3) The claim shall relate to the later year.

(4) Subject to sub-paragraph (5) below, the claim shall be for an amount equal to the difference between—

(*a*) the amount in which the person is chargeable to tax for the earlier year ("amount A"); and

(*b*) the amount in which he would be so chargeable on the assumption that effect could be, and were, given to the claim in relation to that year ("amount B").

(5) Where effect has been given to one or more associated claims, amounts A and B above shall each be determined on the assumption that effect could have been, and had been, given to the associated claim or claims in relation to the earlier year.

(6) Effect shall be given to the claim in relation to the later year, whether by repayment or set-off, or by an increase in the aggregate amount given by section 59B(1)(*b*) of this Act, or otherwise.

(7) For the purposes of this paragraph, any deduction made under section 62(2) of the 1992 Act (death: general provisions) in respect of an allowable loss shall be deemed to be made in pursuance of a claim requiring relief to be given in respect of that loss.

GENERAL NOTE

Where a claim is made to carry back relief for a loss incurred or a payment made in a later year to an earlier year, the claim is for the later year. Such a claim need not be made in the claimant's return. The claim is for the amount of the reduction in the tax chargeable for the earlier year if effect were given to the claim in that year, but relief is given for the later year by repayment or set-off or otherwise. Where effect has been given to an associated claim, the reduction in the tax chargeable for the earlier year is calculated as if effect had been given to the associated claim for that year. Where, as a result of death, a capital gains allowable loss incurred in the year of death is carried back against gains of the three preceding years, there is to be deemed to be a claim for that loss, which means that any relief is given for the year of death.

Relief for fluctuating profits of farming etc

3 (1) This paragraph applies where a person who is or has been carrying on a trade of farming or market gardening claims that subsection (2) or (3) of section 96 of the principal Act shall have effect in relation to his profits from that trade for two consecutive years of assessment ("the earlier year" and "the later year").

(2) The claim shall relate to the later year.

(3) Subject to sub-paragraph (4) below, in so far as the claim relates to the profits of the earlier year, the claim shall be for an amount equal to the difference between—

(*a*) the amount in which the person is chargeable to tax for the earlier year ("amount A"); and
(*b*) the amount in which he would be so chargeable on the assumption that effect could be, and were, given to the claim in relation to that year ("amount B").

(4) Where effect has been given to one or more associated claims, amounts A and B above shall each be determined on the assumption that effect could have been, and had been, given to the associated claim or claims in relation to the earlier year.

(5) In so far as the claim relates to the profits of the earlier year, effect shall be given to the claim in relation to the later year by an increase in the amount of tax payable or, as the case may require, in the aggregate amount given by section 59B(1)(*b*) of this Act.

(6) Where this paragraph applies twice in relation to the same year of assessment, the increase or reduction in the amount of tax payable for that year which is required by sub-paragraph (5) above on the earlier application shall be disregarded in determining amounts A and B above for the purposes of the later application.

GENERAL NOTE
A claim to average farming profits of two successive years under TA 1988 s 96 is a claim for the later year. The claim is for the difference between the tax chargeable for the earlier year and what it would have been if effect had been given to the claim in that year. This amount could be an increase or a decrease depending on which of the two years had the higher profit; any increase will increase the tax payable in the later year and any decrease will give rise to repayment or adjustment under TMA 1970 s 59B(1)(*b*).
Where there is an associated claim, the same provisions as in para 2 apply.
Where the later year in one claim becomes the earlier year in a subsequent claim, any increase or reduction in the liability for that year in respect of the first claim is ignored in calculating relief on the later claim.

Relief claimed by virtue of section 96(9)

4 (1) This paragraph applies where—

(*a*) a person who claims that subsection (2) or (3) of section 96 of the principal Act shall have effect for two consecutive years of assessment ("the earlier year" and "the later year") makes or amends a claim for relief under any other provision of the Income Tax Acts for either of those years; and
(*b*) the making or amendment of the claim would be out of time but for subsection (9) of that section.

(2) The claim or amendment shall relate to the later year.

(3) Subject to sub-paragraph (4) below, in so far as the claim or amendment relates to income of the earlier year, the amount claimed, or (as the case may be) the increase or reduction in the amount claimed, shall be equal to the difference between—

(*a*) the amount in which the person is chargeable to tax for the earlier year ("amount A"); and
(*b*) the amount in which he would be so chargeable on the assumption that effect could be, and were, given to the claim or amendment in relation to that year ("amount B").

(4) Where effect has been given to one or more associated claims, amounts A and B above shall each be determined on the assumption that effect could have been, and had been, given to the associated claim or claims in relation to the earlier year.

(5) In so far as the claim or amendment relates to income of the earlier year, effect shall be given to the claim or amendment in relation to the later year by an increase in the amount of tax payable or, as the case may require, in the aggregate amount given by section 59B(1)(*b*) of this Act.

(6) In this paragraph "amend" includes revoke and "amendment" shall be construed accordingly.

GENERAL NOTE
Where a claim has been made for average farming profits of two successive years, any other claim for relief for either of those years may be made or amended within two years after the end of the later year. If such a claim would otherwise be out of date, it is to be taken as a claim for the later year. The increase or reduction of the amount of the other claim is calculated in the way described in para 3.

Carry-back of post-cessation etc receipts

5 (1) This paragraph applies where a person who has received a sum to which section 108 of the principal Act applies (election for carry-back) makes an election under that section requiring tax to be charged as if the sum were received on the date on which the discontinuance took place or, as the case may be, on the last day of the period at the end of which the change of basis took place; and in this paragraph—

"the earlier year" means the year in which the sum is treated as received;
"the later year" means the year in which the sum is received.

(2) The claim shall relate to the later year.

(3) Subject to sub-paragraph (4) below, the claim shall be for an amount equal to the difference between—

(*a*) the amount in which the person is chargeable to tax for the earlier year ("amount A"); and
(*b*) the amount in which he would be so chargeable on the assumption that effect could be, and were, given to the claim in relation to that year ("amount B").

(4) Where effect has been given to one or more associated claims, amounts A and B above shall each be determined on the assumption that effect could have been, and had been, given to the associated claim or claims in relation to the earlier year.

(5) In computing amount B for the purposes of this paragraph, no further deduction or relief shall be made or given in respect of any loss or allowance deducted in pursuance of section 105 of the principal Act.

(6) Effect shall be given to the claim in relation to the later year by an increase in the amount of tax payable.

GENERAL NOTE
TA 1988 s 108 allows an election to be made to treat post-cessation receipts as assessable for the year of discontinuance (the earlier year) instead of for the year of receipt (the later year). The election is treated as a claim for the later year, and the tax payable for that year is increased by the difference between the amount chargeable for the earlier year and what that amount would have been if the receipt had been assessable for that year. In making this comparison, no further deduction is to be made in respect of any loss or allowance deducted under TA 1988 s 105. Where effect has been given to an associated claim, the notional increase in the tax chargeable for the earlier year is calculated as if effect had been given to the associated claim for the earlier year.

Backward spreading of certain payments

6 (1) This paragraph applies where a person who has received a payment to which any of the following sections applies, namely–

(*a*) section 534 of the principal Act (relief for copyright payments etc);
(*b*) section 537A of that Act (relief for payments in respect of designs); and
(*c*) section 538 of that Act (relief for painters, sculptors and other artists),

makes a claim under subsection (1) of that section requiring that effect be given to the following provisions of that section in connection with that payment.

(2) The claim shall relate to the year of assessment in which the payment in question is receivable ("the payment year"); and for the purposes of this sub-paragraph a payment shall be regarded as receivable in the year of assessment in computing the amount of the profits or gains of which it would, but for the relevant section, be included.

(3) Subject to sub-paragraph (4) below, in so far as the claim relates to the profits or gains of a year of assessment earlier than the payment year ("the earlier year"), the claim shall be for an amount equal to the difference between—

(*a*) the amount in which the person is chargeable to tax for the earlier year ("amount A"); and

(*b*) the amount in which he would be so chargeable on the assumption that effect could be, and were, given to the claim or amendment in relation to that year ("amount B").

(4) Where effect has been given to one or more associated claims, amounts A and B above shall each be determined on the assumption that effect could have been, and had been, given to the associated claim or claims in relation to the earlier year.

(5) In so far as the claim relates to the profits or gains of the earlier year, effect shall be given to the claim in relation to the payment year by an increase in the amount of tax payable.

GENERAL NOTE

This paragraph relates to claims to spread back payments for copyright (TA 1988 s 534), for designs (TA 1988 s 537A) and for sales of paintings and other works of art (TA 1988 s 538). Such a claim is a claim for the year in which the payment is receivable, and the tax payable for that year is increased by the difference between the amount chargeable for the earlier year and what that amount would have been if part of the receipt had been included in the profits of that year. Where effect has been given to an associated claim, the notional increase in the tax chargeable for the earlier year is calculated as if effect had been given to the associated claim for the earlier year.

Section 132 ## SCHEDULE 18

OVERDUE TAX AND EXCESSIVE PAYMENTS BY THE BOARD

The Taxes Management Act 1970

1 In section 55 of the Taxes Management Act 1970 (recovery of tax not postponed) in subsection (1) (which specifies the appeals to which section 55 applies) for paragraph (*b*) (assessments under section 29) there shall be substituted–

"(*b*) an assessment to tax made otherwise than under section 9 of this Act,".

GENERAL NOTE
TMA 1970 s 55 provides for recovery of tax following an appeal in specified circumstances so far as it is not the subject of a postponement application. One of the circumstances is an appeal against an assessment made following a discovery of loss of tax due to fraud or neglect (TMA 1970 s 29). This paragraph extends that circumstance to any assessment other than a self-assessment.

2 (1) Section 59A of the Taxes Management Act 1970 (payments on account of income tax) shall be amended in accordance with the following provisions of this paragraph.

(2) In subsection (2) (requirement to make payments on account and determination, subject to subsections (4) and (4A) of the amount of such payments) for "(4) and (4A)" there shall be substituted "(4) to (4B)".

(3) In subsection (4A) (determination, subject to subsections (3) and (4), of amount of payments on account in the case of late or amended assessments), after "subsections (3) and (4) above" there shall be inserted "and subsection (4B) below".

(4) After subsection (4A) there shall be inserted–

"(4B) If as regards the year immediately preceding the year of assessment the taxpayer is assessed to income tax under section 29 of this Act in any amount, then, subject to subsections (3) and (4) above and to any subsequent application of this subsection, the amount of each payment on account shall be, and shall be deemed always to have been, the total of—

(*a*) the amount which, immediately before the making of the assessment under section 29, is the amount of that payment, and
(*b*) an amount equal to 50 per cent of the amount in which he is assessed under that assessment;

and if that assessment is varied, the amount in which he is assessed under it shall be taken for the purposes of paragraph (*b*) above to be the amount of the assessment as varied."

(5) In subsection (5) (adjustments to be made where subsection (4A) applies) after "subsection (4A)" there shall be inserted "or (4B)".

GENERAL NOTE
This paragraph inserts new s 59A(4A) into TMA 1970 which specifies a further matter to be taken into consideration in determining the amount of income tax to be paid on account for a year of assessment. Where, for the year preceding the year of assessment, an assessment has been made following a discovery by the Revenue that tax has been lost, the tax charged in that assessment is to be included in the calculation of the payment on account. Any variation in the amount of the Revenue assessment is to be reflected in the amount of the payment on account.

3 (1) Section 86 of the Taxes Management Act 1970 (interest on overdue income tax and capital gains tax) shall be amended in accordance with the following provisions of this paragraph.

(2) In subsection (4) (subsection (5) to apply with respect to interest in cases where taxpayer makes a claim under section 59A(3) or (4) but an amount becomes payable by him under certain provisions of section 59B) in paragraph (*b*), after "payable by him" there shall be inserted "(i)" and at the end of that paragraph there shall be added

"or

(ii) in accordance with section 59B(6) of this Act in respect of income tax assessed under section 29 of this Act."

(3) In subsection (6) (determination of what amount is payable in accordance with section 59B(3), (4) or (5)) after "section 59B(3), (4) or (5) of this Act" there shall be inserted "or, in respect of income tax assessed under section 29 of this Act, in accordance with section 59B(6) of this Act".

GENERAL NOTE
Where a taxpayer claims to reduce the amount of a payment on account because he considers that his liability will be less, interest on unpaid tax will be charged in respect of any addition to the amount of the payment on account made in accordance with para 2 above.

4 (1) Section 88 of the Taxes Management Act 1970 (which relates to interest on tax recovered to make good loss due to the taxpayer's fault and which is superseded by section 86 of that Act, as substituted by the Finance Act 1995) shall cease to have effect.

(2) In consequence of the repeal of section 88 of the Taxes Management Act 1970—

(*a*) section 88A of that Act (determinations under section 88) shall cease to have effect;
(*b*) in section 91 of that Act (effect of interest on reliefs) in subsection (1)—

(i) the words "or section 88" shall cease to have effect; and
(ii) for the words "those provisions", in each place where they occur, there shall be substituted "that section"; and

(*c*) in section 113 of that Act (form of returns and other documents) subsection (1C) shall cease to have effect.

GENERAL NOTE
This paragraph repeals TMA 1970 s 88 which is superseded by TMA 1970 new s 86. In consequence TMA 1970 ss 88A and 113(1C) will cease to have effect and references to s 88 in TMA 1970 s 91(1) are deleted.

The Taxes Act 1988

5 In section 307 of the Taxes Act 1988 (enterprise investment scheme and business expansion scheme: withdrawal of relief) in subsection (6) (application of section 86 of the Taxes Management Act 1970 to assessments made by virtue of section 307 as if the reckonable date were as specified in that subsection) for "the reckonable date" there shall be substituted "the relevant date".

GENERAL NOTE
This paragraph amends TA 1988 s 307 (charge of interest on withdrawal of relief under the enterprise investment scheme) the relevant date is substituted for the reckonable date to take account of the change of wording in TMA 1970 s 86.

6 (1) Section 369 of the Taxes Act 1988 (MIRAS) shall be amended in accordance with the following provisions of this paragraph.

(2) In subsection (7)—

(*a*) for paragraph (*a*) (which applies section 29(3)(*c*) of the Taxes Management Act 1970) there shall be substituted—

"(*a*) section 29(1)(*c*) (excessive relief) as it has effect apart from section 29(2) to (10) of that Act;";

(*b*) in paragraph (*b*) (which applies section 30 of the Taxes Management Act 1970) after the words in parentheses there shall be inserted "apart from subsection (1B)";
(*c*) in paragraph (*c*) (which applies section 88 of the Taxes Management Act 1970) for "section 88" there shall be substituted "section 86"; and
(*d*) in the words following paragraph (*d*) after "as if it had been repaid" there shall be inserted "as respects a chargeable period".

(3) After subsection (7) there shall be inserted—

"(8) In the application of section 86 of the Management Act by virtue of subsection (7) above in relation to sums due and payable by virtue of an assessment made for the whole or part of a year of assessment ('the relevant year of assessment') under section 29(1)(c) or 30 of that Act, as applied by that subsection, the relevant date—

(a) is 1st January in the relevant year of assessment in a case where the person falling within subsection (6) above has made a relevant interim claim; and

(b) in any other case, is the later of the following dates, that is to say—

(i) 1st January in the relevant year of assessment; or

(ii) the date of the making of the payment by the Board which gives rise to the assessment.

(9) In this section–

'financial year', in relation to any person, means a financial year of that person for the purposes of the relevant regulations;

'interim claim' means an interim claim within the meaning of the relevant regulations;

'relevant interim claim' means, in relation to an assessment made for a period coterminous with, or falling wholly within, a person's financial year, an interim claim made for a period falling wholly or partly within that financial year; and

'the relevant regulations' means regulations made under section 378(3) for the purposes of subsection (6) above."

GENERAL NOTE
Subparagraph (2) makes minor amendments to TA 1988 s 369(7) (MIRAS) which deals with an overpayment of tax to the lender to bring it into line with changes of procedure introduced for the self-assessment scheme. Subparagraph (3) inserts new s 369(8) and (9) into TA 1988 which provide for interest to be charged on tax assessed to recover excess relief or overpayment. Such interest runs from the later of—

(a) 1 January in the relevant year of assessment; or

(b) the date of the payment by the Revenue,

except that where the lender has made an interim claim for its financial year (or a period falling wholly within its financial year) interest runs from 1 January in the relevant year of assessment.

7 In section 374A of the Taxes Act 1988 (interest which never has been relevant loan interest etc) in subsection (4) (which provides for the application of the Taxes Management Act 1970 to an assessment under subsection (3) of that section as if it were an assessment to income tax and as if certain other things were the case) the words from "and as if" onwards shall be omitted.

GENERAL NOTE
Where interest has never qualified as MIRAS interest, an assessment may be made to recover from the borrower any tax which he has deducted (TA 1988 s 374A). The provisions of TMA 1970 apply to such an assessment as if it were an income tax assessment for the year in which the deduction was made (TA 1988 s 374A(4)). That subsection also provided that other conditions had to be satisfied for TMA 1970 to apply; this paragraph deletes these conditions.

8 In section 375 of the Taxes Act 1988 (interest ceasing to be relevant loan interest etc) in subsection (4) (which provides for the application of the Taxes Management Act 1970 to an assessment under subsection (3) of that section as it applies by virtue of section 374A(4) to an assessment under section 374A(3)) for "as it applies, by virtue of subsection (4) of section 374A, to an assessment under subsection (3) of that section" there shall be substituted "as if it were an assessment to income tax for the year of assessment in which the deduction was made".

GENERAL NOTE
This paragraph makes a similar amendment to that in para 7 in the case of interest ceasing to be MIRAS interest.

9 In section 412(4) of the Taxes Act 1988 (group relief: power to assess under section 412(3) is without prejudice to the making of assessments under section 29(3)(c) of the

Taxes Management Act 1970) for "section 29(3)(*c*)" there shall be substituted "section 29(1)(*c*)".

GENERAL NOTE
  See note to para 10.

10 In section 588 of the Taxes Act 1988 (training courses: employee and employer may be assessed under section 29(3) of the Taxes Management Act 1970 if employee fails to comply with conditions for relief) for "section 29(3)" there shall be substituted "section 29(1)".

GENERAL NOTE
  What was TMA 1970 s 29(3)(*c*) has become TMA 1970 new s 29(1). Paragraphs 9 and 10 make the necessary amendments in TA 1988 ss 412(4) and 588.

11 (1) Schedule 14 to the Taxes Act 1988 (life assurance premium relief: provisions ancillary to section 266) shall be amended in accordance with the following provisions of this paragraph.

(2) In paragraph 6(2) (which provides for the application of the Taxes Management Act 1970 to an assessment under paragraph 6 of that Schedule as if it were an assessment to tax for the year of assessment in which the relief was given and as if certain other things were the case) the words from "and as if" onwards shall be omitted.

(3) In paragraph 7(3) (which applies specified provisions of the Taxes Management Act 1970 to the payment of a sum claimed under section 266(5)(*b*)—

(*a*) for paragraph (*a*) (which applies section 29(3)(*c*) of the Taxes Management Act 1970) there shall be substituted—

"(*a*) section 29(1)(*c*) (excessive relief) as it has effect apart from section 29(2) to (10) of that Act;";

(*b*) in paragraph (*b*) (which applies section 30 of the Taxes Management Act 1970) after the words in parentheses there shall be inserted "apart from subsection (1B)";
(*c*) in paragraph (*c*) (which applies section 88 of the Taxes Management Act 1970) for "section 88" there shall be substituted "section 86"; and
(*d*) for the words following paragraph (*d*) there shall be substituted—

"shall apply in relation to an amount which is paid to any person by the Board as an amount recoverable by virtue of section 266(5)(*b*) but to which that person is not entitled as if it were income tax which ought not to have been repaid and, where that amount was claimed by that person, as if it had been repaid as respects a chargeable period as a relief which was not due."

(4) After paragraph 7(3) there shall be added—

"(4) In the application of section 86 of the Management Act by virtue of sub-paragraph (3) above in relation to sums due and payable by virtue of an assessment made for the whole or part of a year of assessment ('the relevant year of assessment') under section 29(1)(*c*) or 30 of that Act, as applied by that sub-paragraph, the relevant date—

(*a*) is 1st January in the relevant year of assessment in a case where the person falling within section 266(5)(*b*) has made a relevant interim claim; and
(*b*) in any other case, is the later of the following dates, that is to say—

(i) 1st January in the relevant year of assessment; or
(ii) the date of the making of the payment by the Board which gives rise to the assessment.

(5) In this paragraph—

'financial year', in relation to any person, means a financial year of that person for the purposes of the relevant regulations;
'interim claim' means an interim claim within the meaning of the relevant regulations;
'relevant interim claim' means, in relation to an assessment made for a period

coterminous with, or falling wholly within, a person's financial year, an interim claim made for a period falling wholly or partly within that financial year;
'the relevant regulations' means regulations made under sub-paragraph (1) above."

GENERAL NOTE
  This paragraph makes amendments to TA 1988 Sch 14 (relief for insurance premiums) similar to those described under para 6 above.

The Finance Act 1989

12 (1) Section 57 of the Finance Act 1989 (medical insurance: supplementary) shall be amended in accordance with the following provisions of this paragraph.

(2) In subsection (3) (which applies specified provisions of the Taxes Management Act 1970 to the payment of an amount claimed under section 54(6)(*b*))—

(*a*) for paragraph (*a*) (which applies section 29(3)(*c*) of the Taxes Management Act 1970) there shall be substituted—

  "(*a*) section 29(1)(*c*) (excessive relief) as it has effect apart from section 29(2) to (10) of that Act;";

(*b*) in paragraph (*b*) (which applies section 30 of the Taxes Management Act 1970) after the words in parentheses there shall be inserted "apart from subsection (1B)";
(*c*) in paragraph (*c*) (which applies section 88 of the Taxes Management Act 1970) for "section 88" there shall be substituted "section 86"; and
(*d*) for the words following paragraph (*d*) there shall be substituted—

"shall apply in relation to an amount which is paid to any person by the Board as an amount recoverable by virtue of section 54(6)(*b*) above but to which that person is not entitled as if it were income tax which ought not to have been repaid and, where that amount was claimed by that person, as if it had been repaid as respects a chargeable period as a relief which was not due."

(3) After subsection (3) there shall be inserted—

"(3A) In the application of section 86 of the Taxes Management Act 1970 by virtue of subsection (3) above in relation to sums due and payable by virtue of an assessment made under section 29(1)(*c*) or 30 of that Act, as applied by that subsection, the relevant date—

(*a*) in a case where the person falling within section 54(6) above has made any interim claim, within the meaning of regulations made under subsection (1) and section 54(4) above, as respects some part of the year of assessment for which the assessment is made, is 1st January in that year of assessment; and
(*b*) in any other case, is the later of the following dates, that is to say—

(i) 1st January in the year of assessment for which the assessment is made; or
(ii) the date of the making of the payment by the Board which gives rise to the assessment."

GENERAL NOTE
  Where medical insurance relief is given by way of deduction of tax from premiums, the insurer is entitled to claim from the Revenue the amount of tax deducted. If the payer ceases to be entitled to relief, the Revenue may recover from the insurer any tax over-repaid. This paragraph makes amendments to TA 1988 s 57 similar to those described under para 6 above.

13 In section 178 of the Finance Act 1989 (setting rates of interest) in subsection (2)(*f*) (which specifies the provisions of the Taxes Management Act 1970 to which the section applies) the words "88" shall be omitted.

GENERAL NOTE
  This paragraph deletes the reference to TMA 1970 s 88 (which is repealed by para 4 above) in FA 1989 s 178(2)(*f*) (which sets rates of interest).

The Finance Act 1991

14 (1) Section 33 of the Finance Act 1991 (vocational training) shall be amended in accordance with the following provisions of this paragraph.

(2) In subsection (3) (which applies specified provisions of the Taxes Management Act 1970 to the payment of an amount claimed under section 32(5)(*b*))—

(*a*) for paragraph (*a*) (which applies section 29(3)(*c*) of the Taxes Management Act 1970) there shall be substituted—

"(*a*) section 29(1)(*c*) (excessive relief) as it has effect apart from section 29(2) to (10) of that Act;";

(*b*) in paragraph (*b*) (which applies section 30 of the Taxes Management Act 1970) after the words in parentheses there shall be inserted "apart from subsection (1B)";
(*c*) in paragraph (*c*) (which applies section 88 of the Taxes Management Act 1970) for "section 88" there shall be substituted "section 86"; and
(*d*) for the words following paragraph (*d*) there shall be substituted—

"shall apply in relation to an amount which is paid to any person by the Board as an amount recoverable by virtue of section 32(5)(*b*) above but to which that person is not entitled as if it were income tax which ought not to have been repaid and, where that amount was claimed by that person, as if it had been repaid as respects a chargeable period as a relief which was not due."

(3) After subsection (3) there shall be inserted—

"(3A) In the application of section 86 of the Taxes Management Act 1970 by virtue of subsection (3) above in relation to sums due and payable by virtue of an assessment made under section 29(1)(*c*) or 30 of that Act, as applied by that subsection, the relevant date—

(*a*) in a case where the person falling within section 32(5) above has made any interim claim, within the meaning of regulations made under subsection (1) above, as respects some part of the year of assessment for which the assessment is made, is 1st January in that year of assessment; and
(*b*) in any other case, is the later of the following dates, that is to say—

(i) 1st January in the year of assessment for which the assessment is made; or
(ii) the date of the making of the payment by the Board which gives rise to the assessment."

GENERAL NOTE
A person entitled to relief under FA 1991 s 32 for payments for vocational training obtains the relief by deducting tax from the payments and the recipient is entitled to repayment by the Revenue of the tax deducted. If the recipient has received a repayment to which he was not entitled, the Revenue may recover from the recipient any tax over-repaid. This paragraph makes amendments to FA 1991 s 33 similar to those described under para 6 above.

The Taxation of Chargeable Gains Act 1992

15 (1) Section 281 of the Taxation of Chargeable Gains Act 1992 (payment by instalments of tax on gifts) shall be amended in accordance with the following provisions of this paragraph.

(2) In subsection (5), for paragraph (*a*) (tax payable by instalments to carry interest in accordance with Part IX of the Taxes Management Act 1970, except section 88) there shall be substituted—

"(*a*) tax payable by instalments by virtue of this section carries interest in accordance with Part IX of the Management Act as that Part applies where no election is made under subsection (2) above, and".

(3) In subsection (6) (power to pay at any time unpaid tax payable by instalments, with interest to the date of payment) after "with interest" there shall be inserted "(determined in accordance with subsection (5)(*a*) above)".

(4) In subsection (7) (cases where tax payable by instalments, with interest to the date of payment, becomes due and payable immediately) after "with interest" there shall be

inserted "(determined in accordance with subsection (5)(*a*) above as if the tax were tax payable by instalments by virtue of this section)".

GENERAL NOTE
Where an election is made under TCGA s 281 to pay by instalment CGT on a gift, this paragraph substitutes new sub-s (5)(*a*) which provides that interest is chargeable under TMA 1970 Part IX as though no claim to pay by instalments had been made. Interest is calculated in accordance with new sub-s (5)(*a*) where the taxpayer clears unpaid instalments in advance of the due date(s), or where, under TCGA 1992 s 281(7), tax payable by instalments becomes payable immediately with interest.

The Finance Act 1995

16 In section 73(4) of the Finance Act 1995 (power to apply certain provisions of the Taxes Management Act 1970 in relation to certain sums payable in connection with venture capital trusts)—

(*a*) for "section 29(3)(*c*)" there shall be substituted "section 29(1)(*c*)";
(*b*) for "section 88" there shall be substituted "section 86"; and
(*c*) after paragraph (*d*) there shall be added—

"and section 86 of that Act may be so applied with such modifications as respects the relevant date as may be specified in the regulations."

GENERAL NOTE
This paragraph makes the necessary amendments to FA 1995 s 73(4) (venture capital trusts) consequent on the repeal of TMA 1970 s 88.

Commencement

17 (1) Paragraphs 1 to 3, 6(2)(*a*) and (*b*), 8, 10, 11(3)(*a*) and (*b*), 12(2)(*a*) and (*b*), 14(2)(*a*) and (*b*) and 16(*a*) above have effect, subject to sub-paragraph (2) below—

(*a*) for the purposes of income tax and capital gains tax, as respects the year 1996–97 and subsequent years of assessment; and
(*b*) for the purposes of corporation tax, as respects accounting periods ending on or after the day appointed under section 199 of the Finance Act 1994 for the purposes of Chapter III of Part IV of that Act (self-assessment management provisions).

(2) Paragraphs 1, 3, 6(2)(*a*) and (*b*), 10, 11(3)(*a*) and (*b*), 12(2)(*a*) and (*b*) and 14(2)(*a*) and (*b*) above, so far as relating to partnerships whose trades, professions or businesses are set up and commenced before 6th April 1994, has effect as respects the year 1997–98 and subsequent years of assessment.

(3) Paragraphs 4, 5, 6(2)(*c*) and (3), 11(3)(*c*) and (4), 12(2)(*c*) and (3), 13, 14(2)(*c*) and (3), 15 and 16(*b*) and (*c*) above have effect, subject to sub-paragraph (4) below—

(*a*) as respects the year 1996–97 and subsequent years of assessment; and
(*b*) in relation to any income tax or capital gains tax which—

(i) is charged by an assessment made on or after 6th April 1998; and
(ii) is for the year 1995–96 or any earlier year of assessment;

and where sub-paragraph (4) of paragraph 11, sub-paragraph (3) of paragraph 12, or sub-paragraph (3) of paragraph 14 has effect by virtue of paragraph (*b*) of this sub-paragraph it shall have effect with the substitution, in the provision inserted by that sub-paragraph, for "section 29(1)(*c*)" of "section 29(3)(*c*)".

(4) Paragraphs 4, 6(2)(*c*) and (3), 11(3)(*c*) and (4), 12(2)(*c*) and (3), 13 and 14(2)(*c*) and (3) above, so far as relating to partnerships whose trades, professions or businesses were set up and commenced before 6th April 1994 have effect—

(*a*) as respects the year 1997–98 and subsequent years of assessment; and
(*b*) in relation to any income tax which—

(i) is charged by an assessment made on or after 6th April 1998; and
(ii) is for the year 1995–96 or any earlier year of assessment.

(5) Paragraphs 7 and 11(2) above have effect—

(*a*) as respects the year 1996–97 and subsequent years of assessment; and (*b*) subject to sub-paragraphs (6) and (7) below, in relation to any income tax or capital gains tax which–

    (i) is charged by an assessment made on or after 6th April 1998; and

    (ii) is for the year 1995–96 or any earlier year of assessment.

(6) Sub-paragraph (5)(*b*) above does not apply to paragraph 7 above so far as paragraph 7 provides for the omission of—

    (*a*) paragraph (*a*) of subsection (4) of section 374A of the Taxes Act 1988, and

    (*b*) the words "and as if" so far as they relate to paragraph (*a*) of that subsection.

(7) Sub-paragraph (5)(*b*) above does not apply to paragraph 11(2) above so far as paragraph 11(2) provides for the omission of—

    (*a*) the words "sections 55(1) (recovery of tax not postponed) and", and

    (*b*) the words "and as if—

        (*a*) the assessment were among those specified in"

so far as those words relate to the words mentioned in paragraph (*a*) of this sub-paragraph.

(8) Paragraphs 6(2)(*d*), 11(3)(*d*), 12(2)(*d*) and 14(2)(*d*) above shall not apply in relation to any payment if the payment, or the claim on which it is made, was made before the day on which this Act is passed.

(9) Paragraph 9 above has effect as respects accounting periods ending on or after the day appointed under section 199 of the Finance Act 1994 for the purposes of Chapter III of Part IV of that Act (self-assessment management provisions).

(10) Any power to make regulations exercisable by virtue of an amendment made by any of the preceding provisions of this Schedule may be exercised so as to make provision having effect in relation to any year of assessment in relation to which that provision has effect in accordance with sub-paragraphs (1) to (9) above.

GENERAL NOTE

    This paragraph sets out the dates from which the various provisions of Sch 18 are to take effect.

Section 133 # SCHEDULE 19

SELF-ASSESSMENT: CLAIMS AND ENQUIRIES

Introductory

1 The Taxes Management Act 1970, as it has effect—

(*a*) for the purposes of income tax and capital gains tax, as respects the year 1996–97 and subsequent years of assessment, and

(*b*) for the purposes of corporation tax, as respects accounting periods ending on or after the day appointed under section 199 of the Finance Act 1994 for the purposes of Chapter III of Part IV of that Act (self-assessment management provisions),

shall be amended in accordance with the following provisions of this Schedule.

GENERAL NOTE
The amendments made to TMA 1970 by this Schedule apply from the commencement of the self-assessment scheme.

Matters subject to enquiry

2 In each of sections 9A(1), 11AB(1), 12AC(1), 19A(1), 28A(1) and 28B(1) (matters subject to enquiry), after paragraph (*b*) there shall be inserted "or

(*c*) any claim or election included in the return (by amendment or otherwise)".

GENERAL NOTE
In addition to enquiring into a return and an amendment of a return, a Revenue officer may enquire into a claim included in a return or amended return.

Power to call for documents

3 (1) In section 19A (power to call for documents for the purposes of certain enquiries), after subsection (2) there shall be inserted the following subsection—

"(2A) The officer of the Board may also (whether or not he imposes a requirement under subsection (2) above), by a notice in writing, require the taxpayer, within such time (which shall not be less than 30 days) as may be specified in the notice—

(*a*) to produce to the officer such documents as are in the taxpayer's possession or power and as the officer may reasonably require for the purpose of making a determination for the purposes of section 28A(7A)(*d*) or 28B(6A)(*d*) of this Act, and

(*b*) to furnish the officer with such accounts or particulars as he may reasonably require for that purpose."

(2) In subsections (3), (5), (7), (9)(*a*) and (10) of that section, for the words "subsection (2)", in each place where they occur, there shall be substituted "subsection (2) or (2A)".

(3) In subsection (4) of that section, for "subsection (2) or" there shall be substituted "subsection (2), (2A) or".

(4) In section 97AA(1) (penalty for failure to comply with notice), for "section 19A(2) or (3)" there shall be substituted "section 19A(2), (2A) or (3)".

GENERAL NOTE
This paragraph inserts new s 19A(2A)into TMA 1970 which empowers a Revenue officer to issue a notice requiring production of such documents, accounts or particulars as he may require to enable him to decide between possible alternative treatments of a receipt (see paras 4 and 5 below). Failure to comply with the notice will attract penalties under TMA 1970 s 97AA.

Further amendments of section 28A

4 (1) In section 28A (amendment of self-assessment where enquiries made in the case of individuals, trustees and companies)—

(*a*) in each of subsections (2)(*a*) and (4)(*b*), for "subsection (1)(*b*) above" there shall be substituted "subsection (1)(*b*) or (*c*) above";

(*b*) in subsection (4)(*a*), for "the tax contained in the taxpayer's self-assessment" there shall be substituted "any amount set out in the return"; and
(*c*) in subsection (5)(*b*), at the end there shall be inserted "and as to any claims or elections into which he has enquired".

(2) After subsection (4) of that section there shall be inserted the following subsections—

"(4A) If—

(*a*) any claim or election is included in the return,
(*b*) the officer is of opinion that the claim or election should be disallowed in whole or in part but that its disallowance to the extent he thinks appropriate would not require any amendment of the taxpayer's self-assessment, and
(*c*) the claim or election, so far as the officer thinks it should be disallowed, is not, before the end of the period mentioned in subsection (3) above, amended to the officer's satisfaction or withdrawn,

the officer shall, before the end of the period mentioned in subsection (4) above, give notice to the taxpayer of the extent to which he is disallowing the claim or election.

(4B) Subsection (4A)(*c*) above is without prejudice to any provision by virtue of which any claim or election is irrevocable or unamendable."

(3) Immediately before subsection (8) of that section there shall be inserted the following subsections—

"(7A) Where, in the case of any return made in respect of any chargeable period—

(*a*) alternative methods are allowed by the Tax Acts for bringing amounts into account in that return,
(*b*) the return is made or amended using one of those methods,
(*c*) a return could have been made in that case using an alternative method, and
(*d*) an officer of the Board determines which of the alternative methods is to be used by the Board in relation to the taxpayer for that period,

any enquiry into that return or into an amendment of it shall be conducted, and this section shall have effect, as if the only method allowed for the purposes of the Tax Acts were the method determined by the officer.

(7B) For the purposes of subsection (7A) above the cases where the Tax Acts allow alternative methods for bringing amounts into account in a return are—

(*a*) the case where those amounts may be brought into account either—

(i) in making a computation for the purposes of Case I or II of Schedule D; or
(ii) in making a computation for the purposes of any of Cases III to V of that Schedule; and

(*b*) the case where the computation in which amounts are brought into account may be either—

(i) a computation for the purposes of Case I of Schedule D; or
(ii) a computation for the purpose of applying the basis (commonly called the I minus E basis) under which a company carrying on life assurance business or capital redemption business may be charged to tax on that business otherwise than under Case I of Schedule D.

(7C) In subsection (7B) above—

'life assurance business' includes annuity business within the meaning of Chapter I of Part XII of the principal Act; and
'capital redemption business' means any capital redemption business, within the meaning of section 458 of that Act, which is business to which that section applies."

GENERAL NOTE
TMA 1970 s 28A provides that a Revenue officer, on conclusion of his enquiries into a return, must give notice to the taxpayer of the amount of tax which should be included in the self-assessment and (if the taxpayer does not do so within 30 days of the issue of the notice) may amend the self-assessment accordingly. This procedure is extended to amendment of the self-assessment following an enquiry into a claim made in a return.

Subparagraph (2) inserts new s 28A(4A) and (4B) into TMA 1970 which deal with the position where the Revenue officer considers that a claim or election included in a return should be disallowed in whole or in part, but the disallowance does not require amendment of the taxpayer's self-assessment. If the claim or election is not amended within 30 days of the completion of the Revenue enquiries, the officer must within a further 30 days give notice to the taxpayer of the extent to which the claim or election is being disallowed. This is without prejudice to any provision making the claim irrevocable or unamendable.

Subparagraph (3) inserts new s 28A(7A), (7B) and (7C) into TMA 1970 which deal with the situation where there are alternative ways of bringing amounts into account in a return, namely—

(*a*) where an amount may be included in a computation under Schedule D Cases I or II or under Schedule D Cases III–V;
(*b*) in the case of life assurance business, an amount may be included in a computation under Schedule D Case I or in a computation under the I minus E basis.

Where a Revenue officer makes an enquiry into a return in a case where these alternatives exist, he must determine which alternative to use; any amendment to the self-assessment must be made in accordance with that alternative.

Further amendments of section 28B

5 ·(1) In section 28B (amendment of partnership statement following enquiry)—

(*a*) in subsection (3)(*b*), for "subsection (1)(*b*) above" there shall be substituted "subsection (1)(*b*) or (*c*) above"; and
(*b*) in subsection (5)(*b*), at the end there shall be inserted "and as to any claims or elections into which he has enquired."

(2) After subsection (6) of that section there shall be inserted the following subsections—

"(6A) Where, in the case of any return made in relation to any period of account—

(*a*) alternative methods are allowed by the Tax Acts for bringing amounts into account in that return,
(*b*) the return is made or amended using one of those methods,
(*c*) a return could have been made in that case using an alternative method, and
(*d*) an officer of the Board determines which of the alternative methods is to be used by the Board in relation to the partnership for that period,

any enquiry into that return or into an amendment of it shall be conducted, and this section shall have effect, as if the only method allowed for the purposes of the Tax Acts were the method determined by the officer.

(6B) In subsection (6A) above 'period of account' has the same meaning as in section 12AB of this Act; and subsection (7B) of section 28A of this Act applies for the purposes of subsection (6A) above as it applies for the purposes of subsection (7A) of that section."

GENERAL NOTE
This paragraph inserts new s 28B(6A) and (6B) into TMA 1970 which make identical provisions to those in para 4 in the case of an enquiry into a partnership return.

Right of appeal against notice disallowing claim in return

6 (1) In subsection (1) of section 31 (appeals)—

(*a*) after paragraph (*a*) there shall be inserted the following paragraph—

"(*aa*) a decision contained in a notice under section 28A(4A) of this Act disallowing a claim or election in whole or in part, or";

and

(*b*) in the words after paragraph (*c*), for "amendment or" there shall be substituted "amendment, the notice under section 28A(4A) of this Act or, as the case may be, the notice of".

(2) After that subsection there shall be inserted the following subsection—

"(1AA) The matters that may be questioned on any appeal against—

(*a*) an amendment under subsection (2) or (4) of section 28A of this Act, (*b*) a decision contained in a notice under subsection (4A) of that section disallowing a claim or election in whole or in part, or

(*c*) an amendment under section 28B(3) or 30B(1) of this Act,

do not include any determination made for the purposes of section 28A(7A)(*d*) or 28B(6A)(*d*) of this Act."

(3) In subsection (5) of that section, the words "against any assessment" shall be omitted.

GENERAL NOTE
Subparagraph (1) amends TMA 1970 s 31(1) to allow an appeal against a notice of disallowance of the whole or part of a claim or election (see paras 4 and 5 above).
Subparagraph (2) inserts new s 31(1AA) into TMA 1970 which provides that any appeal against a disallowance of a claim does not include an appeal against the decision to use a particular alternative method of computation.
Subparagraph (3) makes it clear that the right of appeal is not confined to an appeal against an assessment.

7 In section 50 (procedure on appeals), after subsection (7) there shall be inserted the following subsection—

"(7A) If, on appeal, it appears to the Commissioners that a claim or election specified in a notice under section 28A(4A) of this Act should have been allowed or disallowed to an extent different from that specified in the notice, the claim or election shall be allowed or disallowed accordingly to the extent that appears to them appropriate, but otherwise the decision in the notice shall stand good."

GENERAL NOTE
This paragraph inserts new s 50(7A) into TMA 1970, which provides that on an appeal against a notice disallowing a claim or election, the Commissioners may amend the disallowance as appears to them to be appropriate, otherwise the disallowance in the notice will stand.

Claims not included in returns

8 (1) In Schedule 1A (claims not included in returns), in paragraph 4 (giving effect to claims and amendments), in sub-paragraph (1) for "(1A) and (3)" there shall be substituted "(1A), (3) and (4)".

(2) In sub-paragraph (2) of that paragraph, for "sub-paragraph (3)" there shall be substituted "sub-paragraphs (3) and (4)".

(3) After sub-paragraph (3) there shall be inserted the following sub-paragraph—

"(4) Nothing in this paragraph applies in relation to a claim or an amendment of a claim if the claim is not one for discharge or repayment of tax."

GENERAL NOTE
This paragraph inserts new Sch 1A para 4(4) into TMA 1970 which makes it clear that para 4 does not apply unless the claim is for a discharge or repayment of tax.

9 (1) In paragraph 7 of Schedule 1A (amendment of claims where enquiries made), after sub-paragraph (3), there shall be inserted the following sub-paragraphs—

"(3A) If, in the case of a claim which is not a claim for discharge or repayment of tax—

(*a*) the officer is of opinion that the claim should be disallowed in whole or in part, and

(*b*) the claim, so far as the officer thinks it should be disallowed, is not, before the end of the period mentioned in sub-paragraph (2) above, amended to the officer's satisfaction or withdrawn,

the officer shall, before the end of the period mentioned in sub-paragraph (3) above, give notice to the taxpayer of the extent to which he is disallowing the claim.

(3B) Sub-paragraph (3A)(*b*) above is without prejudice to any provision by virtue of which any claim is irrevocable or unamendable."

(2) In sub-paragraph (4)(*b*) of that paragraph, for "the amount which" there shall be substituted "whether the claim should be allowed in whole or in part and as to what amount (if any)".

Subparagraph (1) inserts new Sch 1A para 7(3A) into TMA 1970. This deals with the case where there has been a Revenue enquiry into a claim which is not included in a return and the officer considers that it should be disallowed in whole or in part. If the claim is not amended within 30 days of the completion of the Revenue enquiries, the officer must within a further 30 days give notice to the taxpayer of the extent to which the claim is being disallowed. This is without prejudice to any provision making the claim irrevocable or unamendable.
Subparagraph (2) amends TMA 1970 Sch 1A para 7(4) to provide that the officer's enquiries into the claim are completed when he states a conclusion as to whether the claim should be allowed in whole or in part and as to what (if any) amount.

Right of appeal against notice disallowing claim not in return

10 (1) In paragraph 9 of Schedule 1A (appeals), for sub-paragraph (1) there shall be substituted the following sub-paragraph—

"(1) An appeal may be brought against—

(*a*) an amendment under paragraph 7(3) above, or

(*b*) a decision contained in a notice under paragraph 7(3A) above,

by giving notice to the officer within 30 days after the date on which the notice of amendment or, as the case may be, the notice under paragraph 7(3A) above was issued."

(2) In sub-paragraph (2) of that paragraph, for "making of the amendment under paragraph 7(3) above" there shall be substituted "date mentioned in sub-paragraph (1) above".

(3) In sub-paragraph (3) of that paragraph, for "under this paragraph" there shall be substituted "against an amendment under paragraph 7(3) above".

(4) After sub-paragraph (4) of that paragraph there shall be inserted the following sub-paragraph—

"(5) If, on appeal, it appears to the Commissioners that a claim specified in a notice under paragraph 7(3A) above should have been allowed or disallowed to an extent different from that specified in the notice, the claim shall be allowed or disallowed accordingly to the extent that appears to them appropriate, but otherwise the decision in the notice shall stand good."

Subparagraph (1) amends TMA 1970 Sch 1A para 9(1) by inserting a right of appeal against a decision in a notice under TMA 1970 Sch 1A para 7(3A) (see para 9 above). The appeal is to be made within 30 days after the issue of the notice of refusal.
Subparagraph (2) fixes the extended time limit for an appeal (in special circumstances) at three months from the normal time limit.
Subparagraphs (3) and (4) set out the powers of the Commissioners on appeal similar to those in para 7 above.

SCHEDULE 20   Section 134

SELF-ASSESSMENT: DISCRETIONS EXERCISABLE BY THE BOARD ETC

GENERAL NOTE

This Schedule makes amendments to 71 different provisions in the Taxes Acts (listed in the Schedule). The general import of the amendments is to delete references to—

(*a*) the need to produce proof of statements made in support of claims;

(*b*) the need to satisfy the Board or the inspector of certain matters or circumstances;

(*c*) the need to prove that certain circumstances do not exist (where their existence would negate a claim);

(*d*) the right of the Revenue (or, on appeal, the Commissioners) to determine what is just and reasonable.

The Revenue have powers under the self-assessment rules to challenge any claim or statement if they are not satisfied with it.

The Taxes Act 1988

1 In section 24(2) of the Taxes Act 1988 (presumption as to sums being paid by way of premium unless the contrary is shown) for "is" there shall be substituted "can be".

2 In section 38(4) of the Taxes Act 1988 (assumptions as to benefits and payments relating to leases) in the words after paragraph (*b*), for "is" there shall be substituted "can be".

3 In section 65(4) of the Taxes Act 1988 (assessments under Cases IV and V of Schedule D: subsections (1) to (3) not to apply to a person who satisfies the Board that he is not domiciled in the United Kingdom etc) for "on a claim made to the Board, satisfies the Board" there shall be substituted "makes a claim to the Board stating".

4 In section 74(1)(*j*) of the Taxes Act 1988 (Case I or II of Schedule D: no deduction in respect of debts), in sub-paragraph (i) (deduction allowed for a bad debt proved to be such) the words "proved to be such" shall cease to have effect.

5 (1) In section 109A of the Taxes Act 1988 (relief for post-cessation expenditure) in subsection (4) (relief for debt taken into account in computing profits or gains and later released or proved to be bad), in the first sentence, for the words following "entitled" there shall be substituted "is released in whole or in part as part of a relevant arrangement or compromise (within the meaning of section 74), he shall be treated as making a payment to which this section applies of—

(*a*) an amount equal to the amount released, or

(*b*) if he was entitled to only part of the benefit of the debt, an amount equal to an appropriate proportion of that amount."

(2) After that subsection there shall be inserted—

"(4A) Where a trade, profession or vocation carried on by a person has been permanently discontinued and subsequently an unpaid debt which was taken into account in computing the profits and gains of that trade, profession or vocation and to the benefit of which he is entitled, proves to be bad, then if—

(*a*) in making a claim for a year of assessment under subsection (1) above he gives notice that the debt was bad in any part of that year, and

(*b*) he has not given such a notice in respect of that debt in the making of any other such claim,

he shall be treated as making in that year a payment to which this section applies of an amount equal to the amount of the debt or, if he was entitled to only part of the benefit of the debt, to an appropriate proportion of that amount.

If any sum is subsequently received by him in payment of a debt for which relief has been given by virtue of this subsection, the sum shall be treated as one to which section 103 applies; and no deduction shall be made under section 105 in respect of any sum."

6 In section 132(1) of the Taxes Act 1988 (emoluments for period of absence treated as emoluments for duties performed in the UK except in so far as it is shown that but for that absence they would have been emoluments for duties performed outside the UK) for "it is shown that, but for that absence, they would" there shall be substituted "they would, but for that absence".

7 In section 145(7) of the Taxes Act 1988 (living accommodation provided for employee deemed to be provided by reason of his employment for the purposes of section 145(1) unless it can be shown that it is a case falling within paragraph (*a*) or (*b*)) in paragraphs (*a*) and (*b*) the words "it can be shown that" shall cease to have effect.

8 In section 159 of the Taxes Act 1988 (pooled cars)—

(*a*) in subsection (1) (which provides that the section is to apply to any car in the case of which the inspector is satisfied, whether on a claim under that section or otherwise, that it has been included in a car pool) for the words from "in the case" to "that it" there shall be substituted "which"; and

(*b*) subsections (4) to (6) (claims and appeals) shall cease to have effect.

9 In section 161 of the Taxes Act 1988 (exceptions from charge under section 160 on beneficial loans)—

(*a*) in subsection (3) (exception for certain loans if it is shown that the interest rate is of a certain description) the words "it is shown that" shall cease to have effect; and

(*b*) in subsection (4) (exception for loan to employee's relative from which employee shows that he derived no benefit) the words "shows that he" shall cease to have effect.

10 (1) In section 168 of the Taxes Act 1988 (interpretative provisions) in subsection (3) (exception from charge under Chapter II of Part V for any such payment or provision made by employer as can be shown to have been made in normal course of his domestic, family or personal relationships) for the words following "any such payment or provision" there shall be substituted "which is made by the employer, being an individual, in the normal course of his domestic, family or personal relationships".

(2) In subsection (6) of that section—

(*a*) in paragraph (*b*) (exception from charge for car made available by employer where it can be shown that the car was made available in normal course of his domestic, family or personal relationships) for "it can be shown that the car was" there shall be substituted "the car is"; and

(*b*) in paragraph (*d*) (similar exception for vans) for "it can be shown that the van was" there shall be substituted "the van is".

11 In section 186(10) of the Taxes Act 1988 (value of the proceeds of certain disposals—

(*a*) for paragraph (*b*) there shall be substituted the following paragraph—

"(*b*) any other disposal falling within that subsection is not at arm's length;"; and

(*b*) in paragraph (*c*) for "that sub-paragraph" there shall be substituted "that subsection".

12 In section 231(3A) of the Taxes Act 1988 (restriction of tax credit where certain arrangements made by close investment-holding companies)—

(*a*) in the words preceding paragraph (*a*), the words "it appears to the inspector that" shall cease to have effect; and

(*b*) in the words following paragraph (*b*), for "appears to the inspector to be" there shall be substituted "is".

13 In section 257 of the Taxes Act 1988 (personal allowance)—

(*a*) in subsection (2) (claimant entitled to deduction if he proves that he is 65 or over), and

(*b*) in subsection (3) (claimant entitled to deduction if he proves that he is 75 or over),

the words "proves that he" shall cease to have effect.

14 (1) Section 257A of the Taxes Act 1988 (married couple's allowance) shall be amended in accordance with the following provisions of this paragraph.

(2) In subsection (1) (claimant entitled to reduction if he proves that he is a married man whose wife is living with him) for the words from the beginning to "he is" there shall be substituted "If the claimant is, for the whole or any part of the year of assessment,".

(3) In—

(*a*) subsection (2) (claimant entitled to reduction if he proves that he is a married man whose wife is living with him and that either of them is 65 or over), and

(*b*) subsection (3) (similar provision on proof that claimant or wife is 75 or over),

for the words from the beginning to "and that" there shall be substituted "If the claimant is, for the whole or any part of the year of assessment, a married man whose wife is living with him, and".

15 In section 257E(1) of the Taxes Act 1988 (claimant entitled to relief if his wife lives with him and he proves that for the year 1989–90 he was entitled as described in paragraph (*a*) or (*b*))—

(*a*) the words "he proves" shall cease to have effect; and

(*b*) the word "that", in the first and third places where it occurs in each of paragraphs (*a*) and (*b*), shall cease to have effect.

16 (1) Section 257F of the Taxes Act 1988 (transitional relief: effect of preceding sections where claimant who does not live with his wife proves that paragraphs (*a*) to (*c*) apply) shall be amended in accordance with the following provisions of this paragraph.

(2) The words "the claimant proves" shall cease to have effect.

(3) In paragraph (*a*)—

(*a*) for "that he" there shall be substituted "the claimant"; and

(*b*) the word "that" in the second place where it occurs shall cease to have effect.

(4) In paragraph (*b*) the word "that" in the first place where it occurs shall cease to have effect.

(5) In paragraph (*c*) the word "that" in the first and third places where it occurs shall cease to have effect.

17 (1) Section 259 of the Taxes Act 1988 (additional relief in respect of children) shall be amended in accordance with the following provisions of this paragraph.

(2) In subsection (2) (claimant entitled to reduction if he proves that a qualifying child is resident with him) for the words from "if the claimant" to "he shall be entitled" there shall be substituted "if—

(*a*) the claimant is a person to whom this section applies, and

(*b*) a qualifying child is resident with him for the whole or a part of a year of assessment,

the claimant shall be entitled".

(3) In subsection (6) (circumstances in which the reference in subsection (5) to a child receiving full-time instruction includes a child undergoing training for a trade, profession or vocation) the second paragraph (inspector's power to require particulars of training) shall cease to have effect.

18 In section 261A(1) of the Taxes Act 1988 (person who proves that a qualifying child is resident with him in the year in which he and his wife separate is entitled to relief) for "who proves that a qualifying child is resident with him" there shall be substituted "with whom a qualifying child is resident".

19 In section 265(1) of the Taxes Act 1988 (claimant entitled to blind person's allowance if he proves that he is a registered blind person) the words "proves that he" shall cease to have effect.

20 In section 274(4) of the Taxes Act 1988 (effect of war insurance premiums on the limit on relief under section 266 or 273) in the second paragraph (definition of war insurance premiums: to include any part of any premium paid in respect of a life insurance policy which appears to the inspector to be attributable to risks arising from war or war service abroad) for "appears to the inspector to be" there shall be substituted "is".

21   In section 278(2) of the Taxes Act 1988 (bar on relief for non-residents not to apply to an individual who satisfies the Board that he or she is a Commonwealth citizen etc) the words "satisfies the Board that he or she" shall cease to have effect.

22   In section 306(2) of the Taxes Act 1988 (claim for relief in respect of eligible shares must be accompanied by a certificate issued by the company) for the words from the beginning to "accompanied by" there shall be substituted "No claim for relief in respect of eligible shares in a company may be made unless the person making the claim has received from the company".

23   In section 311(4) of the Taxes Act 1988 (application of section 306(2) to claims in respect of shares issued to the managers of an approved fund) for the words from "as if it required" to "accompanied by" there shall be substituted—

   "(*a*) as if it required the certificate referred to in that section to be issued by the company to the managers; and
   (*b*) as if it provided that no claim for relief may be made unless the person making the claim has received from the managers".

24   In section 381(4) of the Taxes Act 1988 (no relief unless it is shown that trade was on a commercial basis) the words "it is shown that" shall cease to have effect.

25   (1)   In section 384 of the Taxes Act 1988 (restrictions on right of set-off) in subsection (1) (no relief unless it is shown that trade was on a commercial basis and with a view to the realisation of profits) the words "it is shown that" shall cease to have effect.

(2)   For subsection (9) of that section (conclusive evidence that a trade was carried on with a view to the realisation of profits) there shall be substituted—

   "(9)   Where at any time a trade is carried on so as to afford a reasonable expectation of profit, it shall be treated for the purposes of subsection (1) above as being carried on at that time with a view to the realisation of profits".

26   In section 393A of the Taxes Act 1988 (losses: set-off against profits of the same or an earlier accounting period)—

   (*a*) in subsection (3)(*b*) (no relief unless trade was on commercial basis and with a view to the realisation of gain) for "it is shown that for" there shall be substituted "for"; and
   (*b*) in subsection (4), for paragraph (*a*) (conclusive evidence that a trade was carried on with a view to the realisation of gain) there shall be substituted—

      "(*a*) where at any time a trade is carried on so as to afford a reasonable expectation of gain, it shall be treated as being carried on at that time with a view to the realisation of gain; and".

27   In section 397(3) of the Taxes Act 1988 (farming and market gardening: relief not to be restricted in certain cases)—

   (*a*) for ", if it is shown by the claimant" there shall be substituted "in any case"; and
   (*b*) for the word "that", at the beginning of each of paragraphs (*a*) and (*b*), there shall be substituted "where".

28   (1)   Section 488 of the Taxes Act 1988 (co-operative housing associations) shall be amended in accordance with the following provisions of this paragraph.

(2)   For subsection (9) (which provides for a claim to be made to the inspector within two years and excludes the operation of section 42 of the Taxes Management Act 1970) there shall be substituted—

   "(9)   A claim under this section may be made at any time not later than two years after the end of the year of assessment or accounting period to which, or to a part of which, it relates."

(3) In subsection (10) (no claim under the section to have effect unless it is proved that the conditions there specified are complied with) for the words from "no claim" to "it is proved that" there shall be substituted "no claim shall be made under this section unless".

(4) For subsection (11) (power of Board to direct that a claim shall have effect if they are satisfied that the conditions in subsection (10) are substantially complied with, and power to revoke the direction on subsequent information) there shall be substituted—

"(11) A housing association may make a claim under this section notwithstanding anything in subsection (10) above, if the association reasonably considers that the requirements of that subsection are substantially complied with.

(11A) If as a result of an enquiry—

(*a*) under section 11AB of the Management Act into a return, or an amendment of a return, in which a claim under this section by a housing association is included, or

(*b*) under paragraph 5 of Schedule 1A to that Act into a claim under this section by a housing association, or an amendment of such a claim,

an amendment is made to the association's self-assessment or, as the case may be, to the claim, the liability of all persons concerned to tax for all relevant years or accounting periods may also be adjusted by the making of assessments or otherwise."

(5) For subsection (12) (particulars required to be included in a claim may include an authority granted by the members for the use of information in their tax returns for determining the claim) there shall be substituted—

"(12) A housing association making a claim under this section may be required under or by virtue of section 11(1) of, or paragraph 2(5) of Schedule 1A to, the Management Act to deliver an authority, granted by all members of the association, for any relevant information contained in any return made by a member under the provisions of the Income Tax Acts to be used by an officer of the Board in such manner as he may think fit in connection with any enquiry under section 11AB of, or paragraph 5 of Schedule 1A to, the Management Act, so far as relating to the association's claim under this section."

29 (1) Section 489 of the Taxes Act 1988 (self-build societies) shall be amended in accordance with the following provisions of this paragraph.

(2) For subsection (7) (which excludes the operation of section 42 of the Taxes Management Act 1970 but provides for a claim to be made to the inspector within two years) there shall be substituted—

"(7) A claim under this section may be made at any time not later than two years after the end of the year of assessment or accounting period to which, or to a part of which, it relates."

(3) In subsection (8) (no claim under the section to have effect unless it is proved that the conditions there specified are complied with) for the words from "no claim" to "it is proved that" there shall be substituted "no claim shall be made under this section unless".

(4) For subsection (9) (power of Board to direct that a claim shall have effect if they are satisfied that the conditions in subsection (8) are substantially complied with, and power to revoke the direction on subsequent information) there shall be substituted—

"(9) A self-build society may make a claim under this section notwithstanding anything in subsection (8) above, if the society reasonably considers that the requirements of that subsection are substantially complied with.

(9A) If as a result of an enquiry—

(*a*) under section 11AB of the Management Act into a return, or an amendment of a return, in which a claim under this section by a self-build society is included, or

(*b*) under paragraph 5 of Schedule 1A to that Act into a claim under this section by a self-build society or an amendment of such a claim,

an amendment is made to the society's self-assessment or, as the case may be, to the claim, the society's liability to tax for all relevant years or accounting periods may also be adjusted by the making of assessments or otherwise."

30   In section 503(6) of the Taxes Act 1988 (apportionments where a letting relates only in part to holiday accommodation) for "appear to the inspector, or on appeal the Commissioners, to be" there shall be substituted "are".

31   In section 570(2) of the Taxes Act 1988 (schemes for rationalizing industry: treatment of certain payments made under such schemes)—

(*a*)   the words "on a claim it is shown in accordance with the provisions of Part II of Schedule 21 that" shall cease to have effect;

(*b*)   after "the Tax Acts" there shall be inserted "and a claim is made to that effect,";

(*c*)   for "that Schedule", where those words first occur, there shall be substituted "Schedule 21"; and

(*d*)   at the end there shall be added—

"and paragraph 6 of that Schedule applies for the purposes of this subsection as it applies for the purposes of that Schedule."

32   In section 582(2)(*b*) of the Taxes Act 1988 (cases where retention of funding bonds is impracticable)—

(*a*)   the words "the Board are satisfied that" shall cease to have effect; and

(*b*)   in sub-paragraph (i), for the words from the beginning to "them" there shall be substituted—

"(i) any such person shall be relieved from the obligation to retain bonds and account for income tax under that paragraph, on his furnishing to the Board".

33   (1) Section 584 of the Taxes Act 1988 (relief for unremittable overseas income) shall be amended in accordance with the following provisions of this paragraph.

(2)   For subsections (2) and (3) (the account to be taken of overseas income which the Board are satisfied is unremittable) there shall be substituted—

"(2) Subject to subsection (2A) below, where a person so chargeable makes a claim under this subsection in relation to any overseas income—

(*a*)   which is unremittable; and

(*b*)   to which subsection (1)(*a*) above will continue to apply notwithstanding any reasonable endeavours on his part,

then, in the first instance, account shall not be taken of that income, and tax shall be assessed, or, in the case of corporation tax, assessable, and shall be charged on all persons concerned and for all periods accordingly.

(2A) If on any date paragraph (*a*) or (*b*) of subsection (2) above ceases to apply to any part of any overseas income in relation to which a claim has been made under that subsection—

(*a*)   that part of the income shall be treated as income arising on that date, and

(*b*)   account shall be taken of it, and of any tax payable in respect of it under the law of the territory where it arises, according to their value at that date."

(3)   In subsection (4) (company chargeable to corporation tax in respect of source of income that it has ceased to possess) for "a company becomes chargeable to corporation tax in respect of income from any source by virtue of subsections (2) and (3)" there shall be substituted "a person becomes chargeable to income tax or corporation tax in respect of income from any source by virtue of subsection (2) or (2A)".

(4)   In subsection (5) (where payment made by ECGD in respect of income, conditions in subsection (2) treated as not satisfied) for the words following "treated as income" there shall be substituted "to which paragraphs (*a*) and (*b*) of subsection (2) above do not apply (and accordingly cannot cease to apply)".

(5)   For subsection (6) (delivery of notices under subsection (2) and making of assessments required by such notices) there shall be substituted—

"(6) A claim under subsection (2) above—

(*a*)   for the purposes of income tax, shall be made on or before the first anniversary of the 31st January next following the year of assessment in which the income arises;

(*b*) for the purposes of corporation tax, shall be made no later than two years after the end of the accounting period in which the income arises."

(6) In subsection (7) (charge to tax on executors and administrators) after "(2)" there shall be inserted "or (2A)".

(7) In subsection (8) (how to determine the amount of unremittable overseas income) for "(3)" there shall be substituted "(2A)".

34 In section 585(1) of the Taxes Act 1988 (relief for delayed remittances: claim may be made on showing that the conditions in paragraphs (*a*) to (*c*) are satisfied) for the words from "by making a claim" to "that is to say" there shall be substituted ", if the relevant conditions are satisfied, by making a claim require that the following provisions of this section shall apply; and for this purpose the relevant conditions are—".

35 In section 717(9) of the Taxes Act 1988 (which provides for section 713 to have effect for certain cases with the substitution of a new provision for subsections (3) to (6)) in the substituted subsection, for "an inspector decides is just and reasonable; and the jurisdiction of the General Commissioners or the Special Commissioners on any appeal shall include jurisdiction to review such a decision of the inspector" there shall be substituted "is just and reasonable".

36 In section 731(3) of the Taxes Act 1988 (cases of purchase and sale of securities where sections 732 to 734 do not apply)—

(*a*) in paragraph (*b*) (it is shown to the satisfaction of the Board that certain conditions are satisfied in relation to the purchase and sale) for the words from "it is shown" to "and that" there shall be substituted "the purchase and sale were each effected at the current market price, and"; and

(*b*) the words following paragraph (*b*) (appeals) shall cease to have effect.

37 In section 769(2)(*d*) of the Taxes Act 1988 (acquisitions of shares on death and certain gifts of shares to be left out of account in applying the rules in subsection (1) for ascertaining change in ownership of company)—

(*a*) for "and, if it is shown that the gift" there shall be substituted ", and any gift of shares which"; and

(*b*) the words "any gift of shares" shall cease to have effect.

38 (1) Section 812 of the Taxes Act 1988 (withdrawal of right to tax credit of certain non-resident companies connected with unitary states) shall be amended in accordance with the following provisions of this paragraph.

(2) In subsection (4), paragraph (*a*) (one of the conditions for the withdrawal of the right to tax credit treated as being satisfied unless, on making a claim under section 213(3), the claimant proves otherwise to the satisfaction of the Board) shall cease to have effect.

(3) In subsection (7) (power to substitute one of two sets of provisions for subsections (3) and (4)) for the words following "there shall be substituted" there shall be substituted "either the following subsection—

'(3) A company shall be treated as having a qualifying presence in a unitary state if it is liable in such a state to a tax charged on its income or profits by whatever name called for any period ending after the relevant date for which that state charges tax.';

or the following subsections—

'(3) A company shall be treated as having a qualifying presence in a unitary state if it has its principal place of business in such a state at any time after the relevant date.

(4) For the purposes of subsection (3) above the principal place of business of a company shall include both the place where central management and control of the company is exercised and the place where the immediate day-to-day management of the company as a whole is exercised.'."

39 In section 815A of the Taxes Act 1988 (transfer of a non-UK trade) for subsections (2) to (4) there shall be substituted—

"(2) Where gains accruing to company A on the transfer would have been chargeable to tax under the law of the relevant member State but for the Mergers Directive, this Part, including any arrangements having effect by virtue of section 788, shall apply as if the amount of tax, calculated on the required basis, which would have been payable under that law in respect of the gains so accruing but for that Directive, were tax payable under that law."

40 In Schedule 6 to the Taxes Act 1988 (taxation of directors and others in respect of cars) in sub-paragraphs (1) and (2) of paragraph 2 (reduction for use of car for business travel) for "it is shown to the inspector's satisfaction that the employee was required by the nature of his employment to use, and did use" there shall be substituted "the employee is required by the nature of his employment to use and does use".

41 In Schedule 7 to the Taxes Act 1988 (taxation of benefit from loans obtained by reason of employment) in paragraph 1(5) (benefit of loan not obtained by reason of employment if made by an individual and shown to have been made in normal course of his domestic, family or personal relationships) the words "and shown to have been made" shall cease to have effect.

42 In Schedule 12 to the Taxes Act 1988 (foreign earnings) in paragraph 2(2) (emoluments in respect of which deduction under section 193(1) allowed not to exceed such proportion as is shown to be reasonable) the words "shown to be" shall cease to have effect.

43 In Schedule 21 to the Taxes Act 1988 (tax relief in connection with schemes for rationalizing industry and other redundancy schemes), paragraph 3 (no relief in respect of payments under schemes unless certain amounts are shown) shall cease to have effect.

The Capital Allowances Act 1990

44 In section 29(3) of the Capital Allowances Act 1990 (apportionments where a letting relates only in part to holiday accommodation) for "appear to the inspector, or on appeal the Commissioners, to be" there shall be substituted "are".

The Taxation of Chargeable Gains Act 1992

45 In the following provisions of this Schedule "the Gains Act" means the Taxation of Chargeable Gains Act 1992.

46 In section 30(4) of the Gains Act (section not to apply if it is shown that there was no tax avoidance purpose) for "if it is shown that" there shall be substituted "in a case where".

47 In each of—

(*a*) subsections (5) and (6) of section 30 of the Gains Act (consideration to be increased or reduced by such amount as appears to the inspector etc to be just and reasonable),

(*b*) section 32(4)(*b*) of the Gains Act (costs in cases of part disposal to be such proportion as appears to the inspector etc to be just and reasonable), and

(*c*) subsections (7) and (8) of section 33 of the Gains Act (amounts to be reduced to such amount as appears to the inspector etc to be just and reasonable),

for "appears to the inspector, or on appeal the Commissioners concerned, to be" there shall be substituted "is".

48 In section 48 of the Gains Act (consideration due after time of disposal and irrecoverable consideration) for the words following "if any part of the consideration so brought into account" there shall be substituted "subsequently proves to be irrecoverable, there shall be made, on a claim being made to that effect, such adjustment, whether by way of discharge or repayment of tax or otherwise, as is required in consequence."

49 In section 49 of the Gains Act (contingent liabilities) for subsection (2) (adjustment to be made if it is shown to the satisfaction of the inspector that a contingent liability has become enforceable) there shall be substituted—

"(2) If any such contingent liability subsequently becomes enforceable and is being or has been enforced, there shall be made, on a claim being made to that effect, such adjustment, whether by way of discharge or repayment of tax or otherwise, as is required in consequence."

50   In section 52(4) of the Gains Act (apportionments by such method as appears to the inspector etc to be just and reasonable) the words "such method as appears to the inspector or on appeal the Commissioners concerned to be" shall cease to have effect.

51   In section 116(13) of the Gains Act (subsection (12) not to apply where inspector, being satisfied sum is comparatively small, so directs) the words "the inspector is satisfied that" and "and so directs," shall cease to have effect.

52   (1) In section 122 of the Gains Act (distribution which is not a new holding) in subsection (2) (treatment of distributions which the inspector is satisfied are comparatively small) the words "the inspector is satisfied that" and "and so directs" shall cease to have effect.

(2) Subsection (3) of that section (appeals from decisions of inspectors under subsection (2)) shall cease to have effect.

(3) In subsection (4)(*a*) of that section (subsections (2) and (3) not to apply in certain cases) for "subsections (2) and (3)" there shall be substituted "subsection (2)".

53   (1) In section 133 of the Gains Act (premiums on conversion of securities) in subsection (2) (treatment of premiums which the inspector is satisfied are comparatively small) the words "the inspector is satisfied that" and "and so directs" shall cease to have effect.

(2) Subsection (3) of that section (appeals from decisions of inspectors under subsection (2)) shall cease to have effect.

(3) In subsection (4)(*a*) of that section (subsections (2) and (3) not to apply in certain cases) for "subsections (2) and (3)" there shall be substituted "subsection (2)".

54   In each of sections 150(10)(*a*) and 150A(9)(*a*) of the Gains Act (reductions in relief to be apportioned in such a way as appears to the inspector etc to be just and reasonable) for "such a way as appears to the inspector, or on appeal to the Commissioners concerned, to be" there shall be substituted "a way which is".

55   In section 164F(8)(*a*) of the Gains Act (section not to apply where it is shown that winding up etc is bona fide) the words "it is shown that" shall cease to have effect.

56   In section 164FG of the Gains Act (multiple claims for reductions under section 164A(2) or 164F(10A) of the Gains Act) in subsection (2) (reductions to be treated as claimed separately in such sequence as the claimant elects or an officer of the Board in default of an election determines) the words "or an officer of the Board in default of an election determines" shall cease to have effect.

57   (1) In each of subsections (4) and (6) of section 176 of the Gains Act (losses or gains on disposals where there have been depreciatory transactions to be reduced to such extent as appears to the inspector etc to be just and reasonable) for "appears to the inspector, or, on appeal, the Commissioners concerned, to be" there shall be substituted "is".

(2) In subsection (5) of that section (footing on which decision under subsection (4) is to be made) for "The inspector or the Commissioners shall make the decision under subsection (4) above" there shall be substituted "A reduction under subsection (4) above shall be made".

58   In section 181(1)(*b*) of the Gains Act (sections 178 and 179 not to apply where it is shown that merger was bona fide) the words "it is shown that", and the word "that" in the second place where it occurs, shall cease to have effect.

59   (1) Section 222 of the Gains Act (relief on disposal of residence and land up to the permitted area, which is 0.5 of a hectare) shall be amended in accordance with the following provisions of this paragraph.

(2) For subsection (3) (which provides for the permitted area in certain cases to be such area, larger than 0.5 of a hectare, as the Commissioners may determine) there shall be substituted—

"(3) Where the area required for the reasonable enjoyment of the dwelling-house (or of the part in question) as a residence, having regard to the size and character of the dwelling-house, is larger than 0.5 of a hectare, that larger area shall be the permitted area."

(3) In subsection (5) (determination of individual's main residence)—

(*a*) paragraph (*b*) (which, subject to conclusive notice by the individual under paragraph (*a*), provides for the question to be determined by an inspector), and
(*b*) the words following that paragraph (right of appeal against inspector's determination),

shall cease to have effect.

(4) In subsection (6), paragraph (*b*) (further provision about the right of appeal against determinations under subsection (5)(*b*)) and the word "and" immediately preceding it shall cease to have effect.

60 In section 224(2) of the Gains Act (adjustment of relief given by section 223 for changes occurring during period of ownership) for "may be adjusted in such manner as the Commissioners concerned may consider to be just and reasonable" there shall be substituted "may be adjusted in a manner which is just and reasonable".

61 In section 226 of the Gains Act (relief in respect of private residence occupied by dependent relative before 6th April 1988) subsection (5) (power of inspector, before granting a claim for relief under that section, to require claimant to show that granting the claim will not preclude relief to claimant's wife or husband) shall cease to have effect.

62 In section 241(7) of the Gains Act (apportionments where a letting relates only in part to holiday accommodation) for "appear to the inspector, or on appeal the Commissioners, to be" there shall be substituted "are".

63 (1) In section 271 of the Gains Act (miscellaneous exemptions) in subsections (1)(*g*) and (2), for "such extent as the Board are satisfied" there shall be substituted "the extent".

(2) In subsection (2) of that section, in the second paragraph, the words "the Board are satisfied that" shall cease to have effect.

64 In section 279(1) of the Gains Act (claimant for deduction in respect of gains accruing from the disposal of foreign assets must show that conditions in subsection (3) are satisfied) for paragraph (*b*) there shall be substituted—

"(*b*) the person charged or chargeable makes a claim, and
(*c*) the conditions set out in subsection (3) below are, so far as applicable, satisfied as respects those gains ('the qualifying gains');".

65 In section 280 of the Gains Act (payment of tax by instalments where consideration payable by instalments) for "if the person making the disposal satisfies the Board that he would otherwise suffer undue hardship, the tax on a chargeable gain accruing on the disposal may, at his option," there shall be substituted "at the option of the person making the disposal, the tax on a chargeable gain accruing on the disposal may".

66 (1) Schedule 6 to the Gains Act (retirement relief) shall be amended in accordance with the following provisions of this paragraph.

(2) In paragraph 3, in sub-paragraphs (1), (3) and (4) (under each of which a person is treated as having retired on ill-health grounds if, on production of such evidence as the Board may reasonably require, the Board are satisfied as there mentioned)—

(*a*) the words "on production of such evidence as the Board may reasonably require, the Board are satisfied" shall cease to have effect, and
(*b*) for "that he" (in each place where those words occur) there shall be substituted "he".

(3) At the end of that paragraph there shall be added—

"(5) In any case where—

(*a*) an officer of the Board gives notice to any person under section 9A(1) of, or paragraph 5(1) of Schedule 1A to, the Management Act (notice of intention to enquire into a return or claim or an amendment of a return or claim), and

(*b*) the enquiry to any extent relates to the question whether or not a person falls to be treated as having retired on ill-health grounds by virtue of the foregoing provisions of this paragraph,

then, without prejudice to any other powers of such an officer in relation to such an enquiry, an officer of the Board may at the same or any subsequent time by notice in writing require that person, within such time (which shall not be less than 30 days) as may be specified in the notice, to produce such evidence relating to the question mentioned in paragraph (*b*) above as may reasonably be specified in the notice."

(4) In paragraph 10 (limitation of retirement relief in certain cases)—

(*a*) in sub-paragraph (1) for "appears to the Board to be" there shall be substituted "is"; and

(*b*) in sub-paragraph (2) for "the Board shall have regard" there shall be substituted "regard shall be had".

67 In Schedule 8 to the Gains Act (leases) in paragraph 10(2) (presumption as to sums being paid by way of premium unless the contrary is shown) for the words following "in so far as" there shall be substituted "other sufficient consideration for the payment can be shown to have been given".

The Finance Act 1993

68 (1) In section 144 of the Finance Act 1993 (irrecoverable debts) in paragraph (*b*) of each of subsections (1) and (2) (cases where inspector is satisfied as to whole, or part, of a debt being irrecoverable) the words "the inspector is satisfied,", and the word "that" in the first place where it occurs, shall cease to have effect.

(2) In subsection (3)(*b*) of that section (debt to be treated as reduced by amount which was irrecoverable in the inspector's opinion) the words "in the opinion of the inspector" shall cease to have effect.

(3) Subsection (4) of that section (construction, for the purposes of appeals, of references in the section to the inspector) shall cease to have effect.

69 (1) In section 145 of the Finance Act 1993, in subsections (1)(*c*) and (4)(*b*) (requirements that inspector is satisfied as to the recoverability of the outstanding amount) the words "the inspector is satisfied that" shall cease to have effect.

(2) In subsections (2)(*b*), (3)(*b*) and (5) of that section (opinion of inspector as to recoverability of the outstanding amount) the words "in the opinion of the inspector" shall cease to have effect.

(3) Subsection (6) of that section (construction, for the purposes of appeals, of references in the section to the inspector) shall cease to have effect.

70 In Schedule 15 to the Finance Act 1993 (exchange gains and losses: alternative calculations) in paragraph 3(4) (meaning of unremittable income), for paragraphs (*a*) to (*c*) there shall be substituted—

"(*a*) a claim under subsection (2) of section 584 of the Taxes Act 1988 (relief for unremittable income) has been made in relation to the income,

(*b*) paragraphs (*a*) and (*b*) of that subsection apply to it, and

(*c*) those paragraphs have not ceased to apply to it."

The Finance Act 1994

71 (1) Section 163 of the Finance Act 1994 (interest rate and currency contracts: irrecoverable payments) shall be amended in accordance with the following provisions of this paragraph.

(2) In subsection (1) (application of subsections (2) and (3) where inspector is satisfied

as to irrecoverability of qualifying payment) for the words from "where" to "made" there shall be substituted "where a qualifying company—

(*a*) is entitled to a right to receive a qualifying payment, and
(*b*) makes a claim".

(3) In subsections (2) and (3) (treatment of irrecoverable amounts) in paragraph (*a*) (amount is considered to have become irrecoverable in the period), for "is considered to have" there shall be substituted "may reasonably be regarded as having".

(4) In subsection (4) (treatment of amounts later recovered), in paragraph (*b*) (the whole or any part of so much of the qualifying payment as was considered irrecoverable is recovered in a later accounting period) for "was considered irrecoverable" there shall be substituted "fell within paragraphs (*a*) and (*b*) of that subsection".

SCHEDULE 21

Section 135

SELF-ASSESSMENT: TIME LIMITS

This Schedule is aimed at standardising time limits for claims, elections, notices etc to fit in with the introduction of self-assessment. The new time limits to be applied in the provisions listed in paras 2–48 are—

(*a*) as regards income tax, the 31 January following the end of the year of assessment concerned (or an anniversary of that date);

(*b*) as regards corporation tax, an anniversary of the end of the accounting period concerned.

In appropriate provisions, references to "an inspector" are amended to "an officer of the Board" as the person to whom claims etc should be made.

The Taxes Act 1988

1 In section 62A(3) of the Taxes Act 1988 (time limit for giving notice of a change of basis period) for the words following "The second condition is" there shall be substituted—

"(*a*) in the case of a trade, profession or vocation carried on by an individual, that notice of the accounting change is given to an officer of the Board in a return under section 8 of the Management Act on or before the day on which that return is required to be made and delivered under that section;

(*b*) in the case of a trade, profession or vocation carried on by persons in partnership, that notice of the accounting change is given to an officer of the Board in a return under section 12AA of that Act on or before the day specified in relation to that return under subsection (2) or (3) of that section."

2 (1) Section 84 of the Taxes Act 1988 (relief for gifts to educational establishments) shall be amended in accordance with the following provisions of this paragraph.

(2) In subsection (3), in the words following paragraph (*b*) (relief not available unless donor makes claim within two years of making the gift) for "two years of making the gift" there shall be substituted "the period specified in subsection (3A) below".

(3) After that subsection there shall be inserted—

"(3A) The period mentioned in subsection (3) above is—

(*a*) in the case of a claim with respect to income tax, the period ending with the first anniversary of the 31st January next following the year of assessment in whose basis period the gift is made;

(*b*) in the case of a claim with respect to corporation tax, the period of two years beginning at the end of the accounting period in which the gift is made.

(3B) In paragraph (*a*) of subsection (3A) above 'basis period' means—

(*a*) in relation to a year of assessment for which a basis period is given by sections 60 to 63, that basis period,

(*b*) in relation to a year of assessment for which no basis period is given by those sections, the year of assessment."

3 (1) Section 101 of the Taxes Act 1988 (valuation of work in progress at discontinuance of profession or vocation) shall be amended in accordance with the following provisions of this paragraph.

(2) In subsection (2) (election may be made within 12 months after discontinuance) for "12 months after the discontinuance" there shall be substituted "the period specified in subsection (2A) below".

(3) After that subsection there shall be inserted—

"(2A) The period mentioned in subsection (2) above is—

(*a*) in the case of an election for the purposes of income tax, the period ending with the first anniversary of the 31st January next following the year of assessment in which the profession or vocation is discontinued;

(*b*) in the case of an election for the purposes of corporation tax, the period of two years beginning at the end of the accounting period in which the profession or vocation is discontinued."

427

4 In section 257BB(5)(*a*) of the Taxes Act 1988 (notice to be given not later than six years after the end of the year of assessment to which it relates) for "not later than six years after" there shall be substituted "on or before the fifth anniversary of the 31st January next following".

5 In section 257D(9)(*a*) of the Taxes Act 1988 (notice to be given not later than six years after the end of the year of assessment to which it relates) for "not later than six years after" there shall be substituted "on or before the fifth anniversary of the 31st January next following".

6 In section 265(5)(*a*) of the Taxes Act 1988 (notice to be given not later than six years after the end of the year of assessment to which it relates) for "not later than six years after" there shall be substituted "on or before the fifth anniversary of the 31st January next following".

7 In section 306(1) of the Taxes Act 1988 (claim for relief in respect of eligible shares) as it has effect in relation to shares issued on or after 1st January 1994 (the enterprise investment scheme) for paragraph (*b*) (claim to be made not later than twelve months after the inspector authorises the issue of a certificate) there shall be substituted—

"(*b*) not later than the fifth anniversary of the 31st January next following that year of assessment".

8 (1) Section 356B of the Taxes Act 1988 (residence basis: married couples) shall be amended in accordance with the following provisions of this paragraph.

(2) In subsection (2)(*a*) (election to be made before the end of the period of twelve months beginning with the end of the first year of assessment for which it is made or such longer period as the Board may in any particular case allow) for the words following "shall be made" there shall be substituted "on or before—

(i) the first anniversary of the 31st January next following the first year of assessment for which it is made, or
(ii) such later date as the Board may in any particular case allow,".

(3) In subsection (4)(*b*) (notice of withdrawal not to be given after the end of the period of twelve months beginning with the end of the first year of assessment for which it is given or such longer period as the Board may in any particular case allow) for the words following "shall not be given after" there shall be substituted—

"(i) the first anniversary of the 31st January next following the year of assessment for which it is given, or
(ii) such later date as the Board may in any particular case allow, and".

9 In section 356C(6) of the Taxes Act 1988, for paragraph (*a*) (election to have effect for the period in which it is made and subsequent periods) there shall be substituted—

"(*a*) shall be made on or before the first anniversary of the 31st January next following the year of assessment in which falls the first period for which it is made and shall have effect for that period and subsequent periods,".

10 In section 381(1) of the Taxes Act 1988 (claim to be made by notice given within two years after year of assessment in which loss sustained) for "within two years after" there shall be substituted "on or before the first anniversary of the 31st January next following".

11 In section 392(5) of the Taxes Act 1988 (claim to be made within six years after the year of assessment in question)—

(*a*) for "within six years after" there shall be substituted "on or before the fifth anniversary of the 31st January next following"; and
(*b*) for "not later than six years after" there shall be substituted "on or before the fifth anniversary of the 31st January next following".

12 In section 471 of the Taxes Act 1988 (exchange of securities in connection with conversion operations, nationalisation etc) for subsection (2) (tax treatment under subsection (1) not to apply to a person who gives notice to the inspector that he desires not to be treated as mentioned in that subsection) there shall be substituted—

"(2) Subsection (1) above shall not apply to a person who elects, by notice given to an officer of the Board, not to be treated as mentioned in that subsection.

(2A) A notice under subsection (2) above—

(*a*) for the purposes of income tax, shall be given on or before the first anniversary of the 31st January next following the year of assessment in whose basis period the exchange takes place;

(*b*) for the purposes of corporation tax, shall be given no later than two years after the end of the accounting period in which the exchange takes place.

(2B) In paragraph (*a*) of subsection (2A) above 'basis period' means—

(*a*) in relation to a year of assessment for which a basis period is given by sections 60 to 63, that basis period;

(*b*) in relation to a year of assessment for which no basis period is given by those sections, the year of assessment."

13 (1) In section 472 of the Taxes Act 1988 (distribution of securities issued in connection with nationalisation etc) in subsection (1) (dealer to be treated for tax purposes in the manner specified in subsections (2) and (3), unless he gives notice to the inspector that he desires not to be so treated) for "gives notice to the inspector not later than two years after the end of the chargeable period in which the distribution takes place that he desires" there shall be substituted "elects, by notice given to an officer of the Board,".

(2) After subsection (3) of that section there shall be inserted—

"(3A) A notice under subsection (1) above—

(*a*) for the purposes of income tax, shall be given on or before the first anniversary of the 31st January next following the year of assessment in whose basis period the distribution takes place;

(*b*) for the purposes of corporation tax, shall be given no later than two years after the end of the accounting period in which the distribution takes place.

(3B) In paragraph (*a*) of subsection (3A) above 'basis period' means—

(*a*) in relation to a year of assessment for which a basis period is given by sections 60 to 63, that basis period;

(*b*) in relation to a year of assessment for which no basis period is given by those sections, the year of assessment."

14 (1) Section 504 of the Taxes Act 1988 shall be amended in accordance with the following provisions of this paragraph.

(2) In subsection (6) (claim to be made within two years after the year of assessment or accounting period in which holiday accommodation is let) for "two years after that year or period" there shall be substituted "the time specified in subsection (6A) below".

(3) After subsection (6) there shall be inserted—

"(6A) The time mentioned in subsection (6) above is—

(*a*) in the case of a claim for the purposes of income tax, the period ending with the first anniversary of the 31st January next following the year of assessment in which the accommodation was let;

(*b*) in the case of a claim for the purposes of corporation tax, the period of two years beginning at the end of the accounting period in which the accommodation was let."

15 (1) Section 524 of the Taxes Act 1988 (taxation of receipts from sale of patent rights) shall be amended in accordance with the following provisions of this paragraph.

(2) In subsection (2) (election to be made by notice served on the inspector not later than two years after end of chargeable period in which sum received)—

(*a*) for "the inspector not later than two years after the end of the chargeable period in which the sum was received" there shall be substituted "an officer of the Board within the period specified in subsection (2A) below"; and

(*b*) for "that chargeable period" there shall be substituted "the chargeable period in which it was received".

(3) After that subsection there shall be inserted—

"(2A) The period mentioned in subsection (2) above is—

(*a*) in the case of an election for the purposes of income tax, the period ending with the first anniversary of the 31st January next following the year of assessment in which the sum was received;

(*b*) in the case of an election for the purposes of corporation tax, the period of two years beginning at the end of the accounting period in which the sum was received."

(4) In subsection (4) (election to be made not later than two years after the end of the year of assessment in which the sum is paid) for "not later than two years after the end of" there shall be substituted "on or before the first anniversary of the 31st January next following".

16 In section 585(6) of the Taxes Act 1988 (no claim may be made more than six years after the end of the year of assessment in which the income to which it relates is received in the United Kingdom) for "more than six years after the end of" there shall be substituted "after the fifth anniversary of the 31st January next following".

17 In section 619(4) of the Taxes Act 1988 (election to be made before the end of the year of assessment in which qualifying premium paid) for "before the end of" there shall be substituted "on or before the 31st January next following".

18 In section 641(4) of the Taxes Act 1988 (election to be made not later than three months after the end of the year of assessment in which contributions are actually paid) for "not later than three months after the end of" there shall be substituted "on or before the 31st January next following".

19 In section 691(4) of the Taxes Act 1988 (election to be made within two years of the end of the year of assessment to which it relates) for "within two years of the end of" there shall be substituted "on or before the first anniversary of the 31st January next following".

20 In section 700(3) of the Taxes Act 1988 (time for making assessments, adjustments or claims shall not expire before the end of the third year following the year of assessment in which the administration of the estate was completed) for "third year" there shall be substituted "period of three years beginning with the 31st January next".

21 (1) Section 781 of the Taxes Act 1988 (assets leased to traders and others) shall be amended in accordance with the following provisions of this paragraph.

(2) In subsection (8) (adjustment may be made at any time not more than six years from end of chargeable period in which payment made) for the words following "at any time" there shall be substituted "within the period specified in subsection (8A) below".

(3) After that subsection there shall be inserted—

"(8A) The period mentioned in subsection (8) above is—

(*a*) in the case of adjustments with respect to income tax, the period ending with the fifth anniversary of the 31st January next following the year of assessment in which the payment was made;

(*b*) in the case of adjustments with respect to corporation tax, the period of six years beginning at the end of the accounting period in which the payment was made."

22 In section 804(7) of the Taxes Act 1988 (claim for credit against tax for any year of assessment to be made within six years of the end of that year of assessment) for "within six years of the end of", in each place where those words occur, there shall be substituted "on or before the fifth anniversary of the 31st January next following".

23 In section 806(1) of the Taxes Act 1988 (claim to be made not later than six years from end of chargeable period for which income or gain falls to be charged to tax) for the words following "any income or chargeable gain" there shall be substituted—

"(*a*) shall, in the case of any income or chargeable gain which—

(i) falls to be charged to income tax for a year of assessment, or

(ii) would fall to be charged to income tax for a year of assessment if any income tax were chargeable in respect of the income or gain,

be made on or before the fifth anniversary of the 31st January next following that year of assessment;

(*b*) shall, in the case of any income or chargeable gain which—

(i) falls to be charged to corporation tax for an accounting period, or
(ii) would fall to be charged to corporation tax for an accounting period if any corporation tax were chargeable in respect of the income or gain,

be made not more than six years after the end of that accounting period."

24 In Schedule 11 to the Taxes Act 1988, in paragraph 12 (election to be made by notice given to the inspector within six years after the year of assessment in which payment made) for "the inspector within six years after" there shall be substituted "an officer of the Board on or before the fifth anniversary of the 31st January next following".

The Finance Act 1988 (c 39)

25 In section 39(2)(*b*) of the Finance Act 1988 (election to be made not later than twelve months after the end of the first year of assessment for which it is to have effect) for "not later than twelve months after the end of" there shall be substituted "on or before the first anniversary of the 31st January next following".

The Capital Allowances Act 1990 (c 1)

26 (1) Section 25 of the Capital Allowances Act 1990 (qualifying expenditure) shall be amended in accordance with the following provisions of this paragraph.

(2) In subsection (3) (election to be made by notice given to the inspector not later than two years after the end of the chargeable period related to the incurring of expenditure) for "the inspector not later than two years after the end of that chargeable period" there shall be substituted "an officer of the Board within the period specified in subsection (3A) below".

(3) After subsection (3) there shall be inserted—

"(3A) The period mentioned in subsection (3) above is—

(*a*) for the purposes of income tax, the period ending with the first anniversary of the 31st January next following the year of assessment in which ends the chargeable period related to the incurring of the expenditure;
(*b*) for the purposes of corporation tax, the period of two years beginning at the end of the chargeable period related to the incurring of the expenditure."

27 (1) Section 30 of the Capital Allowances Act (ships: first-year allowances) shall be amended in accordance with the following provisions of this paragraph.

(2) In subsection (1) (notices that may be given where first-year allowance falls to be made) for "the inspector not later than two years after the end of the period" there shall be substituted "an officer of the Board within the period specified in subsection (1A) below".

(3) After subsection (1) there shall be inserted—

"(1A) The period mentioned in subsection (1) above is—

(*a*) for the purposes of income tax, the period ending with the first anniversary of the 31st January next following the year of assessment in which ends the period of account for which the allowance mentioned in that subsection falls to be made;
(*b*) for the purposes of corporation tax, the period of two years beginning at the end of the accounting period for which the allowance mentioned in that subsection falls to be made."

28 For section 31(3) of the Capital Allowances Act (ships: notice to postpone writing-down allowance) there shall be substituted—

"(3) Where the shipowner has qualifying expenditure for a chargeable period in respect of his single ship trade, he may by notice given to an officer of the Board require the postponement of—

(*a*) the whole of the writing-down allowance to be made to him for that chargeable period, or

(*b*) so much of it as is specified in the notice.

(3A) A notice under subsection (3) above—

(*a*) for the purposes of income tax, shall be given on or before the first anniversary of the 31st January next following the year of assessment in which ends the chargeable period mentioned in that subsection;

(*b*) for the purposes of corporation tax, shall be given no later than two years after the end of the chargeable period mentioned in that subsection.''

29 (1) Section 33 of the Capital Allowances Act 1990 (ships: exclusion of section 31) shall be amended in accordance with the following provisions of this paragraph.

(2) For subsection (1) (notice to exclude section 31) there shall be substituted—

''(1) The shipowner may by notice given to an officer of the Board require that, with effect from the beginning of a chargeable period of a single ship trade, not being the chargeable period relating to the permanent discontinuance of that trade, section 31 shall not, or as the case may be, shall no longer apply.''

(3) For subsection (4) (notice to have expenditure in respect of single ship trade attributed to actual trade) there shall be substituted—

''(4) The shipowner may by notice given to an officer of the Board require that an amount of expenditure specified in the notice, being less than the amount which, apart from this subsection, would be his qualifying expenditure in respect of a single ship trade for a chargeable period of that trade, shall be attributed to his actual trade.''

(4) After subsection (5) there shall be substituted—

''(5A) A notice under subsection (1) or (4) above—

(*a*) for the purposes of income tax, shall be given on or before the first anniversary of the 31st January next following the year of assessment in which ends the chargeable period mentioned in that subsection;

(*b*) for the purposes of corporation tax, shall be given no later than two years after the end of the chargeable period mentioned in that subsection.''

30 (1) Section 37 of the Capital Allowances Act 1990 (election for certain machinery or plant to be treated as short life assets) shall be amended in accordance with the following provisions of this paragraph.

(2) In subsection (2) (elections)—

(*a*) in paragraph (*c*) (election may not be made more than two years after the end of the chargeable period in which the capital expenditure was incurred) for the words following ''may not be made'' there shall be substituted ''after the end of the period specified in subsection (2A) below''; and

(*b*) the words following paragraph (*d*) shall cease to have effect.

(3) After that subsection there shall be inserted—

''(2A) The period mentioned in subsection (2) above is—

(*a*) for the purposes of income tax, the period ending with the first anniversary of the 31st January next following the year of assessment in which ends the chargeable period related to the incurring of the capital expenditure concerned;

(*b*) for the purposes of corporation tax, the period of two years beginning at the end of the chargeable period related to the incurring of the capital expenditure concerned;

and if different parts of the capital expenditure are incurred at different times, only that part of the expenditure which is first incurred shall be taken into account for the purposes of this subsection.''

31 (1) Section 53 of the Capital Allowances Act 1990 (expenditure incurred by equipment lessor) shall be amended in accordance with the following provisions of this paragraph.

(2) In subsection (2) (election to be made by notice given to the inspector before the expiry of the period of two years beginning at the end of the chargeable period related to the incurring of the expenditure)—

(a) for "the inspector" there shall be substituted "an officer of the Board"; and

(b) for "of two years beginning at the end of the chargeable period related to the incurring of the expenditure referred to in subsection (1)(a) above" there shall be substituted "specified in subsection (2A) below".

(3) After that subsection there shall be inserted—

"(2A) The period mentioned in subsection (2) above is—

(a) for the purposes of income tax, the period ending with the first anniversary of the 31st January next following the year of assessment in which ends the chargeable period related to the incurring of the expenditure referred to in subsection (1)(a) above;

(b) for the purposes of corporation tax, the period of two years beginning at the end of the chargeable period related to the incurring of the expenditure referred to in subsection (1)(a) above."

32 (1) Section 68 of the Capital Allowances Act 1990 (exclusion of certain expenditure relating to films, tapes and discs) shall be amended in accordance with the following provisions of this paragraph.

(2) In subsection (5) (claim to be made not later than two years after the end of the relevant period) for "not later than two years after the end of that period" there shall be substituted "within the period specified in subsection (5A) below".

(3) After that subsection there shall be inserted—

"(5A) The period mentioned in subsection (5) above is—

(a) for the purposes of income tax, the period ending with the first anniversary of the 31st January next following the year of assessment in which ends the relevant period mentioned in that subsection;

(b) for the purposes of corporation tax, the period of two years beginning at the end of the relevant period mentioned in that subsection."

(4) In subsection (9A)(b) (election to be made by giving notice to the inspector not later than two years after the end of the relevant period in which the film etc is completed)—

(a) for "the inspector" there shall be substituted "an officer of the Board"; and

(b) for "not later than two years after the end of the relevant period in which the film, tape or disc is completed" there shall be substituted "within the period specified in subsection (9AA) below".

(5) After subsection (9A) there shall be inserted—

"(9AA) The period mentioned in subsection (9A)(b) above is—

(a) in the case of an election for the purposes of income tax, the period ending with the first anniversary of the 31st January next following the year of assessment in which ends the relevant period in which the film, tape or disc is completed;

(b) in the case of an election for the purposes of corporation tax, the period of two years beginning at the end of the relevant period in which the film, tape or disc is completed."

(6) In subsection (9B) for "(9A)(b)" there shall be substituted "(9AA)".

33 In section 129(2) of the Capital Allowances Act 1990 (election to be made by notice given to the inspector not more than two years after the end of the chargeable period related to the occurrence of the event) for the words following "by notice given to" there shall be substituted "an officer of the Board; and—

(a) an election under this subsection for the purposes of income tax shall be made on or before the first anniversary of the 31st January next following the year of assessment in which ends the chargeable period related to the occurrence of the event; and

(b) an election under this subsection for the purposes of corporation tax shall be made not more than two years after the end of the chargeable period related to the occurrence of the event.''

34 In section 141(3) of the Capital Allowances Act 1990, in the second paragraph (election as respects an allowance for any year of assessment to be made by giving notice to the inspector not later than two years after the end of that year of assessment) for ''the inspector not later than two years after the end of'' there shall be substituted ''an officer of the Board on or before the first anniversary of the 31st January next following''.

The Taxation of Chargeable Gains Act 1992 (c 12)

35 In section 35(6) of the Taxation of Chargeable Gains Act 1992 (elections under section 35(5) to be made by notice to the inspector within period ending 2 years after the end of the year of assessment or accounting period in which the disposal is made or at such later time as the Board may allow)—

(*a*) for ''the inspector'' there shall be substituted ''an officer of the Board''; and
(*b*) for paragraphs (*a*) and (*b*) there shall be substituted—

''(*a*) in the case of an election for the purposes of capital gains tax, with the first anniversary of the 31st January next following the year of assessment in which the disposal is made;
(*aa*) in the case of an election for the purposes of corporation tax, 2 years after the end of the accounting period in which the disposal is made; or
(*b*) in either case, at such later time as the Board may allow;''.

36 In section 161 of the Taxation of Chargeable Gains Act 1992 (appropriations to and from stock) after subsection (3) there shall be inserted—

''(3A) An election under subsection (3) above shall be made—

(*a*) for the purposes of capital gains tax, on or before the first anniversary of the 31st January next following the year of assessment in which ends the period of account in which the asset is appropriated for the purposes of the trade as trading stock;
(*b*) for the purposes of corporation tax, within 2 years after the end of the accounting period in which the asset is appropriated for the purposes of the trade as trading stock;

and in paragraph (*a*) above 'period of account' means a period for which the accounts of the trade are made up.''

37 In section 242 of the Taxation of Chargeable Gains Act 1992 (small part disposals) after subsection (2) there shall be inserted—

''(2A) A claim under subsection (2) above shall be made—

(*a*) for the purposes of capital gains tax, on or before the first anniversary of the 31st January next following the year of assessment in which the transfer is made;
(*b*) for the purposes of corporation tax, within 2 years after the end of the accounting period in which the transfer is made.''

38 In section 243 of the Taxation of Chargeable Gains Act 1992 (part disposal to authority with compulsory powers) after subsection (2) there shall be inserted—

''(2A) A claim under subsection (2) above shall be made—

(*a*) for the purposes of capital gains tax, on or before the first anniversary of the 31st January next following the year of assessment in which the transfer is made;
(*b*) for the purposes of corporation tax, within 2 years after the end of the accounting period in which the transfer is made.''

39 In section 244 of the Taxation of Chargeable Gains Act 1992 (part disposal: consideration exceeding allowable expenditure) after subsection (2) there shall be inserted—

''(3) An election under subsection (2)(*b*) above shall be made—

(*a*) for the purposes of capital gains tax, on or before the first anniversary of the

31st January next following the year of assessment in which the part disposal is made;

(*b*) for the purposes of corporation tax, within 2 years after the end of the accounting period in which the part disposal is made."

40 In section 253 of the Taxation of Chargeable Gains Act 1992 (relief for loans to traders) after subsection (4) there shall be inserted—

"(4A) A claim under subsection (4) above shall be made—

(*a*) for the purposes of capital gains tax, on or before the fifth anniversary of the 31st January next following the year of assessment in which the payment was made;

(*b*) for the purposes of corporation tax, within 6 years after the end of the accounting period in which the payment was made."

41 In section 279 of the Taxation of Chargeable Gains Act 1992 (foreign assets: delayed remittances) for subsection (5) (no claim under section 279 to be made more than 6 years after end of year of assessment in which chargeable gain accrues) there shall be substituted—

"(5) No claim under this section in respect of a chargeable gain shall be made—

(*a*) in the case of a claim for the purposes of capital gains tax, at any time after the fifth anniversary of the 31st January next following the year of assessment in which the gain accrues; or

(*b*) in the case of a claim for the purposes of corporation tax, more than 6 years after the end of the accounting period in which the gain accrues."

42 (1) Schedule 2 to the Taxation of Chargeable Gains Act 1992 shall be amended in accordance with the following provisions of this paragraph.

(2) In paragraph 4 (election for pooling) in sub-paragraph (11) (election to be made by notice to the inspector not later than the expiration of 2 years from the end of the year of assessment or accounting period of a company in which the first relevant disposal is made, or such further time as the Board may allow) for the words following "notice to" there shall be substituted "an officer of the Board given—

(*a*) in the case of an election for the purposes of capital gains tax, on or before the first anniversary of the 31st January next following the year of assessment in which the first relevant disposal is made;

(*b*) in the case of an election for the purposes of corporation tax, not later than the expiration of 2 years from the end of the accounting period in which the first relevant disposal is made; or

(*c*) in either case, within such further time as the Board may allow."

(3) In paragraph 17 (election for valuation at 6th April) in sub-paragraph (3) (election to be made by notice to the inspector given within 2 years from the end of the year of assessment or accounting period of a company in which the disposal is made, or such further time as the Board may by notice allow) for the words following "by notice to" there shall be substituted "an officer of the Board given—

(*a*) in the case of an election for the purposes of capital gains tax, on or before the first anniversary of the 31st January next following the year of assessment in which the disposal is made;

(*b*) in the case of an election for the purposes of corporation tax, within 2 years from the end of the accounting period in which the disposal is made; or

(*c*) in either case, within such further time as the Board may by notice allow."

43 In Schedule 4 to the Taxation of Chargeable Gains Act 1992 (deferred charges on gains before 31st March 1982) in paragraph 9(1) (time for making claims)—

(*a*) in paragraph (*b*)—

(i) for "any other case" there shall be substituted "the case of a disposal made by, or a gain treated as accruing to, a person chargeable to corporation tax"; and

(ii) the words "year of assessment or" shall be omitted;

(*b*) after paragraph (*b*) there shall be inserted—

"*(c)* in the case of a disposal made by, or a gain treated as accruing to, a person who is chargeable to capital gains tax, on or before the first anniversary of the 31st January next following the year of assessment in which the disposal in question is made or the gain in question is treated as accruing,"; and

(c) in the words following paragraph *(b)*, after "period" there shall be inserted "or (as the case may be) on or before such later date".

44 (1) Schedule 6 to the Taxation of Chargeable Gains Act 1992 (retirement relief etc) shall be amended in accordance with the following provisions of this paragraph.

(2) In paragraph 2(1) (election to be made by notice given to the Board not more than 2 years after the end of the year of assessment in which the disposal occurred) for "not more than 2 years after the end of" there shall be substituted "on or before the first anniversary of the 31st January next following".

(3) In paragraph 5(2) (claim for relief to be made not later than 2 years after the end of the year of assessment in which the disposal occurred) for "not later than 2 years after the end of" there shall be substituted "on or before the first anniversary of the 31st January next following".

(4) In paragraph 12(5)*(b)* (election to be made by giving notice to the inspector not later than 2 years after the end of the year of assessment in which capital distribution received)—

(a) for "not later than 2 years after the end of" there shall be substituted "on or before the first anniversary of the 31st January next following"; and
(b) for "the inspector" there shall be substituted "an officer of the Board".

(5) In paragraph 16 (aggregation of spouse's interest in the business: election to be made by giving notice to the inspector not later than 2 years after the end of the year of assessment in which material disposal occurred)—

(a) in sub-paragraph (1)*(e)* for "not later than 2 years after the end of" there shall be substituted "on or before the first anniversary of the 31st January next following"; and
(b) in sub-paragraph (2) for "the inspector" there shall be substituted "an officer of the Board".

The Finance (No 2) Act 1992 (c 48)

45 For section 41(6) of the Finance (No 2) Act 1992 (claim to be made not later than two years after the end of the relevant period in which the expenditure to which it relates becomes payable) there shall be substituted—

"(6) A claim under this section shall be made—

(a) for the purposes of income tax, on or before the first anniversary of the 31st January next following the year of assessment in which ends the relevant period in which the expenditure to which it relates becomes payable;
(b) for the purposes of corporation tax, not later than two years after the end of the relevant period in which the expenditure to which it relates becomes payable."

46 For section 42(6) of the Finance (No 2) Act 1992 (claim to be made not later than two years after the end of the relevant period to which it relates) there shall be substituted—

"(6) A claim under this section shall be made—

(a) for the purposes of income tax, on or before the first anniversary of the 31st January next following the year of assessment in which ends the relevant period to which the claim relates,
(b) for the purposes of corporation tax, not later than two years after the end of the relevant period to which the claim relates,

and shall be irrevocable."

47 (1) Schedule 10 to the Finance (No 2) Act 1992 (furnished accommodation) shall be amended in accordance with the following provisions of this paragraph.

(2) In paragraph 10(4) (election or notice to be made or given by notice in writing to

the inspector before the end of the period of one year beginning with the end of the year of assessment concerned or such longer period as the Board may in any particular case allow)—

(*a*) in paragraph (*a*) for the words following "must be made or given" there shall be substituted "on or before—

(i) the first anniversary of the 31st January next following the year of assessment concerned, or

(ii) such later date as the Board may in any particular case allow, and"; and

(*b*) in paragraph (*b*) for "the inspector" there shall be substituted "an officer of the Board".

(3) In paragraph 10, in sub-paragraph (5) (assessment not to be out of time if made before the end of the period of one year beginning with the day when the election was made or the notice given) for "before the end of the period of one year beginning with the day when" there shall be substituted "on or before the first anniversary of the 31st January next following the year of assessment in which".

(4) In paragraph 12(2) (election must be made in writing to the inspector before the end of the period of one year beginning with the end of the year of assessment for which it is made or such longer period as the Board may in any particular case allow)—

(*a*) in paragraph (*b*) for the words following "must be made" there shall be substituted "on or before—

(i) the first anniversary of the 31st January next following the year of assessment for which it is made, or

(ii) such later date as the Board may in any particular case allow, and"; and

(*b*) in paragraph (*c*) for "the inspector" there shall be substituted "an officer of the Board".

(5) In paragraph 12(4) (notice of withdrawal to be given in writing to the inspector before the end of the period of one year beginning with the end of the year of assessment for which it is given or such longer period as the Board may in any particular case allow)—

(*a*) in paragraph (*a*) for the words following "must be given" there shall be substituted "on or before—

(i) the first anniversary of the 31st January next following the year of assessment for which it is given, or

(ii) such later date as the Board may in any particular case allow,"; and

(*b*) in paragraph (*b*) for "the inspector" there shall be substituted "an officer of the Board".

(6) In paragraph 12, in sub-paragraph (6)(*b*) (notice of withdrawal deemed to be given on the last day of the period of one year beginning with the end of the year of assessment concerned) for "last day of the period of one year beginning with the end of" there shall be substituted "first anniversary of the 31st January next following".

(7) In paragraph 12, in sub-paragraph (7) (assessment not to be out of time if made before the end of the period of one year beginning with the day when the election was made or the notice was given) for "before the end of the period of one year beginning with the day when" there shall be substituted "on or before the first anniversary of the 31st January next following the year of assessment in which".

The Finance Act 1994 (c 9)

48 (1) Section 118 of the Finance Act 1994 (expenditure on machinery or plant: notification) shall be amended in accordance with the following provisions of this paragraph.

(2) In subsection (3) (condition fulfilled with respect to a chargeable period if notice given to the inspector not later than two years after the end of the period) for "the inspector, in such form as the Board may require, not later than two years after the

end of that period" there shall be substituted "an officer of the Board, in such form as the Board may require, within the period specified in subsection (3A) below".

(3) After subsection (3) there shall be inserted—

"(3A) A notice under subsection (3) above—

(*a*) for the purposes of income tax, shall be given on or before the first anniversary of the 31st January next following the year of assessment in which ends the chargeable period mentioned in that subsection;

(*b*) for the purposes of corporation tax, shall be given no later than two years after the end of the chargeable period mentioned in that subsection."

SCHEDULE 22

SELF-ASSESSMENT: APPEALS

The Taxes Management Act 1970

1 The Taxes Management Act 1970 shall be amended in accordance with paragraphs 2 to 10 below.

2 In section 19A (power to call for documents for purposes of certain enquiries), for subsection (11) there shall be substituted the following subsection—

"(11) The determination of the Commissioners of an appeal under subsection (6) above shall be final and conclusive (notwithstanding any provision having effect by virtue of section 56B of this Act)."

GENERAL NOTE
Where an appeal is made under TMA 1970 s 19A(6) against a notice to produce documents etc, the decision of the Commissioners is final and conclusive, notwithstanding TMA 1970 s 56B.

3 In section 28A (amendment of self-assessment where enquiries made), for subsections (6) and (7) there shall be substituted the following subsections—

"(6) At any time before a notice is given under subsection (5) above, the taxpayer may apply for a direction that the officer shall give such a notice within such period as may be specified in the direction.

(6A) Subject to subsection (7) below, an application under subsection (6) above shall be heard and determined in the same way as an appeal against an amendment of a self-assessment under subsection (2) or (4) above.

(7) The Commissioners hearing the application shall give the direction applied for unless they are satisfied that the officer has reasonable grounds for not giving the notice."

GENERAL NOTE
This paragraph amends TMA 1970 s 28A(6), (7), which deals with the situation where a Revenue officer has commenced enquiries into a self-assessment return and has not given notice that the enquiries are completed. At such a time, the taxpayer may apply for a direction that the officer shall (within a specified time) give such a notice. The application for a direction is to be heard by the Commissioners in the same way as an appeal against a Revenue amendment of a self-assessment, and unless they are satisfied that the officer has reasonable grounds for continuing his enquiries, they must give the direction applied for.

4 In section 31 (appeals in connection with assessments), for subsection (3) there shall be substituted the following subsection—

"(3) An appeal against an assessment made—

(*a*) by the Board, or
(*b*) under section 350 of the principal Act,

shall be to the Special Commissioners."

GENERAL NOTE
TMA 1970 s 31(3) lists cases where an appeal against an assessment can only be to the Special Commissioners. This paragraph deletes from that list appeals against assessments under the settlements anti-avoidance provisions and those dealing with estates in course of administration, but TMA 1970 new s 46B(4) (see under para 7 below) restores the position. An assessment under TA 1988 s 350 (annual payments made out of profits or gains not charged to tax) is added to the list.

5 In section 33A (error or mistake in partnership statement), for subsection (8) there shall be substituted the following subsections—

"(8) Subject to subsection (8A) below, the determination of the Special Commissioners of an appeal under subsection (6) above shall be final and conclusive (notwithstanding any provision having effect by virtue of section 56B of this Act).

(8A) Subsection (8) above does not apply in relation to a point of law arising in connection with the computation of profits.''

GENERAL NOTE

TA 1988 s 33A(8) provides that where an appeal is made against the refusal of an "error or mistake" claim relating to a partnership statement, the decision of the Commissioners is final and conclusive. This paragraph inserts TA 1988 new s 33A(8A) which allows an appeal to the High Court on a point of law in connection with the computation of profits.

6   Section 42(12) and Schedule 2 (Commissioners to whom appeal lies where appeal is against amendment of claim not included in return) shall be omitted.

GENERAL NOTE

See note to para 8.

7   For section 47 there shall be substituted the following sections—

"46B   Questions to be determined by Special Commissioners

(1) In so far as the question in dispute on an appeal to which this section applies is a question which under this section is to be determined by the Special Commissioners, the question shall be determined by them.

(2) This section applies to—

(*a*) an appeal against an amendment under section 28A(2) or (4) of this Act of a self-assessment;
(*b*) an appeal against a decision contained in a notice under section 28A(4A) of this Act disallowing a claim or election in whole or in part;
(*c*) an appeal against an amendment under section 28B(3) or 30B(1) of this Act of a partnership statement;
(*d*) an appeal against an assessment to tax which is not a self-assessment;
(*e*) an appeal against an amendment under paragraph 7(3) of Schedule 1A to this Act of a claim or election made otherwise than by being included in a return;
(*f*) an appeal against a decision contained in a notice under paragraph 7(3A) of Schedule 1A to this Act disallowing in whole or in part a claim or election made otherwise than by being included in a return.

(3) Any question—

(*a*) of the value of any shares or securities in a company resident in the United Kingdom, other than shares or securities quoted in The Stock Exchange Daily Official List, and
(*b*) arising in relation to the taxation of chargeable gains (whether under capital gains tax or corporation tax) or in relation to a claim under the 1992 Act,

is a question to be determined by the Special Commissioners.

(4) Any question as to the application of any of the following provisions of the principal Act is a question to be determined by the Special Commissioners—

(*a*) Chapter IA or IB of Part XV (settlements);
(*b*) Part XVI (administration of estates);
(*c*) sections 740 and 743(1) (liability in respect of transfer of assets abroad);
(*d*) section 747(4)(*a*) (liability in respect of controlled foreign company).

(5) Any question as to the application of—

(*a*) section 830 of the principal Act, or
(*b*) section 276 of the 1992 Act,

(liability in relation to territorial sea and designated areas) is a question to be determined by the Special Commissioners.

46C   Jurisdiction of Special Commissioners over certain claims included in returns

(1) In so far as the question in dispute on an appeal to which this section applies concerns a claim made—

(*a*) to the Board, or

(*b*) under any of the provisions of the principal Act listed in subsection (3) below,

the question shall be determined by the Special Commissioners.

(2) This section applies to—

(*a*) an appeal against an amendment under section 28A(2) or (4) of this Act of a self-assessment;

(*b*) an appeal against an amendment under section 28B(3) or 30B(1) of this Act of a partnership statement.

(3) The provisions of the principal Act mentioned in subsection (1) above are—

(*a*) section 121(1) and (2) (management expenses of owner of mineral rights);

(*b*) sections 459 and 460 (exemption for certain friendly societies);

(*c*) section 467 (exemption for certain trade unions and employers' associations);

(*d*) sections 527, 534, 536 and 538 (reliefs in respect of royalties, copyright payments etc);

(*e*) Chapter I of Part XVIII.

46D   Questions to be determined by Lands Tribunal

(1) In so far as the question in dispute on an appeal to which this section applies—

(*a*) is a question of the value of any land or of a lease of land, and

(*b*) arises in relation to the taxation of chargeable gains (whether under capital gains tax or corporation tax) or in relation to a claim under the 1992 Act,

the question shall be determined by the relevant Lands Tribunal.

(2) This section applies to—

(*a*) an appeal against an amendment under section 28A(2) or (4) of this Act of a self-assessment;

(*b*) an appeal against a decision contained in a notice under section 28A(4A) of this Act disallowing a claim or election in whole or in part;

(*c*) an appeal against an amendment under section 28B(3) or 30B(1) of this Act of a partnership statement;

(*d*) an appeal against an assessment to tax which is not a self-assessment;

(*e*) an appeal against an amendment under paragraph 7(3) of Schedule 1A to this Act of a claim or election made otherwise than by being included in a return;

(*f*) an appeal against a decision contained in a notice under paragraph 7(3A) of Schedule 1A to this Act disallowing in whole or in part a claim or election made otherwise than by being included in a return.

(3) In this section 'the relevant Lands Tribunal' means—

(*a*) in relation to land in England and Wales, the Lands Tribunal;

(*b*) in relation to land in Scotland, the Lands Tribunal for Scotland;

(*c*) in relation to land in Northern Ireland, the Lands Tribunal for Northern Ireland.''

GENERAL NOTE
See note to para 8.

8   In section 57(3)(*c*) (power to make regulations authorising conditional decisions where more than one tribunal is determining questions in the proceedings), for "section 47" there shall be substituted "section 46B, 46C or 46D".

GENERAL NOTE
Paragraph 6 repeals TMA 1970 s 42(12) and Sch 2, which specify to which Commissioners an appeal is to be made against a refusal or amendment of a claim in a return. Those provisions are replaced by TMA 1970 new ss 46B, 46C inserted by para 7. They provide that where an appeal is

to the General Commissioners, any question involving any of the provisions listed in the new sections is to be determined by the Special Commissioners; presumably any other question raised by the appeal will be determined by the General Commissioners. Paragraph 7 also inserts new s 46D into TMA 1970 which sets out matters to be determined by the Lands Tribunal. Paragraph 8 makes a consequential amendment to TMA 1970 s 57(3)(*c*) (regulations about appeals concerning chargeable gains).

9 In Schedule 1A (claims not included in returns), after paragraph 9 there shall be inserted the following paragraphs—

"**10** An appeal against an amendment under paragraph 7(3) above of a claim made—

    (*a*) to the Board,
    (*b*) under Part XVI of the principal Act (administration of estates), or
    (*c*) under any of the provisions of the principal Act listed in section 46C(3) of this Act,

shall be to the Special Commissioners.

11 (1) Subject to paragraph 10 above and the following provisions of this paragraph, an appeal under paragraph 9(1) above shall be to the General Commissioners.

(2) The appellant may elect (in accordance with section 46(1) of this Act) to bring the appeal before the Special Commissioners.

(3) Such an election shall be disregarded if—

    (*a*) the appellant and the officer of the Board agree in writing, at any time before the determination of the appeal, that it is to be disregarded; or
    (*b*) the General Commissioners have given a direction under sub-paragraph (5) below and have not revoked it.

(4) At any time before the determination of an appeal in respect of which an election has been made an officer of the Board after giving notice to the appellant may refer the election to the General Commissioners.

(5) On any such reference the Commissioners shall, unless they are satisfied that the appellant has arguments to present or evidence to adduce on the merits of the appeal, give a direction that the election be disregarded.

(6) If, at any time after the giving of such a direction (but before the determination of the appeal) the General Commissioners are satisfied that the appellant has arguments to present or evidence to adduce on the merits of the appeal, they shall revoke the direction.

(7) Any decision to give or revoke such a direction shall be final.

(8) If—

    (*a*) a person bringing an appeal under paragraph 9(1) above has another appeal pending to either body of Commissioners concerning an assessment on him, and
    (*b*) the appeals relate to the same source of income,

the appeal under paragraph 9(1) above shall be to the body of Commissioners before whom the appeal concerning the assessment is being brought.

(9) This paragraph is subject to provision made by or under Part V of this Act."

GENERAL NOTE
This paragraph inserts new Sch 1A paras 10 and 11 into TMA 1970, which deal with appeals against amendments of claims not included in returns; these are not covered by the lists in TMA 1970 ss 46B–46D (see para 7 above).

TMA 1970 new Sch 1A para 10 lists appeals which can only be made to the Special Commissioners.

TMA 1970 new Sch 1A para 11 provides that other appeals are to be made to the General Commissioners, with the right of election to have it heard by the Special Commissioners. Where such an election has been made, and before the appeal has been determined, a Revenue officer may refer the election to the General Commissioners (after giving notice to the appellant).

Unless the General Commissioners are satisfied that the appellant has arguments or evidence to put forward, they must rule that the election be disregarded, ie they will hear the appeal themselves. If they subsequently become satisfied that the appellant has arguments or evidence to put forward, they must revoke the earlier ruling, which means that the appeal will be transferred to the Special Commissioners.

Where the appellant against an amendment of a claim has another appeal pending concerning an assessment, and both appeals relate to the same source of income, the appeal regarding the claim is to be heard by the same body of Commissioners as the appeal against the assessment.

Subject to the above, an appeal against an amendment of a claim is dealt with in accordance with the general appeal rules in TMA 1970 Part V.

10 The following Schedule shall be substituted for Schedule 3—

''SCHEDULE 3
RULES FOR ASSIGNING PROCEEDINGS TO GENERAL COMMISSIONERS

Introductory

1 In this Schedule—

'the relevant place' means the place referred to in section 44(1) of this Act, which is used to identify the General Commissioners before whom proceedings are to be brought; and

'the taxpayer', in relation to any proceedings, means the party to the proceedings who is neither the Board nor an officer of the Board.

General rule for income and capital gains tax proceedings

2 (1) In the case of any proceedings relating to income tax or capital gains tax the relevant place is whichever of the places specified in sub-paragraph (2) below is identified—

(*a*) except where the proceedings are commenced by an officer of the Board, by an election made by the taxpayer; and

(*b*) where the proceedings are so commenced, by an election made by the officer.

(2) Those places are—

(*a*) the place (if any) in the United Kingdom which, at the time when the election is made, is the taxpayer's place of residence;

(*b*) the place (if any) which at that time is the taxpayer's place of business in the United Kingdom;

(*c*) the place (if any) in the United Kingdom which at that time is the taxpayer's place of employment;

and, in the case of a place of employment, it shall be immaterial for the purposes of this paragraph whether the proceedings in question relate to matters connected with the employment of the taxpayer.

(3) Where the taxpayer fails to make an election for the purposes of this paragraph before the time limit given by paragraph 5 below, an officer of the Board may elect which of the places specified in sub-paragraph (2) above is to be the relevant place.

(4) In sub-paragraph (2)(*a*) above 'place of residence' means—

(*a*) in relation to an election made by the taxpayer, his usual place of residence; and

(*b*) in relation to an election made by an officer of the Board, the taxpayer's usual place of residence or, if that is unknown, his last known place of residence.

(5) In sub-paragraph (2)(*b*) above 'place of business' means—

(*a*) the place where the trade, profession, vocation or business with which the proceedings are concerned is carried on, or

(*b*) if the trade, profession, vocation or business is carried on at more than one place, the head office or place where it is mainly carried on.

(6) This paragraph does not apply in the case of any proceedings to which paragraph 3, 4 or 7 below applies.

PAYE appeals

3 (1) In the case of an appeal in exercise of a right of appeal conferred by regulations under section 203 of the principal Act, the relevant place is—

(*a*) except in a case falling in paragraph (*b*) below, the place determined by the regulations, and

(*b*) if the appellant elects for one of the places specified in paragraph 2(2) above to be the relevant place instead, the place identified by the election.

(2) This paragraph does not apply in the case of any proceedings to which paragraph 4 or 7 below applies.

Corporation tax etc

4 (1) In the case of the proceedings mentioned in sub-paragraph (2) below the relevant place is whichever of the places specified in sub-paragraph (3) below is identified—

(*a*) except where the proceedings are commenced by an officer of the Board, by an election made by the company or other body corporate which is a party to the proceedings ('the corporate taxpayer'); and

(*b*) where the proceedings are so commenced, by an election made by the officer.

(2) The proceedings are—

(*a*) proceedings relating to corporation tax;

(*b*) proceedings relating to income tax which are proceedings to which a company resident in the United Kingdom and within the charge to corporation tax is a party;

(*c*) proceedings relating to tax assessable under sections 419 and 420 of the principal Act (close company loans).

(3) The places are—

(*a*) the place where, at the time when the election is made, the corporate taxpayer carries on its trade or business;

(*b*) the place where, at that time, the head office or principal place of business of the corporate taxpayer is situated;

(*c*) the place where, at that time, the corporate taxpayer resides.

(4) Where the corporate taxpayer fails to make an election for the purposes of this paragraph before the time limit given by paragraph 5 below, an officer of the Board may elect which of the places specified in sub-paragraph (3) above is to be the relevant place.

(5) This paragraph does not apply in the case of any proceedings to which paragraph 7 below applies.

Procedure for making elections, etc

5 (1) An election by a taxpayer for the purposes of this Schedule shall be made by notice in writing to an officer of the Board.

(2) The time limit for the making of such an election in relation to proceedings is—

(*a*) the time when the taxpayer gives notice of appeal or, if the proceedings are not an appeal, otherwise commences the proceedings; or

(*b*) such later date as the Board allows.

(3) Such an election shall be irrevocable.

6 An election by an officer of the Board for the purposes of this Schedule shall be made by notice in writing served on the taxpayer.

Partnerships

7 In the case of proceedings relating to a partnership to which a partner of that partnership is a party, the relevant place is—

(*a*) the place where the trade, profession or business of the partnership is carried on, or

(*b*) if the trade, profession or business is carried on at more than one place, the place where it is mainly carried on.

Directions by the Board

8 (1) The Board may give a direction in relation to any class of proceedings specified in the direction that, notwithstanding the preceding provisions of this Schedule, the relevant place shall be taken to be a place in a division specified in the direction.

(2) A direction given under this paragraph shall not have effect in relation to any proceedings unless an officer of the Board has served on the taxpayer a notice in writing stating the effect of the direction in relation to those proceedings.

(3) A direction given under this paragraph shall not have effect if the taxpayer gives a notice in accordance with sub-paragraph (4) below objecting to the direction.

(4) The taxpayer gives a notice in accordance with this sub-paragraph if he gives it in writing to the Board within the period of 30 days beginning with the day on which the notice under sub-paragraph (2) above was served on him.

9 (1) The Board may give directions for determining the relevant place in cases where—

(*a*) the proceedings fall within paragraph 2, 4 or 7 above, but there is no place falling within paragraph 2(2), 4(3) or, as the case may be, paragraph 7; or

(*b*) the relevant place would, apart from the direction, be a place outside the United Kingdom.

(2) A direction given under this paragraph by the Board shall not have effect in relation to any proceedings unless an officer of the Board has served on the taxpayer a notice in writing stating the effect of the direction in relation to those proceedings.

(3) A direction under sub-paragraph (1) above may be given in relation to—

(*a*) proceedings falling within that sub-paragraph;

(*b*) any class of such proceedings specified in the direction; or

(*c*) proceedings specified in the direction.

Other provisions

10 The provisions of this Schedule have effect subject to sections 44(2), 46A and 57 of this Act, sections 102(1), 113(5), 343(10) and 783(9) of the principal Act and section 151 of the Capital Allowances Act 1990.''

GENERAL NOTE

This paragraph inserts new Sch 3 into TMA 1970 (Rules for assigning proceedings to General Commissioners) to replace the existing Sch 3, which was largely in the form of a table. General Commissioners are appointed for a geographical area (a "division"), and the proceedings will be assigned to the Commissioners for the division in which falls the "relevant place". New Sch 3 sets out how the relevant place is determined.

INCOME TAX AND CAPITAL GAINS TAX: GENERAL RULE

The taxpayer may elect to have the proceedings heard by choosing as the relevant place (which must be in the UK) his place of residence, his place of business or his place of employment at the time of the election. If the proceedings are not commenced by the taxpayer or if he does not make an election, the choice is made by a Revenue officer. Place of residence and place of business are defined. This rule does not apply to PAYE appeals or to appeals by a company or a partnership (TMA 1970 Sch 3 para 2).

PAYE APPEALS

Unless the taxpayer elects for one of the places mentioned in TMA 1970 Sch 3 para 2, the relevant place is determined by the PAYE regulations (TMA 1970 Sch 3 para 3).

CORPORATION TAX ETC

This rule applies to proceedings relating to—

(*a*) corporation tax;

(*b*) income tax which are proceedings involving a UK resident company;
(*c*) close company loans.

The company may elect to have the proceedings heard by choosing as the relevant place the place where it carries on its business, the place where its head office is situated or the place where it resides. If the proceedings are not commenced by the company, or if the company fails to make an election, the choice is made by a Revenue officer (TMA 1970 Sch 3 para 4).

PROCEDURE FOR MAKING ELECTIONS
An election by the taxpayer to adopt a relevant place must be made in writing to a Revenue officer at the time the appeal is made or when proceedings are commenced (unless the Revenue allow a later time limit), and cannot be revoked. An election by a Revenue officer must be made by written notice to the taxpayer (TMA 1970 Sch 3 para 5).

PARTNERSHIPS
The relevant place for partnership proceedings to which a partner is a party is the place where its trade, profession or business is carried on (or mainly carried on) (TMA 1970 Sch 3 para 7).

DIRECTIONS BY THE BOARD
Notwithstanding the right of a taxpayer in most cases to elect for a particular relevant place, the Revenue may give and serve on the taxpayer a direction specifying a relevant place of their choice. The Revenue direction will not have effect if, within 30 days of service of the notice, the taxpayer objects in writing (TMA 1970 Sch 3 para 8).
Where the proceedings fall under TMA 1970 new Sch 3 paras 2, 4 or 7 and there is no place which falls within the available options (or if the place would be outside the UK), the Revenue may give directions for determining the relevant place, which will only be valid if it has been notified in writing to the taxpayer (TMA 1970 Sch 3 para 9).

OTHER PROVISIONS
TMA 1970 Sch 3 will not apply where there is a specific provision in another section of the Taxes Acts governing the choice of Commissioners in the particular circumstances where that section applies (TMA 1970 Sch 3 para 10).

TA 1988 S 102
TMA 1970 Sch 3 para 11 makes a cosmetic change to TA 1988 s 102(1)(*a*).

COMMENCEMENT
The Schedule has effect from the introduction of the self-assessment scheme (TMA 1970 Sch 3 para 12).

Section 102 of the Taxes Act 1988

11   In section 102(1)(*a*) of the Taxes Act 1988 (cases where jurisdiction exercised by General Commissioners) for "both the trades, professions or vocations" there shall be substituted "each of the persons whose trade, profession or vocation is one of those".

Commencement of Schedule

12   This Schedule has effect in relation to—

(*a*) any proceedings relating to the year 1996–97 or any subsequent year of assessment, and
(*b*) any proceedings relating to an accounting period ending on or after the day appointed under section 199 of the Finance Act 1994 for the purposes of Chapter III of Part IV of that Act (self-assessment).

SCHEDULE 23

SELF-ASSESSMENT: SCHEDULES 13 AND 16 TO THE TAXES ACT 1988

INTRODUCTION

Paragraphs 3, 4, 5, 6, 9, 11, 13 of this Schedule do no more than substitute "an officer of the Board" for "the inspector" in various provisions of TA 1988 Schs 13 and 16. This change is in line with similar changes made in FA 1994 in other areas affected by the move to self-assessment.

PART I

SCHEDULE 13 TO THE TAXES ACT 1988

BACKGROUND NOTE

Under TA 1988 Sch 13 companies are required to make quarterly returns of franked payments and account for ACT. Under self-assessment this obligation will continue in very much the same way as it does now (although it is notable that the Revenue have been consulting over the design of form CT 61), except in one respect, the treatment of qualifying distributions or payments whose nature is not clear.

1 Schedule 13 to the Taxes Act 1988 (collection of advance corporation tax) shall be amended in accordance with the following provisions of this Part of this Schedule.

2 In paragraph 2 (contents of returns) in sub-paragraph (2) (specification of particular matters to be included in a return) after "The return shall specify" there shall be inserted "(*a*)" and at the end of that sub-paragraph there shall be inserted—

"(*b*) whether any estimated amount of franked payments is included under that paragraph by virtue of paragraph 7(2) below and, if so, the amount so included;
(*c*) whether any estimated amount of advance corporation tax is included under paragraph (*c*) of sub-paragraph (1) above by virtue of paragraph 7(2) below and, if so, the amount so included."

GENERAL NOTE

This paragraph inserts TA 1988 new Sch 13 para 2(*b*), (*c*). Further information to be shown on an ACT return is the amount (if any) of estimated franked payments included and the amount (if any) of the estimated amount of ACT included by virtue of TA 1988 new Sch 13 para 7(2) (see para 7 below).

3 In paragraph 3(3) (power of the inspector to make an assessment in certain cases)—

(*a*) for "the inspector", where first occurring, there shall be substituted "an officer of the Board"; and
(*b*) for "or if the inspector is dissatisfied with any return, he may" there shall be substituted "or if an officer of the Board is of the opinion that a return is incorrect, any such officer may".

4 (1) In sub-paragraph (1) of paragraph 3B (power of the inspector to make an assessment where he is not satisfied that there is a reasonable basis for the company treating itself as an international headquarters company)—

(*a*) for "the inspector is not satisfied that there was a reasonable basis" there shall be substituted "an officer of the Board is of the opinion that there was not a reasonable basis"; and
(*b*) for "he may" there shall be substituted "any such officer may".

(2) In sub-paragraph (3) of that paragraph for "the inspector" there shall be substituted "an officer of the Board".

5 In paragraph 5 (certain deemed claims for set-off in respect of franked investment income to be supported by such evidence as the inspector may reasonably require) for "the inspector" there shall be substituted "an officer of the Board".

6 In paragraph 6A(1) (certain deemed claims for set-off in respect of foreign income dividends to be supported by such evidence as the inspector may reasonably require) for "the inspector" there shall be substituted "an officer of the Board".

7 (1) Paragraph 7 (special provision for qualifying distributions which are not payments and payments whose nature is not clear) shall be amended as follows.

(2) For sub-paragraph (2) (no amount to be shown under paragraph 2(1)(a) or (c) in respect of those qualifying distributions or payments) there shall be substituted—

"(2) No amount is required to be shown under paragraph 2(1)(a) or (c) above in respect of the qualifying distribution or payment and, unless estimated amounts are shown by virtue of paragraph (a) below, paragraph 3(1) above shall not apply in relation to advance corporation tax in respect thereof; but—

(a) the company making the return may include under paragraph 2(1)(a) and (c) above estimated amounts in respect of the qualifying distribution or payment; and
(b) if it does so, paragraph 3(1) above shall apply in relation to advance corporation tax in respect thereof as it applies in relation to advance corporation tax in respect of franked payments which are required to be included in the return."

(3) In sub-paragraph (3) (particulars of the qualifying distribution or payment to be given separately in the return) at the beginning there shall be inserted "Whether or not estimated amounts are also included under paragraph 2(1)(a) or (c) above in respect of the qualifying distribution or payment,".

(4) For sub-paragraph (4) (assessment of advance corporation tax) there shall be substituted—

"(3A) Sub-paragraph (4) below applies—

(a) if an estimated amount is not included under paragraph 2(1)(a) or (c) above in respect of the qualifying distribution or payment; or
(b) if an officer of the Board is of the opinion that an estimated amount which is included under paragraph 2(1)(a) or (c) above in respect of the qualifying distribution or payment is incorrect.

(4) Where this sub-paragraph applies, any advance corporation tax payable in respect of the qualifying distribution or payment shall be assessed on the company and shall be so assessed without regard to any franked investment income received by the company, but—

(a) relief shall be given in accordance with sub-paragraph (4A) or (4B) below;
(b) for the purposes of the application of paragraph 2(3) above to any subsequent return period, the amount of the franked payment comprising the qualifying distribution or payment shall be taken to be the amount calculated as mentioned in sub-paragraph (4A) or (4B) below, as the case may be; and
(c) any advance corporation tax due under an assessment made by virtue of this sub-paragraph shall be treated for the purposes of interest on unpaid tax as having been payable at the time when it would have been payable if correct amounts had been included under paragraph 2(1)(a) and (c) above in respect of the qualifying distribution or payment.

(4A) Where sub-paragraph (4) above applies by virtue of sub-paragraph (3A)(a) above, relief shall be given from the tax assessed (by discharge thereof) to the extent, if any, to which that tax exceeds the tax that would have been payable if the amount of the franked payment comprising the qualifying distribution or payment, calculated on the amount or value thereof shown in the assessment, had been included in the return under sub-paragraph (1)(a) of paragraph 2 above and the tax had been calculated in accordance with sub-paragraph (4) of that paragraph.

(4B) Where sub-paragraph (4) above applies by virtue of sub-paragraph (3A)(b) above, relief shall be given from the tax assessed (by discharge thereof) to the extent, if any, to which that tax exceeds the tax that would have been payable if the excess (if any) of—

(a) the amount of the franked payment comprising the qualifying distribution or payment, calculated on the amount or value thereof shown in the assessment, over (*b*) the estimated amount specified under paragraph 2(2)(*b*) above in respect of that franked payment,

had been included in the return under sub-paragraph (1)(*a*) of paragraph 2 above and the tax had been calculated in accordance with sub-paragraph (4) of that paragraph."

GENERAL NOTE
This paragraph amends TA 1988 Sch 13 para 7, which deals with qualifying distributions which are not payments and payments whose nature is not clear.

Schedule 13 para 7(2) as amended provides that the company may include estimated amounts in respect of such items in the return and pay the appropriate amount of ACT. It is, however, under no obligation to do so.

It should be noted that under TA 1988 Sch 13 para 7(3) as inserted by Sch 23 para 7(3) of the Act even if the company chooses to pay an estimated amount of ACT with the quarterly return in respect of a distribution, it is still under an obligation to make a separate disclosure of that distribution on the appropriate section of the CT 61.

Schedule 13 para 7(3) requires particulars of such payments to be given separately in the ACT return whether or not estimated amounts have been included.

New Sch 13 paras 3A, 4, 4A and 4B apply where no estimated amounts in respect of such payments are included in the main part of the CT 61 or where a Revenue officer is not satisfied with such estimate. Any ACT due in respect of the payment is assessed on the company without regard to franked investment income received, but the amount of tax payable is reduced to what it would have been if the payment had been included in the main part of the return. Interest on unpaid tax is payable as if the ACT on these payments had been due in the main part of the return. This is a charge from the current position, where interest runs only from 14 days after the issue of an assessment (Sch 13 para 10(2)). In calculating the ACT liability for a subsequent period, any surplus franked investment income forward is reduced by any deduction for franked investment income in the calculation of the assessment on the payments described above.

8 After paragraph 7 there shall be inserted—

"Amended return where company becomes aware of an error

7A (1) If a company becomes aware—

(*a*) that anything which ought to have been included in a return made by it under this Schedule for any return period has not been so included,
(*b*) that anything which ought not to have been included in a return made by it under this Schedule for any return period has been so included,
(*c*) that an estimated amount included by virtue of paragraph 7(2)(*a*) above in a return under this Schedule for any period is incorrect, or
(*d*) that any other error has occurred in a return made by it under this Schedule for any return period,

it shall forthwith supply to the collector an amended return for that return period.

(2) The duty imposed by sub-paragraph (1) above is without prejudice to any duty that may also arise under paragraph 7A of Schedule 16.

(3) Where an amended return is supplied under this paragraph, all such assessments, adjustments, set-offs or payments or repayments of tax shall be made as may be required for securing that the resulting liabilities to tax (including interest on unpaid or overpaid tax) whether of the company or any other person are the same as they would have been if a correct return had been made."

GENERAL NOTE
At present there are no specific rules to deal with the situation where a company becomes aware that there is an error in a CT 61.

This paragraph inserts TA 1988 new Sch 13 para 7A introducing a new reporting requirement. This requires a company to supply the collector with an amended ACT return "forthwith" (this term is not specifically defined) if the company becomes aware of—

(*a*) any ommission from the original return;
(*b*) the inclusion of anything which should not have been included;
(*c*) an incorrect estimate of the special payments described in para 7; or
(*d*) any other error in the return.

A similar requirement applies to a return under TA 1988 Sch 16 (see para 12 below).

Where an amended return is supplied, all necessary adjustments are to be made by way of assessment, adjustment, set-off, payments or repayments of tax to ensure tha the amount payable (including interest on paid or overpaid tax) is what it would have been if the original return had been correct.

9 In paragraph 8 (power of inspector to make assessments etc where items are included in returns under the Schedule in error) for "the inspector" there shall be substituted "an officer of the Board".

PART II
SCHEDULE 16 TO THE TAXES ACT 1988

10 Schedule 16 to the Taxes Act 1988 (collection of income tax on company payments which are not distributions) shall be amended in accordance with the following provisions of this Part of this Schedule.

11 In paragraph 4(2) (cases where the inspector may make an assessment)—

(*a*) for "the inspector", where first occurring, there shall be substituted "an officer of the Board"; and

(*b*) for "or if the inspector is dissatisfied with any return, he may" there shall be substituted "or if an officer of the Board is of the opinion that a return is incorrect, any such officer may".

12 After paragraph 7 there shall be inserted—

"Amended return where company becomes aware of an error

7A (1) If a company becomes aware—

(*a*) that anything which ought to have been included in a return made by it under this Schedule for any period has not been so included,

(*b*) that anything which ought not to have been included in a return made by it under this Schedule for any period has been so included, or

(*c*) that any other error has occurred in a return made by it under this Schedule for any period,

it shall forthwith supply to the collector an amended return for that period.

(2) The duty imposed by sub-paragraph (1) above is without prejudice to any duty that may also arise under paragraph 7A of Schedule 13.

(3) Where an amended return is supplied under this paragraph, all such assessments, adjustments, set-offs or payments or repayments of tax shall be made as may be required for securing that the resulting liabilities to tax (including interest on unpaid or overpaid tax) whether of the company or any other person are the same as they would have been if a correct return had been made."

GENERAL NOTE
This paragraph inserts TA 1988 new Sch 16 para 7A, which requires a company to supply the collector with an amended Sch 16 return "forthwith" (again this is not specifically defined) if the company becomes aware of—

(*a*) any omission from the original return;

(*b*) the inclusion of anything which should not have been included; or

(*c*) any other error in the return.

Where an amended return is supplied, all necessary adjustments are to be made by way of assessment, adjustment, set-off, payments or repayments of tax to ensure that the amount payable (including interest on paid or overpaid tax) is what it would have been if the original return had been correct.

13 In paragraph 8 (power of inspector to make assessments etc where items are included in returns under the Schedule in error) for "the inspector" there shall be substituted "an officer of the Board".

SCHEDULE 24   Section 138

SELF-ASSESSMENT: ACCOUNTING PERIODS ETC

INTRODUCTION

Although TA 1988 s 12 gives detailed rules to determine when a company's corporation tax accounting period begins and ends, there are nonetheless occasions when there is uncertainty about the precise commencement and cessation of an accounting period. It may be because of geniune technical difficulties (for instance, a dispute over when the date on which a trade commenced), but it will often be because a company has not supplied any information to allow an inspector to form a judgement.

There is already a provision in TA 1988 s 12(8) for the inspector to make an assessment for the period which he thinks is the accounting period and for that assessment to stand as an assessment for the true accounting period if the latter is subsequently established. This legislation has recently been tested in *Kelsey v Stipplechoice Ltd* [1995] STC 681, where the Revenue were defeated in an attempt to change the accounting period to which an assessment related. Given that accounting periods are fundamental to the operation of corporation tax and to returns under Pay and File, which will (from the appointed day) have to include self-assessments, it is clearly important—at least from the Revenue's point of view—that the operation of the law in this area should be clarified. Some procedural changes were almost certainly necessary in any case because of the way that self-assessment operates, but *Stipplechoice* must have given the matter a higher priority.

First (adopting the approach taken by the Chancellor in his Budget speech), it should be made clear what has not changed. There is no alteration to the rules which define the start and finish of an accounting period. This is still governed by s 12.

What has been clarified is the Revenue's enquiry and amendment powers where there is a dispute over the true accounting period.

PART I

AMENDMENTS OF THE TAXES MANAGEMENT ACT 1970

Introductory

1   The Taxes Management Act 1970 shall be amended in accordance with this Part of this Schedule.

2   In section 11 (return of profits), after subsection (9) there shall be inserted the following subsection—

"(10) In the following provisions of this Act 'section 11 notice' means a notice under this section."

Power to enquire into return for wrong period, etc

3   In section 11AA (return of profits to include self-assessment), after subsection (4) there shall be inserted the following subsections—

"(5) This section, except subsection (4) above, applies in relation to a return for a period—

(*a*) which ends in or at the end of the period specified in the section 11 notice;
(*b*) which in the return is treated as an accounting period; but
(*c*) which is not, or may not be, an accounting period.

(6) In relation to such a return, 'the filing date' means, in this section and section 11AB of this Act, the day which would be the day mentioned in section 11(4) of this Act if the period for which the return is made were an accounting period."

GENERAL NOTE

Under self-assessment the Revenue must give formal notice of their intention to enquire into a return. Under the original rule in TMA 1970 s 11AB(1) the enquiry was limited to the basis on which the return or amended return was made. This paragraph inserts TMA 1970 new s 11AA(5), (6), which allows for an enquiry where a company makes a self-assessment for a period—

(*a*) which ends in or at the end of the period specified in the notice requiring the return;
(*b*) which is treated as an accounting period; but
(*c*) which is not, or may not be, an accounting period.

The filing date is fixed by reference to the end of the period for which the return is made as though that was an accounting period.

4 (1) In section 11AB(1) (power to enquire into return of profits), after paragraph (*c*) (which is inserted by paragraph 2 of Schedule 19 to this Act), there shall be inserted "or

(*d*) if it appears to the officer that a return delivered in response to a section 11 notice—

(i) is or may be a return for the wrong period, or
(ii) has become a return for the wrong period as a result of a direction under section 12(5A) of the principal Act,

the period for which the return should have been made,".

(2) After subsection (3) of that section there shall be inserted the following subsections—

"(4) For the purposes of subsection (1)(*d*) above a return is a return for the wrong period in each of the cases set out below.

(5) The first case is where—

(*a*) the return is made for a period which ends in or at the end of the period specified in the section 11 notice and which in the return is treated as an accounting period; but
(*b*) the period for which the return is made is not an accounting period of the company.

(6) The second case is where—

(*a*) the return is made for a part of the period specified in the section 11 notice which in the return is treated as not falling within an accounting period of the company; but
(*b*) there is an accounting period ending in or at the end of the period specified in the section 11 notice."

GENERAL NOTE
This paragraph inserts TMA 1970 new s 11AB(1)(*d*), (4)–(6). It defines a return for a wrong period as—

(*a*) one described in para 3 above; or
(*b*) one made for part of the period specified in the notice, which in the return is treated as not falling within an accounting period, but where there is an accounting period ending in (or at the end of) the period specified in the notice.

Where a return has been made for a wrong period, a Revenue officer may make enquiries into the period for which the return should have been made.

5 In section 19A(1) (cases where officer has power to call for documents), after paragraph (*c*) (which is inserted by paragraph 2 of Schedule 19 to this Act) there shall be inserted "or

(*d*) the period for which a return should have been made."

GENERAL NOTE
This paragraph inserts TMA 1970 new s 19A(1)(*d*) which allows a Revenue officer to call for documents to assist him in his enquiries into the correctness of the period for which the return is made.

Amendment of return for wrong period

6 After section 28A there shall be inserted the following sections—

"28AA   Amendment of return of profits made for wrong period

(1) Where an officer of the Board gives notice under section 11AB(1) of this Act to a company of his intention to enquire into the period for which a return should have been made, the officer's enquiries shall be treated as completed at such time as he by notice—

(*a*) informs the company that he has completed his enquiries; and
(*b*) states his conclusions on the subject of his enquiries.

(2) Subsections (3) and (4) below apply where the officer in the conclusions stated under subsection (1) above designates a period, in accordance with subsections (6) to (8) below, as the accounting period for which the return should have been made.

(3) At any time in the period of 30 days beginning with the day on which the officer's enquiries are completed, the company may amend the return for the purpose of making it a return appropriate to the designated period.

(4) At any time in the period of 30 days beginning immediately after the period mentioned in subsection (3) above, the officer may by notice to the company amend the return for the purpose of making it a return appropriate to the designated period.

(5) The power under subsections (3) and (4) above to amend a return includes the power to amend a self-assessment so as to make clear that it is a self-assessment for the designated period.

(6) If there is only one accounting period ending in or at the end of the period specified in the section 11 notice, the only period which the officer may designate is that period.

(7) If there is more than one accounting period ending in or at the end of the period specified in the section 11 notice, the only period which the officer may designate is the earliest of those accounting periods for which no return has been delivered.

(8) In designating a period, the officer must specify the dates on which the period begins and ends.

28AB   Provisions supplementary to section 28AA

(1) On an application made by the company, the Commissioners shall direct the officer to give a notice under section 28AA(1) of this Act within a period specified in the direction, unless they are satisfied that the officer has reasonable grounds for not giving such a notice.

(2) Proceedings under subsection (1) above shall be heard and determined in the same way as an appeal.

(3) An appeal may be brought against an amendment made under section 28AA(4) of this Act within the period of 30 days beginning with the date on which the notice of the amendment was issued.

(4) The provisions of this Act relating to appeals shall have effect in relation to an appeal under subsection (3) above as they have effect in relation to an appeal against an assessment to tax.

(5) Subsection (6) below applies where—

(*a*) a return is delivered in response to a section 11 notice;
(*b*) following a statement of conclusions under section 28AA of this Act, a period is finally determined to be the accounting period for which the return should have been made;
(*c*) the effect of the determination is that there is a period ('a further period') which—

(i) before the determination was not an accounting period ending in or at the end of the period specified in the section 11 notice, and
(ii) as a result of the determination, becomes a period so ending;

and

(*d*) there is no return which can be amended under section 28AA of this Act so as to become a return for that further period.

(6) Where this subsection applies, the section 11 notice shall be taken to require a return for the further period before the postponed final day.

(7) The postponed final day is whichever is the later of—

(*a*) the final day determined under section 11(4) of this Act; and (*b*) the last day of the period of 30 days beginning with the day on which the accounting period for the return mentioned in subsection (5)(*a*) above is finally determined.

(8) In relation to any return for the further period the provisions of this Act shall have effect as if any reference to the filing date in relation to that return were a reference to the postponed final day.''

GENERAL NOTE
Under self-assessment an enquiry into a return has to be formally opened and closed. An enquiry is ended when the officer informs the company of that fact and makes a statement of his conclusions (TMA 1970 s 28A).

This paragraph inserts TMA 1970 new ss 28AA (amendment of return of profits made for wrong period) and 28AB (supplementary provisions) which gives details of how an enquiry into the correctness of the accounting period is to be resolved.

On the completion of an enquiry into a return for a wrong period, the Revenue officer may designate a period as the accounting period for which the return should have been made (s 28A(1), (2)).

The period which may be designated is—

(*a*) if there is only one accounting period ending within the period specified in the notice, that period; or
(*b*) if there is more than one such period, the earliest of them (s 28AA(6), (7)).

The company may, within 30 days of the date of completion of the enquiries, amend the return to make it apply to the designated period; if it does not, the Revenue officer may, within a further 30 days, make that amendment. The power to amend the return in this way includes the power to amend the self-assessment based on it, which amendment must make it clear that it is a self-assessment for the designated period (s 28AA(3)–(5)).

EXAMPLE
Pashley Ltd is a trading company which makes its accounts up to 31 December each year.
A return notice for the 12 months to 31 December 1988 is issued in June 1999. The company submits the return on 1 December 1999 on the basis that there was an accounting period from 1 January 1998 to 31 December 1998.
In March 2000 an officer of the Board takes the view that on 1 July 1998 the company changed its status from a trading company to an investment company, and thus that there were two accounting periods in the 12 months to 31 December 1988—

(*a*) 1.1.1998–30.6.1998;
(*b*) 1.7.1998–31.12.1998.

On 1 April 2000 she therefore issues a notice under s 11AB(1)(d) of her intention to enquire into the period of which the return is made. On 1 December 2000 she informs the company by notice that her enquiries are complete and that her conclusions are that there were indeed two accounting periods in 1998. Under TMA 1970 s 28AA(7) she is able to designate that the return issued in June 1999 is for the accounting period 1 January 1998 to 30 June 1998.
There is now no proper return for the accounting period 1 July 1998 to 31 December 1998. Under TMA 1970 s 28AB(5) the company is required to make a return for that period (no new s 11 notice has to be issued). This return has to be made by 1 May 2000.

The company has the same right to seek an early determination of the designated period as in the case of other enquiries into a return, the proceedings to be heard in the same way as an appeal (s 28AB(1), (2)). There is also a right to appeal against a determination by a Revenue officer of a designated period, which is dealt with in the same way as an appeal against an assessment (s 28AB(3), (4)).

The determination of the correct accounting period may have the consequence that there is a further period within the period specified in the original notice which becomes an accounting period; there will be no return which can be amended in respect of it. In that situation, the original notice is treated as requiring a return for the further period. The further return has to be delivered before the later of—

(*a*) the original date for compliance with the notice; or
(*b*) 30 days after the determination of the designated period.

That date will become the filing date for the further return (s 28AB(5)–(8)).

Failure to deliver return: determinations

7   After section 28C there shall be inserted the following sections—

"28D Determination of corporation tax where no return delivered

(1) Where—

(*a*) a section 11 notice has been served on a company, and
(*b*) no return is delivered to an officer of the Board in response to the notice before the relevant day,

the officer may make a determination of the amounts in which, to the best of his information and belief, the company is chargeable to corporation tax for the relevant period.

(2) In subsection (1) above 'the relevant period' means—

(*a*) if there is only one accounting period ending in or at the end of the period specified in the section 11 notice, that accounting period;
(*b*) if there is more than one accounting period ending in or at the end of the period so specified, each of those accounting periods;
(*c*) if the officer has insufficient information to identify the accounting periods of the company, such period or periods ending in or at the end of the period so specified as he may determine.

(3) Subject to subsections (4) and (5) below, a determination under subsection (1) above shall have effect for the purposes of Parts VA, VI, IX and XI of this Act as if—

(*a*) it were a self-assessment made under section 11AA of this Act; and
(*b*) (where subsection (2)(*c*) above applies) the period for which the determination is made were an accounting period of the company.

(4) If—

(*a*) the company delivers a return for a period ending in or at the end of the period specified in the section 11 notice,
(*b*) the period is, or is treated in the return as, an accounting period, and
(*c*) the return includes a self-assessment under section 11AA of this Act,

the self-assessment shall supersede the determination under subsection (1) above or, if there is more than one determination under that subsection, the determination for the period which is, or most closely approximates to, the period for which the return is made.

(5) If the company shows—

(*a*) that there is no period ending in or at the end of the period specified in the section 11 notice which is an accounting period of the company, or
(*b*) that it has delivered a return containing a self-assessment for the accounting period, or each accounting period, ending in or at the end of the period specified in the section 11 notice,

any determination under subsection (1) above shall be of no effect.

28E Determination of corporation tax where notice complied with in part

(1) Where—

(*a*) a company delivers a return for an accounting period ending in or at the end of the period specified in a section 11 notice served on the company, but
(*b*) there is another period so ending (an 'outstanding period') which it appears to an officer of the Board is or may be an accounting period but for which no return has been delivered before the relevant day,

the officer may make a determination of the amounts in which, to the best of his information and belief, the company is chargeable to corporation tax for the outstanding period.

(2) Subject to subsections (3) and (4) below, a determination under subsection (1) above shall have effect for the purposes of Parts VA, VI, IX and XI of this Act as if—

(*a*) it were a self-assessment made under section 11AA of this Act; and

(b) where the officer has insufficient information to determine whether the outstanding period is an accounting period, the period for which the determination is made were an accounting period of the company.

(3) If, after the determination is made—

(a) the company delivers a further return for a period ending in or at the end of the period specified in the section 11 notice,

(b) the period is, or is treated in the return as, an accounting period, and

(c) the return includes a self-assessment under section 11AA of this Act,

the self-assessment shall supersede the determination under subsection (1) above.

(4) If the company shows that it has delivered a return containing a self-assessment for the accounting period, or each accounting period, ending in or at the end of the period specified in the section 11 notice, the determination under subsection (1) above shall be of no effect.

28F Corporation tax determinations: supplementary

(1) Notice of any determination under section 28D or 28E of this Act shall be served on the person in respect of whom it is made and shall state the date on which it is issued.

(2) No determination may be made under section 28D or 28E of this Act after the end of the period of five years beginning with the relevant day.

(3) A self-assessment shall not supersede a determination under section 28D or 28E of this Act if it is made after whichever is the later of—

(a) the end of the period of five years beginning with the relevant day; and

(b) the end of the period of twelve months beginning with the date of the determination.

(4) Where—

(a) an officer of the Board has commenced any proceedings for the recovery of any tax charged by a determination under section 28D or 28E of this Act, and

(b) before those proceedings are concluded, the determination is superseded by a self-assessment,

those proceedings may be continued as if they were proceedings for the recovery of so much of the tax charged by the self-assessment as is due and payable and has not been paid.

(5) In sections 28D and 28E of this Act and this section 'the relevant day' means, in relation to a section 11 notice—

(a) if the final day for the delivery of any return required by the notice can be ascertained in accordance with section 11(4) of this Act, that day;

(b) in any other case, the day determined in accordance with subsection (6) below.

(6) The day is whichever is the later of—

(a) the last day of the period of 30 months from the end of the period specified in the section 11 notice; and

(b) the last day of the period of three months from the day on which the section 11 notice was served."

GENERAL NOTE
Under self-assessment, the Revenue have powers to issue a determination of the amount of tax payable where a company has failed to make a return. Unless superseded by a "real" self-assessment made by the taxpayer, this determination is treated as his self-assessment.

The rules in TMA 1970 s 28C, which introduced this concept, already refer to companies as well as to individuals, but they have been extended in Sch 24 para 7 of the Act in order to ensure (to quote the Treasury background notes issued with the Act) "that the rules under the self-assessment system for determination of tax where no return is made will operate properly for companies".

The legislation has been strengthened to cover the situation where there may be more than one accounting period in the return period or where there is uncertainty about the dates of the accounting period(s).

This paragraph inserts TMA 1970 new ss 28D–28F.

Where, following the issue of a notice, a company fails to deliver a return within the time stipulated, the Revenue officer may determine the amount for which the company is chargeable to corporation tax (s 28D(1)). If there is only one accounting period ending within the period specified in the notice, the determination will relate to that period. If there is more than one accounting period ending within the period specified in the notice, the determination will relate to each of them. If the officer has insufficient information about the accounting periods, he may determine the amount for any period or periods ending within the period specified in the notice (s 28D(2)). Such a determination has effect as if it were a self-assessment for the purposes of appeals, payment of tax, interest and penalties (s 28D(3)).

If a company delivers a return, including a self-assessment, for a period ending within the period specified in the notice which is treated in the return as an accounting period, that self-assessment supersedes any determination under s 28D(1) (s 28D(4)). Such a determination has no effect if the company shows—

(*a*) that there is no accounting period ending within the period specified in the notice; or
(*b*) that it has delivered a return and self-assessment for each accounting period ending within the period specified in the notice (s 28D(5)).

EXAMPLE

Hallett Ltd is an investment company which makes its accounts up to 30 April each year.

On 1 September 1998 it is issued with a TMA 1970 s 11 notice requiring it to make a return for the year to 30 April 1998. This return should have been made by 30 April 1999, but no return was made and so the officer makes a determination on 1 July 1999 for the accounting period 1 May 1997 to 30 April 1998.

This determination prompts Hallet Ltd into action, and on 1 September 1999 it submits a return in response to the original s 11 notice. This reveals that the company disposed of its final investments on 31 January 1998, since when it has been dormant and thus not within the charge to corporation tax. Hallett Ltd's self-assessment under the return is therefore for the accounting period 1 May 1997 to 31 January 1998. There is no other accounting period in the period covered by the return. The officer does not enquire into his self-assessment.

Hallett Ltd's self-assessment for the accounting period 15 May 1997 to 31 January 1998 will supersede the officer's determination for the 12 months to 30 April 1988.

Where the company delivers a return for an accounting period ending within the period specified in the notice, but which does not cover the whole of that period, and a Revenue officer considers that the missing period may be an accounting period, he may make a determination of his estimate of the corporation tax liability for the missing period (s 28E(1)). Such a determination has effect as a self-assessment for that period (s 28F(2)). If, after the determination has been made, the company delivers a return and self-assessment covering the missing period, that return supersedes the determination (s 28E(3)). Similarly, the determination will have no effect if the company can show that it has already delivered a return and self-assessment for all accounting periods ending in the period specified in the notice (s 28E(4)).

EXAMPLE

King Ltd is a trading company which makes up its accounts to 31 March each year. On 1 September 1998 it is issued with a return for the period 1 April 1997 to 31 March 1998. It makes a return on 1 February 1999. This is prepared on the basis that the company ceased trading on 30 June 1997 and was dormant until it commenced a new trade in May 1998. (It prepared accounts to 31 March 1998.)

The officer dealing with the case forms the view that the trade in fact commenced on 1 March 1998 and that there is a one-month accounting period from 1 March 1998 to 31 March 1998. As no return has been made for this period he issues a determination for that period.

The officer eventually accepts the view that the new trade did not commence until May 1998. The determination for 1 March 1998 to 31 March 1998 is therefore deemed to be of no effect.

Notice of any determination under these provisions must be served on the company (s 28F(1)). A determination must be made within five years of the relevant day (see below) (s 28F(2)). A self-assessment will not supersede a determination unless it is made within five years from the relevant day or 12 months from the date of the determination, whichever is the later (s 28F(3)). Where, after proceedings for collection of tax charged by a determination have been commenced, the determination is superseded by a self-assessment, the proceedings may be continued to collect any amount unpaid on the self-assessment (s 28F(4)).

The relevant day means, in relation to a notice, the final day for delivery of any return required by the notice if it can be ascertained under TMA 1970 s 11(4). If it cannot be so determined, it is the later of—

(*a*) 30 months from the end of the period specified in the notice; or
(*b*) three months from the date of issue of the notice (s 28F(5)).

Commencement

8 (1) Paragraphs 3 to 6 above have effect in relation to returns made for periods ending on or after the day appointed under section 199 of the Finance Act 1994 for the purposes of Chapter III of Part IV of that Act (self-assessment).

(2) Paragraph 7 above has effect in relation to notices under section 11 of the Taxes Management Act 1970 specifying a period ending on or after the day so appointed.

GENERAL NOTE
    Paragraphs 3–6 have effect from the day appointed for the commencement of self-assessment. Paragraph 7 has effect for notices specifying a period ending after that day.

PART II
OTHER AMENDMENTS

General

9 In this Part of this Schedule "the appointed day" means the day appointed as mentioned in paragraph 8(1) above.

GENERAL NOTE
    This paragraph defines the appointed day for the purposes of paras 11–12 as that described in para 8.

Repeal of section 8A of the Taxes Act 1988

10 Section 8A of the Taxes Act 1988 (resolutions to reduce corporation tax) shall cease to have effect.

GENERAL NOTE
    When self-assessment is introduced, TA 1988 s 8A, which effectively brought the principle of the Provision Collection of Taxes Act 1968 into the administration of corporation tax, will be abolished (FA 1996 Sch 24 para 10). The connection is not immediately obvious. The reason appears to be that as s 8A is couched in terms of the making of assessments by the Revenue it will become obsolete once the responsibility of making assessments passes to a taxpayer company.

Determination of accounting date

11 (1) Section 12 of the Taxes Act 1988 (basis of, and periods for, assessment) shall be amended as follows.

(2) In subsection (5)—

(*a*) at the beginning there shall be inserted "Subject to subsection (5A) below"; and
(*b*) for the words "as the Board may determine" there shall be substituted "as the company may determine".

(3) After subsection (5) there shall be inserted the following subsection—

"(5A) If the Board is of the opinion, on reasonable grounds, that a date determined by a company for the purposes of subsection (5) above is inappropriate, they may by notice direct that the accounting date of such other of the trades referred to in that subsection as appears to them to be appropriate shall be used instead."

(4) This paragraph has effect where each of the different dates referred to in section 12(5) of the Taxes Act 1988 occurs on or after the appointed day.

GENERAL NOTE
    Where a company carries on more than one trade and makes up accounts for any of them to different dates, TA 1988 s 12(5) provided that the Revenue could determine the company's accounting date for corporation tax purposes. This paragraph amends that provision to allow the company to determine its accounting date (sub-para (1)). It also inserts TA 1988 new s 12(5A), which allows the Revenue to amend (by direction in a notice) the date chosen by the company if they consider, on reasonable grounds, that the date chosen by the company is inappropriate. The change applies where all the dates fall after the appointed day.

Companies in liquidation

12 (1) Section 342 of the Taxes Act 1988 (companies in liquidation) shall be amended as follows.

(2) In subsection (5) (assumption as to commencement date of final accounting period where company being wound up), for the words "the inspector may, with the concurrence of the liquidator" there shall be substituted "the liquidator may".

(3) In subsection (6) for the words from "as if" to the end there shall be substituted "as if the winding-up had commenced with the beginning of that new accounting period".

(4) This paragraph has effect in relation to the winding up of a company if the date on which the affairs of the company are completely wound up does not occur before the appointed day.

GENERAL NOTE

A similar charge is made in relation to companies in liquidation. TA 1988 s 342(5) provided that the inspector could make an assumption as to the date when the winding up would be completed. Subparagraph (2) allows the liquidator to make this assumption without reference to the Revenue. Subparagraph (3) amends TA 1988 s 342(6), and provides that where the actual date of completion is later than that assumed, a new accounting period will begin on the day following the assumed date and will end on the actual date of completion.

These changes apply only where the completion of the winding up occurs after the appointed day (sub-para (4)).

Construction of references to assessments

13 In section 197(1) of the Finance Act 1994 (construction of certain references), in paragraph (*b*) after "28C" there shall be inserted ", 28D or 28E".

GENERAL NOTE

TA 1988 s 197(1) provides that a reference to a person being assessed or charged to tax by an assessment includes a determination under TMA s 28C. This paragraph extends that reference to a determination under TMA 1970 ss 28D and 28E (see para 7 above).

SCHEDULE 25

SELF-ASSESSMENT: SURRENDERS OF ADVANCE CORPORATION TAX

INTRODUCTION

This Schedule contains a comprehensive code for the surrender to a subsidiary company of surplus ACT. The putting in of a proper procedure for the withdrawal of claims is to be welcomed, although this will almost certainly have the effect that the informal arrangements under which many large groups currently operate will have to be revised to a statutory, and perhaps less flexible, basis.

Amendments of section 240 of the Taxes Act 1988

1 (1) Section 240 of the Taxes Act 1988 (set-off of company's advance corporation tax against subsidiary's liability to corporation tax) shall be amended as follows.

(2) For subsection (1) there shall be substituted the following subsections–

"(1) Where a company ('the surrendering company') has paid an amount of advance corporation tax in respect of a dividend or dividends paid by it in an accounting period, it may under this section surrender the benefit of so much of that amount as is available for surrender, or any part of that amount that is available for surrender, to any company which was a subsidiary of it throughout that accounting period.

(1A) The surrender shall take effect on the surrendering company making a claim in accordance with Schedule 13A.

(1B) A claim to surrender an amount exceeding the amount the benefit of which, at the time the claim is made, is available for surrender shall be of no effect."

(3) For subsections (6) and (7) there shall be substituted the following subsections—

"(5A) A claim under subsection (1A) above may be withdrawn by the surrendering company with the consent of the subsidiary to whom the surrender was made.

(5B) The withdrawal of a claim under subsection (1A) above to make a surrender for an accounting period of the surrendering company shall not prevent the making of a further claim under that subsection for that accounting period (whether to the same or a different subsidiary).

(5C) Where the surrendering company withdraws a claim by virtue of which an amount of advance corporation tax was treated under subsection (2) above as paid by its subsidiary in respect of a distribution made on a date determined under that subsection—

(*a*) the subsidiary shall be treated as if it had not paid that amount in respect of a distribution made by it on the date so determined; and

(*b*) subject to the effect of any further claim, the surrendering company shall be treated as having paid a corresponding amount of advance corporation tax in respect of a distribution made by it on the date so determined.

(5D) The amount of advance corporation tax the benefit of which is at any time available for surrender is the amount referred to in subsection (1) above less any amount which at that time falls within subsection (5E) below.

(5E) The amounts are—

(*a*) any amount which has been repaid to the surrendering company;

(*b*) any amount which has been dealt with under section 239(3);

(*c*) any amount surrendered under a claim for that period which has not been withdrawn.

(5F) Subject to subsection (5C)(*b*) above, no amount of advance corporation tax the benefit of which has been surrendered under this section shall be treated for the purposes of section 239 as advance corporation tax paid by the surrendering company."

(4) After subsection (13) there shall be inserted the following subsection—

"(14) Schedule 13A (which makes supplementary provision with respect to surrenders of advance corporation tax) shall have effect."

GENERAL NOTE

Subparagraph (2) amends TA 1988 s 240(1) and inserts TA 1988 new s 240(1A), (1B). A company which has paid ACT in respect of dividends paid in an accounting period may surrender the benefit of all or part of such ACT which is available for surrender (see below) to any company which was a subsidiary throughout that accounting period. The procedure for making a claim to surrender is set out in new TA 1988 Sch 13A (see para 2 below). A claim to surrender more than the amount available will be of no effect. Concern was expressed that the effect of this provision would be to invalidate the whole of the claim, not just the surrender of the excess. However, during the course of the Committee State the Financial Secretary to the Treasury clarified that only the excess element would be invalidated (HC Official Report, Standing Committee E (Finance Bill), 20 February 1996, cols 434, 435).

Subparagraph (3) repeals TA 1988 s 240(6), (7) which is superseded by TA 1988 new Sch 13A. It also inserts TA 1988 new s 240(5A)–(5F).

New sub-s (5A) provides that a claim may be withdrawn with the consent of the subsidiary concerned.

New sub-s (5B) provides that such a withdrawal does not prevent a further claim for surrender for the same accounting period, to the same or a different subsidiary.

New sub-s (5C) provides that, where a claim is withdrawn, both the surrendering company and the subsidiary are treated as regards ACT as though the claim had never been made.

New sub-s (5D) and new sub-s (5E) define the amount of ACT available for surrender; it is the amount paid in respect of dividends paid in the accounting period, less—

(a) any amount which has been repaid;

(b) any surplus ACT brought forward from an earlier period; and

(c) any amount already surrendered under a claim which has not been withdrawn.

This definition makes no substantive change to the calculation of the amount of ACT which can be surrendered, other than to make specific reference to claims which have been withdrawn.

Subparagraph (4) inserts TA 1988 new s 240(14) which introduces TA 1988 new Sch 13A.

The new Schedule 13A to the Taxes Act 1988

2 After Schedule 13 to the Taxes Act 1988 there shall be inserted the following Schedule—

"SCHEDULE 13A
SURRENDERS OF ADVANCE CORPORATION TAX

General

1 (1) In this Schedule any reference to a claim is to a claim under section 240(1A).

(2) In this Schedule 'the relevant accounting period of the surrendering company' means, in relation to a claim by the surrendering company, the accounting period referred to in section 240(1).

Multiple claims

2 (1) Surrenders to different subsidiaries or to the same subsidiary at different times shall be treated as made by separate claims (however the claims are presented).

(2) Where a surrendering company makes more than one claim at the same time, the claims shall be treated as made in such sequence as the surrendering company at that time elects or as, in default of such an election, an officer of the Board determines.

Content of claims etc

3 (1) A claim must specify—

(a) the amount the benefit of which is surrendered; and

(b) the subsidiary to whom the surrender is made.

(2) The amount specified in compliance with sub-paragraph (1)(a) above must be an amount which is quantified at the time when the claim is made.

Time limit for claims

4 A claim by the surrendering company must be made within the period of six years from the end of the relevant accounting period of the surrendering company.

Claim to be included in return where possible

5 (1) Where a claim could be made by being included in a return under section 11 of the Management Act, or an amendment of such a return, it must be so made.

(2) Section 42 of and Schedule 1A to the Management Act (procedure for making claims) shall not apply to the making of claims.

6 (1) A claim not included in a return or an amendment of a return must be made to an officer of the Board and must be supported by such documents as the officer may require.

(2) The claim shall be made in such form as the Board may determine.

(3) The form of claim shall provide for a declaration to the effect that all the particulars given in the form are correctly stated to the best of the information and belief of the person making the claim.

Contents of notices of withdrawal, etc

7 (1) A claim shall not be withdrawn except by a notice given to an officer of the Board in such form as the Board may determine.

(2) A notice withdrawing a claim must specify—

(*a*) the surrendering company which made the claim;
(*b*) the amount the benefit of which was surrendered under the claim;
(*c*) the subsidiary to whom the surrender was made; and
(*d*) the relevant accounting period of the surrendering company in relation to the claim.

(3) A notice withdrawing a claim must be accompanied by a notice signifying the consent required by section 240(5A).

(4) Where a claim included in a return is withdrawn and the withdrawal could be made by an amendment of the return, it must be so made.

Simultaneous claims and withdrawals of claims

8 Where—

(*a*) a claim ('claim A') is withdrawn, and
(*b*) at the time when claim A is withdrawn, another claim ('claim B') is made,

claim A shall be treated as being withdrawn before claim B is treated as made.

Time limit for withdrawing claims

9 (1) Subject to sub-paragraph (3) below, a claim shall not be withdrawn after the earlier of—

(*a*) the end of the period of six years from the end of the relevant accounting period of the surrendering company; and
(*b*) the date on which an assessment for any relevant accounting period of the subsidiary in whose favour the claim was made becomes final.

(2) In this paragraph 'relevant accounting period of the subsidiary' means, in relation to a claim, any period in which a distribution is treated under section 240(2) as made by virtue of the claim.

(3) In the circumstances given by sub-paragraph (4) below, a claim may be withdrawn at any time before the end of the period of six years from the end of the relevant accounting period of the surrendering company.

(4) The circumstances are that—

(*a*) the claim was made—

(i) after the date on which an assessment for a relevant accounting period of the subsidiary in whose favour the claim is made becomes final; and
(ii) after a further assessment has been made on the subsidiary for that period by an officer of the Board or the Board; and

(*b*) immediately before the claim is withdrawn, none of the advance corporation tax which, by virtue of the claim, is treated as paid by the subsidiary has been finally dealt with to the subsidiary's advantage.

(5) For the purposes of sub-paragraph (4) above, advance corporation tax is finally dealt with to the subsidiary's advantage if—

(*a*) it is set against any liability of the subsidiary under any assessment to corporation tax which has become final; or
(*b*) any of it is repaid to the subsidiary.

No amendment of claims

10   Nothing in the Management Act shall be read as allowing a claim to be amended.

Further self-assessments by the surrendering company

11   (1) Where—

(*a*) a claim is made after an assessment to corporation tax for the relevant accounting period of the surrendering company has become final,
(*b*) under section 239(1), advance corporation tax has been set against the company's liability to corporation tax for that period, and
(*c*) the claim is a claim to surrender the benefit of an amount which is or includes the whole or a part of the amount set-off,

the claim must be accompanied by an assessment (a self-assessment) of the corporation tax due as a result of the claim.

(2) The tax shall be treated as due and payable, in accordance with section 59D of the Management Act, on the day following the expiry of nine months from the end of the relevant accounting period.

(3) The standard provisions about enquiries into self-assessments (given by paragraph 14 below) apply to self-assessments provided under this paragraph.

12   (1) Where—

(*a*) by virtue of section 239(4), advance corporation tax paid in the relevant accounting period of the surrendering company has been set against the company's liability to corporation tax for a later accounting period,
(*b*) the claim is made after assessments to corporation tax for both periods have become final, and
(*c*) the claim is a claim to surrender the benefit of an amount which is or includes the whole or a part of the amount set-off,

the claim must be accompanied by an assessment (a self-assessment) of the corporation tax due as a result of the claim.

(2) The tax shall be treated as due and payable, in accordance with section 59D of the Management Act, on the day following the expiry of nine months from the end of the later accounting period.

(3) The standard provisions about enquiries into self-assessments (given by paragraph 14 below) apply to self-assessments provided under this paragraph.

(4) For the purposes of sub-paragraph (1)(*a*) above, advance corporation tax which was in fact paid in the relevant accounting period of the surrendering company shall be treated as set against the liability of the company to corporation tax for the later accounting period after any other advance corporation tax available to be so treated.

Further self-assessments by subsidiary

13   (1) Sub-paragraph (3) below applies where—

(*a*) under section 239(1), advance corporation tax has been set against the subsidiary's liability to corporation tax for an accounting period ('the relevant accounting period'),

(*b*) the advance corporation tax is, includes or is part of advance corporation tax which is treated as paid by the subsidiary in respect of that period on the assumption that section 240(2) required that treatment, and

(*c*) after an assessment to corporation tax for that period has become final, the subsidiary becomes aware of facts ('the true facts') which, by virtue of section 240(1B), make that treatment incorrect.

(2) Sub-paragraph (3) below also applies where—

(*a*) by virtue of section 239(4), advance corporation tax has been set against the subsidiary's liability to corporation tax for an accounting period ('the relevant accounting period'),

(*b*) the advance corporation tax is, includes or is part of advance corporation tax which is treated as paid by the subsidiary in respect of a previous accounting period on the assumption that section 240(2) required that treatment, and

(*c*) after an assessment to corporation tax for that period has become final, the subsidiary becomes aware of facts ('the true facts') which, by virtue of section 240(1B), make that treatment incorrect.

(3) The subsidiary must, before the end of the period of three months beginning with the day on which it becomes aware of the true facts, provide an officer of the Board with an assessment (a self-assessment) of the amount of corporation tax which was due for the relevant accounting period on the basis of the true facts.

(4) The tax shall be treated as due and payable, in accordance with section 59D of the Management Act, on the day following the expiry of nine months from the end of the relevant accounting period of the subsidiary.

(5) The standard provisions about enquiries into self-assessments (given by paragraph 14 below) apply to self-assessments provided under this paragraph.

(6) For the purposes of this paragraph it shall be assumed that advance corporation tax actually paid (or correctly treated as paid) by the subsidiary has been set against the subsidiary's liability to corporation tax before any advance corporation tax incorrectly treated as paid by the subsidiary.

Standard provisions about enquiries into self-assessments

14 (1) The standard provisions about enquiries into self-assessments (which correspond, in general terms, to certain provisions of section 28A of the Management Act) are as follows.

(2) An officer of the Board may, at any time before the end of the period of one year beginning with the day on which the self-assessment is received, give notice of his intention to enquire into the self-assessment.

(3) The officer's enquiries shall end on such day as he by notice—

(*a*) informs the company that he has completed his enquiries, and

(*b*) states his conclusions as to the amount of tax which should be contained in the company's self-assessment.

(4) At any time in the period of 30 days beginning with the day on which the enquiries end, the company may amend its self-assessment so as to make good any deficiency or eliminate any excess in the amount of tax contained in the self-assessment.

(5) At any time in the period of 30 days beginning immediately after the period mentioned in sub-paragraph (4) above, the officer may by notice to the company amend the company's self-assessment so as to make good any deficiency or eliminate any excess in the amount of tax contained in the self-assessment.

(6) The provisions of the Management Act apply to an amendment of a self-assessment under sub-paragraph (5) above as they apply to an amendment of a self-assessment under section 28A(4) of that Act.

(7) At any time before a notice is given under sub-paragraph (3) above, the company may apply for a direction that the officer shall give such a notice within such period as may be specified in the direction.

(8) Subject to sub-paragraph (9) below, an application under sub-paragraph (7) above shall be heard and determined in the same way as an appeal against an amendment of a self-assessment under section 28A(2) or (4) of the Management Act.

(9) The Commissioners hearing an application under sub-paragraph (7) above shall give the direction applied for unless they are satisfied that the officer has reasonable grounds for not giving the notice.

Repayments

15 (1) Where—

(*a*) a claim is withdrawn after an assessment for the relevant accounting period of the surrendering company has become final, and
(*b*) an amount of corporation tax paid by the surrendering company in respect of that period would not have been payable if the claim had not been made,

the surrendering company shall be entitled by notice to claim repayment of that amount.

(2) Where—

(*a*) a claim is made after the date on which an assessment for any relevant accounting period of the subsidiary in whose favour the claim is made becomes final, and
(*b*) an amount of corporation tax paid by the subsidiary in respect of that period would not have been payable if the claim had not been made,

the subsidiary shall be entitled by notice to claim repayment of that amount.

(3) In this paragraph 'relevant accounting period of the subsidiary' has the same meaning as in paragraph 9.''

GENERAL NOTE
This paragraph inserts new TA 1988 Sch 13A.

TA 1988 Sch 13A para 1
This paragraph defines a claim as a claim under TA 1988 s 240(1A) and the relevant accounting period as the period for which a claim is made.

TA 1988 Sch 13A para 2
This paragraph provides that surrenders to different subsidiaries at different times are treated as separate claims. If more than one claim is made at the same time, the company may elect in what sequence they are to be taken. (TA 1988 s 1A presumably requires separate claims for surrender to more than one subsidiary.) If the company does not specify the sequence, the Revenue will decide. This is an important point. Because claims cannot be varied, only withdrawn, and because the amount of ACT which is available to surrender is deemed after taking account of any earlier claims to surrender to be ACT for that accounting period, claims will be dealt with in the strict order in which they are made. This may mean that if a group gets the sequence of claims wrong it may have no alternative but to withdraw all of the claims and resubmit in the correct order, assuming of course that it is still within the time limit. Under the new regime there will no longer be a requirement for the subsidiary company to consent to receive the ACT.

TA 1988 Sch 13A para 3
This paragraph provides that a claim must specify the amount surrendered (which must be quantified at the time) and the subsidiary to whom the surrender is made. It is significant that the reference is to "quantified" and not "quantifiable". This would appear to rule out any sort of formula claims eg "the maximum amount available under TA 1988 s 240(1) after first giving effect to a surrender to ABC Ltd", although there must be a possibility that the Revenue will issue a statement of practice on this point as they have, for instance, on group relief under Pay and File (SP 10/93).

TA 1988 Sch 13A para 4
This paragraph provides that a claim by the surrendering company must be made within six years from the end of the relevant accounting period.

TA 1988 Sch 13A para 5
This paragraph provides that if a claim could be made in a corporation tax return, or an amendment of such return, it must be so made. TMA s 42 and Sch 1A do not apply.

TA 1988 Sch 13A para 6
This paragraph provides that if a claim not included in a return or an amended return is to be made to a Revenue officer in such form as the Board determine and must be supported by such documents as the officer may require. The form must include a declaration that the particulars are correct to the best of the knowledge and belief of the claimant.

TA 1988 Sch 13A para 7
This paragraph introduces specific provision dealing with withdrawals of claims. A withdrawal must be by way of notice to a Revenue officer in such form as the Board determine, and must specify the surrendering and subsidiary companies, the amount surrendered under the claim and the relevant accounting period of the subsidiary. It must be accompanied by the written consent of the subsidiary. Where the claim was made in a return and the withdrawal could be made in an amended return, it must be so made.

TA 1988 Sch 13A para 8
This paragraph provides that where a one claim is withdrawn and at the same time another claim is made, the withdrawal is treated as made before the new claim is made.

TA 1988 Sch 13A para 9
This paragraph provides that the basic time limit for the withdrawal of a claim is the *earlier* of—

(*a*) six years from the end of the accounting period of the surrendering company in which the ACT was paid; and
(*b*) the date on which an assessment for an accounting period of the subsidiary in which the surrendered ACT is deemed to be paid under TA 1988 s 240(2) becomes final.

Note: The legislation may be ambiguous in that under TA 1988 s 239 ACT carried forward is deemed to be paid in the succeeding accounting period in which it is used. This deeming rule also applies to ACT surrendered to a subsidiary under s 240(2). Thus it is possible to construe the time limit in two ways: either by reference solely to the assessment for the accounting period of the subsidiary in which the ACT is actually surrendered, or to an assessment for any accounting period of the subsidiary in which the surrendered ACT is actually used. Given that the ACT could, at least in theory, be carried forward in the subsidiary almost indefinitely, it would seem that the former interpretation would be favoured by the courts, but it is unsatisfactory to have this ambiguity.
The concept of an assessment becoming final is familiar from the existing system, but under self-assessment it will have a different connotation. Unless the TMA 1970 s 29 (as revised) powers of discovery are invoked, the only assessment which will exist for an accounting period will be a company's own self-assessment. A self-assessment is clearly an assessment for these purposes (TMA 1970 s 11AA).
Such an assessment will become final and conclusive at the later of—

(*a*) the expiry of the time period during which the officer can issue a formal notice of his intention to enquire into the return (which will normally be 12 months after the filing date (TMA 1970 s 11AB); and
(*b*) if the officer issues such a notice, 30 (or in some case 60) days after the officer has given formal notice of the completion of his enquiries into the return (TMA 1970 s 28A).

In order for the extended time limit for a withdrawal of a claim to operate all of the following conditions have to be present—

(*a*) the claim was made after the date on which an assessment for the accounting period of the subsidiary in which the ACT is deemed to be paid became final and conclusive;
(*b*) a further assessment for that accounting period was made by the Revenue;
(*c*) the ACT has neither been set against the corporation tax liability of the subsidiary for any period for which an assessment has become final and conclusive, nor has been repaid to the subsidiary.

It will be readily appreciated that this situation will not arise very often as further assessments will only be issued where the Revenue have made a discovery. In fact the effect of this provision is to give the taxpayer a "second bite at the cherry" in terms of reliefs when the Revenue assesses further tax. To that extent they mirror the extended time limits for claims to relief in TMA 1970 s 36(3) which are allowed when an assessment is raised under the fraudulent and negligent conduct.

TA 1988 Sch 13A para 10
If a company wishes to amend a claim it will have to withdraw the claim and make a new claim, assuming of course that the time limit for making the claim has not expired. This paragraph provides that a claim cannot be amended.

TA 1988 Sch 13A para 12
This paragraph provides that—

(a) where ACT paid in the relevant accounting period of the surrendering company has been set off against its corporation tax liability for a later period;
(b) the corporation tax assessments for both periods have become final; and
(c) a claim is made to surrender all or part of ACT which has been set off.

the claim must be accompanied by a self-assessment of the tax due as a result of withdrawing the set-off of the ACT surrendered in the claim. Such tax is treated as due and payable nine months after the end of the later accounting period. In these circumstances, any ACT paid in the relevant accounting period is treated as set off against the corporation tax liability of the later period after any other ACT available for set-off.

EXAMPLE

Howell Ltd is a trading company which makes up its accounts to 30 September each year. It has a 100% subsidiary Pegg Ltd.

Howell pays a dividend on 1 January 1988 and accounts for ACT of £10,000. In its self-assessment accompanying the return for the year to 30 September 1998 it sets the whole of this ACT against its own corporation tax liability.

Pegg Ltd's self-assessment for 1997–98 shows a nil corporation tax liability. However, the officer raises an enquiry into the return. The outcome of this is that certain items which were treated as repairs are now agreed to be capital. After making the necessary amendments to its self-assessment Pegg Ltd is left with a corporation tax liability of £20,000. Howell Ltd decides to surrender the whole of the ACT paid on 1 January 1998 to Pegg Ltd. The time limit for making the claim is 30 September 2004.

Howell Ltd will have to submit a revised self-assessment with the claim to surrender the ACT and will have to pay the additional tax due arising from the surrender. Interest will run from the normal due date for the 1997–98 liability, ie 30 June 1999. Pegg Ltd will be entitled to claim repayment of the tax which will arise as a result of the ACT set-off: this will attract repayment interest. (It would be open to the group to make a claim under FA 1989 s 102.)

TA 1988 Sch 13A para 13
This paragraph deals with the situation where a subsidiary which has received the surrender of ACT under TA 1988 s 240(2) becomes aware that it has obtained relief to which it is not entitled. This could arise because the surrendering company has purported to surrender ACT in excess of the amount available for surrender (the excess relief being given in the year of surrender or by carry forward to a later year under TA 1988 s 239(4)). Within three months of the day on which the subsidiary company becomes aware of the error it must provide a Revenue officer with a self-assessment on the basis of the true facts. The tax in this self-assessment is treated as due and payable nine months after the end of the relevant accounting period of the subsidiary. For the purpose of this provision, it is to be assumed that any ACT availability paid (or correctly treated as paid) has been set off before the unallowable ACT. The provisions described in Sch 13A para 14 below regarding enquiries into self-assessments apply.

TA 1988 Sch 13A para 14
This paragraph provides that a Revenue officer may, within one year of receiving a self-assessment under Sch 13A, give notice of his intention to enquire into it. The procedure is similar to that which applies to an enquiry into a return (TMA 1970 s 28A).

TA 1988 Sch 13A para 15
Subparagraph (1) provides that a claim is withdrawn after the assessment on the surrendering company for the relevant accounting period has become final, the company may by notice claim repayment of any tax which would not have been payable if the surrender had not been made. Subparagraph (2) provides that where a claim is made after an assessment on the subsidiary for any relevant period (see para 9 above) has become final, the subsidiary may by notice claim repayment of any tax paid which would not have been payable if the claim had not been made.

Note that the repayment is not automatic.

3 Paragraphs 1 and 2 above have effect where the accounting period of the surrendering company ends on or after the day appointed under section 199 of the Finance Act 1994 for the purposes of Chapter III of Part IV of that Act (self-assessment).

GENERAL NOTE
The provisions in paras 1 and 2 have effect where the accounting period of the surrendering company ends on or after the day appointed for the introduction of self-assessment.

Other amendments

4 Section 239(5) of the Taxes Act 1988 (manner in which claims under section 239(1) and (4) to be given effect) shall cease to have effect in relation to accounting periods ending on or after the day appointed as mentioned in paragraph 3 above.

GENERAL NOTE
This paragraph repeals TA 1988 s 239(5) which is superseded by this Schedule.

5 In the Table in section 98 of the Taxes Management Act 1970 (penalties in respect of certain information provisions), after the entry in the second column relating to Schedule 13 to the Taxes Act 1988, there shall be inserted the following entry—

"Schedule 13A, paragraphs 11, 12 and 13;".

GENERAL NOTE
This paragraph applies the penalty provisions of TMA 1970 s 98 to assessments under TA 1988 new Sch 13A paras 11–13.

SCHEDULE 26   Section 150

DAMAGES AND COMPENSATION FOR PERSONAL INJURY

INTRODUCTION

Measures were introduced in FA 1995 (TA 1988 ss 329A and 329B as inserted by FA 1995 s 142) to alleviate the possible tax charge on so-called structured settlements, that is agreements in personal injury cases to make regular payments to the injured party rather than a single once-and-for-all lump sum. Under the tax law as it stood before FA 1995 many of these payments would have been treated as taxable annual payments (and subject to deduction of tax at source), whereas a single lump sum payment would have been exempt from both income tax and CGT.

The provisions in FA 1995 went a long way towards dealing with the problem by providing a tax exemption from tax payments under a structured settlement made out of court, but they did not specifically deal with structured settlements made by a court order. Neither did they deal with cases where payments were made to or by a third party. Both of these situations are covered in the new legislation.

METHOD OF MAKING THE CHANGES

The Government has widened the scope of the relief not, as might have been expected, by amending the FA 1995 legislation but by completely re-writing all of the provisions. Although the new rules cover a wider variety of circumstances than the old ones, they are in fact expressed in more concise, yet perfectly clear, language, a welcome move given the number of occasions elsewhere in this Act where the opposite is true.

THE SCOPE OF THE RELIEF

The new rules apply to damages for personal injury, which for the purpose of this Act includes not only injuries as generally understood, but also diseases and the impairment of a person's physical condition. Relief for income tax (as well as from the obligation to deduct income tax at source) is given in personal injury cases where there is—

(*a*) an agreement to settle a claim for damages (TA 1988 s 329AA(1)(*a*)); or
(*b*) a court order awarding damages (TA 1988 s 329AA(1)(*b*)); or
(*c*) a compensation award under the Criminal Injuries Compensation Scheme (TA 1988 s 329AB(1)),

which is payable wholly or partly in the form of periodical payments.

THE PAYER AND THE PAYEE

The exemption applies whether the payment is made to the individual who was injured, to a person who receives the payment on his or her behalf, or to the trustees of a settlement in which the injured person has the sole life interest. In this last case any payments made by the trustees to the beneficiary are also exempt from income tax.

The tax exemption also applies where payment is not made by the person causing the injury (or his insurance company) but where instead a third party purchases an annuity to fund payments to the injured party. The Press Release introducing the new provision (Press Release of 29 February 1996) gives as an example of this the purchase of an annuity by the Motor Insurers' Bureau where the motorist causing the injury was not insured.

EXTENSION OF THE RELIEF

The legislation is widely drawn, so that the exemption will apply in as many cases of periodic payment for personal injury as possible. Thus, interim payments made by order of a court are included, as are interim payments made voluntarily by a defendant on account of damages which may be awarded against him. The Treasury is also given power to bring within the scope of the tax exemption any future type of scheme (whether statutory or not) which may provide for similar periodic payments in personal injury cases.

COMING INTO FORCE

The reliefs for payments under voluntary agreements and for payments made under a court order come into effect for payments received after Royal Assent, regardless of when the agreement or order under which the payments are made came into effect. This means that payments which may not currently qualify for relief will achieve tax exempt status from Royal Assent.

Payments under the Criminal Injuries Compensation Act 1995 qualify for tax exemption from the passing of that Act, ie the new relief will operate retrospectively.

The repeals notice makes it clear that the tax-free status under the original FA 1995 legislation of payments already made is not affected by the widening of the tax exemption.

CONCLUSION

Taken together the new rules should mean that tax exemption should apply to all payments for personal injury in structured settlement cases. This is a sensible reform which is greatly to be welcomed, removing as it does a taxation charge which was surely never designed to apply to such payments: it is only the very wide scope of the annual payments legislation which created the problem in the first place.

The sections inserted after section 329 of the Taxes Act 1988 by section 150 of this Act are as follows—

"329AA   Personal injury damages in the form of periodical payments

(1) Where—

(*a*) an agreement is made settling a claim or action for damages for personal injury on terms whereby the damages are to consist wholly or partly of periodical payments; or
(*b*) a court awarding damages for personal injury makes an order incorporating such terms,

the payments shall not for the purposes of income tax be regarded as the income of any of the persons mentioned in subsection (2) below and accordingly shall be paid without any deduction under section 348(1)(*b*) or 349(1).

(2) The persons referred to in subsection (1) above are—

(*a*) the person ("A") entitled to the damages under the agreement or order;
(*b*) any person who, whether in pursuance of the agreement or order or otherwise, receives the payments or any of them on behalf of A;
(*c*) any trustee who, whether in pursuance of the agreement or order or otherwise, receives the payments or any of them on trust for the benefit of A under a trust under which A is during his lifetime the sole beneficiary.

(3) The periodical payments referred to in subsection (1) above, or any of them, may, if the agreement or order mentioned in that subsection or a subsequent agreement so provides, consist of payments under one or more annuities purchased or provided for, or for the benefit of, A by the person by whom the payments would otherwise fall to be made.

(4) Sums paid to, or for the benefit of, A by a trustee or trustees shall not be regarded as his income for the purposes of income tax if made out of payments which by virtue of this section are not to be regarded for those purposes as income of the trustee or trustees.

(5) In this section "personal injury" includes any disease and any impairment of a person's physical or mental condition.

(6) For the purposes of this section a claim or action for personal injury includes—

(*a*) such a claim or action brought by virtue of the Law Reform (Miscellaneous Provisions) Act 1934;
(*b*) such a claim or action brought by virtue of the Law Reform (Miscellaneous Provisions) Act (Northern Ireland) 1937;
(*c*) such a claim or action brought by virtue of the Damages (Scotland) Act 1976;
(*d*) a claim or action brought by virtue of the Fatal Accidents Act 1976;
(*e*) a claim or action brought by virtue of the Fatal Accidents (Northern Ireland) Order 1977.

(7) In relation to such an order as is mentioned in paragraph (*b*) of subsection (1) above "damages" includes an interim payment which the court, by virtue of rules of court in that behalf, orders the defendant to make to the plaintiff; and where, without such an order, the defendant agrees to make a payment on account of the damages that may be awarded against him in such an action as is mentioned in paragraph (*a*) of that subsection, that paragraph shall apply to the payment and the agreement as it applies to damages and to such an agreement as is there mentioned.

(8) In the application of subsection (7) above to Scotland for references to the plaintiff and the defendant there shall be substituted references to the pursuer and the defender.

329AB   Compensation for personal injury under statutory or other schemes

(1) Section 329AA applies to annuity payments under an award of compensation made under the Criminal Injuries Compensation Scheme as it applies to payments of damages in that form under such an agreement or order as is mentioned in subsection (1) of that section.

(2) In subsection (1) above "the Criminal Injuries Compensation Scheme" means—

(*a*) the scheme established by arrangements made under the Criminal Injuries Compensation Act 1995; or

(*b*) arrangements made by the Secretary of State for compensation for criminal injuries and in operation before the commencement of that scheme.

(3) If it appears to the Treasury that any other scheme or arrangement, whether established by statute or otherwise, makes provision for the making of periodical payments by way of compensation for personal injury within the meaning of section 329AA, the Treasury may by order apply that section to those payments with such modifications as the Treasury consider necessary."

SCHEDULE 27
FOREIGN INCOME DIVIDENDS

INTRODUCTION

The concept of a foreign income dividend was introduced by FA 1994 s 138 and Sch 16, which inserts ss 246A–246Y into TA 1988.

Any company can, on paying a dividend, declare it to be a foreign income dividend. Generally, the company accounts for ACT in the normal manner (ss 246A and 246B). However, at the end of the accounting period the ACT on the foreign income dividend is repayable to the company insofar as the ACT is covered by "notional foreign source advance corporation tax" for the accounting period. That is, broadly, that the dividend itself can be shown to be the passing on of profits received from foreign companies (ss 246N and 246P).

Where the UK company making the payment of the foreign income dividend falls within the definition of an international headquarters company (an IHC), as given in TA 1988 s 246S, the company is not required to pay ACT on making the payment of the dividend (s 246T). However, if events later in the accounting period cause the company to lose its status as an IHC, ACT in respect of the dividend is then payable, with interest (s 246V).

For the recipient, a foreign income dividend is treated as if it carries the same tax credit as is available for a conventional dividend from a UK company, except that no repayment of the tax credit is available (ss 246D and 246C).

This Schedule remedies various technical deficiencies that have been identified with the original legislation. Also, the definition of an IHC is widened to include a subsubsidiary.

Companies that pay FIDs

1 (1) In section 246A(1) of the Taxes Act 1988 (foreign income dividends) after "a company" there shall be inserted "resident in the United Kingdom".

(2) This paragraph has effect in relation to dividends paid on or after 28th November 1995.

GENERAL NOTE

For a dividend paid on or after 28 November 1995, treatment as a foreign income dividend is denied unless the payer company is resident in the United Kingdom. It is, thus, no longer possible for a foreign company with a liability to UK corporation tax, perhaps by virtue of a branch in the UK, to avoid the payment of ACT by matching a dividend with foreign income. It would appear, however, that FID treatment remains available to a dual resident company, even where the operation of a double taxation agreement has the effect that the company is treated as if it were not resident in the UK.

Recipients of FIDs

2 Section 246D(5) of that Act (exclusion of section 233(1) and (1A) in the case of foreign income dividends) shall have effect, and be deemed always to have had effect, as if at the end there were inserted "to which an individual is beneficially entitled, a foreign income dividend paid to personal representatives or a foreign income dividend paid to trustees in a case in which the dividend is income to which section 686 applies."

GENERAL NOTE

This is a retrospective amendment aimed to link the FID treatment afforded to the recipient to the beneficial ownership of the dividend. Thus, the exclusion of the treatment normally applied to a non-qualifying distribution (such as a bonus redeemable share) by TA 1988 s 233, applies also to the non-corporate recipient of an FID unless the recipient is within one of the following categories—

(*a*) the recipient is an individual who is the beneficial owner of the dividend;
(*b*) the recipients are personal representatives of a deceased individual;
(*c*) the recipients are trustees who are, in respect of that FID, subject to the special tax rate for trusts that is applied to discretionary trusts and accumulation trusts.

Calculation of the distributable foreign profit and the notional foreign source ACT

3 (1) In section 246I(6) of that Act, for the words from "an amount equal" onwards there shall be substituted "the amount of corporation tax payable, before double taxation relief is afforded, in respect of the foreign source profit."

(2) In section 246P(2) of that Act (assumptions to apply for the purposes of calculating the notional foreign source ACT), the following paragraph shall be inserted before the "and" at the end of paragraph (*e*)—

"(*ea*) where any of the matched foreign source profits represent an amount ('a gross profit') reduced by one or more such deductions as are mentioned in section 246I(2), the amount of double taxation relief which is to be taken, in finding the amount of corporation tax falling finally to be borne, to have been available (after the reduction) to be allowed by reference to the amount representing the gross profit was equal to the amount that would have been available to be so allowed had no reduction been made;".

(3) In section 246P of that Act, after subsection (12) there shall be inserted the following subsection—

"(12A) In this section 'double taxation relief' has the same meaning as in section 246I."

(4) Subject to sub-paragraph (5) below, this paragraph has effect in relation to accounting periods ending after 28th November 1995.

(5) This paragraph, so far as applicable as respects authorised unit trusts, has effect in relation to any distribution period ending after 28th November 1995.

GENERAL NOTE
For a dividend to be treated as a foreign income dividend, it is necessary to identify foreign source profits that equal or exceed the distribution made by the UK company. TA 1988 s 246I(4) requires that the foreign profits are reduced by the "relevant amount of tax" that is borne by those profits. Section 246I(5) deals with the situation where the foreign tax exceeds the UK corporation tax; in such a case, the amount treated as distributable foreign source profit is the amount net of the foreign tax.

Subparagraph (1) amends the treatment where the foreign tax is less than the UK corporation tax. Where foreign tax attributed to a dividend is less than the UK corporation tax that would be suffered on profits of that sum, the distributable foreign profit is treated as the foreign source profit less the UK corporation tax that would be payable, if no double taxation relief is available.

Subparagraph (2) provides that, in making the calculation of distributable foreign profit, the corporation tax liability is computed ignoring any deductions from profit for charges on income, expenses of management, or other deductions where the company can choose the class of income against which the deduction is put.

Subparagraph (3) provides a definition of "double taxation relief" for the purpose of TA 1988 s 246P as, arguably, the Taxes Acts had not given a definition of this phrase for the purpose of that section.

This paragraph has effect for accounting periods ending after 28 November 1995; there is, thus, potentially retrospection for up to one year. In the case of an authorised unit trust the effect is in relation to a distribution period ending after that date.

International headquarters company

4 (1) Section 246S of that Act (conditions for treatment as international headquarters company) shall be amended as follows.

(2) In subsection (3) (wholly-owned subsidiary of foreign quoted parent company), in paragraph (*a*), for "wholly owned by" there shall be substituted "a 100 per cent subsidiary of".

(3) Subsection (8) (extension of subsection (3)) shall cease to have effect.

(4) After subsection (10) there shall be inserted the following subsection—

"(10A) For the purposes of this section a company is a 100 per cent subsidiary of another if and so long as it is a body corporate all of whose share capital would fall to be treated for the purposes of section 838 as owned directly or indirectly by the other and that other is a body corporate; but for this purpose references in that section to owning share capital shall be construed in accordance with subsection (12) below."

(5) Subject to sub-paragraph (6) below, this paragraph has effect in relation to any accounting period ending after 28th November 1995.

(6) Where—

(*a*) this paragraph has effect under sub-paragraph (5) above in relation to an accounting period in which a dividend is paid, and

(*b*) the immediately preceding period ended on or before 28th November 1995,

subsection (9) (requirement to be international headquarters company in the period before that in which a dividend is paid) shall have effect in the case of that dividend as if this paragraph also had effect in relation to that immediately preceding period.

GENERAL NOTE

This paragraph tidies up some details of the legislation relating to international headquarters companies, that was enacted by FA 1994 Sch 16, which gave a special regime for international headquarters companies by inserting ss 246S–246W into TA 1988. A company that qualifies as an international headquarters company is entitled to elect to treat a distribution as a foreign income dividend and to make the payment of that dividend without accounting for ACT (s 246T). The definition of an IHC requires that, broadly, the conditions are fulfilled, not only throughout the accounting period in which the FID is paid, but also during the period of 12 months immediately preceding that accounting period (s 246S(3)).

TA 1988 s 246S(3) required that the IHC is "wholly owned by" a non-resident company. Paragraph 4(2)–(5) substitutes the requirement that the IHC be "a one hundred per cent subsidiary" of a non-resident company. Thus, the definition of "a one hundred per cent subsidiary" is that applied by TA 1988 s 838, this being the same definition as is used to determine the membership of a group for the purpose of group relief, etc. TA 1988 s 246S(12) requires that the test is the percentage of the votes that the parent company would be capable of casting if there were an annual general meeting of the subsidiary on the date in question (para 4(4)).

As the definition of TA 1988 s 838(1) is incorporated into the IHC legislation, it is unnecessary to have the deeming provisions of s 246S(8) to deal with a string of companies. Section 246S(8) is, thus, repealed and, in its place, the treatment for a string of companies is given by TA 1988 s 838(2)–(9).

These provisions have effect for any accounting period ending after 28 November 1995. As the definition of an international headquarters company requires that conditions are fulfilled for the preceding accounting period, in order for a distribution paid on or after 28 November 1995 to be treated as an FID made by an IHC, the conditions imposed by this amending legislation must be fulfilled not only for the period in which the dividend is paid, but also for the whole of the immediately preceding accounting period. Thus, a company that has annual accounting periods to 30 November and which makes a distribution on 29 or 30 November 1995 is required to fulfil the amended requirements of para 4 with effect from 1 December 1993 if the distribution is to be treated as a foreign income dividend paid by an international headquarters company. As the treatment of a distribution as a foreign income dividend is only available for a dividend paid on or after 1 July 1994 (TA 1988 s 246Y(2)), this retrospection will mean, for many companies, that the new provisions completely replace the original provisions.

Life assurance business charged under Case I of Schedule D

5 (1) In section 440B of that Act (modifications for life assurance business charged under Case I of Schedule D), after subsection (1) there shall be inserted the following subsection—

"(1A) Nothing in section 208 shall prevent foreign income dividends from being taken into account in any computation of the profits of the company's life assurance business charged in accordance with Case I of Schedule D."

(2) This paragraph has effect in relation to accounting periods beginning on or after 1st January 1996.

GENERAL NOTE

For an accounting period beginning on or after 1 January 1996, a foreign income dividend is brought into account as a receipt, where the recipient is a life assurance business charged under Schedule D Case I.

Foreign income distributions to corporate unit holders

6 (1) In section 468R of that Act (foreign income distributions to corporate unit holders), after subsection (3) there shall be inserted the following subsection—

"(4) No repayment shall be made of any tax which is deemed to have been deducted by virtue of the application of paragraph (*b*) of section 468Q(2) in relation to a foreign income distribution."

(2) This paragraph applies in relation to any distribution period ending on or after 28th November 1995.

GENERAL NOTE

For any distribution period ending on or after 28 November 1995, a corporate holder of units in an authorised unit trust is denied repayment of the notional tax credit affixing to a foreign income dividend.

SCHEDULE 28

FOTRA SECURITIES: CONSEQUENTIAL AMENDMENTS

This Schedule is introduced by s 154 and makes consequential changes in respect of FOTRA gilts.

The Taxes Act 1988

1 Section 47 of the Taxes Act 1988 (FOTRA securities) shall cease to have effect.

GENERAL NOTE
This paragraph repeals TA 1988 s 47, which provides for the claim to exemption to tax in respect of FOTRA gilts. It is superseded in part by s 154.

2 Section 474(2) of that Act (which prevents the deduction of expenses in respect of securities the income on which is exempt from tax) shall cease to have effect.

GENERAL NOTE
This paragraph repeals TA 1988 s 474(2), which denies the deduction for expenses in connection with FOTRA gilts where there the income is exempt (for this purpose the term expenses excludes interest on borrowed money, but this is subject to s 475—see para 3 below). Section 474(2) applies to banking business, insurance business or a business consisting wholly or partly in dealing in securities, carried on in the UK by a person not ordinarily resident. It is superseded in part by s 154. (See also para 3 below.)

3 (1) In section 475 of that Act (tax-free securities: exclusion of interest on borrowed money), for subsection (1) there shall be substituted the following subsection—

"(1) This section has effect where a banking business, an insurance business or a business consisting wholly or partly in dealing in securities—

(*a*) is carried on in the United Kingdom by a person not ordinarily resident there; and

(*b*) in computing for any of the purposes of the Tax Acts the profits arising from, or loss sustained, in the business, any amount which would otherwise be brought into account is disregarded by virtue of a condition subject to which any 3½% War Loan 1952 or after was issued;

and for this purpose insurance business includes insurance business of any category."

(2) In subsections (3) and (8) of that section for the words "tax-free Treasury securities", in each place where they occur, there shall be substituted "3½% War Loan 1952 or after"

(3) Subsections (6) and (7) of that section shall cease to have effect.

GENERAL NOTE
This paragraph amends TA 1988 s 475.
TA 1988 s 475 applies in the circumstances described in s 474(2) (see para 2 above) to deny relief for interest expense. This paragraph amends s 475, the conditions in s 474(2) (which subsection was deleted by para 2) continue to apply for the purposes of s 475, but subject to amendment. It provides that it only applies to 3.5% War Loan Stock 1952 and applies equally to all categories of insurance business.

4 In paragraph 5 of Schedule 19AA to that Act (designation of certain assets of overseas life assurance fund), for sub-paragraph (7) there shall be substituted the following sub-paragraph—

"(7) For the purposes of sub-paragraph (5)(*d*) above, the reference to securities issued with a FOTRA condition is a reference to any FOTRA security within the meaning of section 154 of the Finance Act 1996."

GENERAL NOTE
This paragraph amends the definition of FOTRA securities in TA 1988 Sch 19AA para 5(7) (which applies to overseas life assurance funds) to that provided by s 154.

5 In paragraph 5C of Schedule 19AC to that Act (modification for overseas life insurance companies in relation to tax-free securities), for sub-paragraph (2) there shall be substituted the following sub-paragraphs—

"(2) Where, in computing the income to which this paragraph applies, any profits and gains arising from a FOTRA security, or from any loan relationship represented by it, are excluded by virtue of the tax exemption condition of that security, the amount which by virtue of section 76 is to be deductible by way of management expenses shall be reduced in accordance with sub-paragraph (3) below.

(3) That amount shall be reduced so that it bears to the amount which would be deductible apart from this sub-paragraph the same proportion as the amount of the income to which this paragraph applies (after applying the provisions of section 154(2) to (7) of the Finance Act 1996) bears to what would be the amount of that income if the tax exemption condition were disregarded.

(4) Subsection (8) of section 154 of the Finance Act 1996 (meaning of 'FOTRA security' and 'tax exemption condition') shall apply for the purposes of this paragraph as it applies for the purposes of that section."

GENERAL NOTE
This paragraph amends the definition of FOTRA security in TA 1988 Sch 19AC para 5C (which applies to overseas life insurance companies) to that provided by s 154. It also makes consequential amendments.

6 In paragraph 1(3) of Schedule 24 to that Act and in paragraph 5(5) of Schedule 27 to that Act (amount taken into account in computing tax of company on the assumption that it is resident in the United Kingdom), for "by virtue of section 47 or 48" there shall be substituted, in each case, "and have been so received by virtue of section 154(2) of the Finance Act 1996".

GENERAL NOTE
This paragraph provides for amendments consequential to the repeal of TA 1988 s 47 (see para 1 above). The changes relate to Sch 24 para 1(3) (which refers to the calculation of chargeable profits of non-UK resident companies) and TA 1988 Sch 27 para 5(5) (which provides for the calculation of UK equivalent profits for the purposes of the offshore fund provisions of Sch 27).

The Inheritance Tax Act 1984 (c 51)

7 In section 6(2) of the Inheritance Tax Act 1984 (FOTRA securities to be excluded property in specified circumstances), for the words from "neither" to "United Kingdom" there shall be substituted "of a description specified in the condition".

GENERAL NOTE
This paragraph provides for amendment to IHTA 1984 s 6(2) which defines "excluded property" so as to alter the requirement that the person is not domiciled nor ordinarily resident in the UK. This condition is replaced with the definition "of a description specified in the condition".

8 In each of paragraphs (*a*) and (*b*) of section 48(4) of that Act (excluded property in the case of settlements), for the words from "neither" to "United Kingdom" there shall be substituted "of a description specified in the condition in question".

GENERAL NOTE
This paragraph provides for amendment to IHTA 1984 s 48(4) which defines "excluded property" in respect of a "reversionary interest". It alters the requirement that the relevant persons are not domiciled nor ordinarily resident in the UK. This condition is replaced with the definition "of a description specified in the condition in question".

SCHEDULE 29

PAYING AND COLLECTING AGENTS ETC

INTRODUCTION

This Schedule inserts a new Chapter VIIA in Part IV of TA 1988, dealing with the collection of tax on public revenue dividends (such as interest on gilts) and foreign dividends or interest. The new provisions result from the new rules for corporate debt (see FA 1996 ss 80–105), the abolition of Schedule C and the repeal of TA 1988 s 123 and Sch 3 (see FA 1996 s 79 and Sch 7). Under the new Chapter, collection agents, such as banks and stockbrokers, who do no more than arrange to clear a cheque in respect of a foreign dividend, will no longer have to deduct tax from the dividend. There are also clearer rules to allow specified investors, such as non-residents and UK charities, to receive foreign dividends or interest without a tax deduction. The changes apply from the date of Royal Assent to FA 1996 (see Budget Press Release, 28 November 1995, "Paying and collecting agents for foreign dividends—changes to the scheme for deduction of tax", *Simon's Weekly Tax Intelligence* 1995, p 1872).

The structure of the new sections inserted in TA 1988 in outline is as follows—

(*a*) TA 1988 s 118A contains definitions;

(*b*) TA 1988 s 118B determines the persons who are paying agents and defines "relevant payment";

(*c*) TA 1988 s 118C determines the persons who are collecting agents and defines "relevant receipt";

(*d*) TA 1988 s 118D defines the relevant payments which are chargeable payments and the relevant receipts which are chargeable receipts, by reference to the provisions of TA 1988 s 118G and other factors;

(*e*) TA 1988 s 118E sets out the liability of a paying agent to deduct tax from a chargeable payment and the liability of a collecting agent to account for tax in respect of a chargeable receipt;

(*f*) TA 1988 s 118F is concerned with the payment of tax in respect of chargeable payments and chargeable receipts;

(*g*) TA 1988 s 118G provides that certain relevant payments are not to be chargeable payments, and that certain relevant receipts are not to be chargeable receipts;

(*h*) TA 1988 s 118H contains administrative provisions relating to the reliefs in s 118G;

(*i*) TA 1988 s 118I is concerned with deduction of tax at a reduced rate;

(*j*) TA 1988 s 118J contains provisions to prevent double accounting;

(*k*) TA 1988 s 118K relates to regulations.

PART I

THE NEW CHAPTER

1   In Part IV of the Taxes Act 1988 (provisions relating to the Schedule D charge) the following Chapter shall be inserted after Chapter VII—

"CHAPTER VIIA

PAYING AND COLLECTING AGENTS

118A   Definitions

In this Chapter—

(*a*) except in the terms 'agent concerned', 'collecting agent' and 'paying agent', references to an 'agent' include a person acting as nominee or sub-agent for an agent;

(*b*) 'bank' has the meaning given by section 840A;

(*c*) the 'chargeable date'—

(i) in the case of a relevant payment, has the meaning given by section 118B(5); and

(ii) in the case of a relevant receipt, has the meaning given by section 118C(4);

(*d*) 'collecting agent' has the meaning given by section 118C(1), and in relation to any relevant receipt or chargeable receipt, a reference to the collecting agent is a reference to the collecting agent by virtue of whose performance of a relevant function that receipt was received or arose;

(*e*) in relation to any dividends, references to 'coupons' include warrants for and bills of exchange purporting to be drawn or made in payment of those dividends;

(*f*) references to a depositary include references to a person acting as agent or nominee for a depositary;

(*g*) except in paragraph (*h*) below, references to 'dividends' are references to foreign dividends, United Kingdom public revenue dividends or relevant dividends as the context requires;

(*h*) 'foreign dividends' means any annual payments, interest or dividends payable out of or in respect of foreign holdings;

(*i*) 'foreign holdings' means the stocks, funds, shares or securities of any body of persons not resident in the United Kingdom or of a government or public or local authority in a country outside the United Kingdom;

(*j*) 'gilt-edged securities' means any securities which—

(i) are gilt-edged securities for the purposes of the 1992 Act; or

(ii) will be such securities on the making of any order under paragraph 1 of Schedule 9 to that Act the making of which is anticipated in the prospectus under which they were issued;

(*k*) 'international organisation' has the meaning given by section 51A(8);

(*l*) references to a 'nominee' include a person acting as agent or nominee for a nominee;

(*m*) 'paying agent' has the meaning given by section 118B(1);

(*n*) 'prescribed' means prescribed in regulations made by the Board under this Chapter or prescribed by the Board in accordance with such regulations;

(*o*) 'quoted Eurobond' means a quoted Eurobond within the meaning of section 124 the interest on which is chargeable to tax under Case III of Schedule D, and 'quoted Eurobond interest' means interest on such a quoted Eurobond;

(*p*) 'relevant dividends' means foreign dividends and quoted Eurobond interest;

(*q*) 'relevant holdings' means foreign holdings and quoted Eurobonds;

(*r*) 'relevant payment' has the meaning given by section 118B(5);

(*s*) 'relevant receipt' has the meaning given by section 118C(2);

(*t*) 'securities' includes any loan stocks or similar securities, whether secured or unsecured; and

(*u*) 'United Kingdom public revenue dividends' means income from securities which is payable out of the public revenue of the United Kingdom or Northern Ireland.

118B   Paying agents

(1) A person specified in column 1 of Table A below shall be a paying agent for the purposes of this Chapter in relation to such dividends as are—

(*a*) of a description set out in column 2 of that Table opposite his specification; and

(*b*) entrusted to him for payment or distribution.

TABLE A

1	2
1 Any person in the United Kingdom.	United Kingdom public revenue dividends
2 The Bank of England	United Kingdom public revenue dividends paid on securities entered in the register of the Bank of Ireland in Dublin
3 Any person in the United Kingdom	foreign dividends which are payable to persons in the United Kingdom and do not fall within subsection (4) below

(2) The Bank of England and the Bank of Ireland shall be treated as paying agents for the purposes of this Chapter in relation to United Kingdom public revenue dividends which are payable to them.

(3) The National Debt Commissioners shall be treated as paying agents for the purposes of this Chapter in relation to United Kingdom public revenue dividends payable by them.

(4) Foreign dividends fall within this subsection if they are payable out of, or in respect of, the stocks, funds, shares or securities of an organisation which is for the time being designated for the purposes of this subsection pursuant to section 582A(1).

(5) Any payment in relation to which a person is a paying agent shall be a relevant payment for the purposes of this Chapter; and the chargeable date is—

(*a*) in relation to such a payment as is mentioned in subsection (2) above, the date on which the payment is received; and
(*b*) in relation to any other relevant payment, the date on which the payment is made.

118C   Collecting agents

(1) Subject to subsection (3) below, a person described in column 1 of Table B below shall be a collecting agent for the purposes of this Chapter in relation to such functions performed by him as are set out in that description, which shall be relevant functions for the purposes of this Chapter.

(2) Such dividends or proceeds of sale or other realisation as—

(*a*) are set out in column 2 of Table B below opposite the description of a collecting agent in column 1; and
(*b*) are received or arise by virtue of that collecting agent's performance of a relevant function comprised in that description

shall be relevant receipts for the purposes of this Chapter.

TABLE B

1	2
1 Any person in the United Kingdom who, in the course of a trade or profession, acts as custodian of any relevant holdings	any relevant dividends in respect of those relevant holdings which are received by him or are paid to another person at his direction or with his consent
2 Any person in the United Kingdom who, in the course of a trade or profession, by means of coupons collects or secures payment of or receives relevant dividends for another person	the relevant dividends which he so collects or receives or of which he so secures payment
3 Any person in the United Kingdom who, in the course of a trade or profession, otherwise acts for another person in arranging to collect or secure payment of relevant dividends	the relevant dividends which he so collects or of which he so secures payment
4 Any bank in the United Kingdom which sells or otherwise realises coupons for relevant dividends and pays over the proceeds or carries them into an account	the proceeds of sale or other realisation of those coupons

1	2
5 Any dealer in coupons in the United Kingdom who purchases any coupons for relevant dividends otherwise than from a bank or another dealer in coupons	the proceeds of sale of those coupons

(3) Neither the clearing of a cheque, nor the arranging for the clearing of a cheque, shall of itself be a relevant function.

(4) The chargeable date, in relation to a relevant receipt, is—

(*a*) in the case of a relevant receipt falling within paragraph 4 or 5 of Table B above, the date on which the sale or realisation is effected, and

(*b*) in any other case, the date on which the dividends are paid.

(5) For the purposes of paragraph 1 of Table B above, a person acts as a custodian of relevant holdings if he holds them, or an entitlement to them, for another person.

(6) The Board may by regulations provide for the application of the provisions of this Chapter relating to collecting agents where—

(*a*) a person in the United Kingdom—

(i) holds, beneficially or otherwise, a right (the relevant right) which is a right to delivery of, or to amounts representing the whole or substantially the whole of the value of, a specified quantity of shares or securities comprised in a relevant holding which is held by a person outside the United Kingdom, and

(ii) is entitled to receive income (the relevant income) which is derived from, or which represents, foreign dividends or quoted Eurobond interest on that quantity of shares or securities; and

(*b*) apart from the provisions of the regulations, the relevant right is not a relevant holding, or the relevant income does not constitute foreign dividends or quoted Eurobond interest.

(7) Regulations under subsection (6) above may—

(*a*) treat the relevant right as a foreign holding or, as the case may be, a holding of quoted Eurobonds (the notional holding); and

(*b*) treat the relevant income as foreign dividends or, as the case may be, quoted Eurobond interest paid on the notional holding.

118D Chargeable payments and chargeable receipts

(1) For the purposes of this Chapter, every relevant payment shall be a chargeable payment unless—

(*a*) it is made in respect of a foreign dividend—

(i) which is payable on foreign holdings held in a recognised clearing system; and

(ii) in respect of which any conditions imposed by virtue of subsection (8) below are satisfied; or

(*b*) it is a payment of interest on an exempted certificate of deposit; or

(*c*) the making of the payment is excluded from being a chargeable payment by subsections (4), (5) or (6) below or by section 118G.

(2) For the purposes of this Chapter, every relevant receipt shall be a chargeable receipt, unless—

(*a*) it arises in respect of relevant holdings which are held in a recognised clearing system and—

(i) the collecting agent pays or accounts for the relevant receipt directly or indirectly to the recognised clearing system, and

(ii) any conditions imposed by virtue of subsection (8) below are satisfied; or

(*b*) it arises in respect of relevant holdings which are held in a recognised clearing system for which the collecting agent is acting as depositary; or
(*c*) it is excluded from being a chargeable receipt by subsection (7) below or by section 118G.

(3) In subsection (1)(*b*) above, 'exempted certificate of deposit' means a certificate of deposit (within the meaning of section 56(5)) issued by a person in the United Kingdom relating to a deposit with a branch in the United Kingdom through which a company resident outside, and not resident in, the United Kingdom carries on a trade.

(4) The payment of United Kingdom public revenue dividends on securities the interest on which is, by virtue of directions given (or treated by section 51 as having been given) under section 50(1), payable without deduction of income tax shall not be a chargeable payment unless the interest is for the time being payable under deduction of income tax pursuant to an application made (or treated by section 51 as having been made) under section 50(2).

(5) The payment of United Kingdom public revenue dividends in respect of securities standing in the name of the official custodian for charities, or in respect of which there is given to the paying agent a certificate from the Board to the effect that the dividends are subject only to charitable trusts and are exempt from tax, shall not be a chargeable payment.

(6) In a case where—

(*a*) foreign dividends are entrusted by a company which at the time they are entrusted (the 'relevant time') is not resident in the United Kingdom,
(*b*) they are entrusted for payment to a company which at the relevant time is resident in the United Kingdom, and
(*c*) at the relevant time the company mentioned in paragraph (*b*) above directly or indirectly controls not less than 10 per cent of the voting power in the company mentioned in paragraph (*a*) above,

the payment of those dividends shall not be a chargeable payment.

(7) In a case where—

(*a*) foreign dividends are payable by a company which at the time of the payment (the 'relevant time') is not resident in the United Kingdom,
(*b*) payment of those dividends is collected, received or secured, or coupons for those dividends are realised, on behalf of a company which at the relevant time is resident in the United Kingdom, and
(*c*) at the relevant time the company mentioned in paragraph (*b*) above directly or indirectly controls not less than 10 per cent of the voting power in the company mentioned in paragraph (*a*) above,

those dividends or, as the case may be, the proceeds of realisation of those coupons shall not be a chargeable receipt.

(8) The Board may by regulations provide that subsection (1)(*a*) above does not apply in respect of a relevant payment or that subsection (2)(*a*) above does not apply in respect of a relevant receipt, unless the paying agent or, as the case may be, the collecting agent has obtained a declaration from the recognised clearing system or its depositary in such form, and containing such information, as may be required by those regulations.

(9) The Board may by regulations make such provision as they may consider appropriate for requiring paying agents and collecting agents to deliver returns setting out particulars of—

(*a*) any relevant payments made by them which would have been chargeable payments but for the provisions of section 118D(1)(*a*);
(*b*) any relevant receipts which would have been chargeable receipts but for the provisions of section 118D(2)(*a*) or (*b*);

and for the keeping and production to, or to an officer of, the Board of any document in which any such declaration as is mentioned in subsection (8) above is contained.

118E Deduction of tax from chargeable payments and chargeable receipts

(1) Subject to subsection (2) below, where a paying agent makes a chargeable payment—

(*a*) he shall, on making the payment, deduct from it a sum representing the amount of income tax thereon;

(*b*) he shall become liable to account for that sum;

(*c*) the person to whom the chargeable payment is made shall allow the deduction on receipt of the residue of the payment, and the paying agent shall be acquitted and discharged of so much money as is represented by the deduction, as if that sum had actually been paid; and

(*d*) the deduction shall be treated as income tax paid by the person entitled to the chargeable payment.

(2) In relation to United Kingdom public revenue dividends payable to the Bank of Ireland out of the public revenue of the United Kingdom, or which are entrusted to the Bank of Ireland for payment and distribution and are not payable by that Bank out of its principal office in Belfast, subsection (1) above shall not apply, but—

(*a*) the money which, apart from this subsection, would be issuable to the Bank of Ireland under section 14 of the National Debt Act 1870, or otherwise payable to the Bank of Ireland for the purpose of dividends on securities of the United Kingdom government entered in the register of the Bank of Ireland in Dublin, shall be issued and paid to the Bank of England;

(*b*) the Bank of England shall deduct from the money so issued and paid to it a sum representing the amount of income tax on the dividends payable to the Bank of Ireland, and on the dividends on the securities of the United Kingdom government entered in the register of the Bank of Ireland in Dublin, and shall become liable to account for the same under section 118F(1);

(*c*) the Bank of England shall pay to the Bank of Ireland the residue of the money so issued and paid to it, to be applied by the Bank of Ireland in payment of the dividends; and

(*d*) the deduction shall be treated as income tax paid by the person entitled to the dividends, and the Bank of England and the Bank of Ireland shall be acquitted and discharged of so much money as is represented by the deduction, as if that sum had actually been paid.

(3) Where a collecting agent performs a relevant function—

(*a*) he shall on the chargeable date become liable to account for a sum representing the amount of income tax on any chargeable receipt in relation to which he is the collecting agent;

(*b*) he shall be entitled—

(i) to be indemnified by the person entitled to the chargeable receipt against the income tax for which he is liable to account in accordance with paragraph (*a*) above; and

(ii) to deduct out of the chargeable receipt or to retain from any other sums otherwise due from him to the person entitled to the chargeable receipt, or received by him on behalf of that person, amounts sufficient for meeting any liability to account for such income tax which he has discharged or to which he is subject;

(*c*) the person entitled to the chargeable receipt shall allow the deduction or retention on receipt of the residue of the chargeable receipt, and the collecting agent shall be acquitted and discharged of so much money as is represented by the deduction, as if that sum had actually been paid; and

(*d*) the amount for which the collecting agent is liable to account shall be treated as income tax paid by the person entitled to the chargeable receipt.

(4) A paying agent who makes a chargeable payment, or a collecting agent who is required to account for tax on a chargeable receipt, shall, if the person entitled to the chargeable payment or, as the case may be, the chargeable receipt so requests in

writing, furnish him within thirty days after receiving that request with a certificate showing—

(*a*) the gross amount of the payment or receipt;
(*b*) the amount of income tax treated as paid by him;
(*c*) the actual amount actually paid or accounted for to him; and
(*d*) the chargeable date.

(5) The Board may by regulations—

(*a*) require a certificate furnished pursuant to subsection (4) above to contain information additional to that set out in paragraphs (*a*) to (*d*) of that subsection or a declaration made by or on behalf of the paying agent or collecting agent;
(*b*) make provision for the form of such a certificate or declaration.

(6) The duty imposed by subsection (4) above shall be enforceable at the suit or instance of the person requesting the certificate.

118F   Accounting for tax on chargeable payments and chargeable receipts

(1) Income tax in respect of United Kingdom public revenue dividends for which the Bank of England, the Bank of Ireland, the National Debt Commissioners or any public office or department of the Crown are liable to account pursuant to section 118E(1) or (2) shall become due and payable on the seventh day after the chargeable date and shall be paid into the general account of the Board at the Bank of England or, in the case of the Bank of Ireland, at the Bank of Ireland.

(2) Any other income tax for which a paying agent is liable to account under section 118E(1), and any income tax for which a collecting agent is liable to account under section 118E(3), shall become due and payable on the fourteenth day from the end of the month in which the chargeable date falls.

(3) Any tax due under subsection (1) or (2) above shall carry interest, at the rate applicable under section 178 of the Finance Act 1989, from the date on which it becomes due until it is paid.

(4) The Board may by regulations make such provision as they may consider appropriate—

(*a*) for requiring paying agents and collecting agents to deliver returns setting out particulars of—

(i) chargeable payments made by them;
(ii) chargeable receipts in respect of which they are liable to account for tax;
(iii) any relevant payments made by them which would have been chargeable payments but for the provisions of section 118G;
(iv) any relevant receipts which would have been chargeable receipts but for the provisions of section 118G;
(v) the amount of any tax accounted for by them, or for which they are liable to account, in relation to chargeable payments or chargeable receipts;
(vi) in the case of relevant payments falling within sub-paragraph (iii) above, the paragraphs of subsection (3) or (4) of section 118G that applied to them;
(vii) in the case of relevant receipts falling within sub-paragraph (iv) above, the paragraphs of subsection (4) of section 118G that applied to them;
(viii) the names and addresses of the persons entitled to the relevant payments or relevant receipts;

(*b*) with respect to the furnishing of information by paying agents or collecting agents, including the inspection of books, documents and other records on behalf of the Board;
(*c*) for the assessment under the regulations of amounts due and for appeals against such assessments;
(*d*) for the repayment in specified circumstances of amounts paid (or purporting to be paid) under this Chapter.

118G Relevant securities of eligible persons

(1) Subject to subsection (2) below, and to the provisions of any regulations under section 118H—

(*a*) any relevant payment to which subsection (3) or (4) below applies shall not be a chargeable payment; and

(*b*) any relevant receipt to which subsection (4) below applies shall not be a chargeable receipt.

(2) Regulations made under paragraph (*g*), (*h*) or (*i*) of subsection (4) below may provide that only one of paragraphs (*a*) and (*b*) of subsection (1) above is to apply by virtue of those regulations in relation to relevant payments or relevant receipts of a particular kind or from a particular source.

(3) This subsection applies to payments of United Kingdom public revenue dividends so long as—

(*a*) they are exempt from tax by virtue of section 46, 49, 516 or 517;

(*b*) they are payable in respect of gilt-edged securities which for the time being are treated by section 51A as issued subject to the condition that interest on them is paid without deduction of income tax;

(*c*) they are payable in respect of securities which have been issued with such a condition as is authorised by section 22(1) of the Finance (No 2) Act 1931 and which are for the time being beneficially owned by a person who is not ordinarily resident in the United Kingdom;

(*d*) they are eligible for relief from tax by virtue of section 505(1)(*c*) or (*d*), or would be so eligible but for section 505(3);

(*e*) they are eligible for relief from tax by virtue of section 592(2), 608(2)(*a*), 613(4), 614(2), (3) or (4) or 643(2); or

(*f*) they are payable in respect of securities held by or on behalf of a person of such a description as may be prescribed.

(4) This subsection applies to relevant payments (not being payments of United Kingdom public revenue dividends) and relevant receipts—

(*a*) to which a person who, at the chargeable date—

(i) is not resident in the United Kingdom, and

(ii) beneficially owns the relevant holdings from which they are derived,

is beneficially entitled;

(*b*) which consist of, or of the proceeds of sale or other realisation of coupons for, interest (other than quoted Eurobond interest) to which a bank which, at the chargeable date—

(i) is resident in the United Kingdom, and

(ii) beneficially owns the foreign holdings from which they are derived,

is beneficially entitled;

(*c*) which arise to the trustees of a qualifying discretionary or accumulation trust in their capacity as such in respect of relevant holdings held on the trusts thereof;

(*d*) which are eligible for relief from tax by virtue of section 505(1)(*c*) or (*d*), or would be so eligible but for section 505(3);

(*e*) which are eligible for relief from tax by virtue of section 592(2), 608(2)(*a*), 613(4), 614(2), (3) or (4), 620(6) or 643(2);

(*f*) which consist of, or of the proceeds of sale or other realisation of coupons for, dividends payable out of the public revenue of the Republic of Ireland or out of or in respect of shares or securities issued by or on behalf of any Republic of Ireland company, society, adventure or concern;

(*g*) to which a person of such a description as may be prescribed and who, at the chargeable date, beneficially owns the securities from which they are derived, is beneficially entitled;

(*h*) which are derived from relevant holdings held by or on behalf of a person of such a description as may be prescribed;

(*i*) which are of such a description as may be prescribed; or (*j*) which fall to be treated as the income of, or of the government of, a sovereign power or of an international organisation.

(5) For the purposes of subsection (4)(*c*) above, a trust is a qualifying discretionary or accumulation trust if—

(*a*) it is such that some or all of any income arising to the trustees would fall (unless treated as income of the settlor or applied in defraying expenses of the trustees) to be comprised for the year of assessment in which it arises in income to which section 686 (liability to additional rate tax of certain income of discretionary trusts) applies;

(*b*) the trustees are not resident in the United Kingdom; and

(*c*) none of the beneficiaries of the trust is resident in the United Kingdom.

(6) The persons who are to be taken for the purposes of subsection (5) above to be the beneficiaries of a discretionary or accumulation trust shall be every person who, as a person falling wholly or partly within any description of actual or potential beneficiaries, is either—

(*a*) a person who is, or will or may become, entitled under the trust to receive the whole or any part of any income under the trust; or

(*b*) a person to or for the benefit of whom the whole or any part of such income may be paid or applied in exercise of any discretion conferred by the trust;

and for the purposes of this subsection references, in relation to a trust, to income under the trust shall include references to so much (if any) of any property falling to be treated as capital under the trust as represents amounts originally received by the trustees as income.

(7) The Board may by regulations provide that a paying agent who is entrusted with the payment or distribution of—

(*a*) United Kingdom public revenue dividends on securities which are held by a nominee approved for the purposes of this subsection, or

(*b*) foreign dividends on foreign holdings held by such a nominee,

shall treat those dividends as not being chargeable payments.

(8) For the purpose of giving relief from tax pursuant to arrangements which have effect by virtue of section 788, the Board may by regulations provide that a paying agent who is entrusted with the payment or distribution of United Kingdom public revenue dividends on gilt-edged securities held by a nominee approved for the purposes of this subsection shall—

(*a*) treat those dividends as not being chargeable payments, or

(*b*) deduct tax from them at such reduced rates (being lower than the rate that would otherwise be applicable by virtue of section 118E(1)) as may be prescribed.

(9) Where, pursuant to subsection (7) or (8) above, dividends are paid without deduction of tax, or subject to deduction of tax at a reduced rate, the provisions of this Chapter shall apply, subject to subsection (10) below and to the provisions of regulations under section 118H, as though the nominee was the paying agent in relation to those dividends and the chargeable date was the date on which he received them.

(10) Where tax has been deducted from dividends at a reduced rate pursuant to regulations under subsection (8) above, the tax for which the nominee is liable to account by virtue of subsection (9) above shall not exceed the difference between the amount of tax on those dividends at the rate that is applicable by virtue of section 118E(1) and the tax already deducted from them.

118H   Relevant securities of eligible persons: administration

(1) The Board may by regulations provide that section 118G(1) shall not apply as regards relevant payments or relevant receipts—

(*a*) unless such conditions as may be prescribed are fulfilled;

(*b*) where the Board have reason to believe that section 118G(3) does not apply to, or to the whole of, any relevant payments; or (*c*) where the Board have reason to believe that section 118G(4) does not apply to, or to the whole of, any relevant payments or relevant receipts.

(2) In subsection (3) below, references to the relevant exclusion are to exclusion from being a chargeable payment or chargeable receipt pursuant to section 118G(1) or regulations made under section 118G(7) or (8), or to the deduction of tax at a reduced rate pursuant to regulations under section 118G(8), as the case may be; and references to the agent concerned are to the paying agent or collecting agent or, as the case may be, to the nominee approved for the purpose of section 118G(7) or (8).

(3) Regulations under this section or section 118G(7) or (8) may—

(*a*) disapply the relevant exclusion in respect of any relevant payments or relevant receipts derived from any securities or relevant holdings unless the appropriate person has made a declaration in writing to the agent concerned, in such form as may be prescribed or authorised by the Board, confirming that the requirements for the exclusion are satisfied;

(*b*) require the person who makes such a declaration to undertake in the declaration to notify the agent concerned if the circumstances set out in the declaration change;

(*c*) require the agent concerned to consider the accuracy of any declaration made pursuant to a requirement imposed by virtue of paragraph (*a*) above;

(*d*) impose obligations—

(i) on persons having any rights in relation to relevant payments or relevant receipts in respect of which the relevant exclusion applies or is claimed to apply; and

(ii) on persons who are the agents concerned in relation to such relevant payments or relevant receipts as are mentioned in sub-paragraph (i) above

as to the provision of information, and the production of documents, to the Board or, on request, to an officer of the Board;

(*e*) provide for notices to be issued by the Board to persons who fail to comply with requirements for the provision of information or documents mentioned in paragraph (*d*) above, disapplying the relevant exclusion in relation to relevant payments or relevant receipts in relation to which they have any rights or in relation to which they are the agents concerned;

(*f*) impose requirements as to—

(i) the form and contents of any declaration to be made in accordance with the regulations under this section;

(ii) the appropriate person to make such a declaration;

(iii) the form and manner in which, and the time at which, any declaration is to be made or provided; and

(iv) the keeping and production to, or to an officer of, the Board of any document in which any such declaration is contained;

(*g*) provide for notices to be issued by the Board to such persons as may be described in the regulations where the Board are satisfied that the relevant exclusion applies, or where the Board are satisfied or have reason to believe that the relevant exclusion does not apply.

(4) Regulations under section 118G(7) or (8) may—

(*a*) prescribe conditions for the inclusion of securities or foreign holdings in arrangements established under that subsection;

(*b*) set out procedures for the approval of nominees for the purpose of that subsection and for the withdrawal of such approval.

118I Deduction of tax at reduced rate

The Board may make regulations which provide for the amount of any income tax which a paying agent would otherwise be liable to deduct under section 118E(1)(*a*), or for which a collecting agent would otherwise be liable to account under section 118E(3)(*a*), to be reduced by reference to liabilities for such tax paid under the law of a territory outside the United Kingdom as may be prescribed.

118J   Prevention of double accounting

(1) A relevant dividend the payment of which is a chargeable payment shall not be a chargeable receipt for the purpose of this Chapter.

(2) Subsection (1) above does not prevent the proceeds of sale or other realisation of a coupon from being a chargeable receipt.

(3) The Board may make regulations—

(*a*) for preventing more than one collecting agent from being liable to account for tax on the same dividend; or
(*b*) which provide that—

(i) where more than one person is a collecting agent in relation to a dividend, those persons may agree between themselves which one of their number shall be treated as the collecting agent in relation to that dividend; and
(ii) the person so identified shall for all the purposes of this Chapter be treated as the sole collecting agent in relation to that dividend.

118K   Regulations

(1) Any power to make regulations under this Chapter—

(*a*) may be exercised as regards prescribed cases or descriptions of case; and
(*b*) may be exercised differently in relation to different cases or descriptions of case, or in relation to different persons or descriptions of person.

(2) Regulations under this Chapter may include such supplementary, incidental, consequential or transitional provisions as appear to the Board to be necessary or expedient.

(3) No specific provision of this Chapter about regulations shall prejudice the generality of subsections (1) and (2) above.''

GENERAL NOTE
This paragraph contains the new Chapter VIIA which is inserted into TA 1988.

TA 1988 S 118A
This section is concerned with definitions. With regard to the liability of paying agents, "foreign dividends" are any annual payments, interest or dividends payable in respect of foreign holdings. As regards the liability of collecting agents, "relevant dividends" means foreign dividends and quoted eurobond interest. A quoted eurobond for this purpose is a quoted eurobond as defined in TA 1988 s 124, but subject to the condition that the interest arising is taxable under Schedule D Case III.

TA 1988 S 118B
This section provides that the following are paying agents—

(*a*) any person in the UK in relation to UK public revenue dividends entrusted to him for payment or distribution;
(*b*) the Bank of England in relation to UK public revenue dividends which are paid on securities entered in the register of the Bank of Ireland in Dublin, and which are entrusted to the Bank of England for payment or distribution;
(*c*) the Bank of England and the Bank of Ireland in relation to UK public revenue dividends payable to them;
(*d*) the National Debt Commissioners in relation to UK public revenue dividends payable by them;
(*e*) any person in the UK in relation to foreign dividends which are entrusted to him for payment or distribution, and which are payable to persons in the UK, except where the foreign dividends relate to securities of an international organisation which is designated for this purpose under TA 1988 s 582A(1).

Any payment in relation to which a person is a paying agent is a "relevant payment" (sub-s (5)), and is thus potentially chargeable to tax, subject to the provisions of s 118D and s 118G.
The "chargeable date" applicable to a relevant payment, which determines the date for payment of tax under s 118F, is the date on which the payment is made, except for payments within (*c*) above, in which case it is the date on which the payment is received.

TA 1988 s 118C
A "collecting agent" is defined by reference to the functions undertaken by him. Where a person performs any of the following "relevant functions", he is a collecting agent in relation to that function—

(a) any person in the UK who, in the course of a trade or profession, acts as custodian of any relevant holdings (as defined in s 118A);
(b) any person in the UK who, in the course of a trade or profession, collects, secures payment of or receives relevant dividends for another person, whether by means of coupons or otherwise;
(c) any bank in the UK which sells or otherwise realises coupons for relevant dividends and pays over the proceeds or carries them to an account;
(d) any dealer in coupons in the UK who purchases coupons for relevant dividends otherwise than from a bank or another dealer in coupons.

It is specifically provided that simply clearing a cheque, or arranging for a cheque to be cleared, is not a relevant function (sub-s (3)).
The "relevant receipts" of a collecting agent, which are potentially chargeable to tax, subject to the provisions of s 118D and s 118G, are the following amounts which are received or arise by virtue of the collecting agent's performance of a relevant function (sub-s (2))—

(a) in relation to a relevant function within (a) above, any relevant dividends in respect of the relevant holdings concerned, which are received by him or are paid to another person at his direction or with his consent;
(b) in relation to other relevant functions, the relevant dividends which he collects or receives, or whose payment he secures, or the proceeds of sale or other realisation of the coupons, as appropriate.

The "chargeable date" applicable to a relevant receipt, which determines the date for payment of the tax under s 118F, is the date on which the dividend is paid, except where the relevant receipt relates to a relevant function within (c) or (d) above, in which case it is the date on which the sale or other realisation of the coupons is effected.
There is provision for regulations to extend the scope of this section to cases where a person in the UK has a right to delivery of a quantity of securities comprised in a relevant holding which is held by a person outside the UK, and also has a right to income which is representative of foreign dividends or quoted eurobond interest on that quantity of securities (sub-s (6)).

TA 1988 s 118D
The basic rule is that relevant payments and relevant receipts are chargeable payments and chargeable receipts respectively, and thus chargeable to tax under s 118E. However, there are exceptions to this rule, as follows—

(a) an exclusion relating to securities held in a recognised clearing system, subject to the applicable conditions;
(b) exclusion from chargeable payments of a payment of interest on a certificate of deposit which relates to a deposit with a UK branch of a non-resident company, and which comes within sub-s (3);
(c) exclusion from chargeable payments of interest on government securities which is payable gross, as specified in sub-s (4);
(d) exclusion from chargcable payments of UK public revenue dividends which have charitable status under the rules in sub-s (5);
(e) an exclusion for foreign dividends payable to, or entrusted to, a resident company which controls at least ten per cent of the voting power of the non-resident company which paid, or entrusted, the dividends, as specified in sub-ss (6) and (7) (these subsections may be compared with the previous TA 1988 s 123(7) and (8));
(f) the exclusions which are specified by s 118G.

Regulations may be made to supplement the provisions of this section (sub-ss (8) and (9)).

TA 1988 s 118E
When a paying agent makes a chargeable payment, he is required to deduct income tax and account for this under s 118F. The deduction is treated as income tax paid by the person entitled to the chargeable payment (sub-s (1)).
There is an exception to this for UK public revenue dividends payable to the Bank of Ireland out of UK public revenue, or which are entrusted to the Bank of Ireland for payment and distribution otherwise than out of its principal office in Belfast. In this case, the Bank of England deducts income tax from the public revenue dividends concerned and remits the balance of the dividends to the Bank of Ireland (sub-s (2)).
When a collecting agent performs a relevant function (as defined in s 118C), he is liable to account for income tax under s 118F on any chargeable receipt in relation to which he is the collecting agent. He is entitled to deduct that income tax from the chargeable receipt or from other monies due from him to the person who is entitled to the chargeable receipt. The tax for

which the collecting agent is liable to account is treated as income tax paid by the person entitled to the chargeable receipt (sub-s (3)).

Tax deduction certificates must be provided by paying agents and collecting agents, on request (sub-ss (4)–(6)).

TA 1988 s 118F

Income tax for which a paying agent or collecting agent is liable to account under s 118E is due and payable on the fourteenth day from the end of the month in which the chargeable date (as defined in s 118B or s 118C) falls (sub-s (2)).

This is subject to an exception for income tax on UK public revenue dividends which is to be accounted for under s 118E by the Bank of England, the Bank of Ireland, the National Debt Commissioners or any public office or department of the Crown. In this case, the tax is payable on the seventh day after the chargeable date (sub-s (1)).

The tax carries interest from the due date at the rate applicable under FA 1989 s 178 (sub-s (3)).

The following are to be governed by regulations (sub-s (4))—

(*a*) returns by paying agents and collecting agents;
(*b*) the furnishing of information;
(*c*) the inspection of records on behalf of the Board;
(*d*) assessments and appeals;
(*e*) repayment of tax in appropriate circumstances.

TA 1988 s 118G

This section is concerned with the exclusion of relevant payments and relevant receipts from chargeable payments and chargeable receipts in particular circumstances (see also s 118D).

Subject to regulations, a payment of a UK public revenue dividend is not a chargeable payment where (sub-s (3))—

(*a*) it is eligible for relief as being applicable to a charity;
(*b*) it is eligible for relief as relating to an approved pension fund;
(*c*) it is payable in respect of securities held by or on behalf of a person of a prescribed description;
(*d*) it is payable in respect of gilts on which the interest is paid gross under TA 1988 s 51A;
(*e*) it is payable in respect of securities issued with a condition authorised by F(No2)A 1931 s 22(1) and which are beneficially owned by a person who is not ordinarily resident in the UK;
(*f*) it is exempt from tax by virtue of TA 1988 s 46 (Savings certificates and tax reserve certificates), s 49 (Stocks and dividends in name of Treasury etc), s 516 (Government securities held by non-resident central banks), or s 517 (Issue departments of the Reserve Bank of India and the State Bank of Pakistan).

Subject to regulations, a relevant payment, other than payment of a UK public revenue dividend, or a relevant receipt is not a chargeable payment or a chargeable receipt where (sub-s (4))—

(*a*) the person who is beneficially entitled to the dividend or sale proceeds is non-resident, and beneficially owns the relevant holding concerned;
(*b*) the amount concerned is the sale proceeds of coupons for interest (other than quoted eurobond interest), and the person beneficially entitled to the amount is a bank which is resident in the UK, and which beneficially owns the foreign holding concerned;
(*c*) the amount arises to the trustees of a discretionary or accumulation trust in respect of a relevant holding of the trust, where the trustees are non-resident, none of the beneficiaries is UK resident, and the trust otherwise satisfies the conditions set out in sub-ss (5) and (6);
(*d*) the amount is eligible for relief as being applicable to a charity;
(*e*) the amount is eligible for relief as relating to an approved pension fund;
(*f*) the amount relates to dividends payable out of the public revenue of the Republic of Ireland, or payable in respect of shares or securities of a Republic of Ireland company or other concern;
(*g*) the amount falls to be treated as the income of, or of the government of, a sovereign power, or of an international organisation as defined in TA 1988 s 51A(8);
(*h*) the person who is beneficially entitled to the amount is a person of a prescribed description who beneficially owns the securities concerned;
(*i*) the amount is derived from a relevant holding held by or on behalf of a person of a prescribed description;
(*j*) the amount is of a prescribed description.

Regulations may provide for a paying agent to treat a relevant payment as not being a chargeable payment where the securities concerned are held by an approved nominee (sub-s (7)). Further regulations may provide for relief under double taxation agreements in relation to interest on gilts, where the securities are held by an approved nominee, by allowing the paying agent to deduct tax at a lower rate, or to treat the interest as not being a chargeable payment (sub-s (8)).

Where dividends are paid without deduction of tax, or subject to deduction of tax at a reduced rate, under these regulations, the nominee may be treated as a paying agent, with the chargeable date being taken as the date when he receives the dividends (sub-s (9)). In such a case, the nominee will be given credit against his liability for tax which has been deducted at a reduced rate (sub-s (10)).

TA 1988 s 118H
This section provides for regulations to be made to exercise control over the exclusions contained in s 118G. Obligations may be imposed on the persons concerned to provide requisite information, to determine whether the requirements for exclusion are satisfied. The relevant exclusion may be disapplied if there is reason to believe that the requirements are not satisfied.

TA 1988 s 118I
This section provides for regulations to be made to reduce the rate of tax deductible, so as to take account of overseas tax paid.

TA 1988 s 118J
This section is concerned with prevention of double accounting for tax. If a relevant dividend is a chargeable payment, it is not to be a chargeable receipt. However, this does not prevent the proceeds of sale of a coupon from being a chargeable receipt.
Regulations may be made to deal with the situation where more than one collecting agent may be liable to account for tax on the same dividend.

TA 1988 s 118K
This is a general section in relation to the power to make regulations.

PART II
OTHER PROVISIONS

Penalties

2 (1) In section 98 of the Taxes Management Act 1970 (penalties in respect of certain information provisions) the words "regulations under section 118D, 118F, 118G, 118H or 118I;" shall be inserted—

(*a*) in column 1 of the Table, after "regulations under section 42A"; and
(*b*) in column 2 of the Table, after "regulations under section 51B".

(2) In the same section—

(*a*) the words "regulations under section 124(3);" shall be inserted in column 1 of the Table after the words inserted by sub-paragraph (1)(*a*) above; and
(*b*) for the words "section 124(3)" in column 2 of the Table there shall be substituted "regulations under section 124(3)".

GENERAL NOTE
Relevant provisions of the new Chapter VIIA are inserted into the Table in TMA 1970 s 98 (penalties relating to special returns etc). In addition, references are also inserted into the Table to regulations under TA 1988 s 124(3), such regulations being provided for by the amendments in para 4.

Amendments of the Taxes Act 1988

3 The Taxes Act 1988 shall be amended in accordance with paragraphs 4 to 7 below.

GENERAL NOTE
This paragraph introduces the incidental amendments to TA 1988.

4 For section 124(2) to (5) there shall be substituted—
"(2) The conditions are—
(*a*) that a person who—
(i) is not resident in the United Kingdom, and
(ii) beneficially owns the quoted Eurobond
is beneficially entitled to the interest;

(*b*) that the quoted Eurobond is held in a recognised clearing system.

(3) The Board may by regulations provide that subsection (1)(*b*) above shall be taken not to apply to a payment of interest unless—

(*a*) the person by or through whom the payment is made (the relevant payer) has received a declaration confirming that one of the conditions of subsection (2) above is satisfied, or

(*b*) they have issued a notice to the relevant payer stating that they consider that one (or both) of those conditions is satisfied.

(4) Regulations under subsection (3) above may—

(*a*) impose requirements as to—

(i) the contents of any declaration to be made in accordance with regulations under subsection (3)(*a*) above,

(ii) the form and manner in which any declaration is to be provided in accordance with any such regulations, and

(iii) the keeping and production to, or to an officer of, the Board of any document in which any such declaration is contained;

(*b*) make provision for any such declaration to be made by the person entitled to the interest (or, as the case may be, the depositary for the recognised clearing system) or by such other person as may be prescribed by the regulations;

(*c*) require the relevant payer to consider the accuracy of any such declaration;

(*d*) make provision for notices to be issued by the Board to such persons as may be described in the regulations where the Board consider that—

(i) one (or both) of the conditions of subsection (2) above, or

(ii) neither of those conditions

is satisfied in relation to interest paid on any holding or quoted Eurobonds;

(*e*) make provision with respect to the furnishing of information by relevant payers, including the inspection of books and other records on behalf of the Board;

(*f*) require relevant payers to deliver returns setting out particulars of payments made by them to which subsection (1)(*b*) above applies and the names and addresses of the persons entitled to them;

(*g*) contain such supplementary, incidental, consequential or transitional provisions as appear to the Board to be necessary or expedient.''.

GENERAL NOTE
This paragraph makes associated changes to TA 1988 s 124 in relation to deduction of tax from interest on quoted eurobonds, as defined in TA 1988 s 124(6). One result of this is that the exemption from deduction of tax at source afforded by TA 1988 s 124(1)(*b*) is subject to conditions to be imposed by regulations under TA 1988 s 124(3).

5 (1) In section 348(3) and in section 349(1), at the end there shall be inserted ''or to any payment which is a relevant payment for the purposes of Chapter VIIA of Part IV''.

(2) In section 349(3), the following paragraph shall be inserted after paragraph (*d*)—

''(*e*) to any payment which is a relevant payment for the purposes of Chapter VIIA of Part IV; or''

GENERAL NOTE
The amendment in this paragraph ensures that relevant payments are outside the scope of TA 1988 s 348 and s 349(1) and (2) (deduction of tax at source).

6 In section 582A (designated international organisations: miscellaneous exemptions), in subsection (1) for ''(2) to (6) below'' there shall be substituted ''(2) and (4) to (6) below and section 118B(4)''.

GENERAL NOTE
This paragraph makes a consequential amendment to TA 1988 s 582A (designated international organisations).

7 In paragraph 4(8) of Schedule 23A (manufactured overseas dividends), for the words "subsection (2) or (3) of section 123 or under Part III, as the case may be, and for Parts III and IV of Schedule 3" there shall be substituted "Chapter VIIA of Part IV and for that Chapter".

GENERAL NOTE
This paragraph amends TA 1988 Sch 23A para 4(8) (manufactured overseas dividends) by substituting a reference to the new Chapter VIIA for the reference to TA 1988 Part III s 123 and Sch 3.

Amendment of the Finance Act 1989

8 In section 178 of the Finance Act 1989 (setting rates of interest), in subsection (2)(*m*), before "160" there shall be inserted "118F,".

GENERAL NOTE
This paragraph amends FA 1989 s 178, so that that section applies to interest chargeable under the new TA 1988 s 118F(3).

SCHEDULE 30

INVESTMENTS IN HOUSING

INTRODUCTION

The Government's intention to make tax provision for housing investment trusts was announced in the White Paper "Our future homes" published on 27 June 1995. Previously, TA 1988 s 842 provided that an investment trust company could not be approved by the Revenue unless its income arose wholly or mainly from shares or securities. This rule is amended so that approved investment trusts are additionally able to invest, either wholly or partly, in certain categories of residential property to be let on assured tenancies. Net rental income accruing to an investment trust in respect of such housing is taxed at the small companies' rate of corporation tax, and the normal exemption of investment trusts from tax on capital gains applies to their disposals of the properties.

The change is effective for accounting periods beginning on or after the day on which FA 1996 is passed (see Budget Press Release, 28 November 1995, "Housing investment trusts", *Simon's Weekly Tax Intelligence* 1995, p 1855).

Reduced rate of corporation tax

1 After section 508 of the Taxes Act 1988 there shall be inserted the following sections—

"508A   Investment trusts investing in housing

(1) Where any company that is an investment trust has eligible rental income for any accounting period—

(*a*) the rate of corporation tax chargeable for any financial year on the trust's housing investment profits for that period shall be deemed to be the small companies' rate for that year; and

(*b*) its housing investment profits for that period shall be treated for the purposes of section 13 as excluded from its basic profits for that period.

(2) For the purposes of this section—

(*a*) a company's eligible rental income for any period is so much of its income for that period as consists in rents or other receipts deriving from lettings by the company of eligible properties; and

(*b*) its housing investment profits for any period are so much of its profits for that period as represents the amount chargeable to tax under Schedule A in respect of its eligible rental income for that period.

(3) In computing the amount mentioned in subsection (2)(*b*) above for any period, deductions shall be made which (except in so far as they exceed the amount from which they are deducted) are, in aggregate, not less than the sum of the following amounts—

(*a*) every amount which is both—

(i) deductible (otherwise than as a debit brought into account under Chapter II of Part IV of the Finance Act 1996) in the computation of any income of the company, or of its total profits, for that period, and

(ii) referable to, or to activities connected with, the letting by the company on assured tenancies of dwelling-houses that are eligible properties when so let,

and

(*b*) any amount that is so referable that would represent a non-trading deficit on the company's loan relationships for that period.

(4) For the purposes of subsection (3) above any question—

(*a*) whether for any period there is an amount referable to any matter that would represent a non-trading deficit on a company's loan relationships, or

(*b*) as to what that amount is for that period,

shall be determined by computing whether and to what extent there would for that period have been a non-trading deficit on the company's loan relationships if debits and credits fell to be brought into account under Chapter II of Part IV of the Finance Act 1996 to the extent only that they are referable to that matter.

508B Interpretation of section 508A

(1) In section 508A 'eligible property', in relation to a company, means (subject to the following provisions of this section) any dwelling-house as respects which the following conditions are satisfied—

(*a*) the company first acquired an interest in the dwelling-house on or after 1st April 1996;
(*b*) that interest was not, at the time when it was acquired, subject to any letting or to any statutory tenancy;
(*c*) at that time no arrangements had been made by the company or any person connected with it for the letting of the dwelling-house;
(*d*) the interest of the company in the dwelling-house is a freehold interest or an interest under a long lease at a low rent;
(*e*) the consideration given by the company for the acquisition of its interest in the dwelling-house did not exceed—

(i) £125,000, in the case of a dwelling-house in Greater London, or
(ii) £85,000, in any other case;

(*f*) the dwelling-house is let by the company under an assured tenancy and is neither—

(i) let by the company in consideration of a premium within the meaning of Schedule 8 to the 1992 Act, nor
(ii) a dwelling-house in respect of which the person to whom it is let or any associate of his has been granted any option to purchase.

(2) For the purposes of paragraph (*b*) of subsection (1) above, no account shall be taken of any shorthold tenancy or statutory shorthold tenancy to which the interest became subject before the time when it was acquired.

(3) For the purposes of paragraph (*c*) of subsection (1) above, no account shall be taken of any arrangements made by a person connected with the company in question before the time when the interest was acquired by the company if—

(*a*) that person had an interest in the dwelling-house when he made those arrangements;
(*b*) that person did not dispose of his interest at any time after the arrangements were entered into and before the company acquired its interest; and
(*c*) the arrangements were such as to confer a relevant entitlement on a person who, at the time when the company acquired its interest, was a tenant under any shorthold tenancy of the dwelling-house (or any part of it).

(4) For the purposes of subsection (3)(*c*) above a relevant entitlement is an entitlement of a tenant under a shorthold tenancy of any premises, on the coming to an end of that tenancy, to such a further tenancy of the same or substantially the same premises as will itself be a shorthold tenancy.

(5) For the purposes of this section the consideration given by a company for the acquisition of an interest in a dwelling-house shall be taken (subject to subsection (6) below) to include—

(*a*) any amount expended by the company on the construction or renovation of the dwelling-house or on any conversion by virtue of which that dwelling-house came to be usable as such;
(*b*) any amount so expended by a person connected with the company; and
(*c*) any consideration given by a person connected with the company for the acquisition of any such interest in the dwelling-house as—

(i) is subsequently acquired by the company, or
(ii) is held by such a person at the same time as the company holds its interest in the premises.

(6) Where a company has acquired any interest in a dwelling-house from a person connected with that company—

(*a*) amounts expended by that person as mentioned in paragraph (*a*) of subsection (5) above, and

(*b*) the amount of any consideration given by that person for an interest in the dwelling-house,

shall be treated by virtue of that subsection as included in the consideration given by the company to the extent only that the aggregate of those amounts exceeds the consideration given by that company to that person for the interest acquired from that person by the company.

(7) In section 508A and this section—

'associate' has the meaning given by subsections (3) and (4) of section 417;
'assured tenancy' means—

(*a*) any letting which is an assured tenancy for the purposes of the Housing Act 1988 or the Housing (Scotland) Act 1988, or

(*b*) any tenancy in Northern Ireland which complies with such requirements or conditions as may be prescribed by regulations made by the Department of the Environment for Northern Ireland;

'letting' includes a letting by virtue of an agreement for a lease or under a licence, and 'let' shall be construed accordingly;
'long lease', in relation to the interest of a company in any dwelling-house, means a lease for a term of years certain of which at least 21 years remains unexpired at the time when that interest was acquired by the company;
'low rent' means a rent at an annual rate not exceeding—

(*a*) £1,000, in the case of a dwelling-house in Greater London; and

(*b*) £250, in any other case;

'rent' has the same meaning as it has for the purposes of Schedule A in its application to companies within the charge to corporation tax;
'shorthold tenancy' means any letting which is an assured shorthold tenancy for the purposes of the Housing Act 1988 or a short assured tenancy for the purposes of the Housing (Scotland) Act 1988;
'statutory shorthold tenancy' means—

(*a*) a statutory periodic tenancy within the meaning of the Housing Act 1988 which arose on the coming to an end of an assured shorthold tenancy which was a fixed term tenancy, or

(*b*) a statutory assured tenancy within the meaning of the Housing (Scotland) Act 1988 which arose on the coming to an end of a short assured tenancy;

'statutory tenancy'—

(*a*) in relation to England and Wales, has the same meaning as in the Rent Act 1977;

(*b*) in relation to Scotland, has the same meaning as in the Rent (Scotland) Act 1984; and

(*c*) in relation to Northern Ireland, has the same meaning as in the Rent (Northern Ireland) Order 1978.

(8) Section 839 shall apply for the purposes of this section.

(9) Section 508A shall have effect where—

(*a*) a company acquires an interest in any dwelling-house, and

(*b*) a person connected with the company has previously acquired an interest in the dwelling-house, being an interest subsequently acquired by the company or one held by that person at the same time as the company holds its interest,

as if references in this section (except in subsection (3) above) to the time when the company first acquired an interest in the premises included references to the time when the person connected with the company first acquired his interest.

(10) The Treasury may, if they think fit, by order vary the figures for the time being

specified in paragraph (*e*) of subsection (1) above; and an order under this subsection may make different provision for different localities in Greater London or elsewhere.

(11)   In the application of this section to Scotland—

(*a*)   references to acquiring an interest shall be construed, if there is a contract to acquire the interest, as references to entering into that contract;

(*b*)   references to the freehold interest shall be construed as references to the estate or interest of the proprietor of the *dominium utile* or, in the case of property other than feudal property, of the owner;

(*c*)   in the definition of 'long lease' in subsection (7) above, the word 'certain' shall be omitted.

(12)   Regulations made for the purposes of paragraph (*b*) of the definition of 'assured tenancy' in subsection (7) above shall be made by statutory rule for the purposes of the Statutory Rules (Northern Ireland) Order 1979, and shall be subject to negative resolution within the meaning of section 41(6) of the Interpretation Act (Northern Ireland) 1954.''

GENERAL NOTE

This paragraph inserts new ss 508A and 508B into TA 1988. These sections contain the rules for the taxation of income from eligible properties and for determining whether a property is eligible.

TA 1988 S 508A

This section provides that the small companies' rate of corporation tax applies to the housing investment profits of an approved investment trust company (sub-s (1)). The housing investment profits are also excluded from "basic profits" for the purposes of TA 1988 s 13. The effect of these provisions of sub-s (1) would seem to be that, whilst the housing investment profits enjoy the lower rate of tax, the existence of those profits may increase the rate of tax payable by the company on its other profits. The calculation of the marginal relief under TA 1988 s 13(2) will be affected by the exclusion of the housing investment profits from "basic profits".

The housing investment profits are defined as the amount chargeable under Schedule A in respect of eligible rental income (sub-s (2)), less amounts deductible from total profits which relate to the company's letting of eligible properties (sub-s (3)). Eligible rental income consists of rents or other receipts from the letting of eligible properties (sub-s (2)).

TA 1988 S 508B

This section contains the definition of "eligible property" (sub-ss (1)–(6)) and other definitions (sub-s (7)), together with incidental provisions (sub-ss (8)–(12)).

Only dwelling-houses costing £85,000 or less (£125,000 in Greater London) can be eligible properties, and the following conditions must also be satisfied. The interest acquired by the company must be either the freehold or a long lease at a low rent, and that interest must not have been subject to any letting or statutory tenancy (other than a shorthold tenancy or statutory shorthold tenancy) at the time of acquisition. There must have been no arrangements by the company or a connected person to let the property at the time when it was acquired (subject to a limited exception for a shorthold tenancy resulting from arrangements previously made by a connected person), but the property must be let by the company under an assured tenancy. The assured tenancy must not be in consideration of a premium, and there must be no option to purchase the property granted to the tenant or an associate. The property must have been acquired by the company after 31 March 1996, and, for this purpose, the time of earlier acquisition by a connected person may be taken in certain circumstances.

With regard to the maximum cost of the property, the amount of the consideration given by the company for the acquisition of the interest is taken to include (sub-s (5))—

(*a*)   amounts spent by the company, or by a person connected with the company, on construction or renovation of the dwelling-house, or on conversion of the property to a usable dwelling-house;

(*b*)   the cost to a person connected with the company of the acquisition of an interest in the dwelling-house which has either been subsequently acquired by the company, or is held by the connected person at the same time as the company holds its interest.

However, where the company has acquired an interest in the property from a connected person, the costs incurred by the connected person within (*a*) and (*b*) above are only deemed to be included in the consideration for the property given by the company to the extent that those costs exceed the consideration given by the company to the connected person in respect of the interest acquired from that person (sub-s (6)).

The figures for the maximum cost of eligible properties may be varied by Treasury order (sub-s (10)).

A property is considered to be any unit of accommodation, so that three separate flats in the same building represent three properties (Budget Press Release, 28 November 1995, "Housing investment trusts", *Simon's Weekly Tax Intelligence* 1995, p 1855).

Investments in housing by investment trusts

2 (1) Section 842 of the Taxes Act 1988 (investment trusts) shall be amended as follows.

(2) In subsection (1) (conditions as to a company's income for approval as an investment trust)—

(*a*) in paragraph (*a*), for "derived wholly or mainly from shares or securities" there shall be substituted "consists wholly or mainly of eligible investment income"; and
(*b*) in paragraph (*e*), for "the income it derives from shares or securities" there shall be substituted "its eligible investment income".

(3) After that subsection there shall be inserted the following subsection—

"(1AA) Income is eligible investment income for the purposes of this section in so far as it is either—

(*a*) income deriving from shares or securities, or
(*b*) eligible rental income, within the meaning of section 508A."

GENERAL NOTE
TA 1988 s 842 is concerned with the conditions for approval of investment trust companies. The changes to that section, to permit investment trusts to invest in eligible properties, are contained in this paragraph.

The eligible investment income of an investment trust will be either income from shares or securities, or eligible rental income as defined in TA 1988 s 508A.

Commencement

3 This Schedule has effect in relation to accounting periods beginning on or after the day on which this Act is passed.

GENERAL NOTE
This Schedule applies for accounting periods beginning on or after the date of Royal Assent.

SCHEDULE 31   Section 163

LIFE ASSURANCE BUSINESS LOSSES

BACKGROUND NOTE

This Schedule makes a number of important changes to the rules for the calculation of and relief for losses incurred in life insurance business which were brought in by FA 1995 s 51 and Sch 8 para 16. That legislation limited or prevented relief for losses arising out of additions of capital to the long-term fund, often on the transfer of business between companies. Such losses were an artificial creation of the arithmetic of the then existing rules. Genuine losses, often funded by injections of capital by the parent company, could however occur in the early years of operation of a new company, and the new rules provide for relief to be available in some such circumstances. On the other hand, it was found that the 1995 legislation could be circumvented by ensuring that the loss arose in a different accounting period from the injection of capital, and the new rules prevent relief for losses created artificially in this way. The new legislation also prevents effective double relief for the same loss, clarifies the interaction of loss relief and the spreading of new business acquisition expenses and makes a number of minor technical amendments.

Expenses of management

1 In section 76 of the Taxes Act 1988 (expenses of management: insurance companies) in subsection (1) (which applies section 75 of that Act with specified exceptions) before paragraph (*a*) there shall be inserted—

"(*aa*) where the whole or any part of a loss arising to the company in respect of its life assurance business in an accounting period is set off under section 393A or 403(1), there shall be deducted from the amount treated as the expenses of management for that period an amount equal to so much of the loss as, in the aggregate, is so set off, reduced by the amounts by which any losses for that period under section 436, 439B or 441 fall to be reduced under section 434A(2)(*b*); and
(*ab*) section 75(1) shall have effect with the substitution for 'in computing profits apart from this section' of—

'(*a*) in computing income for the purposes of Schedule A, or
  (*b*) by virtue of section 121(3) in computing income from the letting of rights to work minerals in the United Kingdom'; and".

GENERAL NOTE

This paragraph amends TA 1988 s 76 with the insertion of sub-para (1)(*aa*) and (*ab*).

The new s 76(1)(*aa*) provides that where a loss on life insurance business is set against the company's profits for the same or an earlier accounting period, or is claimed as group relief, the company's management expenses for the same period are reduced by the aggregate amount of the reliefs so given less the restriction made to pension, life reinsurance and overseas life assurance business losses in respect of charges.

Section 76(1)(*ab*) modifies the operation of s 75(1) so that relief (now limited to basic life assurance and general annuity business) is not excluded by the deduction of expenses in a loss or notional Case I computation, and prevents relief being given both as a management expense and under Schedule A or in computing the income from the letting of mineral rights.

Computation of losses and limitation on relief

2 (1) In relation to accounting periods beginning on or after 1st January 1996 and ending after 31st March 1996, section 434A of the Taxes Act 1988 (life assurance business: computation of losses and limitation on relief) shall be amended as follows—

(*a*) for subsection (2) there shall be substituted the subsection (2) set out in sub-paragraph (2) below; and
(*b*) in subsection (2A) (which is inserted by paragraph 23(2) of Schedule 14 to this Act) for "(2)(*c*)" there shall be substituted "(2)(*a*)(ii)".

(2) The subsection (2) set out in this sub-paragraph is as follows—

"(2) Where for any accounting period the loss arising to an insurance company from its life assurance business falls to be computed in accordance with the provisions of this Act applicable to Case I of Schedule D—

499

(*a*) the loss resulting from the computation shall be reduced (but not below nil) by the aggregate of—

(i) the aggregate amount treated as a charge on income in computing for the period, otherwise than in accordance with those provisions, the profits or losses of the company's life assurance business; and
(ii) any relevant non-trading deficit for that period on the company's debtor relationships; and

(*b*) if the whole or any part of that loss as so reduced is set off—

(i) under section 393A, or
(ii) under section 403(1),

any losses for that period under section 436, 439B or 441 shall be reduced to nil, unless the aggregate of those losses exceeds the total of the amounts set off as mentioned in sub-paragraphs (i) and (ii) above, in which case each of those losses shall be reduced by an amount which bears to that total the proportion which the loss in question bears to that aggregate.''

(3) In relation to accounting periods beginning on or after 1st January 1996 and ending on or before 31st March 1996, for subsection (2) of section 434A of the Taxes Act 1988 there shall be substituted the subsection (2) set out in sub-paragraph (2) above, but with the following amendments to paragraph (*a*), that is to say—

(*a*) in the words preceding sub-paragraph (i), the words ''the aggregate of '' shall be omitted;
(*b*) in sub-paragraph (i), for ''aggregate amount treated as a charge on income'' there shall be substituted ''amount of interest and annuities treated as charges on income''; and
(*c*) sub-paragraph (ii) shall be omitted.

GENERAL NOTE
Subparagraphs (1) and (2) amend TA 1988 s 434A, as substituted by FA 1995 Sch 8 para 20, for accounting periods beginning after 31 December 1995 and ending after 31 March 1996. Under s 434A(2) as amended, a loss computed under Case I provisions is to be reduced by the amount treated as a charge and any non-trading deficit on debtor relationships (both of which are relieved separately). Where any part of such a loss is relieved against other profits or by way of group relief, any Case VI losses referable to pension, life reinsurance or overseas life assurance business are reduced to nil, unless in aggregate they exceed the aggregate reliefs in respect of the Case I loss in which case they are proportionately reduced. This provision reverses the previous order of priority—under TA 1988 s 434A(2)(*a*) as originally enacted, the Case I loss available for relief was reduced by the Case VI losses relating to the categories of business mentioned above. Subparagraph 2(1)(*b*) makes a consequential amendment to a cross-reference.
Subparagraph (3) provides for the exceptional case of an accounting period wholly within the period from 1 January to 31 March 1996 by excluding the references in the new s 434A(2) to loan relationships (the legislation on which only applies to accounting periods ending after the latter date).

Spreading of relief for acquisition expenses

3 (1) In section 86 of the Finance Act 1989 (spreading of relief for acquisition expenses) in subsection (1), for the words from ''less any such repayments'' to the end there shall be substituted—

''reduced by the items specified in subsection (1A) below.''

(2) After that subsection there shall be inserted—

''(1A) Those items are—

(*a*) the appropriate portion of any deduction falling to be made under paragraph (*aa*) of subsection (1) of section 76 of the Taxes Act 1988 for the period in question;
(*b*) any such repayments or refunds falling within paragraph (*c*) of that subsection as are received in that period;
(*c*) any reinsurance commissions falling within paragraph (*ca*) of that subsection.

(1B) For the purposes of paragraph (*a*) of subsection (1A) above, 'the appropriate portion' of the deduction there mentioned is the amount which bears to the whole of that deduction the proportion which the acquisition expenses, without making the reduction required by subsection (1) above, would bear to the whole of the expenses of management, without making the deductions required by paragraphs (*aa*), (*a*), (*c*) and (*ca*) of section 76(1) of the Taxes Act 1988.''

GENERAL NOTE
This paragraph amends the rules for spreading acquisition expenses, in FA 1989 s 86, to reflect the changes made to TA 1988 s 76 (relief for management expenses) by para 1 of this Schedule. The new s 86(1A) ensures that the amount of acquisition costs spread forward is calculated by reference to the net amount after deducting part of the reduction made in respect of the losses referable to basic life assurance and general annuity business. The amount to be deducted is in the ratio of gross acquisition costs to gross management expenses (FA 1989 new s 86(1B)).

Ascertainment of losses

4 In section 83 of the Finance Act 1989 (receipts to be brought into account) for subsection (3) (ascertainment of losses) there shall be substituted—

''(3) In ascertaining whether or to what extent a company has incurred a loss in respect of that business in a case where an amount is added to the company's long term business fund as part of or in connection with—

(*a*) a transfer of business to the company, or
(*b*) a demutualisation of the company not involving a transfer of business,

that amount shall (subject to subsection (4) below) be taken into account, for the period for which it is brought into account, as an increase in value of the assets of that fund within subsection (2)(*b*) above.

(4) Subsection (3) above does not apply where, or to the extent that, the amount concerned—

(*a*) would fall to be taken into account as a receipt apart from this section,
(*b*) is taken into account under subsection (2) above otherwise than by virtue of subsection (3) above, or
(*c*) is specifically exempted from tax.

(5) Any amount which is to be taken into account pursuant to subsection (3) above for a period of account shall be so taken into account—

(*a*) after the making of any reduction under subsection (6) of section 83AA below in relation to that period, but
(*b*) before the making of any reduction under subsection (3) of that section in relation to an accounting period of the company ending in or with that period.

(6) In subsection (3) above 'transfer of business' means—

(*a*) a transfer of the whole or part of the long term business of an insurance company in accordance with a scheme sanctioned by a court under Part I of Schedule 2C to the Insurance Companies Act 1982;
(*b*) a qualifying overseas transfer, within the meaning of paragraph 4A of Schedule 19AC to the Taxes Act 1988; or
(*c*) the making of a contract of reinsurance which, in whole or in part, constitutes or forms part of a total reinsurance by the reinsured, unless the reinsurer under the contract falls within section 439A of the Taxes Act 1988 (pure reinsurance).

(7) For the purposes of subsection (3)(*a*) above, a transfer of business falling within subsection (6)(*c*) above shall be treated as a transfer of business to the company which is the reinsurer under the contract of reinsurance.

(8) In this section—

'add', in relation to an amount and a company's long term business fund, includes transfer (whether from other assets of the company or otherwise);
'demutualisation' means the conversion, under the law of any territory, of a company which has been carrying on insurance business without having a share capital into a company with a share capital, without any change of legal personality;
'total reinsurance' means the reinsurance (whether effected by a single contract of

501

reinsurance or by two or more such contracts, taken together, whether or not made with the same reinsurer) of the whole, or substantially the whole, of the reinsured's risk—

(*a*) under policies of a particular description issued in respect of insurances made in the course of carrying on life assurance business before the making of the contract of reinsurance (or, in a case where there are two or more contracts of reinsurance, the last of them); or

(*b*) under contracts of a particular description so made."

GENERAL NOTE

This paragraph amends FA 1989 s 83, itself amended by FA 1996 Sch 8 para 16. The changes, together with the new ss 83AA and 83AB inserted by para 5 and the changes made to s 83A by para 6 of this Schedule, enact the new refined approach to losses arising from additions of capital to the long-term fund. It should be noted that FA 1989 s 83(3) as amended applies only to the calculation of and relief for a loss, and not to the computation of profit for any purpose. The treatment of additions to capital which do not create a loss, or which exceed the loss which would otherwise arise, is to be found in FA 1989 new ss 83AA and 83AB inserted by para 5. It should also be noted that as s 83 is concerned with receipts that are to be brought into account in a computation of profits or losses for Case I purposes, the term "loss" is presumed to mean a loss as computed or in the course of computation for tax purposes, and not to an actuarial deficit (or to the result shown by the technical account for life assurance business required by article 34 of the EC Insurance Accounts Directive 91/674/EEC).

FA 1989 s 83(3) is replaced by the new sub-ss (3)–(8) which targed losses arising from injections of capital made in connection with a transfer of business to the company or the demutualisation of the company not involving a transfer of business. "Transfer" is defined by sub-s (6) and comprises not only transfers sanctioned by the regulatory legislation but also "total reinsurance", except where the reinsurer is a pure reinsurer. As the legislation is concerned with additions to the fund, the loss targeted by the inclusion of reinsurance is a loss incurred by a reinsurer, but the exclusion of a pure insurer from the scope of the legislation ensures that the ordinary operation of the reinsurance market is unimpeded (a pure insurer is only assessable under Case I following TA 1988 s 439A). "Total reinsurance" means the cession of the primary insurer's whole liability under a policy or category of policy (sub-s (8), which also defines "demutualisation"). Subsection (5) links the calculation with the provisions of the new s 83AA.

Application of surplus in reduction of certain losses

5 After section 83 of the Finance Act 1989 there shall be inserted—

"83AA Amounts added to long term business fund of a company in excess of that company's loss

(1) If one or more relevant amounts are brought into account for a period of account of a company and either—

(*a*) the aggregate of those amounts exceeds the loss which, after the making of any reduction under subsection (6) below but before any application of section 83(3) above in relation to that period, would have arisen to the company in that period in respect of its life assurance business, or

(*b*) no such loss would have so arisen,

the surplus for that period shall be applied in accordance with the following provisions of this section and section 83AB below.

(2) In this section—

'relevant amount' means so much of any amount which is added to the long term business fund of a company as mentioned in subsection (3) of section 83 above as does not fall within any of the paragraphs of subsection (4) of that section;

'surplus', in relation to a period of account of a company, means (subject to section 83AB(2) below)—

(*a*) if the aggregate of the relevant amounts brought into account for that period exceeds the amount of any loss which, after the making of any reduction under subsection (6) below but before any application of section 83(3) above in relation to that period, would have arisen to the company in that period in respect of its life assurance business, the amount of the excess; or (*b*) if no such loss would have so arisen, the aggregate of the relevant amounts brought into account for that period.

(3) Where, apart from section 83AB(2) below, there is a surplus for a period of account of a company for which there are brought into account one or more relevant amounts which were added to the company's long term business fund as part of, or in connection with, a particular transfer of business, the appropriate portion of the surplus for that period shall be treated as reducing (but not below nil) so much of any loss arising to the transferor company in the relevant accounting period as, on a just and reasonable apportionment of the loss, is referable to the business which is the subject of that particular transfer.

(4) For the purposes of subsection (3) above, the appropriate portion of the surplus for a period of account of a company is, in the case of any particular transfer of business, the amount which bears to that surplus (apart from any additions by virtue of section 83AB(2) below) the proportion which A bears to B, where—

A is the aggregate of such of the relevant amounts added to the company's long term business fund as part of, or in connection with, that particular transfer of business as are brought into account for that period, and
B is the aggregate of the relevant amounts brought into account for that period.

(5) Any reduction pursuant to subsection (3) above of the loss arising to the transferor company in the relevant accounting period shall be made after—

(*a*) the making of any reduction under subsection (6) below, and
(*b*) any application of section 83(3) above,

in relation to the period of account of that company in which falls the date of the particular transfer of business in question.

(6) Any loss arising to a company in respect of its life assurance business in a period of account subsequent to one for which there is a surplus shall be reduced (but not below nil) by so much of that surplus as cannot be applied—

(*a*) under subsection (3) above;
(*b*) under this subsection, in the reduction of a loss arising to the company in an earlier period of account; or
(*c*) under section 83AB below, in relation to a transfer of business from the company in that or any earlier period of account.

(7) Any reduction pursuant to subsection (6) above of a loss arising to a company in a period of account shall be made—

(*a*) before any application of section 83(3) above in relation to that period, and
(*b*) if the company is also the transferor company in relation to a particular transfer of business, before the making of any reduction under subsection (3) above in relation to that one of its accounting periods which is the relevant accounting period in relation to that transfer.

(8) A surplus in respect of an earlier period of account shall be applied under subsection (6) above before a surplus in respect of a later period of account.

(9) All such adjustments to the liability to tax of any person shall be made, whether by assessment or otherwise, as may be required to give effect to this section.

(10) In this section—

'add' has the same meaning as in section 83 above;
'the relevant accounting period' means the accounting period of the transferor company which—

(*a*) ends on the date of the transfer of business mentioned in subsection (3) above, or
(*b*) if that transfer of business falls within section 83(6)(*c*) above and no accounting period of the transferor company ends on that date, ends next after that date;

'transfer of business' has the same meaning as in section 83(3) above;

'the transferor company' means the company from which the transfer of business mentioned in subsection (3) above is effected.

(11) A transfer of business falling within section 83(6)(c) above shall be treated for the purposes of this section as a transfer of business from the company which is the reinsured under the contract of reinsurance.

83AB Treatment of surplus where there is a subsequent transfer of business from the company etc

(1) If an amount is added to the long term business fund of a company as part of or in connection with a transfer of business to the company, or a demutualisation of the company not involving a transfer of business, and—

(a) there is a surplus for the period of account of the company for which that amount is brought into account,

(b) at any time after the transfer of business or demutualisation, there is a transfer of business from the company (the 'subsequent transfer'), and

(c) at the end of the relevant period of account there remains at least some of the surplus mentioned in paragraph (a) above which cannot be applied—

(i) under subsection (3) of section 83AA above,

(ii) under subsection (6) of that section, in the reduction of a loss arising to the company in an earlier period of account, or

(iii) under this section, in relation to an earlier subsequent transfer,

so much of the surplus falling within paragraph (c) above as, on a just and reasonable apportionment, is referable to business which is the subject of the subsequent transfer shall be applied under this section.

(2) An amount of surplus which is to be applied under this section shall be so applied by being treated as an amount of surplus (additional to any other amounts of surplus) for the period of account of the transferee company which last precedes the period of account of that company in which the subsequent transfer is effected, whether or not there is in fact any such preceding period of account.

(3) If, in a case where an amount is treated under subsection (2) above as an amount of surplus for a period of account of a company, the period is not one for which there is brought into account an amount added to the company's long term business fund in connection with the subsequent transfer, subsection (1) above shall have effect in relation to any transfer of business from the company subsequent to that transfer as if an amount had been so added and had been brought into account for that period.

(4) Any question as to what is a just and reasonable apportionment in any case for the purposes of subsection (1) above shall be determined by the Special Commissioners who shall determine the question in the same manner as they determine appeals; but any person affected by the apportionment shall be entitled to appear and be heard or make representations in writing.

(5) A surplus in respect of an earlier period of account shall be applied under this section before a surplus in respect of a later period of account.

(6) All such adjustments to the liability to tax of any person shall be made, whether by assessment or otherwise, as may be required to give effect to this section.

(7) In this section—

'add' has the same meaning as in section 83 above;

'demutualisation' has the same meaning as in section 83 above;

'the relevant period of account' means the period of account of the company from which the subsequent transfer is effected which consists of or includes the accounting period of that company which—

(a) ends with the day on which the subsequent transfer is effected; or

(b) if the subsequent transfer is a transfer of business falling within section 83(6)(c) above and no accounting period of the company ends on that day, ends next after that day;

'surplus' has the same meaning as in section 83AA above;

'transfer of business' has the same meaning as in section 83(3) above;
'transferee company' means the company to which the subsequent transfer of
   business is effected.

(8) Where it is necessary for any purpose of this section to identify the time at which
a demutualisation of a company takes place, that time shall be taken to be the time
when the company first issues shares.

(9) A transfer of business falling within section 83(6)(*c*) above shall be treated for the
purposes of this section as a transfer of business from the company which is the
reinsured under the contract of reinsurance to the company which is the reinsurer
under that contract.''

GENERAL NOTE
Since FA 1989 s 83(3), as amended, applies only to the computation of a loss, the legislation
goes on to provide, in FA 1989 new ss 83AA and 83BB inserted by this paragraph, for cases where
the bringing into account of additions to the fund has no effect on the tax computation, or is only
partially reflected therein. The legislation provides for the deduction, in computations of the
company's losses for other periods, or of losses arising to a transferor or transferee, depending on
the circumstances, of the whole part of the "surplus". This term is slightly misleading—it does
not refer to an actuarial surplus but to a figure calculated in accordance with FA 1989 new
s 83AA(2).

FA 1989 s 83AA
Subsection (1) sets out the circumstances in which a "surplus" has to be calculated and applied
in accordance with the following subsections and the provisions of s 83AB. One or more "relevant
amounts", that is additions to the fund caught by s 83(3), must have been brought to account and
either (*a*) the aggregate of those amounts exceeds the loss which would otherwise have arisen or
(*b*) there would not have been a loss.
The "surplus" is one of two numbers (s 83AA(2)):

(*a*) the excess of "relevant amounts" over the amount of the loss (calculated after deducting a
"surplus" brought forward but before taking account of the "relevant amounts") or
(*b*) if there would not have been a loss calculated as in (*a*), the aggregate of the "relevant
amounts".

Subsections (3)–(8) set out how the "surplus" is to be dealt with in the case of transfers
(including reinsurance). The "surplus", or the part of it referable to a particular transfer, reduces
any loss of the transferor referable to the transfer in question. Where several "relevant amounts"
are brought into account, the surplus is allocated in the proportion that the "relevant amount",
referable to the particular transfer, bears to the total "relevant amounts". The reduction of the
loss is made after the addition of amounts added to the fund under s 83(3) as amended and any
reduction in respect of a "surplus" brought forward under sub-s (6). Amounts of "surplus" which
cannot be applied against the loss of the transferor for the relevant accounting period are set
against the losses of subsequent accounting periods until exhausted. The losses against which the
"surplus" is set are the losses calculated before the addition of transfers to the fund or any
reduction to be made where the company is itself a transferor company affected by s 83AA(3).
"Surpluses" are dealt with in the order of the accounting periods to which they relate.
Subsection (9) provides for the adjustment of tax liabilities and sub-ss (10) and (11) contain
definitions and interpretation.

FA 1989 s 83AB
This section sets out the treatment of a "surplus", referable to either a transfer (including
reinsurance) or demutualisation, where there is a subsequent transfer of the business in question.
The unapplied "surplus", insofar as it relates to the business transferred, is treated as if it were
a "surplus" of the transferee for the accounting period preceding the transfer, so that it can be
carried forward against any loss of the transferee for the accounting period of the transfer
(sub-ss (1) and (2)). If necessary, an amount transferred to the fund is deemed to have been
brought into account, so that s 83AA is triggered (sub-s (3)).
Subsections (4)–(9) provide for the adjudication of disputes, give the priority of set-offs, allow
adjustments of liabilities, and provide the relevant definitions and interpretation.

Meaning of "brought into account" in sections 83AA and 83AB

6 (1) In section 83A of the Finance Act 1989, in subsection (1) (meaning of "brought
into account" in section 83)—

(*a*) for "In section 83" there shall be substituted "In sections 83 to 83AB"; and
(*b*) for "that section" there shall be substituted "those sections".

(2) In subsection (2) of that section (the accounts which are recognised for the purposes of that section) for "that section" there shall be substituted "those sections".

Enactments disapplying section 83(3) of the Finance Act 1989

7 (1) The following provisions of the Taxes Act 1988 (each of which provides for section 83(3) of the Finance Act 1989 not to apply in certain cases) shall cease to have effect—

(a) section 436(3)(aa);
(b) section 439B(3)(b); and
(c) section 441(4)(aa).

(2) In consequence of sub-paragraph (1)(b) and (c) above, the word "and" shall be added at the end of section 439B(3)(a) and section 441(4)(a) of the Taxes Act 1988.

Overseas life insurance companies

8 (1) Schedule 8A to the Finance Act 1989 (modifications of sections 83 and 89 in relation to overseas life insurance companies) shall be amended in accordance with the following provisions of this paragraph.

(2) In the heading "Modifications of sections 83 and 89 in relation to overseas life insurance companies" after "83" there shall be inserted "to 83A".

(3) In paragraph 1(1), for "sections 83 and 83A" there shall be substituted "sections 83 to 83A".

(4) In paragraph 1A, in sub-paragraph (4)—

(a) for the words from "being transferred" to "added to that fund" there shall be substituted "being added to the company's long term business fund"; and
(b) in the second sentence, for "a transfer" and "transferred" there shall be substituted respectively "an addition" and "added".

(5) After that sub-paragraph there shall be added—

"(5) Any reference in section 83AA(2), (3) or (4) or 83AB(1) or (3) to an amount being added to the relevant company's long term business fund shall be construed in accordance with sub-paragraph (4) above."

(6) In paragraph 1C(4), for "transfer" there shall be substituted "addition".

Transitional provisions

9 (1) In the application of section 83AA or 83AB of the Finance Act 1989 in a case where one or more relevant amounts added to a company's long term business fund on or before 25th March 1996 are brought into account for a period of account beginning on or after 1st January 1996—

(a) the amount of any loss which, before any application of section 83(3) of that Act in relation to that period, would have arisen to the company in that period shall be treated as reduced (but not below nil) by the aggregate of those relevant amounts; and
(b) except as provided by paragraph (a) above, those relevant amounts shall be disregarded.

(2) In the application of sub-paragraph (1) above in relation to an overseas life insurance company, any reference to an amount added to a company's long term business fund shall be taken as a reference to any assets which became assets of the long term business fund of an overseas life insurance company used or held for the purposes of the company's United Kingdom branch or agency, having immediately previously been—

(*a*) held by the company otherwise than as assets of that fund, or
(*b*) used or held otherwise than for those purposes.

(3) If the relevant accounting period mentioned in subsection (3) of section 83AA of the Finance Act 1989 is a period beginning before 1st January 1996, only the appropriate portion of the eligible loss shall be reduced pursuant to that subsection; and for the purposes of this sub-paragraph—

(*a*) "the eligible loss" means so much of the loss arising to the transferor company in the relevant accounting period as, on a just and reasonable apportionment of the loss for the purposes of that subsection, is referable to the business which is the subject of the particular transfer of business in question; and
(*b*) "the appropriate portion" of the eligible loss is the amount which bears to the eligible loss the proportion which A bears to B where—

A is the number of days in the relevant accounting period which fall on or after 1st January 1996; and
B is the total number of days in the relevant accounting period.

(4) Paragraph 10(2) below shall not prevent—

(*a*) an amount of surplus for a period of account of a company beginning on or after 1st January 1996, or
(*b*) an amount of surplus for any period of account of a company which, by virtue of the operation of this sub-paragraph, derives from an amount of surplus falling within paragraph (*a*) above,

from being treated by virtue of section 83AB of the Finance Act 1989 as an amount of surplus for the period of account of another company last preceding its earliest period of account ending on or after 1st January 1996 (whenever beginning) or from being applied accordingly under section 83AA(6) or 83AB of that Act.

(5) In this paragraph—

"add" has the same meaning as in section 83 of the Finance Act 1989;
"brought into account" has the same meaning as it has in sections 83 to 83AB of that Act by virtue of section 83A of that Act;
"relevant amount" has the same meaning as in section 83AA of that Act;
"surplus" has the same meaning as in sections 83AA and 83AB of that Act.

GENERAL NOTE
Subparagraphs (1) and (2) provide for cases where "relevant amounts" added to the fund in the period from 1 January to 25 March 1996 are brought into account for a period of account beginning after 31 December 1995. The loss, before the s 83(3) addition which would have arisen is treated as reduced by the "relevant amounts" but they are otherwise disregarded, so they do not enter into any computation of "surplus". In the case of an overseas life insurance company, addition to the long-term business fund means the appropriation to or use for the UK branch or agency business of assets which were not previously so used or held (such a company may not have a separate identifiable UK fund, and even if it does the assets referable to the UK business are separately determined under the provisions of TA 1988 s 444B and Sch 19C inserted by FA 1993 s 97(1) and Sch 9 para 1).
Subparagraph (3) provides for the apportionment *pro rata temporis* of a transferee's loss, vulnerable to reduction under s 83AA(3), in respect of an accounting period beginning before 1 January 1996.
Subparagraph (4) ensures that the commencement provisions in para 10 do not prevent an amount of surplus from being treated under s 83AB as an amount arising to a transferee in a preceding period of account (and then carried forward), and sub-para (5) applies relevant definitions.

Commencement

10 (1) Subject to paragraph 2(1) and (3) above, paragraphs 1 to 3 above have effect in relation to accounting periods beginning on or after 1st January 1996.

(2) Subject to paragraph 9 above, paragraphs 4 to 8 above have effect in relation to periods of account beginning on or after 1st January 1996.

COMMENCEMENT
The amendments and new provisions take effect for accounting periods beginning after 31 December 1995, subject to the particular application of paras 2(1) and (3) and 9.

SCHEDULE 32

EQUALISATION RESERVES

BACKGROUND NOTE

This Schedule lays down the proposed tax treatment of compulsory equalisation reserves to be made by general insurance companies in respect of certain categories of business. In general the term "equalisation reserve" is used to describe a reserve made out of profits in order to provide a cushion against adverse results from future insurance transactions, or against unexpected deterioration in the emerging results of business already effected but in respect of which claims remain outstanding. Such reserves are therefore to be distinguished from the specific calculated reserves made in the light of previous experience in respect of outstanding claims, including claims incurred but not reported. They are "intended to form part of an insurer's protection against the inherent volatility of some types of . . . business. Claims equalisation reserves are used to set aside funds in good years to assist the meeting of losses in bad ones, resulting in a smoothing of insurers' underwriting results over time. By setting aside [such amounts] . . . the company puts itself in a stronger position to meet [exceptional] claims" (DTI press release P/95/699 of 19 October 1995, "Equalisation reserves consultation document published").

The introduction of compulsory equalisation reserves for regulatory purposes follows a lengthy period of consultation in which industry representatives first sought a tax deduction in respect of such reserves (the Revenue regarded equalisation reserves, not being made in respect of specific calculable liabilities, as inadmissible on ordinary Case I principles). Attention was drawn to the tax treatment of such reserves in other EC member states. The Government view was that it was not willing to allow a tax deduction for any reserves which were not made to meet regulatory requirements. A joint Revenue and DTI consultation document was issued in July 1993 and following further discussions a second joint consultation document, containing proposals for the calculation of and tax treatment of compulsory equalisation reserves, was issued in April 1995. In July 1995 the Insurance Companies (Reserves) Act 1995 became law. This Act inter alia inserted a new s 34A in the Insurance Companies Act 1982 requiring insurance companies to make equalisation reserves in respect of types of business to be specified by and calculated in accordance with regulation.

The detailed tax rules, reflecting the regulatory provisions, will be included in regulations, which are expected to be made in the summer of 1996.

1 In Chapter I of Part XII of the Taxes Act 1988 (insurance companies and capital redemption business), after section 444B there shall be inserted the following sections—

"Equalisation reserves

444BA   Equalisation reserves for general business

(1) Subject to the following provisions of this section and to sections 444BB to 444BD, the rules in subsection (2) below shall apply in making any computation, for the purposes of Case I or V of Schedule D, of the profits or losses for any accounting period of an insurance company whose business has at any time been or included business in respect of which it was required, by virtue of section 34A regulations, to maintain an equalisation reserve.

(2) Those rules are—

(*a*) that amounts which, in accordance with section 34A regulations, are transferred into the equalisation reserve in respect of the company's business for the accounting period in question are to be deductible;

(*b*) that amounts which, in accordance with any such regulations, are transferred out of the reserve in respect of the company's business for that period are to be treated as receipts of that business; and

(*c*) that it must be assumed that all such transfers as are required by section 34A regulations to be made into or out of the reserve in respect of the company's business for any period are made as required.

(3) Where an insurance company having any business in respect of which it is required, by virtue of section 34A regulations, to maintain an equalisation reserve ceases to trade—

(*a*) any balance which exists in the reserve at that time for the purposes of the

Tax Acts shall be deemed to have been transferred out of the reserve immediately before the company ceases to trade; and

(*b*) that transfer out shall be deemed to be a transfer in respect of the company's business for the accounting period in which the company so ceases and to have been required by section 34A regulations.

(4) Where—

(*a*) an amount is transferred into an equalisation reserve in respect of the business of an insurance company for any accounting period,

(*b*) the rule in subection (2)(*a*) above would apply to the transfer of that amount but for this subsection,

(*c*) that company by notice in writing to an officer of the Board makes an election in relation to that amount for the purposes of this subsection, and

(*d*) the notice of the election is given not more than two years after the end of that period,

the rule mentioned in subsection (2)(*a*) above shall not apply to that transfer of that amount and, instead, the amount transferred (the 'unrelieved transfer') shall be carried forward for the purposes of subsection (5) below to the next accounting period and (subject to subsection (6) below) from accounting period to accounting period.

(5) Where—

(*a*) in accordance with section 34A regulations, a transfer is made out of an equalisation reserve in respect of an insurance company's business for any accounting period,

(*b*) the rule in subsection (2)(*b*) above would apply to the transfer but for this subsection, and

(*c*) the accounting period is one to which any amount representing one or more unrelieved transfers has been carried forward under subsection (4) above,

that rule mentioned in subsection (2)(*b*) above shall not apply to that transfer except to the extent (if any) that the amount of the transfer exceeds the aggregate of the amounts representing unrelieved transfers carried forward to that period.

(6) Where in the case of any company—

(*a*) any amount representing one or more unrelieved transfers is carried forward to an accounting period in accordance with subsection (4) above, and

(*b*) by virtue of subsection (5) above the rule in subsection (2)(*b*) above does not apply to an amount representing the whole or any part of any transfer out of an equalisation reserve in respect of the company's business for that period,

the amount mentioned in paragraph (*a*) above shall not be carried forward under subection (4) above to the next accounting period except to the extent (if any) that it exceeds the amount mentioned in paragraph (*b*) above.

(7) To the extent that any actual or assumed transfer in accordance with section 34A regulations of any amount into an equalisation reserve is attributable to arrangements entered into wholly or mainly for tax purposes—

(*a*) the rule in subsection (2)(*a*) above shall not apply to that transfer; and

(*b*) the making of that transfer shall be disregarded in determining, for the purposes of the Tax Acts, whether and to what extent there is subsequently any requirement to make a transfer into or out of the reserve in accordance with section 34A regulations;

and this subsection applies irrespective of whether the insurance company in question is a party to the arrangements.

(8) For the purposes of this section the transfer of an amount into an equalisation reserve is attributable to arrangements entered into wholly or mainly for tax purposes to the extent that the arrangements to which it is attributable are arrangements—

(*a*) the sole or main purpose of which is, or

(*b*) the sole or main benefit accruing from which might (but for subsection (7) above) be expected to be,

the reduction by virtue of this section of any liability to tax.

(9) Where—

(*a*) any transfer made into or out of an equalisation reserve maintained by an insurance company is made in accordance with section 34A regulations in respect of business carried on by that company over a period ('the equalisation period'), and

(*b*) parts of the equalisation period are in different accounting periods,

the amount transferred shall be apportioned for the purposes of this section between the different accounting periods in the proportions that correspond to the number of days in the equalisation period that are included in each of those accounting periods.

(10) The Treasury may by regulations provide in relation to any accounting periods ending on or after 1st April 1996 for specified transitional provisions contained in section 34A regulations to be disregarded for the purposes of the Tax Acts in determining how much is required, on any occasion, to be transferred into or out of any equalisation reserve in accordance with the regulations.

(11) In this section and sections 444BB to 444BD 'section 34A regulations' means regulations made under section 34A of the Insurance Companies Act 1982 (equalisation reserves in respect of general business).

444BB   Modification of s 444BA for mutual or overseas business and for non-resident companies

(1) The Treasury may by regulations make provision modifying section 444BA so as, in cases mentioned in subsection (2) below—

(*a*) to require—

(i) sums by reference to which the amount of any transfer into or out of an equalisation reserve falls to be computed, or
(ii) the amount of any such transfer,

to be apportioned between different parts of the business carried on for any period by an insurance company; and

(*b*) to provide for the purposes of corporation tax for the amounts taken to be transferred into or out of an equalisation reserve to be computed disregarding any such sum or, as the case may be, any such part of a transfer as is attributed, in accordance with the regulations, to a part of the business described for the purpose in the regulations.

(2) Those cases are cases where an insurance company which, in accordance with section 34A regulations, is required to make transfers into or out of an equalisation reserve in respect of any business carried on by that company for any period is carrying on, for the whole or any part of that period—

(*a*) any business the income and gains of which fall to be disregarded in making a computation of the company's profits in accordance with the rules applicable to Case I of Schedule D, or

(*b*) any business by reference to which double taxation relief is afforded in respect of any income or gains.

(3) Section 444BA shall have effect (subject to any regulations under subsection (1) above) in the case of an equalisation reserve maintained by an insurance company which—

(*a*) is not resident in the United Kingdom, and

(*b*) carries on business in the United Kingdom through a branch or agency,

only if such conditions as may be prescribed by regulations made by the Treasury are satisfied in relation to that company and in relation to transfers into or out of that reserve.

(4) Regulations under this section prescribing conditions subject to which section 444BA is to apply in the case of any equalisation reserve maintained by an insurance company may—

(*a*) contain conditions imposing requirements on the company to furnish the

Board with information with respect to any matters to which the regulations relate, or to produce to the Board documents or records relating to any such matters; and

(*b*) provide that, where any prescribed condition is not, or ceases to be, satisfied in relation to the company or in relation to transfers into or out of that reserve, there is to be deemed for the purposes of the Tax Acts to have been a transfer out of that reserve of an amount determined under the regulations.

(5) Regulations under this section may—

(*a*) provide for apportionments under the regulations to be made in such manner, and by reference to such factors, as may be specified or described in the regulations;

(*b*) make different provision for different cases;

(*c*) contain such supplementary, incidental, consequential and transitional provision as the Treasury may think fit;

(*d*) make provision having retrospective effect in relation to accounting periods beginning not more than one year before the time when the regulations are made;

and the powers conferred by this section in relation to transfers into or out of any reserve shall be exercisable in relation to both actual and assumed transfers.

(6) In this section 'double taxation relief', means—

(*a*) relief under double taxation arrangements which takes the form of a credit allowed against corporation tax, or

(*b*) unilateral relief under section 790(1) which takes that form;

and 'double taxation arrangements' here means arrangements having effect by virtue of section 788.

444BC   Modification of s 444BA for non-annual accounting etc

(1) The Treasury may by regulations make provision modifying the operation of section 444BA in relation to cases where an insurance company has, for the purpose of preparing the documents it is required to prepare for the purposes of section 17 of the Insurance Companies Act 1982, applied for any period an accounting method described in paragraph 52 or 53 of Schedule 9A to the Companies Act 1985 (accounting on a non-annual basis).

(2) Subsection (5) of section 444BB applies for the purposes of this section as it applies for the purposes of that section.

444BD   Application of s 444BA rules to other equalisation reserves

(1) The Treasury may by regulations provide for section 444BA to have effect, in such cases and subject to such modifications as may be specified in the regulations, in relation to any equivalent reserves as it has effect in relation to equalisation reserves maintained by virtue of section 34A regulations.

(2) For the purposes of this section a reserve is an equivalent reserve if—

(*a*) it is maintained, otherwise than by virtue of section 34A regulations, either—

(i) by an EC company carrying on business in the United Kingdom through a branch or agency, or

(ii) in respect of any insurance business (within the meaning of the Insurance Companies Act 1982) which is carried on outside the United Kingdom by a company resident in the United Kingdom; and

(*b*) the purpose for which, or the manner in which, it is maintained is such as to make it equivalent to an equalisation reserve maintained by virtue of section 34A regulations.

(3) For the purposes of this section a reserve is also an equivalent reserve if it is maintained in respect of any credit insurance business in accordance with requirements imposed either—

(*a*) by or under any enactment, or

(*b*) under so much of the law of any territory as secures compliance with the requirements of Article 1 of the credit insurance directive (equalisation reserves for credit insurance).

(4) Without prejudice to the generality of subsection (1) above, the modifications made by virtue of that subsection may—

(*a*) provide for section 444BA to apply in the case of an equivalent reserve only where such conditions as may be specified in the regulations are satisfied in relation to the company maintaining the reserve or in relation to transfers made into or out of it; and

(*b*) contain any other provision corresponding to any provision which, in the case of a reserve maintained by virtue of section 34A regulations, may be made under sections 444BA to 444BC.

(5) Subsections (4) and (5) of section 444BB shall apply for the purposes of this section as they apply for the purposes of that section.

(6) Without prejudice to the generality of section 444BB(5), the transitional provision which by virtue of subsection (5) above may be contained in regulations under this section shall include—

(*a*) provision for treating the amount of any transfers made into or out of an equivalent reserve in respect of business carried on for any specified period as increased by the amount by which they would have been increased if no transfers into the reserve had been made in respect of business carried on for an earlier period; and

(*b*) provision for excluding from the rule in section 444BA(2)(*b*) so much of any amount transferred out of an equivalent reserve as represents, in pursuance of an apportionment made under the regulations, the transfer out of that reserve of amounts in respect of which there has been no entitlement to relief by virtue of section 444BA(2)(*a*).

(7) In this section—

'credit insurance business' means any insurance business falling within general business class 14 of Schedule 2 to the Insurance Companies Act 1982 that is not reinsurance business;

'the credit insurance directive' means Council Directive 87/343/EEC of 22nd June 1987 amending, as regards credit insurance and suretyship insurance, First Directive 73/239 on the coordination of laws, regulations and administrative provisions relating to the taking-up and pursuit of the business of direct insurance other than life assurance; and

'EC company' has the same meaning as in the Insurance Companies Act 1982.''

GENERAL NOTE

This paragraph inserts in TA 1988 new ss 444BA–444BD which contain the principal provisions determining the deductibility of amounts transferred to or from equalisation reserves, and enabling powers in respect of matters which are to be dealt with by regulation.

TA 1988 s 444BA

Subsections (1)–(3) set out the basic rules for the treatment, in both Case I and VI computations, of transfers in and out of equalisation reserves. Transfers to such reserves are deductible and transfers out of such reserves are treated as business receipts. For this purpose it is to be assumed that the insurer makes the transfers to and from the reserves which are required by the DTI regulations (the draft tax regulations published in November 1995 make provision for situations where this is not the case). Where a company ceases to trade, any balance in the reserve is treated as having been required to be transferred out of the reserve, and to have been so transferred, immediately before cessation. These measures apply only, in the first instance, to equalisation reserves required by the DTI regulations (which are described as "section 34A regulations" after the enabling power in the Insurance Companies Act 1982 under which they are made).

Subsections (4)–(6) allow an insurer to elect not to deduct the whole or part of sums which would otherwise be deductible under sub-s (2)(*a*). Such an election must be made within two years of the end of the accounting period. The amount not relieved is to be carried forward and set against the amount assessable under sub-s (2)(*b*) in respect of a transfer out of the same reserve, any further carry forward being limited to the excess of the original unrelieved transfer to the reserve over the amount transferred out of the reserve. This measure allows insurers to forego a deduction which would displace other reliefs not available to carry forward against a later assessment, for example relief for foreign tax on branch profits.

Subsections (7) and (8) contain an anti-avoidance measure denying the benefit of the above provisions in the case of transfers attributable to arrangements whose sole or main purpose is, or where the resulting sole or main benefit might be expected to be the reduction in the company's tax liability.

Subsection (9) provides for apportionment between accounting periods where transfers are required by the DTI regulations in respect of a period, described as an "equalisation period", which falls into more than one accounting period.

Subsection (10) enables the Treasury to provide, by regulation, for specified transitional provisions in the DTI regulations to be disregarded, insofar as they relate to accounting periods ending after 31 March 1996.

Subsection (11) defines "section 34A regulations".

TA 1988 s 444BB

This section provides for the modification, by regulation, of s 444BA in its application to mutual or overseas business and to non-resident companies.

Subsections (1) and (2) allow the regulations to provide for apportionment of transfers, or the sums by reference to which they are calculated, to different parts of a company's business, or for amounts attributable to specified parts of the business to be disregarded. This provision applies to cases where the income and gains are disregarded for Case I purposes (for example, certain business transacted on a mutual basis) or the tax charge is subject to relief for overseas tax (overseas branch business).

Subsection (3) allows additional conditions to be imposed by regulation in the case of non-resident companies carrying on business in the UK through a branch or agency.

Subsections (4) and (5) set out the permitted scope of regulations made under this section, including information powers, deemed transfers out of the reserves, apportionments and so on. Such regulations may have retrospective effect to the extent that they may affect accounting periods beginning not more than 12 months before the time they are made.

Subsection (6) provides the definition of "double taxation relief" for the purposes of this section, including both agreement and unilateral relief which is given by way of credit (reliefs given by way of exemption are therefore excluded).

TA 1988 s 444BC

This section provides for the modification, by regulation, of s 444BA in cases where business is not accounted for on an annual basis (for example, on the basis of a three-year closing account).

TA 1988 s 444BD

Subsections (1)–(3) provide for the extension, by regulation, of the relief afforded by s 444BA to "equivalent reserves". These are reserves having the same purpose as equalisation reserves within the DTI regulations and which are made—

(a) by an EC company carrying on business in the UK through a branch or agency;
(b) by a UK resident company in respect of business carried on outside the UK; or
(c) in respect of credit insurance, including reserves made under a law securing compliance with Article I of the Credit Insurance Directive (Council Directive 87/343/EEC of 22 June 1987 amending the First Non-life Insurance Directive, 73/239/EEC of 24 July 1973).

Subsections (4)–(6) set out the scope of the regulations made under this section, including information powers, deemed transfers out of the reserves, apportionments and so on.

Subsection (7) defines the terms used in this section; in particular the term "EC Company" carries the same meaning as in the Insurance Companies Act 1982, that is, including companies incorporated in member states of the European Economic Area.

2 In the second column of the Table in section 98 of the Taxes Management Act 1970 (penalties in respect of certain information provisions), after the entry relating to regulations under section 431E(1) or 441A(3) of the Taxes Act 1988 there shall be inserted the following entries—

"regulations under section 444BB;

regulations under section 444BD;".

GENERAL NOTE

This paragraph provides penalties for failure to provide information required by regulations made under the enabling powers in new ss 444BB and 444BD.

SCHEDULE 33

MANAGEMENT EXPENSES OF CAPITAL REDEMPTION BUSINESS

Amendment of section 76 of Taxes Act

1 (1) In section 76 of the Taxes Act 1988 (management expenses of companies carrying on life assurance business), after subsection (5) there shall be inserted the following subsection—

"(5A) In the preceding provisions of this section references to life assurance business and references to basic life assurance and general annuity business shall be deemed, in each case, to include references to capital redemption business."

(2) In subsection (6) of that section, at the end there shall be inserted "or to any capital redemption business carried on by the company at or through that branch or agency."

(3) In subsection (8) of that section, before the definition of "investment business" there shall be inserted the following definition—

"'capital redemption business' means any capital redemption business, within the meaning of section 458, which is business to which that section applies;".

GENERAL NOTE
This amendment provides statutory relief (which was previously given by concession) for the management expenses of post-1937 capital redemption business. It does not apply to pre-1938 business, which is not segregated by TA 1988 s 458 as amended, and which therefore continues to be assessed under Schedule D Case I. As all the rules in TA 1988 s 76(1)–(5) apply the relief is subject to a *notional Case I* restriction. The amendment to s 76(6) extends the relief to overseas life insurance companies in respect of UK capital redemption business.

Treatment of capital redemption business

2 In subsection (1) of section 458 of the Taxes Act 1988 (capital redemption business), at the end there shall be inserted "and where section 76 applies by virtue of subsection (5A) of that section, it shall apply separately to capital redemption business".

GENERAL NOTE
The amendment to TA 1988 s 458(1) ensures that the *I minus E* figures for capital redemption business remain separate from those for basic life assurance and general annuity business.

Overseas life insurance companies

3 In sub-paragraph (1) of paragraph 5 of Schedule 19AC to the Taxes Act 1988 (modification of section 76), at the end of paragraph (*a*) of the subsection (6A) which is treated as inserted by that sub-paragraph there shall be inserted "or capital redemption business".

GENERAL NOTE
This paragraph amends the notionally inserted TA 1988 s 76(6A) to include a reference to capital redemption, insofar as carried on by an overseas life insurance company through a branch or agency in the UK.

Commencement

4 This Schedule has effect as respects accounting periods ending on or after the day appointed under section 199 of the Finance Act 1994 for the purposes of Chapter III of Part IV of that Act (self-assessment management provisions).

GENERAL NOTE
The provisions of this Schedule follow those of the principal provision in s 168 and come into force for accounting periods ending on or after the day appointed for the commencement of self-assessment for corporation tax.

Section 169

SCHEDULE 34

PROVISIONAL REPAYMENTS IN CONNECTION WITH PENSION BUSINESS

BACKGROUND NOTE
This Part of the Schedule amends the existing provision relating to quarterly repayments to fit with the new self-assessment procedures for corporation tax.

PART I

AMENDMENTS OF SCHEDULE 19AB TO THE TAXES ACT 1988

1 (1) Paragraph 1 (entitlement to certain payments on account) shall be amended in accordance with the following provisions of this paragraph.

(2) In sub-paragraph (1) (entitlement to payment of an amount equal to the aggregate there mentioned) after "equal" there shall be inserted ", subject to paragraph 2 below,".

(3) For sub-paragraphs (3) and (4) (ascertainment of the "provisional fraction") there shall be substituted—

"(3) In the application of subsections (5) to (9) of section 432A for the purpose of determining the amounts to which a company is entitled by way of provisional repayments in the case of any accounting period of the company, the reference in subsection (5) to 'the relevant fraction' shall be taken as a reference to the provisional fraction for that accounting period.

(4) For the purposes of this paragraph—

(*a*) the provisional fraction for an accounting period of a company is the fraction which would, on the basis of the company's latest section 11 return, be the relevant fraction for the purposes of section 432A(5) for the accounting period to which that return relates; but

(*b*) if there is no section 11 return on the basis of which that fraction can be ascertained, the provisional fraction shall be taken to be nil;

but this sub-paragraph is subject to paragraph 2 below."

(4) In sub-paragraph (5) (meaning of "the appropriate portion") in paragraph (*b*) (company carrying on more than one category of long term business) for sub-paragraph (ii) (income arising from assets not linked to pension business) there shall be substituted—

"(ii) if and to the extent that the payment or distribution in question is income which is not referable to a category of business by virtue of subsection (3) or (4) of section 432A, the provisional fraction; and

(iii) except as provided by sub-paragraph (i) or (ii) above, none."

(5) For sub-paragraph (6) (inspector not to give effect to claim unless he is satisfied he has been given sufficient information) there shall be substituted—

"(6) Section 42 of the Management Act (claims) shall not apply to a claim for a provisional repayment.

(6A) A claim for a provisional repayment shall be in such form as the Board may determine and the form of claim shall provide for a declaration to the effect that all the particulars given in the form are correctly stated to the best of the knowledge and belief of the person making the claim."

(6) For sub-paragraph (7) (provisional repayments to be treated as payments on account of certain payments or repayments which will eventually fall to be made in respect of income tax and tax credits) there shall be substituted—

"(7) A provisional repayment for a provisional repayment period shall be regarded as a payment on account of the amounts (if any) which the company would, apart from this Schedule, be entitled to be paid or repaid in respect of its pension business for the accounting period in which that provisional repayment period falls, in respect of—

(*a*) income tax borne by deduction on payments received by the company in that accounting period and referable to its pension business, and

(*b*) tax credits in respect of distributions received by the company in that accounting period and referable to its pension business,

on a claim such as is mentioned in section 7 of this Act or section 42(4) of the Management Act in respect of that accounting period.''

(7) Sub-paragraph (8) (which relates to any case where an election is made under section 438(6) as respects franked investment income and which, having regard to amendments made by this Schedule, is unnecessary) shall cease to have effect.

(8) For sub-paragraph (10) (definitions) there shall be substituted—

"(10) In this paragraph—

'latest section 11 return', in the case of an accounting period of a company ('the current accounting period'), means, subject to sub-paragraph (11) below, the section 11 return for the latest preceding accounting period of the company for which such a return has been delivered before the making of the first claim for a provisional repayment for the current accounting period;

'section 11 return', in the case of any company, means a return delivered by the company pursuant to section 11 of the Management Act and includes a reference to any accounts, statements or reports delivered pursuant to that section together with the return;

'self-assessment' means an assessment included in a return under section 11 of the Management Act by virtue of section 11AA of that Act and includes a reference to such an assessment as amended under section 11AA(2) or 28A(3) or (4) of that Act.

(11) In any case where—

(*a*) there is a section 11 return which would, apart from this sub-paragraph, be the latest section 11 return in the case of an accounting period of a company,

(*b*) the self assessment required to be included in that return pursuant to section 11AA of the Management Act has been amended under section 11AA(2) or 28A(3) or (4) of that Act, and

(*c*) that amendment was made before the making of the first claim for a provisional repayment for the accounting period mentioned in paragraph (*a*) above,

the return which is to be regarded as the latest section 11 return in the case of that accounting period shall be that return as it stands amended immediately after the making of that amendment of the self-assessment (or, if the self-assessment has been so amended more than once, that return as it stands amended immediately after the making of the last such amendment) but ignoring amendments which do not give rise to any change in the fraction which, on the basis of the return as it has effect from time to time, would be the relevant fraction for the purposes of section 432A(5) for the accounting period to which the return relates.''

GENERAL NOTE

Subparagraphs (1)–(3)
The repayments are to be calculated by reference to s 11 returns rather than information held by the Inspector. If there is no s 11 return from which the provisional fraction can be derived it is taken as nil, as before, but information in some other form will no longer suffice.

Subparagraph (4)
The amendment follows the new, simplified, attribution rules in TA 1988 s 432A as amended by FA 1995 Sch 8.

Subparagraph (5)
The Board may prescribe the form in which a claim for provisional repayment should be made.

Subparagraphs (6) and (7)
A provisional repayment is to be treated as a payment on account of any amounts due under a claim made, under the new self-assessment provisions, for repayment of income tax or tax credit. The reference to TMA 1970 s 42(4) is to that section in the form substituted by FA 1994 Sch 19

para 13. The present references to the final determination of assessments will no longer be appropriate.

Subparagraph (8)
The new sub-para (10) of Sch 19AB provides the necessary definitions and cross-references to the self-assessment legislation, and makes clear which s (11) returns, or amended returns, are to be used as the source of the provisional fraction when making a provisional repayment.

2 (1) Paragraph 2 (changes in the provisional fraction) shall be amended in accordance with the following provisions of this paragraph.

(2) For sub-paragraphs (1) and (2) (cases where the paragraph applies, and consequences of its application) there shall be substituted—

"(1) This paragraph applies in any case where—

(*a*) a claim has been made for a provisional repayment for at least one provisional repayment period in an accounting period of a company;
(*b*) subsequently, a further such claim is made for a provisional repayment period falling within that accounting period; and
(*c*) had that further claim been the first claim made for a provisional repayment for that accounting period, the provisional fraction for the accounting period would have been a different fraction (whether in consequence of the delivery of a section 11 return for a later preceding accounting period or the application of paragraph 1(11) above);

and in this paragraph the 'substituted provisional fraction' means the different fraction mentioned in paragraph (*c*) above.

(2) Where this paragraph applies—

(*a*) the amount of any provisional repayment to which the company is entitled for the provisional repayment period mentioned in sub-paragraph (1)(*b*) above shall be an amount determined in accordance with sub-paragraph (3) below or such lesser amount as may be specified in the claim; and
(*b*) in relation to any later provisional repayment period in the same accounting period, the substituted provisional fraction shall, subject to any further application of this paragraph, be treated as the provisional fraction for the accounting period."

(3) In sub-paragraph (3), in the definition of "total entitlement", for the words following paragraph (*b*) there shall be substituted—

"had the substituted provisional fraction been the provisional fraction for the accounting period as from the beginning of that period; and".

GENERAL NOTE
This paragraph makes the corresponding amendments to para 2 of Sch 19AB, which provides for the cumulative repayments for an accounting period to take account of changes in the provisional fraction (because of submission of a later return or an amendment to a return).

3 (1) Paragraph 3 (repayment, with interest, of excessive provisional repayments) shall be amended in accordance with the following provisions of this paragraph.

(2) In sub-paragraph (1), for paragraphs (*a*) and (*b*) (which respectively refer to the company's assessment to corporation tax being finally determined and the amount referred to in paragraph 1(7)) there shall be substituted—

"(*a*) an insurance company's self-assessment for an accounting period becomes final, and
(*b*) the aggregate amount of the provisional repayments made to the company for that accounting period exceeds the appropriate amount,".

(3) After that sub-paragraph there shall be inserted—

"(1A) For the purposes of sub-paragraph (1)(*b*) above, the appropriate amount for an accounting period of a company is the amount (if any) which, on the assumptions in sub-paragraphs (1B) and (1C) below and disregarding any provisional repayments, the company would be entitled to be paid or repaid, when its self-assessment for the period becomes final, in respect of its pension business for that accounting period on a claim such as is mentioned in section 7 of this Act or section 42(4) of the Management Act in respect of—

(*a*) income tax borne by deduction on payments received by the company in that accounting period and referable to its pension business, and

(*b*) tax credits in respect of distributions received by the company in that accounting period and referable to its pension business.

(1B) The first assumption is that no payments or repayments have been made to the company in respect of—

(*a*) income tax such as is mentioned in paragraph (*a*) of sub-paragraph (1A) above, or

(*b*) tax credits such as are mentioned in paragraph (*b*) of that sub-paragraph,

before the company's self-assessment for the accounting period in question becomes final.

(1C) The second assumption is that in making any set off under—

(*a*) section 7(2),

(*b*) paragraph 5 of Schedule 16, or

(*c*) regulations made by virtue of section 51B,

income tax borne by deduction on income which is not referable to pension business is set off before income tax so borne on income which is referable to pension business.

(1D) In its application by sub-paragraph (1) above, section 30 of the Management Act shall have effect as if, instead of the provision made by subsection (5), it provided that an assessment under that section by virtue of sub-paragraph (1) above is not out of time under section 34 of that Act if it is made no later than the end of the accounting period following that in which the self-assessment mentioned in paragraph (*a*) of that sub-paragraph becomes final.''

(4) In sub-paragraph (3) (application of section 87A of the Taxes Management Act 1970) in paragraph (*b*) (which provides for the specified words in subsection (1) of that section to be disregarded) for '''(in accordance with section 10 of the principal Act)''' there shall be substituted '''(in accordance with section 59D of this Act)'''.

(5) In sub-paragraph (4) (amount of principal outstanding to be determined in accordance with sub-paragraphs (5) to (7)) for ''(7)'' there shall be substituted ''(8)''.

(6) After sub-paragraph (7) there shall be added—

''(8) For the purposes of subsection (7) above, any repayment made by the company in respect of an amount paid or repaid to it in respect of—

(*a*) income tax such as is mentioned in paragraph (*a*) of sub-paragraph (1A) above, or

(*b*) tax credits such as are mentioned in paragraph (*b*) of that sub-paragraph,

shall be treated as a repayment in respect of the principal, taking an earlier such repayment by the company before a later.

(9) In this paragraph 'self-assessment' means an assessment included in a return under section 11 of the Management Act by virtue of section 11AA of that Act and includes a reference to such an assessment as amended.''

GENERAL NOTE

This paragraph amends para 3 of Sch 19AB which provides for the recovery, with interest, of repayments which are ultimately found to have been excessive. The amended text substitutes the terminology of and references to the new self-assessment procedures where appropriate.

4 (1) Paragraph 6 (interpretation) shall be amended in accordance with the following provisions of this paragraph.

(2) In sub-paragraph (1), for the definition of ''provisional fraction'' there shall be substituted—

'''provisional fraction' shall be construed in accordance with paragraphs 1(4) and 2 above;''.

(3) Sub-paragraph (3) (which makes transitional provision for cases where an insurance company has not made a return under section 11 of the Taxes Management Act 1970 as amended by section 82 of the Finance (No 2) Act 1987) shall cease to have effect.

(4) After that sub-paragraph there shall be added—

"(4) Sub-paragraph (5) below applies in any case where an insurance company—

(*a*) which has delivered a return under section 11 of the Management Act for an accounting period ending before the self-assessment appointed day, but
(*b*) which has not delivered its first return under that section for an accounting period ending on or after that day,

makes the first claim for a provisional repayment for a particular accounting period ending on or after that day.

(5) Where this sub-paragraph applies—

(*a*) the provisional fraction for the accounting period to which the claim mentioned in sub-paragraph (4) above relates shall be determined in accordance with paragraph 1(3), (4), and (6) and sub-paragraph (3) above, as they have effect in relation to accounting periods ending before that day; and
(*b*) paragraph 2 above, as originally enacted, shall have effect in relation to that accounting period as it has effect in relation to accounting periods ending before that day.

(6) In this paragraph 'the self-assessment appointed day' means the day appointed under section 199 of the Finance Act 1994 for the purposes of Chapter III of Part IV of that Act (self-assessment management provisions)."

GENERAL NOTE
This paragraph makes the consequential changes to the interpretation provisions in para 6 of Sch 19AB, and adds a transitional provision, in new sub-paras (4) and (5), to allow provisional fractions in claims made after the coming into force of the self-assessment provisions but before a new-style s 11 return has been made to be calculated under the old rules until a return has been made under the new procedures.

PART II
AMENDMENTS OF SCHEDULE 19AC TO THE TAXES ACT 1988

This Part of the Schedule makes consequential amendments to the provisions relating to overseas life insurance companies.

5 (1) Paragraph 15 (modification of Schedule 19AB) shall be amended in accordance with the following provisions of this paragraph.

(2) Sub-paragraph (1) (which relates to paragraph 1(8) of Schedule l9AB) shall cease to have effect.

(3) At the end there shall be added—

"(3) In paragraph 3(1C) of Schedule 19AB, for paragraph (*a*) there shall be substituted—

'(*a*) section 11(3),'."

GENERAL NOTE
Paragraph 15 of Sch 19AC is amended by the omission of sub-para (1) which is no longer needed (para 1(8) of Sch 19AB having been made redundant) and the addition of a new sub-para (3) modifying the new para 3(1C) of Sch 19AB (itself inserted by para 3 of this Schedule) to refer to TA 1988 s 11(2), which provides for the set-off of income tax by a non-resident company, instead of s 7(2) which applies only to UK resident companies.

SCHEDULE 35   Section 179

ROLL-OVER RELIEF IN RESPECT OF SHIPS

INTRODUCTION

This Schedule is concerned with the relief which allows a balancing charge on disposal of a ship to be deferred, in whole or in part, provided that a further ship is purchased within the following six years. The relief was introduced by FA 1995 and is contained in CAA 1990 ss 33A–33F. As originally enacted, the relief requires the disposal and purchase of the ships to be undertaken by the same person in respect of the same trade, subject to a limited relaxation for particular cases where there has been a change in the persons carrying on the trade. The amendments effected by this Schedule allow the relief to apply, subject to the relevant conditions, where the disposal and purchase are undertaken by different members of a 75 per cent group of companies in relation to their respective trades (see Inland Revenue Press Release, 26 March 1996, "Ships: rollover relief for balancing charges—extension across groups of companies", *Simon's Weekly Tax Intelligence* 1996, p 586). The extended relief applies with regard to disposals of ships occurring on or after the date of Royal Assent, although the relief cannot actually be claimed until a date to be appointed by the Treasury by order.

Preliminary

1 The Capital Allowances Act 1990 shall be amended as follows.

GENERAL NOTE

This paragraph introduces the amendments to CAA 1990.

Amendment of provisions relating to roll-over relief in respect of ships

2 (1) In subsection (3) of section 33A (relief limited to expenditure on new shipping incurred or to be incurred by the shipowner), for paragraph (*b*) there shall be substituted the following paragraph—

"(*b*) the amount of any expenditure incurred or to be incurred by qualifying persons in the period of six years beginning with the day on which the event mentioned in subsection (1)(*b*) above occurs, so far as that expenditure is, or (when incurred) will be, expenditure to which an addition made under this section in respect of that event may be attributed in accordance with subsection (5) below;".

(2) In subsection (4) of that section (relief not to apply where expenditure on new shipping not incurred by the shipowner within six years), for the words from the beginning of paragraph (*b*) onwards there shall be substituted the following—

"(*b*) circumstances arise in which the whole or any part of the addition ceases (otherwise than by being attributed) to be an amount that may be attributed in accordance with subsection (5) below, to expenditure on new shipping incurred by qualifying persons in the period of six years mentioned in subsection (3)(*b*) above,

the shipowner shall be assumed not to have been entitled to so much of the addition as will not be so attributed."

(3) For subsection (5) of that section (attribution of relief to expenditure on new shipping) there shall be substituted the following subsections—

"(5) Subject to subsection (5A) below and to section 33D(6), where—

(*a*) an addition is made under this section to the shipowner's qualifying expenditure for the relevant period in respect of his actual trade, and

(*b*) expenditure on new shipping is incurred by a qualifying person in the period of six years mentioned in subsection (3)(*b*) above,

the shipowner may, by notice to an officer of the Board, attribute to that expenditure so much of the addition as is equal to so much of the expenditure as is not already the subject of an attribution under this subsection.

(5A) A notice under subsection (5) above shall not have effect in a case where the shipowner and the qualifying person to whose expenditure the notice relates are not the same person unless that person joins with the shipowner in the giving of that notice."

(4) After subsection (7) of that section there shall be inserted the following subsection—

"(8) In this section and the following provisions of this Chapter references to a qualifying person, in relation to any expenditure, are references to—

(*a*) the shipowner; and

(*b*) where the shipowner is a company, any company which, at the time when the expenditure is or is to be incurred, is or (as the case may be) would be a member of the same group of companies as the shipowner;

and for the purposes of this subsection two companies are members of the same group of companies at any time if, at that time, they are treated as members of the same group of companies for the purposes of Chapter IV of Part X of the principal Act (group relief)."

GENERAL NOTE

This paragraph amends CAA 1990 s 33A to reflect the fact that the expenditure on new shipping, as required by s 33A(3)(*b*), may be incurred by a different group member.

The persons who are able to incur qualifying expenditure on new shipping are determined by the definition of "qualifying person" in s 33A(8) (inserted by sub-para (4)). The following are qualifying persons—

(*a*) the person who disposed of the old ship (the shipowner); and

(*b*) if the shipowner is a company, a member of the same 75 per cent group, as defined for group relief purposes.

The group relationship must exist at the time when the expenditure is, or is to be incurred. In addition, as a result of s 33D(2A) (inserted by para 4(3)), the relief will not be available in respect of expenditure by a different group member unless the group relationship is maintained throughout the period of three years or more from the date when the expenditure is incurred until the expiry of three years from the time when the ship is first brought into use.

The relief operates by adding an amount to the shipowner's qualifying expenditure (to offset the balancing charge which is to be deferred). This addition is then attributed to specified expenditure on new shipping, and the deferred charge is effectively recovered through a deemed disposal value which offsets the specified expenditure for capital allowances purposes.

The attribution of the addition to expenditure on new shipping is dealt with through s 33A(5). As amended by sub-para (3), this subsection requires a notice to the Revenue to effect the attribution, when the expenditure has been incurred, whereas there was previously the possibility of either identification of the expenditure (actual or proposed) by the shipowner, or a determination by the Revenue. In its amended form, s 33A(5) indicates that the addition may be attributed to expenditure on new shipping incurred by either the shipowner or another qualifying person. Where the person undertaking the expenditure is not the shipowner, the notice to the Revenue in respect of the attribution must be made jointly by the shipowner and the qualifying person incurring the expenditure (s 33A(5A) inserted by sub-para (3)).

The amount of relief which may be claimed is limited to the lowest of the various figures specified in s 33A(3). The amount referred to by s 33A(3)(*b*), which was previously the expenditure on new shipping to be incurred by the shipowner in the permitted six-year period, is amended by sub-para (1). This subsection now refers to expenditure by qualifying persons, to which an attribution under s 33A(5) may be made.

Where projected expenditure on new shipping does not, in fact, arise within the permitted period, the relief is effectively withdrawn. This is dealt with by s 33A(4). Under the extended relief, the proposed expenditure may, of course, be expenditure by the shipowner or by another qualifying person. However, the amendment of s 33A(4), effected by sub-para (2), appears to go slightly further than this, the relief being withdrawn if any circumstances arise under which the addition to qualifying expenditure ceases to be capable of attribution to the expenditure concerned. This may envisage a possible situation where expenditure on new shipping has been incurred by a group member, but that group member does not wish to join in a notice to the Revenue under s 33A(5A) to effect the attribution to that expenditure.

In this respect, it should be noted that s 33D(6) provides that expenditure cannot be used for attribution if there is previously occurring expenditure within the permitted period which could have been used. This restriction applies even if the other expenditure cannot actually be used for attribution, due to an election not to apply the single ship trade provisions of CAA 1990 s 31. Following amendment by para 4(5), s 33D(6) now covers previously occurring expenditure by any qualifying person. It would thus seem that, even where the shipowner has itself incurred expenditure on new shipping within the permitted period, that expenditure could be unavailable for attribution due to prior expenditure by another group member which does not, in fact, wish to use its own expenditure for attribution.

In connection with the definition of "qualifying person", it is necessary also to have regard to the fact that, where there is a change in the persons carrying on the shipowner's trade, expenditure by the successors may, in appropriate circumstances, be treated as expenditure by the shipowner, under the separate provision in s 33D(7). In certain such cases, it would seem to be the shipowner, rather than the person incurring the expenditure, who is entitled to give the attribution notice to the Revenue under s 33A(5), although it may be possible for the successors to vary such a notice under s 33F(4) as supplemented by s 33F(7).

3 (1) In subsection (1) of section 33C (re-imposition of deferred charge)—

(*a*) in paragraph (*b*), for "the shipowner" there shall be substituted "a qualifying person"; and

(*b*) for paragraph (c) there shall be substituted the following paragraph—

"(*c*) the expenditure is expenditure the whole or any part of which is expenditure to which the whole or any part of the addition is attributed in accordance with section 33A(5)."

(2) In subsection (2) of that section—

(*a*) the words "to be", in the first place where they occur, shall be omitted; and

(*b*) in paragraph (*b*), for "the shipowner" there shall be substituted "the qualifying person in question".

GENERAL NOTE

This paragraph makes consequential amendments to CAA 1990 s 33C, which deals with the reimposition of the deferred charge by reference to the attributed expenditure.

References to the "shipowner" are replaced by references to a "qualifying person" in appropriate places. Under s 33C(2)(*b*), as amended, the deemed disposal value arising is taken into account in respect of the single ship trade of the qualifying person incurring the expenditure on new shipping.

4 (1) In section 33D (definition of expenditure on new shpping), in subsection (1)—

(*a*) in paragraph (*a*), for "the shipowner's actual trade" there shall be substituted "a trade carried on by the person who incurs that expenditure"; and

(*b*) in paragraph (*b*), for "the shipowner" there shall be substituted "that person".

(2) In subsection (2) of that section—

(*a*) in paragraph (*a*), for "the shipowner" there shall be substituted "the person who incurred the expenditure"; and

(*b*) in paragraph (*c*)(ii), for "the shipowner" there shall be substituted "the person who incurred the expenditure".

(3) After subsection (2) of that section there shall be inserted the following subsections—

"(2A) Subject to subsection (2B) below, expenditure incurred by a qualifying person other than the shipowner on the provision of a ship shall not be, and shall be deemed never to have been, expenditure on new shipping if—

(*a*) at any time after the time when the ship first belongs to that person in consequence of that expenditure, it ceases to belong to that person without having been brought into use for the purposes of a trade of that person;

(*b*) the ship is brought into use for the purposes of a trade of that person and an event falling within section 24(6)(*c*) occurs with respect to the ship before the end of the period of three years beginning with the time when it is first brought into use; or

(*c*) there is a time falling—

(i) after the expenditure is incurred, and

(ii) where the ship is brought into use for the purposes of a trade of that person, before the end of the period of three years beginning with the time when it is first so brought into use,

when the shipowner and that person do not fall to be treated as members of the same group of companies for the purposes of Chapter IV of Part X of the principal Act (group relief).

(2B) Subsection (2A) above shall not apply by virtue of paragraph (*a*) or (*b*) of that subection in any case if the event by virtue of which the case falls within that paragraph is, or is the result of—

(*a*) the total loss of the ship; or

(*b*) damage to the ship that puts it in a condition in which it is impossible, or not commercially worthwhile, for the repair required for restoring it to its previous use to be undertaken;

and that subsection shall have effect, where anything falling within paragraph (*a*) or (*b*) above occurs, as if times falling after the occurrence of the total loss or, as the case may be, after the occurrence of the damage were to be disregarded for the purposes of paragraph (*c*) of that subsection."

(4) In subsection (4) of that section—

(*a*) in paragraphs (*a*) and (*b*), for the words "the shipowner", in each place where they occur, there shall be substituted "the person who incurred the expenditure"; and

(*b*) in paragraph (*c*)(i), for "the shipowner's actual trade" there shall be substituted "a trade carried on by the person who incurred that expenditure".

(5) In subsection (6) of that section, for "by the shipowner" there shall be substituted "by a qualifying person".

(6) In subsection (7) of that section—

(*a*) for "any trade previously carried on by the shipowner" there shall be substituted "the shipowner's actual trade"; and

(*b*) in paragraph (*a*), for the words "by the persons for the time being carrying on that trade" there shall be substituted "for the purposes of that trade by the persons for the time being carrying it on".

(7) For subsection (8) of that section there shall be substituted the following subsection—

"(8) For the purposes of this section a person is connected with another person at any time if, at that time—

(*a*) he is, within the terms of section 839 of the principal Act, connected either with that other person or with a person who is connected with that other person by virtue of paragraph (*b*) below; or

(*b*) he is carrying on a trade previously carried on by that other person in a case in which the only changes in the persons engaged in carrying on that trade between—

(i) the time when it was previously carried on by that other person, and

(ii) the time in question,

are changes in respect of which the trade is to be treated by virtue of section 113(2) or 343(2) of the principal Act as not having been discontinued;

and the persons who shall be taken for the purposes of this section, in relation to expenditure incurred by a person who is not the shipowner, to be connected at any time with the person by whom the expenditure is or has been incurred shall include every person who at that time is connected (in accordance with the preceding provisions of this subsection) with the shipowner."

GENERAL NOTE

The amendments made by this paragraph relate to the definition of "expenditure on new shipping" in CAA 1990 s 33D. Only expenditure on new shipping is available for attribution (and thus for the relief) under s 33A(5).

It was formerly a requirement of s 33D(1) that the expenditure on a qualifying ship (as defined in s 33E) should be incurred for the purposes of the trade of the person who disposed of the old ship (the shipowner). This is amended by sub-para (1), so that the expenditure must now relate to the trade of the qualifying person incurring the expenditure. Thus, the old ship and the new ship may be used for different trades. It should be noted that, where Group Company A incurs the expenditure on the new ship, the ship must be used for the purposes of Group Company A's trade. If Group Company A, as a non-trading finance company, incurs expenditure on a new ship for use in Group Company B's trade, then the expenditure would not seem to be available to support a claim to relief.

In s 33D(1)(*b*), which requires the expenditure on the ship to be taken into account for the purposes of a single ship trade under CAA 1990 s 31, the former reference to the shipowner is replaced by a reference to the person incurring the expenditure (sub-para (1)). A corresponding amendment is made to the wording of s 33D(2), dealing with the possible disqualification of expenditure for the purposes of the relief if the ship ceases to be a qualifying ship within a specified time (sub-para (2)).

Where expenditure on a ship is incurred by a qualifying person other than the shipowner, s 33D(2A) and s 33D(2B), inserted by sub-para (3), provide that the expenditure does not qualify as expenditure on new shipping if any of the following circumstances apply—

(*a*) the ship ceases to belong to the qualifying person concerned without having been brought into use in his trade, except where this situation arises due to the total loss of the ship or substantial damage which puts it beyond repair;

(*b*) a disposal or deemed disposal of the ship occurs within the three years from the time when it is brought into use, except where this situation is due to the total loss of the ship or substantial damage which puts it beyond repair; or

(*c*) the group relationship (as defined for group relief purposes) between the qualifying person concerned and the shipowner is broken at any time before the expiry of three years from the time when the ship is brought into use, but excluding from the length of this period any time after the total loss of the ship or the occurrence of any substantial damage which puts it beyond repair.

As originally enacted, s 33D(4) provided that expenditure on a ship was not expenditure on new shipping if the ship had previously belonged to the shipowner or a connected person within a specified period, or if one of the main objects of the provision of the ship was to obtain relief under s 33A. Subparagraph (4) amends this subsection to encompass previous ownership by the person incurring the expenditure (whether the shipowner or not) or a connected person.

Under s 33D(6), as amended by sub-para (5), expenditure on new shipping may not be available for attribution under s 33A(5) (and thus may not be available to support a claim for relief) if there is preceding expenditure on provision of a ship by any qualifying person, which has not been used for attributions.

The opportunity has been taken to tighten up the wording of s 33D(7) with regard to a change in the persons carrying on the shipowner's former trade (sub-para (6)).

The definition of connected persons for the purposes of s 33D is amended through the substitution of s 33D(8) by sub-para (7). In relation to expenditure on a ship incurred by a person other than the shipowner, the persons who are treated as connected with the person incurring the expenditure include any person who is connected with the shipowner.

5 (1) In section 33E (definition of a qualifying ship), after subsection (8) there shall be inserted the following subsection—

"(9) Subsections (5), (6) and (8) above shall have effect for the purposes of section 33D in relation to any ship on the provision of which expenditure is incurred on or after the passing of the Finance Act 1996 as if the references in those subsections to the shipowner included references to the person incurring that expenditure."

GENERAL NOTE
This paragraph makes a consequential amendment to CAA 1990 s 33E, which deals with the definition of a qualifying ship. A new sub-s (9) is inserted into s 33E to provide that, in the specified subsections, references to the shipowner are to include a reference to the person incurring the expenditure on a ship.

6 (1) In section 33F (procedural provisions), in subsection (4)—

(*a*) for "An attribution made for the purposes of section 33A(5) or 33C" there shall be substituted "Subject to subsection (4A) below, an attribution in accordance with section 33A(5)"; and

(*b*) for "the person giving the notice" there shall be substituted "the shipowner".

(2) After that subsection there shall be inserted the following subsection—

"(4A) A notice by the shipowner under subsection (4) above shall not have effect in a case where the shipowner and the qualifying person to whose expenditure the notice relates are not the same person unless that person joins with the shipowner in the giving of that notice."

GENERAL NOTE
This paragraph amends CAA 1990 s 33F in relation to a notice to the Revenue to vary an attribution under s 33A(5). Following a claim for relief under s 33A, the attribution of the amount of the relief to expenditure on new shipping determines that the relief is to be recouped by reference to that expenditure.

However, s 33F(4) provides that an attribution notice may be varied by the shipowner. In a case where the attribution relates to expenditure on a new ship which is incurred by a qualifying

525

person other than the shipowner, s 33F(4A), inserted by sub-para (2), provides that the qualifying person concerned must join with the shipowner in giving the notice to vary the attribution. This corresponds to s 33A(5A), which requires the original attribution notice in such a situation to be given by the shipowner and the other qualifying person jointly.

It should also be noted that, where there has been a change in the persons carrying on the shipowner's trade, such that expenditure by the successors is treated as if it were incurred by the shipowner under s 33D(7), a notice to vary the attribution would be given by the successors rather than the shipowner, as set out in s 33F(7).

Commencement

7 (1) Subject to sub-paragraph (2) below, this Schedule shall have effect in relation to any case in which the event mentioned in section 33A(1)(*b*) occurs on or after the day on which this Act is passed.

(2) Subject to sub-paragraph (3) below, this Schedule shall not apply for the purposes of claims, assessments and adjustments made on or after the day on which this Act is passed but before such day as the Treasury may by order appoint.

(3) Sub-paragraph (2) above shall not prevent the making on or after the day appointed under that sub-paragraph of any claims, assessments or adjustments in respect of the application of this Schedule, in accordance with sub-paragraph (1) above, in relation to times before that day; and nothing in any provision relating to the period within which any claim or assessment must be made shall prevent any such claim, assessment or adjustment from being made by reference to this Schedule if it is made no more than twelve months after the day so appointed.

GENERAL NOTE

The amendments effected by this Schedule apply in relation to disposals of old ships on or after the date of Royal Assent (sub-para (1)). However, it will not be possible to make claims for the extended relief until a day to be appointed by the Treasury by order (sub-para (2)). Once the day has been appointed, claims, assessments or adjustments can be made in accordance with the provisions of this Schedule, and with regard to disposals of ships occurring from the date of Royal Assent. It will be possible to make claims, assessments or adjustments by reference to this Schedule within the 12 months after the appointed day, regardless of any time limit for such claims or assessments specified elsewhere (sub-para (3)).

SCHEDULE 36

CONTROLLED FOREIGN COMPANIES

GENERAL NOTE

The anti-avoidance legislation relating to controlled foreign companies was introduced in 1984 following a very long drawn out consultation process which began in 1981. The main aim of the legislation is to attribute a proportionate share of the income (but not capital gains) of an overseas company (resident in a jurisdiction where it is subject to a low rate of tax and which is controlled by UK resident persons) to UK resident companies having at least a 10 per cent interest in the overseas company. An overseas company whose income may be attributed in this way is referred to as a controlled foreign company ("CFC").

In order to moderate the unpopularity of the original legislation care had been taken to remove as many genuine cases as possible from the ambit of the CFC charge. This was achieved by setting up a number of alternative exemption conditions and if the overseas resident company could meet one of them, that would be sufficient to take it out of the TA 1988 s 747 charge.

A list was issued of jurisdictions for which it could automatically be assumed that a company resident there was not subject to a low rate of tax. If the overseas company was not resident in one of the listed "excluded territories", it could still be exempted from the CFC charge if its income (measured as for UK taxation purposes) for a 12-month accounting period was less than £20,000. If this exemption did not apply, the company could still qualify for exemption from the CFC charge if it carried on exempt activities. Alternatively, it could qualify for exemption if more than 35 per cent (by voting power) of the overseas company's shares were publicly held, were quoted on a recognised stock exchange and were actively dealt in on the exchange.

If none of these exemptions apply, the company can still qualify for exemption if it can be demonstrated that the company was not set up to avoid UK taxation and that no transactions or series of transactions carried out by the company in the accounting period were undertaken to avoid UK taxation or that there was no reduction or only a minimal reduction in UK taxation achieved by the transactions. This condition is popularly referred to as the "motive test". It is generally very difficult to rely on the motive test for exemption from the CFC charge.

Even if none of the above exemptions apply, the CFC charge can still be avoided if the company can meet the "acceptable distribution policy" ("ADP") test. Under the original legislation, the company would be pursuing an ADP if a dividend was paid up to the UK within 18 months of the CFC's year end, amounting to at least 90 per cent of a non-trading CFC's or 50 per cent of a trading CFC's profits available for distribution (as shown in their accounts). However, if it could be demonstrated that the CFC was prevented from paying such a dividend under the laws of the territory, it could still avoid the CFC charge.

Apportionments of CFC income to UK resident companies are not automatic and require a direction to be issued by the Board of Inland Revenue. That is not surprising given the many uncertainties which can arise under this legislation. However, the retention of direction making powers by the Revenue does not sit too well with "pay and file" and self-assessment for corporation tax. A Revenue consultative document was issued on 28 November 1995 which explores ways in which the CFC legislation could be amended to fit into the self-assessment regime. It argues against the retention of the Revenue's direction making power (on the grounds of its incompatibility with self-assessment) and, broadly, proposes to replace it with wider reporting requirements and the abolition of the ADP exemption. The other exemptions would remain but would become claims which the UK company could make. This system is to be linked to the system of advance clearances announced in a Revenue Press Release on 9 November 1994.

In recent years it has become clear that the Government has become unhappy with the workings of the ADP test. In FA 1994, applying to accounting periods ended on or after 30 November 1993, the 90 per cent ADP standard applying to non-trading companies was amended to substitute "net chargeable profits" (ie profits computed for UK tax purposes) for "available [accounting] profits". The ADP standard for trading companies will be brought into line with that for non-trading companies for accounting periods beginning on or after 28 November 1995.

The proposal in the consultative document is that, if the ADP exemption is abolished, the UK shareholder's liability would be computed on a current year basis on a roughly equivalent amount of income as calculated for the ADP standard but discounted to take into account the fact that the tax liability is advanced by almost two years (the figure would be something like 80 per cent of taxable profit). It is also proposed that the charge should only apply to UK companies having a 20 per cent or greater interest in a CFC. The deadline for responses to the consultative document was 29 March 1996.

Many critics of the proposals have focused on the heavy extra compliance burden that this extension of the legislation is likely to cause and have wondered whether that will be balanced by advantages to the Exchequer. In the Finance Bill debate, the Treasury Minister dismissed the issue by pointing to the relatively small number of companies involved ("no more than 500") operated by "people who know what they are doing".

THE AMENDMENTS
These amendments apply to accounting periods beginning on or after 28 November 1995.

CHANGES TO THE ACCEPTABLE DISTRIBUTION POLICY STANDARD
The main amendments to TA 1988 s 747A and Schs 24 and 25 are to remove references to "trading company" since, in respect of accounting periods beginning on or after 28 November 1995, all companies will be subject to the same ADP test. This, now considerably simplified, test is to be found in TA 1988 Sch 25 para 2(1) and requires 90 per cent of the taxable income (computed on UK taxation principles) to be distributed to the UK.
A new defined term is introduced, an "ADP exempt period" (para 3(3) of this Schedule inserts a new TA 1988 Sch 24 para 1(6)) which is an accounting period of a CFC which began on or after 28 November 1995 and in respect of which the company pursued an acceptable distribution policy (as that will now be defined). This definition is used in a number of contexts but always in such a way as to make it clear that the company is required to compute its "chargeable profits" (ie profits computed as for UK tax purposes under the assumptions set out in TA 1988 Sch 24) in order to arrive at either—

(*a*) the amount which will be attributable to UK resident companies having at least a 10 per cent interest in the CFC; or
(*b*) the amount of income which will need to be distributed if the company is to pursue an ADP.

In consequence of the above changes, the time limit for claims to be made in calculating the taxable profits of an ADP exempt period is set at 20 months following the accounting period (para 3(7) of this Schedule inserts a new TA 1988 Sch 24 para 4(2A)).

CHANGES TO THE MOTIVE TEST
The opportunity has been taken to tighten up the definition of associated operations which have as their effect the reduction of UK taxation. In TA 1988 s 748(3)(*a*) and in Sch 25(16) references to "two or more transactions taken together" have been extended by adding "the results of at least one of which are so reflected" (ie in the profit and loss account for the period).

CHANGES TO THE EXEMPT ACTIVITIES TEST
Again there has been some tightening up of the definition of "wholesale, distributive or financial business" (in TA 1988 Sch 25 para 6(2)(*b*)). Under the original formulation the exempt activities test is failed where the operations of the company include such business and the gross trading receipts in an accounting period is derived as to 50 per cent or more from connected or associated persons. The tainted transactions are extended to include transactions not just with connected or associated persons but also with all persons who have an interest in the overseas company at any time in the accounting period.

1 (1) Section 747A of the Taxes Act 1988 (special rule for computing chargeable profits: currency) shall be amended as follows.

(2) Subsection (7) (first relevant accounting period of a trading company where subsection (6) does not apply) shall be omitted.

(3) In subsection (8) (first relevant accounting period of a company which is not a trading company—

(*a*) the words "the company is not a trading company and" shall be omitted;
(*b*) for "its", where first occurring, there shall be substituted "the company's"; and
(*c*) after paragraph (*b*) (cases where direction under section 747 would have been given had the company not pursued an acceptable distribution policy) there shall be added—

"unless the company is a trading company, in which case paragraph (*b*) above shall be disregarded in the case of its accounting periods beginning before 28th November 1995."

2 In section 748(3) of the Taxes Act 1988 (direction under section 747(1) not to be given in cases where reduction in United Kingdom tax was not the main purpose etc) in paragraph (*a*), for "or any two or more of those transactions taken together" there shall be substituted "or any two or more transactions taken together, the results of at least one of which are so reflected,".

3 (1) Schedule 24 to the Taxes Act 1988 (assumptions for calculating chargeable profits etc) shall be amended in accordance with the following provisions of this paragraph.

(2) In paragraph 1 (general) after sub-paragraph (3) there shall be inserted—

"(3A) In any case where—

(*a*) it is at any time necessary for any purpose of Chapter IV of Part XVII to determine the chargeable profits of the company for an accounting period, and
(*b*) at that time—

(i) no direction has been given under section 747(1) with respect to that or any earlier accounting period of the company, and
(ii) it has not been established that that or any earlier accounting period of the company is an ADP exempt period,

in determining the chargeable profits of the company for the accounting period mentioned in paragraph (*a*) above it shall be assumed, for the purpose of any of the following provisions of this Schedule which refer to the first accounting period in respect of which a direction is given under section 747(1) or which is an ADP exempt period, that that period (but not any earlier period) is an accounting period in respect of which such a direction is given or which is an ADP exempt period."

(3) After sub-paragraph (5) of that paragraph there shall be inserted—

"(6) Any reference in this Schedule to an 'ADP exempt period', in the case of any company, is a reference to an accounting period of the company—

(*a*) which begins on or after 28th November 1995; and
(*b*) in respect of which the company pursued, within the meaning of Part I of Schedule 25, an acceptable distribution policy."

(4) In paragraph 2(1) (company assumed to have become resident in the United Kingdom at the beginning of the first accounting period in respect of which a direction is given under section 747(1) and to have continued so resident etc) for "in respect of which a direction is given under section 747(1) and" there shall be substituted—

"(*a*) in respect of which a direction is given under section 747(1), or
(*b*) which is an ADP exempt period,

and".

(5) In paragraph 4 (maximum reliefs assumed to have been claimed etc unless notice requesting other treatment is given by UK resident company or companies with a majority interest) after sub-paragraph (1) there shall be inserted—

"(1A) Sub-paragraph (2) below applies to any accounting period of the company—

(*a*) in respect of which a direction is given under section 747(1); or
(*b*) which is an ADP exempt period."

(6) In sub-paragraph (2) of that paragraph (notice to be given not later than the expiry of the time for making an appeal under s 753 or within such longer period as the Board may allow—

(*a*) at the beginning there shall be inserted "Where this sub-paragraph applies to an accounting period of the company, then"; and
(*b*) for "the time for the making of an appeal under section 753" there shall be substituted "the appropriate period".

(7) After that sub-paragraph there shall be inserted—

"(2A) For the purposes of sub-paragraph (2) above, 'the appropriate period'—

(*a*) in the case of an accounting period in respect of which a direction is given under section 747(1), means the time for the making of an appeal under section 753; and
(*b*) in the case of an accounting period which is an ADP exempt period, means the period of twenty months following the end of the accounting period."

(8) After sub-paragraph (3) of that paragraph (which defines the UK resident company or companies with a majority interest) there shall be inserted—

"(3A) Sub-paragraph (3) above shall apply in relation to an accounting period which is an ADP exempt period as it would apply if—

(*a*) that accounting period had instead been one in respect of which a direction had been duly given under section 747(1), and (*b*) such apportionments and assessments as are mentioned in sub-paragraph (3) above had been made."

(9) In paragraph 9(1)(*c*) (losses incurred in accounting periods in which, among other things, the company was not resident in the United Kingdom) after "was not resident" there shall be inserted ", and is not to be assumed by virtue of paragraph 2(1)(*b*) above to have been resident,".

(10) In paragraph 10 (capital allowances for expenditure incurred on machinery or plant before the first accounting period in respect of which a direction is given under section 747(1)) for "in respect of which a direction is given under section 747(1), the" there shall be substituted—

"(*a*) in respect of which a direction is given under section 747(1), or
(*b*) which is an ADP exempt period,

the".

(11) In paragraph 11 (write-down of allowances for certain years preceding the first for which a direction is given under section 747(1)) in sub-paragraph (2) (which defines the starting period as the first accounting period for which a direction is given and makes provision in respect of claims under paragraph 9(3)) for "in respect of which a direction is given under section 747(1) and" there shall be substituted—

"(*a*) in respect of which a direction is given under section 747(1), or
(*b*) which is an ADP exempt period,

and".

4 (1) Schedule 25 to the Taxes Act 1988 (cases excluded from direction-making powers) shall be amended as follows.

(2) In paragraph 2 (acceptable distribution policy)—

(*a*) in sub-paragraph (1)(*d*) (amount of the dividend etc paid to persons resident in the United Kingdom) for "50 per cent. of the company's available profits" there shall be substituted "90 per cent. of the company's net chargeable profits";
(*b*) in sub-paragraph (6) (computation of appropriate portion of profits in cases where there are two classes of issued shares) in the definition of "X", for "available profits" there shall be substituted "net chargeable profits".

(3) In paragraph 2A (further provisions to determine whether a controlled foreign company which is not a trading company pursues an acceptable distribution policy—

(*a*) in sub-paragraph (1) (application) the words "which is not a trading company" shall be omitted;
(*b*) in sub-paragraph (5)(*c*) (which modifies the definition of "X" in paragraph 2(6) for certain purposes) for "available profits" there shall be substituted "net chargeable profits";
(*c*) sub-paragraphs (6) and (7) (which are superseded by amendments made to paragraph 2 by this Schedule) shall be omitted.

(4) In paragraph 3 ("available profits" and "net chargeable profits" for purposes of Part I of the Schedule)—

(*a*) sub-paragraphs (1) to (4) (ascertainment of "available profits") shall be omitted;
(*b*) in sub-paragraph (5) (certain dividends to be left out of account in determining available profits or, where the company is not a trading company, chargeable profits) the words "the available profits or, where the company is not a trading company," shall be omitted.

(5) In paragraph 6 (exempt activities) in sub-paragraph (2)(*b*) (less than 50 per cent. of gross trading receipts from wholesale, distributive or financial business to be derived from connected or associated persons) after "connected or associated persons" there shall be added "or persons who have an interest in the company at any time during that accounting period."

(6) In paragraph 16(2) (reductions in United Kingdom tax: extended meaning of "transaction" in paragraphs 17 and 18)—

(*a*) in paragraph (*a*), after "transaction" there shall be inserted "the results of which are"; and

(*b*) in paragraph (*b*), for "two or more such transactions taken together" there shall be substituted "two or more transactions taken together, the results of at least one of which are so reflected".

SCHEDULE 37
                              BANKS

GENERAL NOTE
   The general interpretation provisions of TA 1988 (ss 831–842) are to include a new s 840A which
gives a formal definition of "bank". This definition includes a European bank within the meaning
of the Banking Co-ordination (Second Council Directive) Regulations 1992 which has complied
with the regulations regarding the establishment of a UK branch. It also includes any other
international organisation of which the UK is a member and which is designated a bank by the
Treasury.
   The above definition applies in particular to the provision of information relating to distributions,
to the "charges" legislation, to the "transfers of assets abroad" legislation and to the double
taxation relief legislation.
   There are consequential amendments to the provisions dealing with the deduction of tax at
source from annual payments etc under s 349 and the requirements of TMA 1970 for banks to
make special returns of interest credited to accounts and to provide information relating to income
from securities. As regards s 349(3)(*a*), a payment of interest to a non-resident bank may be made
gross only if the bank is within the charge to corporation tax as respects that interest. Where the
interest is paid to a UK branch, it may well be necessary for that branch to be a permanent
establishment under the terms of the relevant double taxation agreement.
   The new definition also applies for IHT purposes in relation to non-residents' bank accounts.

                              PART I
              "BANK" RE-DEFINED FOR CERTAIN PURPOSES

1   (1) After section 840 of the Taxes Act 1988 there shall be inserted the following
section—

"840A   Banks

(1) In any provision in relation to which it is provided that 'bank' has the meaning
given by this section 'bank' means—

   (*a*) the Bank of England;
   (*b*) an institution authorised under the Banking Act 1987;
   (*c*) a relevant European institution; or
   (*d*) a relevant international organisation which is designated as a bank for the
   purposes of that provision by an order made by the Treasury.

(2) For the purposes of subsection (1) above, an institution is a relevant European
institution if—

   (*a*) it is a European authorised institution within the meaning of the Banking Co-
   ordination (Second Council Directive) Regulations 1992; and
   (*b*) the requirements of paragraph 1 of Schedule 2 to those regulations have been
   complied with in relation to its establishment of a branch.

(3) For the purposes of subsection (1) above, a relevant international organisation is
an international organisation of which the United Kingdom is a member."

(2) In section 828 of the Taxes Act 1988 (regulations and orders), in subsection (4), for
"or 791" there shall be substituted "791 or 840A(1)(*d*)".

                              PART II
              AMENDMENTS OF THE TAXES ACT 1988

           Provisions in which new meaning of "bank" applies

2   (1) The following subsection—

   "( ) In this section 'bank' has the meaning given by section 840A.",

shall be inserted in the Taxes Act 1988 in accordance with sub-paragraph (2) below.

(2) The subsection shall be inserted—

(*a*) in section 234A (information relating to distributions), after subsection (8), as subsection (8A);
(*b*) in section 349 (payment of interest under deduction of tax, etc), after subsection (3), as subsection (3AA);
(*c*) in section 745 (obligation to furnish information not to apply to banks), after subsection (5), as subsection (5A);
(*d*) in section 816 (obligation to disclose certain particulars to apply to banks), after subsection (3), as subsection (3A).

(3) In Schedule 20 to the Taxes Act 1988 (charities: qualifying investments and loans), in paragraph 7 (certain deposits with banks to be qualifying investments), after sub-paragraph (2), there shall be inserted the following sub-paragraph—

"(3) In this paragraph 'bank' has the meaning given by section 840A."

(4) The provisions of paragraph 10 of that Schedule shall become sub-paragraph (1) of that paragraph and after that sub-paragraph there shall be inserted the following sub-paragraph—

"(2) In this paragraph 'bank' has the meaning given by section 840A."

Related amendments

3   In section 349(3) of the Taxes Act 1988—

(*a*) in paragraph (*a*), for the words from "in the United Kingdom" to the end there shall be substituted "on an advance from a bank, if at the time when the interest is paid the person beneficially entitled to the interest is within the charge to corporation tax as respects the interest";
(*b*) in paragraph (*b*), for "such a bank in the ordinary course of that" there shall be substituted "a bank in the ordinary course of its".

4   After subsection (3AA) of section 349 of the Taxes Act 1988 (inserted by paragraph 2 above) there shall be inserted the following subsection—

"(3AB) An order under section 840A(1)(*d*) designating an organisation as a bank for the purposes of paragraph (*a*) of subsection (3) above may provide that that paragraph shall apply to the organisation as if the words from 'if,' to the end were omitted."

5   In Schedule 20 to the Taxes Act 1988, in paragraphs 7(1) and 10, for "an institution authorised under the Banking Act 1987" there shall in each case be substituted "a bank".

Application

6   The amendments of the Taxes Act 1988 made by paragraphs 2 to 5 above apply as mentioned in paragraphs 7 to 10 below.

7   The amendment of section 234A applies in relation to payments made on or after the day on which this Act is passed.

8   (1) The amendment of subsection (3)(*a*) of section 349, and inserted subsection (3AA) of that section so far as it relates to subsection (3)(*a*), apply in accordance with sub-paragraphs (2) to (6) below.

(2) The amendments do not apply in relation to interest payable before the day on which this Act is passed.

(3) In the case of an institution which—

(*a*) immediately before the day on which this Act is passed, is treated for the purposes of section 349(3)(*a*) as a bank carrying on a bona fide banking business in the United Kingdom, and
(*b*) on that day, falls within the definition of "bank" given by section 840A(1),

the amendments apply in relation to interest payable on an advance made before that day as well as in relation to interest payable on an advance made on or after that day.

(4) In the case of an institution which—

533

(*a*) immediately before the day on which this Act is passed, is not treated for the purposes of section 349(3)(*a*) as a bank carrying on a bona fide banking business in the United Kingdom, and

(*b*) on that day, falls within the definition of "bank" given by section 840A(1),

the amendments apply only in relation to interest payable on an advance made on or after that day.

(5) Sub-paragraph (6) below applies in the case of an institution which—

(*a*) immediately before the day on which this Act is passed, is treated for the purposes of section 349(3)(*a*) as a bank carrying on a bona fide banking business in the United Kingdom; and

(*b*) on that day does not fall within the definition of "bank" given by section 840A(1).

(6) The amendments apply in relation to—

(*a*) interest payable on an advance made on or after the day on which this Act is passed; and

(*b*) interest payable on an advance made before that day, if at the time when the interest is paid the person beneficially entitled to the interest is not within the charge to corporation tax as respects the interest.

(7) The amendment of subsection (3)(*b*) of section 349, and inserted subsection (3AA) of that section so far as it relates to subsection (3)(*b*), apply in relation to interest paid on or after the day on which this Act is passed on an advance made on or after that day.

(8) In relation to interest paid on an advance made before the day on which this Act is passed, section 349(3)(*b*) shall have effect as if for the words "such a bank" there were substituted "a bank carrying on a bona fide banking business in the United Kingdom" (and section 349(3AA) shall be disregarded).

9 The amendments of sections 745 and 816 apply in relation to requirements imposed on or after the day on which this Act is passed.

10 The amendments of paragraphs 7 and 10 of Schedule 20 apply in relation to deposits made or, as the case may be, money placed on or after the day on which this Act is passed.

PART III
OTHER AMENDMENTS

Amendments of the Management Act

11 (1) The following subsection—

"( ) In this section 'bank' has the meaning given by section 840A of the principal Act.",

shall be inserted in the Taxes Management Act 1970 in accordance with sub-paragraph (2) below.

(2) The subsection shall be inserted—

(*a*) in section 17 (returns from banks etc), after subsection (1), as subsection (1A);

(*b*) in section 18 (obligation to supply certain information not to apply to banks), after subsection (3), as subsection (3AA);

(*c*) in section 24 (obligation to disclose certain particulars not to apply to banks), after subsection (3), as subsection (3A).

(3) In section 17(1) of that Act, for "person carrying on the trade or business of banking" there shall be substituted "such person who is a bank".

(4) In section 18(3) of that Act for the words from "carrying on" to the end there shall be substituted "in respect of any interest paid by the bank in the ordinary course of its business".

(5) This paragraph applies as follows—

(*a*) the amendments of section 17 apply in relation to interest paid on or after the day on which this Act is passed; and

(*b*) the amendments of sections 18 and 24 apply in relation to requirements imposed on or after the day on which this Act is passed.

Amendments of the Inheritance Tax Act 1984

12 (1) In section 157 of the Inheritance Tax Act 1984 (non-residents' bank accounts), in subsection (5), for "the Bank of England, the Post Office or an authorised institution" there shall be substituted "a bank or the Post Office".

(2) After that subsection there shall be inserted the following subsection—

"(6) In this section 'bank' has the meaning given by section 840A of the Taxes Act 1988."

(3) This paragraph applies in relation to deaths occurring on or after the day on which this Act is passed.

SCHEDULE 38
QUOTATION OR LISTING OF SECURITIES

GENERAL NOTE

The word "quoted" in relation to shares and securities occurs many times in IHTA 1984, TA 1988 and TCGA 1992. It is to be replaced by the word "listed" as from 1 April 1996. Similarly, the word "quotation" is replaced by "listing" and "quoted on" the Stock Exchange is replaced by "listed in the official list of" the Stock Exchange. To avoid confusion, where the word "listed" appears (eg listed in the SEDOL) it is replaced by "quoted".

The Finance Act 1973

1 (1) In section 38(2)(*c*) of the Finance Act 1973 (disposals of exploration or exploitation rights to include disposals of shares deriving their value from such rights), for "quoted" there shall be substituted "listed".

(2) This paragraph has effect in relation to disposals of shares on or after 1st April 1996.

The Inheritance Tax Act 1984

2 (1) For the second and the last occurrences of the word "quoted" in each of—

(*a*) sections 105(1ZA) and 113A(3B) of the Inheritance Tax Act 1984 (meaning of "quoted" etc), and

(*b*) the paragraph in section 272 of that Act (general interpretation) which defines "quoted" and "unquoted",

there shall be substituted "listed".

(2) This paragraph has effect—

(*a*) in relation to transfers of value on or after 1st April 1996; and

(*b*) for the purposes of any charge to tax by reason of an event occurring on or after 1st April 1996, in relation to transfers of value before that date.

3 (1) In section 180(3) of that Act (whether two investments are of the same description), for "quoted" there shall be substituted "listed".

(2) This paragraph has effect in relation to any time falling on or after 1st April 1996.

4 (1) In section 178(2) of that Act (shares or investments whose quotation is suspended at time of death)—

(*a*) for "quotation" there shall be substituted "listing"; and

(*b*) for "quoted" there shall be substituted "so listed or dealt in".

(2) In section 186B(1) of that Act (shares or investments whose quotation is suspended at the end of the relevant period), for "quotation" there shall be substituted "listing".

(3) This paragraph has effect in relation to investments sold, or treated as sold, on or after 1st April 1996.

5 (1) In each of sections 227(1AA) and 228(5) of that Act (meaning of "unquoted"), for the word "quoted" there shall be substituted "listed".

(2) This paragraph has effect—

(*a*) in relation to transfers of value on or after 1st April 1996; and

(*b*) for the purposes of any charge to tax by reason of an event ocurring on or after 1st April 1996, in relation to transfers of value before that date.

The Taxes Act 1988

6 (1) In each of the provisions of the Taxes Act 1988 listed in sub-paragraph (2) below, for "quoted" (wherever occurring) there shall be substituted "listed".

(2) The provisions referred to in sub-paragraph (1) above are—

(*a*) paragraph (*b*) of the definition of "quoted Eurobond" in section 124(6);

(*b*) section 209(2)(*e*)(ii);

(*c*) section 246S(3)(*c*) and (*e*);
(*d*) section 254(11);
(*e*) section 349(3A)(*b*);
(*f*) section 415(1)(*b*);
(*g*) section 477A(1A);
(*h*) section 576(4);
(*j*) paragraph 11(*a*) and (*c*) of Schedule 9;
(*k*) paragraph (*c*) of paragraph l(5C) of Schedule 18;
(*l*) paragraph 5 of Schedule 20; and
(*m*) paragraph 13(2)(*c*) of Schedule 25.

(3) So far as relating to the provision mentioned in sub-paragraph (2)(*a*) above, sub-paragraph (1) above has effect in relation to any interest paid on a quoted Eurobond on or after 1st April 1996.

(4) So far as relating to the provision mentioned in sub-paragraph (2)(*b*) above, sub-paragraph (1) above has effect in relation to any interest paid or other distribution made on or after 1st April 1996.

(5) So far as relating to the provisions mentioned in sub-paragraph (2)(*c*) and (*m*) above, sub-paragraph (1) above has effect in relation to accounting periods ending on or after 1st April 1996.

(6) So far as relating to the provision mentioned in sub-paragraph (2)(*d*) above, sub-paragraph (1) above has effect in relation to securities issued on or after 1st April 1996.

(7) So far as relating to the provisions mentioned in sub-paragraph (2)(*e*) and (*g*) above, sub-paragraph (1) above has effect in relation to dividends or interest which become payable on or after 1st April 1996.

(8) So far as relating to the provision mentioned in sub-paragraph (2)(*f*) above, sub-paragraph (1) above has effect in relation to periods of 12 months ending on or after 1st April 1996.

(9) So far as relating to the provision mentioned in sub-paragraph (2)(*h*) above, sub-paragraph (1) above has effect in relation to relevant periods ending on or after 1st April 1996.

(10) So far as relating to the provisions mentioned in sub-paragraph (2)(*j*) and (*k*) above, sub-paragraph (1) above has effect in relation to any time falling on or after 1st April 1996.

(11) So far as relating to the provision mentioned in sub-paragraph (2)(*l*) above, sub-paragraph (1) above has effect in relation to chargeable periods ending on or after 1st April 1996.

7 (1) In each of the provisions of that Act listed in sub paragraph (2) below, for "quoted on" there shall be substituted "listed in the Official List of".

(2) The provisions referred to in sub-paragraph (1) above are—

(*a*) paragraph (*b*) of the definition of "preference shares" in section 210(4);
(*b*) section 842(1)(*c*); and
(*c*) section 842AA(2)(*e*).

(3) Sub-paragraph (1) above, so far as relating to the provision mentioned in sub-paragraph (2)(*a*) above, has effect in relation to share capital repaid on or after 1st April 1996.

(4) Sub-paragraph (1) above, so far as relating to the provisions mentioned in sub-paragraph (2)(*b*) and (*c*) above, has effect in relation to accounting periods ending on or after 1st April 1996.

8 (1) In section 251(5) of that Act (application of section 272(3) of the Taxation of Chargeable Gains Act 1992), for "listed" there shall be substituted "quoted".

(2) This paragraph has effect where the relevant date falls on or after 1st April 1996.

9 (1) In section 735(3) of that Act (meaning of the "appropriate proportion")—

(*a*) after "the appropriate proportion" there shall be inserted ", in relation to securities listed in the Official List of the Stock Exchange,";

(*b*) in paragraph (*a*), for "first listed in The Stock Exchange Daily Official List at a price excluding the value of," there shall be substituted ", in accordance with announcements made by The Stock Exchange, first to be dealt in without carrying rights to"; and

(*c*) in paragraph (*b*), for "quoted in that List at a price excluding the value of" there shall be substituted ", in accordance with such announcements, first to be dealt in without carrying rights to".

(2) In section 735(4) of that Act (application of section 753(3) to securities purchased before their first interest payment), for "quoted" there shall be substituted "to be dealt in".

(3) In section 735(5) of that Act (application of section 735(3) to securities not listed in the Stock Exchange Daily Official List)—

(*a*) for "Stock Exchange Daily Official List" there shall be substituted "Official List of The Stock Exchange"; and

(*b*) after "shall have effect" there shall be inserted "as it has effect in relation to securities which are so listed but".

(4) This paragraph has effect in relation to cases where the first buyer purchases securities on or after 1st April 1996.

The Taxation of Chargeable Gains Act 1992

10 (1) In each of the provisions of the Taxation of Chargeable Gains Act 1992 listed in sub-paragraph (2) below, for the word "quoted" (wherever occurring) there shall be substituted "listed".

(2) The provisions referred to in sub-paragraph (1) above are—

(*a*) section 144(8)(*b*);
(*b*) the definition of "unquoted company" in section 164N(1);
(*c*) section 165(2)(*b*)(i);
(*d*) section 276(2)(*c*) and (6);
(*e*) section 281(3)(*c*); and
(*f*) paragraph 2(2)(*b*)(i) of Schedule 7.

(3) So far as relating to the provisions mentioned in sub-paragraph (2)(*a*) and (*c*) to (*f*) above, sub-paragraph (1) above has effect in relation to disposals on or after 1st April 1996.

(4) So far as relating to the provision mentioned in sub-paragraph (2)(*b*) above, sub-paragraph (1) above has effect in relation to acquisitions of qualifying investments (within the meaning of section 164A of that Act) on or after 1st April 1996.

11 (1) In section 146(4)(*b*) of that Act (definition of "quoted shares and securities"), for the words "have a quoted market value" there shall be substituted the words "are listed".

(2) This paragraph has effect in relation to disposals of options on or after 1st April 1996.

12 (1) In section 272(3) of that Act (market value of certain listed shares or securities), for "listed" there shall be substituted "quoted".

(2) In Schedule 11 to that Act (transitional provisions and savings), in paragraph 7(1)(*a*) (modification of section 272(3) when ascertaining market values before 25th March 1973), for "listed" there shall be substituted "quoted".

(3) This paragraph has effect where the relevant date falls on or after 1st April 1996.

SCHEDULE 39

Section 201

ENACTMENT OF CERTAIN INLAND REVENUE EXTRA-STATUTORY CONCESSIONS

PART I

INCOME TAX AND CORPORATION TAX

Capital Allowances

1 (1) The Capital Allowances Act 1990 ("the 1990 Act") shall be amended as follows.

(2) The following section shall be inserted after section 15 of the 1990 Act:

"15A Balancing charge after cessation of trade

(1) This section applies where:

(*a*) a balancing charge falls to be made as provided in section 15 on any person in respect of a building or structure which is temporarily out of use but is deemed by virtue of subsection (1) of that section still to be an industrial building or structure; and

(*b*) when the building or structure was last in use, it was in use as an industrial building or structure for the purposes of a trade which was carried on by that person but which has since been permanently discontinued.

(2) Where this section applies, the amount of the balancing charge shall be treated for the purposes of section 105 of the principal Act (allowable deductions) as a sum received by that person which is chargeable to tax under section 103 or 104(1) of the principal Act (charges on receipts after discontinuance), and accordingly any loss, expense, debit or capital allowance such as is referred to in section 105(1) may be deducted from the amount of the balancing charge.

(3) Nothing in subsection (2) above shall prevent any amounts allowable under any other provisions of the Tax Acts from being deducted from the amount of the balancing charge.

(4) Section 15(3) shall apply for the purposes of this section."

(3) Section 35 of the 1990 Act (contributions to expenditure, and hiring of cars) shall be amended by the insertion of the following subsection after subsection (2):

"(2A) Where subsection (2) has operated to reduce any expenditure on the hiring of a motor car, and subsequently either any rebate (by whatever name called) of the rentals is made or any transaction occurs with regard to any rentals that falls within section 94 of the principal Act (debts deducted and subsequently released), then the amount otherwise taxable in respect of the rebate or transaction shall be reduced in the same proportion as the expenditure on hiring was reduced."

(4) The amendment made by subparagraph (2) above shall have effect where the balancing charge falls to be made on or after the day on which this Act is passed, and the amendment made by subparagraph (3) above shall have effect in relation to rebates made and transactions occurring on or after the day on which this Act is passed.

SUBPARAGRAPH (2)

ESC B19

This is enacted in the form of a new CAA 1990 s 15A. It provides that where a balancing charge arises on the disposal of an industrial building after the cessation of the trade in which it was used, that balancing charge is treated as a post-cessation receipt. This means that unused trading losses may be brought forward for set off against it under TA 1988 s 105.

SUBPARAGRAPH (3)

ESC B28
Where a car costing more than £12,000 is leased, part of the lease rentals is disallowed under CAA 1990 s 35(2). Where this happens, a corresponding proportion of any rebate is exempt from tax.

Contributions to overseas pension schemes

2 (1) Section 76 of the Finance Act 1989 (non-approved retirement benefits schemes) shall be amended as follows.

(2) At the beginning of each of subsections (2), (3), (5) and (6), for "Expenses" there shall be substituted "Subject to subsection (6A) below, expenses".

(3) The following subsections shall be inserted after subsection (6):

"(6A) Expenses to which subsection (6B) or (6C) below applies shall be treated as not falling within any of subsections (2), (3), (5) or (6) above.

(6B) This subsection applies to expenses of paying any sum, or of providing benefits, pursuant to a superannuation fund which satisfies the requirements of section 615(6) of the Taxes Act 1988.

(6C) This subsection applies to expenses of paying any sum, or of providing benefits, pursuant to a retirement benefits scheme which is established outside the United Kingdom and which the Board are satisfied corresponds to such a scheme as is mentioned in paragraphs (*a*), (*b*) or (*c*) of section 596(1) of the Taxes Act 1988, where the expenses are incurred for the benefit of:

(*a*) employees whose emoluments are foreign emoluments within the meaning of section 192 of the Taxes Act 1988; or
(*b*) employees who are not resident in the United Kingdom and whose duties are performed wholly outside the United Kingdom (and for this purpose duties performed in the United Kingdom the performance of which is merely incidental to the performance of other duties outside the United Kingdom shall be treated as performed outside the United Kingdom)."

(4) The amendments made by this paragraph shall have effect in relation to expenses incurred on or after the day on which this Act is passed.

ESC B39
FA 1989 s 76 disallows expenses of providing benefits under non-approved pension schemes. This disallowance will not apply to foreign pension schemes which correspond to approved schemes in relation to expenses incurred (eg contributions) after Royal Assent.

PART II
CHARGEABLE GAINS

Treatment of compensation and insurance money

3 (1) Section 23 of the Taxation of Chargeable Gains Act 1992 (receipt of compensation and insurance money not treated as a disposal) shall be amended as follows.

(2) The following subsections shall be substituted for subsection (6):

"(6) If a building ('the old building') is destroyed or irreparably damaged, and all or part of a capital sum received by way of compensation for the destruction or damage, or under a policy of insurance of the risk of the destruction or damage, is applied by the recipient in constructing or otherwise acquiring a replacement building situated on other land ('the new building'), then for the purposes of subsections (4) and (5) above each of the old building and the new building shall be regarded as an asset separate from the land on which it is or was situated and the old building shall be treated as lost or destroyed.

(7) For the purposes of subsection (6) above:

(*a*) references to a building include references to any permanent or semi-permanent structure in the nature of a building; and

(*b*) the reference to a sum applied in acquiring the new building does not include a reference to a sum applied in acquiring the land on which the new building is situated; and

(*c*) all necessary apportionments shall be made of any expenditure, compensation or consideration, and the method of apportionment shall be such as is just and reasonable.

(8) This section shall apply in relation to a wasting asset with the following modifications:

(*a*) paragraphs (*b*) and (*c*) of subsection (1) above, and subsection (2) above, shall not apply; and

(*b*) in subsections (1) and (3) above, the amount of the expenditure from which the deduction is to be made shall be the amount which would have been allowable under Chapter III of this Part if the asset had been disposed of immediately after the application of the capital sum.''

(3) The amendments made by this paragraph shall have effect in relation to capital sums received on or after 6th April 1996.

ESC D19, D1

TCGA 1992 s 23(4) provides that where an asset is lost or destroyed and the insurance compensation is applied in acquiring a replacement asset, the gain under s 23 can be rolled over into the replacement asset. For this purpose, if the asset is a building, it is to be treated as a separate asset from the land on which it stands. Under the general law, the building is part of the land on which it stands, and land is not lost or destroyed. The effect of the provision is to allow a rollover claim where it would otherwise not be allowed. Similarly, if the lessee of a short lease uses the recovery to make good damage to the property, that recovery is not treated as a capital sum under s 22.

Assets of negligible value

4 (1) Section 24 of the Taxation of Chargeable Gains Act 1992 (disposals where assets lost or destroyed, or become of negligible value) shall be amended by the substitution of the following subsection for subsection (2):

''(2) Where the owner of an asset which has become of negligible value makes a claim to that effect:

(*a*) this Act shall apply as if the claimant had sold, and immediately reacquired, the asset at the time of the claim or (subject to paragraphs (*b*) and (*c*) below) at any earlier time specified in the claim, for a consideration of an amount equal to the value specified in the claim.

(*b*) An earlier time may be specified in the claim if:

(i) the claimant owned the asset at the earlier time; and

(ii) the asset had become of negligible value at the earlier time; and either

(iii) for capital gains tax purposes the earlier time is not more than two years before the beginning of the year of assessment in which the claim is made; or

(iv) for corporation tax purposes the earlier time is on or after the first day of the earliest accounting period ending not more than two years before the time of the claim.

(*c*) Section 93 of and Schedule 12 to the Finance Act 1994 (indexation losses and transitional relief) shall have effect in relation to an asset to which this section applies as if the sale and reacquisition occurred at the time of the claim and not at any earlier time.''

(2) The amendment made by this paragraph shall have effect in relation to claims made on or after 6th April 1996.

ESC D28

This paragraph enacts the concession whereby a negligible value claim under TCGA 1992 s 24 can be related back up to two years from the beginning of the year in which the claim is made.

541

The wording of the provisions makes it clear that the asset must have negligible value both at the time of the claim and at the earlier date specified in the claim.

Settled Property

5 (1) Section 72 of the Taxation of Chargeable Gains Act 1992 (termination of life interest on death of person entitled) shall be amended as follows.

(2) In subsections (1), (2) and (5), for the words "a life" wherever they occur, there shall be substituted "an" and, in subsection (5), the word "life", in the third place where it occurs, shall be omitted.

(3) For subsections (3) and (4) there shall be substituted the following subsections:

"(3) This section shall apply on the death of the person entitled to any annuity payable out of, or charged on, settled property or the income of settled property as it applies on the death of a person whose interest in possession in the whole or any part of settled property terminates on his death.

(4) Where, in the case of any entitlement to an annuity created by a settlement some of the settled property is appropriated by the trustees as a fund out of which the annuity is payable, and there is no right of recourse to, or to the income of, settled property not so appropriated, then without prejudice to subsection (5) below, the settled property so appropriated shall, while the annuity is payable, and on the occasion of the death of the person entitled to the annuity, be treated for the purposes of this section as being settled property under a separate settlement."

(4) The amendments made by this paragraph shall have effect in relation to deaths occurring on or after 6th April 1996.

6 (1) Section 73 of the Taxation of Chargeable Gains Act 1992 (death of life tenant: exclusion of chargeable gain) shall be amended as follows.

(2) In subsection (1), for the words from "termination" to "that interest" there shall be substituted "death of a person entitled to an interest in possession in the settled property".

(3) In subsection (2), the word "life" shall be omitted.

(4) In subsection (3), for the words from "subsection (5)" to "subsection (2) above" there shall be substituted "subsections (3) to (5) of that section shall apply for the purposes of this section".

(5) The amendments made by this paragraph shall have effect in relation to deaths occurring on or after 6th April 1996.

ESC D43
 The tax-free uplift to market value of settled property on the termination of a life interest (TCGA 1992 s 72) is extended to cover the termination of any other interest in possession and the death of an annuitant. If the annuity is payable out of an earmarked fund, that fund is treated as a separate settlement. There are consequential amendments to s 73.

Retirement Relief

7 (1) Paragraph 14 of Schedule 6 to the Taxation of Chargeable Gains Act 1992 shall be amended as follows.

(2) In subparagraph (2), the word "original" shall be inserted before "qualifying period".

(3) The following subparagraphs shall be inserted at the end:

"(7) In relation to the expression 'the original qualifying period', the questions whether a disposal is a qualifying disposal and whether the period relating to that disposal is a qualifying period shall be determined without regard to the requirement that the length of the period be at least one year.

(8) This paragraph shall not apply if the extended qualifying period resulting from the operation of subparagraphs (1) to (7) would be a period of less than one year."

(4) The amendments made by this paragraph shall have effect in relation to disposals made on or after 6th April 1996.

ESC D48

The provisions relating to the aggregation of earlier business periods (TCGA 1992 Sch 6 para 14) apply even when the asset currently being disposed of was not held for the 12 months minimum period, provided that the disposal was in all other respects a qualifying disposal.

Relief for loans to traders

8 (1) Section 253 of the Taxation of Chargeable Gains Act 1992 (relief for loans to traders) shall be amended as follows.

(2) In subsection (3):

(*a*) for the words from the beginning until "is satisfied that" there shall be substituted "Where a person who has made a qualifying loan makes a claim and at that time"; and

(*b*) for the words "when the claim was made" there shall be substituted "at the time of the claim or (subject to subsection (3A) below) any earlier time specified in the claim."

(3) The following subsection shall be inserted after subsection (3):

"(3A) For the purposes of subsection (3) above, an earlier time may be specified in the claim if:

(*a*) the amount to which that subsection applies was also irrecoverable at the earlier time; and either

(*b*) for capital gains tax purposes the earlier time falls not more than two years before the beginning of the year of assessment in which the claim is made; or

(*c*) for corporation tax purposes the earlier time falls on or after the first day of the earliest accounting period ending not more than two years before the time of the claim."

(4) In subsection (4) for the words from the beginning until "is satisfied that" there shall be substituted "Where a person who has guaranteed the repayment of a loan which is, or but for subsection (1)(*c*) above would be, a qualifying loan makes a claim and at that time."

(5) The amendments made by this paragraph shall have effect in relation to claims made on or after 6th April 1996.

ESC D36

This enacts the concession whereby a claim for a CGT loss on a qualifying loan to a trader can be related back up to two years from the beginning of the year in which the claim is made. However, the conditions for relief must be satisfied at the time the claim is made as well as at the time specified in the claim (TCGA 1992 s 253).

Relief for debts on qualifying corporate bonds

9 (1) Section 254 of the Taxation of Chargeable Gains Act 1992 (relief for debts on qualifying corporate bonds) shall be amended as follows.

(2) In subsection (2):

(*a*) for the words from the beginning until "is satisfied that" there shall be substituted "Where a person who has made a qualifying loan makes a claim and at that time"; and

(*b*) for the words "when the claim was made" there shall be substituted "at the time of the claim or (subject to subsection (8A) below) any earlier time specified in the claim".

(3) In subsections (6) and (7), the words "the inspector is satisfied that" shall be omitted.

(4) In subsection (8), the words "in the inspector's opinion" shall be omitted.

(5) The following subsection shall be inserted after subsection (8):

"(8A) For the purposes of subsection (2) above, an earlier time may be specified in the claim if:

(*a*) the condition which was fulfilled at the time of the claim was also fulfilled at the earlier time; and either

(*b*) for capital gains tax purposes the earlier time falls not more than two years before the beginning of the year of assessment in which the claim is made; or

(*c*) for corporation tax purposes the earlier time falls on or after the first day of the earliest accounting period ending not more than two years before the time of the claim.''

(6) In subsection (11), the words ''the inspector was satisfied that'', ''by the inspector'' and ''he was satisfied that'' shall be omitted.

(7) The amendments made by this paragraph shall have effect in relation to claims made on or after 6th April 1996.

ESC D36
Similarly, a claim for relief under s 254 on a QCB may be related back up to two years.

PART III

STAMP DUTY

Lost or spoiled instruments

10 (1) The Stamp Duties Management Act 1891 (''the Management Act'') shall be amended as follows.

(2) In section 9 of the Management Act (procedure for obtaining allowance), subsection (7), paragraph (*e*), the words ''which is inadvertently and undesignedly spoiled, and in lieu whereof another instrument made between the same parties and for the same purpose is executed and duly stamped, or'' shall be omitted.

(3) The following section shall be inserted after section 12 of the Management Act:

''Allowance for lost or spoiled instruments

12A   Lost or spoiled instruments

(1) This section applies where the Commissioners are satisfied that:

(*a*) an instrument which was executed and duly stamped ('the original instrument') has been accidentally lost or spoiled; and

(*b*) in place of the original instrument, another instrument made between the same persons and for the same purpose ('the replacement instrument') has been executed; and

(*c*) an application for relief under this section is made to the Commissioners; and either

(*d*) where the original instrument has been lost, the applicant undertakes to deliver it up to the Commissioners to be cancelled if it is subsequently found; or

(*e*) where the original instrument has been spoiled:

(i) the application is made within two years after the date of the original instrument, or if it is not dated, within two years after the time when it was executed, or within such further time as the Commissioners may allow; and

(ii) no legal proceeding has been commenced in which the original instrument has been or could or would have been given or offered in evidence; and

(iii) the original instrument is delivered up to the Commissioners to be cancelled.

(2) Where this section applies:

(*a*) the replacement instrument shall not be chargeable with any duty, but shall be stamped with the duty with which it would otherwise have been chargeable in accordance with the law in force at the time when it was executed, and shall be deemed for all purposes to be duly stamped; and

(*b*) if any duty, interest, fine or penalty was paid in respect of the replacement instrument before the application was made, the Commissioners shall pay to such person as they consider appropriate an amount equal to the duty, interest, fine or penalty so paid.

(3) For the purposes of this section the Commissioners may require the applicant to produce such evidence by statutory declaration or otherwise as they think fit.''

(4) Subject to subparagraph (5) below, the amendments made by this paragraph shall have effect from the day on which this Act is passed.

(5) The amendments made by this paragraph shall not apply in relation to an instrument which has been accidentally spoiled if an application for allowance under section 9 of the Management Act was made before the day on which this Act is passed.

LOST OR SPOILED DOCUMENTS (ESC G1, G2)

Exemption from duty is granted where a document is lost or spoiled and a replacement document is executed. The replacement document must be submitted for adjudication and will be stamped with the duty which would otherwise be payable. A spoiled document must be surrendered to the Stamp Office. A lost document must be surrendered if it is subsequently found (SDMA 1891 new s 12A).

Section 202 # SCHEDULE 40

GILT STRIPPING: TAXATION PROVISIONS

GENERAL NOTE

The Accrued Income Scheme rules are amended to deal with the situation where a gilt is exchanged for a stripped version of the same gilt. This is deemed to be a transfer of the gilt with accrued interest for the purposes of the scheme, so the accrued income up to the date of exchange is brought into charge. However, the acquisition of strips is not treated as an acquisition of gilts with accrued interest for the purposes of the scheme (TA 1988 new s 722A).

Similarly, where strips are exchanged for a single gilt consolidating those strips, that is an acquisition of the single gilt with accrued interest, but the strips are not treated as transferred with accrued interest.

As far as dealers in gilts are concerned, when a gilt is exchanged for strips, it is treated as redeemed at market value. Each strip is then deemed to be acquired at a proportionate part of that value. Similarly, where strips are consolidated, they are treated as redeemed at market value and the consolidated gilt is treated as acquired at the aggregate market value. These rules do not, however, apply for corporation tax, where the new rules dealing with loan relationships apply (see TA 1988 new s 730C).

For CGT purposes, a strip of a gilt is also a gilt (TCGA 1992 Sch 9 new para 1A).

The Stamp Act 1891 (c 39)

1 In the definition of "stock" in section 122(1) of the Stamp Act 1891, after "Bank of Ireland," there shall be inserted "any strip (within the meaning of section 47 of the Finance Act 1942) of any such stocks or funds,".

2 (1) At the end of paragraph (1) of the general exemptions at the end of Schedule 1 to the Stamp Act 1891 (exemption for Government stocks etc) there shall be inserted "or strips (within the meaning of section 47 of the Finance Act 1942) of such stocks or funds".

(2) Where any day is appointed as the abolition day for the purposes of sections 107 to 110 of the Finance Act 1990, sub-paragraph (1) above shall cease to have effect in accordance with the provisions of that Act for the coming into force of the repeal of the paragraph mentioned in that sub-paragraph.

The Taxes Act 1988

3 (1) At the end of subsection (5) of section 710 of the Taxes Act 1988 (meaning of "transfer"), there shall be inserted—

"(b) except as otherwise provided by subsections (1) and (3) of section 722A, does not include any transaction forming part of any such exchange as is mentioned in either of those subsections.".

(2) After subsection (13) of that section there shall be inserted the following subsections—

"(13A) Where a security is deemed to have been transferred by virtue of section 722A(1), the interest period in which the exchange in question takes place shall be treated as ending on the day on which it would have ended had the exchange not taken place.

(13B) Where a security is deemed to have been transferred by virtue of section 722A(3), the interest period in which the exchange in question takes place shall be treated as having begun on such day as shall for that purpose be specified in the security."

4 In section 711 of the Taxes Act 1988 (interpretation of sections 710 and 712 to 728 of that Act), after subsection (6) there shall be inserted the following subsection—

"(6A) In any case where section 722A(1) or (3) applies, the deemed transfer shall be treated as made—

(a) without accrued interest in any such case where the exchange in question is made at any time after the balance has been struck for a dividend on the security but before the day on which that dividend is payable;

(*b*) with accrued interest in any other such case."

5 In section 712(4) of the Taxes Act 1988 (meaning of "settlement day", after "722" there shall be inserted ", 722A".

6 In the Taxes Act 1988, the following section shall be inserted after section 722—

"722A Gilt strips: deemed transfer

(1) For the purposes of sections 710 to 728, where a gilt-edged security is exchanged by any person for strips of that security the security shall be deemed to have been transferred by that person.

(2) Nothing in subsection (1) above shall have effect to cause any person to be treated as the transferee of any securities for the purposes of section 713(2)(*b*).

(3) For the purposes of sections 710 to 728, where strips of gilt-edged securities are exchanged by any person for a single gilt-edged security consolidating those strips, that security shall be deemed to have been transferred to that person.

(4) Nothing in subsection (3) above shall have effect to cause any person to be treated as the transferor of any securities for the purposes of section 713(2)(*a*).

(5) In this section—

'gilt-edged security' has the same meaning as in section 51A; and
'strip' means anything which, within the meaning of section 47 of the Finance Act 1942, is a strip of a gilt-edged security."

7 In the Taxes Act 1988, the following section shall be inserted after section 730B—

"730C Exchanges of gilts: traders etc

(1) This section has effect for the purposes of computing the profits and gains arising from any trade, profession or vocation carried on by any person in so far as the computation is such as to require amounts in respect of the acquisition or redemption of a gilt-edged security (including any strip) to be brought into account.

(2) Where a gilt-edged security is exchanged by any person for strips of that security—

(*a*) the security shall be deemed to have been redeemed at the time of the exchange by the payment to that person of its market value; and
(*b*) that person shall be deemed to have acquired each strip for the amount which bears the same proportion to that market value as is borne by the market value of the strip to the aggregate of the market values of all the strips received in exchange for the security.

(3) Where strips of a gilt-edged security are consolidated into a single security by being exchanged by any person for that security—

(*a*) each of the strips shall be deemed to have been redeemed at the time of the exchange by the payment to that person of the amount equal to its market value; and
(*b*) that person shall be deemed to have acquired the security for the amount equal to the aggregate of the market values of the strips given in exchange for the security.

(4) References in this section to the market value of a security given or received in exchange for another are references to its market value at the time of the exchange.

(5) Subsections (3) and (4) of section 473 shall not apply in the case of any exchange to which subsection (2) or (3) above applies.

(6) Without prejudice to the generality of any power conferred by section 202 of the Finance Act 1996, the Treasury may by regulations make provision for the purposes of this section as to the manner of determining the market value at any time of any gilt-edged security (including any strip).

(7) Regulations under subsection (6) above may—

(*a*) make different provision for different cases; and

(b) contain such incidental, supplemental, consequential and transitional provision as the Treasury may think fit.

(8) This section does not apply for the purposes of corporation tax.

(9) In this section—

'gilt-edged security' has the same meaning as in section 51A; and
'strip' means anything which, within the meaning of section 47 of the Finance Act 1942, is a strip of a gilt-edged security.''

The Taxation of Chargeable Gains Act 1992 (c 12)

8 In Schedule 9 to the Taxation of Chargeable Gains Act 1992 (gilt-edged securities), after paragraph 1 there shall be inserted the following paragraph—

"1A (1) Any security which is a strip of a security which is a gilt-edged security for the purposes of this Act is also itself a gilt-edged security for those purposes.

(2) In this paragraph 'strip' has the same meaning as in section 47 of the Finance Act 1942.''

SCHEDULE 41   Section 205

REPEALS

PART IV
VALUE ADDED TAX

(1) FISCAL WAREHOUSING

Chapter	Short title	Extent of repeal
1994 c. 23.	The Value Added Tax Act 1994.	In section 62(1)(*a*), the words "or" at the end of sub-paragraph (i) and "and" at the end of sub-paragraph (ii).

This repeal has effect in accordance with section 26(2) of this Act.

(2) WORK ON MATERIALS

Chapter	Short title	Extent of repeal
1994 c. 23.	The Value Added Tax Act 1994.	Section 22. In section 55(5)(*a*), the word "or" at the end of the paragraph. Section 97(4)(*b*). In Schedule 4, paragraph 2.

(3) VALUE OF IMPORTED GOODS

Chapter	Short title	Extent of repeal
1994 c. 23.	The Value Added Tax Act 1994.	In section 21(2)(*a*), the word "and" at the end of the paragraph.

This repeal has effect in accordance with section 27(4) of this Act.

(4) CONSTRUCTION AND CONVERSION OF BUILDINGS

Chapter	Short title	Extent of repeal
1995 c. 4.	The Finance Act 1995.	Section 33(2).

This repeal has effect in accordance with section 30(4) of this Act.

(5) GROUPS

Chapter	Short title	Extent of repeal
1994 c. 23. 1995 c. 4.	The Value Added Tax Act 1994. The Finance Act 1995.	Section 43(1A). In section 25(2), the words from the beginning to the word "and" immediately after the subsection (1A) inserted in section 43 of the Value Added Tax Act 1994.

These repeals have effect in accordance with section 31(5) of this Act.

PART V

INCOME TAX, CORPORATION TAX AND CAPITAL GAINS TAX

(1) APPLICATION OF LOWER RATE TO INCOME FROM SAVINGS

Chapter	Short title	Extent of repeal
1988 c. 1.	The Income and Corporation Taxes Act 1988.	Section 207A. Sections 468E and 468EE. In section 469— (*a*) in subsection (1), paragraph (*b*) and the word "and" immediately preceding it; and (*b*) the second paragraph of subsection (3).
1990 c. 29.	The Finance Act 1990.	Section 51.
1992 c. 48.	The Finance (No 2) Act 1992.	Section 19(4).
1993 c. 34.	The Finance Act 1993.	Section 77(1) and (2). Section 79(3). In Schedule 6, paragraph 14.
1994 c. 9.	The Finance Act 1994.	Section 111.

1 Subject to note 2 below, these repeals come into force in accordance with section 73 of, and Schedule 6 to, this Act.

2 The repeals in section 469 of the Taxes Act 1988 come into force for distribution periods ending on or after 6th April 1996.

(2) TRANSFER OF SCHEDULE C CHARGE ETC

Chapter	Short title	Extent of repeal
1970 c. 9.	The Taxes Management Act 1970.	In the Table in section 98— (*a*) in the first column, the entry relating to paragraph 13(1) of Schedule 3 to the Taxes Act 1988; and (*b*) in the second column, the entry relating to paragraph 6C of that Schedule
1988 c. 1.	The Income and Corporation Taxes Act 1988.	Section 17. In section 18(3), in Case IV, the words "except such income as is charged under Schedule C". Sections 44 and 45. Section 48. In sections 50(1) and 51A(1), the words "but shall be chargeable to tax under Case III of Schedule D". Section 52. Section 123. In section 124— (*a*) in subsection (6), the definitions of "recognised clearing system" and "relevant foreign securities", and the word "and" immediately preceding those definitions; and

Chapter	Short title	Extent of repeal
1988 c. 1. —(*contd*)	The Income and Corporation Taxes Act 1988.—(*contd*)	(*b*) subsection (7). In section 322(1), the words "and he shall be treated as not resident in the United Kingdom for the purposes of sections 48 and 123(4)". In section 398(*b*), the words "C or". Section 474(1) and (3). Section 505(1)(*c*)(i). Section 582A(3). In section 832(1), the definition of "recognised clearing system". Schedule 3.
1988 c. 39.	The Finance Act 1988.	Section 76(1), (2), (3) and (5).
1989 c. 26.	The Finance Act 1989.	In section 178(2)(*m*), the words "and paragraph 6B of Schedule 3 to".
1992 c. 48.	The Finance (No 2) Act 1992.	Section 30. In Schedule 11, paragraphs 1, 2, 4 and 5.
1993 c. 34.	The Finance Act 1993.	In Schedule 6, paragraphs 17 and 25(5).
1995 c. 4.	The Finance Act 1995.	In section 128(3)(*a*), the words "Schedule C".

These repeals have effect—

(*a*) in accordance with Schedule 7 to this Act; and

(*b*) without prejudice to paragraph 25 of Schedule 6 to this Act.

(3) LOAN RELATIONSHIPS

Chapter	Short title	Extent of repeal
1970 c. 9.	The Taxes Management Act 1970.	In section 42 (as substituted by paragraph 13 of Schedule 19 to the Finance Act 1994), in subsection (7)(*a*), "484,".
1988 c. 1.	The Income and Corporation Taxes Act 1988.	Section 57. Section 78. Sections 88A to 88C. Sections 126 and 126A. In section 242, in each of subsections (2)(*b*) and (8)(*b*), the words "or paragraph 5 of Schedule 4". In section 337— (*a*) in subsection (2), the words "to subsection (3) below and"; and (*b*) subsection (3). In section 338— (*a*) in subsection (3), the words from "and" at the end of paragraph (*a*) to the end of the subsection; (*b*) in subsection (4), paragraphs (*b*) and (*c*); (*c*) in subsection (5)(*a*), the words ", not being interest"; and (*d*) subsection (6).

Chapter	Short title	Extent of repeal
1988 c. 1. —(*contd*)	The Income and Corporation Taxes Act 1988.—(*contd*)	Section 338A. Section 340. Section 341. Section 401(1A). In section 404(6)(*c*)(ii), the words "or paragraph 5(2) of Schedule 4". In section 477A, subsections (3A) to (3C). Sections 484 and 485. In section 494(3), the words "not consisting of a payment of interest". Section 714(6). Section 724. In section 804A(3), in paragraph (*b*) of the definition of "B", the words "and interest". Schedule 4. In Schedule 19AC, in paragraph 5B(2)(*b*), the words "or paragraph 5 of Schedule 4". In Schedule 23A, paragraphs 6(3), (4), (6) and (7). In Schedule 26, the word "and" at the end of paragraph 1(3)(*d*).
1989 c. 15.	The Water Act 1989.	Section 95(10).
1989 c. 26.	The Finance Act 1989.	Sections 93 to 95. Section 116. Schedules 10 and 11.
1990 c. 29.	The Finance Act 1990.	Section 56. Sections 58 and 59. Section 74. Schedule 10.
1991 c. 31.	The Finance Act 1991.	Section 52(2) and (3). In Schedule 12, paragraphs 3 and 4.
1992 c. 12.	The Taxation of Chargeable Gains Act 1992.	Section 108(1)(*b*). Section 117(2A), (3), (9) and (10). Section 118. In Schedule 10, paragraphs 14(6), (29) and (57), 19(6) and 22(4).

1992 c. 48.	The Finance (No 2) Act 1992.	Section 33.
		In section 65(2)—
		  (*a*) paragraphs (*b*) and (*c*); and
		  (*b*) in paragraph (*f*), the words "to (*c*)".
		Schedule 7.

1993 c. 34.	The Finance Act 1993.	Sections 61 to 66.
		Section 103(4).
		Section 129(5) and (6).
		Section 152(2).
		Section 153(6) and (11A).
		Section 164(12).
		Section 176(3)(*b*) to (*d*).
		In Schedule 6—
		  (*a*) paragraph 18;
		  (*b*) in paragraph 20, the words "and in paragraph 11(1) of Schedule 11 to that Act"; and

Chapter	Short title	Extent of repeal
1993 c. 34.—(*contd*)	The Finance Act 1993.—(*contd*)	(*c*) paragraph 21. In Schedule 17, paragraphs 4 to 6. In Schedule 18, paragraphs 3 and 7.
1994 c. 9.	The Finance Act 1994.	Section 171. Section 251(12). In Schedule 18, in paragraph 4— (*a*) the definition of "the I minus E basis"; and (*b*) the words after the definition of "non-life mutual business". In Schedule 24, in paragraph 9— (*a*) the words "and 254" and the words "or 254", in each place where they occur; and (*b*) in sub-paragraph (9), the words "and subsection (10) of section 254 of that Act".
1995 c. 4.	The Finance Act 1995.	Section 42(6). Section 50. Section 87(6). Sections 88 and 89. Schedule 7. In Schedule 8, paragraphs 10 and 12(1)(*c*). In Schedule 24, paragraphs 4 to 6.

These repeals come into force in accordance with the provisions of Chapter II of Part IV of this Act.

(4) PROVISION OF LIVING ACCOMMODATION

Chapter	Short title	Extent of repeal
1988 c. 1.	The Income and Corporation Taxes Act 1988.	In section 145(1), the words "and is not otherwise made the subject of any charge to him by way of income tax".

This repeal has effect in accordance with section 106 of this Act.

(5) SHARE OPTION SCHEMES ETC

Chapter	Short title	Extent of repeal
1988 c. 1.	The Income and Corporation Taxes Act 1988.	In section 187(8), paragraph (*b*) and the word "and" immediately preceding it. In Schedule 9, in paragraph 21(1), the word "and" immediately preceding paragraph (*e*), paragraph 28(2) and (4) and paragraph 29(8).
1989 c. 26.	The Finance Act 1989.	In Schedule 5, in paragraph 4(5)(*a*), the words "not less than one year and".
1992 c. 12.	Taxation of Chargeable Gains Act 1992.	Section 149A(4). Section 238(4).

1 The repeal in section 187 of the Taxes Act 1988 has effect in accordance with section 117 of this Act.

2 The repeal in paragraph 21 of Schedule 9 to that Act has effect in accordance with section 113 of this Act.

3 The repeals in paragraphs 28 and 29 of that Schedule have effect in accordance with section 114 of this Act.

4 The repeal in the Finance Act 1989 has effect in accordance with section 119 of this Act.

5 The repeal of section 149A(4) of the Taxation of Chargeable Gains Act 1992 has effect in accordance with section 111(6) of this Act.

6 The repeal of section 238(4) of that Act has effect in accordance with section 112(2) and (3) of this Act.

(6) SELF-ASSESSMENT: RETURNS ETC

Chapter	Short title	Extent of repeal
1970 c. 9.	The Taxes Management Act 1970.	In section 8(1A), the words from "and the amounts referred to" to the end. In section 8A(1A), the words from "and the amounts referred to" to the end. In section 12AA(7)(*a*), the words "any part of". Section 12AC(6). In section 28C(3), the words "or 11AA". In section 42, subsections (3A) and (3B) and, in subsection (7)(*a*), the words "534, 535, 537A, 538".
1988 c. 1.	The Income and Corporation Taxes Act 1988.	In section 108, the words from "and, in any such case" to the end. In section 535, in subsection (4), the words "Subject to subsection (5) below", subsections (5) and (7) and, in subsection (6), the words from "unless the author" to the end. In section 547(5)(*a*), the words from "no assessment" to "but". In section 599A, in subsection (6), the words from "subject" to "and" and subsection (7).
1992 c. 12.	The Taxation of Chargeable Gains Act 1992.	In section 246, the words from "or, if earlier" to the end.
1994 c. 9.	The Finance Act 1994.	In Schedule 19, paragraph 23.

1 The repeals of subsections (3A) and (3B) of section 42 of the Taxes Management Act 1970 and the repeals in sections 108 and 535 of the Income and Corporation Taxes Act 1988 have effect in accordance with section 128(11) of this Act.

2 The repeal in subsection (7)(*a*) of section 42 of the Taxes Management Act 1970 has effect in accordance with section 128(12) of this Act.

3 The other repeals have effect in accordance with section 121(8) of this Act.

(7) SELF-ASSESSMENT: NOTICES

Chapter	Short title	Extent of repeal
1970 c. 9.	The Taxes Management Act 1970.	In section 42, in subsection (7), in paragraph (*a*), "62A," and "401,", and in paragraph (*c*), "30,", "33,", "48, 49," and "124A," and in subsection (10) the words "and notices".

These repeals have effect in accordance with section 130 of this Act.

(8) OVERDUE TAX AND EXCESSIVE PAYMENTS BY THE BOARD

Chapter	Short title	Extent of repeal
1970 c. 9.	The Taxes Management Act 1970.	Section 88. Section 88A. In section 91(1), the words "or section 88". Section 113(1C).
1971 c. 68.	The Finance Act 1971.	In Schedule 6, paragraph 87.
1975 c. 45.	The Finance (No 2) Act 1975.	Section 46(4).
1980 c. 48.	The Finance Act 1980.	Section 61(4), so far as relating to section 88(5)(*c*) and (*d*) of the Taxes Management Act 1970.
1988 c. 1.	The Income and Corporation Taxes Act 1988.	In section 374A(4), the words from "and as if" onwards. In Schedule 14, in paragraph 6(2) the words from "and as if" onwards. In Schedule 29, in paragraph 32, the entries relating to section 88(2), section 88(5)(*b*) and section 88(5)(*c*) of the Taxes Management Act 1970.
1989 c. 26.	The Finance Act 1989.	Section 159. Section 160(1), (2) and (4). Section 161. In section, 178(2)(*f*), the words "88". In section 179(1)(*b*)(i), the words "and 88(1)".

These repeals have effect in accordance with paragraph 17 Schedule 18 to this Act.

(9) SELF-ASSESSMENT: CLAIMS AND ENQUIRIES

Chapter	Short title	Extent of repeal
1970 c. 9.	The Taxes Management Act 1970.	In section 31(5), the words "against any assessment".

This repeal has effect in accordance with Schedule 19 to this Act.

(10) SELF-ASSESSMENT: DISCRETIONS ETC

Chapter	Short title	Extent of repeal
1988 c. 1.	The Income and Corporation Taxes Act 1988.	In section 74(1)(*j*)(i), the words "proved to be such".
		In section 145(7)(*a*) and (*b*), the words "it can be shown that".
		Section 159(4) to (6).
		In section 161, in subsection (3), the words "it is shown that" and, in subsection (4), the words "shows that he".
		In section 231(3A), the words "it appears to the inspector that".
		In section 257(2) and (3), the words "proves that he".
		In section 257E(1) the words "he proves" and, in each of paragraphs (*a*) and (*b*), the word "that" in the first and third places where it occurs.
		In section 257F, in the words preceding paragraph (*a*), the words "the claimant proves", and the word "that" in the second place where it occurs in paragraph (*a*), the first place where it occurs in paragraph (*b*) and the first and third places where it occurs in paragraph (*c*).
		In section 259(6), the second paragraph.
		In section 265(1), the words "proves that he".
		In section 278(2), the words "satisfies the Board that he or she".
		In section 381(4), the words "it is shown that".
		In section 384(1), the words "it is shown that".
		In section 570(2), the words "on a claim it is shown in accordance with the provisions of Part II of Schedule 21 that".
		In section 582(2)(*b*), the words "the Board are satisfied that".
		In section 731(3), the words following paragraph (*b*).
		In section 769(2)(*d*), the words "any gift of shares".
		In section 812(4), paragraph (*a*).
		In Schedule 7, in paragraph 1(5), the words "and shown to have been made".
		In Schedule 12, in paragraph 2(2), the words "shown to be".
		In Schedule 21, paragraph 3.

Chapter	Short title	Extent of repeal
1992 c. 12.	The Taxation of Chargeable Gains Act 1992.	In section 52(4), the words "such method as appears to the inspector or on appeal the Commissioners concerned to be". In section 116(13), the words "the inspector is satisfied that" and "and so directs,". In section 122, in subsection (2), the words "the inspector is satisfied that" and "and so directs" and subsection (3). In section 133, in subsection (2), the words "the inspector is satisfied that" and "and so directs" and subsection (3). In section 164F(8)(*a*), the words "it is shown that". In section 164FG(2), the words "or an officer of the Board in default of an election determines". In section 181(1)(*b*), the words "it is shown that" and the word "that" in the second place where it occurs. In section 222, in subsection (5), paragraph (*b*) and the words following it and, in subsection (6), paragraph (*b*) and the word "and" immediately preceding it. Section 226(5). In section 271(2), in the second paragraph, the words "the Board are satisfied that". In Schedule 6, in paragraph 3, in sub-paragraphs (1), (3) and (4), the words "on production of such evidence as the Board may reasonably require, the Board are satisfied".
1993 c. 34.	The Finance Act 1993.	In section 144, in subsections (1)(*b*) and (2)(*b*), the words "the inspector is satisfied," and the word "that", in the first place where it occurs, and, in subsection (3)(*b*), the words "in the opinion of the inspector" and subsection (4). In section 145, in subsection (1)(*c*), the words "the inspector is satisfied that", in subsections (2)(*b*) and (3)(*b*), the words "in the opinion of the inspector", in subsection (4)(*b*), the words "the inspector is satisfied that" and in subsection (5), the words "in the opinion of the inspector" and subsection (6).

These repeals have effect in accordance with section 134 of, and Schedule 20 to, this Act.

(11) SELF-ASSESSMENT: TIME LIMITS

Chapter	Short title	Extent of repeal
1990 c. 1.	The Capital Allowances Act 1990.	In section 37(2), the words following paragraph (*d*).
1992 c. 12.	The Taxation of Chargeable Gains Act 1992.	In Schedule 4, in paragraph 9(1)(*b*), the words "year of assessment or".
1994 c. 9.	The Finance Act 1994.	In Schedule 15, paragraph 21(*a*)(ii).

These repeals have effect in accordance with section 135 of, and Schedule 21 to, this Act.

(12) SELF-ASSESSMENT: APPEALS

Chapter	Short title	Extent of repeal
1970 c. 9.	The Taxes Management Act 1970.	Section 42(12). In section 44— (*a*) subsections (1A) and (1B), and (*b*) in subsection (2), the words "and any direction under subsection (1A) above". Schedule 2.
1975 c. 7.	The Finance Act 1975.	Section 54.
1975 c. 45.	The Finance (No. 2) Act 1975.	Section 66.
1976 c. 40.	The Finance Act 1976.	In Schedule 9, paragraph 11.
1984 c. 43.	The Finance Act 1984.	In Schedule 22, paragraph 3(2).
1988 c. 1.	The Income and Corporation Taxes Act 1988.	In the Table in paragraph 32 of Schedule 29, the entries relating to Schedule 3 to the Taxes Management Act 1970.
1988 c. 39.	The Finance Act 1988.	Section 133(1).
1989 c. 26.	The Finance Act 1989.	Section 160(6). Section 168(8).
1990 c. 1.	The Capital Allowances Act 1990.	In Schedule 1, paragraph 1(4).
1994 c. 9.	The Finance Act 1994.	In Schedule 19, paragraph 36.
1995 c. 4.	The Finance Act 1995.	In Schedule 17, in paragraph 22, the words "(including that provision as proposed to be substituted by paragraph 7 of Schedule 19 to the Finance Act 1994)".

These repeals have effect in accordance with Schedule 22 to this Act.

(13) SELF-ASSESSMENT: ACCOUNTING PERIODS ETC

Chapter	Short title	Extent of repeal
1988 c. 1.	The Income and Corporation Taxes Act 1988.	Section 8A.
1993 c. 34.	The Finance Act 1993.	Section 206(2).

(14) SELF-ASSESSMENT: ADVANCE CORPORATION TAX

Chapter	Short title	Extent of repeal
1988 c. 1.	The Income and Corporation Taxes Act 1988.	Section 239(5).

This repeal has effect in accordance with Schedule 25 to this Act.

(15) CLASS 4 CONTRIBUTIONS

Chapter	Short title	Extent of repeal
1988 c. 1.	The Income and Corporation Taxes Act 1988.	Section 617(5).
1992 c. 4.	The Social Security Contributions and Benefits Act 1992.	In Schedule 2, in paragraph 3(2), the words "(*e*) section 617(5) (relief for Class 4 contributions)".
1992 c. 7.	The Social Security Contributions and Benefits (Northern Ireland) Act 1992.	In Schedule 2, in paragraph 3(2), the words "section 617(5) (relief for Class 4 contributions)".

These repeals have effect in accordance with section 147 of this Act.

(16) PERSONAL INJURY DAMAGES AND COMPENSATION

Chapter	Short title	Extent of repeal
1988 c. 1.	The Income and Corporation Taxes Act 1988.	Sections 329A to 329C.
1995 c. 4.	The Finance Act 1995.	Section 142.
1995 c. 53.	The Criminal Injuries Compensation Act 1995.	Section 8.

(17) FOREIGN INCOME DIVIDENDS

Chapter	Short title	Extent of repeal
1988 c. 1.	The Income and Corporation Taxes Act 1988.	In section 246S— (*a*) in subsection (3), the words after paragraph (*e*); and (*b*) subsection (8).

These repeals have effect in accordance with Schedule 27 to this Act.

(18) FOTRA SECURITIES

Chapter	Short title	Extent of repeal
1988 c. 1.	The Income and Corporation Taxes Act 1988.	Section 47. Section 474(2). In section 475— (*a*) in subsection (5), the words "Subject to subsection (6) below,"; (*b*) subsections (6) and (7); and

Chapter	Short title	Extent of repeal
1988 c. 1. —(*contd*)	The Income and Corporation Taxes Act 1988.—(*contd*)	(*c*) in subsection (8), the words from "and this subsection" onwards. In section 715— (*a*) in subsection (1), paragraphs (*g*) and (*h*); and (*b*) in subsection (8), the definition of "FOTRA securities".
1993 c. 34.	The Finance Act 1993.	In section 174— (*a*) subsection (6); and (*b*) in subsection (7), the definitions of "FOTRA securities" and "non-resident United Kingdom trader".
1994 c. 9.	The Finance Act 1994.	Section 222(6) and (7).

These repeals come into force in accordance with section 154(9) of this Act.

(19) PAYING AND COLLECTING AGENTS

Chapter	Short title	Extent of repeal
1988 c. 39.	The Finance Act 1988.	Section 76(4) and (6).

(20) ACCRUED INCOME SCHEME

Chapter	Short title	Extent of repeal
1988 c. 1.	The Income and Corporation Taxes Act 1988.	Section 721(1) and (4).

These repeals come into force in accordance with section 158 of this Act.

(21) MANUFACTURED PAYMENTS, REPOS, ETC.

Chapter	Short title	Extent of repeal
1970 c. 9.	The Taxes Management Act 1970.	In the first column of the Table in section 98, the entry relating to section 729(11) of the Taxes Act 1988.
1988 c. 1.	The Income and Corporation Taxes Act 1988.	Section 729. Section 732(3). In section 737(5AA)(*b*), the words from "and the words" onwards. Section 737A(2)(*b*). Section 786(4). In Schedule 23A, paragraph 4(7A).
1994 c. 9.	The Finance Act 1994.	Section 124.
1995 c. 4.	The Finance Act 1995.	Section 80(2).

1 Subject to note 2 below, these repeals have effect in accordance with section 159(1) of this Act.

2 The repeals in section 737 of, and Schedule 23A to, the Taxes Act 1988, and the repeal of section 124 of the Finance Act 1994, come into force on the day on which this Act is passed.

(22) VENTURE CAPITAL TRUSTS

Chapter	Short title	Extent of repeal
1988 c. 1.	The Income and Corporation Taxes Act 1988.	In Schedule 28B, in paragraph 9, in sub-paragraph (1) the words "subject to sub-paragraph (2) below" and sub-paragraph (2).

These repeals have effect in accordance with section 161 of this Act.

(23) LIFE ASSURANCE BUSINESS LOSSES

Chapter	Short title	Extent of repeal
1988 c. 1.	The Income and Corporation Taxes Act 1988.	Section 436(3)(*aa*). Section 439B(3)(*b*). Sections 441(4)(*aa*).
1995 c. 4.	The Finance Act 1995.	In Schedule 8, paragraph 16(4) and (5).

These repeals have effect in accordance with paragraph 10(2) of Schedule 31 to this Act.

(24) MANAGEMENT EXPENSES OF INSURANCE COMPANIES

Chapter	Short title	Extent of repeal
1988 c. 1.	The Income and Corporation Taxes Act 1988.	In section 434(1)(*b*), the words from "of the tax" onwards. In section 434D(8), in paragraph (*b*) of the second sentence, the words from "of the tax" onwards. In section 442(3), the words "otherwise than for the purposes of section 76(2)". In section 473, subsection (5). In Schedule 19AC— (*a*) in paragraph 5(1), in the subsection (6B) deemed to be inserted in section 76, the words "and subsections (2) and (3)(*b*) above"; and (*b*) in paragraph 9, in the subsection (1A) deemed to be inserted in section 434, the words from "of the tax" onwards.
1992 c. 12.	The Taxation of Chargeable Gains Act 1992.	In Schedule 10, in paragraph 14(27)(*a*), the words "and (5)".

These repeals come into force in accordance with section 164(5) of this Act.

(25) ANNUAL PAYMENTS UNDER INSURANCE POLICIES

Chapter	Short title	Extent of repeal
1988 c. 1.	The Income and Corporation Taxes Act 1988.	Section 434B(1).

This repeal has effect in accordance with section 165 of this Act.

(26) INDUSTRIAL ASSURANCE BUSINESS

Chapter	Short title	Extent of repeal
1988 c. 1.	The Income and Corporation Taxes Act 1988.	In section 431(2)— (a) the definitions of "industrial assurance business" and of "ordinary long term business" and "ordinary life assurance business"; and (b) in the definition of "long term business fund", the words from "or, where" to "so maintained". Section 432(2). In section 458(3), the words "or industrial assurance business".
1989 c. 26.	The Finance Act 1989.	Section 83A(5).
1990 c. 29.	The Finance Act 1990.	In Schedule 6, paragraph 3.

These repeals come into force in relation to accounting periods beginning on or after 1st January 1996.

(27) PROVISIONAL REPAYMENTS IN CONNECTION WITH INSURANCE COMPANIES' PENSION BUSINESS

Chapter	Short title	Extent of repeal
1988 c. 1.	The Income and Corporation Taxes Act 1988.	In Schedule 19AB, in paragraph 1(5)(b), the word "and" immediately preceding sub-paragraph (ii) and paragraphs 1(8) and 6(3). In Schedule 19AC, paragraph 15(1).

These repeals have effect in accordance with section 169 of, and Schedule 34 to, this Act.

(28) FRIENDLY SOCIETIES

Chapter	Short title	Extent of repeal
1992 c. 48.	The Finance (No 2) Act 1992.	In Schedule 9, paragraph 14(2).

This repeal has effect in accordance with section 171 of this Act.

(29) LOANS TO PARTICIPATORS ETC

Chapter	Short title	Extent of repeal
1988 c. 1.	The Income and Corporation Taxes Act 1988.	In section 419(6), the words "and to a company not resident in the United Kingdom".

This repeal has effect in accordance with section 173(6) of this Act.

(30) CHARGEABLE GAINS: NON-RESIDENT COMPANIES

Chapter	Short title	Extent of repeal
1992 c. 12.	The Taxation of Chargeable Gains Act 1992.	Section 13(5)(*a*) and (6). In Schedule 5, paragraph 8(10).

These repeals come into force in relation to gains accruing on or after 28th November 1995.

(31) CANCELLATION OF TAX ADVANTAGES: TRANSACTIONS IN CERTAIN SECURITIES

Chapter	Short title	Extent of repeal
1996 c. 8.	The Finance Act 1996.	In section 175, subsections (2) and (3) and, in subsection (4), the words "Except as provided by subsection (3) above,".

These repeals have effect in accordance with section 175(3) of this Act.

(32) SUB-CONTRACTORS IN THE CONSTRUCTION INDUSTRY

Chapter	Short title	Extent of repeal
1988 c. 1.	The Income and Corporation Taxes Act 1988.	In section 566(2), the words "and any such regulations may make different provision for different circumstances."

(33) CAPITAL ALLOWANCES: ROLL-OVER RELIEF IN RESPECT OF SHIPS

Chapter	Short title	Extent of repeal
1990 c. 1.	The Capital Allowances Act 1990.	In section 33C(2), the words "to be", in the first place where they occur.

(34) CONTROLLED FOREIGN COMPANIES

Chapter	Short title	Extent of repeal
1988 c. 1.	The Income and Corporation Taxes Act 1988.	In section 747A, subsection (7) and, in subsection (8), the words "the company is not a trading company and". In Schedule 25, in paragraph 2A, in sub-paragraph (1), the words "which is not a trading company" and sub-paragraphs (6) and (7) and, in paragraph 3, sub-paragraphs (1) to (4) and, in sub-paragraph (5), the words "the available profits or, where the company is not a trading company,".

These repeals have effect in accordance with section 182 of this Act.

PART VI

INHERITANCE TAX

Chapter	Short title	Extent of repeal
1984 c. 51.	The Inheritance Tax Act 1984.	In section 105— (*a*) in subsection (1), "109A", the words "shares in or" in paragraph (*b*), and paragraph (*c*); (*b*) subsections (1A) and (1B); (*c*) in subsection (2), the words "(*b*) or"; and (*d*) subsection (2A). In section 107(4), the words "and section 109A below". Section 109A. Section 116(2A).
1987 c. 16.	The Finance Act 1987.	In Schedule 8, paragraphs 5 to 7.
1995 c. 4.	The Finance Act 1995.	Section 155(2).

1 Subject to note 2 below, these repeals have effect in accordance with section 184(6)(*b*) of this Act.

2 The repeal in section 116 of the Inheritance Tax Act 1984, and the related repeal in section 155 of the Finance Act 1995, have effect in accordance with section 185(3) and (6) of this Act.

PART VII

STAMP DUTY AND STAMP DUTY RESERVE TAX

Chapter	Short title	Extent of repeal
1986 c. 41.	The Finance Act 1986.	In section 87, in subsection (2), the words "the expiry of the period of two months beginning with" and the words from "unless" to the end and subsections (4), (5) and (8). Section 88(2) and (3). Section 94(8). Section 96(12). Section 97(2).
1996 c. 8.	The Finance Act 1996.	Sections 186 to 196.

1 The repeals in sections 87 and 88 of the Finance Act 1986 have effect in accordance with sections 188 and 192 of this Act.

2 The repeals in sections 94 and 96 of the Finance Act 1986 have effect in accordance with section 194 of this Act.

3 The repeal in section 97 of the Finance Act 1986 has effect in accordance with section 196(4) of this Act.

4 The repeals in the Finance Act 1996 have effect—

(*a*) so far as relating to stamp duty, in accordance with section 108 of the Finance Act 1990; and
(*b*) so far as relating to stamp duty reserve tax, in accordance with section 110 of the Finance Act 1990.

PART VIII
MISCELLANEOUS
(1) RATES OF INTEREST

Chapter	Short title	Extent of repeal
1994 c. 9.	The Finance Act 1994.	In Schedule 6, paragraph 11. In Schedule 7, paragraph 21(5).
1994 c. 23.	The Value Added Tax Act 1994.	Section 74(6).

Subsection (7) of section 197 of this Act applies in relation to these repeals as it applies in relation to subsection (6) of that section.

(2) BANKS

Chapter	Short title	Extent of repeal
1984 c. 51.	The Inheritance Tax Act 1984.	In section 157(5), paragraph (*b*) and the word "and" immediately preceding it.
1987 c. 22.	The Banking Act 1987.	In Schedule 6, paragraph 17.

These repeals have effect in accordance with Schedule 37 to this Act.

(3) QUOTATION AND LISTING OF SECURITIES

Chapter	Short title	Extent of repeal
1992 c. 12.	The Taxation of Chargeable Gains Act 1992.	Section 288(4).

This repeal has effect in relation to times falling on or after 1st April 1996.

(4) ENACTMENT OF EXTRA-STATUTORY CONCESSIONS

Chapter	Short title	Extent of repeal
1891 c. 38.	The Stamp Duties Management Act 1891.	In section 9(7)(*e*), the words from "which is inadvertently" to "executed and duly stamped, or".
1992 c. 12.	The Taxation of Chargeable Gains Act 1992.	In section 72(5), the word "life" in the third place where it occurs. In section 73(2), the word "life". Section 75. In section 254— (*a*) in subsections (6) and (7), the words "the inspector is satisfied that"; (*b*) in subsection (8), the words "in the inspector's opinion"; and (*c*) in subsection (11), the words "the inspector was satisfied that", "by the inspector" and "he was satisfied that".

These repeals have effect in accordance with Schedule 39 to this Act.

INDEX

All references are to FA 1996 unless otherwise stated

571

572

I

LANDFILL TAX—*cont.*
representative of another person, power to assess, s 50(4), (8)
samples, power to take, s 60, Sch 5 para 10
security for tax, s 60, Sch 5 para 31
sequestered estate, carrying on business of person with, s 58(4)
service of notices etc, s 60, Sch 5 paras 38, 39
set-off of amounts, s 60, Sch 5 para 42
taxable activities, s 69
taxable disposal,
   invoice issued in respect of, s 61
   meaning, s 40(1)
   regulations, power to make, s 62
time for payment, s 49
transfer of business as going concern, s 58(5), (6)
unincorporated body,
   registration, s 58(2)
   regulations, power to make, s 58(1)

LIFE INSURANCE POLICY
removal of certification requirements, s 162

LOAN
beneficial. *See* BENEFICIAL LOAN
limit on relief for interest on, s 76
meaning, s 103(1)

LOAN RELATIONSHIP
accounting methods,
   application of, s 86
   authorised, ss 85, 103(1)
   changes of, s 90
   connected parties, ss 87, 88
   inconsistent application of, s 89
amounts brought into account in respect of certain assets, s 92
"carried-forward debit": meaning, s 83(3)
chargeable assets, linked to the value of, s 93
collective investment schemes,
   authorised unit trusts, s 98, Sch 10 para 2
   investment trusts, s 98, Sch 10 para 1
   non-qualifying investments test, s 98, Sch 10 para 8
   offshore funds,
      company holdings in, s 98, Sch 10 paras 4–6
      distributing, s 98, Sch 10 para 3
      meaning, s 98, Sch 10 para 7
   orders, power to make, s 98, Sch 10 para 9
   unit trusts,
      authorised, s 98, Sch 10 para 2
      company holdings in, s 98, Sch 10 paras 4–6
computational provisions. *See* credits and debits, computing *below*
connected parties, ss 87, 88
convertible securities etc, s 92
creditor relationship,
   meaning, s 103(1)
   party to, s 103(2)
credits and debits, computing,
   bad debts,
      connection, parties having, s 84, Sch 9 para 6
      generally, s 84, Sch 9 para 5
      loss period: meaning, s 84, Sch 9 para 9(1)
      overseas sovereign debt, s 84, Sch 9 paras 8, 9
      overseas State authority: meaning, s 84, Sch 9 para 8(9)
      relevant overseas debt: meaning, s 84, Sch 9 para 8(7)
   capital expenditure, treatment as, s 84, Sch 9 para 14
   close companies, discounted securities of, s 84, Sch 9 para 18
   discounted securities where companies having a connection, s 84, Sch 9 para 17
   distributions, s 84, Sch 9 para 1
   foreign exchange gains and losses, s 84, Sch 9 para 4

N

NON-RESIDENT EEA NATIONAL
tax relief, s 145

NOTICE
procedure for giving, s 130

O

OFFSHORE FUND
collective investment schemes. *See under* LOAN RELATIONSHIP
meaning, s 98, Sch 10 para 7
qualifying corporate bonds, holdings excluded from treatment as, s 104, Sch 14 para 62

OIL LICENCE
disposal,
    alternative tax treatment, election for, s 180
    generally, s 180
overseas petroleum, provisions relating to, s 181
undeveloped area, in relation to, s 181(2)

OVERDUE TAX
interest on, s 131
statutory amendments, s 132, Sch 18

OVERSEAS ELECTORS
domicile for tax purposes, s 200

OVERSEAS PENSION SCHEME
contributions to, s 201, Sch 39 para 2

P

PARTNERSHIP
tax liability, s 123

PAYE
regulations as to payments on account of income tax, s 126
settlement agreements, s 110

PENALTY
Sch D charge, statutory amendments, s 156, Sch 29 para 2
VAT,
    failure to notify, for, s 37
    repeated misdeclaration, for, s 36

PENSION BUSINESS
provisional repayments in connection with, s 169, Sch 34

PERSONAL ALLOWANCES
1996–97,
    blind person's allowance, s 75
    generally, s 74

PERSONAL INJURY
damages and compensation for, s 150, Sch 26

PERSONAL PENSION
mis-sold, s 148

PERSONAL PENSION SCHEME
return of contributions on or after death of member, s 172

PROFIT SHARING SCHEME
appropriate allowance, s 118
appropriate percentage, s 117
release date, s 116

581

Index

V

VALUE ADDED TAX
default surcharge, payments on account etc, s 35
EC Second VAT Simplification Directive, s 25
failure to notify, penalties for, s 37
fiscal warehousing. *See* FISCAL WAREHOUSING
imported goods, value of, s 27
invoices and accounting, s 38
refunds in connection with construction and conversion, s 30
repeals, s 205, Sch 41 Part IV
repeated misdeclaration penalty, s 36
small gifts, s 33
surcharge, default, s 35
work on materials, s 29
zero-rated supply of services, s 29

VENTURE CAPITAL TRUST
control of companies etc, s 161

VOCATIONAL TRAINING RELIEF
claim for, s 129
generally, s 144